554

P9-BYB-330

A CENTURY OF WEALTH IN AMERICA

A CENTURY *of*

WEALTH *in*

AMERICA

Edward N. Wolff

THE BELKNAP PRESS OF HARVARD UNIVERSITY PRESS

Cambridge, Massachusetts and London, England · *2017*

Library of Congress Cataloging-in-Publication Data

Names: Wolff, Edward N., author.
Title: A century of wealth in America / Edward N. Wolff.
Description: Cambridge, Massachusetts : The Belknap Press of Harvard University Press,
    2017. | Includes bibliographical references and index.
Identifiers: LCCN 2017011157 | ISBN 9780674495142 (alk. paper)
Subjects: LCSH: Wealth—United States—History—20th century. | Wealth—United
    States—History—21st century. | Households—Economic aspects—United States—
    History—20th century. | Households—Economic aspects—United States—History—
    21st century. | United States—Economic conditions—20th century. | United States—
    Economic conditions—2001–2009. | United States—Economic conditions –2009 -
Classification: LCC HC110.W4 W6469 2017 | DDC 339.20973/0904—dc23
    LC record available at https://lccn.loc.gov/2017011157

For my son, Spencer, and daughter, Ashley

Cent'unni!

"The truth is out there."

—THE X-FILES

Contents

Preface

This book is almost entirely empirical in orientation. There is very little theory except, perhaps, in Chapter 6, which analyzes the life cycle model. The orientation is to rely heavily on data analysis to draw out conclusions regarding patterns of wealth accumulation and wealth trends. The work follows the Baconian method of inductive reasoning from empirical observation rather than Descartes's method of using mathematical reasoning to develop an overarching theoretical framework. This book documents and analyzes trends in both wealth accumulation patterns and wealth inequality in the United States from 1900 to 2013. International comparisons are also provided where comparable data permits. The data presented in this book is the culmination of over forty years of research on this topic.

In some respects, work on this book began in 1972 when I was hired by Nancy and Richard Ruggles as a research assistant at the National Bureau of Economic Research in New Haven. (I was a PhD student at Yale at the time.) The project was called the Measurement of Economic and Social Performance (MESP) and was funded by the National Science Foundation. My primary responsibility was to develop and implement a procedure for the statistical matching of micro databases. One outgrowth of this work was the development of the so-called MESP database, which was the product of three statistical matches and two sets of imputations and contains asset and liability information, as well as detailed demographic data, for a sample of 63,457 households. The database was developed from October 1972 through October 1977.

Five articles on household wealth were based on this project: (1) "The Distributional Effects of the 1969–75 Inflation on Holdings of Household Wealth in the United States," 1979; (2) "Estimates of the 1969 Size Distribution of Household Wealth in the United States from a Synthetic Database," 1980; (3) "The Accumulation of Wealth Over the Life-Cycle: A Microdata Analysis,"

1981; (4) "Effect of Alternative Imputation Techniques on Estimates of Household Wealth in the U.S. in 1969," 1982; and (5) "The Distribution of Household Disposable Wealth in the United States," 1983.

Subsequent work relied more and more heavily on the Federal Reserve Board's Survey of Consumer Finances (SCF), starting with its 1983 survey. Some fifty articles were published from this source, including: (1) "Estimates of Household Wealth Inequality in the United States, 1962–83," 1987; (2) "Changing Inequality of Wealth," 1992; (3) "Trends in Household Wealth in the United States, 1962–1983 and 1983–1989," 1994; (4) "Recent Trends in the Size Distribution of Household Wealth," 1988; (5) "Wealth Accumulation by Age Cohort in the U.S., 1962–1992: The Role of Savings, Capital Gains and Intergenerational Transfers," 1999; (6) "Recent Trends in Wealth Ownership, from 1983 to 1998," 2001; (7) "Changes in Household Wealth in the 1980s and 1990s in the U.S.," 2006; (8) "Recent Trends in Household Wealth in the U.S.: Rising Debt and the Middle Class Squeeze," 2011; (9) "Household Wealth Trends in the United States, 1983–2010," 2014; (10) "The Asset Price Meltdown and Household Wealth over the Great Recession in the United States," 2014; and (11) "The Middle Class: Losing Ground, Losing Wealth," 2014.

A few words should be said to differentiate this book from my 1995 "best-seller" *Top Heavy* (reprinted in 1996 and then reprinted in an updated and expanded edition in 2002). Whereas *Top Heavy* was aimed at a relatively general audience and had very little in the way of technical detail, the current volume is aimed at a more scholarly audience and includes much more technical discussion of the methodological issues associated with measuring and analyzing household wealth. Another major difference is that the data series in my previous book ended in 1998, whereas the current volume extends it to 2013. Moreover, the current volume presents work that was only briefly touched upon in the previous work, including: (1) the development of a long-term time series on the growth in average household wealth; (2) an analysis of the role of Social Security and pension wealth on household wealth accumulation and inequality; (3) comparisons of estimates of household wealth from alternative wealth surveys; (4) more comprehensive international comparisons of household wealth inequality; (5) an econometric analysis of the life cycle model; (6) an extensive investigation of the role of bequests in household wealth accumulation; (7) a discussion of trends in asset poverty in the United States; (8) a decomposition analysis and a more extended time-series analysis of the factors that have caused the rise in wealth inequality in the United States over the last thirty years; and (9) an investigation of wealth trends over the period that included the so-called Great Recession.

Eleven sets of findings in particular are highlighted in this volume. The first is the remarkable growth in household wealth over the twentieth century and, in particular, over the 1980s, 1990s, and early and mid-2000s. What is particularly surprising is that despite the well-publicized decline in personal savings rates since the early 1980s, the growth in household wealth continued unabated over this period. Chapter 5 helps to unravel this seeming contradiction.

The second is the sharp increase in wealth inequality in the United States over the last four decades. The wealth share of the richest 1 percent of households almost doubled between the mid-1970s and 2013. During the 1980s, 1990s, and 2000s, almost the entire growth in household wealth accrued to the richest 20 percent of households and almost two-thirds to the richest 1 percent alone. There is clear evidence of a growing bifurcation in the United States between the "favored fifth" and almost all the rest (see Chapter 2).

The third is the incredible run-up of debt by the middle class. Between 1983 and 2007, these households' debt more than doubled from 67 to 157 percent of their income, and their ratio of debt to net worth climbed from 37 to 61 percent. The bulk of this debt was secured by real estate in the form of home mortgages. This made the middle class particularly vulnerable when the financial crisis hit in 2007 (see Chapter 3).

The fourth is the precipitous decline in the wealth of the average family that occurred over the Great Recession, from 2007 to 2013. Indeed, by 2013 median household wealth was back to where it had been in 1969! There were two key factors at play here. First, middle-class families had reached a high level of indebtedness by 2007. Second, over three-fifths of their wealth was tied up in their own homes. As a result, the steep plunge in housing prices of 24 percent was leveraged into an even greater decline in their wealth of 44 percent. There is also evidence of substantial dissavings among the middle class over these years. Differential leverage between the top 1 percent and the middle class also played a key role in accounting for movements in wealth inequality over time (see Chapter 3).

The fifth is that tremendous shifts occurred in the wealth holdings of different demographic groups in the United States. Elderly families witnessed a steady growth in their relative wealth holdings over the postwar period. In contrast, young families and families with children saw their relative economic status decline almost continuously over the last thirty years or so. The average wealth of black families was about the same relative to white families in 2007 as in 1983 (a ratio of 0.19), but by 2013 the ratio had slipped to 0.13. Moreover, in 2013, the racial wealth gap was still more than three times as great as the corresponding income gap (see Chapter 9).

The sixth confronts the recent argument that with the huge growth in pension wealth, particularly defined contribution plans, stock ownership was spreading widely in U.S. society. Chapter 3 documents a significant increase in the percentage of families that had an interest in the stock market either directly or indirectly through various pension plans from 1962 to 2001. After 2001, however, stock ownership rates fell off. Moreover, the concentration of stock ownership in America was still as great in 2013 as it had been in 1983.

The seventh concerns the role of Social Security and defined benefit pension wealth on trends in overall wealth inequality. It has long been known that including Social Security wealth along with conventional wealth in the household balance sheet will reduce measured wealth inequality. Moreover, given the tremendous growth of Social Security wealth relative to conventional wealth since the program began (in 1937), the equalizing effect increased over time. However, wealth based on private pensions became more unequally distributed in recent years. Because private pension wealth was the fastest growing component of total wealth, the net equalizing effect of total retirement wealth has actually declined since 1983 (see Chapter 8).

The eighth is the amazing turnabout in the level of inequality of the United States relative to other countries at a similar level of economic development. By almost any conceivable index—household income, equivalent income, poverty, and household wealth—the United States is today the most unequal country (or nearly so) among the advanced industrialized nations of the world. This has not always been the case. In the early part of this century and even in the 1950s, the United States ranked among the more equal in this group of countries. Chapter 4 will document these disturbing changes with regard to personal wealth inequality.

The ninth is that the standard model of savings—the life cycle model—explains only a small fraction of the variation of wealth among households—on the order of 5 to 10 percent (see Chapter 6). In contrast, there is direct survey evidence that intergenerational transfers of wealth may explain upwards of 40 percent of the total household lifetime accumulation of wealth (see Chapter 7). If this is the case, we are led to the rather bleak conclusion that the United States is not a land of equal opportunity for all but rather one in which social class plays a very important role.

The tenth is the remarkable persistence of "asset poverty," defined as the lack of financial resources to provide for normal consumption over a period of three months, over years 1983 to 2007 despite a sharp increase in median household net worth. The Great Recession, perhaps not surprisingly, witnessed a substantial spike in the incidence of asset poverty (see Chapter 11).

The eleventh, on a positive note, is the enormous increase in household wealth over the long term. Real marketable wealth per household enjoyed a fourfold increase from 1900 to 2013 and real per capita wealth mushroomed by a factor of 7.5 over these years (Chapter 12). A note to readers: If you prefer not to plod through all of the technical details, I recommend that you skip to Chapter 15 first, which contains an apt summary of principal findings.

A CENTURY OF WEALTH IN AMERICA

I

Recent Developments
in Personal Wealth

1

Plan of the Book and Historical Backdrop

This chapter provides an overview of trends in the standard of living, the poverty rate, income inequality, labor earnings, and the wage share of national income since 1947.[1] With this historical backdrop in mind, the rest of the book focuses on household wealth.

Part I looks at recent developments in personal wealth in the United States and several other advanced economies. Chapter 2 documents trends in mean and median household net worth and net worth inequality over the half century from 1962 to 2013. Relying on calculations from the Survey of Consumer Finances (SCF) from the Federal Reserve Board in Washington, DC, as well as several other household surveys, particular attention is devoted to developments during the event usually referred to as the Great Recession (2007 to 2013).

Before proceeding to the statistical analysis, Chapter 2 addresses three preliminary issues. Historical background on trends in asset prices and the like between 2001 and 2013 is followed by several rationales for looking at household wealth as an indicator of personal well-being. The primary data sources used for Chapter 2 are SCFs covering the years 1983 to 2013. Each survey consists of a core representative sample combined with a high-income supplement. Data were also drawn from the 1962 Survey of Financial Characteristics of Consumers (SFCC), which was conducted by the Federal Reserve Board and was a precursor to the SCF. This is also a stratified sample that over-samples high-income households. The second is the 1969 MESP (Measurement of Economic and Social Performance) database, a synthetic dataset constructed from income tax returns and information provided in the 1970 U.S. Census of Population. Property income flows (such as dividends) in the tax data were then capitalized into corresponding asset values (such as stocks) to obtain estimates of household wealth.

The statistical analysis in Chapter 2 documents time trends in both median and mean wealth from 1962 to 2013, with special attention paid to the Great Recession period, from 2007 to 2013. In particular, the chapter reports that after robust growth in median wealth (in real terms), there followed a massive destruction of household wealth, with median wealth plunging by a staggering 44 percent from 2007 to 2010. This analysis is followed by a look at trends in wealth inequality over the same period. The estimates show that wealth inequality in 1983 was quite close to its level in 1962. After rising steeply between 1983 and 1989, it remained virtually unchanged from 1989 to 2007. The years 2007 to 2010 saw another sharp elevation in wealth inequality. Comparisons with income inequality movements are also presented.

The investigation of inequality continues with calculation of the share of total wealth gains accruing to different wealth groups. All in all, the greatest gains in wealth over these years were enjoyed by the upper 20 percent, particularly the top 1 percent, of the wealth distributions. A review of time trends using alternative wealth concepts and measures and makes comparisons with another data source: The first part considers how the inclusion of the value of autos and other vehicles affects measured wealth trends. The second part presents comparisons of post-2000 trends between SCF data and data from the Panel Study of Income Dynamics (PSID).

Chapter 3 analyzes changes in the portfolio composition of household wealth from 1983 to 2013 (the period for which consistent data exists) and computes rates of return on household wealth over the same period. It also looks at developments in ownership rates for various asset classes, such as stocks and defined contribution (DC) plans. A notable finding is the sharp rise in relative indebtedness, with the overall ratio of debt to net worth climbing from 15 percent in 1983 to 18 percent in 2013 and the overall debt-income ratio surging from 68 percent in 1983 to 107 percent in 2013. A portfolio composition analysis by wealth class then indicates that there are marked class differences in how middle-income families and the rich save their income. In 2013, about three-fifths of middle-class wealth was invested in primary residences and another 20 percent went into monetary savings of one form or another. Their debt to net worth was very high, 0.64, and their debt-income ratio was 1.25. In contrast, the top 1 percent invested over 80 percent of their savings in investment vehicles. Their debt to net worth ratio was 0.026 and their debt-income ratio was 0.38, both ratios substantially lower than for the middle class.

The rather staggering debt level of the middle class in 2013 raises the question of whether this was a recent phenomenon or whether it was going on for some time. Chapter 3 documents a sharp rise in middle-class indebtedness between 1983 and 2013 as well as deterioration in the financial resources available to the middle class. Ownership of investment assets is concentrated in the top 10 percent of families, accounting for about 85 to 90 percent of stocks, bonds, trusts, and business equity, and over three-quarters of non-home real estate. Detail is presented on what happened in the housing market from 2007 to 2013.

Calculations of rates of return on household portfolios show that differences in portfolio composition, particularly leverage (indebtedness), between wealth classes translates into large disparities in rates of return on household wealth. Differences in returns between the top 1 percent and the middle three quintiles were quite substantial in some years. In the 2001–2007 period, when asset prices were generally rising, the average annual return on net worth was 5.6 percent for the latter and 3.9 percent for the former—a difference of 1.7 percentage points. In contrast, over years 2007 to 2010, when asset prices declined, the return was −6.5 percent for the top 1 percent and −10.6 percent for the middle group—a differential of 4.1 percentage points in favor of the top 1 percent.

Chapter 3 then considers stock ownership. The percentage of families that had an interest in the stock market either through direct ownership of stock shares or indirectly through pension accounts and the like surged from 32 to 52 percent between 1989 and 2001 but then fell off to 46 percent in 2013. This analysis is followed by a look at trends in ownership rates and the value of defined contribution pension accounts.

How does U.S. wealth inequality compare with that of other countries? How have relative levels of inequality changed over time? How does the U.S. level of median and mean wealth compare to those of other advanced economies? These issues provide an international context for the experiences in the United States. Chapter 4 presents international comparisons of personal wealth inequality for a number of countries and over time. There is recent historical data on personal wealth inequality available for Canada, France, Germany, Japan, Sweden, and the United Kingdom.

The evidence shows that the rise in wealth inequality during the 1980s observed for the United States was not general among industrialized countries (at least among those for which the requisite data are available). In contrast, the rise in *income* inequality seems to be more widespread. Second, the evidence suggests that in comparison with other advanced countries with comparable data, the United States by the 1980s ranked as the most unequal country in terms of wealth inequality. This same was true for income inequality. The situation was basically unchanged by 2000 and 2010.

Third, the relatively high U.S. wealth inequality today appears to be a marked turnaround from the early part of the twentieth century, when the country appeared considerably more equal in terms of wealth ownership than European countries such as Great Britain and Sweden. It also contrasts with the early 1970s when wealth inequality in the United States appeared to be comparable with levels in other industrialized countries. Fourth, the results also indicate that while the United States ranked highest in terms of mean wealth per adult around the year 2000 among countries for which comparable data are available, the country ranked relatively low in terms of *median* wealth per adult. By 2010, the United States had slipped to third place among eight countries in terms of mean wealth but last place in terms of median net worth.

Part II of the book considers some of the mechanisms behind changing wealth inequality. Chapter 5 "deconstructs" wealth trends over the period from 1922 to 2013. Two methods are used to analyze trends in wealth inequality. The first relies on decomposition analysis from 1983 to 2013. The change in wealth over a period can be decomposed into capital revaluation, savings, and net intergenerational transfers. The same decomposition can be used for different parts of the wealth distribution such as the top 1 percent and the middle three wealth quintiles.

Here, capital revaluation explains about 80 percent or more of the change in overall simulated mean net worth over the 1983–1989, 1989–2001, 2001–2007, 2007–2010, and 2010–2013 periods. This finding was true for all households, the top 1 percent, and the middle three wealth quintiles.

For changes in inequality, I look at changes in the ratio of net worth between the top 1 percent and the middle three wealth quintiles. Trends in this "P99/P2080" ratio were influenced mainly by differentials in rates of return and savings rates between the two groups, with the former generally lowering inequality and the latter raising it. Over years 1983 to 1989, savings rate differences explained over 100 percent of the rise in the P99/P2080 ratio. Over years 1989 to 2001, the higher rate of return of the middle group lowered the rise in the ratio by 45 percent, while the higher savings rate of the top group raised it by 137 percent. Over years 2001 to 2007, the higher rate of return of the middle group offset their lower savings rate.

Between 2007 and 2010 both factors contributed positively to the rise in the P99/P2080 ratio and each explained about half. From 2010 to 2013, the higher savings rate of the top group added positively to the rise in the P99/P2080 ratio while the higher returns on wealth of the middle group made a negative contribution.

The second method is regression analysis to analyze the factors that seem to play an important role in movements in household wealth inequality over time over the period from 1922 to 2013. The dependent variable is the share of wealth of the top 1 percent of wealth holders. Three explanatory variables appear to be particularly important. The first is the income share of the top 1 percent of income recipients, whose estimated coefficient is positive and significant at the 1 percent level. The second is the ratio of stock to home prices, whose estimated coefficient is also positive and significant at the 10 percent level. The third is the ratio of total debt to net worth, which has a negative coefficient significant at the 1 percent level.

Chapter 5 also confronts Piketty's "law," which states that wealth inequality rises if the rate of return on capital is greater than the rate of real output growth. Evidence for the United States in the years 1983 to 2013 finds no confirmation of this law. Instead, it is argued that wealth inequality generally rises if the rate of return on wealth is greater for the top 1 percent than for the middle class.

Another approach to understanding wealth inequality is based on the so-called life cycle model, in which it is argued that households accumulate wealth during working years in order to ensure adequate consumption during retirement years. This theory implies a rising level of wealth with age until retirement followed by a continuous decline. Chapter 6 provides an econometric analysis of the life cycle model and considers its implications for wealth accumulation. The chapter begins with a brief survey of the literature on the life cycle model.

Econometric analysis is then applied to the life cycle model using traditional concepts of household wealth. The results suggest that although the coefficients of such a model are statistically significant, the model itself explains only a very small fraction of the variation in household wealth (at most, on the order of 5 to 10 percent). When confined to the middle class, the model performs much better. The implication is that the life cycle model provides a useful explanation of wealth accumulation motives for the middle class. In particular, it suggests that this class acquires wealth for retirement, liquidity, and consumption purposes. The upper classes, however, are more likely to accumulate wealth for other reasons—perhaps power and prestige—and bequest models are more appropriate for explaining the distribution of wealth within this class.

Pension and Social Security wealth can be incorporated quite directly into the life cycle model of household wealth accumulation since they are forms of retirement wealth. The question arises as to how much their inclusion into the household wealth portfolio improves the explanatory power of the life cycle model. Cross-sectional regression analysis is then performed using alternative concepts of pension and Social Security wealth. Results tend to confirm the above conclusions. The performance of the model for the total population is not substantially improved, but for the middle class it accounts for substantial improvement in the degree of variation in total household wealth accounted.

Another important factor accounting for disparities in wealth among households is wealth transfers—collectively, inheritances and inter vivos gifts. Chapter 7 analyzes wealth transfers in relation to the distribution of wealth from 1989 to 2013. They come into play in two ways here. First, they influence time trends in median and mean household wealth. Second, they impact the household distribution of wealth and overall wealth inequality.

Chapter 7 begins with a review of some of the background literature. Direct survey evidence is available from the SCF on the receipt of inheritances and gifts, as well as the amount *given* in the form of gifts and donations. The survey evidence does show that bequests and gifts play a major role in wealth accumulation, as documented in the remainder of the chapter.

The results reported in Chapter 7 show that on average over the period from 1989 to 2013, about one-fifth of American households at a given point of time reported wealth transfers and these accounted for quite a sizable figure, about a quarter of their net worth. From 1989 to 2013, wealth transfers as a proportion of current net worth fell sharply, from 29 to 24 percent. There was little evidence of an inheritance "boom."

Wealth transfers tend to be equalizing in terms of the distribution of household wealth, though a number of caveats apply to this result. The rationale is that while it is true that the value of wealth transfers climbs sharply with both household income and wealth, wealth transfers as a *proportion* of wealth declines almost monotonically with both income and wealth level. As a result, net worth excluding wealth transfers is negatively correlated with wealth transfers themselves. Since the two are negatively correlated, adding wealth transfers to net worth actually reduces overall wealth inequality.

Chapter 7 also includes calculations of *net* wealth transfers—the difference between inheritances and gifts received and gifts and donations made to others. Net wealth transfers are important in understanding trends in median and mean wealth and are also used in the wealth simulations in Chapters 5 and 9.

Chapter 8 considers the roles of Social Security and private pensions in the household accumulation of wealth. It has now become standard to include both Social Security and private defined benefit (DB) pension wealth in the household balance sheet. This chapter addresses two main issues with regard to the wealth created by the retirement system. First: Are the time trends in mean and median wealth that are reported in Chapter 2 altered when these two additional components are included in the definition of household wealth to create augmented wealth? Second: Are time trends in wealth inequality the same for augmented wealth as for the standard wealth measure?

The three decades from 1983 to 2013 saw the gradual elimination of the traditional DB pension system, which is relatively equal, and the offsetting rise of DC pension coverage, which is relatively unequal. Social Security wealth, which is the most equal component of augmented wealth, was a stable presence throughout the period from 1983 to 2013.

The period from 1983 to 2007 saw robust growth in standard net worth, with the median value rising by 63 percent in real terms among households headed by middle-aged people (ages 47 to 64). The addition of DB pension wealth and Social Security wealth resulted in a smaller gain of 33 percent. From 2007 to 2013, on the other hand, median net worth plummeted by 52 percent for this age group but median augmented wealth was down by "only" 27 percent because of the relative increase in Social Security wealth over these years and its concentration in the middle of the wealth distribution.

It is perhaps no surprise that including Social Security wealth along with conventional wealth in the household balance sheet reduces the degree of measured wealth inequality. However, what is not well known is that defined benefit pension wealth is almost as unequally distributed as conventional household wealth. Its inclusion in the household portfolio thus has a much smaller equalizing effect.

Chapter 8 also shows that the equalizing effects of defined benefit pension wealth and Social Security wealth lessened between 1983 and 2007. Net worth inequality among people aged 47 to 64 years shows an increase of 0.033 Gini points from 1983 to 2007. In contrast, the Gini coefficient for augmented wealth climbed by 0.076 points. On the other hand, from 2007 to 2013, while the Gini coefficient for net worth rose by 0.043, that for augmented wealth went up by only 0.015 points. The explanation for this was the rising share of Social Security wealth in augmented wealth over the Great Recession period. Since Social Security wealth was much more equally distributed than net worth, its relative increase acted as a moderating influence on the increase in wealth inequality over these years.

Part III identifies the individuals who constitute the rich and poor classes in America. Chapter 9 portrays wealth differences among socioeconomic groups. It is well known that there are important differences in income among different demographic groups. This chapter documents similar differences in wealth holdings. This chapter analyzes basic trends and employs decomposition analysis to isolate the sources of differences in average wealth holdings between groups. The decomposition analysis is based on differences in capital revaluation, savings rates, and net wealth transfers between selected groups (see Chapter 5 for details). Another approach used in this chapter is to standardize the composition of households by their average share in the population in consecutive years to analyze trends in overall mean wealth and wealth inequality.

Chapter 9 also investigates wealth differences across income classes. Perhaps paramount among socioeconomic variables is income class. The chapter finds that mean net worth increases with income level. The ratio in mean net worth between the top 1 percent and middle-income quintile was 89 in 2013. The percentage gain in mean net worth between 1983 and 2013 also rose almost monotonically with income level, indicating a fanning out of wealth differences over this period. Another notable finding is that median net worth and financial resources fell in absolute terms for the bottom three income quintiles from 1983 to 2013. By 2013 the median figure for financial resources was close to zero for the bottom two income quintiles and only $11,000 for the middle quintile.

Next, the chapter considers age patterns in household wealth. The standard life cycle model predicts that wealth will rise with age until retirement age and then decline. Cross-sectional age-wealth profiles for various years verify this general pattern. It is especially striking that these profiles were not invariant over time. In particular, there was a steady shift in relative wealth holdings away from younger households and toward older Americans between 1983 and 2013. This section finds that the ratio of net worth between households under age 35 and all households fell from 0.21 in 1983 to 0.11 in 2010. In constant dollar terms, their mean net worth plunged by 46 percent from 2007 to 2010. The ratio of the net worth of age group 35 to 44 to overall net worth declined from 0.71 in 1983 to 0.42 in 2010. In constant dollar terms, their net worth was down by 39 percent from 2007 to 2010. Capital losses almost fully accounted for the downward trend in simulated mean net worth for these two age groups between 2007 and 2010.

In regard to racial and ethnic difference in household wealth, Chapter 9 finds that the wealth gap between black and white households was almost exactly the same in 2007 as in 1983. The ratio of mean wealth between the two groups from 2007 to 2010 declined from 0.19 to 0.14. Blacks were much more leveraged than whites, and this discrepancy led to a large spread in rates of return over the 2007–2010 period, which largely accounted for the relative loss. In contrast, the ratio of mean wealth between Hispanic and white households grew from 0.16 to 0.26 between 1983 and 2007. Hispanic net worth collapsed in half from 2007 to 2010 and the ratio of mean net worth with white households declined from 0.26 to 0.15. Hispanic households, like blacks, were heavily leveraged, and as a result, there was a wide differential in returns over years 2007 to 2010, which largely accounted for the relative collapse of Hispanic wealth.

Another division is by educational group. The data presented in this chapter indicate that the mean net worth of college graduates was ten times the wealth of households with fewer than four years of high school and six times the wealth of high school graduates in 2013. Between 1983 and 2013, the mean net worth of college graduates gained 52 percent, while it was down by 12 percent for those with fewer than four years of high school and by 7 percent for high school graduates. In 2013, the median figures for financial resources were almost zero for high school drop-outs and only $3,900 for high school graduates.

Another socioeconomic dimension is household type. Chapter 9 divides the population into three basic household types—married couples, single males, and single females—and further distinguishes for married couples and single females between those with children and those without. This section reports that in 2013, married couples as a group possessed the highest mean net worth and single females with children the lowest. The ratio of mean net worth between married couples and single mothers was almost 14 to 1. From 1983 to 2013 single mothers experienced a 22 percent decline in their mean net worth and a 93 percent decline in median net worth to only $500 in 2013. Median financial resources remained basically at zero over the whole time period for single mothers.

Chapter 10 investigates the demographic and workforce characteristics of the rich. Who are the rich? Do they tend to be elderly or middle-aged? What is their racial makeup? Are they all highly educated? Do they work for others or do they own their own businesses? What occupations and industries are they found in? Have these patterns changed over time? Has there been a shift from "rentier" wealth to entrepreneurial wealth? How do their demographics and workforce behavior compare to the general population? The empirical analysis covers selected years between 1983 and 2013.

Several questions are of particular interest. First, with the substantial increase of inequality over this period and especially with the record-high salaries recorded on Wall Street and among professional workers in general, has there been a shift in the composition of the rich away from the classic "coupon-clippers" toward entrepreneurs? Second, along with this trend, has there been a shift toward finance and professional services as the main sources of employment of the rich? Third, with the growth in Wall Street wealth, has there been a corresponding change in the composition of the rich toward younger workers and away from middle-aged and older groups? Fourth, with the large incomes recorded in the entertainment and sports industries, do we find an increasing proportion of African Americans in the ranks of the rich? Fifth, given the rising premium to education observed since the decade of the 1980s, has there been a notable shift in the composition of the rich toward college-educated workers?

Looking first at the period from 1983 to 1992, there were notable increases in the share of young families in the ranks of the very rich. Second, despite significant growth in the overall educational attainment of the population between 1983 and 1992, there was no corresponding increase in the educational attainment of the top wealth and income percentile. Third, the proportion of black households among the very rich actually fell during this period, while the proportion of Hispanics remained essentially unchanged. Fourth, there was evidence that entrepreneurial activity played a significant role in gaining entry to the ranks of the very rich, with self-employed workers as a fraction of total employment among the top wealth percentile almost doubling between 1983 and 1992, as did the corresponding share in the top income percentile, from 27 to 64 percent.

Updated results through 2013 indicate that some of these trends continued but others were reversed. First, the very rich became decidedly older between 1992 and 2013. Second, the very rich became better educated. Third, the rich continued to remain an almost exclusively white enclave. Fourth, the number of self-employed workers as a share of the total number of employed in the top wealth percentile continued to advance.

Chapter 11 focuses on the other end of the wealth spectrum and, in particular, on the persistence of asset poverty. As such, the chapter looks into the wealth holdings of the poor (yes, the poor do own wealth!). The chapter covers the years 1962 through 2013. The first part of the chapter reports that the wealth holdings of families below the poverty line relative to those above declined from 1962 to 2001 but recovered in 2013. Second, families below the poverty line were generally equally bad off in terms of net worth as in terms of income relative to families above the poverty line. Third, the addition of defined benefit pension wealth to the household portfolio had relatively little effect on the ratio of mean wealth between the poor and the non-poor population. Fourth, in contrast, the level of Social Security wealth in the household portfolio raised the ratio of average wealth between the two groups.

In the second part of the chapter, I define asset poverty as the unavailability of financial resources to provide for normal consumption over a period of three months. This section documents the remarkable persistence of asset poverty over the last three decades despite a sharp increase in median household net worth (at least until 2007), and the spike in asset poverty rates over the Great Recession.

Asset poverty rates for minorities are found to be over twice the rate for whites. They also fell monotonically with both age and education; were much higher for renters than homeowners; and among family types ranged from a low of about 5 percent for elderly couples to 50 to 65 percent for female single parents, depending on the year.

Results on asset poverty are discouraging in that very high rates of asset poverty for the U.S. population are revealed. In 2007, even before the onset of the Great Recession, one-fourth of American families had insufficient net worth to enable them to get by for three months at a poverty-line level of living, and over two-fifths had insufficient liquid assets to support poverty-level living for a three-month period. Rates of asset poverty were even higher for particular subgroups: 55 percent for minorities; 74 percent for families with heads aged less than 25 years; 48 percent for those with less than a high school degree; 70 percent for renters; and 65 percent for nonelderly female heads with children.

Part IV looks at long-term trends in household wealth. Chapter 12 first discusses methodological issues and then investigates developments in aggregate wealth and portfolio composition. The statistical analysis begins with a broad picture of twentieth-century trends, with regard to both aggregate household wealth and its composition. The purpose of this chapter is to provide a historical context for the developments in recent years. It documents the remarkable growth in mean family wealth, which averaged 1.26 percent per year in real terms from 1900 to 2013, slightly outpacing growth of disposable personal income. The fastest growth was from 1989 to 2007, averaging 2.76 percent per year, a rate over one and a half percentage points greater than disposable personal income growth.

There were also rather dramatic changes in the composition of household wealth over the 113 years studied. Unincorporated business equity fell considerably as a proportion of total household wealth, while deposits in financial institutions increased sharply. In addition, while the homeownership rate increased steadily over the twentieth century (at least until 2004), owner-occupied housing increased only moderately as a proportion of total assets. Corporate stock had the most volatile behavior in the household portfolio, reflecting price movements in the stock market. Debt as a proportion of total assets rose from 5 percent in 1910 to 18 percent in 2013. Finally, both pension reserves and Social Security wealth increased relative to marketable assets, from virtually zero in 1900 to 12 and 48 percent, respectively, in 1983, though both shares did decline after that point.

Chapter 13 then examines wealth inequality trends over the long term, piecing together from various sources the historical record on overall wealth concentration in the United States from 1922 to 2013. Data points from 1922 to 1983 are based on estate tax records. In addition, more detailed estimates are provided from microdata sources for the years 1962, 1969, 1983, 1989, 1992, 1995, 1998, 2001, 2004, 2007, 2010, and 2013. This chapter shows that after a somewhat erratic downward trend in wealth concentration between 1929 and the late 1970s, as measured here by the wealth share of the top 1 percent of households, wealth inequality rose very sharply through 1998, fell off from 1998 to 2001, and then rose gradually through 2013.

Part V provides an analysis of a possible wealth tax, as well as the overall conclusions to the book. Chapter 14 is a policy chapter, which examines the possibility of direct wealth taxation in the United States. Both the high level of wealth inequality in the United States and its increase in recent years provide some urgency to a consideration of potential policy remedies.

Personal wealth is currently taxed at the federal level in two ways: realized capital gains (as part of personal income taxes) and estate taxation. Should we also think about the direct taxation of household wealth? Almost a dozen European countries have or have had such a system in place, including Germany, the Netherlands, Sweden, and Switzerland. On equity grounds, the combination of income and the stock of wealth provides a better gauge of the ability to pay taxes than income alone. Moreover, there is no evidence from other advanced economies that the imposition of a modest direct tax on household wealth has had any deleterious effect on personal savings or overall economic growth.

The previous book *Top Heavy* proposed a very modest tax on wealth modeled after the Swiss wealth tax system (a $100,000 exemption with marginal tax rates running from 0.05 to 0.3 percent). In it, calculations for year 1989 showed that such a tax structure would yield an average tax rate on household wealth of 0.2 percent and would reduce the average yield on household wealth by only 6 percent. Even the top marginal tax rate of 0.30 percent would reduce the average yield by only 9 percent. These figures suggest that disincentive effects on personal savings would be very modest indeed. Such a tax could raise $50 billion in additional revenue and have a very small impact on the tax bills of 90 percent of American families.

This chapter provides updated estimates for 2013. Using the same "Swiss-style" tax structure adjusted for inflation (from the CPI-U), I estimate that $121 billion would be raised in 2013, about 4.4 percent of total federal tax receipts for that year. Moreover, the average tax rate on household wealth would still be 0.2 percent, and the new tax would reduce the average yield on household wealth by only 6.2 percent. Even the top marginal tax rate of 0.3 percent would reduce the average yield by only 9.7 percent. These results suggest that disincentive effects, if any, on personal savings would be very modest.

Chapter 15 ties together the major findings and themes of the preceding chapters.

Three appendices are also provided at the end of the book. Appendix 1 describes the statistical adjustments and imputations made to the 1962 SFCC, and the 1983, 1989, 1992, and 1995 SCF. Appendix 2 details the construction of the 1969 MESP file. Appendix 3 provides methodological details on the construction of estimates for both Social Security wealth and defined benefit pension wealth.

Recent Trends in Income, Poverty, Earnings, Income Inequality, and the Wage Share

The early years of the twenty-first century have witnessed a struggling middle class despite relatively robust growth in the overall American economy. During the first six years of the George W. Bush administration, from 2001 to 2007, gross domestic product (GDP) in real dollars expanded by 16.4 percent despite a brief recession in 2001 and labor productivity (real GDP divided by full-time equivalent employees) grew at an annual pace of 2.2 percent. Both figures were close to their post–World War II highs for similar periods.

Then the Great Recession hit. The Great Recession began in December 2007 and "officially" ended in June 2009.[2] Over this period, real GDP fell by 4.3 percent and then from the second quarter of 2009 to the second quarter of 2013 it gained 9.2 percent. After that it grew by another 6.8 percent through the third quarter of 2016.[3] The unemployment rate shot up from 4.4 percent in May 2007 to a peak of 10 percent in October 2009; but by October 2016 it was down to 4.9 percent.[4]

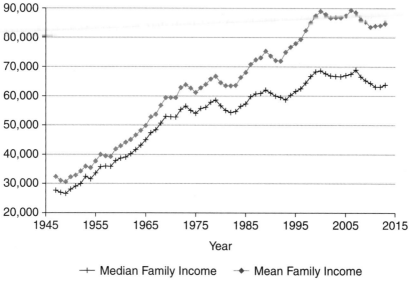

Figure 1.1. Median and Mean Family Income, 1947–2013
(2013 dollars, CPI-U-RS adjusted)

What happened to living standards since 2007? What happened to poverty? What happened to wages? What happened to inequality? What happened to the wage and profit share? Is there a connection between inequality and the profit share? These are the primary themes of the second section of this chapter. But first, I will put recent events in the context of historical data for the United States going back to the end of World War II (the so-called postwar period).

Income and Earnings Stagnate while Poverty Remains Unchanged

Despite the booming economy, the most common metric used to assess living standards, *real median family income* (the income of the average family, found in the middle of the distribution when families are ranked from lowest to highest in terms of income, deflated by the Consumer Price Index), actually *rose by a paltry 1.9 percent* from 2001 to 2007.[5] From 1973 to 2001, it gained 20 percent, so that from 1973 to 2007 its total percentage gain amounted to 22 percent. In contrast, between 1947 and 1973, median family income more than doubled (see Figure 1.1).

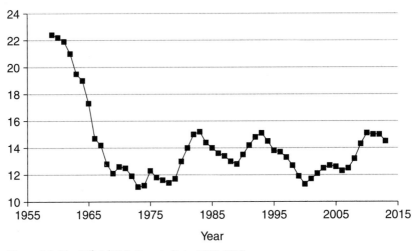

Figure 1.2. The Official U.S. Poverty Rate, 1959–2013
(Percentage)

Then the Great Recession hit. From 2007 to 2013, real median family income *fell by 7.4 percent,* despite the recovery officially beginning in June 2009. In fact, from 2000 to 2013, it was down by 7 percent. Median income in 2013 was back where it was in 1997!

The story is a bit different for *mean* family income. It likewise doubled between 1947 and 1973, but then increased by 38 percent from 1973 to 2001. It then rose by a mere 0.7 percent from 2001 to 2007, for a total gain of 39 percent from 1973 to 2007. This is less than the increase over the preceding quarter century but greater than the rise in median family income. The disparity between the two series means that while mean and median income rose at about the same pace before 1973, mean income grew at a much faster rate than median income after 1973. The discrepancy reflects rising inequality since the early 1970s. Real mean family income also fell during the Great Recession. It declined by 4.4 percent from 2007 to 2013, less than the median.

Another troubling problem is poverty. Between 1959 and 1973, there was great success in reducing poverty in America, with the overall poverty rate declining by more than half from 22.4 to 11.1 percent (see Figure 1.2). After that, the poverty rate has stubbornly refused to go any lower. It has generally followed the business cycle. After 1973, it generally trended upward, climbing to 15.1 percent in 1993, then fell back to 11.3 percent in 2000, only slightly

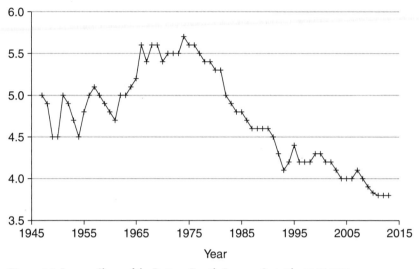

Figure 1.3. Income Share of the Bottom Family Income Quintile, 1947–2013 (Percentage)

above its nadir, and then rose to 12.5 percent in 2007. During the Great Recession, poverty once again rose, reaching 15 percent in 2012 and then falling to 14.5 percent in 2013.

Another indicator of the well-being of lower income families is the share of total income received by the bottom quintile (20 percent) of families (see Figure 1.3). At first, the share declined, from 5 percent in 1947 to 4.7 percent in 1961, but then it rose rather steadily over time, reaching 5.7 percent in 1974. It then fell off sharply, to 4.1 percent in 2007. Over the Great Recession it continued to fall, reaching 3.8 percent in 2013.

A related statistic is the mean income of the poorest 20 percent of families (in constant dollars), which shows the absolute level of income (whereas the share of income shows the *relative* level of income). Their average income more than doubled between 1947 and 1974 but then gained almost nothing more by 2007. The difference in post-1974 trends between this series and the share of income of the bottom quintile, which fell sharply, is that mean income was rising in the general population after 1974. Then from 2007 to 2013 the mean income of the bottom quintile fell by an astounding 10.8 percent, to $16,100 in 2013 dollars. This was back at the level it was in 1984!

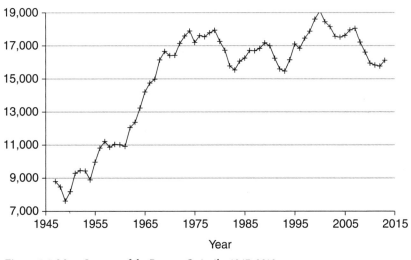

Figure 1.4. Mean Income of the Bottom Quintile, 1947–2013
(2013 dollars, CPI-U-RS adjusted)

The main reason for stagnating family incomes and recalcitrant poverty is the failure of wages to rise significantly. From 2001 to 2007, real hourly wages gained a measly 2.6 percent, based on the Bureau of Labor Statistics (BLS) hourly wage series.[6] This is the series most relevant to middle-class wages. Indeed, between 1973 and 2000, real hourly wages *fell by 6.8 percent,* so that between 1973 and 2007 real wages were down by 4.4 percent (see Figure 1.5). This contrasts with the preceding years, 1947 to 1973, when real wages grew by 75 percent. Indeed, in 2007, the hourly wage was $19.59 per hour (in 2013 dollars), about the same level as in 1971 (in real terms).

Somewhat surprisingly, real wages actually rose over the Great Recession. From 2007 to 2013, they were up by 2.1 percent. This time trend likely reflects the fact that the workers who were laid off over these years were lower paid and less skilled.

Two other measures of worker pay are shown in Figure 1.5.[7] The results also show a marked slowdown after 1973. Average wages and salaries per full-time equivalent employee (FTEE) grew by 2.3 percent per year from 1947 to 1973 and then by only 0.4 percent per year from 1973 through 2007. Average employee compensation (including fringe benefits) per FTEE increased by 2.6 percent per year during the first of these two periods and then

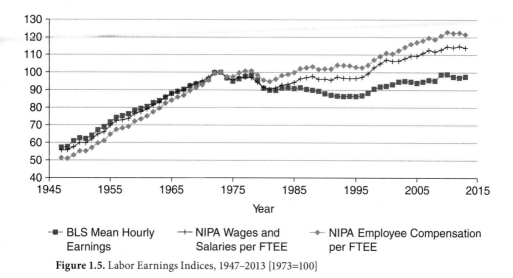

Figure 1.5. Labor Earnings Indices, 1947–2013 [1973=100]

by 0.5 percent per year in the second. From 2007 to 2013, the former rose at an annual rate of 0.2 percent and the latter at 0.3 percent per year.

Despite falling real wages, living standards were maintained by the growing labor force participation of wives, which increased from 41 percent in 1970 to 57 percent in 1988.[8] Married women entered the labor force more slowly starting in 1989, and by 2007 their labor force participation rate increased to only 61 percent. This trend was accompanied by a slowdown in the growth of real living standards. From 2007 to 2011, the participation rate of married women actually fell to 60.2 percent.[9]

Income Inequality Rises Sharply

The United States has also seen rising inequality during the early twenty-first century, as reflected, first, by the Gini index for family income (see Figure 1.6). The Gini index is the most widely used measure of inequality and ranges from a value of zero to one hundred, with a low value indicating less inequality and a high value indicating more. Between 1947 and 1968, the Gini index generally trended downward, reaching its lowest value in 1968, at 34.8. Since then, it experienced an upward ascent, gradual at first and then more steep in the 1980s and 1990s, reaching a value of 43.2 in 2007.[10] What

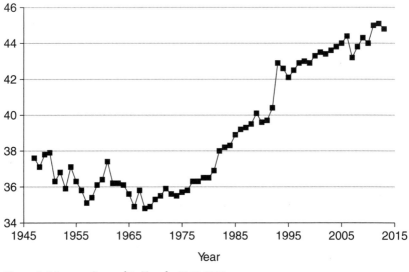

Figure 1.6. Income Inequality Trends, 1947–2013
(Gini index, family income)

happened during the Great Recession? Inequality continued to rise, according to the CPS figures, to a Gini of 44.8 in 2013. Though property income fell over this period, the middle and lower classes were hit even harder by unemployment and a reduction in hours worked.

A second index, the share of total income received by the top 5 percent of families, has a similar time trend (see Figure 1.7). It declined gradually, from 17.5 percent in 1947 to 14.8 percent in 1974, and then rose after this point, especially in the 1990s, reaching 20.1 percent in 2007. It then increased even further to 21.2 percent in 2013, close to its highest value over the postwar period. Moreover, according to data available in the World Top Incomes Database, based on IRS tax returns, the top 10 percent of income recipients took in almost half (49 percent) of the country's total income in 2013, close to the highest level recorded since the government began collecting the relevant data a century ago, when the federal government instituted an income tax. The income share of the top 1 percent in 2012 returned to the same level as before the Great Recession (and even the Great Depression)— 18.9 percent, up from 18.3 percent in 2007, though it did fall to 17.5 percent in 2013.[11]

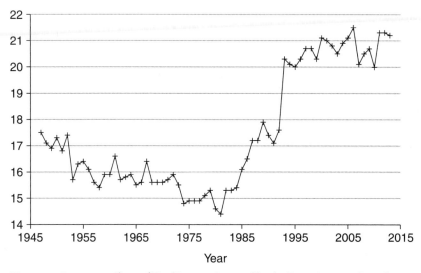

Figure 1.7. Percentage Share of Total Income Received by the Top 5 Percent of Families, 1947–2013

What Has Happened to Tax Rates?

Trends in marginal tax rates of the federal personal income tax also affect the well-being of families as well as inequality (see Figure 1.8).[12] The first series is the top marginal tax rate (the marginal tax rate faced by the richest tax filers). In 1944, the top marginal tax rate was 94 percent! After the end of World War II, the top rate was reduced to 86.5 percent (in 1946), but during the Korean War it was back to 92 percent (in 1953). Even in 1960, it was still at 91 percent. This generally declined over time, as Congress implemented tax legislation. It was first lowered to 70 percent in 1966, then raised to 77 percent in 1969 to finance the war in Vietnam, then lowered again to 70 percent in 1975, then to 50 percent in 1983 (Reagan's first major tax act), and then again to 28 percent in 1987 (through the Tax Reform Act of 1986). After that, it trended upward to 31 percent in 1991 (under the first President Bush) and then to 39.6 percent in 1993 (under President Clinton) but by 2007 it was back down to 35 percent (under President George W. Bush), where it remained until 2013, when Preside Obama raised it back to 39.6 percent.[13]

The other two series show the marginal tax rates at $67,000 and $33,000, both in 1995 dollars. The time patterns are quite different for these than the

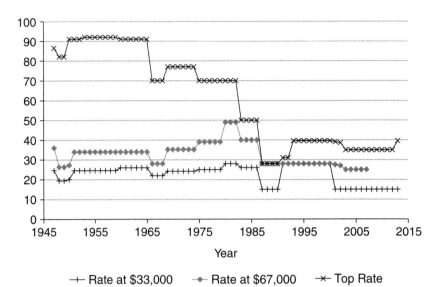

Figure 1.8. Marginal Tax Rates, Selected Income Levels in 1995 Dollars, 1947–2013 (Percentage)

first. The marginal tax rate at $67,000 (about the sixtieth percentile) was relatively low in 1946, at 36 percent, and generally trended upward, reaching 49 percent in 1980, before declining to 28 percent in 1986, where it remained until 2000 before falling to 25 percent in 2007 (and 2013). The marginal tax rate at $33,000 (about the thirtieth percentile) was also relatively low in 1946, at 25 percent, but it actually increased somewhat over time, reaching 28 percent in 1991 where it remained through 2000 before dropping to 15 percent from 2001 onward.

All in all, tax cuts over the postwar period have generally been more generous for the rich, particularly the super-rich. Since 1946, the top marginal tax rate has fallen by a huge 47 percentage points (or by 54 percent), the marginal rate at $67,000 by 11 percentage points (or by 31 percent), and the rate at $33,000 by 10 percentage points (or by 39 percent).

Rising Profit Is the Key

Where did the increased output go over the last thirty years or so? Another anomaly that arose regarding the relation between productivity and earn-

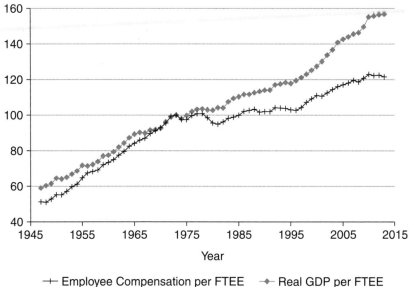

Figure 1.9. Real Labor Earnings and Labor Productivity, 1947–2013
(Index, 1973 = 100)

ings helps to explain. In particular, the historical connection between labor productivity growth and real wage growth also broke down after 1973.[14]

From 1947 to 1973, average real worker compensation (a broader concept than wages, including social insurance and fringe benefits) grew almost in tandem with overall labor productivity growth (see Figure 1.9).[15] While the latter averaged 2.4 percent per year, the former ran at 2.6 percent per year. Labor productivity growth plummeted after 1973. The period from 1973 to 1979, in particular, witnessed the slowest growth in labor productivity during the postwar period, 0.5 percent per year (the so-called productivity slowdown), and the growth in real employee compensation per worker actually turned negative during this period. From 1979 to 2001, the U.S. economy experienced a modest revival in labor productivity growth, which averaged 1.1 percent per year, while the growth in real employee compensation per worker (full-time equivalent employee) recovered to only 0.5 percent per year. From 2001 to 2007, labor productivity growth surged upward to 2.2 percent per year but the latter still rose less, at 1.6 percent per year.

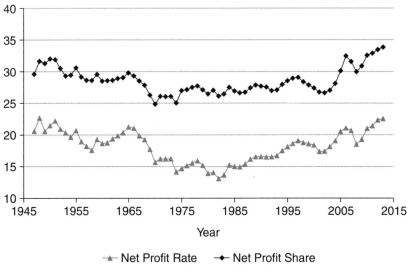

Figure 1.10. Net Profit Rate and Net Profit Share, 1947–2013 (Percentage)

Then the Great Recession hit. From 2007 to 2010, real GDP fell by 3.2 percent (in total, not per year) and surprisingly, employment fell even more, so that labor productivity actually advanced by 6.6 percent. Indeed, from 2007 to 2013, labor productivity grew by 7.7 percent or at an annual rate of 1.2 percent, close to its historical average. In contrast, average employee compensation gained only 1.7 percent (in total), so that the gap between productivity and employee compensation widened even further.

If productivity rose faster than earnings after 1973, where did the excess go? The answer is increased profitability. The basic data are from the U.S. Bureau of Economic Analysis (BEA) National Income and Product Accounts. For the definition of net profits, I use the BEA's definition of total net property-type income, including corporate profits, interest, rent, and half of proprietors' income. (The definition excludes the Capital Consumption Allowance, or CCA).[16] The net rate of profit is defined as the ratio of total net property income to total private net fixed capital. The net profit rate declined by 7.5 percentage points between 1947 and its nadir of 13.1 percent in 1982 (see Figure 1.10). It then climbed by 6 percentage points from 1982 to 1997 but fell off by 1.7 percentage points between 1997 and 2001. It surged upward after 2001, reaching 20.7 percent in 2007. Then, over the Great Recession, the

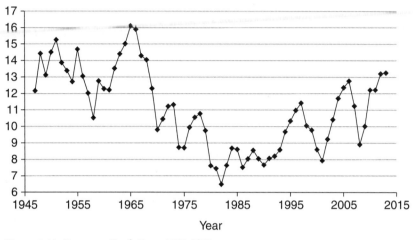

Figure 1.11. Corporate Profit Rate, 1947–2013
(Percentage)

profit rate surged even more, attaining a figure of 22.5 percent in 2013, close to its postwar peak.

Figure 1.10 also shows trends in the net profit share in national income, which is defined as the ratio of total net property income to net national income. The net profit share fell by 4.8 percentage points between 1947 and its low point of 24.8 percent in 1970. It then generally drifted upward, rising by 1.9 percentage points between 1970 and 2001. During the George W. Bush years, from 2001 to 2007, the profit share jumped up by another 4.9 percentage points to reach 31.6 percent in 2007. Finally, over the Great Recession, the profit share jumped by another 1.5 percentage points to attain 33.8 percent, its highest point over the postwar period. The results clearly show that the stagnation of labor earnings in the United States since the early 1970s translated into rising profits in the economy.

Trends are very similar for corporate profits. The corporate profit rate (the ratio of corporate profits to the capital stock owned by the corporate sector) declined from 10.9 percent in 1947 to 6.5 percent in 1982 (its low point) and then bounced back to 11.1 percent in 2007 (see Figure 1.11). After falling sharply to 8.9 percent in 2008, it then rebounded to 13.3 percent in 2013, though still below its peak of 16.1 percent in 1965. Corporate profits as a share of national income fell from 11.1 percent in 1947 to 9.2 percent in 1970 and then rose to 12.4 percent in 2007 (see Figure 1.12). After nosediving to

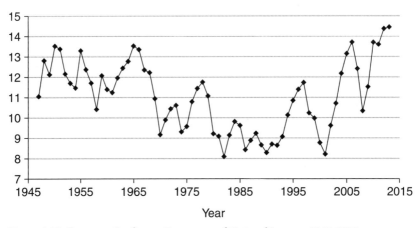

Figure 1.12. Corporate Profits as a Percentage of National Income, 1947–2013

10.3 percent in 2008, it jumped back to 14.5 percent in 2013, its high for the postwar period.

What is the connection between inequality and profitability? The relationship can be analyzed in two ways. First, one can compute simple correlation coefficients between the two. As measures of inequality, one can use (1) the Gini coefficient for family income; (2) the share of the top 5 percent as derived from the CPS data; and the shares of (3) the top 1 percent, (4) the top 0.1 percent, and (5) the top 0.01 percent from the World Top Incomes Database.[17] (I also include the U.S. poverty rate.) As measures of profitability, one can use (1) the overall profit share, (2) the overall profit rate, (3) the corporate profit rate, and (4) the corporate profit share.

Income inequality generally climbed upward from the early 1980s to 2013, as did profitability, though both declined during the late 1990s (see Figure 1.13). Moreover, both, after dipping between 2007 and 2008, generally soared to new heights by 2013. The simple correlation coefficient between the Gini index for family income and the net profit rate over the 1947–2013 period is 0.24, significant at the 10 percent level; and between the Gini index and the net profit share it is 0.36, significant at the 1 percent level (see Table 1.1). These relationships do not necessarily indicate causation since the two variables are not defined independently, though a rise in the profit share could, ceteris paribus, lead to an increase in the Gini coefficient for income. This is also true for the other correlations discussed in this section.

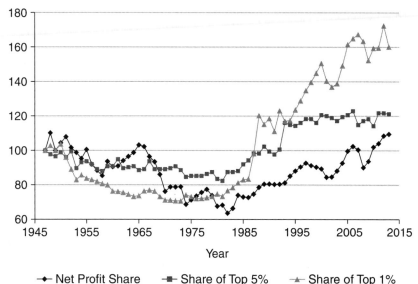

Figure 1.13. Net Profit Share and Top Income Shares, 1947–2013
(Index, 1947 = 100)

The correlation of the Gini index with the corporate profit rate, however, is negative (and significant at the 5 percent level) and that with the corporate profit share is effectively zero.

Correlations with the income share of the top 5 percent are higher: 0.44 and 0.44 with the net profit rate and the net profit share, respectively. Both correlations are significant at the 1 percent level. Its correlations with the corporate profit rate and share, on the other hand, are very low or negative and not significantly different than zero. Similar patterns exist between these three measures of profitability and the share of the top 1 percent, the share of the top 0.1 percent, and that of the top 0.01 percent. The poverty rate is positively correlated with the four profitability measures and these correlation coefficients are all statistically significant.[18]

As shown in Figure 1.13, which juxtaposes the net profit share and the income share of the top 5 percent, both indexed at 100 in 1947, the time trends track very closely after 1993. The two were reasonably close from 1947 to 1956 and again from about 1963 to 1970. The periods when the two differed were from 1957 to 1962 and then again from 1971 to 1992. There also appears to be a break point in the two series around 1980 when they

Table 1.1. Simple correlations between income inequality and profitability

	Period			
	1947–2013		1979–2013	
A. Family Income Gini Index				
1. Overall net profit rate	0.240	#	0.904	**
2. Overall net profit share	0.356	**	0.684	**
3. Corporate profit rate	−0.254	*	0.746	**
4. Corporate profits as a share of national income	0.032		0.646	**
B. Share of Top 5%—CPS				
1. Overall net profit rate	0.435	**	0.872	**
2. Overall net profit share	0.436	**	0.598	**
3. Corporate profit rate	0.032		0.715	**
4. Corporate profits as a share of national income	0.171		0.583	**
C. Share of Top 1%—WTID				
1. Overall net profit rate	0.417	**	0.935	**
2. Overall net profit share	0.504	**	0.747	**
3. Corporate profit rate	−0.093		0.751	**
4. Corporate profits as a share of national income	0.179		0.668	**
D. Share of Top 0.1%—WTID				
1. Overall net profit rate	0.360	**	0.927	**
2. Overall net profit share	0.460	**	0.747	**
3. Corporate profit rate	−0.144		0.743	**
4. Corporate profits as a share of national income	0.138		0.666	**
E. Share of Top 0.01%—WTID				
1. Overall net profit rate	0.333	**	0.930	**
2. Overall net profit share	0.445	**	0.780	**
3. Corporate profit rate	−0.159		0.754	**
4. Corporate profits as a share of national income	0.139		0.696	**
F. Overall Poverty Rate[a]				
1. Overall net profit rate	0.324	*	−0.057	
2. Overall net profit share	0.277	*	0.217	
3. Corporate profit rate	0.418	**	0.000	
4. Corporate profits as a share of national income	0.290	*	0.114	

Abbreviations. CPS, Current Population Survey; WTID, The World Top Incomes Database
a. Series begins in 1959.
Significant at the 10% level. * Significant at the 5% level. ** Significant at the 1% level.

start to trend upward. Results are roughly similar between the net profit share and the income share of the top 5 percent. As a result, Table 1.1 also shows correlation coefficients for the 1979–2013 period (the correlation coefficient attains its maximum value in 1979).

The correlation coefficients between the four profitability measures and the inequality measures are all now stronger in the 1979–2013 period than in the 1947–2013 period and all are significant at the 1 percent level. The correlations reach as high as 0.94. On the other hand, correlations between profitability and the poverty rate are all small (negative in one case) and not statistically significant.

Several interesting patterns emerge. First, the inequality measures are more strongly correlated with the overall profit rate than the overall profit share. Likewise, they have a higher correlation with the corporate profit rate than the corporate profit share. These findings make sense since CEO compensation and compensation of other top executives are generally tied to the profit rate of a company (that is, its return on equity), not to its profit share. Moreover, stock market movements are more strongly related to trends in the profit rate than in the profit share. As a result, the compensation of all professions that are tied to the stock market should be affected by changes in the profit rate more than by changes in the profit share. Second, the corporate profit rate generally has a weaker correlation with the inequality measures than the overall net profit rate and the corporate profit share, and a smaller correlation with the inequality indices than the overall net profit share. These results probably reflect the fact that the corporate sector represents only a relatively small part of the overall economy.

Third, the correlations of the top income shares (the income shares of the top 1, 0.1, and 0.01 percent) with profitability measures are stronger than those involving either the overall Gini coefficient or the share of the top 5 percent and profitability. This pattern is also reasonable because the compensation of the very top income earners is more closely tied to the stock market, and hence movements in profitability, than the lower portions of the earnings distribution.

The second method of relating inequality to profitability is an autoregressive AR(1) regression of the inequality measure on each of the four measures of profitability. Results, shown in Table 1.2, paint a different picture than simple correlation coefficients. Over the full 1947–2013 period, the coefficient

Table 1.2. Time-series regressions of income inequality on profitability, 1947–2013

Independent Variables	Dependent Variable					
	Gini Coeff.	Share Top 5%	Share Top 1%	Share Top 0.1%	Share Top 0.01%	Poverty Rate
A. Net Profit Rate	−0.0837	0.0545	0.2045*	0.1222*	0.0548*	−0.1473
	(0.95)	(0.67)	(2.42)	(2.25)	(2.15)	(1.19)
R^2	0.96	0.93	0.9700	0.96	0.96	0.93
Standard error	0.424	0.390	0.403	0.166	0.035	0.560
Durbin-Watson	1.82	2.31	1.71	1.79	1.80	1.92
Log likelihood	−61.55	−66.34	−64.78	−35.06	14.23	−63.23
Sample size	67	67	67	67	67	55
B. Net Profit Share	0.0192	0.0860	0.1960*	0.1072#	0.0436	0.0056
	(0.20)	(0.97)	(2.06)	(1.83)	(1.55)	(0.05)
R^2	0.96	0.93	0.97	0.96	0.96	0.93
Standard error	0.431	0.387	0.410	0.171	0.390	0.596
Log likelihood	−67.04	−63.06	−65.36	−35.92	13.19	−63.98
Durbin-Watson	1.90	2.28	1.78	1.86	1.87	1.76
Sample size	67	67	67	67	67	55
C. Corp. Profit Rate	−0.0716	0.0227	0.0950	0.0553	0.0244	−0.1022
	(1.02)	(0.34)	(1.38)	(1.25)	(1.16)	(1.06)
R^2	0.96	0.93	0.97	0.96	0.96	0.93
Standard error	0.423	0.392	0.428	0.175	0.040	0.582
Durbin-Watson	1.82	2.28	1.64	1.74	1.78	1.63
Log likelihood	−66.49	−63.51	−66.86	−36.91	12.60	−63.39
Sample size	67	67	67	67	67	55
D. Corp. Profit Share	−0.0553	0.0329	0.1288	0.0723	0.0290	−0.0755
	(0.66)	(0.41)	(1.55)	(1.36)	(1.14)	(0.67)
R^2	0.96	0.93	0.97	0.96	0.96	0.93
Standard error	0.427	0.392	0.425	0.175	0.040	0.597
Durbin-Watson	1.84	2.28	1.66	1.76	1.81	1.67
Log likelihood	−66.83	−63.48	−66.58	−36.75	12.58	−63.75
Sample size	67	67	67	67	67	55

Note: The dependent variable is a measure of family income inequality or poverty. The absolute value of the t-statistic is in parentheses below the coefficient. The constant term is not shown.

The results show Maximum Likelihood Estimates for AR(1), where AR(1): Autoregressive process, First-order: $u_t = e_t + r_1 u_{t-1}$, where u_t is the error term of the original equation and e_t is a stochastic term assumed to be identically and independently distributed.

Significant at the 10% level. * Significant at the 5% level. ** Significant at the 1% level.

of the net profit rate is positive and statistically significant (at the 5 percent level) only for the income shares of the top 1 percent, the top 0.1 percent, and the top 0.01 percent. The coefficient of the net profit rate is not significant for the Gini coefficient, the share of the top 5 percent, and the poverty rate. The coefficient of the net profit share is positive and significant only for the share of the top 1 percent (at the 5 percent level) and the share of the top 0.1 percent (at the 10 percent level). On the other hand, there are no significant coefficients for the corporate profit rate or the corporate share.[19]

Table 1.3 shows similar results covering the period from 1979 to 2013. The coefficient of the net profit rate is positive and statistically significant (at the 5 or 1 percent level) only for the income shares of the top 1 percent, the top 0.1 percent, and the top 0.01 percent. The coefficient estimates are two to three times greater than the corresponding estimates for the full 1947 to 2013 period, and the t-ratios are also higher. The coefficient of the net profit share is significant only for the share of the top 1 percent (at the 10 percent level). Coefficients of the corporate profit rate and the corporate profit share are not significant in any case.

Concluding Comments

The last forty years or so have seen slow-growing earnings and income for the middle class, as well as a stagnating poverty rate and rising inequality. In contrast, the early postwar period witnessed rapid gains in wages and family income for the middle class, in addition to a sharp decline in poverty and a moderate fall in inequality. The "booming" 1990s and early 2000s did not bring much relief to the middle class, with median family income growing by only 3 percent *(in total)* between 1989 and 2013. Personal tax rates generally fell over time but by much more for the rich than the middle class. In sum, the middle class has been squeezed in terms of earnings and income since the early 1970s.

The stagnation of living standards among the middle class over these years is attributable to the slow growth in labor earnings. While the average level of earnings (employee compensation per FTEE) almost doubled between 1947 and 1973, it advanced by only 22 percent from 1973 to 2013. There was no growth in real hourly wages according to the BLS data.

Table 1.3. Time-series regressions of income inequality on profitability, 1979–2013

Independent Variables	Dependent Variable					
	Gini Coeff.	Share Top 5%	Share Top 1%	Share Top 0.1%	Share Top 0.01%	Poverty Rate
A. Net Profit Rate	0.0203	0.1021	0.4807*	0.3292**	0.1609**	−0.1315
	(0.14)	(0.62)	(2.67)	(2.80)	(2.81)	(0.94)
R^2	0.94	0.91	0.95	0.93	0.93	0.74
Standard error	0.439	0.531	0.664	0.285	0.067	0.349
Durbin-Watson	1.37	1.66	1.78	1.88	1.94	1.55
Log likelihood	−35.44	−38.21	−42.20	−27.12	−1.67	−30.55
Sample size	35	35	35	35	35	35
B. Net Profit Share	0.0412	0.0793	0.3040#	0.1921	0.0892	−0.0412
	(0.31)	(0.55)	(1.77)	(1.61)	(1.53)	(0.34)
R^2	0.94	0.91	0.94	0.92	0.92	0.73
Standard error	0.438	0.531	0.740	0.321	0.076	0.036
Durbin-Watson	1.37	1.56	1.61	1.73	1.81	1.45
Log likelihood	−35.40	−38.27	−44.25	−29.43	−4.12	−31.06
Sample size	35	35	35	35	35	35
C. Corp. Profit Rate	0.0120	0.0369	0.1944	0.1252	0.0616	−0.0320
	(0.10)	(0.29)	(1.33)	(1.31)	(1.32)	(0.29)
R^2	0.94	0.91	0.94	0.92	0.92	0.74
Standard error	0.439	0.532	0.761	0.328	0.077	0.363
Durbin-Watson	1.36	1.55	1.50	−1.60	1.68	1.49
Log likelihood	−35.45	−38.37	−44.88	−29.96	−4.49	−31.06
Sample size	35	35	35	35	35	35
D. Corp. Profit Share	0.0021	0.0256	0.1646	0.1048	0.0528	−0.0047
	(0.02)	(0.20)	(1.07)	(1.04)	(1.08)	(0.04)
R^2	0.94	0.10	0.94	0.92	0.92	0.73
Standard error	0.439	0.533	0.775	0.334	0.078	0.364
Durbin-Watson	1.35	1.53	1.48	1.59	1.67	1.52
Log likelihood	−35.45	−38.40	−45.20	−30.27	−4.79	−31.11
Sample size	35	35	35	35	35	35

Note: The dependent variable is a measure of family income inequality or poverty. The absolute value of the t-statistic is in parentheses below the coefficient. The constant term is not shown.

The results show Maximum Likelihood Estimates for AR(1), where AR(1): Autoregressive process, First-order: $u_t = e_t + r_1 u_{t-1}$, where u_t is the error term of the original equation and e_t is a stochastic term assumed to be identically and independently distributed.

\# Significant at the 10% level. * Significant at the 5% level. ** Significant at the 1% level.

Though the Great Recession technically ended in June 2009, the doldrums continued in terms of personal income, particularly for the middle class. Median household income in 2013 was still well below its peak in 2007 (7.4 percent below). In fact, in 2013 its level was back where it was in 1997. It was not until calendar year 2015 that median household income showed any significant growth (5.2 percent in real terms from 2014 to 2015 according to the U.S. Census Bureau).

The main reason for the stagnation of labor earnings derives from a clear shift in national income away from labor and toward capital, particularly since the late 1970s. Many studies have documented rising income inequality in the United States and a rising profit share.[20] This chapter shows that there was a clear connection between the two trends. Over this period, both overall and corporate profitability rose substantially, almost back to postwar highs. The stock market was, in part, fueled by rising profitability. While the capitalist class gained from rising profits, workers experienced almost no progress in terms of wages. On the surface, at least, there appears to be a trade-off between the advances in income made by the rich and the stagnation of income among the working class.

Strong correlations are evident between inequality and profitability, particularly since 1979. Regression analysis shows that only the top income shares (those of the top one percent, the top 0.1 percent, and the top 0.01 percent) are positively and significantly related to profitability. Overall family income inequality, as measured by the Gini coefficient, the income share of the top 5 percent, and the poverty rate are not. Moreover, the net profit rate has a stronger and statistically more significant relationship with the top income shares than does the net profit share or the corporate profit rate or share.

The rationales for these results are, first, that CEO compensation and the compensation of other top executives are generally tied to a company's profit rate (that is, its return on equity) rather than to its profit share. Moreover, the stock market is likely to be related to trends in the profit rate rather than the profit share. As a result, the compensation of all professions that are tied to the stock market is likely to be more connected to changes in the profit rate than changes in the profit share. Second, the corporate sector represents only a relatively small part of the overall economy and so is not significantly related to overall inequality trends. Third, the correlations of the top income shares with profitability are stronger than those between either the overall Gini coefficient or the share of the top 5 percent with profitability because the compensation of the very top income earners is more closely tied to the stock market and hence movements in profitability than the lower portions of the earnings distribution.

The top income shares also have a stronger connection with the net profit rate over the 1979–2013 period than over the whole 1947–2013 period. Both the coefficient estimates and the t-ratios are larger for the former than for the latter. After 1978, the trend in both inequality and profitability was generally upward, whereas before, the trend was generally downward.

The sharp break in both the inequality series and profitability can be traced in part to the ending of the social contract between labor and owners of capital that prevailed from the end of World War II to about 1973 (the so-called Treaty of Detroit). During the "Golden Age" of American capitalism, from 1947 to 1973 or so, unions were strong, there was an implicit social contract between capital, and labor and productivity gains were about equally shared between the two. As a result, real wages increased substantially. The mid and late 1970s saw a "profit squeeze." These years also saw the birth of neoliberalism and a switch in corporate philosophy from stakeholder value, whereby the interests of shareholders, workers, and clients were balanced to shareholder value, so that maximizing stock prices became the aim of the firm. This period saw the beginning of wage stagnation and the middle-class squeeze. Since 1980 or so, wages have generally risen with inflation but not in real terms.

There are two variants of this argument. According to the first variant, owners of capital became less generous toward (or less solicitous of) labor. Whereas previously at least large corporations entered into a kind of social contract with their workers—one that involved rent sharing and considerable job security—capital unilaterally broke that contract and demanded more of the rents for itself. Labor thus faced a choice between lower wages and fewer jobs, with the latter being used as a threat to achieve the former. The second, and related, variant of the hypothesis envisions a change in the nature of shareholding away from more patient, relationship-oriented stockholders (such as insiders) and toward more impatient, return-oriented stockholders (such as fund managers who must show quarterly results). This second variant can possibly explain the first: More activist shareholders may have demanded that management focus on creating shareholder value to the detriment of labor and other stakeholders.

Lazonick has provided background on the change in norms. His work documents the shift in the basic U.S. corporate business model from about 1980 to the present, from an emphasis on stakeholder value to one on shareholder value.[21] Lazonick called this the New Economy Business Model (NEBM), and noted its radical alteration of the terms on which workers were employed in the United States. The rise of the NEBM was also connected to the widespread adoption and diffusion of information and communications technology. Compared to the NEBM, the Old Economy Business Model (OEBM) that dominated the U.S. corporate economy from the end of World War II and into the 1980s offered employment that was much more stable and earnings that were much more equitable. In the OEBM, employees (mainly men) typically secured well-paying jobs right after college in established companies and then worked their way up and around the corporate hierarchy over the next three or four decades of employment. In the NEBM, an employee has no expectation of a lifetime career with any particular enterprise. The NEBM set the stage for the rise in profitability that gained force around 1980. Companies no longer valued worker loyalty; workers were expendable if that increased the bottom line of the income statement.

Another major reason for these shifting norms is that unions have shriveled in the United States, particularly in the private sector. During the 1950s and 1960s, unions were strong and the unionization rate was high (it peaked at 33 percent of the labor force in 1953). By 2012, the overall unionization rate was down to 11.3 percent and that in the private sector down to 6.6 percent.[22] David Gordon documented the decline in the unionization rate as one of the leading causes of stagnating wages for American workers.[23] Cross-national evidence compiled elsewhere also suggests that one of the principal reasons for stagnating U.S. wages, particularly in comparison to other advanced economies, is the low level of unionization in this country and its continuing decline.[24]

The federal government also played a role in this transformation. It once acted as referee between labor and capital, but in the early 1980s it came to favor capital over labor. In particular, the Department of Treasury, which historically represented the interests of Wall Street, became the dominant player in the executive branch. The other major culprit was the Federal Reserve Board, which often raised interest rates, particularly during the 1980s, and used moral suasion to clamp down on the economy once wages began to rise.[25]

The remainder of the book focuses on trends in household wealth and wealth inequality. However, this historical backdrop on trends in income, poverty, earnings, income inequality, and the wage share is useful to place the subsequent findings on wealth trends in a broader context.

2

Trends in Household Wealth, 1962 to 2013

Relying on calculations from the Survey of Consumer Finances (SCF) from the Federal Reserve Board of Washington, as well as several other household surveys, this chapter documents trends in mean and median household net worth and net worth inequality over the half century from 1962 to 2013. Particular attention is devoted to how the middle class fared in terms of wealth developments from 2007 to 2010, during one of the sharpest declines in stock and real estate prices, and from 2010 to 2013 as asset prices recovered. The debt of the middle class exploded from 1983 to 2007, creating a very fragile middle class in the United States. The main question is whether their position deteriorated even more over the "Great Recession."[1] Also important to investigate is what has happened to the inequality of household wealth over these years, particularly from 2007 to 2013.[2]

The period covered is from 1962 to 2013. In particular, results will be provided for 1962, 1969, 1983, 1989, 1992, 1995, 1998, 2001, 2004, 2007, 2009, 2010, and 2013. The choice of years is dictated by the availability of survey data on household wealth. By 2013, it is possible to see what the fallout was from the financial crisis and associated recession and which groups experienced greatest impact.

Trends in household wealth have a direct bearing on household well-being and should therefore be of general public interest. Indeed, since the election of Barack Obama in 2012 and during the presidential campaign of 2016, the fortunes of the middle class have generated a large amount of political interest and media attention.

Asset prices plunged between 2007 and 2010 but then rebounded from 2010 to 2013. The most telling finding in this chapter is that median wealth plummeted by 44 percent over the years 2007 to 2010, almost double the drop in housing prices, and by 2010 was at its lowest level since 1969. The inequality of net worth, as measured by the Gini coefficient, after almost two decades of little movement, increased sharply from 2007 to 2010. Rather remarkably, there was virtually no change in median (and mean) wealth from 2010 to 2013 according to the SCF data despite the rebound in asset prices, which presents a new puzzle.

The next section of this chapter provides some historical background, and the following one presents several rationales for looking at household wealth. Next is a discussion of the measurement of household wealth and a description of the data sources used for this study. Two sections describe time trends on median and average wealth holdings and the inequality of household wealth. For a different perspective on wealth changes, the shares of total wealth growth accruing to different wealth groups are computed using a standard wealth measure, which excludes autos and other vehicles. Finally, a study of how wealth trends differ when the value of vehicles *is* included in net worth compares findings on wealth trends with those derived from the Panel Study of Income Dynamics (PSID). A summary of results and concluding remarks completes the chapter.

Historical Background

The last two decades have witnessed some remarkable events. Perhaps most notable was the housing value cycle, featuring an explosion in home prices and then a collapse, affecting net worth and helping to precipitate the Great Recession, followed by a modest recovery. The median house price remained virtually the same in 2001 as in 1989 in real terms.[3] The homeownership rate shot up from 62.8 to 67.7 percent and the year 2001 saw a recession (albeit a short one). Despite this, house prices suddenly took off. The median sale price of existing single-family homes jumped by 17 percent nationwide. From 2004 to 2007, however, housing prices slowed, with the median price advancing only 1.7 percent. Over the years 2001 to 2007 housing prices gained 19 percent.[4] The homeownership rate continued to expand, though at a somewhat slower rate, from 67.7 to 68.6 percent.

In December 2007 the recession and associated financial crisis hit; the recession "officially" ended in June 2009.[5] By then, real gross domestic product (GDP) fell by 4.3 percent. Subsequently, from the second quarter of 2009 to the second quarter of 2013, it gained 9.2 percent. After that it grew by another 6.8 percent through the third quarter of 2016.[6] The unemployment rate shot up from 4.4 percent in May of 2007 to a peak of 10 percent in October 2009, but by October 2016 it was down to 4.9 percent.[7]

One consequence was that asset prices plummeted. From 2007 to 2010, the median home price nosedived by 24 percent, and the share of households owning their own homes fell off, from 68.6 to 67.2 percent.[8] This was followed by a partial recovery, with median house prices rising 7.8 percent through September 2013—still, however, way below their 2007 value.[9] The homeownership rate continued to contract, eventually falling to 65.1 percent.

The housing price bubble in the years leading up to 2007 was fueled in large part by a generous expansion of credit available for home purchases and refinancing. This took a number of forms. First, many homeowners refinanced their primary mortgages. This, combined with the rise in housing prices, meant that their outstanding mortgage principal increased, thereby extracting equity from their homes. Second, many homeowners took out second mortgages and home equity loans or increased the outstanding balances on these instruments. Third, among new homeowners, credit requirements were softened, and so-called no-doc loans were issued requiring little in the way of income documentation. Many of these loans, in turn, were so-called sub-prime mortgages, characterized by excessively high interest rates and balloon payments made at the expiration of the loans (that is, amounts due when the terms of the loans were up). All told, average mortgage debt per household expanded by 59 percent in real terms between 2001 and 2007, and outstanding mortgage loans as a share of house value rose from 0.334 to 0.349, despite the 19 percent gain in real housing prices. (See Chapter 3 for more details.)

In contrast to the housing market, the stock market boomed during the 1990s. Looking at the Standard & Poor's (S&P) 500 index, stock prices surged 159 percent between 1989 and 2001.[10] Stock ownership spread and by 2001 over half of U.S. households owned stock either directly or indirectly (see Chapter 3). The stock market peaked in 2000 and was down by 11 percent by 2004.

From 2004 to 2007, the stock market rebounded, with the S&P 500 rising 19 percent. From 2001 to 2007, stock prices were up 6 percent and the stock ownership rate fell to 49 percent. Then came the Great Recession. Stock prices crashed from 2007 to 2009 and then partially recovered in 2010 for a net decline of 26 percent. The stock ownership rate also once again declined, to 47 percent. The stock market continued to rise after 2010 and by 2013 was up 39 percent over 2010 and above its previous high in 2007; the stock ownership rate continued to drop, to 46 percent.

Real wages, after stagnating for many years, finally grew in the late 1990s. According to U.S. Bureau of Labor Statistics (BLS) figures, real mean hourly earnings rose by 8.3 percent between 1995 and 2001.[11] From 1989 to 2001, real wages rose by 4.9 percent (in total), and median household income in constant dollars grew by 6 percent (see Table 2.1). Employment also surged over these years, growing by 16.7 percent.[12] The (civilian) unemployment rate remained relatively low over these years, at 5.3 percent in 1989, at 4.7 percent in 2001, at a low point of 4 percent in 2000, and averaging 5.5 percent over these years.[13]

Real wages then rose very slowly from 2001 to 2004, with the BLS mean hourly earnings up by only 1.5 percent, and median household income dropped by 1.6 percent. From 2004 to 2007, real wages rose by only 1 percent. Median income showed some growth over this period, rising by 3.2 percent. From 2001 to 2007 it gained 1.6 percent. Employment also grew more slowly over these years, gaining 6.7 percent. The unemployment rate remained low again, at 4.7 percent in 2001 and 4.6 percent in 2007 with an average value of 5.2 percent over the period.

Real wages picked up from 2007 to 2010, increasing by 3.6 percent. On the other hand, median household income declined by 6.7 percent (see Table 2.1). Moreover, employment contracted over these years, by 4.8 percent, and the unemployment rate surged from 4.6 percent in 2007 to 10.5 percent in 2010. From 2010 to 2013 employment grew by 4.7 percent, and the unemployment rate came down to 7.4 percent in 2013.

There was also an explosion of consumer debt leading up to the Great Recession. Between 1989 and 2001, total consumer credit outstanding in constant dollars surged by 70 percent, and then from 2001 to 2007, it rose by another 17 percent.[14] A number of factors contributed to this. First, credit cards became more generally available. Second, credit standards were relaxed considerably, making more households eligible for credit cards. Third, credit limits were generously increased by banks hoping to make profits out of increased fees from late payments and from higher interest rates.

Another source of new household indebtedness took the form of a huge increase in student loans. This issue has recently received wide attention in the press. According to the SCF data, the share of households reporting an educational loan rose from 13.4 percent in 2004 to 15.2 percent in 2007 and then surged to 19.9 percent in 2013.[15] The mean value of educational loans in 2013 dollars exclusively among loan holders increased by 17 percent between 2004 and 2007, another 14 percent between 2007 and 2010, and then an additional 5 percent (to $29,110) in 2013. The median value of educational loans went up by 19 percent from 2004 to 2007, another 3 percent between 2007 and 2010, and then an added 22 percent (to $17,000) in 2013. These loans were heavily concentrated among younger households and, as we shall see in Chapter 9, constituted one of the factors (though not the principal one) that led to a precipitous decline in their net worth between 2007 and 2010.

Another major change in the 1990s and the decade of the 2000s affecting household wealth was a major overhaul of the private pension system in the United States. As documented in Chapter 8, in 1989 46 percent of all households reported holding a defined benefit (DB) pension plan. DB plans are traditional pensions, such as provided by many large corporations, the federal government, and state and local governments, which guarantee a steady flow of income upon retirement. By 2007, that figure was down to 34 percent. The decline was pronounced among younger households, led by people under the age of 46, from 38 to 23 percent, as well as among middle-aged households, ages 47 to 64, from 57 to 39 percent.

Many of these plans were replaced by defined contribution (DC) pension accounts, most notably 401(k) plans and individual retirement accounts (IRAs). These plans allow households to accumulate savings for retirement purposes directly. The share of all households with DC plans skyrocketed from 24 percent in 1989 to 53 percent in 2007. Among younger households, the share rose from 31 to 50 percent, and among middle-aged households from 28 to 64 percent.

This transformation was even more notable in terms of actual dollar values. While the average value of DB pension wealth among all households crept up by 8 percent from $63,500 in 1989 to $68,800 in 2007, the average value of DC plans shot up more than sevenfold from $11,900 to $86,300 (all figures are in 2013 dollars).[16] Among younger households, average DB wealth actually fell in absolute terms, while DC wealth rose by a factor of 3.3. Among middle-aged households, the mean value of DB pensions also declined, while the average value of DC plans mushroomed by a factor of 6.5.

These changes are important for understanding trends in household wealth because DB pension wealth is *not* included in the standard measure of marketable household wealth whereas DC wealth *is* included. Thus, the substitution of DC wealth for DB wealth is likely to lead to an overstatement in the "true" gains in household wealth, since the displacement in DB wealth is not captured. (See Chapter 8 for more discussion.)

The other big story was household debt, particularly that of the middle class, which skyrocketed during these years. Over the recession, the relative indebtedness of American families continued to rise from 2007 to 2010, though it did fall off from 2010 to 2013.

What have all these major transformations wrought in terms of the distribution of household wealth, particularly over the Great Recession? What impacts have these changes had on different demographic groups, particularly as defined by race, ethnicity, and age? This is the subject of the remainder of this chapter, and also of Chapters 3 and 9.

Why Look at Household Wealth?

Most studies have looked at the distribution of well-being or its change over time in terms of income. Family wealth, however, is also an indicator of well-being, independent of the direct financial income it provides.

There are eight reasons. First, owner-occupied housing provides services directly to its owner. Second, wealth is a source of consumption, independent of the direct money income it provides, because assets can be converted directly into cash and thus provide for immediate consumption needs. Third, the availability of financial assets can provide liquidity to a family in times of economic stress, such as occasioned by unemployment, sickness, or family breakup. Fourth, wealth accumulation is a major source of retirement security (the so-called third pillar along with pensions and Social Security). Fifth, wealth is an important component in measuring poverty as recommended by the National Academy of Sciences.[17]

Sixth, wealth is found to affect household behavior over and above income.[18] Seventh, wealth-generated income does not require the same tradeoffs with leisure as earned income.[19] Eighth, in a representative democracy, as in most forms of government, the distribution of power is often related to the distribution of wealth.

As a result, it is important to consider developments in personal wealth along with both income and poverty when evaluating changes in well-being over time. On the basis of previous research, the three indicators do not always track together, so that wealth may give a different picture of developments in well-being. In this chapter, comparisons will be drawn between wealth and income trends.

Data Sources and Methods

The primary data sources used for this study are the 1983, 1989, 1992, 1995, 1998, 2001, 2004, 2007, 2010, and 2013 SCFs. Each survey consists of a core representative sample combined with a high-income supplement. In 1983, for example, the supplement was drawn from the Internal Revenue Service's Statistics of Income data file. An income cutoff of $100,000 of adjusted gross income was used as the criterion for inclusion in the supplemental sample. Individuals were randomly selected for the sample within predesignated income strata.

In later years, the first sample was selected from a standard multistage area-probability design. This part of the sample was intended to provide good coverage of asset characteristics, such as homeownership, that are broadly distributed. The second sample, the high-income supplement, was selected as a so-called list sample from statistical records (the Individual Tax File) derived from tax data by the Statistics of Income (SOI) Division of the Internal Revenue Service (IRS). In this case, the IRS provided the names and addresses of a sample of very high-income families. This second sample was designed to disproportionately select families that were likely to be relatively wealthy.[20] The advantage of the high-income supplement is that it provides a much "richer" sample of high income and therefore potentially very wealthy families. The presence of a high-income supplement creates some complications, however, because weights must be constructed to meld the high-income supplement with the core sample.[21] Typically, about two-thirds of the cases came from the representative sample and one third from the high-income supplement. In the 2007 SCF the standard multistage area-probability sample contributed 2,915 cases and the high-income supplement contributed another 1,507 cases.[22]

The principal wealth concept used here is marketable wealth (or net worth), which is defined as the current value of all marketable or fungible assets less the current value of debts. Net worth is thus the difference in value between total assets and total liabilities. Total assets are defined as the sum of: (1) the gross value of owner-occupied housing; (2) other real estate owned; (3) cash and demand deposits; (4) time and savings deposits, certificates of deposit, and money market accounts; (5) government bonds, corporate bonds, foreign bonds, and other financial securities; (6) the cash surrender value of life insurance plans; (7) the value of DC pension plans, including IRA, Keogh, and 401(k) plans; (8) corporate stock and mutual fund shares; (9) net equity in unincorporated businesses; and (10) equity in trust funds. Total liabilities are the sum of: (1) mortgage debt, (2) consumer debt, including auto loans, and (3) other debt such as educational loans.

This measure reflects wealth as a store of value and therefore a source of potential consumption. This is the concept that best reflects the level of well-being associated with a family's holdings. Thus, only assets that can be readily converted to cash (that is, "fungible" ones) are included. Though the SCF includes information on the value of vehicles owned by the household, I exclude this from my standard definition of household wealth, since the vehicles' resale value typically far understates the value of their consumption services to the household. The value of other consumer durables such as televisions, furniture, household appliances, and the like are not included in the SCF.[23] Another justification for their exclusion is that this treatment is consistent with the national accounts, where purchase of vehicles and other consumer durables is counted as expenditures, not savings.[24]

Also excluded here is the value of future Social Security benefits the family may receive upon retirement (usually referred to as Social Security wealth), as well as the value of retirement benefits from defined benefit pension plans (DB pension wealth). Even though these funds are a source of future income to families, they are not in their direct control and cannot be marketed.[25]

I also use a more restricted concept of wealth, which I call financial resources, or FR. This is defined as net worth minus net equity in owner-occupied housing (the primary residence only). FR is a more liquid concept than marketable wealth, since one's home is difficult to convert into cash in the short term. Moreover, primary homes also serve a consumption purpose besides acting as a store of value. FR represents what a household can draw down without lowering its standard of living, and thus excludes homes (and vehicles).[26]

Two other data sources are used in this chapter. The first of these is the 1962 Survey of Financial Characteristics of Consumers (SFCC). This survey was also conducted by the Federal Reserve Board of Washington and was a precursor to the SCF.[27] This was also a stratified sample that oversampled high-income households. Though the sample design and questionnaire are different from the SCF, the methodology is sufficiently similar to allow comparisons with the SCF data.[28] The second is the 1969 Measurement of Economic and Social Performance (MESP) database, a synthetic dataset constructed from income tax returns and information provided in the 1970 Census of Population. A statistical matching technique was employed to as-sign income tax returns for 1969 to households in the 1970 census. Property income flows (such as dividends) in the tax data were then capitalized into corresponding asset values (such as stocks) to obtain estimates of household wealth.[29]

Estimates of the size distribution of household wealth are sensitive to the sampling frame used in survey data. The reason is that because of the ex-treme skewness of the distribution of household wealth, the inclusion of a high-income supplement in the sample provides much more reliable estimates than a representative sample. The SFCC and the SCF each has an explicit high-income supplement. The MESP dataset has an implicit high-income supplement since it is based in large part on income data from the IRS tax file, which is *not top-coded* like the Current Population Survey and most other publicly available survey data. Moreover, the accounting framework, the choice of observational unit, and patterns of response error, because of portfolio variation with wealth class, also affect wealth estimates.

Median Wealth Plummets over the Great Recession

Table 2.1 documents a robust growth in wealth from 1983 to 2007, even back to 1962 (also see Figure 2.1). Median wealth increased at an annual rate of

Table 2.1. Mean and median wealth and income, 1962–2013 (in thousands, 2013 dollars)

Variable	1962	1969	1983	1989	1992	1995	1998	2001	2004	2007	2010	2013
A. Net Worth												
1. Median	55.5	68.0	78.0	83.5	71.3	69.7	86.7	96.7	96.0	115.1	64.6	63.8
2. Mean	207.4	248.4	303.8	348.1	338.4	312.6	386.2	500.0	530.9	602.3	505.7	508.7
3. Percent with net worth												
a. Zero or negative	18.2	15.6	15.5	17.9	18.0	18.5	18.0	17.6	17.0	18.6	21.8	21.8
b. Less than $5,000[a]	30.0	20.9	25.4	27.6	27.2	27.8	27.2	26.6	26.8	26.6	32.3	33.5
c. Less than $10,000[a]	34.1	26.0	29.7	31.8	31.2	31.9	30.3	30.1	29.9	30.0	36.2	37.1
B. Financial Resources												
1. Median	15.0	19.0	16.9	19.9	16.7	15.2	25.5	30.5	22.4	26.4	13.5	13.8
2. Mean	165.0	210.8	220.5	259.8	258.0	239.9	303.4	392.6	393.8	450.4	395.5	404.9
3. Percent with zero or negative non-home wealth	25.9	23.5	25.7	26.8	28.2	28.7	25.7	25.5	28.0	27.4	29.4	28.7
C. Income (CPS)[b]												
1. Median	40.9	53.3	46.4	52.4	49.8	51.7	55.5	55.6	54.7	56.4	52.6	51.9
2. Mean	46.4	60.6	56.5	66.2	63.2	68.2	74.0	76.6	74.6	76.0	72.0	72.6

	Annual Growth Rates (%)							Percentage Change	
	1962–1983	1983–1989	1989–2001	2001–2007	2007–2010	2010–2013	1962–2013	2007–2010	2010–2013
Annual Growth Rates (percent)									
A. Net Worth									
1. Median	1.63	1.13	1.22	2.91	–19.27	–0.39	0.28	–43.9	–1.2
2. Mean	1.82	2.27	3.02	3.10	–5.83	0.20	1.76	–16.0	0.6
B. Financial Resources									
1. Median	0.55	2.76	3.57	–2.41	–22.46	0.90	–0.16	–49.0	2.7
2. Mean	1.38	2.74	3.44	2.29	–4.34	0.78	1.76	–12.2	2.4
C. Income (CPS)[b]									
1. Median	0.61	2.03	0.48	0.26	–2.32	–0.45	0.47	–6.7	–1.3
2. Mean	0.93	2.66	1.21	–0.14	–1.78	0.29	0.88	–5.2	0.9

Source: Author's computations from the 1983, 1989, 1992, 1995, 1998, 2001, 2004, 2007, 2010, and 2013 Survey of Consumer Finances. Additional sources are the 1962 SFCC and the 1969 MESP file.

Wealth figures are deflated using the Consumer Price Index (CPI-U).

a. Constant 1995 dollars.

b. Source for household income data: U.S. Census of the Bureau, Current Populations Surveys, available at http://www.census.gov/hhes/www/income/data /historical/household/

The 1962 figures are based on family income and the rate of change of family income between 1962 and 1969.

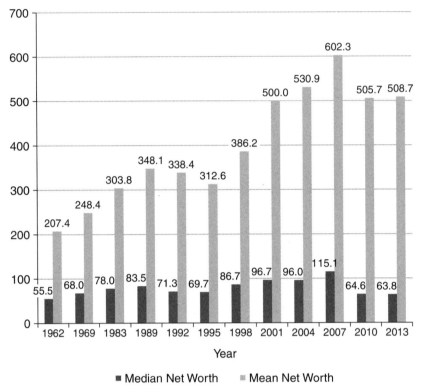

Figure 2.1. Mean and Median Net Worth, 1962–2013
(In thousands, 2013 dollars)

1.63 percent from 1962 to 1983, then slower at 1.13 percent from 1983 to 1989, then a little faster at 1.22 percent from 1989 to 2001, and then much faster at 2.91 percent from 2001 to 2007.[30] Between 2007 and 2010, median wealth plunged by a staggering 44 percent! Indeed, median wealth was actually lower in 2010 than in 1969 (in real terms). The primary reasons, as we shall see in Chapter 3, were the collapse in the housing market and the high leverage of middle-class families. There was virtually no change from 2010 to 2013.[31]

As shown in the third row of Panel A, the percentage of households with zero or negative net worth, after falling from 18.2 percent in 1962 to 15.5 percent in 1983, increased to 17.9 percent in 1989 and 18.6 percent in 2007 (also see Figure 1.2). This was followed by a sharp rise to 21.8 percent in 2010, at which level it remained in 2013. Similar time trends are in evi-

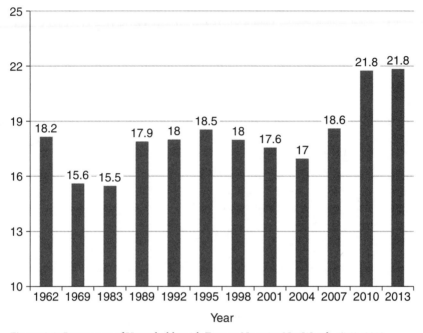

Figure 2.2. Percentage of Households with Zero or Negative Net Worth, 1962–2013

dence for the share of households with net worth less than $5,000 and less than $10,000 (both in 1995 dollars), though in both cases there was a slight increase from 2010 to 2013.

Mean net worth also grew vigorously from 1962 to 1983, at an annual rate of 1.82 percent, a little higher than that of median wealth. Its growth accelerated to 2.27 percent per year over years 1983 to 1989, about double the growth rate of median wealth. Over years 1989 to 2001, the growth rate of mean wealth was 3.02 percent per year, even higher than in the preceding periods. Its annual growth rate then reached 3.1 percent between years 2001 and 2007, largely due to the rapid (19 percent) increase in housing prices. Mean wealth in 2007 was almost double its value in 1983 and about three quarters larger than in 1989. Another point of note is that mean wealth grew about twice as fast as the median between 1983 and 2007, indicating widening inequality of wealth over these years.

The Great Recession also saw an absolute decline in mean household wealth. Although median wealth plunged by 44 percent between 2007 and

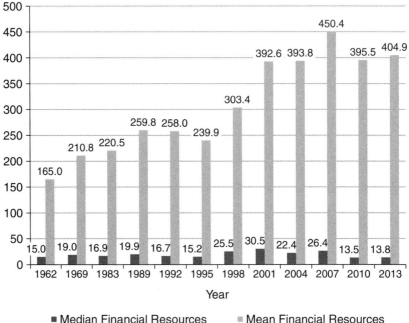

■ Median Financial Resources   ■ Mean Financial Resources

Figure 2.3. Mean and Median Financial Resources, 1962–2013
(In thousands, 2013 dollars)

2010, mean wealth fell by (only) 16 percent.[32] The main cause was falling housing and stock prices (see Chapter 3). Here, too, the faster growth rate in mean wealth than in median wealth (that is, the latter's more moderate decline) was coincident with rising wealth inequality. There was again virtually no change in mean wealth from 2010 to 2013 according to the SCF. However, aggregate data from the Financial Accounts of the United States (FFA) indicated a 27 percent jump in mean net worth over these years. As I shall argue in the next section, there is reason to believe that the SCF data understate average wealth gains over these years and that the aggregate data may be more reliable for these years, at least for mean net worth.

Median financial resources (FR), after expanding at a relatively slow pace of 0.55 percent per year from 1962 to 1983, grew 2.76 percent per year from 1983 to 1989 and 3.57 percent per year from 1989 to 2001, in both cases faster than median net worth (also see Figure 2.3). From 2001 to 2007, median FR fell at an annual rate of 2.41 percent, mainly due to a sluggish stock market and rising nonmortgage debt. All in all, median FR increased by 57 percent from 1983 to 2007, about 10 percentage points more than median net worth.

When the financial crisis hit, median FR nosedived by 49 percent from 2007 to 2010, even more than median net worth, to only $13,500—its lowest level over the fifty-year period! The main reason was across-the-board reductions in asset prices, as well as rising relative indebtedness. This was followed by a slight gain of 2.7 percent between 2010 and 2013.

After holding relatively steady between 1962 and 1983, the fraction of households with zero or negative financial resources expanded from 25.7 percent in 1983 to 27.4 percent in 2007. Thus, the sharp decline in median FR from 2001 to 2007 reflected, in part, the growing nonmortgage debt of the bottom half of the distribution. As asset prices declined in 2010, the share was up again to 29.4 percent. There was a modest reduction in the share from 2010 to 2013, to 28.7 percent.

Mean FR, after expanding at an annual pace of 1.38 percent from 1962 to 1983, grew at 2.74 percent per year from 1983 to 1989 and then at 3.44 percent from 1989 to 2001, in both cases faster than the gains in net worth. The pace then slowed down in the 2001–2007 period to 2.29 percent. Over the entire 1983–2007 period, mean FR increased by 104 percent, slightly more than mean net worth. Increases were almost identical for median and mean FR from 1983 to 2001, but because of the sharp fall-off in median FR from 2001 to 2007, mean FR grew at about double the pace of median FR from 1983 to 2007. The bull market in stocks was largely responsible for the sharp growth in financial resources between 1989 and 2001, while the slow rise in stock prices coupled with rising indebtedness caused the slow growth in average FR from 2001 to 2007.

Once again there was a sharp fall-off of 12 percent in mean FR from 2007 to 2010, but this percentage decline was substantially smaller than that of median FR and less than that of mean net worth. The difference was due to the fact that average net home equity fell by an enormous 28 percent. From 2010 to 2013, there was a slight gain of 2.4 percent in mean FR.

Median household income (based on Current Population Survey data) advanced at a fairly solid pace from 1962 to 1983, at 0.61 percent per year (also see Figure 2.4). After gaining 2.03 percent per annum between 1983 and 1989, its annual growth dipped to only 0.48 percent from 1989 to 2001 and to 0.26 percent from 2001 to 2007, for a net change of 22 percent (overall)

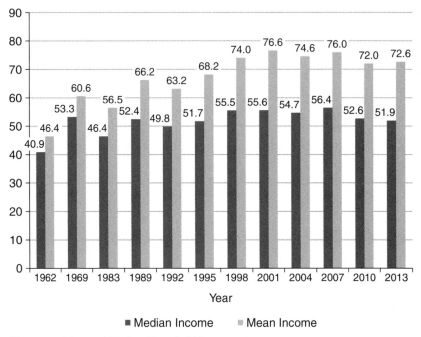

Figure 2.4. Mean and Median Household Income, 1962–2013
(In thousands, 2013 dollars)

from 1983 to 2007. It fell off in absolute terms by 6.7 percent from 2007 to 2010. Though this is not an insignificant amount, the reduction was not nearly as great as that in median wealth (or median FR). From 2010 to 2013, median income slipped by another 1.3 percent.

Mean income, after advancing at an annual rate of 0.93 percent from 1962 to 1983, gained 2.66 percent per year from 1983 to 1989, gained 1.21 percent per year from 1989 to 2001, and then lost 0.14 percent per year from 2001 to 2007, for a total change of 35 percent from 1983 to 2007. Between 1983 and 2007, mean income grew less than mean net worth (and FR), and median income grew at a much slower pace than median wealth. Mean income also dropped in real terms from 2007 to 2010, by 5.2 percent, slightly less than that of median income, but gained 0.9 percent from 2010 to 2013.

In sum, while household income virtually stagnated for the average American household from 1989 to 2007, median net worth and especially median financial resources grew strongly. Between 2001 and 2007, in particular, mean and median income changed very little while mean and median net worth advanced robustly, as did mean FR, though median FR declined. The Great Recession, on the other hand, saw a massive destruction of median net worth (and median FR) but much more modest declines in mean wealth, mean FR, and both median and mean income.

Wealth Inequality Jumps Over the Great Recession

Net worth is highly concentrated, with the richest 1 percent (as ranked by wealth) owning 37 percent of total household wealth in 2013 and the top 20 percent owning 89 percent (see Table 2.2 and Figure 2.5). The figures in Table 2.2 also show that wealth inequality, after rising from 1962 to 1969, returned to its 1962 level in 1983 (also see Figure 2.6).[33] After increasing again from 1983 to 1989, wealth inequality remained virtually unchanged from 1989 to 2007, at least according to the Gini coefficient. The share of wealth held by the top 1 percent rose by 1.4 percentage points from 1983 to 1989 and the Gini coefficient increased from 0.799 to 0.828.

What was behind the uptick in wealth inequality? As Chapters 3 and 5 will explore, two principal factors accounting for changes in wealth concentration are the change in income inequality and the trend in the ratio of stock prices to housing prices. First, there was a huge increase in income inequality between 1983 and 1989, with the Gini coefficient rising by 0.041 points. Second, stock prices increased much faster than housing prices. The stock market boomed and the S&P 500 Index was up by 62 percent, whereas median home prices increased by a mere 2 percent. As a result, the ratio between the two climbed by 58 percent.[34]

Between 1989 and 2007, the share of the top percentile actually declined a bit, from 35.2 to 34.6 percent, though this was more than compensated for by an increase in the share of the next four percentiles.[35] As a result, the share of the top 5 percent increased from 58 percent in 1989 to 61.8 percent in 2007, and the share of the top quintile rose from 83 to 85 percent.[36] The share of the fourth and middle quintiles each declined by about 1 percentage point from 1989 to 2007, while that of the bottom 20 percent increased by 0.2 percentage points. Overall, the Gini coefficient saw a very small rise, from 0.828 in 1989 to 0.834 in 2007.[37]

Table 2.2. The size distribution of wealth and income, 1962–2013

Year	Gini Coefficient	Percentage Share of Wealth or Income Held by									
		Top 1.0%	Next 4.0%	Next 5.0%	Next 10.0%	Top 20.0%	4th 20.0%	3rd 20.0%	2nd 20.0%	Bottom 20.0%	All
A. Net Worth											
1962	0.803	33.4	21.2	12.4	14.0	81.0	13.4	5.4	1.0	-0.7	100.0
1969	0.828	35.6	20.7	12.5	13.8	82.5	12.2	5.0	0.9	-0.6	100.0
1983	0.799	33.8	22.3	12.1	13.1	81.3	12.6	5.2	1.2	-0.3	100.0
1989	0.828	35.2	22.8	11.9	13.2	83.0	12.0	4.7	0.9	-0.7	100.0
1992	0.823	37.2	22.8	11.8	12.0	83.8	11.5	4.4	0.9	-0.5	100.0
1995	0.828	38.5	21.8	11.5	12.1	83.9	11.4	4.5	0.9	-0.7	100.0
1998	0.822	38.1	21.3	11.5	12.5	83.4	11.9	4.5	0.8	-0.6	100.0
2001	0.826	33.4	25.8	12.3	12.9	84.4	11.3	3.9	0.7	-0.4	100.0
2004	0.829	34.3	24.6	12.3	13.4	84.7	11.3	3.8	0.7	-0.5	100.0
2007	0.834	34.6	27.3	11.2	12.0	85.0	10.9	4.0	0.7	-0.5	100.0
2010	0.866	35.1	27.4	13.8	12.3	88.6	9.5	2.7	0.3	-1.2	100.0
2013	0.871	36.7	28.2	12.2	11.8	88.9	9.3	2.7	0.2	-1.1	100.0
B. Financial Resources											
1962	0.838	39.5	22.4	15.0	9.2	86.1	9.5	3.3	2.5	-1.4	100.0
1969	0.841	38.4	22.3	16.9	10.1	87.7	10.3	3.6	0.1	-1.7	100.0
1983	0.893	42.9	25.1	12.3	11.0	91.3	7.9	1.7	0.1	-1.0	99.9
1989	0.920	44.1	25.5	12.1	11.2	92.8	7.4	1.3	0.1	-1.6	100.0

1992	0.903	45.6	25.0	11.5	10.2	92.3	7.3	1.5	0.3	-1.4	100.0
1995	0.914	47.2	24.6	11.2	10.1	93.0	6.9	1.4	0.1	-1.4	100.0
1998	0.893	47.3	21.0	11.4	11.2	90.9	8.3	1.9	0.1	-1.2	100.0
2001	0.888	39.7	27.8	12.3	11.4	91.3	7.8	1.7	0.1	-0.8	100.0
2004	0.902	42.2	26.7	12.0	11.6	92.5	7.3	1.2	0.0	-1.1	100.0
2007	0.908	42.7	29.3	10.9	10.1	93.0	6.8	1.3	0.0	-1.1	100.0
2010	0.921	41.3	29.5	13.3	10.7	94.8	5.9	0.8	0.1	-1.6	100.0
2013	0.923	42.8	29.7	11.9	10.3	94.7	6.0	0.8	0.0	-1.5	100.0

C. Income

1962	0.428	8.4	11.4	10.2	16.1	46.0	24.0	16.6	9.9	3.5	100.0
1969	0.469	10.4	12.4	10.3	15.9	48.9	23.4	16.4	9.5	1.7	100.0
1982	0.480	12.8	13.3	10.3	15.5	51.9	21.6	14.2	8.7	3.7	100.0
1988	0.521	16.6	13.3	10.4	15.2	55.6	20.6	13.2	7.8	2.9	100.0
1991	0.528	15.7	14.8	10.6	15.3	56.4	20.4	12.8	7.4	3.1	100.1
1994	0.518	14.4	14.5	10.4	15.9	55.1	20.6	13.6	8.3	2.4	100.0
1997	0.531	16.6	14.4	10.2	15.0	56.2	20.5	12.8	7.5	3.0	100.0
2000	0.562	20.0	15.2	10.0	13.5	58.6	19.0	12.3	7.4	2.6	100.0
2003	0.540	17.0	15.0	10.9	14.9	57.9	19.9	12.1	7.4	2.8	100.0
2006	0.574	21.3	15.9	9.9	14.3	61.4	17.8	11.1	6.8	2.8	100.0
2009	0.549	17.2	16.5	10.7	14.7	59.1	18.7	14.9	4.3	3.0	100.0
2013	0.574	19.8	16.5	10.8	14.7	61.8	17.8	11.1	6.6	2.8	100.0

Source: Author's computations from the 1983, 1989, 1992, 1995, 1998, 2001, 2004, 2007, 2010, and 2013 Survey of Consumer Finances. Additional sources are the 1962 SFCC and the 1969 MESP file. Income data are from these files.

For the computation of percentile shares of net worth, households are ranked according to their net worth; for percentile shares of financial resources, households are ranked according to their financial resources; and for percentile shares of income, households are ranked according to their income.

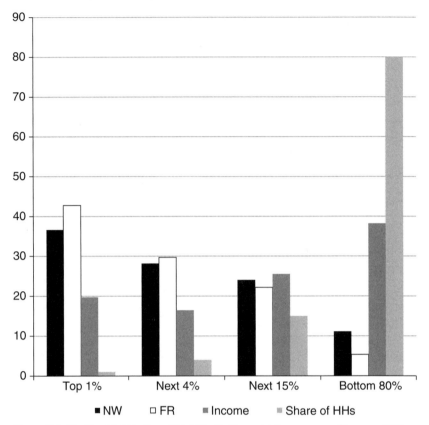

Figure 2.5. The Size Distribution of Net Worth, Financial Resources, and Income, 2013 (Percentage shares)

The years 2007 to 2010 saw a sharp elevation in wealth inequality, with the Gini coefficient rising from 0.834 to 0.866. Interestingly, the share of the top percentile showed a smaller relative gain—less than 1 percent.[38] Most of the rise in wealth share took place in the remainder of the top quintile, and overall the share of wealth held by the top quintile climbed by 3.6 percentage points. The shares of the other quintiles correspondingly dropped, with the share of the second quintile falling by 0.4 and that of the bottom quintile by 0.7 percentage points.

From 2010 to 2013 there was a small rise in the Gini coefficient, from 0.866 to 0.871. The share of the top 1 percent did increase by 1.6 percentage points but there was virtually no change in the share of the top quintile. In constant

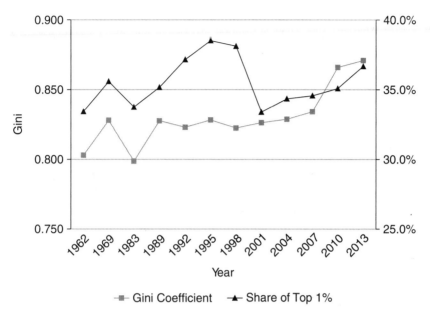

Figure 2.6. Gini Coefficient and the Share of the Top 1 Percent for Net Worth, 1962–2013

dollar terms, the net worth of the top 1 percent grew by 5.9 percent over those years but that of the next 19 percent was down by 1.8 percent. The wealth of the fourth quintile also lost 1.7 percent, that of the middle quintile fell 0.7 percent, and that of the bottom 40 percent declined 5.7 percent.

FR was even more concentrated than net worth, with the richest 1 percent (as ranked by FR) owning 43 percent of total FR in 2013, compared to 37 percent for net worth, and the top 20 percent owning 95 percent, compared to 89 percent for net worth (see Table 2.2 and Figure 2.5). The inequality of FR showed a different time trend than net worth—mainly because of differences in timing between the housing market and the stock market cycles (also see Figure 2.7). The share of the top percentile climbed from 39.5 percent in 1962 to 42.9 percent in 1983 and the Gini coefficient showed a marked increase from 0.838 to 0.893, while the inequality of net worth was about the same in the two years. The share of the top 1 percent then gained by 1.2 percentage points and the Gini coefficient increased from 0.893 to 0.920 between 1983 and 1989—trends, in this case, that mirrored those of net worth.

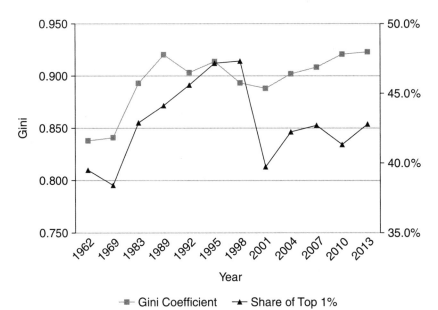

Figure 2.7. Gini Coefficient and the Share of the Top 1 Percent for Financial Resources, 1962–2013

Over the next twelve years, from 1989 to 2001, the share of the richest 1 percent plummeted by 4.4 percentage points, the share of the top five percent fell by 2.0 percentage points, and that of the top quintile by 1.6 percentage points. The share of the fourth quintile increased by 0.4 percentage points, the share of the middle quintile was also up by 0.4 percentage points, that of the second held its own, and that of the bottom quintile rose.[39] As a result, the Gini coefficient fell from 0.920 in 1989 to 0.888 in 2001 and was actually slightly lower in 2001 than in 1983.

The trend reversed between 2001 and 2007, with the share of the top percentile rising by 3 percentage points, that of the top quintile up by 1.7 percentage points, and the shares of the third and four quintiles and the bottom 40 percent all falling. As a result, the Gini coefficient rose from 0.888 in 2001 to 0.908 in 2007, still higher than in 1983 but lower than its previous peak value of 1989. The run-up in inequality from 2001 to 2007 was a reflection of the increase in the share of households with zero or negative financial resources.

From 2007 to 2010, the share of total FR held by the top 1 percent actually declined a bit but the shares of the remaining groups in the top quintile ex-

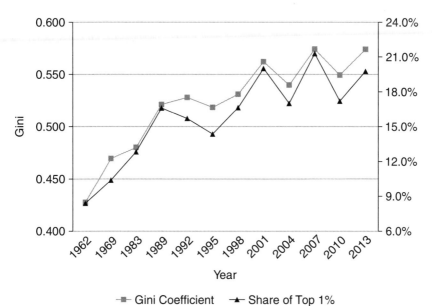

Figure 2.8. Gini Coefficient and the Share of the Top 1 Percent for Household Income, 1962–2013

panded, so that the share of the top quintile rose from 93.0 to 94.8 percent. The shares of the lower four quintiles declined, so that the overall Gini coefficient rose from 0.908 in 2007 to 0.921 in 2010, close to its previous high point in 1989. From 2010 to 2013, there was essentially no change in overall FR inequality as measured by the Gini coefficient, though the share of the top 1 percent increased by 1.5 percentage points.

The top 1 percent of families (as ranked by income on the basis of the SCF data) earned 20 percent of total household income in 2012 and the top 20 percent accounted for 62 percent—large figures but lower than the corresponding wealth shares (also see Figure 2.5).[40] The time trend for income inequality also contrasted with those for net worth and financial resources inequality (also see Figure 2.8). Income inequality showed a sharp rise from 1961 to 1982, with the Gini coefficient expanding from 0.428 to 0.480 and the share of the top 1 percent up from 8.4 to 12.8 percent. Income inequality increased sharply again between 1982 and 1988, with the Gini coefficient rising from 0.480 to 0.521 and the share of the top 1 percent from 12.8 to 16.6 percent.

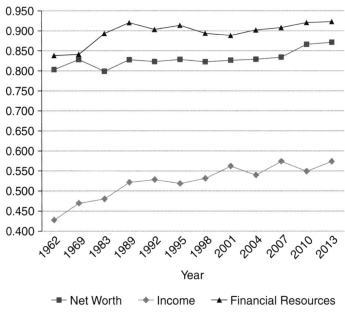

Figure 2.9. Wealth and Income Inequality, 1962–2013
(Gini coefficients)

Inequality again surged from 1988 to 2000, with the share of the top per-centile rising by 3.4 percentage points, the share of the top quintile up by 3 percentage points, the shares of the other quintiles falling again and the Gini index advancing from 0.521 to 0.562. All in all, the years from 1989 to 2001 saw almost the same degree of increase in income inequality as the 1983–1989 period.[41] Inequality once again rose from 2001 to 2007, though the pace slackened. The Gini coefficient increased from 0.562 to 0.574, the share of the top 1 percent was up by 1.3 percentage points, the share of the top quintile was up by 1.7 percentage points, and the shares of the other quintiles fell. All in all, the period from 2001 to 2007 witnessed a moderate increase in income inequality, a small rise in wealth inequality, and a signifi-cant jump in FR inequality (also see Figure 2.9).

Perhaps somewhat surprisingly, the years 2007 to 2010 witnessed a rather sharp contraction in income inequality. The Gini coefficient fell from 0.574 to 0.549 and the share of the top 1 percent dropped sharply from 21.3 to 17.2 percent. Property income and realized capital gains (which are included in the SCF definition of income), as well as corporate bonuses and the value of stock options, plummeted over these years, a process that explains the steep decline in the share of the top percentile. Real wages, as noted earlier, actually rose over these years, though the unemployment rate also increased. As a result, the income of the middle class was down but not nearly as much in percentage terms as that of the high-income groups. In contrast, transfer income such as unemployment insurance rose, so that the bottom also did better in relative terms than the top. As a result, overall income inequality fell over the years 2006 to 2009.[42]

The second half of the Great Recession saw a reversal in this trend, with income inequality once again increasing sharply. The Gini coefficient increased by 0.025 points to 0.574, the same level as in 2007. The share of the top percentile rose to 19.8 percent, somewhat below its 2007 level, while the share of the top quintile was up to 61.8 percent, slightly above its level in 2007. The same set of factors, though in reverse, help explain this turnaround in income inequality. Property income, realized capital gains, and associated income rose sharply over these years as the stock market recovered, accounting for the sharp rise in the share of the top percentile. The unemployment rate fell over these years but real wages were down, according to the BLS figures. As a result, the income of the middle class rose but not nearly as much in percentage terms as that of the high-income groups. Transfer income such as unemployment insurance fell, as the extensions of benefits enacted in the early days of the recession ended.

All in all, income inequality increased much more than either net worth or FR inequality over years 1983 to 2013 (see Figure 2.10). On the basis of the Gini coefficient, net worth inequality was up by 9 percent and FR inequality was up by 3 percent, while income inequality rose by 20 percent.

The results raise three puzzles. The first is that net worth inequality showed a sharp rise over the first part of the Great Recession while income inequality showed an equally sharp decline. A second is that wealth inequality showed a slight increase over the second half of the recession while income inequality surged. A third is that income inequality increased much more than either net worth or FR inequality over years 1983 to 2013. I will return to these puzzles in Chapters 3 and 5.

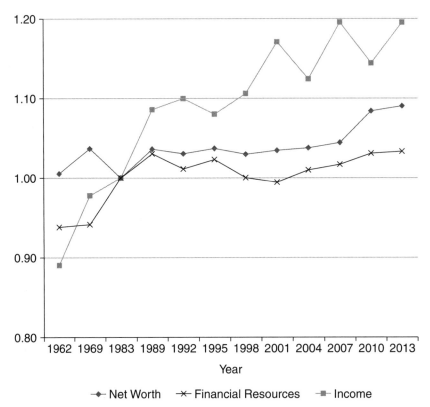

Figure 2.10. Gini Coefficients for Net Worth, Financial Resources, and Income, 1962–2013
[Index, 1983 = 1]

The Upper Strata

Despite the relative stability in overall wealth inequality during the 1990s, there was a near explosion in the number of very rich households (see Table 2.3). The number of millionaires (standardized to 1995 dollars) almost doubled between 1989 and 2001, the number of "pentamillionaires" ($5,000,000 or more) increased three and a half times, and the number of "decamillionaires" ($10,000,000 or more) grew more than fivefold. Much of the growth occurred between 1995 and 2001 and was directly related to the surge in stock prices. The number of the very rich continued to increase between 2001 and 2007 at about the same pace, with the number of million-

Table 2.3. The count of millionaires and multimillionaires, 1983–2013

Year	Total Number of Households (in thousands)	The Number of Households (in thousands) with Net Worth Equal to or Exceeding (in 1995$)		
		1 Million	5 Million	10 Million
1983	83,893	2,411	247.0	66.5
1989	93,009	3,024	296.6	64.9
1992	95,462	3,104	277.4	41.6
1995	99,101	3,015	474.1	190.4
1998	102,547	4,783	755.5	239.4
2001	106,494	5,892	1,067.8	338.4
2004	112,107	6,466	1,120.0	344.8
2007	116,120	7,274	1,466.8	464.2
2010	117,606	7,931	1,073.9	352.3
2013	122,527	7,123	1,314.7	406.5
% Change	46.1	195.4	432.2	511.5

Source: Author's computations from the 1983, 1989, 1992, 1995, 1998, 2001, 2004, 2007, 2010, and 2013 SCFs.

aires growing by 23 percent, the number of pentamillionaires by 37 percent, and the number of decamillionaires by 37 percent as well.

Despite the increase in the share of the top 1 percent of wealth holders, the millionaire count slowed markedly from 2007 to 2010, rising by only 9 percent. Moreover, there was an absolute decline in the number of pentamillionaires and decamillionaires, falling by 27 and 24 percent, respectively. These numbers reflect the steep decline in asset prices over these years, particularly for stocks and business equity (see Chapter 3). From 2010 to 2013, despite the recovery in asset prices, the number of millionaires actually fell by 10 percent. This decline was likely due to the slow recovery in house prices. On the other hand, the number of penta- and decamillionaires rose sharply, by 22 and 15 percent, respectively, reflecting the recovery in stock and business prices.

Searching for the Elusive Top 1 Percent

Another cut on the fortunes of the upper strata of the wealth distribution is provided in Table 2.4, which looks at time trends in the shares of not only the top 1 percent of the wealth distribution but those of the top 0.5 and

Table 2.4. Wealth concentration shares at the top of the wealth distribution, 1962–2013 (percentage)

	Top 1%			Top 0.5%			Top 0.1%			Saez and Zucman (2016)		
	% Share	Threshold[a]	Samp Size	% Share	Threshold[a]	Samp Size	% Share	Threshold[a]	Samp Size	Top 1%	Top 0.5%	Top 0.1%
1962	33.4	$2,344	382	25.6	$3,950	289	13.7	$12,047	110	29.6	21.7	10.1
1969	35.6	$2,417	635	27.8	$4,356	318	15.2	$20,503	64	27.9	20.6	10.0
1983	33.8	$3,628	274	25.7	$6,107	192	13.8	$16,823	71	24.7	18.2	8.0
1989	35.2	$4,387	433	27.0	$6,623	340	14.3	$20,889	153	27.8	21.4	11.5
1992	37.2	$3,789	648	26.0	$5,966	539	11.7	$24,906	315	29.2	22.6	12.2
1995	38.5	$3,834	684	30.0	$7,271	507	14.5	$22,873	251	29.5	22.8	12.3
1998	38.1	$5,383	635	26.3	$8,458	509	12.9	$22,514	286	32.3	25.4	14.5
2001	33.4	$7,679	653	24.2	$11,698	531	10.9	$26,674	324	33.2	26.5	15.7
2004	34.3	$7,636	714	25.3	$11,700	591	12.1	$29,929	355	33.5	26.7	15.5
2007	34.6	$9,249	683	25.5	$13,314	575	12.8	$34,565	349	36.0	29.1	17.7
2010	35.1	$7,153	652	26.0	$11,838	524	12.6	$28,473	312	39.5	32.4	20.7
2013	36.7	$7,767	651	27.4	$11,915	540	13.6	$30,794	318	41.8	34.5	22.0

Source: Author's computations from the 1983, 1989, 1992, 1995, 1998, 2001, 2004, 2007, 2010, and 2013 Survey of Consumer Finances.
Additional sources are the 1962 Survey of Financial Characteristics of Consumers, the 1969 Measurement of Economic and Social Performance (MESP) file, and Emmanuel Saez and Gabriel Zucman, "Wealth Inequality in the United States since 1913: Evidence from Capitalized Income Tax Data," *Quarterly Journal of Economics* 131, no. 2 (May 2016): 519–78.

a. In thousands, 2013 dollars.

b. The unit of analysis is the tax unit. The 2013 figure is for the year 2012.

0.1 percent as well. It is first of note that, as discussed in the previous section, the share of the top percentile, after rising from 1962 to 1969 and returning to its previous level, steadily marched upward to a peak of 38.5 percent in 1995, leveled off through 1998, and then plummeted to 33.4 percent in 2001 (see Figure 2.6). From 2001 onward to 2013 there was a steady advance, reaching 36.7 percent in 2013. Similar time trends are evident for the shares of the top 0.5 and 0.1 percent.

The last set of columns shows comparable top shares from Saez and Zucman. Their series is based on an income capitalization technique and other imputations applied to U.S. income tax data. Total wealth holdings by asset and liability type were then aligned to national balance sheet totals. The unit of analysis is the tax unit. In terms of level, the Saez-Zucman (SZ) series is generally comparable to my own calculations from the SCF, at least through 2001, although time trends are markedly different in some cases. SZ shows a decline in wealth concentration from 1962 through 1983 whereas my data show an initial rise followed by a decline. The SZ data then indicate an almost continuous rise in wealth concentration from 1983 through 2012, whereas the SCF data show a more or less steady increase from 1983 through 1995, a drop from 1995 through 2001, and then a rise through 2013. The SZ series, moreover, shows a much more pronounced jump from 2001 through 2012, with the share of the top 1 percent, for example, climbing by 8.6 percentage points in their series, compared to 3.3 percentage points based on the SCF. The difference in the estimated share of wealth held by the top 1 percent thus expands from −0.2 percentage points to 5.1 percentage points.

It is not entirely clear why the two series track so differently over time. The SZ series was driven mainly by the share of property income (particularly, interest and dividends) received by the top income groups. It is likely that income shares track differently from the share of stocks and financial securities owned by the top wealth groups. The SZ data are also weak in valuing unincorporated business equity, which was an important asset of the top wealth groups. The SZ approach also has problems with valuing 401(k) plans and other tax-deferred DC retirement assets since the income from these sources is not subject to current income tax. The SZ series very likely fails to capture the explosive growth in DC wealth beginning in the mid-1990s. This problem will likely lead to an *overstatement* of the shares of the top groups after 1995 or so since DC accounts are relatively concentrated in the middle of the wealth distribution. This difference would explain why the SCF data show a moderation in wealth concentration from 1995 to 2001 and then a more modest upturn from 2001 through 2013 relative to the SZ series, whereas SZ find a sharp upward trajectory from 1995 through 2012. These factors argue in favor of the SCF data series.[43]

On the other side of the ledger, there are two problems associated with the SCF data in regard to the very top of the wealth distribution—the top 0.5 percent and above. First, as a member of the Federal Reserve team noted in a private conversation, the SCF is not designed to capture the top 0.5 percent of the wealth distribution and above. The SCF data, in contrast, are very reliable for the bottom 99 percent of the wealth distribution. Income tax data, on the other hand, do not have this limitation since families at the very top of the distribution are required to file tax returns. Second, the SCF purposely excludes any member of the so-called Forbes 400, the 400 richest families in the United States as compiled by *Forbes Magazine*.[44] This is true for all survey years. These two factors speak for the greater reliability of the SZ data for the very top of the wealth distribution.

While this might be the case, these factors do not explain why the gap between the SZ and SCF series has widened over time since 2001. As noted earlier, the difference in the estimated wealth share of the top percentile expands from −0.2 percentage points in 2001 to 5.1 percentage points in 2013 (2012 for the SZ series). This result argues for the fact that the SCF is missing the very top of the wealth distribution and that the discrepancy has been growing over time. In other words, it is possible that the distance between Forbes 400 and the SCF survey increased over the years.

Table 2.5 tries to assess this issue. The maximum net worth figure as reported in the SCF was fairly close to the minimum net worth figure required to get onto the Forbes list in the four years for which I could find the pertinent data. Indeed, in three of the four years the maximum SCF figure was greater than the minimum Forbes value. In 2013, for example, the former was $1.324 billion and the latter $1.3 billion. Between 2001 and 2007, the maximum SCF value more than doubled (in 2013 dollars) whereas the minimum Forbes value rose by 85 percent, so that the ratio between the two fell from 1.03 to 0.92. From 2007 to 2010, the former fell by 26 percent and the latter by 31 percent, so that the ratio once again fell. The latter grew much faster than the former from 2010 to 2013, so that the ratio rebounded to 0.98.

Table 2.5. Time trends in the Forbes 400 and a comparison with the Survey of Consumer Finances data, 1983–2013

Variable	1983	1989	2001	2007	2010	2013	% Change 1983–1989	% Change 1989–2001	% Change 2001–2007	% Change 2007–2010	% Change 2010–2013	% Change 1983–2013
A. Maximum SCF Value for Standard Net Worth (in millions, 2013 dollars)	206.4	339.7	763.6	1,586.0	1,168.5	1,324.4	64.6	124.8	107.7	−26.3	13.3	541.8
B. Forbes 400 Values (in millions, 2013 dollars)[a]												
1. Minimum			789.2	1,460.6	1,014.9	1,300.0			85.1	−30.5	28.1	
2. Maximum	5,146	9,769	71,031	66,289	57,690	72,000	89.9	627.1	−6.7	−13.0	24.8	1299.2
C. Ratio between Forbes 400 Value and Maximum SCF Value												
1. Forbes minimum			1.03	0.92	0.87	0.98						
2. Forbes maximum	24.9	28.8	93.0	41.8	49.4	54.4						

Source: Author's computations from the 1983, 1989, 2001, 2007, 2010, and 2013 Survey of Consumer Finances.
a. From http://www.forbes.com/forbes-400/.

In contrast, from 1983 to 1989 the maximum SCF value advanced by 65 percent while the maximum Forbes value gained 90 percent and from 1989 to 2001 the former grew by 125 percent and the latter by a huge 627 percent, so that the ratio between the Forbes figure and the SCF figure skyrocketed from 24.9 in 1983 to 93 in 2001. The maximum SCF value continued its robust gains between 2001 and 2007 while the maximum Forbes value underwent a slight decline, so that the ratio plummeted to 41.8 in 2007. The maximum Forbes figure showed a much smaller loss from 2007 to 2010 and a much greater gain from 2010 to 2013 than the maximum SCF figure so that the ratio rebounded to 54.4 in 2013. Over the full stretch from 1983 to 2013, the maximum Forbes value was up by a factor of 13 while the maximum SCF figure was up by a factor of 5.4. The implication is that over time the SCF data are increasingly losing the very top of the wealth distribution both in terms of the count of very rich families and the value of their wealth.[45]

These results are corroborated by Kennickell.[46] By his calculations (see Table A1) the share of total SCF wealth accounted by the Forbes 400 grew from 1.5 percent in 1989 to 2.3 percent in 2007 (his study covered only this period). In other words, adding the wealth of the Forbes 400 to the SCF data would have increased the share of the top 1 percent by 1.5 percentage points in 1989 but 2.3 percentage points in 2007.

Another point made in a private conversation with Gabriel Zucman is that the concentration of property income (dividends and interest) at the top is higher in the IRS tax data than in the SCF and trends upward more in the tax data than in the SCF. If this is the case, then it is likely that the concentration of stocks and bonds in the SCF is also understated, as is its upward trend over time. These results would again speak in favor of the SZ series over the SCF series.

These findings may also explain why the SZ data, which in principle should be capturing the wealth of the Forbes 400 group, show an almost continuous rise in the share of wealth held by the very top groups from 1983 onward, while the SCF data show a peak in 1995 followed by a fall off from 1995 to 2001 and then a rising trend.

Of particular note is the 2010 to 2013 period. As we will see in Chapter 5, the aggregate balance sheet data from the FFA show a much greater percentage increase in mean net worth from 2010 to 2013 (20.3 percent) than the SCF (0.6 percent). The Forbes group pulled away from the SCF sample

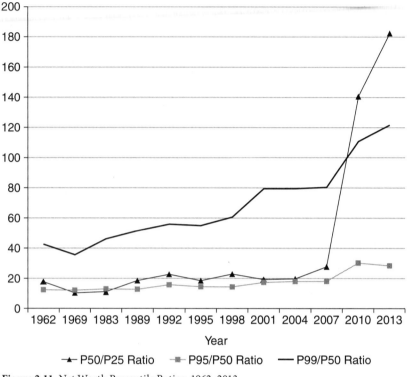

Figure 2.11. Net Worth Percentile Ratios, 1962–2013

both in terms of minimum and maximum value over these years. The ratio of the Forbes minimum value to the SCF maximum value rose from 0.87 to 0.98 while the ratio of the Forbes maximum value to the SCF maximum value advanced from 49.4 to 54.4. The aggregate wealth of the Forbes 400 should, in principle, be captured in the aggregate balance sheet data. This growing discrepancy could also then explain why the aggregate data show a much greater increase in mean wealth over this period than the SCF data. As I argue in Chapter 5, the aggregate data are likely to be more reliable over these years than the SCF.[47]

Another approach for looking at inequality trends is to track net worth percentile ratios over time. Figure 2.11 shows times series on three such ratios: the P99/P50 ratio, the P95/P50 ratio, and the P50/P25 ratio.[48] The first two ratios show what is happening in the upper half of the wealth distribution whereas the P50/P25 ratio indicates what is occurring in the bottom half.[49]

The results are quite dramatic and indicate a different time path for wealth inequality than Gini coefficients or top wealth shares. Looking first at the P99/P50 ratio, we see that after a small dip between 1962 and 1969,[50] the ratio trended sharply upward through 2013. Between 1962 and 2001 the ratio almost doubled, from 42.6 to 79.4, showed a slight upward trajectory from 2001 to 2007, and then climbed by 51 percent from 2007 to 2013, reaching a value of 121.6, almost triple its value in 1962. It is also of note that this metric continued to climb from 2010 to 2013. The P95/P50 ratio also showed an upward course from 1962 to 2013. Over the half century, the ratio advanced by a factor of 2.3, compared to 2.9 for the P99/P50 ratio. The less pronounced rise in the P95/P50 ratio compared to the P99/P50 ratio reflects greater wealth gains among the top 1 percent of the wealth distribution than among the next 4 percent (P95 to P99).

The P50/P25 ratio had a somewhat different path than the first two ratios. Between 1962 and 1969, the P50/P25 ratio plunged by 42 percent, from 17.7 to 10.3. After this point, the ratio generally went upward, reaching 27.7 in 2007, 56 percent greater than its 1962 level. The ratio then skyrocketed, attaining a value of 182.4 in 2013, 10 times as great as in 1962 and 6.6 times as great as in 2007. The reason for this tremendous burst after 2007 was not that P50 (median) wealth grew so rapidly, since it actually declined from 2007 to 2013. Rather it is the fact that P25 absolutely crumbled after 2007, dropping to a mere $350 by 2013. The rise in both the P99/P50 ratio and the P50/P25 ratio indicate that rising wealth inequality reflected increases in inequality in both the top half and the bottom half of the wealth distribution.

The Share of Overall Wealth Gains, 1983 to 2013

Table 2.6 shows absolute changes in wealth and income by quantile between 1983 and 2013. The results are even more striking. Over this period, the largest gains in relative terms were made by the wealthiest households. The top 0.1 percent saw their average wealth (in 2013 dollars) rise by over $27 million, or 65 percent, that of the top 0.5 percent by over $12 million or 79 percent, and that of the top 1 percent by more than $8 million dollars or 82 percent. The remaining part of the top quintile experienced increases from 52 to 110 percent and the fourth quintile by 24 percent, while the middle quintile lost 14 percent and the average wealth of the poorest 40 percent fell by $17,500. By 2013, the average wealth of the bottom 40 percent had fallen to −$10,800.

Another way of viewing this phenomenon is afforded by calculating the proportion of the total increase in real household wealth between 1983 and 2013 accruing to different wealth groups. This is computed by dividing the increase in total wealth of each percentile group by the total increase in household wealth, while holding constant the number of households in that group. If a group's wealth share remains constant over time, then the percentage of the total wealth growth received by that group will equal its share of total wealth. If a group's share of total wealth increases (decreases) over time, then it will receive a percentage of the total wealth gain greater (less) than its share in either year. However, it should be noted that in these calculations, the households found in each group (say the top quintile) may be different in the two years.

The results indicate that the richest 1 percent received 41 percent of the total gain in marketable wealth over the period from 1983 to 2013. This proportion was greater than the share of wealth held by the top 1 percent in any of the intervening thirty years. Indeed, the top 0.1 percent garnered 13.5 percent of the total gains and the top 0.5 percent made off with 30 percent. The next 4 percent (P95 to P99) received 36 percent of the total gain and the next 15 percent 22 percent, so that the top quintile collectively accounted for a little over 100 percent of the total growth in wealth, while the bottom 80 percent accounted for none.

The pattern of results is similar for financial resources. Average FR of the richest 1 percent as ranked by FR climbed 96 percent, that of the next richest 4 percent rose by 132 percent, and that of the next richest 15 percent increased between 84 and 90 percent. Altogether, mean FR of the top quintile gained 104 percent. As in the case of net worth, the fourth quintile showed a positive gain while the third quintile and bottom 40 percent had absolute declines. Of the total growth in non-home wealth between 1983 and 2013, 43 percent accrued to the top 1 percent and almost 100 percent to the top quintile, while the bottom 80 percent collectively accounted for none.

A similar calculation using the SCF income data reveals that the greatest gains in real income from 1982 to 2012 were made by households in the top 1 percent of the income distribution, who saw their incomes grow by

Table 2.6. Mean wealth holdings and income by wealth or income class, 1983–2013 (in thousands, 2013 dollars)

Variable	Top 0.1%	Top 0.5%	Top 1.0%	Next 4.0%	Next 5.0%	Next 10.0%	Top 20.0%	4th 20.0%	3rd 20.0%	Bottom 40.0%	All
A. Net Worth											
1983	41,996	15,624	10,255	1,696	737.7	398.3	1,235.6	191.0	79.3	6.7	303.≡
2013	69,420	27,892	18,623	3,550.8	1,238.9	605.0	2,260.3	236.4	68.1	(10.8)	508.
% change[a]	65.3	78.5	81.6	109.3	67.9	51.9	82.9	23.8	-14.1	–	67.≡
% of gain[a]	13.5	30.2	41.1	36.5	12.3	10.2	100.1	4.5	-1.1	-3.4	100.⊡
B. Financial Resources											
1983	–	–	8,842	1,295	505.9	226.8	940.9	81.4	17.5	(4.5)	206.2
2013	–	–	17,318	3,006.5	963.3	416.0	1,916.3	121.0	16.8	(15.0)	404.9
% change	–	–	95.9	132.2	90.4	83.5	103.7	48.6	-4.2	–	96.4
% of gain[a]	–	–	42.7	34.5	11.5	9.5	98.2	4.0	-0.1	-2.1	100.0
C. Income											
1982	–	–	883.6	228.3	141.8	106.4	178.5	74.5	48.7	21.2	68.8
2012	–	–	1,679	350.5	181.2	120.9	257.2	76.5	46.0	20.3	8≡1
% change	–	–	90.0	53.5	27.8	13.6	44.1	2.7	-5.6	-4.3	2≡6
% of gain[a]	–	–	49.2	31.5	12.9	9.7	103.3	2.6	-3.6	-2.3	10⊡0
Memo: Change in Net Worth by Subperiod											
1962	28,371	10,616	6,934	1,097.7	513.1	290.0	839.5	139.0	56.3	4.9	20⁻.4
1983	41,996	15,624	10,255	1,696.2	737.7	398.3	1,235.6	191.0	79.3	6.7	30⁻.8

% change	48.0	47.2	47.9	54.5	43.8	37.4	47.2	37.4	40.8	35.7	46.5
% of gain[a]	14.4	26.4	35.0	25.2	11.8	11.4	83.5	11.0	4.8	0.7	100.0
1983	41,996	15,624	10,255	1,696.2	737.7	398.3	1,235.6	191.0	79.3	6.7	303.8
1989	49,634	18,820	12,239	1,984.4	830.0	457.9	1,445.3	209.6	81.7	7.8	348.1
% change	18.2	20.5	19.4	17.0	12.5	15.0	17.0	9.7	3.0	-7.2	14.6
% of gain[a]	16.4	34.3	42.6	24.7	9.9	12.8	90.0	8.0	1.0	1.0	100.0
1989	49,634	18,820	12,239	1,984.4	830.0	457.9	1,445.3	209.6	81.7	7.8	348.1
2001	54,387	24,156	16,695	3,226.6	1,233.1	645.0	2,110.9	283.2	98.6	3.8	500.0
% change	9.6	28.4	36.4	62.6	48.6	40.9	46.1	35.1	20.7	-51.9	43.7
% of gain[a]	3.2	17.8	29.8	33.2	13.5	12.5	89.0	9.8	2.3	-1.1	100.0
2001	54,387	24,156	16,695	3,226.6	1,233.1	645.0	2,110.9	283.2	98.6	3.8	500.0
2007	77,255	30,758	20,818	4,107.7	1,349.7	721.2	2,560.5	327.0	119.1	2.5	602.3
% change	42.0	27.3	24.7	27.3	9.5	11.8	21.3	15.4	20.7	-34.1	20.4
% of gain[a]	22.4	32.3	40.3	34.5	5.7	7.5	87.9	8.6	4.0	-0.5	100.0
2007	77,255	30,758	20,818	4,107.7	1,349.7	721.2	2,560.5	327.0	119.1	2.5	602.3
2013	69,420	27,892	18,623	3,550.8	1,238.9	605.0	2,260.3	236.4	68.1	(10.8)	508.7
% change	-10.1	-9.3	-10.5	-13.6	-8.2	-16.1	-11.7	-27.7	-42.8	—	-15.5
% of gain[a]	8.2	15.1	23.1	23.4	5.8	12.2	64.6	19.1	10.7	5.6	100.0

Source: Author's computations from the 1983, 1989, 2001, 2007 and 2013 SCF; and 1962 Survey of Financial Characteristics of Consumers.

For the computation of percentile shares of net worth, households are ranked according to their net worth.

a. The computation is performed by dividing the total increase in wealth of a given group by the total increase of wealth for all households over the period, under the assumption that the number of households in each group remains unchanged over the period. It should be noted that the households found in a given group (such as the top quintile) may be different in each year.

90 percent. Mean incomes increased by over half for the next 4 percent, over a quarter for the next highest 5 percent, and by 14 percent for the next highest 10 percent. The fourth quintile of the income distribution experienced only a 3 percent growth in income, while the middle quintile and the bottom 40 percent had absolute declines. Of the total growth in real income between 1982 and 2012, almost half accrued to the top 1 percent and over 100 percent to the top quintile. These figures were very close to those for net worth and FR.

The second part of Table 2.6 breaks down the growth in mean net worth by subperiod going back to 1962. Over the 1962 to 1983 period, percentage gains in net worth were actually quite similar across the different percentile groups. Even the bottom 40 percent saw a 36 percent growth in their net worth. Over these years, 35 percent of the advance in total wealth accrued to the top 1 percent and 84 percent to the top quintile, figures considerably lower than for the 1983–2013 period as a whole. Years 1983 to 1989 saw higher percentage gains in net worth for the top quintile than the bottom 80 percent of the wealth distribution. Over this period, 43 percent of the total growth in wealth went to the top 1 percent and 90 percent to the top 20 percent. The next period, 1989 to 2001, once again witnessed similar percentage increases in mean net worth across wealth quantiles, with the notable exceptions of the top 0.1 percent whose wealth gained only 9.6 percent and the bottom 40 percent whose mean net worth dropped by 52 percent. Over this time interval, only 30 percent of the total wealth gain accrued to the top 1 percent, much lower than in the 1983–1989 period, but 89 percent to the top quintile, a figure comparable to the preceding period.

Over years 2001 to 2007 the top 0.1 percent enjoyed the highest percentage increase in net worth at 42 percent. The top quintile as a whole experienced a 21 percent gain in mean net worth, the fourth quintile a 15 percent increase, the middle quintile a 21 percent advance, and the bottom two quintiles a 34 percent decrease. Of the total gain in wealth over these years, over a fifth (22 percent) fell into the hands of the top 0.1 percent, a figure higher than that for the 1983–2013 period as a whole, and 40 percent went to the top 1 percent, a figure comparable to that for the 1983–2013 period. The top quintile garnered 88 percent of the total growth, lower than for the whole thirty-year period but comparable to the 1983–1989 and 1989–2001 periods. Years 2007 to 2013 saw a decline in mean net worth. Percentage losses were heavier for the bottom 80 percent than the top quintile. Mean wealth de-

clined by 12 percent for the top 20 percent, 28 percent for the fourth quintile, and 43 percent for the middle quintile. The mean wealth of the bottom
40 percent slipped from slightly positive ($2,500) to a negative $10,800. Over
these years, 23 percent of the total loss in wealth was concentrated among
the top 1 percent and 65 percent among the top quintile. These figures were
considerably lower than comparable figures in the previous four periods
when mean wealth increased. The loss was thus more spread out over the
wealth distribution in this period than the gains of the previous periods.

These results indicate rather dramatically that the despite the Great Recession and its aftermath, growth in the economy during the period from
1983 to 2013 was concentrated in a surprisingly small part of the population—the top 20 percent and particularly the top 1 percent. The growth in
the concentration of wealth was not, however, uniform over time. Two periods, in particular, were characterized by large inequality spurts—1983–1989
and 2001–2007. During the other three periods, the proportion of the total
wealth gains accruing to the top groups was more or less equal to their wealth
share.[51]

Trends in Net Worth with Vehicles Included and a Comparison with the PSID

As shown in Table 2.7 (Panels A and B), including vehicles in the definition
of wealth to form net worth including autos (NWA) not surprisingly increases the value of both median and mean net worth. Time trends for NWA
were remarkably similar to those for net worth (NW) with a couple of exceptions. The first is the 1983–1989 period in which the inclusion of vehicles
resulted in a higher growth in median net worth (11.6 versus 7 percent). The
second was the 2010–2013 period when median NWA showed a 3 percent
increase and median NW a −1.2 percent change. Also, over this period, mean
NWA gained 2.4 percent while mean NW increased by only 0.6 percent.

When comparing inequality trends, we see first that including vehicles in
the definition of wealth results in lower measured inequality according to the
Gini coefficient. This is to be expected since vehicles are important assets of
the lower-income classes and adding vehicles increases the number of
households with positive net worth. Interestingly, the time trend in the Gini

Table 2.7. Time Trends in net worth, with and without vehicles included, 1983–2013

Variable	1983	1989	2001	2007	2010	2013	Change[a] 1983–1989	1989–2001	2001–2007	2007–2010	2010–2013	1983–2013
A. Median Net Worth (in thousands, 2013 dollars)												
1. Without vehicles	78.0	83.5	96.7	115.1	64.6	63.8	7.0	15.8	19.1	−43.9	−1.2	−18.2
2. With vehicles	89.0	99.3	113.3	135.3	79.0	81.4	11.6	14.1	19.5	−41.6	3.0	−8.5
B. Mean Net Worth (in thousands, 2013 dollars)												
1. Without vehicles	303.8	348.1	500.0	602.3	505.7	508.7	14.6	43.7	20.4	−16.0	0.6	67.4
2. With vehicles	315.3	360.6	520.5	623.8	516.0	528.2	14.4	44.3	19.8	−17.3	2.4	67.5
C. Gini Coefficient												
1. Without vehicles	0.799	0.828	0.826	0.834	0.866	0.871	0.029	−0.001	0.008	0.032	0.005	0.072
2. With vehicles	0.779	0.801	0.808	0.816	0.850	0.850	0.022	0.007	0.008	0.034	0.000	0.071
D. Share of Top 1 Percent (percentage)												
1. Without vehicles	33.8	35.2	33.4	34.6	35.1	36.7	1.4	−1.8	1.2	0.5	1.6	2.9
2. With vehicles	35.8	37.3	35.9	36.8	37.9	39.0	1.5	−1.4	0.9	1.1	1.1	3.1
E. Share of Top 5 Percent (percentage)												
1. Without vehicles	56.1	58.0	59.2	61.8	62.5	64.8	1.9	1.2	2.6	0.6	2.3	8.8
2. With vehicles	57.6	59.3	60.8	63.1	64.5	66.0	1.8	1.5	2.3	1.4	1.5	8.4
E. Share of Top 20 Percent (percentage)												
1. Without vehicles	81.3	83.0	84.4	85.0	88.6	88.9	1.7	1.4	0.6	3.6	0.3	7.6
2. With vehicles	82.0	83.6	85.0	85.5	89.3	89.3	1.6	1.4	0.5	3.8	−0.1	7.3

Source: Author's computations from the 1983, 1989, 2001, 2007, 2010, and 2013 Survey of Consumer Finances.
a. Percentage change for Panels A and B

coefficient for NWA matched almost exactly that for NW. Second, somewhat surprisingly, the addition of vehicles to net worth raises the estimated share of wealth held by the top 1, top 5, and, to a lesser extent, the top 20 percent of households. This is because the rich own a higher share of the total value of vehicles than they do of other assets.[52] Once again, time trends in the share of wealth held by these top groups are almost identical for NWA as for NW. The overall conclusion is that the inclusion of the value of vehicles in NW makes very little difference for time trends in net worth.

Another major source of data on household wealth comes from the Panel Study of Income Dynamics (PSID) housed at the Survey Research Center of the University of Michigan. Unlike the SCF, the PSID is basically a representative sample and does not oversample the rich. Nonetheless, it is useful to compare time trends from the two sources, particularly for years 2007 to 2013. The years differ somewhat from the SCF because the PSID has been a biennial survey since 1999. The PSID concept includes vehicles so that the appropriate comparison is with NWA.[53]

Both mean and median NWA are lower in the PSID data than the SCF. In 2007, mean net worth from the PSID was $423,600, compared to $623,800 from the SCF, and median net worth from the PSID was $98,900, compared to $135,300 from the SCF (all figures are in 2013 dollars). Time trends also differ between the two sources. The PSID shows a 43 percent drop in mean wealth and a 51 percent plunge in median wealth from 2007 to 2011 whereas the SCF indicate a 17 percent decline in mean NWA and a 42 percent decrease in median NWA from 2007 to 2010. The former shows a 27 percent rise in the mean and a 16 percent gain in the median from 2011 to 2013 whereas the SCF data indicate little change in either from 2010 to 2013. Over years 2007 to 2013, where we have data from both sources, the PSID shows a 27 percent decline in mean wealth and 43 percent drop in median wealth. The SCF results indicate only a 15 percent fall in mean NWA but a 40 percent reduction in median NWA. Trends in median wealth seem similar between the two sources but trends in mean wealth differ. The likely reason is that the SCF sample has better coverage of high wealth households than does the PSID.

Measured wealth inequality is actually a little higher in the PSID than in the SCF. The Gini coefficient for NWA was 0.832 in the PSID in 2007, compared to 0.816 for NWA in the SCF. This finding seems a bit surprising since the SCF has much better coverage of high wealth households. The PSID also shows a sharp increase in wealth inequality between 2007 and 2009, with the Gini coefficient rising by 0.058. In contrast, the SCF shows a 0.034 jump for NWA. This is followed by 0.011 decline from 2009 to 2011 according to the PSID, for a net change of 0.047 from 2007 to 2011 in comparison to the 0.034 increase for NWA from the SCF (no Gini coefficients are available from the PSID for 2013). Trends in NWA inequality, however, seem roughly similar between the two sources.

Summary and Concluding Remarks

Median household NW showed robust growth from 1962 to 2001, gaining 74 percent or 1.43 percent per year. Over the 2001–2007 period the median increased by 19 percent or 2.91 percent per year, even faster than in the preceding decades. Median income, based on CPS data, had a different time trend, rising by 28 percent or 0.92 percent per year from 1962 to 1989, and then by a mere 7.6 percent (in total) from 1989 to 2007.

Then the Great Recession hit and like a tsunami wiped out forty years of wealth gains. From 2007 to 2010, house prices fell by 24 percent in real terms, stock prices by 26 percent, and median wealth by a staggering 44 percent. By 2010 median wealth was even below where it had been in 1969. The share of households with zero or negative NW rose sharply from 18.6 to 21.8 percent. From 2010 to 2013, asset prices recovered, with stock prices up by 39 percent and house prices by 8 percent. Despite this, median wealth stagnated.

In this chapter, I have measured inequality in four ways: (1) the Gini coefficient, (2) the shares of the top groups, (3) percentile ratios, and (4) the share of total wealth growth accruing to different quantile groups. Results generally agree among the different measures used. According to the first metric, the Gini coefficient, wealth inequality rose sharply from 1983 to 1989 (0.029 Gini point increase). It then remained relatively stable from 1989 to 2007 but showed a steep increase over years 2007 to 2010, with the Gini coefficient climbing from 0.834 to 0.866 and the share of the top 20 percent from 85 to 89 percent. The share of the bottom 40 percent experienced a precipitous drop from 0.2 to −0.8 percent. The Gini coefficient for NW was up slightly form 2010 and 2013, while the share of the top 1 percent was up by 1.6 percent.

In 2013 the Gini coefficient for NW was at its highest level in fifty-one years, at 0.871.

In contrast, the Gini coefficient for income inequality, calculated from the SCF data, showed an almost continuous rise from 1962 to 2000 (a stunning 0.135 Gini point advance), a slight remission from 2000 to 2003, and then another jump of 0.034 Gini points through 2006. By 2006 the Gini coefficient for income had reached 0.574. It then dropped substantially from 2006 to 2009 (a decrease of 0.25 Gini points). But income inequality spiked upward from 2009 to 2012, with the Gini coefficient returning to its 2007 level.

Movements in top shares generally tracked the Gini coefficient. Like the Gini index, the NW shares of the top 1 percent, top 0.5 percent, and top 0.1 percent shot upward from 1983 to 1989. From 1989 to 2007, while the Gini coefficient showed a slight increase, the top shares showed a slight decline. Between 2007 and 2013, as the Gini index showed a sizeable upturn, the shares of the top 1 percent, top 0.5 percent, and top 0.1 percent likewise experienced sizeable gains.

The P99/P50 ratio showed a somewhat contrasting trend. With two exceptions, the P99/P50 ratio increased continuously over time from 46.1 in 1983 to 121.6 in 2013 (by a factor of 2.6). The highest percentage increase in the P99/P50 ratio was 38 percent, recorded between 2007 and 2010. The ratio then rose by 10 percent from 2010 to 2013. The P50/P25 ratio followed a somewhat different course, rising by a factor of 2.5 from 1983 to 2007 and then shooting up over sixfold from 2007 to 2013. The spike from 2007 to 2013 reflected the massive decline in median wealth—a result of the huge deflation in housing prices and concurrent rise in "underwater" homeowners.

The mean wealth of the top 1 percent jumped to 18.6 million dollars in 2013. The percentage increase in NW from 1983 to 2013 was much greater for the top wealth groups than for those lower in the distribution. The average wealth of the poorest 40 percent declined from $6,700 in 1983 to—$10,800 in 2013 (both in 2013 dollars). All in all, the greatest gains in wealth were enjoyed by the upper 20 percent, particularly the top 0.5 and top 1 percent. Between 1983 and 2013, the top 1 percent received 41 percent of the total growth in NW, while the top 20 percent got over 100 percent.

Looking at subperiods, we find that two periods in particular were characterized by large inequality spurts—1983–1989 and 2001–2007. Over those years, the top 1 percent received a disproportionate share of the total wealth growth—42.6 and 40.3 percent, respectively. During the other three periods, the proportion of the total wealth gains accruing to the top groups was more or less equal to their wealth share.

What shall we make of these somewhat different time trends in wealth inequality? First off, there is near universal agreement among the metrics that wealth inequality rose substantially between 1983 and 2013 (and, indeed, between 1962 and 2013). From 1983 to 2013, the Gini coefficient shot upward by 0.072 Gini points, the NW share of the top 5 percent by 8.8 percentage points, and the NW share of the top 20 percent by 7.6 percentage points. The wealth share of the top 1 percent showed a more modest increase of 2.9 percent. The P99 / P50 ratio went up by a factor of 2.6, the P95 / P50 ratio by a factor of 2.2, and the P50 / P25 ratio was up by a factor of 16.3. Moreover, from 1983 to 2013, 41 percent of the total wealth gains accrued to the top 1 percent and 100 percent to the top 20 percent. The Saez and Zucman data also show a tremendous increase in wealth inequality from 1983 to 2012 (the last date available)—with the shares of the top 1 percent, 0.5 percent, and 0.1 percent climbing by 17.1, 16.3, and 13.1 percentage points, respectively.

The main difference among the metrics is in regard to timing. According to the Gini coefficient, there were three large spurts in inequality: (1) 1962–1969 (an increase in the Gini coefficient of 0.025), (2) 1983–1989 (0.029 Gini points), and (3) 2007–2010 (0.032 Gini points). With regard to the very top shares, my calculations show relatively large increases in the wealth shares of the top 1 percent, top 0.5 percent, and 0.1 percent over the 1962–1969 period (gains of 2.2, 2.2, and 1.5 percentage points, respectively), those of the top 1 and 0.5 percent over years 1983 to 1989 (1.4 and 1.3 percentage points, respectively), and those of the top 1 and 0.5 percent over years 2007 to 2013 (2.1 and 1.9 percentage points, respectively). In contrast, the share of the top 5 percent showed spurts in years 1962 to 1969 (1.6 percentage points), 1983 to 1989 (1.9 percentage points) but again in 1989 to 1992 (2.0 percentage points), 2004 to 2007 (2.9 percentage points), and 2010 to 2013 (2.3 percentage points), while the share of the top 20 percent showed particularly strong gains in years 1962 to 1969 (1.5 percentage points), 1983 to 1989 (1.7 percentage points), and in 2007 to 2010 (3.6 percentage points). To complicate matters, we find that the SZ series indicates declining shares of the top 1 percent, 0.5 percent, and 0.1 percent from 1962 to 1969, large gains from 1983 to 1989 (3.1, 3.2, and 2.6 percentage points, respectively), another surge from 1995 to 1998 (2.8, 2.7, and 2.2 percentage points, respectively), and an even larger burst from 2004 to 2012 (8.3, 7.8, and 6.4 percentage points, respectively).

Percentile ratios show a different pattern. The P99/P50, the P95/P50, and the P50/P25 all indicate a surge in inequality from 2007 to 2010—increases of 38 percent, 68 percent, and 408 percent, respectively. The results vary for other periods. The P50/P25 ratio jumped by 65 percent over years 1983 to 1989 but the P99/P50 ratio was up by only 12 percent and the P95/P50 ratio was down slightly. By the P99/P50 there was an inequality burst from 1995 to 2001—up by 44 percent—while the P99/P50 ratio increased 20 percent and the P50/P25 ratio rose only slightly. The share of wealth gains accruing to the top 1 percent was, as noted earlier, particularly strong in the 1983–1989 and 2001–2007 periods—42.6 and 40.3 percent, respectively.

Of the measures presented here, it is probably the case that the Gini coefficient is the most reliable since it reflects the full distribution of wealth. Moreover, it is likely that estimated wealth shares of the top wealth groups are subject to error because, at least in the SCF, both the number of households and their wealth levels in the $100 million and above range are not fully captured. As we saw, this problem affects not only level estimates (actual wealth shares) but, more importantly, trends over time, since the gap between the top SCF value and both the minimum and maximum Forbes 400 value varied considerably over time. The estimated share of total wealth gains accruing to the top 1 percent is also unduly influenced by how well the wealth of this top group is captured in the survey, so that these figures are likely to be less reliable than the Gini coefficient.

The SZ data should in principle capture the very high wealth group but since the SZ estimates are so heavily based on capitalization and other imputation techniques it is likely that their estimates are subject to considerable error. This is particularly so for unincorporated business equity whose value is based on capitalizing unincorporated business income. As we shall see in Chapter 3, business equity is heavily concentrated among rich households. All in all, the SZ series probably gives more reliable estimates of the wealth shares of the top 1 percent and above than the SCF data because of the exclusion of the Forbes 400 from the SCF and the SCF's apparent underreporting of property income at the very top.

Fortunately, the Gini coefficient is not very sensitive to the estimated shares of the top groups. Indeed, as is well known, the Gini coefficient is not very sensitive to either the upper or lower tails of the wealth distribution, since the overwhelming mass of the Lorenz curve lies in the middle of the distribution (see Wolff, *Poverty and Income Distribution* [2009], for example). This is another reason why the Gini coefficient is likely to be the more reliable measure of inequality. Percentile levels (at least up to the 99th percentile) are also likely to be quite reliable, so that percentile ratios like the P99 / P50 ratio should be creditable and offer a complementary measure of inequality to the Gini coefficient. Based on the Gini coefficient, I would conclude that there were three inequality spurts over the fifty-one-year period: 1962–1989, 1983–1989, and 2007–2010. Over the full stretch of time, the Gini coefficient increased by 0.068 points. Interestingly, the P99 / P25 ratio also indicated inequality surges in years 1983–1989 (an 84 percent rise) and, particularly, in years 2007 to 2010 (a sixfold increase!).

As a postscript, it might be useful to comment on the tendency of economists in this field to focus on trends in wealth shares of top groups, when a comprehensive measure like the Gini coefficient seems superior. This body of work emanated from Simon Kuznets's *Shares of Upper Income Groups in Income and Savings* (1953) and Robert Lampman's *The Share of Top Wealth-holders in National Wealth, 1922–56* (1962). In both cases, work on inequality was limited to trends in top shares because of data limitations—in particular, limited income tax coverage in the case of the former and limited estate tax coverage in the case of the latter. Later work on the subject focused on top income and wealth shares because of data limitations.[54] Current work on wealth inequality using survey data might be better off using a comprehensive measure of inequality like the Gini coefficient rather than the wealth shares of top wealth holders.

Appendix Table 2.1. Sample sizes by household characteristic and year, 1983–2013

Category	1983	1989	1992	1995	1998	2001	2004	2007	2010	2013
All Households	4,262	3,143	3,906	4,299	4,305	4,442	4,519	4,418	6,482	6,015
A. Income Level (1998$)										
Under $15,000	999	546	705	717	702	675	644	624	1,196	1,086
$15,000–$24,999	650	362	461	533	513	516	515	490	970	861
$25,000–$49,999	1,173	726	883	1,058	952	979	1,013	939	1,586	1,443
$50,000–$74,999	587	436	499	558	598	612	579	559	861	736
$75,000–$99,999	208	234	251	295	310	294	326	347	410	392
$100,000–$249,999	310	363	484	523	519	527	562	537	659	663
$250,000 or more	335	477	622	615	712	839	880	923	800	833
B. Wealth Level (1998$)										
Under $25,000	1,570	804	1,159	1,259	1,295	1,294	1,418	1,171	2,537	2,246
$25,000–$49,999	406	217	298	306	246	271	273	232	413	368
$50,000–$99,999	584	338	366	454	401	389	348	321	522	473
$100,000–$249,999	725	486	548	590	583	563	534	580	776	739
$250,000–$499,999	308	344	318	369	427	392	392	422	576	517
$500,000–$999,999	203	224	259	300	286	317	346	370	417	422
$1,000,000 or over	466	730	958	1,021	1,068	1,215	1,208	1,322	1,242	1,250
C. Race										
Non-Hispanic whites	3,406	2,558	3,148	3,562	3,498	3,580	3,519	3,518	4,759	4,425
Non-Hispanic African Americans	472	308	358	380	414	462	484	410	790	746
Hispanics[a]	108	161	218	177	251	279	348	313	639	556
Asian and other races	117	116	183	180	143	121	168	177	293	288
D. Age Class[b]										
Under 35	1,157	542	805	886	837	810	757	702	1,178	1,032
35–44	777	688	830	908	926	929	886	812	1,182	1,032
45–54	680	612	775	907	956	1,064	1,081	1,014	1,492	1,327
55–64	673	569	595	657	687	733	919	930	1,362	1,281
65–74	527	452	574	560	522	499	512	549	748	817
75 and over	289	280	327	381	377	407	364	411	520	526
E. Education[c]										
Less than 12 years	1,281	667	613	608	613	615	547	503	658	544
12 years	1,151	787	921	1,086	1,037	1,059	1,057	1,075	1,821	1,601
13–15 years	742	548	737	920	913	874	880	861	1,101	1,028
16 years of more	1,088	1,141	1,635	1,685	1,742	1,894	2,035	1,979	2,902	2,842

Note: Author's computations from the 1983, 1989, 1992, 1995, 1998, 2001, 2004, 2007, 2010, and 2013 Survey of Consumer Finances.

a. Hispanics can be of any race.

b. Households are classified according to the age of the head of household.

c. Households are classified according to the education of the head of household.

3

Changing Portfolio Composition and the Rate of Return on Household Wealth

This chapter analyzes changes in the portfolio composition of household wealth over years 1983 to 2013 (the period for which consistent data exist) and rates of return on household wealth over the same period. It also looks at developments in ownership rates for selected assets and investigates changes in the overall composition of household wealth. Particular attention is paid to developments in the debt to income and the debt to net worth ratio.

Are the rich really different from the rest of the population? This chapter looks at the pattern of wealth holdings of the rich in comparison to the middle class. The rather staggering debt level of the middle class in 2013 raises the question of whether this is a recent phenomenon or has been going on for some time. An investigation into changes in middle class debt and trends in the financial resources available to the middle class over this time period may provide the answer.

Another way of portraying differences between middle class households and the rich is in terms of the share of total assets of different types held by each group. This point of view is examined and further detail is provided on what happened in the housing market from 2007 to 2013. We find that differences in portfolio composition, particularly leverage (indebtedness) between wealth classes, translate into large disparities in rates of return on household wealth over time.

A related issue is whether, as some have suggested, there has been growing ownership of stock in this country. This chapter provides an analysis of this topic and an investigation into whether there has been deterioration in pension accumulations in defined contribution (DC) pension plans over time.

Household Debt Finally Recedes

In 2013, owner-occupied housing was the most important household asset in the average portfolio breakdown for all households shown in Table 3.1, accounting for 29 percent of total assets (also see Figure 3.1). Net home equity—the value of the house minus any outstanding mortgage—amounted to only 17 percent of total assets. Real estate other than owner-occupied housing comprised 10 percent, and business equity another 18 percent.

Demand deposits, time deposits, money market funds, CDs, and the cash surrender value of life insurance (collectively, "liquid assets") made up 7.6 percent and pension accounts 16.5 percent. Bonds and other financial securities amounted to 1.5 percent; corporate stock, including mutual funds, to 12.7 percent; and trust fund equity to 3.2 percent. Debt as a proportion of gross assets was 15 percent, and the debt to net worth ratio was 0.18.

There were some significant changes in the composition of household wealth over years 1983 to 2013. First, the share of housing wealth in total assets, after fluctuating between 28 and 30 percent from 1983 to 2001, jumped to 34 percent in 2004 and then declined to 29 percent in 2013. Two factors explain this movement. The first is the trend in the homeownership rate, which rose from 63 percent in 1983 to 69 percent in 2004 and then fell off to 65 percent in 2013. The second is that the median house price for existing single-family homes rose by 18 percent between 2001 and 2004 and then plunged by 17 percent from 2004 to 2013.[1]

A second and related trend is that net home equity, after falling almost continuously from 24 percent of total assets in 1983 to 18 percent in 1998, picked up to 22 percent in 2004 but then fell again to 17 percent in 2013. The difference between the two series (gross versus net housing values) is attributable to the changing magnitude of mortgage debt on homeowner's property, which increased from 21 percent in 1983 to 37 percent in 1998, fell back to 35 percent in 2004, and then rose again to 39 percent in 2013. Moreover, mortgage debt on principal residences climbed from 9.4 of total assets in 2001 to 12.7 percent in 2010 before receding to 11.2 percent in 2013. The increase in net home equity as a proportion of assets between 2001 and 2004 reflected the strong gains in real estate values over these years, while its sharp decline from 2007 to 2013 reflected the steep fall in housing prices.

Table 3.1. Composition of total household wealth, 1983–2013 (percent of gross assets)

Wealth Component	1983	1989	1992	1995	1998	2001	2004	2007	2010	2013
Principal residence	30.1	30.2	29.8	30.4	29.0	28.2	33.5	32.8	30.7	28.5
Other real estate[a]	14.9	14.0	14.7	11.0	10.0	9.8	11.5	11.3	11.6	10.2
Unincorporated business equity[b]	18.8	17.2	17.7	17.9	17.7	17.2	17.1	20.1	17.7	18.3
Liquid assets[c]	17.4	17.5	12.2	10.0	9.6	8.8	7.3	6.6	7.7	7.6
Pension accounts[d]	1.5	2.9	7.2	9.0	11.6	12.3	11.8	12.1	15.1	16.5
Financial securities[e]	4.2	3.4	5.1	3.8	1.8	2.3	2.1	1.5	1.8	1.5
Corporate stock and mutual funds	9.0	6.9	8.1	11.9	14.8	14.8	11.9	11.8	11.2	12.7
Net equity in personal trusts	2.6	3.1	2.7	3.2	3.8	4.8	2.9	2.3	2.4	3.2
Miscellaneous assets[f]	1.3	4.9	2.5	2.8	1.8	1.8	1.8	1.7	1.7	1.5
Total	100.0	100.0	100.0	100.0	100.0	100.0	100.0	100.0	100.0	100.0
Debt on principal residence	6.3	8.6	9.8	11.0	10.7	9.4	11.6	11.4	12.7	11.2
All other debt[g]	6.8	6.4	6.0	5.3	4.2	3.1	3.9	3.9	4.4	4.0
Total debt	13.1	15.0	15.7	16.3	15.0	12.5	15.5	15.3	17.1	15.2
Selected Ratios in Percent										
Debt / net worth ratio	15.1	17.6	18.7	19.4	17.6	14.3	18.4	18.1	20.6	17.9
Debt / income ratio	68.4	87.6	88.8	91.3	90.9	81.1	115.0	118.7	127.0	107.1
Net home equity / total assets[h]	23.8	21.6	20.1	19.5	18.2	18.8	21.8	21.4	18.1	17.3
Principal residence debt as ratio to house value	20.9	28.6	32.7	36.0	37.0	33.4	34.8	34.9	41.2	39.3
Stocks, directly or indirectly owned as a ratio to total assets[i]	11.3	10.2	13.7	16.8	22.6	24.5	17.5	16.8	17.5	20.7

Source: Author's computations from the 1983, 1989, 1992, 1995, 1998, 2001, 2004, 2007, 2010, and 2013 Survey of Consumer Finances.

a. In 2001, 2004, and 2007, this equals the gross value of other residential real estate plus the *net equity* in nonresidential real estate.

b. Net equity in unincorporated farm and nonfarm businesses and closely held corporations.

c. Checking accounts, savings accounts, time deposits, money market funds, certificates of deposits, and the cash surrender value of life insurance.

d. IRAs, Keogh plans, 401(k) plans, the accumulated value of defined contribution pension plans, and other retirement accounts.

e. Corporate bonds, government bonds (including savings bonds), open-market paper, and notes.

f. Gold and other precious metals, royalties, jewelry, antiques, furs, loans to friends and relatives, future contracts, and miscellaneous assets.

g. Mortgage debt on all real property except principal residence, credit card, installment, and other debt.

h. Ratio of gross value of principal residence less mortgage debt on principal residence to total assets.

i. Includes direct ownership of stock shares and indirect ownership through mutual funds, trusts, and IRAs, Keogh plans, 401(k) plans, and other retirement accounts.

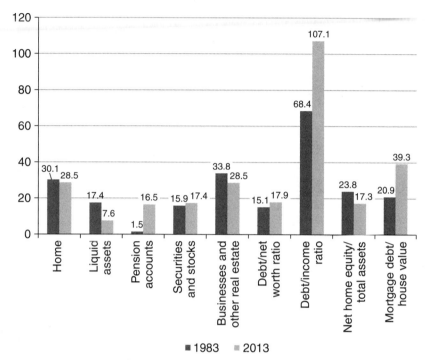

Figure 3.1. Composition of Household Wealth, 1983 and 2013
(Percent of gross assets)

Third, overall relative indebtedness first increased, with the debt to net worth ratio climbing from 15 percent in 1983 to 21 percent in 2010, and then fell off to 18 percent in 2013. Likewise, the debt-income ratio surged almost continuously over time from 68 percent in 1983 to 127 percent in 2010 but then dropped to 107 percent in 2013. If mortgage debt on principal residence is excluded, then the ratio of other debt to total assets actually fell off over time from 6.8 percent in 1983 to 4 percent in 2013.

The large rise in *relative* indebtedness among all households between 2007 and 2010 could be due to a rise in the absolute level of debt and / or a fall-off in net worth and income. As shown in Table 2.1, both mean net worth and mean income fell over the three years. There was also a slight contraction of debt in constant dollars, with mortgage debt declining by 5 percent, other debt by 2.6 percent, and total debt by 4.4 percent (see Table 3.5). Thus, the steep rise in the debt to equity and the debt to income ratios over the three years was entirely due to the reduction in wealth and income. In contrast, from 2010 to 2013, relative indebtedness declined. In this case, both net worth and incomes were relatively unchanged, so that the proximate cause was a sizeable reduction in household debt. In fact, average mortgage debt (in constant dollars) dropped by 13 percent, the average value of other debt by 11 percent, and average household debt by 13 percent.[2]

A fourth change is that pension accounts rose from 1.5 to 16.5 percent of total assets from 1983 to 2013. This increase largely offset the decline in the share of liquid assets in total assets, from 17.4 to 7.6 percent, so that it is reasonable to infer that to a large extent households substituted tax-deferred pension accounts for taxable savings deposits.

Fifth, other (nonhome) real estate fell from 15 percent of total assets in 1983 to 10 percent in 2013, financial securities declined from 4.2 to 1.5 percent of total assets, and unincorporated business equity held more or less steady over time at around 18 percent.[3] Stocks and mutual funds rose from 9 to 13 percent of gross assets over these years. Its year to year trend mainly reflected fluctuations in the stock market. If we include the value of stocks indirectly owned through mutual funds, trusts, IRAs, 401(k) plans, and other retirement accounts, then the value of total stocks owned as a share of total assets more than doubled from 11.3 percent in 1983 to 24.5 percent in 2001, and then tumbled to 17.5 percent in 2010, before rising to 20.7 percent in 2013. The rise during the 1990s reflected the bull market in corporate equities as well as increased stock ownership, while the decline in the 2000s was a result of the sluggish stock market as well as a drop in stock ownership (see Table 3.11b). The increase from 2010 to 2013 reflected the recovery of the stock market.

Portfolio Composition by Wealth Class

The tabulation in Table 3.1 provides a picture of the average holdings of all families in the economy, but there are marked class differences in how middle class families and the rich invest their wealth. As shown in Table 3.2, the richest 1 percent of households (as ranked by wealth) invested almost three-quarters of their savings in investment real estate, businesses, corporate stock, and financial securities in 2013 (also see Figure 3.2). Corporate stocks, either directly owned by the households or indirectly owned through

Table 3.2. Composition of household wealth by wealth class, 2013 (percent of gross assets)

Asset	All Households	Top 1%	Next 19%	Middle 3 Quintiles
Principal residence	28.5	8.7	28.0	62.5
Liquid assets (bank deposits, money market funds, and cash surrender value of life insurance)	7.6	6.1	8.4	8.1
Pension accounts	16.5	9.2	21.7	16.1
Corporate stock, financial securities, mutual funds, and personal trusts	17.4	27.3	16.3	3.4
Unincorporated business equity other real estate	28.5	46.9	24.2	8.6
Miscellaneous assets	1.5	1.9	1.4	1.2
Total assets	100.0	100.0	100.0	100.0
Memo (selected ratios in percent)				
Debt / net worth ratio	17.9	2.6	11.8	64.0
Debt / income ratio	107.1	38.2	96.6	125.0
Net home equity / total assets[a]	17.3	7.3	19.7	31.4
Principal residence debt / house value	39.3	16.5	29.5	49.8
All stocks / total assets[b]	20.7	24.6	22.7	9.5
Ownership Rates (Percent)				
Principal residence	65.1	96.9	95.1	66.7
Other real estate	17.4	75.5	44.0	12.4
Pension assets	49.2	88.7	84.0	44.4
Unincorporated business	10.4	76.6	25.6	6.6
Corporate stock, financial securities, mutual funds, and personal trusts	21.5	84.4	59.5	14.2
Stocks, directly or indirectly owned[b]	46.1	94.0	84.6	41.0
$5,000 or more	36.4	92.9	81.7	30.3
$10,000 or more	32.4	92.8	79.7	25.3

Source: Author's computations from the 2013 Survey of Consumer Finances. Households are classified into wealth class according to their net worth. Brackets for 2013 are as follows:

Top 1 percent: Net worth of $7,766,500 or more.

Next 19 percent: Net worth between $401,000 and $7,766,500.

Quintiles 2 through 4: Net worth between $0 and $401,000.

Also, see notes to Table 3.1.

a. Ratio of gross value of principal residence less mortgage debt on principal residence to total assets.

b. Includes direct ownership of stock shares and indirect ownership through mutual funds, trusts, and IRAs, Keogh plans, 401(k) plans, and other retirement accounts.

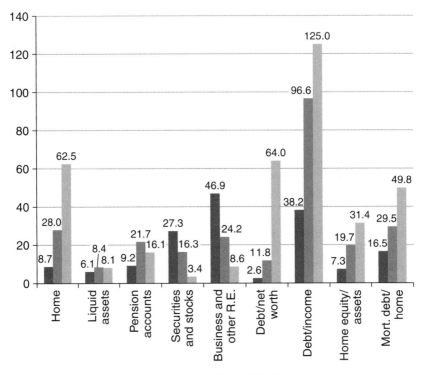

Figure 3.2. Composition of Household Wealth by Wealth Class, 2013
(Percent of gross assets)

mutual funds, trust accounts, or various pension accounts, comprised 25 percent by themselves. Housing accounted for only 9 percent of their wealth (and net equity in housing 7 percent), liquid assets 6 percent, and pension accounts another 9 percent. Their ratio of debt to net worth was only 2.6 percent, their ratio of debt to income was 38 percent, and the ratio of mortgage debt to house value was 17 percent.

Among the next richest 19 percent of U.S. households, housing comprised 28 percent of their total assets (and net home equity 20 percent), liquid assets 8 percent, and pension assets another 22 percent. Investment assets—real estate, business equity, stocks, and bonds—made up 41 percent and 23 percent was in the form of stocks directly or indirectly owned. Debt amounted to 12 percent of their net worth and 97 percent of their income, and the ratio of mortgage debt to house value was 30 percent.

More than three-fifths of the assets of the middle three quintiles of households was invested in their own homes in 2013. Their large mortgage debt was reflected in home equity of only 31 percent of total assets. Another quarter went into monetary savings of one form or another and pension accounts. Together, housing, liquid assets, and pension assets accounted for 87 percent of the total assets of the middle class. The remainder was about evenly split among nonhome real estate, business equity, and various financial securities and corporate stock. Stocks directly or indirectly owned amounted to only 10 percent of their total assets. The ratio of debt to net worth was 64 percent, substantially higher than for the richest 20 percent, and their ratio of debt to income was 125 percent, also much higher than that of the top quintile. Finally, their mortgage debt amounted to about half the value of their principal residences.

Almost all households among the top 20 percent of wealth holders owned their own home, in comparison to 67 percent of households in the middle three quintiles. Three-quarters of very rich households (in the top percentile) owned some other form of real estate, compared to 44 percent of rich households (those in the next 19 percent of the distribution) and only 12 percent of households in the middle 60 percent. Eighty-nine percent of the very rich owned some form of pension asset, compared to 84 percent of the rich and 44 percent of the middle class. A somewhat startling 77 percent of the very rich reported owning their own businesses. The comparable figures were 26 percent among the rich and only 7 percent of the middle class.

Among the very rich, 84 percent held corporate stock, mutual funds, financial securities or a trust fund, in comparison to 60 percent of the rich and only 14 percent of the middle class. Ninety-four percent of the very rich reported owning stock either directly or indirectly, compared to 85 percent of the rich and 41 percent of the middle. If we exclude small holdings of stock, then the ownership rates dropped off sharply among the middle three quintiles, from 41 percent to 30 percent for stocks worth $5,000 or more and to 25 percent for stocks worth $10,000 or more.

Table 3.3 compares the wealth composition of the three wealth classes in 1983 and 2013. There was remarkable stability in the composition of wealth by wealth class over these years. The most notable exception is a substitution of pension assets for liquid assets—a transition that occurred for all three wealth classes but that was particularly marked for percentiles 80–99 and for

Table 3.3. Composition of household wealth by wealth class, 1983 and 2013 (percent of gross assets)

Component	Top 1%		Next 19%		Middle 3 Quintiles	
	1983	2013	1983	2013	1983	2013
Principal residence	8.1	8.7	29.1	28.0	61.6	62.5
Liquid assets (bank deposits, money market funds, and cash surrender value of life insurance)	8.5	6.1	21.4	8.4	21.4	8.1
Pension accounts	0.9	9.2	2.0	21.7	1.2	16.1
Corporate stock, financial securities, mutual funds, and personal trusts	29.5	27.3	13.0	16.3	3.1	3.4
Unincorporated business equity, other real estate	52.0	46.9	32.8	24.2	11.4	8.6
Miscellaneous assets	1.0	1.9	1.6	1.4	1.3	1.2
Total assets	100.0	100.0	100.0	100.0	100.0	100.0
Memo						
Debt / net worth ratio	5.9	2.6	10.9	11.8	37.4	64.0
Debt / income ratio	86.8	38.2	72.8	96.6	66.9	125.0

Note: Author's computations from the 1983 and 2013 Survey of Consumer Finances. Also, see notes to Tables 3.1 and 3.2.

the middle three quintiles. The debt to net worth ratio actually fell by over half for the top 1 percent from 1983 and 2013, as did the debt-income ratio. The debt to net worth ratio increased slightly for the next 19 percent, while the debt-income ratio rose sharply, from 73 to 97 percent. For the middle three wealth quintiles, the debt to net worth ratio as well as the debt-income ratio almost doubled over this period.

More details are provided in Table 3.4 for the middle three wealth quintiles. Perhaps the most striking development was the homeownership rate, which after rising almost continuously over time from 72 percent in 1983 to 78 percent in 2004, plunged by 11 percentage points to 67 percent in 2013.[4] This trend was more pronounced than that among all households, among whom the homeownership rate dropped from 69 percent in 2004 to 65 percent in 2013. A similar trend is evident for the share of home values in the value of total assets, which remained virtually unchanged from 1983 to 2001 but then rose sharply in 2004. This increase was largely a result of rising

Table 3.4. Composition of household wealth of the middle three wealth quintiles, 1983–2013 (percent of gross assets)

Asset	1983	1989	1998	2001	2004	2007	2010	2013
Principal residence	61.6	61.7	59.8	59.2	66.1	65.1	64.8	62.5
Liquid assets (bank deposits, money market funds, and cash surrender value of life insurance)	21.4	18.6	11.8	12.1	8.5	7.8	8.0	8.1
Pension accounts	1.2	3.8	12.3	12.7	12.0	12.9	13.9	16.1
Corporate stock, financial securities, mutual funds, and personal trusts	3.1	3.5	5.5	6.2	4.2	3.6	3.1	3.4
Unincorporated business equity, other real estate	11.4	9.4	8.8	8.5	7.9	9.3	8.9	8.6
Miscellaneous assets	1.3	2.9	1.8	1.2	1.4	1.3	1.3	1.2
Total assets	100.0	100.0	100.0	100.0	100.0	100.0	100.0	100.0
Memo (selected ratios in percent)								
Debt / net worth ratio	37.4	41.7	51.3	46.4	61.6	61.1	69.2	64.0
Debt / income ratio	66.9	83.0	101.6	100.3	141.2	156.7	134.3	125.0
Net home equity / total assets[a]	43.8	39.2	33.3	33.8	34.7	34.8	31.4	31.4
Principal residence debt / house value	28.8	36.5	44.4	42.9	47.6	46.6	51.5	49.8
All stocks / total assets[b]	2.4	3.3	11.2	12.6	7.5	7.0	8.1	9.5
Ownership Rates (Percent)								
Principal residence	71.6	71.5	73.3	75.9	78.2	76.9	68.0	66.7
Other real estate	15.4	15.5	13.7	13.2	13.6	14.7	12.4	12.4
Pension assets	12.2	27.3	48.5	52.9	51.4	53.4	45.8	44.4
Unincorporated business	8.5	8.4	8.5	7.9	8.1	8.8	8.2	6.6
Corporate stock, financial securities, mutual funds, and personal trusts	21.6	24.2	26.7	27.5	27.1	23.1	15.3	14.2
All stocks[b]	16.5	29.4	46.6	51.1	49.7	47.8	41.4	41.0
Mean Debt (thousands, 2013$)								
Debt on principal residence	23.5	34.2	33.2	49.7	71.4	76.1	58.5	52.4
All other debt	12.5	10.5	9.2	12.2	15.1	19.2	13.1	13.3
Total debt	36.0	44.7	42.4	61.9	86.5	95.2	71.6	65.7

Source: Author's computations from the 1983, 1989, 1992, 1995, 1998, 2001, 2004, 2007, 2010, and 2013 Survey of Consumer Finances.

Households are classified into wealth class according to their net worth. Also, see notes to Table 3.1.

a. Ratio of gross value of principal residence less mortgage debt on principal residence to total assets.

b. Includes direct ownership of stock shares and indirect ownership through mutual funds, trusts, and IRAs, Keogh plans, 401(k) plans, and other retirement accounts

house prices and secondarily a consequence of the continued gain in the home-ownership rate. The share then declined from 2004 through 2013 as housing prices fell and the homeownership rate plummeted.

It might seem surprising that despite the steep drop in home prices from 2007 to 2010, housing as a share of total assets actually fell only slightly. The reason is that the other components of wealth fell even more than housing. While mean housing fell by 31 percent in real terms, the mean value of other real estate was down by 39 percent and that of stocks and mutual funds by 47 percent.

Likewise, despite the modest recovery in housing prices from 2010 to 2013, the share of housing in total assets dropped by 2.3 percentage points. The mean value of housing fell by 7.3 percent. Of this, the decline in the home-ownership rate accounted for only 19 percent of the overall decline, while the main culprit was the decline in the mean values of houses, which explained 81 percent. This result seems contrary to the finding that the *median value of existing homes* rose by 8 percent in real terms according to data from the National Association of Realtors (see note 3 in Chapter 2 for the reference). The most likely reason for the difference in results is that the 8 percent figure is based on data for existing homes only whereas the data from the Survey of Consumer Finances (SCF) include the value of homes that were owned by the household prior to the current year as well as newly bought homes. Another difference is that the former include all families whereas my figure is based on households in the middle three wealth quintiles. In fact, according to the SCF data, the *median* value of homes among middle-class households was down by 14 percent in real terms from 2010 to 2013. This result, in turn, may be due to the fact that the new homes bought by families in the SCF sample were cheaper than existing homes.

The share of pension accounts in total assets rose by 15 percentage points from 1983 to 2013, while that of liquid assets declined by 13 percentage points. This trend was more or less continuous over time. This set of changes paralleled that of all households. In contrast, the share of middle-class households holding a pension account, after surging by 41 percentage points, from 12 percent in 1983 to 53 percent in 2007, collapsed by 9 percentage points to 44 percent in 2013. From 2007 to 2010 the mean value of pension accounts fell quite sharply, by 25 percent, though this was less than that of average overall assets, so that the share of pension accounts in total assets rose.

From 2010 to 2013, in contrast, mean pension accounts were up by 12 percent, despite the slight decline in the ownership rate, so that the share of pension accounts in total assets strengthened considerably (by 2.2 percentage points).

The share of all stocks in total assets mushroomed from 2.4 percent in 1983 to 12.6 percent in 2001 and then fell off to 8.1 percent in 2010 as stock prices stagnated and then collapsed and middle-class households divested themselves of stock holdings. The proportion then rebounded to 9.5 percent in 2013 as the stock market recovered. The stock ownership rate among the middle class also shot up quickly from 17 percent in 1983 to 51 percent in 2001, when it peaked. It then declined steeply to 41 percent in 2013. In similar fashion, the share of middle-class households owning either corporate stock, financial securities, mutual funds or a personal trust rose from 22 percent in 1983 to 28 percent in 2001 and then plunged almost by half to 14 percent in 2013. Much of the decline took place between 2007 and 2010, as middle-class households got scared off by the stock market collapse of those years.

The Evolution of Middle-Class Debt

Has the debt level of the middle class always been very high or is this a recent phenomenon? The debt-income ratio peaked in 2010 and then receded in 2013, while the debt to net worth ratio peaked in 2007 and then contracted substantially in 2010 and a bit more in 2013.

There was a sharp rise in the debt to net worth ratio of the middle class from 37 percent in 1983 to 61 percent in 2007. There was a particularly steep uptick between 2001 and 2004, a reflection mainly of rising mortgage debt. The debt to income ratio skyrocketed from 1983 to 2007, more than doubling. Once, again, much of the increase happened between 2001 and 2004. In constant dollar terms, the mean debt of the middle class increased by a factor of 2.6 between 1983 and 2007, mortgage debt by a factor of 3.2, and other debt by a factor of 1.5. The rise in the debt to net worth ratio and the debt-income ratio was much more pronounced than for all households. In 1983, for example, the debt to income ratio was about the same for the middle class as for all households but by 2007 the ratio was much larger for the former.

Table 3.5. The evolution of household debt, 2007–2013 (mean values, in thousands, 2013 dollars)

	2007	2010	2013	% Change		
				2007–2010	2010–2013	2007–2013
A. All Households						
1. Mortgage debt[a]	81.4	77.4	67.2	−5.0	−13.1	−17.4
2. All other debt	27.7	27.0	23.9	−2.6	−11.3	−13.5
a. Educational loans	3.7	5.3	5.8	43.6	10.1	58.1
b. Noneducational debt	24.0	21.7	18.1	−9.6	−16.5	−24.5
3. Total debt	109.1	104.3	91.1	−4.4	−12.6	−16.4
B. Middle Three Wealth Quintiles						
1. Mortgage debt[a]	76.1	58.5	52.4	−23.1	−10.4	−31.1
2. All other debt	19.2	13.1	13.3	−31.6	1.6	−30.5
a. Educational loans	2.7	2.7	3.0	−0.6	11.9	11.2
b. Noneducational debt	16.5	10.4	10.3	−36.7	−1.1	−37.4
3. Total debt	95.2	71.6	65.7	−24.8	−8.2	−31.0

Source: Author's computations from the 2007, 2010, and 2013 Survey of Consumer Finances.
a. Principal residence debt only.

After the Great Recession hit, the debt to net worth ratio continued to rise, reaching 72 percent in 2010, but there was actually a retrenchment in the debt to income ratio, falling to 134 percent in 2010. The reason is that from 2007 to 2010, the mean debt of the middle class actually contracted by 25 percent in constant dollars (see Table 3.5). Average mortgage debt declined by 23 percent, as families paid down their outstanding balances, while the mean value of other debt plummeted by 32 percent, as families paid off credit card balances and other forms of consumer debt. If we separate out educational loans, we find that they actually remained flat over these years whereas noneducational debt soared by 37 percent. Among all households, in contrast, mortgage debt in constant dollars fell by only 5 percent, noneducational debt was down by 10 percent, but student loans climbed by 44 percent. The significant rise in the debt to net worth ratio of the middle class between 2007 and 2010 was due to the steeper drop off in net worth than in debt, while the decline in the debt-income ratio of this group was exclusively due to the sharp contraction of overall debt.

Both the debt to net worth and the debt-income ratios fell from 2010 to 2013 for the middle class. The proximate cause was a decline in overall mean debt, which fell by 8.2 percent in real terms over these years. This, in turn, was due to a decline in average mortgage debt, which dropped by 10.4 percent. The average balance on other debt actually increased slightly, by 1.6 percent. In this case, student loans were up by 12 percent whereas noneducational debt fell by 1 percent. Average overall debt fell even more among all households, by 13 percent, with mortgage debt down by 13 percent and noneducational debt down by 17 percent, whereas student loans increased by 10 percent.

As for all households, net home equity as a percentage of total assets fell for the middle class from 1983 to 2013 and mortgage debt as a proportion of house value rose. The decline in the former between 2007 and 2010 was relatively small despite the steep decrease in home prices, a reflection of the sharp reduction in mortgage debt. There was virtually no change from 2010 to 2013. On the other hand, the rise in the ratio of mortgage debt to house values was relatively large over years 2007 to 2010 because of the fall-off in home prices. This ratio actually contracted somewhat from 2010 to 2013 as outstanding mortgage debt fell.

Nowhere is the "middle-class squeeze" more vividly demonstrated than in their rising debt. As noted earlier, the ratio of debt to net worth of the middle three wealth quintiles rose from 37 percent in 1983 to 46 percent in 2001 and then jumped to 61 percent in 2007. Correspondingly, their debt to income ratio rose from 67 percent in 1983 to 100 percent in 2001 and then zoomed up to 157 percent in 2007! This new debt took two major forms. First, because housing prices went up over these years, families were able to borrow against the now enhanced value of their homes by refinancing their mortgages and by taking out home equity loans (lines of credit secured by their home). In fact, home mortgage debt climbed from 29 percent of total assets in 1983 to 47 percent in 2007, and home equity as a share of total assets fell from 44 to 35. Second, because of their increased availability, families ran up huge debt on their credit cards.

Where did the borrowing go? Some have asserted that was invested in stocks. If this had been the case, then stocks as a share of total assets would have increased over this period, which it did not (it fell from 13 to 7 percent between 2001 and 2007). Moreover, it did not go into other assets. In fact, the rise in housing prices almost fully explains the increase in the net worth of the middle class from 2001 to 2007. Of the $16,400 rise in median wealth, gains in housing prices alone accounted for $14,000 or 86 percent of the growth in wealth. Instead, it appears that middle-class households, experiencing stagnating incomes, expanded their debt in order to finance normal consumption expenditures. Indeed, despite the huge build-up of debt from 2001 to 2007, the average expenditures in constant dollars of the middle-income quintile expanded by a mere 1.7 percent.[5]

The large build-up of debt set the stage for the financial crisis of 2007. When the housing market collapsed in 2007, many households found themselves "underwater," with mortgage debt exceeding the value of the home. This factor, coupled with the loss of income emanating from the recession, led many homeowners to stop paying off their mortgage debt. The resulting foreclosures led, in turn, to steep reductions in the value of mortgage-backed securities. Banks and other financial institutions holding such assets experienced a large decline in their equity, which touched off the financial crisis.

Financial Reserves of Middle-Income Families

Table 3.6 documents a disturbing trend in the financial resources available to middle-income families.[6] Here, I focus on prime working age families (ages 25 to 54). The average prime working age family in 1983 had accumulated only enough financial resources (net worth less home equity) to sustain its normal consumption for a period of 2.3 months in case of income loss and to sustain consumption at 125 percent of the poverty standard for only 4.6 months. Indeed, the next lowest 20 percent of households had only enough savings to keep going for 0.9 months in the event of losing their income, while the bottom 20 percent had no financial reserves. These reserves for the middle class peaked in 1989—3.6 months to sustain normal consumption and 9 months for consumption at 125 percent of the poverty standard. After that, there was a gradual deterioration in their financial reserves. By 2013, the average working age family had only enough reserves to sustain its normal consumption for 0.2 months and consumption at 125 percent of the poverty line for 0.4 months. The bottom 40 percent had virtually no financial reserves.

Concentration of Assets by Asset Type

Another way to portray differences between middle-class households and the rich is to compute the share of total assets of different types held by each

Table 3.6. Accumulated financial resources of prime working age families by income quintile in terms of number of months resources can sustain consumption, 1983–2013

Income Quintile	Number of Months Current Consumption Can be Sustained[a]	Number of Months Consumption at 125% of Poverty Standard Can be Sustained[b]
A. 1983		
Top quintile	16.5	51.4
Fourth quintile	5.7	14.6
Third quintile	2.3	4.6
Second quintile	0.9	1.3
Bottom quintile	0.0	0.0
B. 1989		
Top quintile	18.7	72.6
Fourth quintile	4.7	14.6
Third quintile	3.6	9.0
Second quintile	0.5	0.9
Bottom quintile	0.0	0.0
C. 1995		
Top quintile	19.0	61.3
Fourth quintile	3.5	7.9
Third quintile	1.2	1.8
Second quintile	0.1	0.1
Bottom quintile	0.0	0.0
D. 1998		
Top quintile	25.2	81.5
Fourth quintile	8.2	18.4
Third quintile	2.2	3.4
Second quintile	0.1	0.1
Bottom quintile	0.0	0.0
E. 2001		
Top quintile	33.7	143.5
Fourth quintile	10.4	28.0
Third quintile	2.6	5.1
Second quintile	0.3	0.4
Bottom quintile	0.0	0.0
F. 2007		
Top quintile	26.4	120.6
Fourth quintile	9.0	24.3
Third quintile	1.6	3.2

(*continued*)

Table 3.6. (continued)

Income Quintile	Number of Months Current Consumption Can be Sustained[a]	Number of Months Consumption at 125% of Poverty Standard Can be Sustained[b]
Second quintile	0.0	0.0
Bottom quintile	0.0	0.0
G. 2010		
Top quintile	22.2	92.3
Fourth quintile	2.8	7.0
Third quintile	0.3	0.5
Second quintile	0.0	0.0
Bottom quintile	0.0	0.0
H. 2013		
Top quintile	27.3	113.6
Fourth quintile	5.3	13.0
Third quintile	0.2	0.4
Second quintile	0.0	0.0
Bottom quintile	0.0	0.0

Source: Author's computations from the 1983, 1989, 1995, 1998, 2001, 2007, 2010, and 2013 Survey of Consumer Finances and the Consumer Expenditure Survey for the same years. Calculations from the SCF are for households with age of householder between 25 and 54.

a. Defined as the ratio of median financial resources (net worth less home equity) to the median consumption expenditures for the income group.

b. Defined as the ratio of median financial resources to 125 percent of the poverty line for a family of four.

group (see Table 3.7 and Figure 3.3 and Figure 3.4). In 2013 the richest 1 percent of households held about half of all outstanding stock, financial securities, trust equity, and business equity, and a third of nonhome real estate. The top 10 percent of families as a group accounted for about 85 to 90 percent of stock shares, bonds, trusts, and business equity, and over three-quarters of nonhome real estate. Moreover, despite the fact that 46 percent of households owned stock shares either directly or indirectly through mutual funds, trusts, or various pension accounts, the richest 10 percent of households controlled 81 percent of the total value of these stocks, though less than its 91 percent share of directly owned stocks and mutual funds.

In contrast, owner-occupied housing, deposits, life insurance, and pension accounts were more evenly distributed among households. The bottom 90 percent of households accounted for 59 percent of the value of owner-

Table 3.7. The percent of total assets held by wealth class, 2013

					Share of Top 10%									
Asset Type	Top 1.0%	Next 9.0%	Bottom 90.0%	All	1983	1989	1992	1995	1998	2001	2004	2007	2010	2013
A. Investment Assets														
Stocks and mutual funds	49.8	41.2	9.1	100.0	90.4	86.0	86.3	88.4	85.1	84.5	85.4	89.4	91.2	90.9
Financial securities	54.7	39.6	5.7	100.0	82.9	87.1	91.3	89.8	84.1	88.7	87.9	98.5	93.6	94.3
Trusts	49.5	34.0	16.5	100.0	95.4	87.9	87.9	88.5	90.8	86.7	81.5	79.4	80.9	83.5
Business equity	62.8	31.0	6.2	100.0	89.9	89.8	91.0	91.7	91.7	89.6	90.3	93.3	91.8	93.8
Nonhome real estate	33.7	44.1	22.2	100.0	76.3	79.6	83.0	78.7	74.9	78.5	79.4	76.9	78.9	77.8
Total for group	51.5	37.0	11.5	100.0	85.6	85.7	87.6	87.5	86.2	85.5	85.6	87.8	87.5	88.5
Stocks, directly or indirectly owned[a]	37.8	43.6	18.6	100.0	89.7	80.8	78.7	81.9	78.7	76.9	78.8	81.2	80.6	81.4
B. Housing, Liquid Assets, Pension Assets, and Debt														
Principal residence	9.8	31.1	59.2	100.0	34.2	34.0	36.0	31.7	35.2	37.0	38.0	38.5	40.2	40.8
Deposits[b]	24.8	42.4	32.8	100.0	52.9	61.5	59.7	62.3	51.0	57.2	60.9	57.7	67.5	67.2
Life insurance	30.0	35.3	34.7	100.0	33.6	44.6	45.0	44.9	52.8	46.0	57.3	54.9	54.4	65.3
Pension accounts[c]	17.8	47.5	34.8	100.0	67.5	50.5	62.3	62.3	59.8	60.4	58.3	59.2	65.4	65.2
Total for group	14.5	37.6	47.9	100.0	41.0	43.9	45.2	42.5	44.0	45.9	45.7	45.8	51.0	52.1
Total debt	5.4	21.1	73.5	100.0	31.8	29.4	37.5	28.3	27.0	25.9	27.0	26.6	27.4	26.5

Source: Author's computations from the 1983, 1989, 1992, 1995, 1998, 2001, 2004, 2007, 2010, and 2013 Survey of Consumer Finances.
Households are classified into wealth class according to their net worth. Brackets for 2013 are:

Top 1 percent: Net worth of $7,766,500 or more.
Next 9 percent: Net worth between $980,900 and $7,766,500.
Bottom 90 Percent: Net worth less than $908,900.

a. Includes direct ownership of stock shares and indirect ownership through mutual funds, trusts, and IRAs, Keogh plans, 401(k) plans, and other retirement accounts.
b. Includes demand deposits, savings deposits, time deposits, money market funds, and CDs.
c. IRAs, Keogh plans, 401(k) plans, and other retirement accounts.

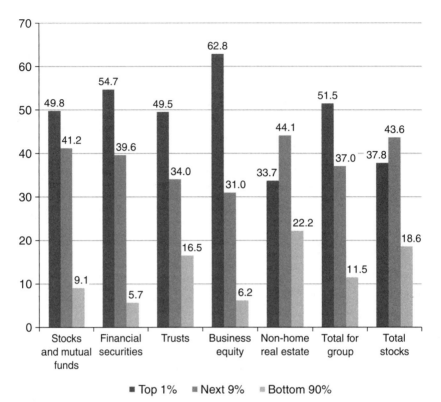

Figure 3.3. Percent of Total Investment Type Assets Held by Wealth Class, 2013

occupied housing, 33 percent of deposits, 35 percent of life insurance cash value, and 35 percent of the value of pension accounts. Debt was the most evenly distributed component of household wealth, with the bottom 90 percent of households responsible for 74 percent of total indebtedness.

The concentration of asset ownership by asset type remained remarkably stable over the three decades despite the dramatic changes in the economy over this time period, with three exceptions: First, the share of total stocks and mutual funds held by the richest 10 percent of households declined from 90 to 85 percent from 1983 to 2004 but then rose back to 91 percent in 2013, while their share of stocks directly or indirectly owned fell from 90 percent in 1983 to 77 percent in 2001 but then rose to 81 percent in 2013. Second, the proportion of total pension accounts held by the top 10 percent fell from 68 percent in 1983 to 51 percent in 1989, reflecting the growing use of IRAs

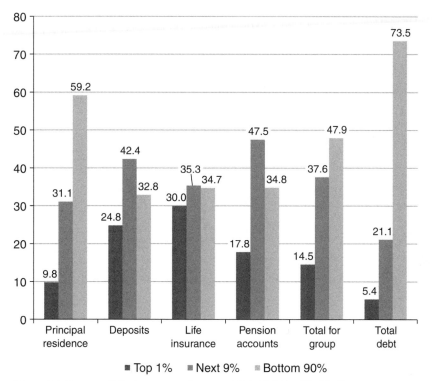

Figure 3.4. Percent of Noninvestment Assets and Debt Held by Wealth Class, 2013

by middle-income families, and then rebounded to 65 percent in 2013 from the expansion of 401(k) plans and their adoption by those with high incomes. Third, the share of total debt held by the top 10 percent declined from 32 to 27 percent between 1983 and 2013.

The Housing Market

It is perhaps no surprise that the housing sector took an especially large hit in the financial crisis—the prime culprits in this crisis were the mortgage industry and the creation of faulty financial instruments by the financial sector that were tied to the fate of the housing market. The housing bubble in the early part of the last decade, which artificially inflated home prices to unprecedented levels, certainly set the stage for a major market correction. Indeed, as noted in Chapter 2, from 2007 to 2010 the median price of existing homes plummeted by 24 percent in real terms. Because housing makes up over 30 percent of total assets for all households and over 60 percent of the assets for the middle class, any economic downturn that affects the housing market will naturally hurt the wealth of the middle class.

The overall homeownership rate declined from 68.6 percent in 2007 to 67.2 percent in 2010 (see Table 3.8). This seems pretty modest, given all the media hype about home foreclosures over these years. Percentage point reductions were sharper for African American and Hispanic households (1.9 percentage points) than for white households (almost no change); for single males (2.6 percentage points) than for married couples or single females (actually a net increase); for high school graduates (4.3 percentage points) than other educational groups; younger age groups in comparison to age group 75 and over (a large net increase); and for households with annual incomes below $25,000 and, surprisingly, above $75,000 than for middle-income households.

The collapse in home values led to a surprisingly modest uptick in the number of families with negative home equity. In 2007, only 1.8 percent of homeowners reported that their net home equity was negative. By 2010, 8.2 percent of homeowners were underwater. As discussed earlier, though housing prices dropped by 24 percent in real terms from 2007 to 2010, there was also a substantial retrenchment of mortgage debt, which accounted for the relatively small share of homeowners underwater in 2010.[7]

Normally, we might think that the poorest households had the greatest incidence of being underwater but this was not always the case. Minorities did have a somewhat higher incidence of negative home equity than whites but the differences were quite small. Interestingly, single females, the poorest of the three family types, and single males had a somewhat lower incidence of negative home equity among homeowners than married couples. The reason for this was likely the lower mortgage debt of single females and single males (that is, they had less expensive houses to begin with). Also, the lowest educational group, those with fewer than twelve years of schooling, had the smallest incidence of negative home equity among their homeowners, only 5 percent.[8] In contrast, the incidence ranged from 8 percent to 11 percent among high school graduates, those with some college, and college graduates.

The age pattern was more consistent with expectations. Homeowners in the youngest age group, under age 35, had by far the highest incidence of negative home equity, 16 percent. The incidence of negative home equity declined almost directly with age, reaching 3 percent for the oldest age group, 75 years and older. This reflected the fact that mortgages were generally paid off as people aged. Moreover, the overall ratio of debt to net worth also declined directly with age.[9]

This pattern by income class is again unexpected. The overall pattern was U-shaped, with the lowest incidence of negative home equity being for the lowest income class (under $15,000 of annual income) and the highest income class ($250,000 or more). The incidence of negative home equity among homeowners peaked at the $50,000 to $75,000 income class. Thus, the middle class was hit hardest by the collapse in housing prices. The reason is that they took out much higher mortgage debt relative to their home values than the poor or the rich, through refinancing, secondary mortgages, and home equity lines of credit (see Tables 3.2 and 3.4).

The average decline in the value of home equity among homeowners from 2007 to 2010 was 29 percent (in constant dollars). This is a surprisingly low figure given the 24 percent decline in real housing prices. If average mortgage debt had remained constant over the three years, average home equity would have dropped by 37 percent.[10] It was only the contraction of average mortgage debt over these years that kept the percentage decline in home equity at 26 percent instead of 37 percent.

Hispanic homeowners suffered by far the largest percentage decline in home equity—47 percent—of the three racial/ethnic groups. Black households experienced a somewhat larger percentage decline than white homeowners. Single female households experienced a somewhat larger decline than single males or married couples. The less schooled households suffered a larger decline than college graduates (only 26 percent for the latter). There was tremendous age variation, with older households more immune to the housing price collapse. The youngest age group experienced a 53 percent fall in home equity while the oldest age group had "only" a 19 percent decline.

There is a U-shaped pattern with regard to household income, with the lowest income class experiencing only a 0.6 percent depreciation in home equity, income class $75,000–$99,999 suffering the greatest percentage

Table 3.8. Share of homeowners with negative home equity and delinquent on their mortgages by household characteristic, 2007–2013

	Homeownership Rate (percentage)			Percent of Homeowners with Negative Home Equity			Percentage Change in Mean Home Equity (2013$) for Homeowners		Percent of Homeowners Delinquent on Mortgage 2009
	2007	2010	2013	2007	2010	2013	2007–2010	2010–2013	
A. All Households	68.6	67.2	65.1	1.8	8.2	6.9	−28.9	−3.8	5.1
B. Race / Ethnicity[a]									
1. Non-Hispanic white	74.8	74.6	73.1	1.7	8.0	5.5	−24.2	−3.4	3.4
2. African American	48.6	47.7	44.0	1.3	9.2	14.2	−26.4	−19.9	11.0
3. Hispanic	49.2	47.3	43.9	2.1	9.1	12.0	−47.0	1.6	15.4
C. Family Type									
1. Married couples	79.0	77.5	75.5	1.9	8.4	7.7	−24.7	−1.6	4.6
2. Single males	51.4	48.9	46.8	3.0	7.5	5.7	−23.4	4.8	3.7
3. Single females	55.1	55.5	53.8	0.9	7.8	5.1	−31.1	−9.9	7.8
D. Years of Schooling[b]									
1. Less than 12 years	52.8	54.3	51.8	0.4	5.0	5.9	−35.9	11.9	11.8
2. 12 Years	68.9	64.6	64.0	2.4	8.4	7.8	−24.5	−11.7	6.0
3. 13–15 years	62.3	61.5	56.4	2.1	10.5	7.5	−34.0	0.3	5.0
4. 16 or more years	77.8	76.5	74.1	1.4	7.8	6.3	−26.0	−3.8	1.6

E. Age Class[b]

1. Under 35	40.7	37.5	35.6	5.5	16.2	9.4	−52.7	24.8	4.6
2. 35–44	66.1	63.8	61.7	2.6	13.8	11.8	−47.8	36.2	6.5
3. 45–54	77.3	75.2	69.1	1.4	8.5	10.1	−28.3	−15.7	5.6
4. 55–64	81.0	78.1	74.2	0.9	5.3	5.9	−14.3	−10.8	4.7
5. 65–74	85.5	82.5	85.8	0.4	3.5	2.8	−29.7	2.7	1.0
6. 75 and over	77.0	81.3	80.1	0.0	2.7	0.4	−18.8	−15.8	3.9

C. Income Class (2007$)

1. Under $15,000	36.3	32.5	35.1	0.8	2.6	3.8	−0.6	−14.6	7.7
2. $15,000–$24,999	53.5	49.5	46.6	1.7	6.4	5.5	−23.3	8.0	5.5
3. $25,000–$49,999	60.9	65.8	61.3	1.9	8.1	9.3	−22.4	−16.8	8.4
4. $50,000–$74,999	76.8	79.4	77.4	1.9	11.7	7.0	−30.2	6.6	6.4
5. $75,000–$99,999	89.2	84.3	86.9	3.2	10.9	8.0	−32.2	−1.1	4.2
6. $100,000–$249,999	92.9	91.3	90.7	1.3	7.4	6.3	−20.5	−11.5	2.7
7. $250,000 or over	97.2	96.1	95.8	0.3	1.4	1.4	−17.7	2.7	0.4

Source: All columns except the last are from authors' computations from the 2007, 2010, and 2013 Survey of Consumer Finances. The last column is author's computations from the 2009 Panel Study of Income Dynamics.
a. Asian and other races are excluded from the table because of small sample sizes.
b. Households are classified by the schooling level and age of the head of household.

decline—32 percent—and the highest income class undergoing an 18 percent loss in home equity. It is likely that this pattern is due to the fact that Hispanic, black, and younger households came later into the home buying market and therefore were more likely to buy when prices were peaking. Indeed, during the early 2000s mortgage companies and banks were using all kinds of devices to permit households with low income and low credit ratings to get into very risky mortgages. This particularly affected minorities and low-income whites.

Generally speaking (though not always) the groups with the highest ownership rates—whites, married people, people with higher education, older people (over age 64), and people with higher income—also had the lowest share of homeowners with negative home equity and the lowest percentage loss in home equity. Here, too, the difference likely reflects when the families in these groups bought their home. Of those who were homeowners, minorities, married individuals, those with some college education, younger people, and people with incomes between $50,000 and $100,000 had the highest percentages with negative home equity. Likewise, among homeowners, Hispanics, single females, those with less than a high school degree and those with some college, younger households, and those with incomes between $75,000 and $990,000 suffered the largest percentage declines in home equity. Young homeowners under the age of 35 (16.2 percent with negative home equity and a 53 percent decline in net home equity) were the hardest hit by the recession.

The Panel Study of Income Dynamics added a special supplement to its 2009 wealth survey on distressed mortgages. In particular, families were asked new questions about mortgage distress in the form of foreclosure activity, falling behind in payments, mortgage modification, and expectations about mortgage payment difficulties in the coming twelve months. Results of this survey on the share of homeowners who were delinquent on their mortgages in 2009 are shown in the last column of Table 3.8.

The interesting feature of these results is that they do not automatically line up with the share of households underwater. That is to say, the mere fact that a family had negative home equity in its home did not necessarily mean that the family would "walk away" from its home by stopping mortgage payments. Indeed, it tended to be the low-income groups that had the highest delinquency rate, which seemed to imply that affordability was the main determinant of mortgage delinquency. This is consistent with reports from the Federal Housing Finance Agency, which suggested that the top five reasons for default were "trigger events" such as income loss (36 percent), excessive obligations such as supporting dependents or high amounts of debt (19 percent), unemployment (8 percent), illness and associated medical costs or loss of income (6 percent), and marital dissolution (3 percent).[11] Individuals who were least able to handle unexpected financial hardships were the most likely to default, regardless of their home equity levels.

The overall delinquency rate among homeowners in 2009 was 5.1 percent and the percent of American homeowners that would likely continue to be behind or fall behind soon was a startling 14.1 percent. Indeed, among all of the demographic characteristics, the percentage of families who would likely fall behind or remain behind on their mortgage was approximately three times the percent of families who were currently behind, suggesting that rates of default and foreclosure continued to rise at least through 2011. Among white households, the percentage was only 3.4 percent but it was 11 percent among blacks and a somewhat startling 15.4 percent among Hispanics (in contrast, the share underwater was slightly higher for blacks than Hispanics). Single females were further behind on mortgage payments (a 7.8 percent delinquency rate) than single males or couples, even though single females had a smaller share of underwater mortgages than married couples.

There was a negative linear relationship between delinquency rate and educational attainment. The lowest education group had a 11.8 percent delinquency rate, compared to 6 percent for high school graduates, 5 percent for those with some college, and a mere 1.6 percent for college graduates. Mortgage delinquency rates did seem to line up fairly well with the percent of homeowners with negative home equity. These relationships probably reflect not much more than the high correlation between income and education. The highest incidence occurred among the nonelderly, with delinquency rates ranging from 4.6 to 6.5 percent. In contrast, among age group 65 to 74, the delinquency rate was only 1 percent. Delinquency rates also tended to line up well with income class, with the lowest income groups having the highest delinquency rates. The bottom income group had a delinquency rate of 7.7 percent, income class $25,000 to $50,000 a rate of 8.4 percent, and income class $50,000 to $75,000 a rate of 6.4 percent, compared to 2.7 percent for the second highest and only 0.4 percent for the highest income class.[12]

An update to 2013 is also provided in Table 3.8. Did the housing situation change by 2013? The overall homeownership rate, as noted earlier, contracted by 2.1 percentage points between 2010 and 2013. Blacks and Hispanics suffered larger declines than whites but declines were about equal among family types. Those with some college, families with a middle-aged head of household, particularly age group 45–54, and middle-income families, especially income class $25,000 to $49,999, experienced the largest drops in homeownership. On the other hand, the homeownership rate picked up among age group 65–74, the lowest income class, and income class $75,000–$99,999.

There was a modest reduction in the overall share of homeowners underwater between 2010 and 2013, from 8.2 to 6.9 percent. The share fell among white households but continued to rise among black and Hispanic households, by 5 and 2.9 percentage points, respectively. By 2013, 14.2 percent of black homeowners had negative home equity, the largest of the three groups. The "underwater rate" fell among the three family types—most strongly among single females. It declined among the educational groups except the lowest one, where it showed a very modest uptick. There was a sizeable decline in the underwater rate among the youngest age group, bringing it down to 9.4 percent from 16.2 percent, and more modest decreases for age groups 35–44 and 75 and over. For the oldest group, the underwater rate was down to 0.4 percent. There were relatively small changes among the other age groups. Changes were also relatively minor by income class, except for middle income, which experienced very substantial declines in the underwater rate (decreases of 4.7 percentage points for income class $50,000–$74,999 and 2.9 percentage points for income class $75,000–$99,999).

Overall, mean home equity declined by 3.8 percent in real terms from 2010 to 2013. Among African Americans, it fell by 20 percent, compared to 3.4 percent for whites, and among Hispanics a slight increase was recorded, offsetting the steep fall-off in the previous three years. Home equity among single males rose by 4.8 percent but dropped by 1.6 percent among married couples and almost 10 percent among single females, compounding the previous precipitous decrease. Net home equity recovered somewhat among those with less than a high school education but fell sharply among high school graduates. Some recovery in net home equity was found for the two youngest age groups but it continued to fall for middle-aged (45–54 and 55–64) households and among the oldest age group. The record was mixed by income classes, though the middle income group ($25,000–$49,999) showed the steepest fall-off in home equity.

The Role of Leverage in Explaining the Trends in Median Wealth and Wealth Inequality

The Six Puzzles

Six puzzles emerge from the analysis presented so far in this chapter and in Chapter 2. Before proceeding to a discussion of these, it is helpful to review previous work on these issues. Wealth inequality is positively related to the ratio of stock prices to housing prices, since the former is heavily concentrated among the rich and the latter is the chief asset of the middle class.[13] A regression was run of a wealth inequality index, measured by the share of marketable wealth held by the top 1 percent of households (WTOP1) on income inequality, measured by the share of income received by the top 5 percent of families (INCTOP5), and the ratio of stock prices (Standard and Poor's 500 index) to median housing prices (RATIO), with 21 data points between 1922 and 1998. It yields:

$$\text{WTOP1} = 5.10 + 1.27 \text{ INCTOP5} + 0.26 \text{ RATIO}, R^2 = 0.64, N = 21 \qquad (3.1)$$
$$\phantom{\text{WTOP1} = }(0.9) \quad (4.2) \qquad\qquad (2.5)$$

with t-ratios shown in parentheses. Both variables are statistically significant (INCTOP5 at the 1 percent level and RATIO at the 5 percent level) and with the expected (positive) sign. Also, the fit is quite good, even for this simple model.[14]

In light of these results, the first puzzle is why median wealth surged from 2001 to 2007 while median income was sluggish. The second is why wealth inequality was flat over these years when income inequality grew. The third is why there was such a steep plunge in median wealth between 2007 and 2010 of 44 percent. This happened despite a moderate drop in median income of 6.4 percent in real terms and steep but less steep declines in housing and stock prices of 24 and 26 percent in real terms, respectively.

The fourth is why there was such a steep increase of wealth inequality, of 0.032 Gini points, over years 2010 to 2013. It is surprising that wealth inequality rose so sharply, given that income inequality dropped by 0.025 Gini points (according to the SCF data) and the ratio of stock to housing prices remained almost unchanged (stock and housing prices declined at about the same rate).

The fifth and, perhaps, most perplexing question is why median (and mean) wealth failed to recover in years 2010 to 2013 when asset prices surged. And finally, why did wealth inequality increase so moderately from 2010 to 2013 when income inequality shot up and the stock to house price ratio climbed by 29 percent.

Leverage is an important factor in explaining changes in median wealth and movements in wealth inequality. The high leverage (that is, debt to net worth ratio) of middle-class households was a crucial factor accounting for the strong gains in median net worth over years 2001 to 2007 and its steep fall over years 2007 to 2010.[15] *Differential leverage* between the rich and the middle class also helps to explain trends in wealth inequality. This factor played an important role in accounting for the constancy of wealth inequality over the 2001–2007 and 2010–2013 periods and its spike over years 2007 to 2010. With regard to the fact that median net worth showed no improvement over years 2010 to 2013, a different explanation is called for. It appeared that substantial dissavings (that is, *negative* savings) over this period accounted for the failure of wealth to grow over these years.

Two Arithmetic Examples

A simple arithmetical example might illustrate the effects of leverage. Suppose average assets are 50 and average debt is zero (see Table 3.9a). Also, suppose that asset prices rise by 20 percent. Then average net worth also rises by 20 percent. Now suppose that average debt is 40 and asset prices once again rise by 20 percent. Then average net worth increases from a base of 10 (50 minus 40) to 20 (60 minus 40) or by *100 percent*. Thus, leverage amplifies the effects of asset price changes.

The converse is also true. Suppose that asset prices decline by 20 percent. In the first case, net worth falls from 50 to 40 or by 20 percent. In the second case, net worth falls from 10 to 0 (40 minus 40) or by 100 percent. Thus, leverage can also magnify the effects of an asset price bust.

Table 3.9a. The effects of leverage on the rate of return: Arithmetic examples

	Year 1	Year 2	% Change
"The Rich"			
Assets	50	60	
Debt	0	0	
Net worth	50	60	20
% increase in asset prices			20
"The Middle Class"			
Assets	50	60	
Debt	40	40	
Net worth	10	20	100
% increase in asset prices			20

Table 3.9b. The effects of differential leverage on the rate of return: Arithmetic examples

	Year 1	Year 2	% Change
"The Rich"			
Stocks	50	40	
Other assets	50	50	
Debt	0	0	
Net worth	100	90	−10
% change in stock prices			−20
"The Middle Class"			
Housing	60	48	
Other assets	10	10	
Debt	30	30	
Net worth	40	28	−30
% increase in house prices			−20

Another arithmetical example might illustrate the effects of differential leverage. Suppose the total assets of the very rich in a given year is 100, consisting of 50 in stocks and 50 in other assets, and its debt is zero, for a net worth of 100 (see Table 3.9b). In contrast, among the middle class, suppose their total assets are 70, consisting of 60 in housing and 10 in other assets, and their mortgage debt is 30, for a net worth of 40. The ratio of net worth between the very rich and the middle is then 2.5 (100 / 40).

Suppose the value of both stocks and housing falls by 20 percent from year 1 to year 2. Then, the total assets of the rich fall to 90 (40 in stocks and 50 in other), for a net worth of 90.[16] The total assets of the middle fall to 58 (48 in housing and 10 in other), but its debt remains exactly the same at 30, for a net worth of 28. As a result, the ratio of net worth between the rich and the middle *rises* to 3.21 (90 / 28). Here it is apparent that even though housing and stock prices fall at the *same rate,* the inequality of wealth goes up. The key is the differential leverage between the rich and the middle class. If asset prices fall, then the rate of return to net worth will be lower than that to assets alone if households are leveraged. In other words, if asset prices decline at the same rate, net worth decreases at an even greater rate for the middle class than the rich, since the ratio of debt to net worth is higher for the middle class than the rich and debt is unchanged in nominal terms.

The converse is also true. If the debt to net worth ratio is higher for the middle class than the rich, then an equal percentage increase in house and stock prices will result in a decrease in wealth inequality.

Rates of Return

Table 3.10 shows average annual *real* rates of return for both gross assets and net worth over the period from 1983 to 2013 (also see Figure 3.5). Results are based on the average portfolio composition over the period and assume that all wealth groups receive the same rate of return, on average, by asset type. In particular, it is assumed that there are no systematic differences in returns on, for example, stocks by wealth class.

What is the evidence supporting this assumption? First, one rather dated study by Blume et al. looked at the relation of dividend yield to household income in 1969.[17] The study found that dividend yield varied inversely with income but the range was very small (2.51 percent to 2.78 percent).[18] Second, Feldstein and Yitzhaki found that high-income investors received a higher rate of return on their investments than individuals with lower incomes.[19] The study, which was based on income tax returns, relied exclusively on capital gains realized on corporate stock.

Third, Johnson, Raub, and Newcomb used micro estate tax data of 2007 decedents matched to 2006 income tax returns to analyze rates of return by wealth class. If anything, they found slightly decreasing rates of returns for

Table 3.10. Average annual real rates of return by period and wealth class, 1983–2013 (percentage)

	1983–1989	1989–2001	2001–2007	2007–2010	2010–2013	1983–2013
A. Gross Assets						
1. All households	2.33	3.33	3.10	−6.38	4.83	2.27
2. Top 1 percent	3.07	3.92	3.75	−6.37	5.91	2.88
3. Next 19 percent	2.33	3.44	2.88	−6.07	4.78	2.29
4. Middle 3 quintiles	1.35	2.32	2.71	−7.07	3.28	1.35
B. Net Worth						
1. All households	3.32	4.35	4.04	−7.28	6.20	3.10
2. Top 1 percent	3.45	4.19	3.92	−6.52	6.16	3.11
3. Next 19 percent	3.00	4.09	3.46	−6.63	5.66	2.83
4. Middle 3 quintiles	3.35	4.67	5.58	−10.55	6.94	3.30
Memo: difference between top 1% and middle quintiles	−0.10	0.48	1.67	−4.04	0.79	0.18

Source: Author's computations from the 1983, 1989, 2001, 2007, 2010, and 2013 Survey of Consumer Finances.
Rates of return by asset type are provided in Appendix Table 3.1.
Households are classified into wealth class according to their net worth.
Calculations are based on household portfolios averaged over the period.
Miscellaneous assets are excluded from the calculation.

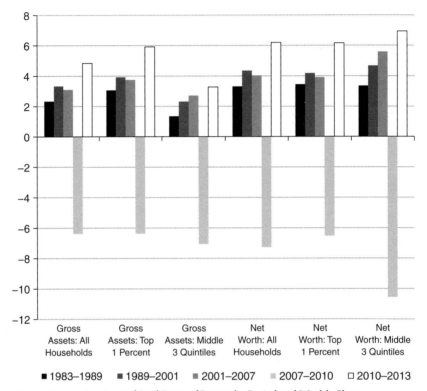

Figure 3.5. Average Annual Real Rates of Return by Period and Wealth Class (Percent)

some asset classes by wealth level.[20] Fourth, much more recently Saez and Zucman provided three pieces of evidence supporting this assumption.[21] They encountered the same issue in their capitalization technique since they also assumed a uniform rate of return across income classes (see Chapters 2 and 12 for a discussion of their methodology). They also used matched estate-income returns (like Johnson et al.) and analyzed three datasets. The first piece of evidence was based on publicly available Statistics of Income (SOI) tabulations of matched estate-income returns for 2008. Saez and Zucman found that within-asset class returns were fairly constant across wealth groups. Although rates of returns varied across individuals, they were similar across wealth groups.

The second source of evidence was the internal SOI matched estate and income tax files over the 1996–2011 period. Saez and Zucman matched the estate tax returns of nonmarried individuals dying in this period to their prior year income tax returns. They found that the interest rate on bonds and deposits did not vary much with wealth level. In 1997, for example, the interest rate was 3.9 percent on aggregate, and between 4.1 and 4.3 percent for all groups of estate tax payers ranging from $0.5–1 million to more than $20 million. The third source was a publicly available sample of estates filed in 1977. Saez and Zucman once again found that rates of return within asset class were very similar across wealth groups. Individuals in the top 0.1 percent and top 0.01 percent had an average dividend yield of 4.7 percent, about the same as the average dividend yield of 5.1 percent among all decedents. The preponderance of the evidence does suggest that there is little systematic variation of rates of return by wealth or income level.

With this in mind, it is of interest to look at the results for all households.[22] The overall average annual rate of return on gross assets rose from 2.33 percent in the 1983–1989 period to 3.33 percent in the 1989–2001 period and then fell slightly to 3.1 percent in the 2001–2007 period before plummeting to −6.38 percent over the Great Recession. This was followed by a substantial recovery to 4.83 percent over years 2010 to 2013.

As shown in Appendix Table 3.1, the largest declines in asset prices over the years 2007 to 2010 occurred for residential real estate and the category businesses and nonhome real estate. The value of financial assets, including stocks, bonds, and other financial securities, registered an annual rate of return of "only" −3.72 percent because interest rates on corporate and foreign bonds continued to remain strong over these years. The value of pension accounts had a −0.34 percent annual rate of return, reflecting the mixture of bonds and stocks held in pension accounts (see Table 3.11c). From 2010 to 2013, all asset classes with the exception of liquid assets made a robust recovery. This was led by financial assets, which recorded a 12.5 percent annual return and businesses and nonhome real estate with a 7.4 percent annual rate of return.

The average annual rate of return on net worth among all households also increased from 3.32 percent in the first period to 4.35 percent in the second, declined somewhat to 4.04 percent in the third and then fell off sharply to −7.28 percent in the 2007–2010 period. Once again, there was a strong recovery to 6.2 percent in the 2010–2013 period. It is first of note that the annual returns on net worth were uniformly higher—by about one percentage

point—than those of gross assets over the first three periods and the last period, when asset prices were rising. The opposite was true in the 2007–2010
period, with the annual return on net worth about one percentage point
lower than that on gross assets. These results illustrate the effect of leverage,
raising the return when asset prices rise and lowering the return when asset
prices fall. Over the full 1983–2013 period, the annual return on net worth
was 0.83 percentage points higher than that on gross assets.[23]

There are striking differences in rates of return by wealth class. The highest
returns on gross assets were registered by the top 1 percent of wealth holders,
followed by the next 19 percent and then by the middle three wealth quintiles. The one exception was the 2007–2010 period when the next 19 percent
was first (the least negative), followed by the top 1 percent and then the
middle three quintiles. The differences were quite substantial. Over the full
1983–2013 period, the average annual return on gross assets for the top
1 percent was 0.59 percentage points greater than that of the next 19 percent
and 1.52 percentage points greater than that of the middle quintiles. The differences reflected the greater share of high yield investment assets like stocks
in the portfolios of the rich and the greater share of housing in the portfolio
of the middle class (see Tables 3.2 and 3.3). Indeed, in the 2010–2013 period,
there was a huge cleavage in returns between the top and middle groups of
2.63 percentage points, reflecting the much higher gains on stocks and investment assets than on housing in those years.

This pattern is almost exactly reversed when we look at returns on net
worth. In this case, in the first three periods and the last when asset prices
were rising, the highest returns were recorded by the middle three wealth
quintiles but in the 2007–2010 period, when asset prices were declining, the
middle group registered the lowest (that is, most negative) rate of return. The
exception was the first period when the top 1 percent had a slightly higher
return than the middle class. The reason was the substantial spread in returns on gross assets between the top 1 percent and the middle group—
1.72 percentage points.

Differences in returns between the top 1 percent and the middle three
quintiles were quite substantial in some years. In the 2001–2007 period, the
average return on net worth was 5.58 percent for the latter and 3.92 percent
for the former—a difference of 1.67 percentage points. The spread was less
over years 2010 to 2013, only 0.79 percentage points. The smaller difference

was due to the much higher returns on the gross assets of the top percentile than of the middle group. On the other hand, over years 2007 to 2010, when asset prices declined, the return on net worth was −6.52 percent for the top 1 percent and −10.55 percent for the middle three quintiles—a differential of 4.04 percentage points in favor of the top 1 percent.

The spread in rates of return between the top 1 percent and the middle three quintiles reflects the much higher leverage of the middle class. In 2013, for example, the debt to net worth ratio of the middle three quintiles was 0.64 while that of the top 1 percent was 0.026. The debt to net worth ratio of the next 19 percent was also relatively low, at 0.118.

The huge negative return on net worth of the middle three quintiles was largely responsible for the precipitous drop in median net worth between 2007 and 2010. This factor, in turn, was due to the steep drop in housing prices and the very high leverage of this group. Likewise, the very high return on net worth of the middle group over the 2001–2007 period played a big role in explaining the robust advance of median net worth, despite the sluggish growth in median income. This in turn, was a result of high leverage coupled with the boom in housing prices. It is somewhat puzzling, however, that the rate of return on net worth of the middle group was very high over the years 2010 to 2013—in fact, the highest of any period—and yet median wealth stagnated over these years. We shall return to this issue later.

The substantial differential in returns on net worth between the middle and top groups (four percentage points lower) is one factor that explains why wealth inequality rose sharply between 2007 and 2010 despite the decline in income inequality. Likewise this differential over the 2001–2007 period (a spread of 1.67 percentage points in favor of the middle quintiles) helps account for the stasis in wealth inequality over these years despite the increase in income inequality. The higher rate of return of the middle than that of the top group over years 2010 to 2013 also helps account for the relative constancy in wealth inequality despite the rise in income inequality.

Stock Ownership First Rises and Then Falls

Tables 3.11a and 3.11b report on overall stock ownership trends from 1983 to 2013 (also see Figure 3.6). The proportion of households that owned corporate

Table 3.11a. Stock ownership, 1983 and 1989 (percent of households holding stocks)

Stock Type	1983	1989	1983–1989
Direct stock holdings only	13.7	13.1	
Stocks and Mutual Funds			
1. Any holdings	24.4	19.9	
2. Holdings worth $5,000 or more[a]	14.5	14.6	
3. Holdings worth $10,000 or more[a]	10.8	12.3	
4. Holdings worth $25,000 or more[a]	6.2	8.4	
Memo:			
Stocks plus mutual funds as a percent of total assets	9.0	6.9	
Percentage change in S&P 500 Index, in constant dollars over period			61.7

Source: Author's computations from the 1983 and 1989 Survey of Consumer Finances.
a. 1995 dollars

stock shares directly declined a bit between 1983 and 1989, from 13.7 to 13.1 percent, while the share that owned any stocks or mutual funds plunged over these years, from 24.4 to 19.9 percent.[24] In contrast, the share of households owning stocks and mutual funds worth $5,000 or more (in 1995 dollars) was stable over this period; and, indeed, the proportion with holdings of $10,000 or more and with $25,000 or more actually rose. These changes over the 1983–1989 period might reflect the steep drop in the stock market in 1987 and the consequent exit of small fund holders after 1987. Yet, despite a 62 percent real increase in stock prices (as measured by the Standard and Poor's 500 index), stocks plus mutual funds as a share of total household assets actually dipped from 9 percent in 1983 to 6.9 percent in 1989—probably because many investors were scared off from the stock market by the mini stock market crash of 1987.

In contrast, the years 1989 to 2001 saw a substantial increase in stock ownership (see Table 3.11b). The share of households with direct ownership of stock climbed from 13.1 to 21.3 percent, while the share with some stock owned either outright or indirectly through mutual funds, trusts, or various pension accounts surged from 31.7 to 51.9 percent. Much of the increase was fueled by the growth in pension accounts like IRAs and 401(k) plans. Between 1989 and 2001, the share of households owning stock through a pension account more than doubled, accounting for the bulk of the overall increase in

Table 3.11b. Stock ownership, 1989–2013 (percent of households holding stocks)

Stock Type	1989	1992	1995	1998	2001	2004	2007	2010	2013	1989–2013
Direct stock holdings only	13.1	14.8	15.2	19.2	21.3	20.7	17.9	15.1	13.8	
Indirect Stock Holdings Only	23.5	29.3	34.8	43.4	47.7	44.0	44.4	43.4	43.1	
1. Through mutual funds	5.9	8.4	11.3	15.2	16.7	14.1	10.6	8.3	7.8	
2. Through pension accounts	19.5	24.8	29.2	37.4	41.4	38.0	40.2	40.0	40.3	
3. Through trust funds	1.6	1.2	1.9	2.4	5.1	4.7	4.1	4.2	4.1	
All Stock Holdings[a]										
1. Any holdings	31.7	37.2	40.4	48.2	51.9	48.6	49.1	46.9	46.1	
2. Stock worth $5,000 or more[b]	22.6	27.3	29.5	36.3	40.1	34.9	34.6	33.6	34.4	
3. Stock worth $10,000 or more[b]	18.5	21.8	23.9	31.8	35.1	29.8	29.6	28.8	29.7	
4. Stock worth $25,000 or more[b]	10.5	13.1	16.6	24.3	27.1	22.5	22.1	21.6	22.5	
Memo:										
Direct plus indirect stocks as a percent of total assets	10.2	13.7	16.8	22.6	24.5	17.5	16.8	17.5	20.7	
Percentage change in S&P 500 Index in constant dollars over period		13.8	20.0	87.3	1.3	−11.2	19.0	−26.6	39.0	179.0

Source: Author's computations from the 1989, 1992, 1995, 1998, 2001, 2004, 2007, 2010, and 2013 Survey of Consumer Finances. The source for stock prices is Table B-96 of the *Economic Report of the President, 2013*, available at http://www.gpoaccess.gov/eop/tables13.html. Updates to 2013 available at http://us.spindices.com/indices/equity/sp-composite-1500.

a. Includes direct ownership of stock shares and indirect ownership through mutual funds, trusts, and IRAs, Keogh plans, 401(k) plans, and other retirement accounts.

b. 1995 dollars

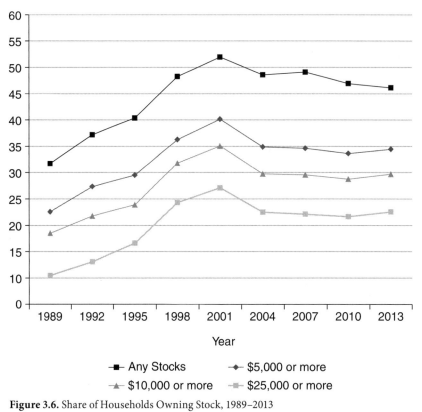

Figure 3.6. Share of Households Owning Stock, 1989–2013 (Percent)

stock ownership. Indirect ownership of stocks through mutual funds also greatly expanded over the 1989–2001 period, from 5.9 to 16.7 percent. All told, the share of households with indirect ownership of stocks more than doubled, from 23.5 to 46.6 percent.

The next twelve years, 2001–2013, generally saw a retrenchment in stock ownership. This trend probably reflected the sharp drop in the stock market from 2000 to 2001, its rather anemic recovery through 2004, its subsequent rebound from 2004 to 2007, and its even sharper fall off from 2007 to 2010. Direct stock ownership plummeted from 21.3 to 13.8 percent, while indirect stock ownership fell from 47.7 to 43.1 percent. The latter trend was largely due to a sharp decline in stock ownership through mutual funds (down by 9 percentage points). Stock ownership through pension accounts was down by

3.4 percentage points from 2001 to 2004 but then rose by 2.2 percentage points from 2004 to 2007 as the stock market recovered. Interestingly, despite the collapse of stock prices from 2007 to 2010, the share of households holding stocks through pension accounts remained essentially unchanged. There was also essentially no change from 2010 to 2013 as the stock market recovered.

By 2004 the share of households that owned stock directly or indirectly dipped below half, down to 48.6 percent, about the same level as in 1998 and down from its peak of 51.9 percent in 2001. The share increased slightly to 49.1 percent in 2007 before dropping to 46.9 percent in 2010 and then 46.1 percent in 2013. Moreover, many of these families had only a minor stake in the stock market in 2013, with only 34.4 percent with total stock holdings worth $5,000 (in 1995 dollars) or more, down from 40.1 percent in 2001; only 29.7 percent owned $10,000 or more of stock, down from 29.8 percent in 2001; and only 22.5 percent owned $25,000 or more of stocks, down from 27.1 percent twelve years earlier.

Direct plus indirect ownership of stocks as a percent of total household assets more than doubled from 10.2 in 1989 to 24.5 in 2001. This increase may reflect in large measure the 171 percent surge in stock prices (in constant dollars) over these years. Between 2001 and 2007 the share plummeted to 16.8 percent, recovering slightly to 17.5 percent in 2010. This change was a result not only of the relative stagnation of the stock market over these years but also of the withdrawal of many families from the stock market. The proportion rose to 20.7 percent in 2010–2013, which reflected the surge in the stock market.

Table 3.11c shows the distribution of total stocks owned by vehicle of ownership. Here there are very marked time trends. Direct stock holdings as a share of total stock holdings fell almost continuously over time, from 54 percent in 1989 to 31.4 percent in 2013. The major deviation occurred in 1998, when direct stock ownership took an upward turn. This may reflect the stock market frenzy of the late 1990s. In contrast, stock held in mutual funds as a share of total stocks rose almost continuously over time from 8.5 percent in 1989 to 21.9 percent in 2004 and then remained more or less flat through 2013, while that held in trust funds declined by 5.6 percentage points from 1989 to 2013.

The most variable pattern was in regard to stock held in DC pension accounts (including IRAs) as a share of total stocks. This trend mainly reflected

Table 3.11c. Distribution of stock ownership by asset type, 1989–2013 (percent of total stock held in each asset type)

Stock Type	1989	1992	1995	1998	2001	2004	2007	2010	2013	Change, 1989–2013
Direct stock holdings	54.0	49.4	36.7	42.6	38.5	37.1	37.1	30.6	31.4	−22.6
Indirect Stock Holdings Only	46.0	50.6	63.3	57.4	61.5	62.9	62.9	69.4	68.6	22.6
1. Through mutual funds	8.5	10.9	17.9	16.3	16.0	21.9	21.3	22.7	21.3	12.8
2. Through pension accounts	24.4	34.1	37.9	32.9	33.5	30.9	31.4	40.2	39.8	15.4
3. Through trust funds	13.2	5.6	7.6	8.2	12.0	8.1	7.2	6.5	7.5	−5.6
Memo:										
Stocks held in pension accounts / total value of pension accounts	32.6	44.8	67.5	64.1	66.3	45.6	43.6	46.8	50.0	17.4

Source: Author's computations from the 1989, 1992, 1995, 1998, 2001, 2004, 2007, 2010, and 2013 Survey of Consumer Finances.

the almost continuously rising share of pension accounts in total assets (from 3 percent in 1989 to 17 percent in 2013) and fluctuations in the stock market. Its share of total stocks increased from 24.4 percent in 1989 to 37.9 percent in 1995, fell off to 31.4 percent in 2007, but then shot up to 40.2 percent in 2010, where it generally remained in 2013. The change from 1989 to 1995 seems to reflect the rise in the stock market, while that from 1995 to 2007 is likely due to a substitution of stock holdings in mutual funds for those in pension plans as investors looked for safer retirement accounts. The big jump from 2007 to 2010 is likely due to two factors. First, interest rates were very low over these years, so that pension holders substituted stocks for bonds in their retirement portfolio, despite the sharp drop in stock prices. Second, the share of pensions in total assets increased from 12 to 15 percent.

The proportion of the total value of pension plans held in the form of stocks showed a parallel movement. It more than doubled between 1989 and 1995, from 32.6 to 67.5 percent, remained at this level through 2001, and then plunged to 43.6 percent in 2007. The sharp tail-off from 2001 to 2004 likely reflected the lethargic performance of the stock market over this period (and its precipitous fall from 2000 to 2002) and the search for more secure investments among plan holders. The share of pensions invested in stocks rose from 43.6 to 46.8 percent from 2007 to 2010 as interest rates dropped sharply, and then to 50 percent in 2013 as the stock market recovered.

Stock ownership is also highly skewed by wealth and income class. As shown in Table 3.12a, 94 percent of the top 1 percent of wealth holders reported owning stock either directly or indirectly in 2013, compared to 43 percent of the middle quintile and 20 percent of the poorest 20 percent. While 93 percent of the top percentile also reported stocks worth $10,000 or more (in current dollars), only 25 percent of the middle quintile and 5 percent of the bottom quintile did so. The top 1 percent of households owned 38 percent of all stocks, the top 5 percent 68 percent, the top 10 percent 81 percent, and the top quintile 92 percent.

Stock ownership is also highly concentrated by income class (see Table 3.12b). Whereas 93 percent of households in the top 4.2 percent of income recipients (those who earned $250,000 or more) owned stock in 2013, 35 percent of the middle class (incomes between $25,000 and $50,000), 18 percent of the lower middle class (incomes between $15,000 and $25,000), and only 8 percent of poor households (income under $15,000) reported stock ownership. The

Table 3.12a. Concentration of stock ownership by wealth class, 2013

Wealth Class	Percent of Households Owning Stock Worth More Than			Percent of Stock Owned		
	0	$4,999	$9,999	Shares	Cumulative	Cumulative −2001
Top 1 percent	94.0	93.7	92.8	37.8	37.8	33.5
Next 4 percent	91.9	91.3	91.0	30.2	67.9	62.3
Next 5 percent	89.2	87.5	86.1	13.5	81.4	76.9
Next 10 percent	79.4	75.4	73.3	10.6	92.0	89.3
Second quintile	60.5	53.2	48.9	6.0	98.0	97.1
Third quintile	42.8	31.1	24.7	1.5	99.5	99.3
Fourth quintile	23.0	9.9	5.9	0.2	99.7	99.8
Bottom quintile	19.6	7.9	4.8	0.3	100.0	100.0
All	46.1	36.9	33.0	100.0		

Source: Author's computations from the 2013 Survey of Consumer Finances.
Note: Includes direct ownership of stock shares and indirect ownership through mutual funds, trusts, and IRAS, Keogh plans, 401(k) plans, and other retirement accounts. All figures are in 2013 dollars.

Table 3.12b. Concentration of stock ownership by income class, 2013

Income Level	Share of Households	Percent of Households Owning Stock Worth More Than			Percent of Stock Owned		
		0	$4,999	$9,999	Shares	Cumulative	Cumulative −2001
$250,000 or more	4.2	92.7	92.2	91.1	52.4	52.4	40.6
$100,000–$249,999	16.2	80.9	74.0	70.7	28.7	81.1	68.6
$75,000–$99,999	10.2	68.3	57.5	50.8	6.4	87.5	77.4
$50,000–$74,999	16.6	55.5	42.4	35.3	6.5	93.9	89.3
$25,000–$49,999	27.5	34.9	22.4	18.7	4.3	98.2	97.6
$15,000–$24,999	14.2	17.5	10.3	8.1	1.0	99.2	98.9
Under $15,000	11.2	8.1	4.4	4.0	0.8	100.0	100.0
All	100.0	46.1	36.9	33.0	100.0		

Source: Author's computations from the 2013 Survey of Consumer Finances.
Note: Includes direct ownership of stock shares and indirect ownership through mutual funds, trusts, and IRAs, Keogh plans, 401(k) plans, and other retirement accounts. All figures are in 2013 dollars.

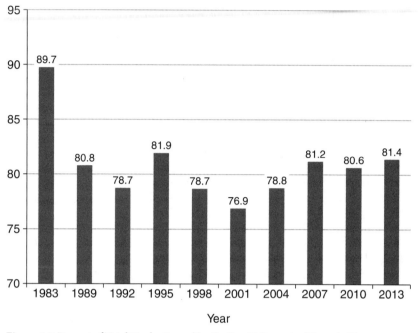

Figure 3.7. Percent of Total Stocks Owned by the Top 10 Percent of Households, 1983–2013

comparable ownership figures for stock holdings of $10,000 or more are 91 percent for the top income class, 19 percent for the middle class, 8 percent for the lower middle class, and 4 percent for the poor. Moreover, 88 percent of all stocks were owned by households earning $75,000 or more (the top 31 percent) and 94 percent by those earning $50,000 or more in terms of income.

Another notable development in the 2000s was an increase in the concentration of stock ownership. The share of total stock owned by the richest 1 percent in terms of wealth increased from 34 percent in 2001 to 38 percent in 2013 and that of the richest 5 percent from 62 to 68 percent. The share of stocks owned by the richest 10 percent of households was 90 percent in 1983, fell to 77 percent in 2001, its lowest level, and then climbed to 81 percent in 2013 (see Figure 3.7). In terms of income, the share of total stock owned by the top income class jumped from 41 to 52 percent (though it should be noted their fraction of total households also rose, from 2.7 to 4.2 percent) and that of the top two income classes from 69 to 81 percent. One result of the stock market bust of the early and late 2000s was a withdrawal of middle-class families from the stock market, whose stock ownership rate fell from 51 percent in 2001 to 41 percent in 2010 (see Table 3.4). There was almost no change in stock ownership from 2010 to 2013 even as the stock market recovered.

Thus, in terms of wealth or income, substantial stock holdings have still not penetrated much beyond the reach of the rich and the upper middle class. The big winners from the stock market boom of the late 1990s and early 2010s (as well as the big losers in the early and late 2000s) were these groups, while the middle class and the poor did not see sizable benefits from the bull market (or losses when the stock market tanked in 2000–2002 and 2007–2010). It was also apparent which groups benefited most from the preferential tax treatment of capital gains.

Defined Contribution Pension Wealth Continues to Rise

Despite the extreme downturn in the stock market from 2007 to 2010, DC pension accounts continued to advance over these years. DC accounts include 401(k) and other employer-provided retirement plans as well as individual retirement accounts (IRAs), Keogh plans, and similar government-sponsored plans. Table 3.13 charts the development of these accounts from 1983 to 2013. There was a huge increase in the share of households holding these accounts from 1983 to 2001, both overall and by individual age group. Overall, the proportion dramatically increased from 11 to 52 percent. The mean value of these plans skyrocketed, almost tripling among account holders and rising by a factor of 13.6 among all households. These time trends partially reflected the history of DC plans. IRAs were first established in 1974, followed by 401(k) plans in 1978 for profit-making companies (403(b) plans for nonprofits are much older); however, 401(k) plans and the like did not become widely available in the workplace until about 1989.

From 2001 to 2007 the share of households with a DC plan leveled off and then from 2007 to 2010 the share fell modestly, from 52.6 to 50.4 percent. The average DC holdings in constant dollars continued to grow after 2001. Overall, it advanced by 21 percent from 2001 to 2007 and then by 11 percent from 2007 to 2010 among account holders and by 22 percent and 7 percent, respectively, among all households. Thus, despite the stock market collapse

Table 3.13. Defined contribution pensions by age group, 1983–2013 (in thousands, 2013 dollars)

	1983	1989	2001	2007	2010	2013	% Change 1983–2013
A. All Households							
1. Percent with a DC account	11.1	24.0	52.2	52.6	50.4	49.2	
2. Mean DC pension wealth (Pension holders only)	46.9	49.5	135.2	163.9	182.5	201.1	328.5
3. Mean DC pension wealth (All households in group)	5.2	11.9	70.6	86.3	91.9	99.0	1,805.7
B. Ages 46 and Under							
1. Percent with a DC account	13.7	31.2	53.8	49.9	47.8	47.3	
2. Mean DC pension wealth (Pension holders only)	24.2	33.2	69.1	69.1	67.4	77.5	220.0
3. Mean DC pension wealth (All households in group)	3.3	10.4	37.1	34.5	32.2	36.6	1,000.3
C. Ages 47–64							
1. Percent with a DC account	12.3	28.3	62.0	63.8	59.6	58.3	
2. Mean DC pension wealth (Pension holders only)	88.6	81.2	205.0	235.8	258.1	242.0	173.2
3. Mean DC pension wealth (All households in group)	10.9	23.0	127.0	150.4	153.8	141.1	1,197.0
D. Ages 65 and Over							
1. Percent with a DC account	2.0	1.3	35.0	40.8	41.1	39.4	
2. Mean DC pension wealth (Pension holders only)	112.7	195.5	201.4	232.9	274.3	374.4	232.2
3. Mean DC pension wealth (All households in group)	2.3	2.6	70.4	95.0	112.8	147.5	6,300.5

Note: Author's computations from the 1983, 1989, 2001, 2007, 2010, and 2013 Survey of Consumer Finances. Defined contribution (DC) pensions include IRAs, Keogh plans, 401(k) plans, and other employer-provided DC plans.

Households are classified into age groups by the age of the head of household.

of 2007–2010 and the 18 percent decline of overall mean net worth, average DC wealth continued to grow after 2007. The reason was that households shifted their portfolios out of other assets and into DC accounts. As noted earlier, the proportion of total assets in pension accounts rose from 12.1 to 15.3 percent over these years (see Table 3.1).[25]

The pattern of change was similar for middle-aged households (ages 47 to 64) and older households (65 and over), but not for younger households (ages 46 and under). The average DC wealth among account holders was unchanged from 2001 to 2007 and then fell by 2.5 percent from 2007 to 2010, whereas among all households in the younger age group, average DC wealth declined by 7 percent from 2001 to 2007 and by another 7 percent from 2007 to 2010 (the difference reflected the reduction in the share of young households holding pension accounts). Thus, in terms of DC accounts, there was no deterioration in retirement preparedness from 2007 to 2010 among middle-aged and older households, though there was among younger households.[26] The fall-off among younger workers was likely due to their high unemployment rate and relatively low wages among those who did have jobs.

There was decline of 1 percentage point in the share of households with DC accounts between 2010 and 2013. By age group, there was a 0.5 percentage point decline among young households, a 1.3 percentage point fall-off among middle-aged households, and a 1.7 percentage point drop among the elderly. This result is consistent with the finding reported in Table 3.4 that pension ownership fell off for the middle three wealth quintiles over these years. Despite this, with the recovery of the stock market, the mean value of DC accounts continued to grow. Overall, it increased by 10 percent among all account holders and 8 percent among all households; 15 and 14 percent, respectively among young households; and 37 and 31 percent, respectively, among elderly ones. The only exception was middle-aged households, among which mean DC wealth fell by 6 percent among account holders and 8 percent among all households in the group. The value of DC plans did recover, and indeed surpassed, its 2007 level among young and elderly households but was still below its 2007 level among middle-aged households.

Summary and Concluding Remarks

Perhaps the most notable development portrayed in this chapter is the sharply rising debt to income ratio between 2001 and 2007, when it reached its highest level in almost 25 years, at 119 percent among all households. The debt to net worth ratio was also way up, from 14.3 to 18.1 percent. Most of the rising debt was from increased home mortgages. From 2007 to 2010 both ratios continued to rise, from 119 to 127 percent for the former and from 18.1 to 20.6 percent for the latter. This occurred despite a moderate retrenchment of overall average debt of 4.4 percent and reflected the drop in both mean wealth and income. Both ratios fell off sharply by 2013, to 107 percent and 17.9 percent, respectively, as outstanding debt continued to shrink, by 13 percent in this case.

While home values as a share of total assets among all households remained relatively unchanged from 1983 to 2013 (around 30 percent), net home equity as a share of total assets fell from 24 to 17. This trend reflected rising mortgage debt on homeowner's property, which grew from 21 percent in 1983 to 39 percent in 2013.

The overall stock ownership rate (either directly or indirectly through mutual funds, trust funds, or pension plans), after rising briskly from 32 percent in 1989 to 52 percent in 2001, fell off to 46 percent in 2013. However, the concentration of investment-type assets generally remained as high in 2013 as it was in the previous three decades. About 90 percent of the total value of stock shares, bonds, trusts, and business equity, and about 80 percent of non-home real estate, were held by the top 10 percent of households. Stock ownership was also highly skewed by wealth class. The top 1 percent of households classified by wealth owned 38 percent of all stocks in 2013, the top 10 percent 81 percent, and the top quintile 92 percent.

Among the middle three wealth quintiles there was a huge increase in the debt-income ratio from 1 in 2001 to 1.57 in 2007 and of the debt to net worth ratio from 0.46 to 0.61. The debt to net worth ratio was also much higher among the middle 60 percent of households in 2007, at 0.61, than among the top 1 percent, at 0.028. The debt to net worth ratio continued to advance to 0.69 percent from 2007 to 2010, but the debt to income ratio actually fell off to 1.34. The reason was the substantial retrenchment of debt among the middle class, with overall debt falling by 25 percent in real terms. The fact that the debt to net worth ratio rose over these years was a reflection of the steep drop in net worth of 44 percent. Both ratios dropped from 2010 to 2013 as outstanding debt levels continued to fall by 8 percent.

In 1989, the average prime working age family had accumulated only enough financial resources to sustain its normal consumption for a period of 3.6 months in case of income loss and to sustain consumption at 125 percent of the poverty standard for 9 months. The average working age family had even lower reserves by 2013—enough to sustain its normal consumption for only 0.2 months and consumption at 125 percent of the poverty line for 0.4 months. The depletion of financial reserves is an important reason for the growing insecurity among the middle class.

The key to understanding the plight of the middle class over the Great Recession was their high degree of leverage and the high concentration of assets in their homes. The steep decline in median net worth between 2007 and 2010 was primarily due to the very high negative rate of return on net worth of the middle three wealth quintiles (−10.6 percent per year). This, in turn, was attributable to the precipitous fall in home prices and their very high degree of leverage. High leverage, moreover, helped explain why median wealth fell more than house prices over these years.

This is not the whole story. On the basis of rates of return computed for the middle three wealth quintiles, a rough estimate is that median wealth should have fallen by only 27 percent, instead of the actual 44 percent. If we ignore net flows of inheritances and gifts over the period,[27] the remaining discrepancy of 17 percent must be due to dissavings.[28] In fact, the homeownership rate plunged by 8.9 percentage points from 2007 to 2010 (see Table 3.14). Ownership of pension accounts also fell by 7.7 percentage points, that of financial assets by 7.8 percentage points, and stock ownership by 6.4 percentage points. These drops were much steeper than among all households. In constant dollar terms, average home values were down by 31 percent, pension assets by 25 percent, financial assets by 41 percent, and total stocks by 19 percent. Middle-class households were draining their assets over these years. I shall analyze the role of capital losses and dissavings more formally in Chapter 5.

With regard to the fact that median net worth showed no improvement over years 2010 to 2013, at least according to the SCF, a different explanation is called for. For the period from 2010 to 2013, the whole story is dissavings. Asset prices more than recovered from 2010 to 2013, except for housing, which was still up by 8 percent (in real terms). On the basis of rates of return computed for the three middle wealth quintiles, median net worth should have increased by *36 percent*. It appears (once again ignoring inheritances and gifts) that substantial dissavings accounted for the failure of wealth to grow over these years. This decomposition is also analyzed in detail in Chapter 5.[29]

The stagnation of median wealth from 2010 to 2013 can be traced to the depletion of assets. In particular, the middle class was using up its assets to pay down its debt, which we saw decreased by 8.2 percent. This showed up,

Table 3.14. The evolution of asset ownership rates, 2007–2013 (percentage)

Asset	2007	2010	2013	Change 2007–2010	2010–2013	2007–2013
A. All Households						
Principal residence	68.6	67.2	65.1	−1.4	−2.1	−3.5
Pension assets	52.6	50.4	49.2	−2.3	−1.1	−3.4
Unincorporated business	12.0	12.1	10.4	0.1	−1.7	−1.6
Financial assets[a]	27.8	22.9	21.5	−4.9	−1.4	−6.3
All stocks[b]	49.1	46.9	46.1	−2.2	−0.8	−3.0
B. Middle Three Wealth Quintiles						
Principal residence	76.9	68.0	66.7	−8.9	−1.4	−10.3
Pension assets	53.4	45.8	44.4	−7.7	−1.3	−9.0
Unincorporated business	8.8	8.2	6.6	−0.7	−1.5	−2.2
Financial assets[a]	23.1	15.3	14.2	−7.8	−1.1	−8.9
All stocks[b]	47.8	41.4	41.0	−6.4	−0.4	−6.8
Memo: Mean Values—Middle Three Wealth Quintiles (in thousands, 2013 dollars)						
Principal residence	$163.4	$113.5	$105.2	−30.5	−7.3	−35.6
Pension assets	$32.3	$24.3	$27.1	−24.8	11.6	−16.0
Unincorporated business	$7.2	$5.7	$4.3	−21.3	−24.5	−40.6
Financial assets[a]	$9.1	$5.4	$5.8	−40.6	6.7	−36.6
All stocks[b]	$17.5	$14.2	$14.9	−18.8	5.3	−14.5

Source: Author's computations from the 2007, 2010, and 2013 Survey of Consumer Finances.
a. Includes corporate stock, financial securities, mutual funds, and personal trusts
b. Includes direct ownership of stock shares and indirect ownership through mutual funds, trusts, and IRAs, Keogh plans, 401(k) plans, and other retirement accounts

in particular, in reduced asset ownership rates. The ownership rate fell from 68 to 66.7 for homes, from 45.8 to 44.4 percent for pensions, from 8.2 to 6.6 percent for unincorporated businesses, and from 15.3 to 14.2 percent for stocks and financial securities. In constant dollar terms, the largest decline in average asset values was for home values, though pension assets and total stocks did show some recovery over these years. Generally speaking, however, the reduction in assets was about equal to the reduction in debt.

The likely reason for the high rate of dissavings of the middle class over both the 2007–2010 and the 2010–2013 periods is income stagnation (actually, a reduction in median income over these years). It appears that the middle class was depleting its assets to maintain consumption. In fact it turns out

that, based on data from the Consumer Expenditure Survey, the average expenditures in real terms of the middle income quintile actually tumbled by
7.7 percent from 2007 to 2010 and by another 3.5 percent from 2010 to 2013.

The evidence, moreover, suggests that middle-class households, experiencing stagnating incomes, expanded their debt (at least until 2007) mainly
in order to finance normal consumption expenditures rather than to increase
their investment portfolio. Indeed, as noted previously, mean consumer expenditures in real terms went up by a mere 1.7 percent from 2001 to 2007
despite the huge increase in indebtedness. Another possible reason is that the
middle class also went into debt to increase their leverage and to raise their
rate of return, at least when asset prices were rising. Of course, the increased
leverage also made them very vulnerable when asset prices collapsed.

The large spread in rates of return on net worth between the middle three
wealth quintiles and the top percentile (over four percentage points) also
largely explained why wealth inequality advanced steeply from 2007 to 2010
despite the decline in income inequality and constancy in the ratio of stock
to housing prices (both declined at about the same rate over these years). It
was thus the case that the middle class took a bigger relative hit on their net
worth from the decline in home prices than the top 20 percent did from the
stock market plunge. This factor is also reflected in the fact that median
wealth dropped much more in percentage terms than mean wealth over the
Great Recession.

In contrast, there was relatively little change in wealth inequality from
2010 to 2013. This was true despite the large increase in income inequality
over these years as well as a sharp rise, of 29 percent, in the ratio of stock to
housing prices. The offsetting factor in this case was the higher rate of return on net worth of the middle class than the top 1 percent (a 0.79 percentage point difference).

Why did household debt, particularly among the middle class, fall so
sharply from 2007 to 2010? A systematic analysis is beyond the scope of the
book. It appears that several factors were involved. First, as noted in
Chapter 2, the housing price bubble in the years before 2007 was fueled in
large part by a generous expansion of available credit for home purchases and
refinancing. This took a number of forms. Many homeowners refinanced
their primary mortgages but, because housing prices rose, they increased the
outstanding mortgage balance and thereby extracted equity from their

homes. In addition, many homeowners took out second mortgages and home equity loans or increased the outstanding balances on these instruments. And finally, among new homeowners, credit requirements softened and so-called no-doc loans were issued requiring little or no income documentation. Many of these loans, in turn, were so-called subprime mortgages, characterized by excessively high interest rates and balloon payments at the end of the loan.

Second, there was an explosion of consumer debt leading up to 2007, and total consumer credit outstanding surged. There were a number of factors responsible for this, including increased availability of credit cards, relaxed credit standards, and increased credit limits.

Third, after the start of the financial crisis, credit tightened considerably in several ways. There was a reduction in the number of new credit cards issued and credit line balances. New mortgage issues fell sharply as banks and other financial institutions increased down payment requirements and credit scores for eligibility. No-doc loans were virtually eliminated. Available home equity credit lines were sharply reduced, which was partly a result of the fact that the value of homes fell sharply and the resultant collateral needed to back up home equity loans consequently declined. And foreclosures and short sales removed mortgage debt from the balance sheets of many households while increased bankruptcy rates further removed household debt.

Fourth, though not usually considered an incentive to save (or dissave) in the standard savings literature, leverage is one mechanism used to obtain a higher rate of return on wealth (see Table 3.10). When asset prices are rising, it would actually be rational for households to increase their outstanding debt in order to augment the return on their balance sheet. Of course, the opposite is the case when asset prices are falling. One possibility is that households burned by the steep fall in asset prices after 2007 and the consequent decline in their net worth may have decided to reduce their debt in order to avoid another similar catastrophe.

Fifth, an offsetting factor is that the inflation rate, as measured by the CPI, showed a substantial drop-off between the 1983–2007 period and the 2007–2013 period—from an average annual rate of 3.05 percent to 1.94 percent. Since inflation reduces outstanding debt balances in real terms, average real debt would have fallen more in the earlier period than the later one from this inflation effect.

Appendix Table 3.1. Average annual nominal rates of return by asset type and period, 1983–2013

Description	Average Nominal Rates of Return by Period (Percentage)					
	1983–2013	1983–1989	1989–2001	2001–2007	2007–2010	2010–2013
Residential real estate	3.54	4.02	4.49	5.84	–7.22	4.92
Business + nonhome real estate	4.53	3.94	4.10	9.75	–5.83	7.39
Liquid assets	3.98	6.70	4.69	3.11	1.28	0.12
Financial assets (including stocks)	9.21	13.32	13.01	2.34	–3.72	12.45
Pension accounts	7.56	11.63	9.60	3.00	–0.34	8.26
Mortgage debt	0.00	0.00	0.00	0.00	0.00	0.00
Nonmortgage debt	0.00	0.00	0.00	0.00	0.00	0.00
Inflation (CPI-U average)	2.88	3.72	3.02	2.66	1.71	2.23

Notes: Real rate of return = (1 + nominal rate) / (1 + ΔCPI) − 1

Owner-occupied housing: The source for years 1989 to 2007 is Table 935 of the *2009 Statistical Abstract*, US Bureau of the Census, available at http://www.census.gov/compendia /statab/. For years after 2007, see National Association of Realtors, "Median Sales Price of Existing Single-Family Homes for Metropolitan Areas," available at: http://www.realtor.org /. The figures are based on median prices of existing houses for metropolitan areas only.

Business and nonhome real estate: Holding gains divided by equity in noncorporate business (from http://www.federalreserve.gov/releases/Z1/20140605, Tables R.100 and B.100.

Liquid assets: The weighted average of the rates of return on checking deposits and cash, time and saving deposits, and life insurance reserves. The weights are the proportion of these assets in their combined total (calculated from http://www.federalreserve.gov/releases/Z1/20140605, Table B.100). The assumptions regarding the rates of return are: zero for checking deposits, the rate of return on a one-month CD (taken from the table "H.15 Selected Interest Rates" published by the Federal Reserve, available at http://www .federalreserve.gov/releases/h15/data.htm) for time and saving deposits, and, one plus the inflation rate for life insurance reserves.

Financial assets: The weighted average of the rates of return on open market paper, U.S. Treasury securities, municipal securities, corporate and foreign bonds, corporate equities, and mutual fund shares. The weights are the proportion of these assets in total financial assets held by the household sector (calculated from Table B.100. noted above). The assumption regarding the rate of return on open market paper is that it equals the rate of return on one-month finance paper (taken from the table H.15 "Selected Interest Rates," http://www.federalreserve.gov/releases/h15/data.htm). The data for the rates of return on other assets are taken from the *Economic Report of the President 2015*, Table B-17, available at https://www.whitehouse.gov/sites/default/files/docs/2015_erp_appendix_b.pdf. The assumptions regarding treasury securities, municipal securities, corporate and foreign bonds, and corporate equities are, respectively, average of treasury security yields, high-grade municipal bond yield, average of corporate bond yields, and annual percent change in the S&P 500 index. Mutual fund shares are assumed to earn a rate of return equal to the weighted average of the rates of return on open market paper, treasury securities, municipal securities, corporate and foreign bonds, and corporate equities. The weights are the proportions of these assets in the total financial assets of mutual funds (calculated from http://www.federalreserve.gov/releases/Z1/20140605, Table L.123).

Stock prices: Table B-96 of the *Economic Report of the President, 2013*, available at http://www.gpoaccess.gov/eop/tables13.html, with updates to 2013 at http://us .spindices.com/indices/equity/sp-composite-1500.

Pension (DC) accounts: Weighted average of returns on stocks, bonds, and money market funds, where the weights are based on the average portfolio composition of DC accounts over the period (for the 1983–1989 period, the weights are based on 1989 data only).

CPI-U: From the *Economic Report of the President 2015*, Table B-10.

4

International Comparisons of Household Wealth Inequality

How does U.S. wealth inequality compare with that of other countries? How have relative levels of inequality changed over time? How does the U.S. level of median and mean wealth compare to those of other advanced economies? These three issues are important to understand in order to provide an international context for the experiences of U.S. citizens. This chapter presents international comparisons of personal wealth inequality for a number of countries and over time. There is now a well-established literature on international comparisons of income distribution. Most of these studies (the more recent ones particularly) are based on the Luxembourg Income Study (LIS), which collects household surveys from most Organisation for Economic Co-operation and Development (OECD) countries and standardizes the income concept, sampling frames, and unit of analysis in order to produce comparable estimates of the size distribution of income.[1] The LIS now has data going back several years.

There are now two comparable databases for household wealth. The first is the Luxembourg Wealth Study (LWS), which like the LIS collects household survey data for a number of OECD countries. An attempt is made to standardize the wealth concept and unit of analysis to make the data comparable across all countries. The second is the Eurosystem Household Finance and Consumption Survey (HFCS), a newly available data source for fifteen European countries in the Eurozone. This differs from the LWS in that a uniform survey instrument is used to collect data for the fifteen countries. Both the LWS and the HFCS have survey data available for only a single year. (Some of the findings from these sources are cited in the section on HFCS data below.)

In this chapter, I present international comparisons of the size distribution of personal wealth.[2] I do not attempt to replicate the work of the LIS in creating conformable income data across countries. Instead, I try to match estimates from different countries on the basis of similar data sources. It should be noted that estimates of personal wealth inequality are very sensitive to the choice of data source, definition of wealth, accounting conventions, unit of analysis, and the sampling frame, particularly the degree of stratification on high-income families or persons.[3] As a result, the international comparisons of household wealth inequality presented here must be treated with some caution. Moreover, I make use of comparable data on the size distribution of household wealth collected for sixteen countries in the year 2000.[4]

Three conclusions emerge from this chapter. First, the sharp rise observed for wealth inequality in the United States from the mid-1970s to about 2000, as documented in Chapters 2 and 13, was not general among industrialized countries (at least among those for which comparable data are available). In particular, wealth inequality increased modestly in Sweden and showed little change or a slight decline in Canada, France, and the United Kingdom through the mid-1980s. Similar findings have been reported for income inequality.[5] Moreover, from the early 1980s to 2000, wealth inequality increased in Canada and Italy, but declined sharply in Germany.

Second, the evidence we do have indicates that in the 1980s the United States ranked as the most unequal country in terms of wealth inequality among eight OECD countries with comparable data—Australia, Canada, France, Germany, Japan, Sweden, the United Kingdom, and the United States. Japan was the most equal, while the other six countries had roughly comparable levels of wealth inequality. This finding again roughly holds for income inequality as well.[6] By 2000 the United States again ranked considerably higher than Canada, Germany and Italy in terms of wealth inequality. Third, the relatively high wealth inequality in the United States today appears to be a marked turnaround from the early 1970s, when the country was comparable with other industrialized countries. In addition, a comparison of time trends for the United States and the United Kingdom indicates that U.S. wealth inequality in the 1980s represented a marked turnaround from the 1920s, when the United States was considerably more equal in terms of wealth ownership than the United Kingdom. Comparative results for the two countries hold for both conventional (marketable) wealth and for augmented wealth, which includes a valuation of public and private pension wealth.

This chapter defines the two concepts of personal wealth used in this study and considers long-term time trends in the concentration of household wealth for three countries—Sweden, the United Kingdom, and the United States. An investigation of recent trends for those three countries, Canada, and France is followed by direct comparisons of wealth inequality among these five countries, as well as Australia, Germany, and Japan. I present some comparisons of income and wealth inequality for selected countries and updated results on the size distribution of wealth to about 2010.

Methodological Issues in Estimating the Distribution of Household Wealth

Official estimates of the size distribution of household income in the United States as well as most other industrialized countries have been compiled by several governmental organizations. The U.S. Bureau of the Census conducts an annual survey in March each year. The Current Population Survey (CPS) provides detailed information on individual and household earnings and income. On the basis of these data, the U.S. Census Bureau constructs its estimates of both family and household income inequality. The CPS has been conducted in the United States since 1947. As a result, there is a consistent time-series on household income distribution that covers almost seven decades.

Unfortunately, no comparable data exist on the size distribution of household wealth for the United States or, for that matter, for any other country in the world. There are no official household surveys conducted on an annual basis for this purpose. As a result, researchers in this field have had to make estimates of household wealth inequality from a variety of sources, which are sometimes inconsistent. Compounding this problem is the fact that household wealth is much more heavily concentrated in the upper percentiles of the distribution than income. Thus, unless surveys or data sources are specifically designed to cover the top wealth groups in a country, it is quite easy to produce biased estimates of the size distribution of wealth, which understate the true level of inequality. The net result is that estimates of household wealth distribution are more problematic than those of income distribution.

The estimates of household wealth contained in this chapter are based mainly on household survey data. When comparing estimates of the size distribution of household wealth from different sources of wealth data, there are four issues of major importance: (1) the sampling frame, (2) the assets and liabilities included in the definition of wealth, (3) the unit of observation, and (4) response errors.

Sample Design

The first issue is the sampling frame. Two different types of samples have been used: random, or representative, samples and stratified samples. The main problem with representative samples is that because household wealth is extremely skewed, the very rich (in the upper tail of the distribution) are often considerably underrepresented in such samples. As a result, estimates of both the mean level of wealth and the degree of wealth inequality are liable to be considerably understated.[7]

A stratified sample, in contrast, may be designed to oversample the rich. For example, in the case of the U.S. 1983 Survey of Consumer Finances (SCF), a "high-income supplement" was drawn from the Internal Revenue Service's Statistics of Income data file. For the 1983 SCF, a cutoff of $100,000 of adjusted gross income was used as the criterion for inclusion in the supplemental sample. Individuals were then randomly selected for the sample within predesignated income strata. The advantage of the high-income supplement is that it provides a much "richer" sample of high-income and therefore potentially very wealthy families. The presence of a high-income supplement creates some complications, however, because there are problems in "weighting" the high-income sample with the core representative sample in order to reflect the actual population distribution.[8]

Another issue concerns the portion of a population included in the sample. For example, in the case of the German survey data used by Hauser and Stein, some of the surveys include only German citizens while others include both German citizens and the resident foreign population.[9]

Accounting Framework

Surveys also differ in the assets and liabilities included in the questionnaire or the wealth concept used. The exclusion of certain assets or liabilities can also make an important difference in estimates of both the level of wealth and the degree of wealth inequality. For example, Kennickell included the value of vehicles in his definition of wealth whereas Wolff excluded their value.[10] The result is that Wolff estimated a higher level of wealth inequality than Kennickell, since automobiles are disproportionately held by lower- and middle-income families. Estimates of median and mean wealth were correspondingly higher in Kennickell's figures, and trends in median wealth were noticeably different in the two sets of results.

In their analysis, Morissette, Zhang, and Drolet did not include the value of assets held in retirement accounts in the Canadian survey data.[11] This omission will likely lead to an upward bias in their estimate of wealth inequality because this type of asset is heavily concentrated in the middle class. In the case of the German data used by Hauser and Stein, the value of business equity was not included in the survey questionnaire and was therefore excluded from the wealth definition. Since business equity is heavily concentrated among wealthy families, this exclusion leads to a downward bias in the estimate of wealth inequality.

Unit of Observation

Estimates of household wealth, like income, are sensitive to the unit of observation. Three are typically used in wealth data analysis: the household, the family, and the individual. The family consists of individuals who are related by marriage or birth (or adoption in the case of children). The household unit is based on place of residence and may include family members as well as other relations and unrelated individuals. Households may also refer to single individuals living by themselves. In income statistics, both mean and median income is typically higher for families than households and the degree of inequality is smaller. The individual is also used as a unit of observation if wealth or income is measured on a per capita basis or if the analysis is based on individual data such as labor earnings or pensions. In the case of wealth, it is often difficult (if not impossible in the case of the United States) to divide assets and liabilities among individuals in a family or household, since most assets and debts are jointly held. The individual is also the basic unit of analysis for estate tax (or duty) data since decedents are by definition individuals. It is often problematic to infer the *household* distribution of wealth from data on wealth holdings of individuals.[12]

Response Error

Household surveys are questionnaires that are given to a sample of households in a population. Their primary advantage is to provide considerable discretion to the interviewer about the information requested of respondents. Their major drawback is that information provided by the respondent is sometimes inaccurate (response error), and, in many cases, the information requested is not provided at all (nonresponse problems). Studies indicate that response error and nonresponse rates are considerably higher among the wealthy than among the middle class.[13]

Definition of Wealth

I use two concepts of wealth in this chapter. I define marketable wealth (or net worth), as the current value of all marketable assets less the current value of debts. Total assets are defined as the sum of the following: (1) owner-occupied housing; (2) other real estate; (3) consumer durables; (4) bank deposits, certificates of deposit, and money market accounts; (5) government bonds, corporate bonds, and other financial securities; (6) the cash surrender value of life insurance plans; (7) defined contribution pension plans, including IRAs and Keogh plans; (9) corporate stock and mutual funds; (10) net equity in unincorporated businesses; and (11) equity in trust funds. Total liabilities are the sum of (1) mortgage debt, (2) consumer debt, and (3) other debt.

A wider definition of household wealth will often add some valuation of pension rights, from both public and private sources, to marketable wealth. One of the major developments in the postwar period among industrialized countries was the enormous growth in both public and private pension systems. Even though such pension funds are not in the direct control of individuals or families, they are a source of future income and thus may be perceived as a form of wealth. The second concept used here is "augmented wealth," defined as the sum of marketable wealth, defined benefit (DB) pension wealth, and Social Security wealth. DB pension wealth is defined as the present value of discounted future pension benefits. In similar fashion, Social Security wealth is defined as the present value of the discounted stream of future Social Security benefits.

Long Term Time Trends in Personal Wealth Inequality

Sweden, the United Kingdom, and the United States: The 1920s through the 1990s

When I originally worked on this subject there were only three countries for which long-term time series were available on household wealth inequality: Sweden, the United Kingdom, and the United States.[14] Data on the size distribution of household wealth in the United States were available principally from estate tax records and cross-sectional household surveys. A reasonably consistent series of estate tax records for the very wealthy collected from federal estate tax records existed for intermittent years between 1922 and 1981. Comparable estimates were also available from the 1962 Survey of Financial Characteristics of Consumers and the 1983, 1986 (a special follow-up of the 1983 survey), 1989, 1992, 1995, and 1998 SCF. In addition, a figure for 1969 was obtained from the MESP dataset of that year and one for 1979 from the Income Survey and Development Program (ISDP) of that year. The construction of this series is detailed in Chapter 13.

The most comprehensive data existed for the United Kingdom. The data are based on estate duty (tax) data and, as a result, use mortality multipliers to obtain estimates of the wealth of the living. Estimates are for the adult population (that is individuals, not households). Figures were available on an almost continuous basis from 1923 to 1990.

Researchers have encountered several problems with the estate data source and methodology for the United Kingdom.[15] First, the estate multiplier method is likely to lead to some bias in estimated wealth shares because of the positive correlation between wealth and life expectancy (wealthier individuals tend to live longer within age-sex groups). Second, the value of household goods and small businesses are likely to be understated in estate data, since their value is considerably greater when in use than when put up for sale. Third, the value of life insurance policies are considerably greater in estates, since they are fully paid out, than comparable policies in the hands of the living. Fourth, except for life insurance policies, the total value of assets based on estate tax data falls far short of national balance sheet figures for the household sector.

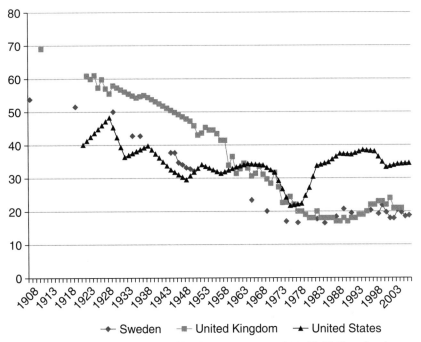

Figure 4.1. Percentage of Wealth Held by the Top 1 Percent of Wealth Holders: Sweden, United Kingdom, United States, 1908–2007

The Swedish data were available on an intermittent basis from 1920 through 1990. The data are based on actual wealth tax returns (Sweden had a wealth tax on current holdings of wealth over these years). Tax return data are subject to error, like other sources of wealth data. The principal problem with tax return information is underreporting due to tax evasion and legal tax exemptions. Other assets, such as housing and stock shares, were extremely well covered because of legal registration requirements in Sweden. Also, the deductibility of interest payments from taxable income made it likely that the debt information was very reliable. On the other hand, bank accounts and bonds were not subject to similar tax controls, and it was likely that their amounts were underreported.

As shown in Figure 4.1, the United States showed a high concentration of wealth throughout the period from 1922 to 2007. A quarter or more of total wealth was owned by the top 1 percent in each of these years except for 1975 to 1980. A comparison of the two end points reveals a higher concentration in 1922 than in 2007: 40.1 versus 34.6 percent. However, this comparison hid important trends over these years.

Between 1922 and 1929 there was a substantial increase in wealth concentration, from 40 to 48 percent. Wealth inequality in 1929 was at its highest point over this entire period. The Great Depression saw a sizable drop in inequality, with the share of the top percentile falling to 36 percent, but by 1939 wealth concentration was almost the same as it was in 1922. There followed a substantial drop in inequality between 1939 and 1949, a result of the leveling effects of World War II and the early postwar period.

The share of wealth held by the richest 1 percent of the population showed a gradual upward trend from 30 percent in 1949 to 34 percent in 1965 and then a rather pronounced fall lasting until 1979. Between 1972 and 1976, in particular, the share of the top percentile fell from 32 to 22 percent.[16] The main reason for the decline in concentration over this four-year period was the sharp drop in the value of corporate stock held by the top wealth holders.

Wealth inequality bottomed out during the late 1970s. A sharp increase in wealth concentration occurred between 1979 and 1983, from a 22 to a 34 percent share, and then again between 1983 and 1989, from 34 to 37 percent, where it remained more or less until 1998.This sharp rise in the concentration of household wealth paralleled the growth in income inequality evident during the 1980s and 1990s.[17]

Figure 4.1 also shows comparative trends among the three countries.[18] For the United Kingdom, there was a dramatic decline in the degree of individual wealth inequality from 1923 to 1974 but little change thereafter. Based on marketable wealth, the share of the top 1 percent of wealth holders dropped from 59 percent in 1923 to 23 percent in 1974. Between 1974 and 1990 there was a relatively minor reduction in the concentration of household wealth, from a 20 percent share of the top percentile to 18 percent.

In Sweden, as in the United Kingdom, there was a dramatic reduction in wealth inequality between 1920 and the mid-1970s. Based on the years for which data were available, the decline appeared to be a continuous process between 1920 and 1975. Over this period, the share of the top percentile declined from 40 to 17 percent of total household wealth. Between 1975 and 1985, there was virtually no change in the concentration of wealth, with the share of the top percentile at 17 percent in these two years. There was a sharp increase in wealth inequality from 1985 to 1990, with the share of the top percentile increasing to 21 percent, a level similar to that of the early 1960s.

Differences among the three countries are rather striking. In all three countries, there was a fairly sizable reduction in wealth concentration between the early 1920s and the late 1970s, though the pattern was much more cyclical in the United States than in the other two countries. Wealth inequality increased in the United States during the 1980s, whereas the trend was almost flat in the United Kingdom. In Sweden, wealth inequality remained relatively constant between the late 1970s and mid-1980s and then showed a fairly substantial jump.

Sweden, the United Kingdom, and the United States: 1908 through 2007

The Swedish data begin in 1908, when the wealth share of the top 1 percent was 54 percent.[19] The new series, like the old one shown in Figure 4.1, shows a dramatic decline in wealth inequality, in this case from 54 percent in 1908 to 16.5 percent in 1985. As in the old series, wealth inequality rose after this point, reaching a 22 percent share in 2000, though it did fall a bit to 19 percent by 2007.

In the case of the United Kingdom, the first data point is now for 1911, with the share of the top percentile an incredible 69 percent. As in the old series, there was an almost continuous decline in the share of the top 1 percent to 23 percent in 1974. The new series now shows a continued decline in the concentration ratio down to 17 percent in 1991. After this point, wealth inequality ticked upward, reaching a 24 percent share in 2002, though by 2005 the share had once again fallen to 21 percent. The extended U.S. series now reveals a modest rise in wealth inequality between 1989 and 1998, with the share of the top percentile increasing from 37.4 to 38.1 percent. There was a sharp drop in the share of the top 1 percent from 1998 to 2001, when it fell to 33.4 percent. After this point wealth inequality ticked upward, reaching 34.6 percent in 2007.[20]

Wealth Inequality Trends, 1970–1992

Household wealth inequality trends from 1970 to 1992 are highlighted in Table 4.1. In addition to Sweden, the United Kingdom, and the United States, data are also available for Canada and France. Again, it should be stressed that the data sources differ among the countries, particularly with regard to the unit of observation. To emphasize this point, I present the time series as an index, with the initial year of the series set to 100.

The results rather dramatically point out the difference between the U.S. experience and that of the other four countries. As noted previously, in the United States there was a very substantial increase in wealth inequality dating from the mid-1970s. Wealth inequality was up by more than 70 percent between 1976 and 1989 and was 17 percent higher in 1992 than in 1972. In the United Kingdom, wealth concentration showed a sizable decline between 1972 and 1975 (perhaps, due to a similar decline in stock prices as in the United States), continued to fall through 1989, and then increased from 1989 through 1992. The share of the top percentile in 1992 was still lower than it was in 1975 (by 20 percent). In the case of Sweden, there was a downward drift from 1970 to 1985 and then a relatively sharp increase until 1990. In 1992, the level of wealth concentration was 3 percent lower than in 1970.

The Canadian data are derived from the Canadian SCF, administered by Statistics Canada. Sample sizes for the three years shown in Table 4.1—1970, 1977, and 1984—were in the range of 12,000 to 14,000 households. There was no special high-income supplement added to the sampling frame, except for the 1977 survey, when an additional 184 special high-income families were included.

The survey results indicate that wealth inequality in Canada declined modestly between 1970 and 1977 and then remained virtually unchanged between 1977 and 1984. There was thus no evidence of rising wealth inequality in Canada between the 1970s and mid-1980s. Moreover, even the decline between 1970 and 1977 may have been due to variability in under-reporting error. In a comparison of total household balance sheets derived from the Canadian SCF with those from the official national balance sheets, Davies computed that the ratio of total net worth between the two sources was 59 percent in 1970, 77 percent in 1977, and 75 percent in 1984.[21] Insofar as estimates of wealth inequality may change as national balance sheet

Table 4.1. Share of marketable net worth held by top percentiles of wealth holders and Gini coefficients, 1970–1990 (Index, initial year of series = 100)

Year	Share of Top 1% U.S.[a]	Share of Top 1% U.K.[b]	Gini Coefficient				
			Sweden[c]	Canada[d]	U.K.[d]	Canada[e]	France[f]
1970		100	100	100		100	
1972	100	107					
1975		76	85				100
1976	68	82			100		
1977		74		95	100	96	
1978		67	83		97		
1979	71	67			98		
1980		64			98		99
1981	85	61			98		
1983	106	67	88		98		
1984		61	84	96	97	96	
1985		61	82		98		
1986	110	61			100		100
1988		57	92				
1989	118	57					
1990		61	103				
1992	117	61	97				92

a. Source: Chapter 13, Table 13.7, Column 8, "Combined Series, Households, Net Worth (NW)."

b. Sources: 1970–1981: A. B. Atkinson, J. P. F. Gordon, and A. Harrison, "Trends in the Shares of Top Wealth-Holders in Britain, 1923–81," *Oxford Bulletin of Economics and Statistics* 51, no. 3 (1989): Table 1. 1982–1991: Board of Inland Revenue, *Inland Revenue Statistics, 1993* (London: HMSO, 1993), Series C, Table 13.5. Results are for adult individuals and are derived from estate duty tax. The 1982–1991 Inland Revenue Series is benchmarked to the 1982 figure.

c. Sources: 1970–1975: Roland Spånt, "Wealth Distribution in Sweden: 1920–1983," in *International Comparisons of the Distribution of Household Wealth*, ed. Edward N. Wolff (New York: Oxford University Press, 1987), Tables 3.7, 3.8, and 3.11. 1975–1990: Statistics Sweden, *Income Distribution Survey in 1992* (Orebro, Sweden: SCB Publishing Unit, 1994), Table 42. Results are for households with wealth valued at market prices, and are derived from wealth tax data. The 1970–1975 data are benchmarked to the Statistics Sweden series.

d. Source: F. J. Good, "Estimates of the Distribution of Personal Wealth," *Economic Trends*, no. 444 (October 1990): 145. Results are for adult individuals and are derived from estate duty data (Series C).

e. Source: James B. Davies, "The Distribution of Wealth in Canada," in *Research in Economic Inequality*, ed. Edward N. Wolff (Greenwich, CT: JAI Press, 1993), Table 1. Results are for households, use unadjusted data, and are derived from the Canadian Survey of Consumer Finances.

f. Sources: 1975 and 1980: Denis Kessler and André Masson, "Personal Wealth Distribution in France: Cross-Sectional Evidence and Extensions," in *International Comparisons of the Distribution of Household Wealth*, ed. Edward N. Wolff (New York: Oxford University Press, 1987), Table 7.6. Results are for households and are derived from the 1975 and 1980 Centre de Recherche sur L'Epargne (CREP) surveys. 1986: Denis Kessler and Edward N. Wolff, "A Comparative Analysis of Household Wealth Patterns in France and the United States," *Review of Income and Wealth* 37, no. 3 (September 1991). Results are for households and are derived from the 1986 Enquete sur les Actifs Financiers conducted by the Institut National de la Statistique et des Etudes Economiques (INSEE). 1992: S. Lollivier and D. Verger, "Le montant de patrimoine et ses disparites," INSEE Working Paper F9508, Paris, 1995, 1. Results are for households and are derived from the 1992 Enquete sur les Actifs Financiers conducted by INSEE.

coverage rates rise (the direction of change depends on the degree of under-reporting by asset type), the measured decline in wealth inequality between 1970 and 1977 might be due to better reporting of assets in the later year.

The last column of Table 4.1 shows results for France in 1975, 1980, 1986, and 1992. The 1975 and 1980 figures are derived from two household surveys conducted by the Centre de Recherche sur L'Epargne (CREP); the 1986 and 1992 figures are derived from household surveys conducted by the Institut National de la Statistique et des Etudes Economiques (INSEE). Though the sample sizes and sample design differ between the 1975 and 1980 CREP surveys and the 1986 and 1992 INSEE surveys, it is still revealing that the results of the four surveys show virtually no difference in wealth inequality in the first three years but a noticeable decline between 1986 and 1992.

Direct Comparisons of Household Wealth Inequality

As noted earlier, one must be cautious in comparing household wealth data drawn from different data sources because of the sensitivity of wealth concentration estimates to definitions of household wealth, sampling frames, and units of analysis. It is possible, however, to make some bilateral comparisons when attention is paid to creating conformable accounting and sampling frameworks.

Estate Tax Data Comparisons

I begin with comparisons derived from estate tax data in the United States and corresponding estate duty data for the United Kingdom and for France (Table 4.2). Concentration figures are for adult individuals and are based on the estate tax multiplier technique. It should be noted that the assets (and liabilities) subject to estate taxation differ somewhat among the three countries, as do the valuation conventions. Despite this, the results are revealing.[22]

The concentration of marketable wealth was much higher in the United Kingdom than in the United States during the 1950s. In 1953, for example, the top percentile owned 44 percent of total wealth in Britain, compared to 34 percent in the United States. During the 1960s and early 1970s, the degree of wealth inequality was comparable in the two countries, while in 1976

Table 4.2. Share of total household wealth held by the richest 1 percent of individual wealth holders on the basis of estate tax (duty) data, 1953–1981

	Marketable Wealth			Augmented Wealth		
Year	U.S.[a]	U.K.[b]	France[c]	U.S.[d]	U.K.[e] Series D	U.K.[e] Series E
1953	34.1	43.5				
1958	31.5	40.9				
1962	33.4	31.9				
1965	34.4	33.3				
1969	31.0	31.3				
1972	31.8	32.0		19.0	18	16
1976	21.8	24.6		13.3	18	13
1977		22.1	19.1			
1981	27.2	22.5		15.5	14	11

a. Source: Chapter 13, Table 13.7, Column 8, "Combined Series, Households, Net Worth (NW)."

b. Sources: Atkinson, Gordon, and Harrison, "Trends in the Shares of Top Wealth-Holders in Britain, 1923–81," Table 1. Results are for adult individuals.

c. Source: Annie Fouquet and Dominique Strauss-Kahn, "The Size Distribution of Personal Wealth in France: A First Attempt at the Estate Duty Method," *Review of Income and Wealth* 30, no. 4 (1984): 403–18.

d. Source: Chapter 13, Table 13.7, Column 7, "Combined Series, Households, Augmented Wealth (W4)." Augmented wealth includes pension reserve wealth and Social Security wealth.

e. Sources: Board of Inland Revenue, *Inland Revenue Statistics, 1993* (London: HMSO, 1993), Table 13.6, Series D, and Table 13.7, Series E. Results are for adult individuals. Series D includes a valuation for occupational pensions. Series E includes a valuation for both occupational and state pensions.

inequality was actually somewhat lower in the United States than in the United Kingdom. U.S. wealth concentration for the top percentile grew in 1981—a 27.2 percent share versus a 22.5 percent.

One data point is also available for France, based on estate tax data for 1977. In 1977 wealth concentration in France was lower than in the United Kingdom—a 19 percent share compared to a 22 percent share—but identical to the U.S. level in 1976.

Results are also shown for augmented wealth. Two series are shown for the United Kingdom. The first includes only occupational pension wealth (Series D) and the second includes both occupational and state pension wealth (Series E). The U.S. data include a valuation based on the expected present value of future Social Security benefits plus a valuation based on pension reserves (though not the expected present value of future defined benefit pension benefits).[23] If a comparable series was derived from the UK data, the estimated share of the top 1 percent of wealth holders would likely lie between the shares estimated from Series D and Series E.

It is at once apparent that the addition of pension and Social Security wealth had a significant effect in lowering measured wealth inequality in the United States. In 1972, for example, there was a 12.8 percentage point gap in the shares of the top percentile between the two series.[24] The effect is similar for the United Kingdom. The addition of both occupational and state pensions lowered the measured share of the top 1 percent by 16 percentage points in 1972.

The share of augmented wealth owned by the top percentile in the United States in 1972 was greater than the comparable shares derived from both Series D and Series E for the United Kingdom. In 1976, in contrast, the share of the top 1 percent in the United States was slightly greater than Series E but considerably less than Series D for the United Kingdom. By 1981 the top percentile share in the United States was again greater than those derived from both Series D and Series E.

Additional data points for augmented wealth are shown in Figure 4.2. In this case, I am using the household unit for the U.S. series and adults for the U.K. series. Moreover, the U.S. series is based on household survey data and the U.K. series on estate duty data.[25] As discussed in Chapter 13, there was a remarkably close correspondence between the share of total wealth owned by the top 1 percent of individuals derived from estate tax data and the share of the top 1 percent of households derived from survey data, at least in the case of the United States. If this relation holds for the United Kingdom, then the three series shown in Figure 4.2 may be on reasonably comparable ground.

Figure 4.2 shows that the concentration of augmented wealth was considerably greater in Britain (from both Series D and Series E) than in the United States in 1971. The comparative degree of inequality quickly changed in 1972, and between 1973 and 1979 the share of the top percentile in the United States was very close to that derived from the United Kingdom's Series E and considerably below the estimated share from Series D. A second crossover point occurred in 1981, and from 1981 through 1991 the inequality of augmented wealth in the United States was clearly greater than that derived from both Series D and Series E. In fact, after 1981, the share of augmented wealth held by the top percentile remained relatively constant in Britain, while it increased sharply in the United States.

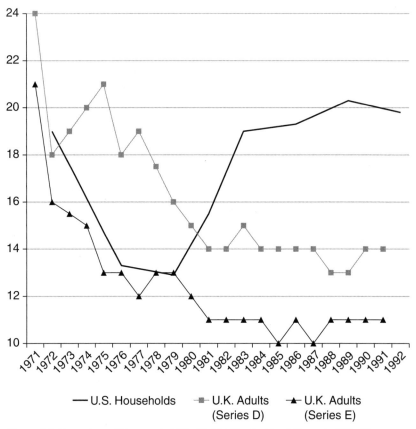

Figure 4.2. Percentage of Augmented Wealth Held by the Top 1 Percent of Wealth Holders, 1971–1992

Comparisons Based on Household Wealth Surveys, 1980s

Estimates of the size distribution of household wealth in the mid-1980s, derived from household surveys in seven OECD countries in the 1980s, are shown in Table 4.3 The first panel shows comparative figures for France and the United States, which were based on a special study to create conformable databases between the two countries.[26] The main difficulty in the study was that survey data in the two countries covered different assets and liabilities (in fact, the French survey did not include any information on household debt). In order to compare the two distributions, it was necessary to create a consistent balance sheet accounts for the two countries.

Panel I shows comparative data for the size distribution of *gross* household wealth in the two countries. The French data come from the 1986 Enquete sur les Actifs Financiers conducted by the INSEE. The sample size was 5,602 families. This survey had a rather complex survey design. It was stratified by various sociodemographic characteristics, but there was no special stratification by high income.

For the United States, I used the 1983 SCF, which had a sample size of 4,262 families. Of these, 3,824 were randomly drawn and thus constituted a representative sample. The other 438 families constituted the so-called high-income supplement. These families were selected on the basis of their high income from a special sample created by the Internal Revenue Service from income tax returns. The U.S. survey data were then adjusted to conform to the coverage of the French survey data. Automobiles and other consumer durables were eliminated from the U.S. data, since these assets were not captured in the French data. Moreover, household debt was not covered in the French survey. As a result, statistics are shown for gross assets instead of net worth (total assets less total debt).

On the basis of the French survey data, the Gini coefficient for gross assets was 0.71, the share of the top 1 percent was 26 percent, and that of the top quintile was 69 percent. On the basis of the original U.S. survey data, the Gini coefficient was 0.77, considerably higher than the French figure. The shares of the top 1, 5, and 20 percent were also considerably higher in the United States, whereas the share of the second quintile was substantially higher in France. The shares of the bottom three quintiles were quite similar in the two countries.

The results indicate that wealth was more unequally distributed in the United States than in France. The differences were considerable. This result was also consistent with the finding that French households had a substantially higher proportion of their wealth in the form of owner-occupied housing, which was more equally distributed among the population than most other assets (particularly, bonds and corporate stock).

There are two other possible explanations for the differences. The first is that there were differences in the degree of underreporting of assets in the two surveys. We were able to check the possible bias for the U.S. survey data by aligning the U.S. survey data with selected assets to national balance sheet totals (see Appendix 1 of the book for details). As shown in Line 1.B.2,

Table 4.3. The size distribution of household wealth in selected OECD countries in the mid-1980s, based on household survey data

Survey	Gini Coeff.	Top 1%	Top 5%	Top Quintile	2nd Quintile	3rd Quintile	4th Quintile	Bot. Quintile
				Percent of Total Wealth Held by				
I. Conformable Databases, Gross Assets[a]								
A. France, 1986 INSEE Survey	0.71	26	43	69	19	9	2	1
B. U.S., 1983 SCF								
1. Original survey data	0.77	33	54	78	14	7	2	0
2. Survey data with selected assets aligned to national balance sheet totals	0.73	30	51	75	14	7	4	1
II. Conformable Databases, Net Worth[b]								
1. Germany, 1988 GSOEP	0.694							
2. U.S., 1988 PSID	0.761							
III. Net Worth, Various Sources								
A. U.S., 1983 SCF[c]								
1. Original survey data	0.79	35	56	80	13	6	2	0
2. Survey data aligned to national balance sheet totals	0.78	33	55	80	13	6	2	0
B. Canada, 1984 SCF[d]								
1. Original survey data	0.69	17	38	69	20	9	2	0
2. Davies estimates		22–27	41–46					
C. Japan[e]								
1. 1981 FSS and SSBM	0.58							
2. 1984 NFIE	0.52		25					
D. Sweden, 1985/1986[f]								
1. HUS (only vehicles included)		16	31	60				
2. HUS (all durables included)		11	24	48				
3. Statistics Sweden (vehicles only)		16.5	37	75				

| E. Australia, 1986 IDS[g] | 19.7 | 41.0 | 72.0 | 20.8 | 7.1 | 0 |

Addendum: Shares of Household Net Worth Derived
from Wealth Tax Data

1. France[b]: Top 0.45% in 1981	9.9%
2. Sweden[i]: Top 0.50% in 1978	11.4%
Top 0.50% in 1983	13.0%

a. Source: Kessler and Wolff, "A Comparative Analysis of Household Wealth Patterns in France and the United States," Table 3. The 1983 SCF was modified to conform with the French accounting conventions used in the 1986 INSEE survey. See the text for details.

b. Richard V. Burkhauser, Joachim R. Frick, and Johannes Schwarze, "A Comparison of Alternative Measures of Economic Well-Being for Germany and the United States," *Review of Income and Wealth* 43, no. 2 (June 1997). The estimates are derived from the GSOEP and the U.S. PSID-GSOEP Equivalent Data File. The wealth figures exclude consumer durables.

c. Source: Edward N. Wolff and Marcia Marley, "Long-Term Trends in U.S. Wealth Inequality: Methodological Issues and Results," in *The Measurement of Saving, Investment, and Wealth*, ed. Robert E. Lipsey and Helen Tice (Chicago: Chicago University Press, 1989), Table 15. The figures include the value of vehicles but exclude other consumer durables.

d. Davies, "The Distribution of Wealth in Canada," 162. The figures include the value of vehicles, but exclude other consumer durables.

e. John Bauer and Andrew Mason, "The Distribution of Income and Wealth in Japan," *Review of Income and Wealth* 38, no. 4 (December 1992): 416–417. The 1981 figure is originally from H. Tachibanaki, *Land Taxation Reform in Japan*, JEI Report No. 28A, Japan Economic Institute, Washington, DC, July 20, 1990, and is derived from the 1981 FSS and the 1981 SSBM. The 1984 figures are originally from N. Takayama, "Household Asset- and Wealthholdings in Japan," in *Aging in the United States and Japan: Economic Trends*, ed. Yukio Noguchi and David Wise (Chicago: Chicago University Press for the National Bureau of Economic Research, 1994) and are based on the 1984 NFIE. The value of major consumer durables is included in these estimates.

f. L. Bager-Sjogren and N. A. Klevmarken, "The Distribution of Wealth in Sweden, 1984–1986," in *Research in Economic Inequality*, ed. Edward N. Wolff (Greenwich, CT: JAI Press, 1993), 208–210. The HUS figures are based on the survey, "Household Market and Non-market Activities" (HUS). The Statistics Sweden figures are originally from K. Jansson and S. Johansson, *Formogenhetsfordelningen 1975–1987* (Stockholm: Statistka Centralbyran, 1988) and are based on a household survey conducted by Statistics Sweden.

g. A. W. Dilnot, "The Distribution and Composition of Personal Sector Wealth in Australia," *The Australian Economic Review* (First Quarter 1990), Table 3. The figures are based on the 1986 IDS, which includes respondents' valuation of housing and mortgage debt. Financial assets and equities are estimated using the income capitalization technique. No estimates of consumer durables are included in household wealth.

h. Fouquet and Strauss-Kahn (1984). This is a minimum estimate based upon declared asset and liability values.

i. Source: Statistics Sweden, *Income Distribution Survey in 1990* (Orebro, Sweden: SCB Publishing Unit, 1992), Table 49.

Abbreviations: FSS, Family Saving Survey; GSOEP, German Socio-Economic Panel; HUS, Household Market and Non-market Activities Survey; IDS, Income Distribution Survey; INSEE, Institut National de la Statistique et des Etudes Economiques; NFIE, National Survey of Family Income and Expenditure; OECD, Organisation for Economic Co-operation and Development; PSID, Panel Survey of Income Dynamics; SCF, Survey of Consumer Finances; SSBM, Survey on Saving Behavior and Motivation.

measured inequality fell in all indices, mainly due to the substantial upward adjustment of the value of demand deposits, time deposits, and insurance savings. Wealth inequality in the United States was still greater than in France, though the differences were not as pronounced. A similar exercise on the French data might have lowered measured wealth inequality in France to a similar degree.

A second possible explanation is that the sampling frame differed between the two surveys. In particular, the U.S. data had a special high-income supplement, which did not exist in the French data. The French survey, as noted previously, had no special stratification by income. It is well known that the better the coverage of high-income household, the higher is *measured* wealth inequality from such a survey. Thus, part of the reason for the finding of greater wealth inequality in the United States than in France might be the greater coverage of wealthy families in the U.S. data.

Panel II shows comparative statistics on the size distribution of wealth drawn from the German Socio-Economic Panel (GSOEP) and the U.S. Panel Survey of Income Dynamics (PS1D)-GSOEP Equivalent Data File for 1988. Burkhauser, Frick, and Schwarze attempted to make the wealth concept used in the two databases consistent by including the same set of assets and liabilities.[27] The sampling frames were also relatively similar, since they are both panel datasets based on representative samples. The results show that the United States was the more unequal of the two countries, with a Gini coefficient of 0.76 for the United States and 0.69 for Germany.

Part B of Panel III shows wealth statistics derived from the 1984 Canadian SCF. Though the sample size for the Canadian SCF was about four times as large as that for the U.S. 1983 SCF, there was no special high-income supplement added to the Canadian SCF as there was for the U.S. data. As a result, as Davies pointed out, there is reason to believe that estimates of the concentration of household wealth may be understated in Canada relative to the United States.

On the basis of the original survey data in the two samples (as well as the U.S. data aligned to national balance sheet totals for the household sector), wealth inequality in the United States was clearly greater than in Canada. The share of the top percentile was 17 percent in Canada and 35 (or 33) percent in the United States and the Gini coefficient was 0.69 for the Canadian data and 0.78 (or 0.79) for the U.S. survey. Davies adjusted the Canadian data on the basis of various outside sources for the upper tail of the distribution. Though Canadian wealth concentration was greater as a result of these adjustments, it was still lower than in the United States.

Estimates for Japan are also shown for 1981, based on the 1981 Family Saving Survey (FSS) and the 1981 Survey on Saving Behavior and Motivation, and for 1984, derived from the 1984 National Survey of Family Income and Expenditure. Neither sample appeared to contain any special high-income supplement but both included major consumer durables. The results suggest that wealth inequality was considerably lower in Japan than in the United States or Canada and, perhaps, Sweden as well. Bauer and Mason suggested that the low wealth concentration in Japan might be due to the extremely large weight owner-occupied housing had in the Japanese household portfolio (total real estate comprised 85 percent of household net worth in 1984).[28]

Three sets of estimates are shown for Sweden in 1985 / 1986. The first two are derived from the survey "Household Market and Non-market Activities" and the third from a household survey conducted by Statistics Sweden at the same time. The asset and liability coverage appeared to be similar to that of the American and Canadian SCFs.[29] There did not appear to be any stratification of either sample by income or wealth level. The figures for the U.S. and Canadian SCF included vehicles but excluded other consumer durables, so that the appropriate comparison is with lines 1 and 3 of the Swedish data. The concentration of wealth appeared to be greater in the United States than in Sweden, which was consistent with the estate tax data comparisons. The original 1984 Canadian SCF data indicated about the same level of wealth concentration in Canada as in Sweden, though Davies' adjusted estimates showed a somewhat higher concentration in Canada.

Panel E shows estimates for Australia based on the 1986 Income Distribution Survey. This was basically an income survey, though it contained information on the value of owner-occupied housing and mortgage debt. Financial assets and equities were estimated using the income capitalization technique, based on reported interest, dividend, and rental income. No estimates of consumer durables were included in household wealth. The inequality of household wealth in Australia appeared to be of the same order of magnitude as Canada but substantially less than in the United States.

One final source of similar data is wealth tax returns in France and Sweden. Though it is hard to say much about the accuracy, asset coverage, and overall comparability of the two data sources, the comparison does suggest that in the early 1980s wealth concentration may have been slightly higher in Sweden than in France (see Table 4.3 addendum).

Comparisons of Wealth Inequality with Income Inequality

Table 4.4 presents LIS data for family income in six countries.[30] The authors first compute the ratio of the income of the tenth percentile to the median income of that country (P10) and then the ratio of the income of the ninetieth percentile to the median income (P90). A small value for P10 indicates that the poor in the country have a relatively low level of income in comparison to the average family in that country. Conversely, a high value for P90

Table 4.4. The ratio of the ninetieth to the tenth percentile of income based on Luxembourg Income Study data, 1979–1987

Country	Year	Ratio of Percentile to Median Income (percent)		Ratio of P90 to P10
		P10	P90	
Australia	1981	46.0	186.3	4.05
	1985	46.5	186.5	4.01
Canada	1981	44.9	182.7	4.07
	1987	45.8	184.2	4.02
France	1979	53.6	186.5	3.48
	1984	55.4	192.8	3.48
Sweden	1981	61.5	150.9	2.45
	1987	55.6	151.5	2.72
U.K.	1979	50.9	179.7	3.53
	1986	51.1	194.1	3.80
U.S.	1979	38.1	187.6	4.92
	1986	34.7	206.1	5.94

Source: Anthony B. Atkinson, Lee Rainwater, and Timothy Smeeding, *Income Distribution in Advanced Economies: The Evidence from the Luxembourg Income Study (LIS)* (Paris: OECD, 1995). PI0 shows the ratio of the income of the tenth percentile to the median income of that country, and P90 shows the ratio of the income of the ninetieth percentile to the median income of that country.

indicates that the rich in the country are particularly relatively well off in comparison to the average family. A summary measure of overall inequality is the ratio of P90 to P10.

In the late 1980s, the United States had by far the highest degree of income inequality among the six countries—a ratio of 5.94. This is consistent with its relative ranking in terms of wealth inequality. In terms of income inequality, the United States was followed by Canada with a ratio of 4.02 and Australia at 4.01. France and the United Kingdom were similar, at 3.48 and 3.79, respectively. The lowest inequality was recorded in Sweden at 2.72. In contrast, all six countries except the United States were quite similar in terms of wealth inequality, with the United States above the rest.

It is also interesting to compare changes in the ratio over time within countries. Here, too, the United States had by far the largest increase of inequality, from a ratio of 4.9 in 1979 to 5.9 in 1986. This also accords with the sharp increase of wealth inequality in this country during the 1980s. Changes were much smaller for other countries. Moreover, of the five countries in the sample, Australia, Canada, and France showed virtually no change in income inequality, while Sweden and the United Kingdom had a slight increase. In terms of wealth inequality, Canada, France, and the United Kingdom were relatively stable while Sweden showed a modest increase in the late 1980s.

Update to 2010

Comparisons from Various Sources

The next two tables provide international comparisons of wealth levels and wealth inequality among selected OECD countries for the years between 1983 and 2001. As shown in Table 4.5, mean wealth was much higher in the United States than in Canada, Germany, Italy, or Finland. Of this group of countries, Italy ranked second (70 percent of the U.S. level in 2000), Canada third (55 percent of the U.S. level in 1999), Germany fourth (45 percent of the U.S. level in 1998), and Finland last (a mere one-sixth of the U.S. level in 1998). Mean wealth also grew much faster in the United States than Canada, Germany, and Finland over the 1980s and 1990s and somewhat faster than in Italy over the 1990s. Median wealth was also higher in the United States than in Canada. The ratio in median wealth between Canada in 1999 and the United States in 1998 was 0.88, which was much higher than the ratio of mean wealth of 0.54. This difference indicates greater wealth inequality in the United States than in Canada. Median wealth grew at almost exactly the same pace in Canada between 1984 and 1999 as in the United States between 1983 and 1998. In fact, the ratio of median wealth between Canada in 1984 and the United States in 1983 was the same as in 1998(1999)—0.88. On the other hand, median wealth was actually higher (by 11 percent) in Sweden than the United States in 1997 (1998), and it was also considerably higher in 1992 and 1995, though lower in 1983. Between 1983 and 1997(1998), median wealth grew almost three times faster in Sweden than the United States (1.90 versus 0.70 percent per year).

Wealth inequality was also much higher in the United States than in the other six countries (see Table 4.6). The Gini coefficient for the United States in 1998 was 0.82, compared to 0.73 in Canada in 1999, 0.64 in Germany in 1998, 0.61 in Italy in 2000, and 0.52 in Finland in 1998. Similar disparities exist with regard to the share of top wealth holders. In the United States, the top 10 percent held 71 percent of all wealth in 1998, compared to a 56 percent share in Canada in 1999, 42 percent in Germany in 1998, and 49 percent in Italy in 2000. Moreover, the shares of wealth held by the fourth and middle quintiles as well as the bottom 40 percent in Canada, Germany, and Italy were considerably higher than the corresponding shares in the United States. The Swedish data show percentile ratios. The P90/P50 ratio for the United States was 7.9, compared to 2.9 for Sweden. Indeed, the P10/p50 ratio was actually negative for the United States, compared to 0.08 for Sweden. By 2000 or so, Finland was by far the most equal of the five countries with comparable data, followed by Italy, Germany, Canada, and then the United States.

It is also of interest that wealth inequality rose in the United States, Canada, Italy, and Finland while it declined sharply in Germany. The Gini coefficient rose by 0.027 in the United States between 1983 and 2001, by 0.036 in Canada from 1984 to 1999, and by 0.060 in Italy between 1989 and 2000. In Germany, in contrast, it plummeted by 0.108 from 1973 to 1998 (and by 0.061 from 1983 to 1998).

The DSSW Study

Table 4.7 shows similar comparisons for the year 2000 based on the work of Davies, Sandström, Shorrocks, and Wolff (DSSW).[31] The objective of the study was to estimate the "world distribution of wealth." DSSW started by assembling estimates for countries with hard data. Data on the distribution of wealth across households or individuals was assembled for twenty countries. One set of figures was selected for each nation, with a preference for the year 2000. In most countries there was only one suitable data source. Where there was a choice DSSW assessed sources in terms of how comprehensive their population and asset coverage were, the unit used (adults being preferred to families or households), and how well they dealt with sampling error, particularly as it affected the upper tail. To assist comparability across countries, a common distribution template was adopted, consisting of the decile shares reported in the form of cumulated quantile shares (that is, Lorenz curve ordinates) plus the shares of the top 10 percent, 5 percent, 2 percent, 1 percent, 0.5 percent and 0.1 percent.

The data differed in various respects. The unit of analysis was most often a household or family, but for France and the United Kingdom it was an adult individual (see Table 4.7). New Zealand used the "economic unit," defined as an unpartnered adult or a couple. Distribution information was sometimes reported by giving all decile shares, together with the shares of the top 5 and 1 percent. But this pattern was far from universal. In some instances information on quantile shares was very sparse. On other occasions, wealth shares were reported for the top 0.5 per cent or even the top 0.1 per cent, as in the cases of Denmark, France, Spain, and Switzerland.

The most important respect in which the data varied across countries was the way in which the information was collected. Household sample surveys were employed in most of the countries. Survey results are affected by sampling and nonsampling error. Nonsampling error tends to reduce estimates of inequality and the shares of the top groups because wealthy households are less likely to respond, and because underreporting is particularly severe for the kinds of financial assets that are especially important for the wealthy—for example, stocks and financial securities.

Other wealth distribution estimates were derived from tax records. The French and U.K. data were based on estate tax returns, while the data for

Table 4.5. Mean and median net worth in selected OECD countries, 1983–2001 (in thousands, 2001 U.S. dollars)

Wealth Definition	Data Source	Sample	Year	Mean Net Worth	Median Net Worth
A. United States: Kennickell[a] Standard wealth definition	SCF	High-income supplement	1989	260.1	
			1992	231.1	
			1995	244.8	
			1998	308.3	
			2001	398.0	
			Annual growth	3.55%	
B. United States: Wolff[b] Standard wealth definition, vehicles excluded	SCF	High-income supplement	1983	231.0	59.3
			1989	264.6	63.5
			1992	257.3	54.2
			1995	237.7	53.0
			1998	293.6	65.9
			2001	380.1	73.5
			Annual growth	2.77%	1.19%
C. Canada: Morissette, et al.[c] Standard wealth definition excluding retirement accounts (RRIFs).	ADS—1984 SFS—1999	Representative High-income supplement	1984	115.2	52.2
			1999	157.4	57.7
			Annual growth	2.08%	0.67%
D. Germany: Hauser and Stein[d] Standard wealth definition excluding consumer durables and business equity	ICS	Representative	1983	112.5	
			1988	117.5	
			1993	146.1	
			1998	132.3	
			Annual growth	1.08%	
E. Italy - Brandolini, et. al.[e] Standard wealth definition excluding retirement accounts and life insurance.	SHIW	Representative	1989	200.3	
			2000	269.0	
			Annual growth	2.68%	
F. Sweden: Klevmarken[f] Standard wealth definition	HUS	Representative	1983		55.8
			1985		55.6
			1992		59.6

			1995	67.2
			1997	72.8
			Annual growth	1.90%
G. Finland: Jäntti[g]				
Standard wealth definition excluding pensions	Statistics Finland Survey	Representative	1987	43.1
			1994	40.3
			1998	50.3
			Annual growth	1.40%

Note: The standard wealth definition, based on U.S. asset and debt components, is given by: Total assets are defined as the sum of the following: (1) owner-occupied housing; (2) other real estate; (3) vehicles; (4) cash and demand deposits; (5) time and savings deposits, certificates of deposit, and money market accounts; (6) government bonds, corporate bonds, foreign bonds, and other financial securities; (7) the cash surrender value of life insurance plans; (8) the value of defined contribution pension plans including IRAs, Keogh, and 401(k) plans; (9) corporate stock and mutual funds; (10) net equity in unincorporated businesses; and (11) net equity in trust funds. Total liabilities are the sum of (1) mortgage debt, (2) consumer debt, including auto loans, and (3) other debt. Net worth equals total assets minus total liabilities.

Note: Figures for Canada, Germany, Italy, Sweden, and Finland are converted to 2001 U.S. dollars using the Penn World Tables Purchasing Power Parities (see http://pwt.econ.upenn.edu/php_site/pwt61_form.php).

a. The source is Arthur Kennickell, "A Rolling Tide: Changes in the Distribution of Wealth in the US, 1998–2001," in *International Perspectives on Household Wealth*, ed. Edward N. Wolff (Cheltenham, U.K.: Edward Elgar Publishing Ltd., 2006), Tables 7 to 10. The figures are based on the family unit.

b. The source is Edward N. Wolff, "Changes in Household Wealth in the 1980s and 1990s in the U.S.," in *International Perspectives on Household Wealth*, Table 1. The figures are based on the household unit.

c. The source is René Morissette, Xuelin Zhang, and Marie Drolet, "The Evolution of Wealth Inequality in Canada, 1984–99," in *International Perspectives on Household Wealth*, Table 1. The figures are based on the family unit.

d. The source is Richard Hauser and Holger Stein, "Inequality of the Distribution of Personal Wealth in Germany, 1973–98," in *International Perspectives on Household Wealth*, Table 1. The figures are based on the household unit and are for West Germany only.

e. The source is Andrea Brandolini et al., "Household Wealth Distribution in Italy in the 1990s," in *International Perspectives on Household Wealth*, Table 6. The figures are based on adjusted data for the household unit.

f. The source is A. Klevmarken, "The Distribution of Wealth in Sweden: Trends and Driving Factors," in *Steigende wirtschaftliche Ungleichheit bei steigendem Reichtum?*, ed. G. Chaloupek and T. Zotter, Tagung der Kammer für Arbeiter und Angestellte für Wien (Vienna: LexisNexis Verlag ARD Orac., 2006) Table 1. The figures are based on the household unit.

g. The source is Markus Jäntti, "Trends in the Distribution of Income and Wealth—Finland 1987–98," in *International Perspectives on Household Wealth*, Table 2. The figures are based on the household unit.

Abbreviations: ADS, Canadian Assets and Debts Survey (1984); HUS, Sweden's household panel survey; ICS, German Income and Consumption Survey; SCF, U.S. Survey of Consumer Finances; SFS—Survey of Financial Security, 1999; SHIW, Italy's Survey of Household Income and Wealth.

Table 4.6. The size distribution of net worth in selected OECD countries, 1983–2001

	Gini Coefficient	P10/P50	P90/P50	Percentage Share of Wealth held by							
Year				Top 1%	Top 5%	Top 10%	Top 20%	4th 20%	3rd 20%	Bottom 40%	All
A. United States: Kennickell[a]											
1989				30.3	54.4	67.4					
1992				30.2	54.6	67.2					
1995				34.6	55.9	67.8					
1998				33.9	57.2	68.6					
2001				32.7	57.7	78.8					
B. United States: Wolff[b]											
1983	0.799			33.8	56.1	68.2	81.3	12.6	5.2	0.9	100.0
1989	0.832			37.4	58.9	70.6	83.5	12.3	4.8	-0.7	100.0
1992	0.823			37.2	60.0	71.8	83.8	11.5	4.4	0.4	100.0
1995	0.828			38.5	60.3	71.8	83.9	11.4	4.5	0.2	100.0
1998	0.822	-0.049	7.829	38.1	59.4	71.0	83.4	11.9	4.5	0.2	100.0
2001	0.826			33.4	59.2	71.5	84.4	11.3	3.9	0.3	100.0
C. Canada: Morissette et al.[c]											
1984	0.691					51.8	69.3	19.7	9.1	1.8	98.1
1999	0.727					55.7	73.1	18.4	7.5	1.1	99.0
D. Germany: Hauser and Stein[d]											
1973	0.748					(NA)	78.0	13.5	5.7	2.8	97.2
1983	0.701					48.8	70.1	23.5	5.5	0.9	99.1
1988	0.668					45.0	66.9	24.7	7.4	1.0	99.0
1993	0.622					40.8	61.0	26.3	10.4	2.3	97.7
1998	0.640					41.9	63.0	25.9	9.5	1.6	98.4

E. Italy: Brandolini et al.[e]

1989	0.553		10.6	27.3	40.2	57.9
1995	0.573		10.7	29.0	42.1	59.5
2000	0.613		17.2	36.4	48.5	63.8

F. Sweden: Klevmarken[f]

1983	0.012	2.716
1985	0.069	2.639
1992	0.055	3.058
1995	0.088	2.887
1997	0.080	2.916

G. Finland: Jäntti[g]

1987	0.470
1994	0.487
1998	0.523

a. The source is Kennickell, "A Rolling Tide: Changes in the Distribution of Wealth in the US, 1998–2001," Table 5. The figures are based on the family unit.

b. The source is Wolff, "Changes in Household Wealth in the 1980s and 1990s in the U.S.," Table 2. The figures are based on the household unit.

c. The source is Morissette, Zhang, and Drolet, "The Evolution of Wealth Inequality in Canada, 1984–99," Tables 3 and 5. The figures are based on the family unit. The rows may not sum to unity because of rounding error.

d. The source is Hauser and Stein, "Inequality of the Distribution of Personal Wealth in Germany, 1973–98," Tables 3 and 4. The figures are based on the household unit. 1973, 1983, and 1988 include only German households, while 1993 and 1998 encompass the total resident population (including foreigners). The rows may not sum to unity because of rounding error.

e. The source is Brandolini et al., "Household Wealth Distribution in Italy in the 1990s," Table 6. The figures are based on adjusted data for the household unit.

f. The source is Klevmarken, "The Distribution of Wealth in Sweden: Trends and Driving Factors," Table 1. The figures are based on the household unit.

g. The source is Jäntti, "Trends in the Distribution of Income and Wealth—Finland 1987–98," Table 2. The figures are based on the household unit.

Table 4.7. Distribution of wealth per adult for selected OECD countries, 2000 (dollar figures are in 2000 USD equivalents)

Country	Quintile Shares					Share of Top		Mean Wealth	Median Wealth	Gini Coeff.	Original Data Source and Unit
	Q1	Q2	Q3	Q4	Q5	10%	1%				
Australia	0.0	4.0	12.0	22.0	62.0	45.0		126,635	75,027	0.622	2002—household survey
Canada			8.0	19.0	70.0	53.0		120,326	45,850	0.688	1999—family survey
Denmark	-17.3	-0.8	2.3	17.1	98.7	76.4	28.8	86,800		0.765	1996—family wealth tax data
Finland	-0.9	3.1	12.8	23.6	61.4	42.3		70,080		0.621	1998—household survey
France						61.0	21.3	126,360	36,975	0.730	1994—adult estate tax return
Germany	-0.2	1.7	7.5	25.0	66.0	44.4		115,325	39,709	0.667	1998—household survey
Ireland	0.2	6.4	12.3	21.5	59.6	42.3	10.4	131,380		0.581	1987—household survey
Italy					63.8	48.5	17.2	150,327	80,043	0.609	2000—household survey
Japan	2.1	6.6	12.0	21.6	57.7	39.3		157,146	93,152	0.547	1999—household survey
New Zealand						51.7		79,589		0.651	2001—economic unit—survey
Norway	0.7	5.1	10.6	18.2	65.4	50.5		106,974		0.633	2000—household wealth tax data
South Korea	1.8	5.6	11.5	21.0	60.1	43.1	14.0	58,314	33,038	0.579	1988—household survey
Spain						41.9	18.3	117,837	72,483	0.570	2002—household survey
Sweden	-6.8	0.2	6.0	20.5	80.1	58.6		103,000		0.776	2002—household survey
Switzerland						71.3	34.8	179,357		0.803	1997—family wealth tax data
United Kingdom						56.0	23.0	172,461	77,439	0.697	2000—adult estate tax returns
United States	-0.2	1.3	4.5	11.8	82.6	69.8	32.7	201,319	41,682	0.801	2001—family survey

Source: James Davies, Susanna Sandström, Anthony Shorrocks, and Edward N. Wolff, "Level and Distribution of Global Household Wealth," *Economic Journal* 121 (March 2011): Table 6, and Davies, Sandström, Shorrocks, and Wolff, "The Global Pattern of Household Wealth," *Journal of International Development* 21, no 8 (November 2009): Appendix IIC.

Denmark, Norway, and Switzerland originated from wealth tax records. These data sources have the advantage that "response" is involuntary, and underreporting is illegal. Underreporting does occur, however, and there are valuation issues that produce analogous problems.

Wealth tax regulations may assign to some assets a fraction of their market value and omit other assets altogether. There are also evident differences in the way that debts are investigated and recorded. For most countries the bottom decile of wealth holders was reported as having positive net worth in the original data, but in Sweden the bottom three deciles each had negative net worth and in Denmark this was true for the bottom four deciles. These negative shares appeared to result partly from measurement problems.[32]

The differences in wealth concentration across countries in Table 4.7 were attributable in part to differences in data quality. In the case of survey data it is important to oversample the upper tail to get the best possible estimates of top wealth shares. This was done in only a few cases—Canada, Germany, Spain, and the United States—in the data used here. The surprisingly low top shares seen here in some countries—for example, Ireland—may reflect this phenomenon.

The original data sources provided a patchwork of quantile shares. In order to move toward an estimate of the world distribution of wealth, more complete and comparable information was needed on the distribution in each country. To achieve this, DSSW first imputed missing cell values.[33] The unit of observation was then converted to an adult base to be consistent among the seventeen countries shown in Table 4.7. In so doing, DSSW assumed that the shape of the adult distribution of wealth at the country level was the same as that of a family- or household-based distribution. Adult and household distributions would indeed have the same shape if children held insignificant assets, the number of adults per household did not vary systematically with wealth, and wealth were equally divided among adults in a household. Children have little wealth, but wealthier households on average had more adults. Although there was a trend toward more equal division of assets within marriage, equal division was not universal. Studies have looked at what happens when, starting with adult data, one "pairs up" a portion of adults into couples and measures inequality on a family basis. This reduces inequality among married people, but increases measured inequality between singles and couples. The effects are to an extent offsetting, but the net effect is to reduce measured inequality somewhat. Finally, the wealth distributions in each country were rebased to year 2000 on the basis of income distribution trends between the base year and 2000.

Table 4.7 shows that estimated wealth concentration varied substantially across countries but was generally very high. Estimated shares of the top 1 percent ranged from a low of 10.4 percent in Ireland to a high of 34.8 percent in Switzerland, with the United States toward the top end of this range at 32.7 percent. The share of the top 10 percent ranged from a low of 39.3 percent in Japan to a high of 76.4 percent in Denmark. Gini coefficients likewise showed a large dispersion, ranging from a low of 0.547 in Japan and a high of 0.803 in Switzerland (the United States was second at 0.801, not far behind Switzerland). The high wealth inequality in Switzerland was probably due to the presence of a large (and lucrative) financial sector in that country. The low inequality in Japan likely reflected social norms in the country that disfavor displays of great wealth and the high share of housing in total wealth.

Table 4.7 also reports figures for mean and median wealth across countries on the basis of Purchasing Power Parity (PPP) exchange rates. One interesting observation is that median wealth rarely exceeded 60 percent of mean wealth. In addition, the rank order of countries changed significantly when medians were used instead of mean values. Of the countries listed in the table, the United States ranked first in mean wealth per adult, followed by Switzerland, the United Kingdom, Japan, and then Italy. Japan ranked first in terms of median wealth per adult, followed by Italy, the United Kingdom, and the United States. Indeed, Japan's median wealth was more than double the figure for the United States although its mean wealth was 22 percent lower. Also, some countries ranked very high in per capita income but were not close to the top of the wealth rankings. This is perhaps most notable for the Nordic countries—Norway, Sweden, Denmark, and Finland. A possible explanation is that a strong public safety net and social programs in these countries make it less necessary for people to build up personal assets than in countries where there is less public wealth and social insurance.

The HFCS Data

The Eurosystem Household Finance and Consumption Survey (HFCS) relies on a uniform survey instrument to collect wealth, income, and demo-

Table 4.8. Wealth inequality in European countries, around 2010

Country	Share of the Top Decile	Gini Coefficient
Austria	61.7	0.762
Belgium	44.0	0.608
Cyprus	56.8	0.697
Finland	45.0	0.664
France	50.0	0.679
Germany	59.0	0.758
Greece	39.0	0.561
Italy	45.0	0.609
Luxembourg	51.3	0.661
Malta	46.8	0.600
The Netherlands	40.1	0.653
Portugal	52.7	0.670
Slovakia	32.8	0.448
Slovenia	35.8	0.534
Spain	43.4	0.580
Euro Area	49.5	0.678

Source: Luc Arrondel, Muriel Roger, and Frédérique Savignac, "Wealth and Income in the Euro Area: Heterogeneity in Households' Behaviours?" European Central Bank Working Paper No. 1709, August 2014.

graphic data from fifteen European countries. The surveys are coordinated by the European Central Bank. Altogether, it has over 63,000 observations representing almost 140 million households in the participating countries. Most countries (though not all) include an oversample of wealthy households based on the SCF design (see Chapter 2 for more details on the SCF "list" sample).

As shown in Table 4.8, Austria ranked highest in terms of wealth inequality among this group of countries (which excludes Switzerland). Its Gini coefficient was 0.762 and the share of the top decile was 61.7 percent. Germany was second, close behind Austria, with a Gini coefficient of 0.758 and a top decile share of 59 percent. The two most equal countries were Slovakia and Slovenia, with Gini coefficients of 0.448 and 0.534 and top decile shares of 32.8 and 35.8 percent, respectively.

Cowell et al. used the same data source to examine wealth levels across European countries.[34] In addition, they included data from Australia, the United Kingdom, and the United States. The results are quite striking, as shown in Table 4.9. In terms of mean wealth, Luxembourg ranked by far the

Table 4.9. Mean and median net worth in selected OECD countries, around 2010 (figures are in thousands of euros)

	Mean	Median	Median Rank
Luxembourg	710.1	401.0	1
Australia	435.0	268.6	2
United States	348.8	49.1	8
Spain	291.4	181.7	3
United Kingdom	290.3	169.3	5
Italy	275.2	175.4	4
France	233.4	114.8	6
Germany	195.2	52.0	7

Source: Frank Cowell et al., "Wealth, Top Incomes and Inequality," in *Wealth: Economics and Policy,* ed. Kirk Hamilton and Cameron Hepburn (Oxford University Press, 2016), Table 1.

highest among this group of countries, with a mean net worth of 710,100 euros. Australia was second at 435,000 euros and the United States third at 348,800 euros. Indeed, Luxembourg's mean wealth was more than twice as high as that of the United States. Interestingly, Germany was the lowest in this group at about half the level of the United States. Luxembourg's high level of wealth corresponds to its high level of GDP per capita, typically ranked first in the world by the Penn World Tables, a database that includes information on per capita GDP for many countries in the world. It also reflects very high property values in the country, as well as a high homeownership rate. In terms of median wealth, the rank order is notably similar to that of mean wealth with the notable exception of the United States, which now ranks dead last, even below Germany. In the case of the United States, very low median net worth largely reflects the very high debt levels of middle-class households (see Chapter 3, for example).[35]

Concluding Remarks

By the mid-1980s, wealth inequality in the United States was considerably higher than in other industrialized countries for which comparable wealth data exist. This finding is in accord with previous studies that have found that by the mid-to-late 1980s, income inequality was greater in the United States than in other industrialized economies. Of the other countries, Australia, Canada, France, Germany, Sweden, and Great Britain all seemed to be roughly on par with each other in terms of their level of personal wealth inequality in the 1980s, while Japan appeared distinctly lower than this group. The situation remained unchanged by 2000 when the United States ranked considerably higher than Canada, Germany, and Italy in terms of wealth inequality. Switzerland ranked the highest according to the DSSW data. Denmark and Sweden also appeared to have very high wealth inequality as well. This result seems surprising given that income inequality was very low in Scandinavian countries. The likely reason is that the extensive welfare system, particularly income support and comprehensive health insurance for the elderly, obviates the need for substantial precautionary saving among poor and middle-class families. Caution must be exercised in international comparisons of wealth inequality between country samples with and without a high-income supplement.

A comparison of long-term time trends for the United Kingdom and the United States indicates that the very high level of wealth inequality in the United States in the 1980s represented a turnaround from the early part of the twentieth century, and even from the 1950s, when the inequality in personal wealth was much larger in the United Kingdom than in the United States. Indeed, in 1911, the wealth share of the top 1 percent in Britain was an incredible 69 percent! A comparison of long-term trends between Sweden and the United States reveals a similar pattern. Two crossover points were evident in the U.S.–U.K. comparison—the 1960s and the early 1980s. During the 1960s and 1970s, personal wealth inequality was roughly comparable in the United Kingdom and the United States. This was true for both marketable wealth and augmented wealth. In the early and mid-1970s the degree of wealth inequality in the United States also appeared comparable to that of Canada, France, and Sweden. By the early 1980s, U.S. wealth inequality began to exceed that of Canada, France, Sweden, and the United Kingdom, and this pattern held at least through 2010.

Another striking difference is the substantial increase in wealth inequality recorded in the United States between the mid-1970s and the late 1980s. This finding is not too surprising in light of the sharp increase in income inequality found for the United States over the same period. Interestingly, a similar rise in wealth inequality did not appear to have occurred in Canada, France, and the United Kingdom. Moreover, from the early 1980s to 2000, wealth inequality continued to rise in the United States. It increased also in Canada from 1984 to 1999 and in Italy from 1989 to 2000 but declined sharply in Germany between 1983 and 1998.

Another important finding is that while the United States ranked highest in terms of mean wealth per adult around the year 2000 among countries for which comparable data are available, the United States ranked relatively low in terms of *median wealth* per adult. The difference reflected the greater degree of wealth inequality in the United States than in these other countries. By 2010, the United States had slipped to third place among eight countries in terms of mean wealth, with Luxembourg by far the highest but last place in terms of median net worth—a result likely due to the very high debt levels among middle-class households in that country.

The results presented in this chapter raise several provocative questions. First, why is wealth inequality today higher in the United States than in other advanced countries? Second, why has wealth inequality recently increased much more sharply in the United States than in other industrialized countries? Are these results due to differences in market forces, demographics, the pattern of savings or inheritances, the behavior of asset markets, institutions, or government policies? With regard to the latter, both the United States and the United Kingdom pursued rather conservative economic policy during the 1980s (Reagan in the United States and Thatcher in the United Kingdom), while the social democrats dominated in Sweden. Moreover, of the three countries, Sweden was the only one with a direct tax on household wealth (at least through 2007).

II

Mechanisms Behind
Changing Wealth Inequality

5

Deconstructing Wealth Trends, 1983–2013

What are the factors that affect movements in mean and median wealth and those of wealth inequality? I analyze these trends in two ways. First, I conduct a decomposition analysis of wealth trends into savings, capital gains, and net wealth transfer components. Second, I rely on econometric analysis to test for the importance of a variety of factors in explaining these movements over the long term, from 1922 to 2013.

With regard to the first of these, recall from Chapter 2 that there was a very steep drop in median net worth of 44 percent between 2007 and 2010. There was also a smaller decline in mean net worth of 16 percent. Rates of returns on net worth were negative over these years (−7.3 percent per year overall and −10.6 percent per year for the middle three wealth quintiles) and that the sharp fall in median net worth of 43.9 percent was largely but not completely due to the very high negative return on net worth. In fact, a rough calculation indicates that this factor would have caused a 26.8 percent fall in median wealth and therefore explained about three-fifths (26.8 / 43.9) of the decline in median net worth. The other two-fifths were presumably due to a very high dissavings rate over these years. Likewise, while mean net worth fell by 16 percent over this period, it should have dropped by 20 percent on the basis of returns on the average household portfolio. In this case, positive savings must have offset the effects of the high negative rate of return.

This chapter begins with description of a model used to decompose movements in wealth levels and wealth inequality into a savings, capital gains, and net wealth transfer component. I then empirically analyze the role of these three components in accounting for wealth movements over time and look into "Piketty's law." The final section introduces a regression model to analyze wealth inequality movements over time.

Decomposition Analysis

I begin with the basic wealth relationship as established in Wolff (1999a):

$$\Delta W_{ct} \equiv W_{ct} - W_{c,t-1} = r_{ct} W_{ct-1} + s_{ct} Y_{ct} + G_{ct}, \tag{5.1}$$

where W_{ct} = net worth (in constant dollars) for age (or birth) cohort c at time t, r = real rate of return on wealth, Y = household income (in constant dollars), s = savings rate out of household income Y, and G = net inheritances and gifts (in constant dollars). With further algebraic manipulation we obtain:

$$s_{ct} = (\Delta W_{ct} - r_{ct} W_{ct-1} - G_{ct}) / Y_{ct} \tag{5.2}$$
$$= S_{ct} / Y_{ct},$$

where S_{ct} is total savings over the period. Equation 5.2 provides the basic formulation for estimating the savings rate.

On the basis of Equation 5.1, the change in wealth over a period can be decomposed into capital revaluation (existing wealth multiplied by the rate of return), savings, and net intergenerational transfers. The analysis will be divided into five subperiods: 1983–1989, 1989–2001, 2001–2007, 2007–2010, and 2010–2013.

The decomposition of mean wealth will also tell us the relative importance of capital gains and savings in explaining changes in wealth over time. Greenwood and Wolff, for example, estimated that about 75 percent of the growth of overall household wealth over the period 1962 to 1983 arose from capital gains (appreciation) of existing wealth and the remaining 25 percent from savings (income less consumption expenditures).[1] Later work confirmed this approximate breakdown between capital gains and savings.[2]

The same decomposition can be used for the wealth of the top 1 percent, the next 19 percent, and the middle three wealth quintiles. I will use changes in the mean wealth of the three middle wealth quintiles as a proxy for understanding the sources of changes in median wealth.[3] For my inequality analysis, I will consider changes over time in the *ratio* of mean wealth of the top 1 percent to that of the middle three wealth quintiles. I can then determine what portion of the change in this difference is due to capital gains and what portion is due to savings and net wealth transfers.

A key feature of the model is that the simulation is conducted by birth cohort for each of the five subperiods enumerated above (1983–1989, 1989–2001, 2001–2007, 2007–2010, 2010–2013). In the initial year of each simulation, households are first divided into the following age groups: 20–24; 25–29; 30–34; 35–39; 40–44; 45–49; 50–54; 55–59; 60–64; 65–69; 70–74; and 75 and over. The simulation then follows the same age group over the period of investigation.

As an example, consider age group 25–29 in 1983. I first compute the mean wealth of the age group in 1983. Second, I calculate the average rate of return on their wealth holdings in 1983. This figure is based on the average portfolio composition of the age group in 1983 and rates of return by asset type over the 1983–1989 period. This calculation leads to total capital gains over the period: $r_{ct}W_{ct-1}$. Third, in 1989 this birth cohort now spans ages 31 to 35. The change in the mean wealth of this birth cohort (ΔW_{ct}) is set equal to the difference between the mean wealth of age group 31–35 in 1989 and age group 25–29 in 1983. Fourth, the total savings of this birth cohort over years 1983 to 1989 can then be computed as $S_{ct} = \Delta W_{ct} - r_{ct}W_{ct-1}$. Fifth, I can then calculate the mean income of this birth cohort over the 1983–1989 period, Y_{ct}, as the average of the mean income of age group 25–29 in 1983 and the mean income of age group 31–35 in 1989. Sixth, the savings rate s_{ct} can be computed according to Equation 5.2.

There are several important methodological issues regarding the implementation of this model that should be addressed before the actual results are shown.

"Pseudo-Panels"

Let us first consider changes in *aggregate* household wealth from time t to t+1. W_t is the total wealth held by households living in the United States at time t and W_{t+1} is the total wealth held by households living in the United States at time t+1. If this were a closed economy, then generally speaking the only sources of change, ΔW_t, would be from savings and capital appreciation.

There may be some "leakages" and additions caused by various circumstances. First, a household could make a charitable contribution, which would subtract from current household wealth. Second, someone could die in this time interval and pay estate taxes or leave a charitable bequest. Third, there may also be outflows if an American resident emigrates from the United States and takes wealth out of the United States over this interval. Fourth, there may be additions to the stock of household wealth if immigrants bring new wealth in. If these effects are small, however, changes in aggregate wealth are due generally to only savings and capital gains on wealth at time t (see Equation 5.1).[4]

In order to analyze the sources of wealth change, it might seem that the appropriate technique is to compare household wealth holdings in time t and t+1. This technique is flawed because over time a given group of households gets older ("ages") and, normally, their wealth rises. A comparison of mean wealth in the two years would thus reflect not only this aging process but also the entry of new households into the population. As a result, the appropriate analysis would be to look at the same group of households in the two years.

The method used here provides us with a "pseudo-panel" over time from multiple cross-sections because we are following up the same birth cohort over time. A very similar technique was first employed by Sabelhaus and Pence.[5] They used six age cohorts beginning in 1989 and followed them over time through 1995. Their results were also based on the U.S. Survey of Consumer Finances (SCF), as well as rates of return estimated from the Flow of Funds Accounts (now called the Financial Accounts of the United States). Their analysis was conducted for the full population of households. What distinguishes the work described here is that I conduct a similar set of decompositions for particular sub-populations. These include a partition of the population by wealth class and, in Chapter 9, by income class, age group, race, education, and household type.[6]

In principle, in the simulation by age group, we want the *same* representative group of households in the second year as in the first. This is not an issue for the simulation involving all households since they are simply being "aged" over time. There are, however, a couple of provisos. First, some deaths may occur between the two years, so that in the second year the group may contain fewer households than in the first year. For the simulation of age group 25–29 in 1983, there may be fewer households in age group 31–35 in 1989 than in age group 25–29 in 1983. Second, more subtly, since households are classified according to the age of the household head, a change in marital status (a couple divorcing, for example) may change the number (and identity) of the households over the period. Third, some households in an age group may emigrate and new households may come into an age group from immigration. Though it is likely that these effects will be relatively small, in order to ensure consistency between the two years I standardize the age distribution in the second year on the basis of the age distribution in the first year. Thus, if 12 percent of households are in age group 25–29 in 1983 (as is the case in actuality), then I standardize the 1989 age distribution so that 12 percent of households are in age group 31–35 in 1989. In other words, in computing overall mean wealth in 1989, I use the age distribution weights of 1983. Overall mean wealth in 1989 is then equal to the mean wealth by age group in 1989 (say, age group 31–35) weighted by the share of households in the corresponding age group in 1983 (in this case, age group 25–29).

In the case of wealth classes, the same issues of attrition and new entrants may apply as in the case of all households for computing the overall mean. In addition, households may shift their wealth class over time. For example, the households in the top 1 percent in 1983 may not be the same as those in the top 1 percent in 1989. There is a regression to the mean over time, and some households in the top 1 percent in 1983 may have slipped to the next 19 percent, for example. As a result, the estimated change in mean wealth over the period, $\Delta \bar{W}$, may, in fact, be less than actual $\Delta \bar{W}$ if we followed exactly the *same households* over time. Since savings is imputed as a residual, this may bias *downward* the estimated savings for that wealth class over the period. Conversely, if households move up into a higher wealth class over the period, the estimated $\Delta \bar{W}$ may be greater than the actual change. This may be the case for the middle three wealth quintiles or the next 19 percent. In that case, estimated savings may be biased upward.

Shifting of wealth classes is not a problem if we are interested in explaining the change in wealth of, for example, the top 1 percent over time.

As noted previously, households in the top 1 percent of the wealth distribution may be different in the two years. In that case, as long as we select households in the second year based on their birth cohort in the first year (for example, age group 31–35 in 1989 and age group 25–29 in 1983) and standardize mean wealth by age group in the second year (age group 31–35 in 1989) by the share of households in the corresponding age group in the first year (ages 25–29 in 1983), then we make sure that the household *groups* in the two years are the same (if not exactly the same households). This procedure will allow us to calculate unbiased estimates of the portions of the *standardized* change in the mean wealth of this group due to capital gains, savings, and net wealth transfers.

In Chapter 9 I perform the same analysis for income classes, age group, race/ethnicity, educational attainment, and family type and parental status. First, with regard to income classes, the same provisos regarding wealth classes apply equally to income classes, since a household may switch income classes over a period. Households in the upper income classes are more likely to shift downward over time while those in lower income classes are more likely to shift upward in the income distribution. These movements will bias the estimates of savings over the period in the same way as for wealth classes if we follow the same households over time. Second, with regard to age classes, birth cohorts remain constant over time so that almost all the same households will appear in the second year as in the first. The only exceptions are due to the death of the household head and marital changes because households are classified into age group on the basis of the age of the household head, emigration, and immigration.

Third, race/ethnicity remains constant over the lifetime for an individual but once again since this category is based on the household head and changes in marital status may affect the classification of a household over time. Fourth, the same may be said of educational attainment (at last after age 25 or so). Fifth, here it is more likely that marital status and parental status may shift over time. Here, the direction of bias is more complicated. If a couple without children has a child over the time interval, then their relative wealth position will likely shift from a higher one to a lower one. The same is true for a single woman who has a child over the period. Two singles who marry over a period will likely shift in relative terms from two lower wealth positions to a higher one, while, conversely, married couples who split up will move down the wealth ladder.

The same pseudo-panel technique should also be valid by socioeconomic group. In particular, following up birth cohorts over time and standardizing by the age distribution of the initial year should produce valid estimates of the *standardized* change in the mean wealth of this group due to capital gains, savings, and net wealth transfers.

Income

The income concept used here is the U.S. Census Bureau's standard gross money measure.[7] More comprehensive income measures have also been used in the literature by Bitler and Hoynes, as well as Armour, Burkhauser, and Larrimore.[8] Their work suggests that the middle of the income distribution as well as the bottom quintile were much more protected from the reduction in market income during and following the Great Recession by substantial gains in in-kind transfers and tax credits that are not captured by standard money income. Without a full accounting for a more comprehensive measure of income one could misinterpret the difference between full income and consumption.

While this is true, unfortunately, data in the SCF do not allow an imputation of in-kind government transfers and tax credits like the Earned Income Tax Credit (EITC). Despite this, total savings S_{ct} as used in Equation 5.1 would not be affected by the use of a more limited or expanded income concept. The income definition would, however, affect the measurement of the savings rate, s_{ct} (see Equation 5.2).

Wealth Levels

I use the SCF wealth data for the standard analysis. However, there appears to be a major discrepancy between the SCF data on household wealth for 2013 and that from the Financial Accounts of the United States (FFA). In particular, the SCF data indicate that mean net worth per household rose only 0.6 percent (in total) over years 2010 to 2013, while the aggregate household balance sheet data based on the FFA shows a 20 percent jump in net worth per household over this interval.[9] While it is beyond the scope of this book to reconcile the two series, this chapter will compare time trends in mean net worth per household from the two sources over the full period from

1983 to 2013 to see whether similar discrepancies exist for other subperiods as well. Moreover, to test the sensitivity of the decomposition results, I will also use the FFA estimates of mean wealth in place of the SCF figures to determine the sensitivity of savings estimates per period to the choice of data source.

Gifts and Inheritances

The SCF contains several questions on (inter vivos) gifts and inheritances received, as well as gifts given to others and donations made to nonprofits and other charitable organizations. Net wealth transfers are defined as gifts and inheritances received minus gifts and donations given. The data are available in the SCF from 1989 onward. On the basis of these variables, one can estimate *net* wealth transfers received by household by period (see Chapter 7 for more details).

Rates of Return

The method used in the simulation assumes a single rate of return by asset type. Differences in rates of return by wealth level are then based solely on differences in portfolio composition. It may also be that rates of return by asset type differ across wealth classes. If the rich receive higher returns on their stock holdings than middle-class households and / or experience higher appreciation on their homes, then rates of return for the rich will be biased downward and those for the middle class will be biased upward. As a consequence, capital appreciation will be understated for the rich and overstated for the middle class and, correspondingly, savings will be overstated for the rich and understated for the middle class.[10]

Decomposition Results

The first set of results is shown in Table 5.1. Note that the simulated change in mean net worth (NW) both overall and by wealth class was greater than the actual change over the period (with one exception) since wealth generally increased with age. Not surprisingly, the differences were larger for the longer time periods. For example, for the 1989–2001 period the simulated change in overall mean NW was $262,200, compared to the actual change of $152,000—a difference of $110,200.

Generally speaking, capital revaluation explained the bulk of the change in overall mean NW (see Panel C). It accounted for 80 percent (22.0/27.6) of the total growth in mean wealth over the 1983–1989 period, 91 percent (68.5/75.3) over years 1989–2001, and 78 percent (27.4/35.4) over the period from 2001 to 2007. From 2007 to 2010, capital losses would have caused mean wealth to decline by 19.6 percentage points, compared to the 10.6 percentage point drop in simulated mean wealth. From 2010 to 2013, capital gains by themselves would have caused mean NW to climb by 20.4 percentage points, whereas simulated mean wealth increased by only 6.4 percentage points.

Net wealth transfers were relatively small in each of the five periods.[11] Savings was then computed as a residual. Its contribution to wealth growth was much lower than that of capital gains in the first three periods, accounting for only 12 percent (3.4/27.6) of the overall growth in mean wealth over years 1983 to 1989, 6.8 percent (5.1/75.3) over 1989–2001, and 15 percent (5.4/35.4) over 2001 to 2007. Over the 2007–2010 period, estimated savings would have caused mean wealth to grow by 9.1 percentage points, offsetting in part the 19.6 percentage point decline emanating from capital losses. In contrast, the results for 2010 to 2013 indicate very high dissavings, causing a 15.5 percentage point fall in mean wealth over these years. This finding seems peculiar and suggests that aggregate FFA data may provide a more realistic view of trends in household wealth over these years.

The implied annual savings rates (the ratio of the annualized savings over the period to the average of the mean income of the first year and the simulated mean income of the second year) do not line up very well with overall savings rates computed from the National Income and Product Accounts (NIPA).[12] It would not be expected that the two are equal for two reasons. First, the NIPA savings rate is defined as income minus consumption expenditure. If a household sells an asset or withdraws cash from a savings account, the NIPA concept would not consider this change in the household's balance sheet as dissavings. It would, however, show up in the SCF concept as dissavings. Likewise, if a household reduces its debt by $1,000, this change would show up as added savings in the SCF concept but would not be captured in the NIPA definition. For these reasons, the SCF savings concept is superior to the NIPA definition.

Second, the NIPA savings rates are computed from annual data whereas my estimates are based on pseudo-panels (over time). Nonetheless, my estimates are quite far from the NIPA benchmark in all five periods, particularly 2007–2010 and 2010–2013. For the last period, my estimated savings rate is actually negative and quite large (−30.8 percent) whereas the NIPA figure is positive. This discrepancy is another indication that the aggregate FFA wealth data may be more reliable for this period.

How do the results for years 2007–2010 and 2010–2013 line up with the data from Chapter 3? Among all households, there was a modest reduction of overall average debt by 4.4 percent in constant dollars from 2007 to 2010 (Table 3.5), so this could be a source of some of the savings indicated earlier. There was also a downward trend in asset ownership over these years (Table 3.14), which was tantamount to dissavings. Over the 2010–2013 period, on the other hand, there was a major retrenchment in average debt (in constant dollars) of 12.6 percent, as well as a continued, though more modest, negative trend in asset ownership. Both these factors should have led to positive savings over these years, in contrast to the negative savings seen in Table 5.1.

Results for the top 1 percent are shown in Panel 2. They are quite similar to those for all households, with capital revaluation accounting for the bulk of wealth growth in the first three periods and savings making a much smaller contribution. Over the 2007–2010 period, capital losses would have caused a 17.8 percentage point decline in the mean wealth of the top percentile but savings would have led to a 6.8 percentage point gain, whereas over years 2010 to 2013, capital gains made a very strong contribution to wealth growth but savings once again had a strong negative effect. Here, too, it is hard to believe that the top 1 percent had such a high negative savings rate.[13]

Among the next 19 percent (percentiles 80 to 99 of the wealth distribution), capital gains accounted for more than 100 percent of their wealth growth over the first three periods, with dissavings making a negative contribution. Over years 2007 to 2010, capital losses would have caused an 18 percentage point decline in their mean wealth (almost exactly the same as that of the top percentile), but savings would have caused a 4.7 percentage point advance. Over the 2010 to 2013 period, capital gains would once again

Table 5.1. Decomposing wealth trends by wealth class, 1983–2013

Wealth Class	1983–1989	1989–2001	2001–2007	2007–2010	2010–20.3	1983–2013
			Period			
A. Actual Change in Mean NW by Wealth Class						
1. All households	44.2	152.0	102.2	−96.6	3.1	204.9
2. Top 1 percent	1,985	4,456	4,123	−3,233	1,038	8,369
3. Next 19 percent	113.5	465.5	256.1	−175.0	−25.9	634.2
4. Middle 3 wealth quintiles	10.8	26.1	22.2	−51.8	−0.8	6.6
B. Simulated Change in Mean NW by Wealth Class						
1. All households	84.0	262.2	177.0	−63.7	32.1	
2. Top 1 Percent	2,855	8,097	4,785	−2,355	1,222	
3. Next 19 percent	132.7	503.5	253.2	−205.6	−22.4	
4. Middle 3 wealth quintiles	17.0	43.8	35.7	−48.2	3.4	
C. Contribution by Component to Percentage Growth in Simulated Mean NW over Period (percentage)						
1. All households						
Percentage growth in simulated mean NW	27.6	75.3	35.4	−10.6	6.4	
Contribution of capital gains (losses)	22.0	68.5	27.4	−19.6	20.4	
Contribution of net wealth transfers	2.3	1.7	2.6	0.0	1.4	
Contribution of savings (implied)	3.4	5.1	5.4	9.1	−15.5	
Memo: Annual savings rate (implied)[a]	2.5	1.9	4.9	20.7	−30.8	
Memo: NIPA personal savings rate (period average)[b]	6.9	4.7	2.5	3.9	4.8	
2. Top 1 percent						
Percentage growth in simulated mean NW	28.3	67.0	28.6	−11.3	6.9	
Contribution of capital gains (losses)	23.0	65.3	26.5	−17.8	20.3	

(continued)

Table 5.1. (continued)

Wealth Class	Period					
	1983–1989	1989–2001	2001–2007	2007–2010	2010–2013	1983–2013
Contribution of net wealth transfers	−1.6	−5.0	−1.1	−0.4	1.9	
Contribution of savings (implied)	6.9	6.7	3.2	6.8	−15.3	
Memo: Annual savings rate (implied)[a]	13.0	6.4	5.6	32.5	−64.6	
3. Next 19 percent						
Percentage growth in simulated mean NW	17.4	57.4	18.9	−12.9	−1.6	
Contribution of capital gains (losses)	19.7	63.3	23.1	−18.0	18.5	
Contribution of net wealth transfers	1.6	3.1	3.2	0.5	1.2	
Contribution of savings (implied)	−3.9	−9.0	−7.5	4.7	−21.3	
Memo: Annual savings rate (implied)[a]	−4.1	−4.7	−9.7	14.4	−60.2	
4. Middle 3 wealth quintiles						
Percentage growth in simulated mean NW	17.7	41.0	26.9	−31.1	3.3	
Contribution of capital gains (losses)	22.3	75.2	39.8	−27.1	23.2	
Contribution of net wealth transfers	1.3	−2.3	3.5	−0.8	2.9	
Contribution of savings (implied)	−5.9	−32.0	−16.4	−3.1	−22.8	
Memo: Annual savings rate (implied)[a]	−1.9	−5.5	−6.4	−3.0	−15.1	

Source: Author's computations from the 1983, 1989, 2001, 2007, 2010, and 2013 Survey of Consumer Finances.
Households are classified into wealth class according to their net worth. Decompositions are then based on the change in the mean wealth of the wealth class over the period. The method is to "age" households over the period. Thus households in age group 25–29 in 2001, for example, are aged to age group 31–35 in 2007. I also assume that the age distribution of the first year (e.g., 2001) remains unchanged over the period (e.g., 2001–2007). Overall mean wealth in 2007 is then equal to the mean wealth by age group in 2007 (for example, age group 31–35) weighted by the share of households in the corresponding age group in 2001 (in this case, age group 25–29).
a. The savings rate is defined as the ratio of the annualized savings over the period to the average of the mean income of the first year and the simulated mean income of the second year.
b. Ratio of NIPA personal savings to NIPA personal income (not personal disposable income).
Abbreviations: NIPA, National Income and Product Accounts; NW, net worth.

have caused a very sizable gain in mean wealth but dissavings in this case more than offset the capital gains effect, causing an overall decline in wealth. The savings rates of this group were uniformly negative over the five periods, except for years 2007 to 2010 when it was positive and quite high.

The results for the middle three wealth quintiles are somewhat different. Capital appreciation once again accounted for more than 100 percent of the change in mean wealth over the first three periods, and dissavings once again provided a negative contribution. The relative magnitudes were larger, with dissavings reducing wealth growth by 32 percentage points in the 1989–2001 period and by 16.4 percentage points over years 2001 to 2007. Over years 2007 to 2010, capital losses accounted for a 27.1 percentage point decline in the mean wealth of this group (87 percent of the total decline) but in this case dissavings added another 3.1 percentage point to the overall decline (10 percent of the total). These results do differ from the rough estimate noted in the introduction to this chapter, which indicates that capital losses accounted for three-fifths of the decrease in median wealth and savings the remaining two-fifths. In the 2010–2013 period, capital gains would have caused mean wealth to rise by 22.8 percentage points by itself but this was almost exactly offset by dissavings over these years. The implied savings rates of the middle wealth group were uniformly negative across the five periods.

How do the savings results for the 2007–2010 and 2010–2013 periods compare to the data on asset holdings and debt of the middle three wealth quintiles from Chapter 3? There was a substantial retrenchment of their average debt by 25 percent in constant dollars from 2007 to 2010 (Table 3.5), so this should have translated into positive savings. There was also a major reduction in asset ownership over these years (see Table 3.14)—for example, 8.9 percentage points for homes and 7.7 percentage point for pension accounts—as well as sizeable declines in the value of these assets. These two changes would have translated into substantial dissavings. It appears that the latter effect dominated debt reduction and led to net dissavings over this period. From 2010 to 2013, there was a more modest decrease in average debt (in constant dollars) of 8 percent, as well as a continued, though more moderate decline in asset ownership. These two factors partially offset each other but led to net dissavings over these years.

Decomposition Results with Data Aligned to the
National Balance Sheets

The same decomposition analysis is also performed with household wealth
data aligned to aggregate time series data of household wealth. This series is
based on the FFA.[14] The procedure is to adjust the household wealth data in
the SCF proportionally by the ratio of the FFA aggregate wealth total to the
SCF wealth total in that year. I use a proportional adjustment since it is not
possible to estimate wealth holding by wealth class or any other characteristic from the FFA balance sheet data.

It is at once apparent that trends in mean household wealth differed between the SCF and the aligned FFA data, particularly for the 1983–1989 and
the 2010–2013 periods. For the first, the SCF data show a 14.6 percent rise in
average NW, while the aligned data indicate a 29.3 percent increase. For the
2010–2013 period, the former indicate a 0.6 percent (total) growth while the
latter show a 20.3 percent advance. There was a less marked difference for
years 1989 to 2001, when the SCF data pointed to a 44 percent increase in
mean NW and the aligned FFA data a 35 percent gain. The trends for the
other two periods were fairly similar. Decomposition results therefore differ
mainly for the earliest, second, and last period.

Table 5.2 indicates that this is largely the case. For the 1983 to 1989 period, savings accounted for 43 percent of the growth in mean wealth for all
households in contrast to 12 percent based on the unaligned SCF data.[15]
Moreover, the implied savings rate leaped from 2.5 to 11.1 percent. For the
1989–2001 period, changes in results were relatively minor. With the aligned
data, savings were negative and would have caused a 5.3 percentage point
decline in mean wealth and the savings rate was –1.7 percent. With the unaligned SCF data, savings were positive and accounted for a mere 6.8 percent
of wealth growth over these years and the savings rate was positive but small,
at 1.9 percent. For the 2010–2013 period, the aligned FFA data indicate positive savings, accounting for 19 percent of the change in mean wealth
(5.1 / 27.2) and a positive savings rate of 8.6 percent. Results from the unaligned data, in contrast, show a huge negative contribution of savings to
wealth growth, accounting for a 15.5 percent drop, and a huge negative savings rate of –30.8 percent.

Table 5.2. Decomposing wealth trends by wealth class on the basis of data aligned to the Financial Accounts of the United States, 1933–2013

	Period					
Wealth Class	1983–1989	1989–2001	2001–2007	2007–2010	2010–2013	1983–2013
A. Actual Change in Mean NW by Wealth Class						
1. All households	69.9	108.7	82.0	−76.6	86.0	270.0
2. Top 1 percent	2,792	3,233	3,295	−2,523	3,928	10,725
3. Next 19 percent	177.6	342.8	204.9	−135.1	207.7	7979
4. Middle 3 wealth quintiles	19.3	16.2	17.7	−42.2	16.2	27.2
B. Simulated Change in Mean NW by Wealth Class						
1. All households	105.1	200.7	143.9	−49.1	115.1	
2. Top 1 percent	3,547	6,129	3,874	−1,823	4,109	
3. Next 19 percent	194.7	374.5	202.5	−160.7	211.2	
4. Middle 3 wealth quintiles	24.8	31.0	28.9	−39.2	20.4	
C. Contribution by Component to Percentage Growth in Simulated Mean NW over Period (percentage)						
1. All Households						
Percentage growth in simulated mean NW	44.0	65.0	34.5	−9.8	27.2	
Contribution of capital gains (losses)	22.0	68.5	27.4	−19.6	20.4	
Contribution of net wealth Transfers	2.9	1.9	3.1	0.0	1.7	
Contribution of savings (implied)	19.1	−5.3	4.0	9.8	5.1	
Memo: Annual savings rate (implied)[a]	11.1	−1.7	3.0	18.6	8.6	
Memo: NIPA personal savings rate (period average)[b]	6.9	4.7	2.5	3.9	4.8	
2. Top 1 Percent						
Percentage growth in simulated mean NW	44.8	57.2	27.8	−10.6	27.9	
Contribution of capital gains (losses)	23.0	65.3	26.5	−17.8	20.3	

(continued)

Table 5.2. (continued)

Wealth Class	Period					
	1983–1989	1989–2001	2001–2007	2007–2010	2010–2013	1983–2013
Contribution of net wealth transfers	−2.0	−5.6	−1.3	−0.5	2.3	
Contribution of savings (implied)	23.8	−2.4	2.6	7.6	5.3	
Memo: Annual savings rate (implied)[a]	35.3	−2.0	3.8	30.3	18.9	
3. Next 19 Percent						
Percentage growth in simulated mean NW	32.4	48.2	18.1	−12.1	17.7	
Contribution of capital gains (losses)	19.7	63.3	23.1	−18.0	18.5	
Contribution of net wealth transfers	2.0	3.5	3.9	0.5	1.5	
Contribution of savings (implied)	10.7	−18.6	−8.9	5.4	−2.3	
Memo: Annual savings rate (implied)[a]	8.8	−8.6	−9.7	13.6	−5.3	
4. Middle 3 Wealth Quintiles						
Percentage growth in simulated mean NW	32.8	32.7	26.0	−30.5	23.6	
Contribution of capital gains (losses)	28.4	84.8	47.7	−32.7	27.7	
Contribution of net wealth transfers	1.7	−2.6	4.2	−1.0	3.5	
Contribution of savings (implied)	2.8	−49.6	−25.9	3.2	−7.7	
Memo: Annual savings rate (implied)[a]	0.7	−7.6	−8.4	2.6	−4.2	

Source: Author's computations from the 1983, 1989, 2001, 2007, 2010, and 2013 SCF and the Financial Accounts of the United States. Households are classified into wealth class according to their net worth. Decompositions are then based on the change in the mean wealth of the wealth class over the period. The method is to "age" households over the period. Thus households in age group 25–29 in 2001 are aged to age group 31–35 in 2007. I also assume that the age distribution of the first year (e.g., 2001) remains unchanged over the period (e.g., 2001–2007). Overall mean wealth in 2007 is then equal to the mean wealth by age group in 2007 (age group 31–35) weighted by the share of households in the corresponding age group in 2001 (in this case, age group 25–29).

a. The savings rate is defined as the ratio of the annualized savings over the period to the average of the mean income of the first year and the simulated mean income of the second year.

b. Ratio of NIPA personal savings to NIPA personal income (not personal disposable income).

Abbreviations: NIPA, National Income and Product Accounts; NW, net worth.

Which results seem more sensible? For the 1983–1989 period, the aligned data, given asset price movements over these years, imply an enormous savings rate, which is not likely. For years 1989 to 2001, the unaligned estimates seem more reasonable since they point toward a positive savings rate over the period, which is more consistent with the NIPA results. Results for the next two periods are quite close from the two simulations. On the other hand, for the 2010–2013 period, the aligned FFA estimates seem much more credible than the unaligned ones since they indicate a positive savings rate over these years whereas the latter show a very high rate of dissavings. I therefore rely on the unaligned estimates for the first four periods but the aligned FFA estimates for years 2010 to 2013.

For the 2010–2013 period, on the basis of the aligned figures, capital gains accounted for 73 percent (20.3 / 27.9) of the growth in the mean wealth of the top 1 percent and savings for 19 percent, and the implied savings rate was 18.9 percent (as opposed to negative for the unadjusted figures). For the next 19 percent, capital gains explained a little over 100 percent of the growth in their mean wealth in years 2010–2013, savings made a very small negative contribution, and the implied savings rate was −5.3 percent (in contrast to −60.2 percent with the unadjusted data). Among the middle three wealth quintiles, capital gains caused their average wealth to grow by 27.7 percentage points over years 2010 to 2013, but this was offset by a 7.7 percentage point reduction in their mean wealth due to dissavings. As with the unadjusted data, their savings rate was negative—in this case, −4.2 percent as opposed to −15.1 percent from the unadjusted data.

Decomposing Changes in Wealth Inequality

The next step is to decompose changes in wealth inequality over time into three components: capital revaluation, savings, and net wealth transfers. As far as I can tell, there is no simple analytical decomposition of Equation 5.1 into these three components. As a result, the technique I use is to set the value of each component equal to its overall average (that is, its value for all households) and then recompute the change in simulated wealth over the period. The difference between the original simulated change and the newly recomputed simulated change is then the measure of the contribution of that component to the simulated change in NW.

The index of wealth inequality that I use in this exercise is the ratio of the mean wealth of the top 1 percent of wealth holders to the mean wealth of the middle three wealth quintiles (60 percent) of wealth holders. I call this the P90/P2080 ratio.[16] This measure seems to provide the most straightforward decomposition compared to alternative measures like the Gini coefficient.

The first concern is how well the actual P90/P2080 ratios line up with the Gini coefficients for NW shown in Table 2.2 of Chapter 2 (see Table 5.3). The former showed a modest increase between 1983 and 1989 (7.7 percent) while the Gini coefficient showed a fairly large rise (0.029 Gini points). Between 1989 and 2001, the P90/P2080 ratio had a larger advance (11.1 percent) while the Gini coefficient declined slightly. Over the 2001–2007 period, the former grew modestly (6.6 percent), while the Gini coefficient had a modest upturn (0.008 Gini points). For years 2007 to 2010, both measures showed an upsurge (the former by 27 percent and the latter by 0.032 Gini points), while over the last three-year period, both rose moderately (6.7 percent and 0.005, respectively). All in all, the two measures lined up surprisingly well over years 1983 to 2013.

The next issue is how well the simulated change in the P90/P2080 compared to the actual change in the P90/P2080 ratio. In this case, also, the two lined up remarkably well (compare lines IIA and IIB).

The third and major issue is how much of the change in inequality is accounted for by the three components. I first consider differences in rates of return on NW between the top 1 percent and the three middle wealth quintiles ("the middle"). As shown in Table 3.10, there was relatively little variation in annual rates of return between the two groups over the 1983–1989 period, though the top 1 percent had a slightly higher return (3.45 versus 3.35 percent). In this period, the percentage change in the P99/P2080 would have been 0.6 percentage points *smaller* (114.4–113.8) if rates of return were the same for the two groups (line IIIC) and, as a result, differences in returns made a small but *positive* 0.6 percentage point contribution to inequality, increasing the percentage change in the ratio in mean wealth between the two groups (the P99/P2080 ratio) by 6.6 percent (line IVA). Over the next period, 1989–2001, there was a larger spread in returns between the two groups—a difference of 0.48 percent per year—but in this case the return was higher for the middle group. If returns had been the same for the two groups,

Table 5.3. Decomposing trends in wealth inequality, 1983–2013

			Year				FFA
	1983	1989	2001	2007	2010	2013	2013
I. Ratio of Mean NW of Top 1% to Mean NW of Middle Three Wealth Quintiles (P99/P2080 Ratio)							
A. Actual ratio	105.0	113.1	125.7	134.0	170.2	181.6	181.6
B. Simulated ratio		114.4	134.0	127.4	172.4	176.2	176.2
C. Simulated ratio with uniform rate of return across wealth classes[a]		113.8	143.4	142.2	152.2	181.2	180.4
D. Simulated ratio with uniform ratio of net wealth transfers to net worth[b]		117.0	135.7	132.0	171.2	178.0	178.0
E. Simulated ratio with uniform ratio of savings to net worth across wealth classes[c]		103.3	105.3	110.6	152.0	163.8	159.5

			Period			FFA
	1983 1989	1989 2001	2001 2007	2007 2010	2010 2013	2010 2013
II. Percentage Change in the P99/P2080 Ratio						
A. Actual ratio	7.7	11.1	6.6	27.0	6.7	6.7
B. Simulated ratio	9.0	18.5	1.4	28.7	3.5	3.5
C. Simulated ratio with uniform rate of return across wealth classes	8.4	26.8	13.1	13.6	6.5	6.0
D. Simulated ratio with uniform ratio of net wealth transfers to net worth	11.5	20.0	5.1	27.7	4.6	4.6
E. Simulated ratio with uniform ratio of savings to net worth across wealth classes	−1.6	−6.8	−12.0	13.4	−3.7	−6.3

(continued)

Table 5.3. (continued)

	Year						FFA
	1983	1989	2001	2007	2010	2013	2013
III. Contribution to the Percentage Change in the P99/P2080 Ratio (in percentage points)[d]							
A. Differences in rates of return		0.6	−8.3	−11.8	15.1	−2.9	−2.5
B. Differences in the ratio of net wealth transfers to net worth		−2.5	−1.5	−3.7	0.9	−1.1	−1.1
C. Differences in the ratio of savings to net worth		10.6	25.3	13.4	15.3	7.3	9.8
total		8.7	15.5	−2.0	31.3	3.3	6.3
IV. Percent of Actual Percentage Change in the Simulated P99/P2080 Ratio[e]							
A. Differences in rates of return		6.6	−44.9	−851.8	52.6	−83.5	−69.5
B. Differences in the ratio of net wealth transfers to net worth		−27.4	−8.2	−267.1	3.3	−30.2	−30.3
C. Differences in the ratio of savings to net worth		117.7	137.0	971.4	53.2	205.9	276.9
residual		3.1	16.1	247.6	−9.1	7.8	−77.2

Source: Author's computations from the 1983, 1989, 2001, 2007, 2010, and 2013 SCF and the FFA.

a. The rate of return of each wealth class is set equal to the overall average rate of return.

b. The ratio of net wealth transfers to net worth of each wealth class is set equal to the overall average ratio. This ratio is defined as the ratio of net wealth transfers to the average net worth over the period, which in turn is equal to the mean of the actual mean net worth of the first year and the simulated net worth of the second year.

c. The ratio of savings to net worth of each wealth class is set equal to the overall average. This ratio is defined as the ratio of savings to the average net worth over the period, which in turn is equal to the mean of the actual mean net worth of the first year and the simulated net worth of the second year.

d. A positive entry indicates that the component increases the P99/P2080 ratio while a negative entry indicates that the component reduces the P99/P2080 ratio.

e. The components (including the residual) sum to 100 percent.

Abbreviations: FFA, Financial Accounts of the United States; NW, net worth.

the P99/P2080 ratio would have risen by 8.3 percentage points more (line IIIA), and, consequently, differences in returns *reduced* wealth inequality by 8.3 percentage points, lowering the percentage increase in the P99/P2080 ratio by 45 percent (line IVA).[17]

Over years 2001–2007, there was an even larger gap in rates of return, 1.67 percentage points, in favor of the middle, and this component lessened the percentage gain in the P99/P2080 ratio by almost 90 percent.[18] Years 2007 to 2010 saw negative returns for the two groups but in this case the annual returns were much lower for the middle group—a discrepancy of 4.04 percentage points. If rates of return had been identical for the two groups, the percentage change in the P99/P2080 ratio would have been 15.1 percentage points smaller. As a consequence, differences in returns augmented inequality over these years, accounting for over half (52.6 percent) of the percentage rise in the P99/P2080 ratio (line IVA).[19] Finally, over years 2010 to 2013, the annual returns became positive again and were greater for the middle than the top percentile—a spread of 0.79 percentage points. This gap reduced the percentage change in the P99/P2080 ratio by 84 percent (line IVA).

How well do these results accord with the analysis of Chapter 3? Here I have speculated that disparities in annual returns between the two groups were a major contributing factor to the spike in wealth inequality from 2007 to 2010 but moderated the rise in inequality in the 2001–2007 and 2010–2013 periods. This new analysis confirms the speculations of Chapter 3.

The next row shows the contribution made by differences in the ratio of net wealth transfers to NW between the two groups.[20] As noted above, the *net* wealth transfers of the top 1 percent were negative except for years 2010 to 2013. This result implies that the very rich gave away more of their wealth in terms of inter vivos gifts and donations than they received in gifts and inheritances.[21] The exception was the period 2010 to 2010, when not surprisingly, inter vivos gifts and donations from the top wealth percentile were down considerably (though the group still received some inheritances and gifts over these years).

The more crucial dimension is the ratio of net wealth transfers to NW. In this case, the net wealth transfer ratio was lower for the top than for the middle across all periods (including 2010–2013) with the sole exception of 2007–2010. Here, the ratio was somewhat higher for the top 1 percent than for the middle group (−0.004 versus −0.010).

As a result, when the ratio of NW transfers to NW is set to the overall average, which was positive in all periods except 2007–2010, the mean wealth of the top 1 percent rose (since wealth transfers are now positive instead of negative). The mean wealth of the middle group also increased, since their net transfers were less than the overall average (except, again, for the 2007–2010 period), and the mean wealth of the former increased more in percentage terms than that of the latter. As a result, setting a uniform ratio of wealth transfers to NW for both wealth groups raised the simulated ratio of mean wealth between the two groups over all periods except for years 2007–2010 (see Line IID). Consequently, the gap in the ratio of net transfers to NW between the two groups had an equalizing effect on the mean ratio (negative entry in Line IVB) except for 2007–2010 when the effect was positive (disequalizing) but very small. The effect of the difference in the net transfer ratio was also relatively small over years 2001–2007 (a difference of 3.7 percentage points in the percentage change in the P99/P2080 ratio, as shown in line IIIB) but the percentage contribution was large because of the very small change in the simulated P99/P2080 ratio over these years (1.4 percentage points, as shown in line IIB).

Simulated savings rates were much higher for richer households than the middle class. If we substitute the aggregate FFA results for the SCF data in the 2010–2013 period, then over the five subperiods, the average savings rate was 15.3 percent for the top 1 percent but only −4.2 percent for the middle three wealth quintiles. The overall average over the five subperiods was 7.7 percent. Equalizing savings rates for the two groups by setting them equal to the overall average lowers the mean wealth of the top percentile and raises the mean wealth of the middle. As a result, this procedure is equalizing in terms of the inequality of wealth, and the *difference* in savings rates contributed positively to inequality.

The results confirm this prediction. Instead of using the savings rate (the ratio of savings to income) in the simulation, I use the ratio of savings to NW in order to be consistent with the other two components (the rate of return and the ratio of net wealth transfers to NW). Over the 1983–1989 period, imposing a uniform savings rate lowered the percentage increase in the simulated P99/P2080 ratio from 9.0 to −1.6 or by 10.6 percentage points (IIIC). Thus, the differential in savings rates between the two groups was disequalizing, accounting for 118 percent of the rise in the P99/P2080 ratio over these years (line IVC). For years 1989–2001, setting a uniform savings rate lowered the rise in the P99/P2080 ratio by 25.3 percentage points (line IIIC), and the disparity in savings rates explained 137 percent of the advance in the P99/P2080 ratio over these years (line IVC). Between 2001 and 2007, the simulated P99/P2080 ratio advanced by 1.4 percent, whereas it would have actually declined by 12 percent if savings rates were equal—a difference of 13.4 percentage points (line IIIC). The discrepancy in savings rates between the two groups in this case accounted for 971 percent (13.4/1.4) of the rise in the P99/P2080 ratio—a high figure because of the very low base.

The period 2007–2010 saw a large jump in wealth inequality, with the simulated P99/P2080 ratio jumping by 28.7 percent. If savings rates were uniform across wealth classes, the P99/P2080 ratio would have risen by only 13.4 percent—a 15.3 percentage point differential (line IIIC). For these years, the differential in savings rates accounted for 53 percent of the rise in the P99/P2080 ratio (line IVC). There was modest growth in inequality over years 2010 to 2013. If savings rates were equal for the two wealth classes, then the P99/P2080 ratio would have decreased by 3.7 percent instead of rising by 3.5 percent, for a 7.3 percentage point difference (line IIIC). The savings rate difference explained 206 percent of the rise in the P99/P2080 ratio over these years (line IVC).

Looking at each period separately, we can now see that the biggest contributor to the upturn in the P99/P2080 ratio in the 1983–1989 period was the difference in savings rates between the top percentile and the middle three wealth quintiles. The higher returns received by the top group also made a slight positive contribution but this was offset by the higher ratio of net wealth transfers to NW of the middle group. Over the 1989–2001 period, the higher rate of return of the middle group relative to the top percentile helped lower the rise in wealth inequality, as did the higher net wealth transfer ratio of the latter. The higher savings rate of the top group relative to the middle added to the upswing in the P99/P2080 ratio. Over the 2001–2007 period, the simulated upswing in the P99/P2080 ratio was very small (1.4 percentage points). Both the higher returns of the middle group and their higher ratio of net wealth transfers to NW relative to the top group helped offset the growth in the P99/P2080 ratio, whereas the higher savings rate of the top group exacerbated the advance.

Over years 2007 to 2010, there was a sharp escalation in wealth inequality. All three factors made positive contributions: the higher (less negative) rate of return of the top 1 percent, their slightly higher net wealth transfer ratio, and their higher savings rate. The two largest contributions came from differences in rates of return and savings rates, each of which accounted for about half of the advance. These results for the 2007–2010 period accord with those of Chapter 3, where it is surmised that these two factors both contributed to the sharp jump in wealth inequality over these years. These new results imply that the two factors made about equal contributions to the explanation for this sharp rise.

Over the period 2010–2013, the P99 / P2080 ratio showed a small enlargement. Both the higher return on the wealth of the middle group and their higher net wealth transfer ratio helped reduce this advance, whereas the higher rate of savings of the top group helped augment the upswing. These results also conform to those of Chapter 3 in which I speculate that rate of return differences contributed negatively to the advance of wealth inequality whereas differences in savings rate had a positive effect.[22]

Confronting Piketty's r > g Proposition

The last topic in this section is a new analysis of Piketty's (2014) now famous "law," which indicates that wealth inequality rises if $r > g$; that is, if the rate of return on capital, r, is greater than the rate of real output growth, g. In fact, I will show that the Piketty condition is not generally met, at least in the case of the United States over years 1983 to 2013.

This finding is evident from Table 5.4. For Piketty's "r" I use my own computation of the average annual rate of return on the household portfolio from Table 3.10. For "g" I use the average annual growth of real GDP derived from the National Income and Product Accounts. A couple of anomalies stand out. First, from 1983 to 1989, r equaled 3.32 percent and g was 4.29 percent, so that the Piketty law would imply a decline in wealth inequality. In fact, the Gini coefficient rose rather sharply (by 0.029 points). Second, over the 2007–2010 period, r was −7.28 percent and g was −0.20 percent, so that again the Piketty law would indicate a drop in wealth inequality. In contrast, the Gini coefficient again showed a vigorous increase of 0.032 points. Indeed, the overall correlation coefficient between the difference $(r - g)$ and the change in the Gini coefficient is actually strongly negative, −0.81. Though

Table 5.4. Confronting Piketty's law

Period	Change in Gini Coeff.	Average Annual Rate of Return[a] (%)			Piketty Variables (%)		
		Top 1% (r_{top})	Middle (r_{mid})	Diff.	r^a	g^b	Diff.
1983–1989	0.029	3.45	3.35	0.10	3.32	4.29	−0.97
1989–2001	−0.001	4.19	4.67	−0.48	4.35	3.06	1.29
2001–2007	0.008	3.92	5.58	−1.67	4.04	2.66	1.38
2007–2010	0.032	−6.52	−10.55	4.04	−7.28	−0.20	−7.08
2010–2013	0.005	6.16	6.94	−0.79	6.20	2.03	4.17
Correl. with Change in Gini Coeff.			0.74				−0.81

a. Source: Chapter 3, Table 3.10.
b. Source: National Income and Product Accounts, Table 1.1.3 Real Gross Domestic Product, Quantity Indexes, available at http://www.bea.gov/iTable/iTable.cfm?ReqID=9&step=1#reqid=9&step=1&isuri=1

these results are hardly definitive since they are based on only five data points and my interpretation of "r" and "g," they do cast some doubt on the reliability of Piketty's law.[23]

A better rule of thumb is to look at the relation between r_{top}, the rate of return on the portfolio of the top 1 percent of wealth holders, and r_{mid}, the rate of return on the portfolio of the middle three wealth quintiles. Instead, it appears that wealth inequality rises if the rate of return on wealth is greater for the top 1 percent than for the middle class. As we saw in Chapter 3, there were striking differences in rates of return on NW between these groups. For example, from 2001 to 2007, when inequality remained relatively stable, the annual real rate of return on NW for the middle three wealth quintiles was 5.6 percent but it was only 3.9 percent for the top percentile (see Table 5.4). In contrast, from 2007 to 2010, when the Gini coefficient for wealth shot up by 0.032, the rate of return for the former was −10.6 percent but "only" −6.5 percent for the latter. In fact, the simple correlation between the difference ($r_{top}, −r_{mid}$) and the change in the Gini coefficient is positive and quite strong, at 0.74. Wealth inequality thus tends to decline or remain stable when the return on wealth for the middle class is greater than that of the very rich and, conversely, increases when the opposite is the case.

Regression Analysis

I next use regression analysis to investigate some of the factors that seem to play an important role in movements in household wealth inequality over time. In Chapter 3, I showed earlier results based on a regression that was run of a wealth inequality index, measured by the share of marketable wealth held by the top 1 percent of households (WTOP1), on income inequality, measured by the share of income received by the top 5 percent of families (INCTOP5), and the ratio of stock prices (the Standard and Poor's 500 index) to median housing prices (RATIO), with 21 data points between 1922 and 1998. It yields:

$$\text{WTOP1} = 5.10 + 1.27 \text{ INCTOP5} + 0.26 \text{ RATIO}, R^2 = 0.64, N = 21 \qquad (5.3)$$
$$\quad\quad (0.9) \quad (4.2) \quad\quad\quad (2.5)$$

with t-ratios shown in parentheses. Both variables are statistically significant (INCTOP5 at the 1 percent level and RATIO at the 5 percent level) and with the expected (positive) sign. Also, the fit is quite good, even for this simple model.

I once again make use of the long-term data developed in Chapter 13, though the model is now extended to 2013. There are 26 data points: 1922, 1929, 1933, 1939, 1945, 1949, 1953, 1958, 1962, 1965, 1969, 1972, 1976, 1979, 1981, 1983, 1986, 1989, 1992, 1995, 1998, 2001, 2004, 2007, 2010, and 2013. Here too a full-fledged model is not possible given the paucity of data points and available variables. As a result, the specification is rather parsimonious.

The dependent variable is the share of marketable wealth held by the top 1 percent of households, drawn from the long-term data in Chapter 13 (WTOP1). An alternative is the share of wealth held of the top 1 percent on the basis of the long-term time series developed by Saez and Zucman in 2016 (SZ-WTOP1). Five explanatory variables are used: (1) the share of income received by the top 1 percent of families drawn from the World Top Incomes Database, based on IRS tax returns, INCTOP1;[24] (2) the ratio of stock prices (the Standard and Poor's 500 index) to median housing prices (RATIO); (3) the ratio of total household debt to NW (DEBT); (4) the ratio of total pension reserves to NW (RPENS); and (5) the ratio of total Social Security wealth to NW (RSSW).

The rationale for including income inequality as an explanatory variable is self-evident: a higher concentration of income among the rich leads to a higher concentration of savings.[25] With regard to the variable RATIO, the major household assets have historically been owner-occupied housing and corporate stock. Evidence suggests that the share of wealth held by the top percentile of the wealth distribution is closely correlated with the stock market, while the share of the middle percentiles tends to move with the median price of housing.

The third explanatory variable is DEBT, the ratio of total household debt to NW. Ideally, I would like to use the *spread* in the ratio of debt to NW between the top and the middle parts of the wealth distribution. The reason is that, as is seen in Chapter 3 and the earlier section in this chapter on changes in wealth inequality, differential leverage translates into a rate of return difference between the two groups. Higher leverage of the middle group relative to the top group will thus tend to lower wealth inequality. Unfortunately, debt-wealth ratios are not available by wealth (or income) class for the full period of analysis. For the seven years that are available (1983, 1989, 1998, 2001, 2007, 2010, and 2013), the correlation between the overall debt to NW ratio and the *difference* in the debt to NW ratio between the top 1 percent and the middle three wealth quintiles is quite strong, 0.74. Overall indebtedness thus seems to be a good proxy for the differential in indebtedness between the two groups.[26]

The last two variables are the ratio of pension reserves to NW (RPENS) and the ratio of Social Security wealth to NW (RSSW).[27] The relative growth in pensions and SSW should have two effects. First, insofar as defined benefit (DB) pensions and SSW substitute for traditional NW, their relative increase should lead to slower growth in NW since families have less need to save for retirement. Second, insofar as DB pensions and SSW are more important for middle wealth than top wealth groups, their relative increase should slow the growth of wealth at the middle of the wealth distribution more than at the top and should thus lead to rising wealth inequality.

Before showing the regression results, it might be helpful to look at the actual time trends of the five variables. Figure 5.1 shows long-term trends in the share of wealth held by the top 1 percent and the share of income received by the top 1 percent. The two variables track quite closely, with the shares generally falling from 1922 to 1976 and then generally rising after that. Figure 5.2 shows trends in WTOP1, RATIO, and DEBT. RATIO and WTOP1 also track well, rising sharply from 1922 to 1929, largely declining from 1929 to 1949, rebounding from 1949 to 1965, falling off again from 1965 to 1976, climbing upward again from 1976 to 1998, dropping off through 2001 (2004 for RATIO), and then generally rising after that point. WTOP1 and DEBT,

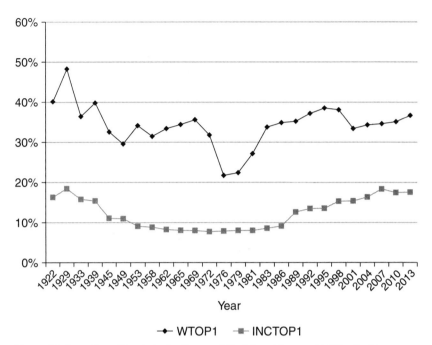

Figure 5.1. Long-Term Trends in the Shares of Wealth and Income Held by the Top 1 Percent, 1922–2013

on the other hand, seem to have very little relationship to each other, with RATIO generally tracking upward over the full period from 1922 to 2013.

Figure 5.3 shows movements in WTOP1 and the share of pension reserves and SSW in NW. Here one would expect that RPENS and RSSW would move in line with WTOP1, but both variables appear to move inversely with respect to WTOP1. Both RPENS and RSSW generally rise between 1922 and the early 1980s whereas wealth inequality generally falls. Both variables then generally trend downward after the early 1980s while WTOP1 largely rises.

The preferred regression results are as follows:[28]

$$WTOP1 = 27.86 + 0.726 \, INCTOP1 + 0.105 \, RATIO - 0.414 \, DEBT, \; R^2 = 0.52, \; N = 26$$
$$\qquad (8.47) \; (2.91) \qquad\qquad (1.33) \qquad\quad (2.19) \qquad\qquad\qquad (5.4)$$

with the absolute value of t-ratios shown in parentheses. In comparison with the original regression results (Equation 5.3), the coefficient of INCTOP1 re-

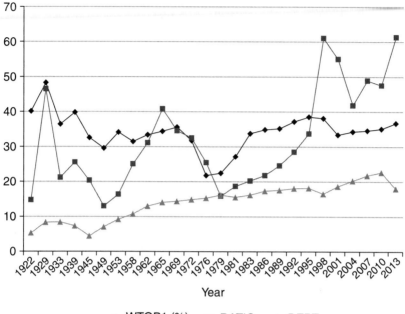

Figure 5.2. Long-Term Trends in the Share of Wealth of the Top 1 Percent, the Ratio of Stock to Home Prices, and the Ratio of Overall Debt to Net Worth, 1922–2013

mains positive and significant at the 1 percent level. On the other hand, the coefficient of RATIO while staying positive is no longer significant. The apparent reason is that RATIO fluctuates rather wildly between 2001 and 2013 while wealth inequality has a steady upward trajectory. The coefficient of the variable DEBT has the predicted negative sign and is significant at the five percent level. The R^2 statistic is lower than in the original results but still quite respectable.[29]

The fit is actually better with SZWTOP1 as the dependent variable:

$$SZWTOP1 = 21.94 + 1.435\ INCTOP1 + 0.102\ RATIO - 0.706\ DEBT, R^2 = 0.86, N = 26$$
$$(8.71)\ (7.69) \qquad\qquad (1.81) \qquad\quad (5.02) \qquad\qquad (5.5)$$

The estimated coefficient of INCTOP1 is again positive and significant at the 1 percent level but is now doubled in value, and the t-ratio is considerably higher.[30] The coefficient of RATIO remains positive but is now marginally significant (at the 10 percent level). The coefficient of DEBT is again negative

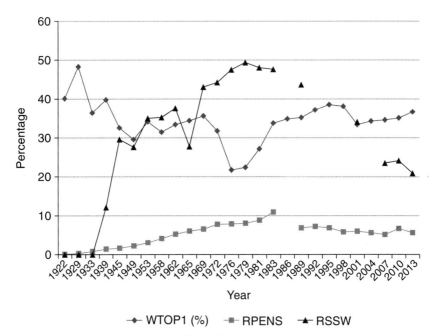

Figure 5.3. Long-Term Trends in the Share of Wealth of the Top 1 Percent and the Ratio of Pension Reserves and Social Security Wealth to Net Worth, 1922–2013

but is now significant at the 1 percent level. The R^2 statistic is much higher, at 0.86.[31]

Summary and Concluding Remarks

On the aggregate level, capital revaluation explained the bulk of the change in overall simulated mean NW—80 percent or more over the 1983–1989, 1989–2001, and 2001–2007 periods on the basis of the unadjusted SCF data and 75 percent over the 2010–2013 period on the basis of the SCF data aligned to the FFA. From 2007 to 2010, capital losses would have lowered mean wealth by 20 percent, compared to the 11 percent drop in simulated mean wealth. Savings accounted for only 12 percent of the overall growth in simulated mean wealth from 1983 to 1989, 7 percent over years 1989–2001, and 15 percent from 2001 to 2007. Over years 2007–2010, savings would have caused mean wealth to grow by 9 percent, in contrast to the 11 percent fall in simulated mean wealth. For years 2010 to 2013, savings made a positive contribution to wealth growth, accounting for 19 percent of the change in mean wealth over this period on the basis of the aligned data.

Results are roughly similar for trends in the mean wealth holdings of the top 1 percent but different for the middle three wealth quintiles. Capital appreciation accounted for more than 100 percent of the change in mean wealth over the first three periods, and dissavings made a negative contribution. Over years 2007 to 2010, capital losses caused a 27 percentage point decline in the mean wealth of this group and dissavings added another −3.1 percentage points. In years 2010–2013, capital gains increased mean wealth by 28 percent on the basis of the FFA aligned data but this was partially offset by dissavings, which lowered wealth by 7.7 percent.

Trends in inequality as measured by the P99/P2080 ratio were largely influenced by differentials in rates of return and differences in savings rates between the two wealth groups. Disparities in returns generally helped lower inequality whereas the variance in savings rates uniformly exacerbated inequality.

Over years 1983–1989, the simulated P99/P2080 ratio rose by 9 percentage points. The biggest contribution to the upturn in the P99/P2080 ratio was from the differential in savings rates, explaining over 100 percent of increased inequality. Over years 1989–2001, the simulated P99/P2080 ratio increased by 18.5 percentage points. The higher rate of return of the middle group on its portfolio relative to the top group lowered the rise in wealth inequality (by 45 percent). The higher savings rate of the top group relative to the middle added substantially to the rise in the P99/P2080 ratio (137 percent). Over the 2001–2007 period, the simulated upturn in the P99/P2080 ratio was very small, due to offsetting effects from the two factors.

Years 2007 to 2010 saw a substantial elevation in wealth inequality, with the simulated P99/P2080 ratio climbing by 28.7 percentage points. In this case, both factors contributed about equally to this phenomenon: the higher (that is, less negative) rate of return of the top 1 percent and their higher savings rate. The simulated P99/P2080 ratio showed a small advance of 6.7 percentage points over years 2010 to 2013. The relatively higher return on the wealth of the middle group slowed the advance by 2.9 percentage points but the higher rate of savings of the top group added 7.3 percentage points.

These findings illustrate the power of leverage, particularly for the middle class. This factor was most evident for the 2001–2007 and 2007–2010 periods. In the first, (real) housing prices advanced at an annual rate of 3.02 percent. The annual real rate of return on the NW of the middle three wealth quintiles averaged 5.58 percent over these years because of high leverage (ratio of debt to NW). As a result, while the simulated mean NW of this group advanced by 26.9 percentage points, capital appreciation by itself would have caused a 39.8 percentage point gain (though this increase was offset by a 16.4 percentage point decline resulting from dissavings). Over years 2007–2010, home prices were down by an annual rate of 8.77 percent per year. The annual return on the NW of the middle group was even lower, –10.55 percent per year, again because of leverage. The simulated NW of this group plummeted by 31.1 percentage points. Capital losses explained 27.1 percentage points or 87 percent of the total decline, with an additional 10 percent due to dissavings. It is of note that this split was much more one-sided than the crude decomposition performed in Chapter 3, which seemed to indicate a 61 percent contribution from the rate of return effect and a 39 percent contribution from the dissavings effect. In other words, leverage coupled with the steep fall in housing prices accounted for fully 87 percent of the collapse of median wealth over these years, instead of 61 percent as calculated in Chapter 3.

With regard to inequality trends as measured by the simulated P99/P2080 ratio, the higher leverage of the middle group relative to the top 1 percent and the strong gains in housing prices led to a 1.67 percentage point divergence in rates of return between the two groups over years 2001 and 2007 and this difference reduced the increase in the P99/P2080 ratio from 11.6 percentage points to 1.4 percentage points or by 88 percent. (The equalizing effect was offset by an even stronger disequalizing effect from differences in savings rates between the two groups, leading to a net rise in inequality over these years.) From 2007 to 2010, the simulated P99/P2080 ratio shot up by 39 percentage points. In this case, high leverage coupled with the housing market collapse led to 4.04 percentage point gap in rates of return in favor of the top 1 percent. This factor accounted for about half the rise in the simulated P99/P2080 ratio over these years, with the other half emanating from differences in savings rates.

On another note, it is useful to consider what implications these simulation results have with regard to savings among the middle class. In Chapter 3

I argue that the middle class, experiencing stagnating incomes, enlarged their debt in order to finance normal consumption expenditures. From 2001 to 2007, despite the huge expansion of debt, the average expenditures in 2013 dollars of the middle income quintile inched up by a mere 1.7 percent (in total).

Implied savings rates (the ratio of savings to the average income over the period) among the three middle wealth quintiles were negative in all five periods used in the analysis: –1.9 percent in 1983–1989, –5.5 percent in 1989–2001, –6.4 percent in 2001–2007, –3.0 percent in 2007–2010, and –4.2 percent in 2010–2013 on the basis of the FFA-aligned data.

The likely reason for the dissavings of the middle class over both the 2007–2010 and 2010–2013 periods was income stagnation (actually, a reduction in median income in both periods). It appears that the middle class was dissaving in order to maintain its normal level of consumption. Data from the Consumer Expenditure Survey (CEX) does indeed show that the average expenditures in real terms of the middle-income quintile actually fell by 7.7 percent from 2007 to 2010 and by another 3.5 percent from 2010 to 2013.[32] Moreover, for the 2001–2007 period average consumer expenditures in real terms rose by only 1.7 percent. So it appeared that the middle class was not exactly splurging over these years.

What about years 1983–1989 and 1989–2001? Again, according to the CEX, average expenditures in real terms were up by 2.6 percent from 1984 to 1989 and by 13.2 percent from 1989 to 2001.[33] The period from 1989 to 2001 is interesting since it alone shows a marked increase in consumer expenditures. It also turns out that this period stands out because there was a 9 percent spurt in real median family income. It thus appears that the consumption expenditures of the middle class rise only when incomes also grow.

This last result leads to the question of whether the middle class will ever save again. This seems possible only if real median income also increases. However, this is only a necessary condition since it is still possible (maybe even likely) that rising income will be absorbed by rising consumption.

In considering Piketty's law, $r > g$, I use my computation of the average annual rate of return on household wealth for r and the average annual growth of real GDP for g. In the case of the United States over years 1983–2013, the correlation coefficient between the difference $(r - g)$ and the change in the Gini coefficient over five periods is actually negative (–0.81). In contrast the simple correlation between the difference in the annual rate of return on the wealth of the top 1 percent and that of the middle three wealth quintiles ($r_{top} - r_{mid}$) and the change in the Gini coefficient is positive and quite strong, at 0.74. This result suggests a better rule of thumb: that wealth inequality tends to decline when the return on wealth for the middle class is greater than that of the rich and, conversely, increases when the opposite is the case.

6

Age-Wealth Profiles and the Life Cycle Model: Implications for Wealth Accumulation

There are two major types of models currently used to explain the size distribution of household wealth. The first is the life cycle model, in which households accumulate wealth during working years in order to ensure adequate consumption during retirement years. This theory implies a rising level of wealth with age until retirement followed by a continuous decline. The second is the intergenerational bequest model, whereby the distribution of wealth of one generation is related to that of the previous generation. This chapter begins with a discussion of these models and their implications concerning wealth inequality.

Empirical testing of the life cycle model, using traditional concepts of household wealth, indicates that although the coefficients of such a model are statistically significant, it explains only a small fraction of variation in household wealth (about 5 to 10 percent). When confined to the middle class, however, the model performs adequately. The implication is that the life cycle model provides a useful explanation of wealth accumulation motives for the middle class. In particular, it suggests that this class acquires wealth for retirement, liquidity, and consumption purposes. People in the upper classes are more likely to accumulate wealth for other reasons—power and prestige, for example—and bequest models are more appropriate for explaining the distribution of wealth within this class.

Pension and Social Security wealth (SSW) can be incorporated directly into the life cycle model of household wealth accumulation because they are forms of retirement wealth. The question arises as to how much their inclusion in the household wealth portfolio improves the explanatory power of the life cycle model. Results of cross-sectional regression analysis using alternative concepts of pension and SSW confirm these conclusions. The performance of the model for the total population is not substantially improved when pension and SSW are incorporated in the definition of household wealth. However, for the middle class, there is substantial improvement in the degree of variation in total household wealth accounted for by the model.[1]

This chapter provides an analysis of these two models. We begin with a brief survey of the pertinent literature and an investigation into the validity of the life cycle model, using standard wealth concepts as an explanation of the variation of wealth holdings among households. The same set of econometric analyses is reproduced in the next section, using an augmented concept of wealth that includes both pension and Social Security wealth.

A Brief Survey of the Life Cycle Literature

Individuals can acquire wealth by gifts, by inheritances, or by saving their own income. Explaining the differences in wealth among individuals and families bears directly on the determinants of the inequality of wealth and equity in the distribution of household resources.

One issue of particular concern throughout this literature is the relative importance of life cycle savings—the tendency of individuals to build up assets as they grow older—versus inheritance in the accumulation of household wealth. Insofar as the former is the major determinant, differences in household wealth can be viewed as the result of the "natural" process of aging and therefore not a major concern of public policy. However, if inheritances play the major role, then issues of fairness and equity come to the fore.

The accumulation of household wealth depends not only on income but also on savings behavior, capital appreciation, and gifts and inheritances. Moreover, wealth is the direct source of property income, which is an important factor in accounting for disparities in family income. This chapter considers some of the factors accounting for differences in wealth among families. The first of these is age. Since individuals work only part of their lives, they have a strong incentive to accumulate wealth for their retirement years. In this chapter, I explore the standard life cycle model that economists have developed to describe this behavior. Other factors, such as gifts and inheritances and capital appreciation, also play a role in wealth accumulation.

This survey of research begins with a presentation of the basic life cycle model. Evidence is presented on the validity of the model, including age-wealth profiles (average wealth by age group), longitudinal analyses, simulation studies, and regression studies. Attempts to expand the life cycle model include the following three extensions: introduction of uncertainty about length of life; the role of retirement wealth; and precautionary savings and liquidity constraints. Analysis of these extensions is followed by a review of pertinent empirical studies[2] and an overall assessment.

The Basic Life Cycle Model

The basic life cycle model (LCM) developed by Modigliani and Brumberg assumes that households save in order to spread out their consumption uniformly over their lifetimes.[3] That is, individuals normally work until age 65 or so and live into their seventies, eighties, and even longer, and therefore will save during their working years to provide for consumption during retirement. This implies that household wealth, defined as accumulated savings, will rise with age until retirement and then decline.

In the simplest form of the model, it is assumed that families earn the same amount in each year until retirement, that lifetime earnings are fully consumed over the lifetime, that age of retirement and longevity are known with certainty at the beginning of work life, and that the interest rate is zero. Under a certain class of utility functions, maximization of lifetime utility leads to a constant annual consumption over the lifetime. The savings pattern that results is a constant savings rate per year until retirement and a constant dissavings rate thereafter. The resulting age-wealth profile is an inverted "V" (see Figure 6.1). Net worth rises linearly with age until retirement and then declines with age in linear fashion.

In a later article, Ando and Modigliani relaxed the assumption of a zero interest rate and assumed that it would be positive and unchanging over time.[4] The resulting profile is an inverted "U," with net worth rising with age until around retirement age and declining thereafter (Figure 6.1). In both cases, the "hump-shaped" profile implies that wealth will decline after retirement, an issue that has received extensive empirical investigation.

James Tobin developed a variant of the LCM that also focuses on savings out of labor earnings as the major source of household wealth.[5] Tobin

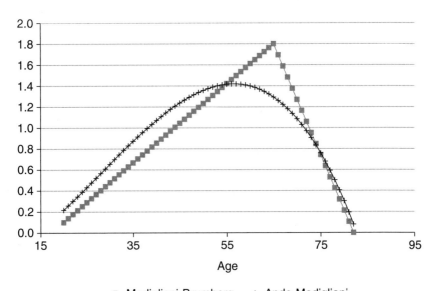

Figure 6.1. Standard Life Cycle Age-Wealth Profiles: Ratio of Wealth by Age Group to Overall Mean Wealth

retained the assumption of a level stream of lifetime consumption and zero net worth at death but added in the possibility that a family might incur debt early in the life cycle to purchase the housing and durables necessary to establish a household. Moreover, the model added a positive rate of return on assets (and debt) as a factor affecting household wealth accumulations. The resulting wealth pattern is shown in Figure 6.2 for contrast. The family dissaves in its early years, saves during its middle years to repay its debt and to accumulate for retirement, and dissaves again in its later years. Thus, in this variant, net worth may start off negative, increase and become positive, and then decline again after retirement.[6]

Age-Wealth Profiles

We begin our survey of empirical work on the LCM with a consideration of age-wealth profiles, which show average wealth by age group. It should be noted at the outset that the LCM is a longitudinal model—that is, it describes the path of wealth accumulation for a given household as it ages over time. On the other hand, age-wealth profiles are "cross-sectional"—that is, they describe the wealth holdings of households of different ages at a *single* point

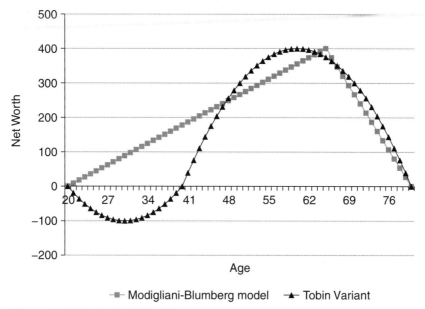

Figure 6.2. Life Cycle Wealth Profiles

in time. There are two biases that may arise from the use of cross-sectional profiles as a validation of the LCM.

First, because real income typically increases over time, the cross-sectional age-wealth profile may be hump-shaped even though the longitudinal profile rises over time.[7] This stems from the fact that if real incomes rise over time, lifetime income may be higher for younger age cohorts than older ones. As a result, in the cross-section (at a given point in time, say 2015), we may observe that 60 year olds have greater wealth than 70 year olds, even though the 70 year olds have greater wealth in 2015 than they had ten years ago, when they were 60. Consequently, accumulated wealth may peak among families whose head of household is in his or her sixties in the cross-section even if each age cohort has continued to save money over time.

Second, a positive correlation exists between wealth and longevity, so that people who live longer will generally be wealthier than those who are deceased.[8] In this case, the cross-sectional profile may slope upward, particularly among the older age cohorts, even though the longitudinal profiles are hump-shaped. The two biases are offsetting, but the net effect of the two is not known.[9]

Table 6.1. Age-wealth profiles for marketable net worth, 1962, 1983, 1989, and 2004 (mean wealth by age group as ratio to the overall mean)

Age Group	1962 SFCC[a]	1983 SCF[b]	1989 SCF[c]	2004 SCF[d]
Under 25	0.13	0.14	0.11	0.05
25–34	0.44	0.35	0.32	0.18
35–44	0.79	0.78	0.71	0.65
45–54	1.05	1.70	1.47	1.21
55–59	1.74	1.78	1.46	1.73
60–64	1.25	1.83	1.71	2.13
65–69	1.65	2.29	1.75	1.47
70–74	1.44	1.52	1.47	1.69
75–79	1.34	1.25	1.37	1.26
80 & over	1.01	0.93	1.30	1.14
Mean	1.00	1.00	1.00	1.00

The statistics are for household wealth. Families are classified into age group according to the age of the head of household.

a. Source: 1962 Survey of Financial Characteristics of Consumers, adjusted to align with national balance sheet totals. See Wolff, "Estimates of Household Wealth Inequality in the United States, 1962–83," *Review of Income and Wealth* series 33, no. 3 (September 1987): 231–56 for details.

b. Source: 1983 Survey of Consumer Finances, adjusted to align with national balance sheet totals. See Wolff, "Estimates of Household Wealth Inequality in the United States," for details.

c. Source: 1989 Survey of Consumer Finances, adjusted to align with national balance sheet totals. See Wolff, "Trends in Household Wealth in the United States, 1962–1983 and 1983–1989," *Review of Income and Wealth* series 40, no. 2 (June 1994): 143–74 for details.

d. Source: 2004 Survey of Consumer Finances.

The early work on age-wealth profiles provided mixed results on the issue of whether families dissave after retirement. Analyzing wealth data for the United Kingdom in 1953, Lydall found almost no difference in mean wealth between families in the age groups 55–64 or 65 and over.[10] Lansing and Sonquist reported that in 1953 average wealth was slightly greater for 63 year olds than 53 year olds in the United States, while in 1962 mean wealth among 62 year olds exceeded that among 52 year olds but was less than the average wealth of 72 year olds.[11] Brittain, using estate tax data for the United States, found wealth increased with age among older Americans.[12]

Table 6.1 shows age-wealth profiles based on some early data for the United States. The wealth concept is marketable net worth.[13] The first column is computed from the 1962 Survey of Financial Characteristics of Consumers. It shows wealth rising steadily with age until age group 55–59, peaking at 1.7

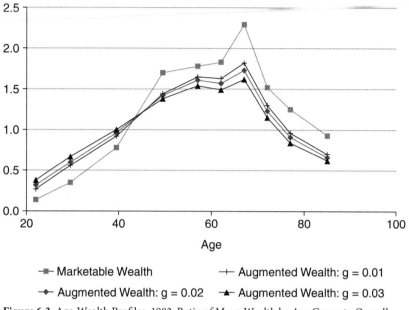

Figure 6.3. Age-Wealth Profiles, 1983: Ratio of Mean Wealth by Age Group to Overall Mean Wealth

times the overall mean for this age cohort, and then generally declining with age thereafter.

The second set of results is based on the 1983 Survey of Consumer Finances (SCF; see also Figure 6.3). The profile shows mean wealth rising steadily with age and peaking in the 65–69 age group at 2.3 times the overall mean and then falling sharply among older age groups. The third set is drawn from the 1989 SCF. The results are quite similar to the 1983 data. Wealth rose with age until the 65–59 age group, where the peak was 1.8 times the mean, followed by a steady decline thereafter. The final set is based on the 2004 SCF. The same hump-shaped profile is in evidence but in this case peak wealth occurred for the 60–64 age group and the peak was 2.1 times the overall mean. It is also of note that the relative mean wealth of the younger age groups (under age 45) slipped rather sharply over time, between 1962 and 2004.

The age-wealth profiles provide general support to the hump-shaped pattern predicted by the LCM. Wealth increased with age, peaked around age 65, and then declined with age. However, two anomalies did appear. First, though wealth declined among older age groups, it did not appear to approach zero, even for households 80 and older. This result was consistent with earlier tests of the LCM.[14]

Second, the data show that the cross-sectional age-wealth profiles became more hump-shaped over the 1962–1983 period and with higher mean wealth at the peak. However, the 1989 profile was flatter than the 1983 one and, indeed, was very close in shape to that of 1962. The age-wealth profile then became sharper again in 2004, with peak wealth rising once again. These results suggest that age-wealth profiles are not static but can change quite substantially over time.

Table 6.2 shows the effect of adding defined benefit (pension) wealth (DBW) and Social Security wealth (SSW) to marketable net worth on the shape of the age-wealth profile (also see Figure 6.3). DBW is defined as the present discounted value of future DB pension benefits. In similar fashion, SSW is defined as the present discounted value of the stream of future social security benefits.[15]

Chapter 8 discusses at some length the concept of augmented household wealth. From the standpoint of an individual a guaranteed future flow of income is in many ways like owning a financial asset. Indeed, there are marketable assets called "annuities" that have precisely the characteristic of providing a steady stream of income after a certain time (or age) is reached. The anticipated Social Security (or DB pension) benefits that an individual will receive after retirement is comparable to such an annuity. In the context of the life cycle model, the main motivation for saving is to guarantee a steady stream of income after retirement, so that SSW (or DBW) may *substitute* for marketable wealth. One implication of this is that there may be a *trade-off* between the accumulation of marketable wealth and that of retirement wealth.

SSW and DBW are constructed to reflect conditional mortality rates, so that there is a built-in bias for mean value to decline with age, particularly after age 70. In other words, since a person's remaining life expectancy declines as the person ages, the total value of his or her remaining SSW will also decline. Despite this, the net effect of including retirement wealth was a flattening of the age-wealth profile (compare, for example, the first two columns of Table 6.2). The younger age cohorts gained relative to the older ones and peak wealth declined. Moreover, the greater the assumed rate of growth of future Social Security benefits (the parameter g), the more the younger groups gained in relative terms and the more the peak flattened. However, all three measures of augmented wealth retained the basic hump shape of the LCM.

Longitudinal Analyses

Although cross-sectional age-wealth profiles generally follow the basic inverted U-shape predicted by the LCM, this cannot be taken as confirmation of the LCM. Shorrocks demonstrated that if real income is growing over time, the cross-sectional age-wealth profile can be hump-shaped even though individuals continue to accumulate wealth over their lifetimes (that is, the longitudinal age-wealth profile slopes upward).[16] A hump-shaped cross-sectional wealth profile is a necessary but not sufficient condition to ensure a hump-shaped wealth profile over the lifetime.

Mirer used actual data on real earnings growth over time to adjust cross-sectional age-wealth profiles for differences in cohort earnings.[17] Using a cross-sectional sample of individuals over age 65 in the United States and adjusting for actual differences in cohort earnings, he found no significant reduction in wealth with advancing age. In other words, even though age-wealth profiles were hump-shaped, the evidence indicated that elderly families did not dissave as they aged. In a follow-up piece, Mirer used a one-year panel from the 1963 and 1964 SFCC (the same families observed in the two years) and calculated a very small dissavings rate for the elderly—a median of 1.2 percent over the year—though it was not statistically significant.[18]

Later work on the LCM used longitudinal (panel) data, which follows the same individuals over time. Diamond and Hausman, using the National Longitudinal Sample (NLS) of older men, found that individuals accumulated wealth up to retirement and then depleted it, though very few individuals in their sample had actually retired.[19] Friedman used the Retirement History Survey (RHS), which covers individuals from age 58 to 73 over a ten-year period.[20] He reported that individuals continued to save in the first four to six years after retirement and then dissavings began.

Hammermesh found from the RHS that spending on consumption items covered in this survey (food, housing, transportation, and health) declined in the first few years after retirement, a finding consistent with Friedman.[21] This finding also confirmed earlier work of Danziger and colleagues based on the cross-sectional 1972–1973 Consumer Expenditure Survey.[22] They

Table 6.2. Age-wealth profiles for marketable and augmented household wealth, 1962 and 1983 (mean wealth by age group as ratio to the overall mean)

Age Group	Marketable Wealth (NWB)	Augmented Household Wealth (AWB)[a]			Ratio: NWB/HK	Ratio: AWB/HK
		g=g'=.01	g=g'=.02	g=g'=.03	k=.01	g=g'=.02; k=.01
A. 1962 SFCC						
Under 25	0.13	0.23	0.28	0.37	0.33	0.62
25–34	0.44	0.50	0.54	0.61	0.71	0.89
35–44	0.79	0.81	0.83	0.86	1.16	1.17
45–54	1.05	1.09	1.09	1.09	1.05	1.06
55–59	1.74	1.63	1.59	1.54	1.42	1.24
60–64	1.25	1.31	1.28	1.23	0.97	0.94
65–69	1.65	1.61	1.56	1.49	1.25	1.11
70–74	1.44	1.35	1.29	1.22	0.93	0.80
75–79	1.34	1.13	1.07	1.01	0.74	0.57
80 & over	1.01	0.82	0.78	0.73	0.95	0.69
Mean	1.00	1.00	1.00	1.00	1.00	1.00

B. 1983 SCF

Under 25	0.14	0.27	0.32	0.38	0.29	0.51
25–34	0.35	0.56	0.60	0.67	0.49	0.56
35–44	0.78	0.92	0.96	1.00	0.98	1.02
45–54	1.70	1.44	1.42	1.38	1.47	1.31
55–59	1.78	1.65	1.61	1.54	1.59	1.69
60–64	1.83	1.63	1.57	1.49	1.48	1.50
65–69	2.29	1.82	1.73	1.62	1.80	1.36
70–74	1.52	1.30	1.23	1.15	1.16	1.16
75–79	1.25	0.96	0.91	0.84	0.73	0.74
80 & over	0.93	0.70	0.66	0.62	0.59	0.50
Mean	1.00	1.00	1.00	1.00	1.00	1.00

Source: Author's calculations from the 1962 Survey of Financial Characteristics of Consumers (SFCC) and the 1983 Survey of Consumer Finances (SCF). The statistics are for household wealth. Households are classified into age group by age of the head of household in 1962 and age of respondent in 1983. HK is estimated human capital.

g' is the assumed rate of growth of Social Security benefits over time for current beneficiaries.

g is the assumed rate of growth of Social Security benefits over time for future beneficiaries.

k is the assumed rate of growth of future labor earnings.

found that the average ratio of consumption expenditures to after-tax income declined with age after age 71. Blinder, Gordon, and Weiss, also using the RHS and introducing a variable for lifetime earnings, found that conventionally measured wealth showed no tendency to decline with age among older people.[23]

However, Hurd, who also used evidence from the RHS, reached the opposite conclusion.[24] Hurd reported that the wealth of the elderly did decline over time, by 22 percent for singles and 2 percent for couples over the period 1969 to 1979. Later, he concluded from the RHS that although a family's consumption declined after retirement as the family aged, so did its wealth.[25]

Borsch-Supan reached a striking conclusion regarding the savings patterns of elderly German families.[26] He found that although wealth holdings declined between families aged 60 and 70, they increased after age 70, and that the very old (80 and older) had the highest savings rate among all age groups. He attributed this finding to two factors. First, the German social security system provided very generous annuities to aged pensioners as well as complete health coverage. Second, consumption expenditures actually declined with age after age 70, presumably reflecting the lessening needs for items such as clothing, transportation and travel, and food. This is similar to the results reported for U.S. households by Hammermesh.[27]

Banks, Blundell, and Tanner and Bernheim, Skinner, and Weinberg also found that consumption appeared to fall after retirement.[28] Bernheim, Skinner, and Weinberg also argued that the standard life cycle model failed to explain the heterogeneity (inequality) of retirement wealth found among households after the age of 65. On the other hand, Engen, Gale, and Uccello argued that the standard life cycle model coupled with stochastic income shocks over the lifetime was not inconsistent with a large level of wealth inequality among retirees.[29]

All in all, econometric studies have generally confirmed the age-wealth profile predicted by the life cycle model, with one or two exceptions. These findings provide further reinforcement to the cross-sectional studies, which have also largely found the inverted U-shape profile of the LCM.

Simulation Analysis
Simulation techniques have also been used to assess the explanatory power of the LCM. In simulation analysis, the researcher attempts to reproduce the

actual characteristics of the wealth distribution on the basis of assumed or estimated parameters of the model.

Atkinson used a simulation to account for the concentration of household wealth in the United Kingdom.[30] He started with the actual distribution of labor earnings and assumed that all wealth accumulation was due to life cycle savings. Using a simulation approach, he estimated that the basic LCM would predict that the top 10 percent of the population would hold only about 20 percent of total wealth, well below the actual concentration ratio of 60 to 70 percent. He then added the assumption that the top 10 percent of the distribution received equal inheritance shares. Even with this added assumption, he calculated that the top 10 percent would hold at most 30 percent of total wealth, still well below the actual share held by the top decile. He concluded that the simple LCM, even with the introduction of some inheritance effects, could not account for the actual concentration of household wealth.

Oulton generalized Atkinson's model to allow the age distribution, individual earnings functions, and the rate of return on assets to vary.[31] Substituting the distribution of earnings estimated from the actual British data into his model and assuming no inheritance, Oulton computed a maximum coefficient of variation of wealth of 0.75, which was substantially less than the actual value of 3.98. He also concluded that the LCM could not by itself adequately explain inequality in individual wealth holdings. In a reply to Oulton, Davies and Shorrocks pointed out that very little can be deduced about the quantitative importance of the life cycle component of saving until, at minimum, a complete model capable of replicating the mean features of saving and wealth behavior observed in actuality has been developed.[32]

Direct survey evidence and econometric tests on household survey data (or probate records) have failed to show a significant effect of bequests on household wealth accumulation. Indirect tests have succeeded in showing this. A model developed by Davies augmented the standard life cycle model with a bequest motive.[33] He began with the actual distribution of wealth in Canada in 1970. He then used actual data on the distribution of inheritances, mortality rates, and other factors to simulate the effects of inheritance on the distribution of wealth in Canada. He concluded that inheritances were a major source of wealth inequality in Canada.

In a follow-up article, Davies and St-Hilaire used the same model to estimate the proportion of total wealth accumulation in Canada that could be traced to inheritances.[34] Without cumulating interest on inheritances, they estimated that 35 percent of total household wealth was traceable to inheritances. With the interest on the inheritances added in, the proportion rose to 53 percent. Laitner calibrated a model incorporating both life cycle saving and inheritance with U.S. data and estimated the share of inherited wealth in the range of 58 to 67 percent.[35]

Two American studies, by White and Kotlikoff and Summers, used simulation to determine whether the LCM could account for the aggregate accumulation of wealth observed in the U.S. economy.[36] Both found that the LCM could explain only a very small proportion of observed household wealth in the United States. White used aggregate household balance sheet data to test whether several variants of the life cycle model accurately predicted the aggregate savings observed in the U.S. economy. Using a wide range of parametric values, White simulated the savings behavior of the population given its actual demographic composition and income flows. She concluded that the assumption that households save for future consumption did not account for the observed aggregate personal saving. At best, the simulated values were approximately 60 percent of the actual. Kotlikoff and Summers used actual age-earnings profiles (showing average earnings by age group) and consumption rates by age group in the United States and calculated that life cycle savings accounted for only about 20 percent of observed U.S. household wealth in 1974. The remainder, by implication, was due to inheritance and intergenerational transfers. In a survey of the literature on the subject, Davies and Shorrocks surmised that between 35 and 45 percent of household net worth can be traced to inheritances and gifts.[37]

In a summary of the literature on consumption patterns after retirement, Hurst concluded that collectively these studies showed there was no puzzle with respect to the spending patterns of households as they transition into retirement.[38] In particular, the literature indicated that there was substantial heterogeneity in expenditure changes at retirement across consumption categories. The declines in spending during retirement for most households were limited to the categories of food and work-related expenses. Expenditures on nearly all other categories of nondurables remained constant or increased. Moreover, even though food spending declined during retirement, actual food intake remained stable. Overall, the studies showed that the standard model of life cycle consumption augmented with home production and uncertain health shocks worked well in explaining the consumption patterns of most households as they transitioned into retirement.

In a more recent review of the literature, De Nardi, French, and Jones concluded that retired American households, particularly high-income ones, decumulate their assets at a slower rate than that implied by the basic LCM, when the time of death is known.[39] This finding raises the question of which additional saving motives explain their behavior. There are two general sets of explanations. The first emphasizes the risks that the elderly face late in life, particularly uncertain life spans and uncertain medical expenses. In fact, the observed patterns of out-of-pocket medical spending, which increases sharply with age during retirement, together with life-span risks, explained a substantial portion of their savings during retirement. The second is the bequest motive, which accounted for a large portion of savings after retirement.

Extensions of the Life Cycle Model

The general findings about individuals not totally exhausting their wealth at time of death and many older individuals not dissaving (reduce their wealth) as they aged raised some questions about the validity of the LCM. The response among economists was to modify the basic model by relaxing one or more of its assumptions. There are four directions in particular: uncertainty, particularly about length of life; the role of SSW and DBW; a bequest motive; and precautionary savings and liquidity constraints. The first two topics are directly related.

The Role of Uncertainty about Death and Lifetime Annuities
In the basic LCM and the Ando-Modigliani version, it is assumed that length of life is known with certainty. However, individuals do not know when they will die. The introduction of uncertainty about length of life can affect the shape of the age-wealth profile, particularly the pattern of dissavings after retirement. Yaari was the first to analyze the effects of uncertainty on life cycle behavior.[40] He demonstrated that uncertainty by itself could lead to increased savings and that (nonaltruistic) individuals will always leave unintended bequests because they will always have savings available should they live longer than expected.

Yaari then introduced annuities into his model. An annuity is a savings instrument that guarantees a fixed annual income until death. At the time of death, the value of this asset becomes zero. An example of this is a pension. Most pensions guarantee a retiree a fixed annual income until time of death (some will also continue the benefit for a surviving spouse). Such an asset removes most of the problems associated with uncertainty about death, since the pension provider assumes the risk about length of life. It thus has considerable advantages over a fixed-value asset such as a bond. Yaari demonstrated that if an annuity is available that is indexed for inflation, the availability of such an indexed annuity would lead to reduced savings in other forms by older individuals and might lead to an exhaustion of wealth at death.

Following Yaari's line of reasoning, Kotlikoff and Spivak estimated that, on the basis of certain parameter values, individuals could leave up to a quarter of their wealth at age 55 unintentionally—that is, without directly planning that it should be left as a bequest to their spouse or children.[41] Davies applied the same argument to explain the slow dissaving by individuals after retirement.[42] In a life cycle model with uncertain longevity, he demonstrated that consumption during retirement would be smaller than in a regime of complete certainty. Using Canadian data, Davies simulated the postretirement consumption and savings patterns of Canadian families and found that savings would still be higher with uncertainty than with certainty about longevity, even with the availability of pensions (a form of annuity). He concluded that uncertainty about length of life could explain the slow dissaving of households after retirement. Using the same data, King and Dicks-Mireaux found that household wealth decreased after retirement but at a rate much slower that predicted by the basic LCM.[43] They attributed this discrepancy to uncertainty over lifetime and the bequest motive.

Others used the model of uncertainty to introduce retirement wealth into the LCM. Sheshinski and Weiss used an overlapping generations model to introduce Social Security as an annuity and demonstrated a depressing effect on private savings.[44] Hubbard extended the theoretical work on uncertain lifetimes. He demonstrated that within a life cycle model an actuarially fair Social Security system would depress household savings by a greater amount than the actual contributions made.[45] He also showed that the household savings rate increased with permanent income.

The Role of Pension and Social Security Wealth

The empirical work on household savings and Social Security dates from Feldstein, who used aggregate time-series data for the United States.[46] He argued that Social Security should reduce household savings because the need to put away money for retirement would be lessened if the government guaranteed future retirement benefits. Feldstein also argued that the payment of Social Security benefits would reduce household disposable income and therefore decrease savings.[47] He estimated that Social Security could reduce personal savings by as much as 50 percent.

Feldstein's analysis generated considerable work on the effects of Social Security on household savings. Cross-sectional evidence was generally mixed. Feldstein and Pellechio, using the 1963 SFCC, found a very strong offset of SSW on private wealth.[48] Blinder, Gordon, and Weiss, using the RHS, estimated that each dollar of SSW substituted for 39 cents of private wealth, though the estimated coefficient had a very large standard error and was quite unstable over alternative specifications.[49] Diamond and Hausman, using the NLS, estimated effects on private wealth as 30 to 50 cents per dollar of SSW.[50] Kotlikoff found that Social Security contributions had a significant negative tax effect on individual savings.[51]

Leimer and Lesnoy, using the same aggregate time-series data as Feldstein, did not find that Social Security had a negative effect on private savings.[52] However, Feldstein's reply reconfirmed his earlier results.[53] Henry Aaron, in a review of the literature, surmised that the wide variation in results on this subject made it difficult to reach any definitive conclusion of the impact of Social Security on savings.[54]

Hubbard, using 1979 and 1980 survey data collected by the U.S. President's Commission on Pension Policy, found that even after controlling for permanent income, both SSW and DBW had statistically significant negative effects on private wealth.[55] SSW was estimated to have an offset of 33 cents per dollar on private wealth, while private pensions had an offset of 16 cents per dollar. As Hubbard noted, the substitution effects were considerably less than the dollar-for-dollar reduction predicted in a standard LCM.

Avery, Elliehausen, and Gustafson provided a similar set of estimates based on the 1983 SCF.[56] Their analysis was confined to households headed by persons 50 years of age or older who were in the labor force. Their computation of net SSW and DBW was based on the difference between the present value of expected benefits less that of anticipated contributions into the respective systems. Standard mortality rates were used to calculate present values. For pensions, expected benefits were based on respondent information, while for Social Security, expected benefits were calculated on the basis of current and future Social Security rates. Current family income was included as an independent variable, though a measure of lifetime earnings or permanent income was not. They reported a substantial substitution between pension and nonpension wealth. A dollar increase in pension wealth offset nonpension wealth by 66 cents. However, coefficients for SSW were small in size and statistically insignificant, indicating little substitution between SSW and marketable wealth.

Another study of direct interest is that of Bernheim.[57] Using the RHS, he first divided his sample into retirees and nonretirees. He computed longitudinal age-wealth profiles for retirees, and found significant dissaving in traditional wealth after retirement. He argued that, with annuities such as Social Security available, the proper concept of wealth is the sum of traditional wealth and the simple discounted value of private pension and Social Security benefits.[58] He found that augmented wealth showed little tendency to decline with age after retirement.

Another study that investigated whether Social Security and pension wealth displaced traditional wealth in the life cycle pattern of accumulation is Gustman and Steinmeier, who used data from the HRS to examine the composition and distribution of total wealth for a group of individuals between 51 and 61 years of age.[59] They focused on the role of pensions in forming retirement wealth and found that pension coverage was widespread. It covered two-thirds of households and accounted for one-quarter of accumulated wealth on average. Social Security benefits accounted for another quarter of total wealth. Gustman and Steinmeier also reported that the ratio of wealth (excluding pensions) to lifetime earnings was the same for individuals with pensions and those without pensions. They concluded that pensions caused very limited displacement of other forms of wealth.

Several papers looked at the issue of whether defined contribution (DC) plans substituted for other forms of wealth and whether there was any net savings derived from DC plans.[60] Poterba, Venti, and Wise used HRS data for 1993 in one study and both macro national accounting data and micro HRS data in another. They concluded that the growth of IRAs and 401(k) plans did not substitute for other forms of household wealth and that they raised household net worth relative to what it would have been without these plans. They found no substitution of DC wealth for either DB wealth or other components of household wealth.[61]

William Gale's research found that very little net savings emanated from DC plans. He concluded that when biases in estimation procedures in the previous literature on the subject were corrected, there was a significant offset of pension wealth on other forms of wealth.[62] Using data from the 1984, 1987, and 1991 SIPP, Engen and Gale estimated that "at best" only a small proportion of 401(k) contributions represent net increments to household savings.[63] In later work, Engen and Gale refined their analysis to look at the substitution effect by earnings groups.[64] Using data from the 1987 and 1991 SIPP, they found that 401(k) plans held by low earners more likely represented additions to net worth than 401(k) plans held by high earners, who held the bulk of this asset. Overall, only between 0 and 30 percent of the value of 401(k) plans represented net additions to private savings. Kennickell and Sunden found a significant negative effect from both DB plan coverage and SSW on nonpension net worth, but concluded that the effects of DC plans, such as 401(k) plans, on other forms of wealth were statistically insignificant.[65]

Precautionary Savings and Liquidity Constraints

Another way to modify the LCM is to introduce capital market imperfections. These usually take one of two forms. First, the interest rate at which a consumer can borrow may differ from the rate at which he or she can lend (the borrowing rate is usually higher than the lending rate). Second, due to credit market restrictions a consumer cannot borrow all that he or she may desire. These two cases are usually referred to as "liquidity constraints." In both cases, the implication is that the consumer cannot carry out his or her optimal lifetime consumption plan, and at some stage desired consumption will be constrained by current resources (in particular, by disposable income and the amount of financial assets). Moreover, since borrowing is constrained, the family will accumulate more wealth than a pure LCM would predict. Tobin and Dolde provided the early theoretical foundations for this approach.[66]

Several studies have suggested the importance of liquidity constraints on wealth accumulation. Hubbard and Judd developed a fifty-five-period simulation model in which young consumers are constrained in terms of borrowing for nine years (from age 20 to 29).[67] They estimated that such liquidity constraints could increase aggregate savings by as much as one-third. However, the age-wealth profiles depicted in Table 6.1 indicated that even families younger than twenty-five had, on average, accumulated positive net worth. As a result, only a fraction of young households might face a liquidity constraint.

A related argument is that consumers will accumulate precautionary savings ("saving for a rainy day"). Individual consumers will accumulate a stock of assets in order to allay the uncertainties associated with their future stream of labor earnings—for example, those related to layoffs, job changes, and illness. In this sense, precautionary savings serve as insurance against potential earnings misfortunes. As a result, when they are young, families will accumulate more wealth than if they were certain of their future income stream. This argument also leads to the hypothesis that consumers will accumulate more wealth than is strictly optimal from a pure life cycle perspective. This motive will also yield a hump-shaped age-wealth profile even in the absence of the standard LCM retirement motive.

There is evidence that precautionary savings explain a sizable fraction of the wealth accumulation observed among households. Zeldes modeled the uncertainty associated with future earnings.[68] He argued that the fear of being liquidity constrained some time in the future (from a shortfall of income) might induce consumers to save more in the present. Using a simulation analysis, Zeldes found that the possibility of future liquidity constraints might raise total savings by as much as 25 percent.[69]

Kotlikoff explored the relation between household saving and uncertainty over future health expenses.[70] He argued that in the absence of full health insurance, families will save as a hedge against uncertain future health expenses. Using simulation analysis, he found that the absence of complete health insurance could exert a substantial positive effect on personal savings. Palumbo also argued that uncertainty about medical expenses could explain the high level of precautionary savings among the elderly and their failure to dissave significantly after retirement.[71]

Caballero calculated from a simulation model that 60 percent of the observed wealth of U.S. households, net of the portion due to strictly life cycle savings, could be attributed to precautionary savings.[72] Jianakoplos, Menchik, and Irvine used data from the NLS of men age 45 to 49 in 1966 over the period 1966 to 1981 to examine determinants of household wealth.[73] They also found that the standard LCM was inadequate to explain the variation of wealth across households. However, once both precautionary and bequest motives were added to the model, they regression fit was considerably better.

Caroll developed a "buffer-stock" model of consumption that emphasizes the importance of precautionary saving in the face of uncertain future income flows. In the standard LCM, current consumption should depend not only on current income but also on future expected income. Carroll found that consumption was closely related to current income but not to future expected income.[74] On the other hand, he found that that the buffer-stock model in which precautionary motives greatly reduce the willingness of prudent consumers to consume out of uncertain future income did a much better job in predicting consumption than the standard LCM.

Caroll and Samwick estimated that as much as 40 percent of aggregate financial (nonhousing, nonbusiness) wealth was held for precautionary motives.[75] Gourinchas and Parker combined the LCM with a buffer-stock model. Using synthetic cohort data derived from the Consumer Expenditure Surveys, they found that young consumers typically behave as buffer-stock agents, with precautionary savings as the primary motive. However, around age 40, the typical household started to accumulate liquid assets for retirement and its behavior conformed most closely to the traditional LCM.[76]

Overall Assessment

This section has provided an overview of previous findings on the LCM. This model predicts that an individual will accumulate wealth over time until retirement age and then reduce wealth holdings. Cross-sectional age-wealth profiles have generally conformed to this prediction, but longitudinal data provided mixed results. Some studies showed the elderly dissaving whereas others indicated little if any dissaving by that age group. One reason for the latter set of findings may be that the very old (over age 75) reduce their consumption expenditures as their needs decline. Moreover, there is no evidence that families draw down their wealth to near zero as they age.

How much does the LCM explain about the distribution of household wealth? Two simulation studies, based on data for the United Kingdom concluded that the LCM could explain at most about one-quarter of the actual concentration of wealth held by the top wealth holders. How much does the LCM explain about wealth accumulation? Two U.S. studies concluded that the LCM could account for only a small part of the growth in household wealth over time.

Partly to overcome deficiencies in the predictive power of the basic LCM, subsequent theoretical and empirical work extended it by modifying one or more of its basic premises. Three modifications were reviewed in this chapter: uncertainty about length of life; the role of SSW and DBW; and liquidity constraints and precautionary savings.

Estimates vary about the importance of each of these other factors. With regard to uncertainty about death, the theoretical work suggests that this factor might account for increased savings and, in particular, the nonexhaustion of wealth at death. One study found that up to a quarter of wealth could be explained by including this factor in the LCM.

Theoretical work indicates that the availability of SSW and DBW should lead to a reduction in the accumulation of traditional (marketable) wealth. Several studies found that SSW and DBW reduced traditional savings, but others found no effect. In the former case, the estimated substitution effects were considerably less than the dollar-for-dollar reduction predicted in the standard LCM.

The presence of liquidity (borrowing) constraints implies that a family will accumulate more wealth than a pure LCM would predict. Precautionary savings serve as a self-insurance device against potential earnings misfortunes, and as a result, consumers will accumulate more wealth than if their future income stream is known with certainty. Some studies estimated that liquidity constraints and precautionary saving could explain as much as one-third of total household wealth.

Econometric Analysis of the Standard Life Cycle Model

Modigliani and Brumberg proposed the LCM as a process for explaining aggregate savings behavior. However, their LCM (and later variants, such as Ando and Modigliani or Tobin), was also a theory of household wealth accumulation. Indeed, the LCM also constituted a theory of the distribution of household wealth, albeit a primitive one. Considerable work was done to test the model's implications concerning the distribution of household wealth using aggregate data, but this aspect of the model was virtually untested using microdata until 1981.[77] This deficiency was particularly surprising because this model describes precisely the process of household wealth accumulation that is presumed to explain the aggregate savings behavior of the economy. Any failure of the LCM to account for the household distribution of wealth would then cast serious doubt on the model's validity as an explanation of savings behavior.

This section investigates the accumulation of wealth over the life cycle using standard measures of household wealth.[78] I find that the model explains only a small fraction of variations in household wealth, even with the inclusion of estimates of household lifetime earnings. Indeed, for certain groups such as nonwhite, rural residents and those with less education, the coefficients of the regression model are insignificant. The explanatory power of the LCM increases markedly when the top wealth holders are removed from the sample and noncash financial and business assets are eliminated from the household portfolios. Essentially, the validity of life cycle wealth accumulation models is restricted to the white, urban, educated middle classes and their accumulation of housing, durables, and cash. The rich appear to have very different motives and sources for saving and the poor earn insufficient income over their lifetimes to accumulate any meaningful amounts of wealth.

This section presents regression results of the LCM estimated on the full sample and selected demographic groups using the 1969 Measurement of Economic and Social Performance (MESP) data set. Several estimates of lifetime earnings are made and introduced into the LCM and the model is applied to different asset groupings.

Microdata Tests of the Basic Life Cycle Model

The empirical analysis presented in this section is based on the 1969 MESP data set. This consists of a cross-section sample of 63,457 U.S. households with demographic, income, and balance sheet information as of the end of 1960.[79]

Since I am interested only in the general explanatory power of the LCM and how it can be applied to different segments of the population, I use several

functional specifications to replicate the LCM age-wealth profile.[80] The first
is a parabolic function on age:

$$NWB_i = \beta_0 + \beta_1 A_i + \beta_2 A_i^2 + u_i \tag{6.1}$$

Where net worth NWB_i is individual household wealth including all consumer durables, A_i is the age of the head of household, and u_i is a random
error term.[81] The LCM predicts: $\beta_1 > 0$ and $\beta_2 < 0$.

This model was estimated on a randomly selected 1 in 10 sample from the
MESP database (sample size of 6,316).[82] The results are shown in line 1 of
Table 6.3. Both coefficients are in the predicted direction and significant at
the 1 percent level. Moreover, the function reaches a maximum at age 62,
close to what the model predicted.

Since the LCM predicts an asymmetrical age-wealth profile, three other
polynomial functions in A were estimated as well:

$$NWB_i = \beta_0 + \beta_1 A_i^2 + \beta_2 A_i^3 + u_i \tag{6.2}$$

$$NWB_i = \beta_0 + \beta_1 A_i^2 + \beta_2 A_i^4 + u_i \tag{6.3}$$

$$NWB_i = \beta_0 + \beta_1 A_i + \beta_2 A_i^3 + u_i \tag{6.4}$$

For each of these functions the coefficient predictions are the same as
above. All the estimated coefficients are in the predicted direction and significant at the 1 percent level (lines 2 through 4 of Table 6.3). Moreover, all
three asymmetrical forms have higher t-ratios than the symmetrical form,
lending further support to the LCM. The ages of maximum wealth are, respectively, 63, 64, and 62. A fifth equation exactly replicates the LCM wealth
profile:

$$NWB_i = \beta_0 + \beta_1 A_i + \beta_2 (A_i D_i) + \beta_3 D_i + u_i \tag{6.5}$$

where D_i is a dummy variable that equals 1 if age is 65 or over and equals
zero otherwise. The coefficient predictions on β_1 and β_2 are the same. Though
the signs are in the predicted direction, only the first coefficient estimator is
significant.[83]

Despite the high t-ratios, particularly in 6.2 and 6.3, the R^2 for these two
forms and the other three are extremely low. These results indicate that the
basic LCM explains only a small part of the overall variation of wealth across
households. This "unexplained" variation is likely due to the three factors

Table 6.3. Full sample estimations of the basic life cycle model

Equation	Constant	A	A^2	A^3	A^4	D	$(A \cdot D)$	R^2	R_a^2
				Independent Variables					
1	−62,508	3870** (3.3)	−31.4** (2.7)	—	—	—	—	0.003	0.003
2	−7,855	—	50.9** (3.8)	−0.537** (3.4)	—	—	—	0.003	0.003
3	156	—	29.1** (4.1)	—	−0.00350** (3.4)	—	—	0.003	0.003
4	42,997	2439** (3.8)	—	−0.211** (2.8)	—	—	—	0.003	0.003
5	−21,857	1492** (4.8)	—	—	—	115,044 (1.2)	−2146 (1.6)	0.004	0.003

Source: Author's computations from the 1969 MESP file.

The dependent variable is household wealth (NWB).

Notes: t-ratios shown in parentheses. Sample size = 6,316.

*Significant at 5 percent level (two-tailed test).

**Significant at 1 percent level (two-tailed test).

Abbreviations: A, age; D, dummy variable, which equals 1 if A ≥ 65; R^2, coefficient of determination; R_a^2, adjusted R^2; NWB, wealth.

discussed earlier in this chapter. It is quite possible that the model performs better for certain subgroups of the population than for others, and part of the unexplained variation in wealth across all households may be due to differences in behavior (like savings) between demographic groups.

The next step is to estimate the LCM on selected subsamples of the population. I use Equation 6.2 because it yields the most significant results for the full sample. The first division is by the race of the head of household. Since race is an unchanging characteristic of an individual, these two samples remain almost mutually exclusive over the life cycle.[84] The results for whites and Asians, who comprise almost 90 percent of the total sample, are nearly identical to those for the whole sample (see Table 6.4). The regression results for blacks and other races show much lower (in absolute value) and insignificant coeffi-

Table 6.4. Regression of wealth on age for selected demographic groups

| Demographic Group | Independent Variables | | | | | |
	Constant	A^2	A^3	R^2	R_a^2	N
Full sample	−7,855	50.9**	−0.537**	0.003	0.003	6,316
		(3.8)	(3.4)			
Whites, Asians	−9,436	54.4**	−0.574**	0.003	0.003	5,617
		(3.7)	(3.3)			
Other racial groups	6,061	22.1	−0.237	0.007	0.004	702
		(1.8)	(1.6)			
Urban, suburban residents	658	38.1**	0.390**	0.008	0.008	4,633
		(4.8)	(4.1)			
Rural residents	−32,193	87.7	−0.953	0.003	0.001	1,543
		(1.2)	(1.7)			
Schooling less than 12 years	−10,384	48.5	0.502	0.002	0.001	2,866
		(1.9)	(1.7)			
12 years schooling	−2,558	41.9*	−0.446	0.004	0.003	1,791
		(2.3)	(1.9)			
Schooling 13–15 years	−8,374	52.7	−0.54	0.01	0.008	788
		(1.8)	(1.5)			
Schooling 16 years or more	−30,168	96.0**	−1.045**	0.02	0.018	868
		(3.4)	(3.9)			

Source: Author's computations from the 1969 MESP file.

Note: Households are classified according to the demographic characteristics of the head of household.

*Significant at the 5 percent level (two-tailed test).

**Significant at the 1 percent level (two-tailed test).

Abbreviations: A, age; N: sample size; R^2, coefficient of determination; R_a^2, adjusted R^2.

cients on A^2 and A^3, which suggests that the life cycle model is not an apt description of the wealth accumulation behavior of minorities (at least in 1969).

The next division is between urban and rural residents. These classifications are not mutually exclusive as some households do move between urban and rural areas over their lifetimes. Despite this, the differences are striking. The coefficients on A^2 and A^3 for urban residents are very significant, whereas those for rural residents are insignificant. Moreover, the R^2 and the adjusted-R^2 statistics are considerably higher for the urban group. The results indicate that the life cycle model is also more appropriate for urban than rural residents.

The third division is by level of schooling. This is a permanent characteristic of individuals after they enter the labor force, except for a small group of people who acquire advanced education after starting to work. The differences are quite striking between these schooling groups. For all the schooling groups except college graduates, the coefficient values on A^2 and A^3 are quite close to those for the full sample, but all the coefficients except one are insignificant. For college graduates, the coefficients on A^2 and A^3 are considerably higher in absolute value and both are significant at the 1 percent level. Moreover, the R^2 and the adjusted R^2 statistics are considerably higher for college graduates than for any other demographic group. These results strongly suggest that the life cycle model is more appropriate for the college-graduate group than for any other educational group (or, indeed, any of the other selected demographic groups).[85]

The Inclusion of Lifetime Earnings

Of the three additional factors discussed earlier that might account for the unexplained variation in household wealth, the one for which it is possible to make estimates with the MESP data set is lifetime earnings (up to current age). If it is assumed that savings rates are constant across households and over time (and, by implication, independent of earnings), then accumulated wealth up to current age should be proportional to lifetime earnings up to current age (assuming a zero interest rate). The revised specification becomes:

$$NWB_i = \beta_0 + \beta_1 A_i^2 + \beta_2 A_i^3 + \beta_3 AE_i + u_i \qquad (6.6)$$

where AE_i is accumulated earnings up to current age for household i.

Cohort-specific earnings functions are estimated separately for each race, gender, and schooling group (see Table 6.5). Two measures of lifetime

Table 6.5. The computation of lifetime earnings for urban, white residents

Subgroup			Regressions on Current Earnings						Age at Maximum Earnings	Undiscounted Lifetime Earnings (to age 65)
				Independent Variables						
Occupation	Schooling (years)	Constant	A	A²	R²	N				
Professionals	0–11	9,975	97.8 (0.4)	-1.65 (0.8)	0.018	181			30	$522,907
	12	-3,169	752.8* (2.5)	-8.11* (2.5)	0.024	255			46	$592,781
	13–15	-13,747	1,214.3** (5.0)	-12.25** (4.6)	0.101	255			50	$609,103
	16+	-21,467	1,648.9** (5.6)	-16.70** (5.0)	0.079	470			49	$676,491
Others	1–11	-4,553	674.9** (8.5)	-7.60** (9.0)	0.087	898			44	$426,408
	12	-231	515.5** (5.9)	-5.72** (5.5)	0.049	711			45	$482,112
	13–15	-4,440	687.9** (4.4)	-7.34** (4.0)	0.097	254			47	$456,820
	16+	-23,847	1,703.9** (4.1)	-17.92** (3.8)	0.062	103			48	$573,220

Source: Author's computations from the 1969 MESP file.

The dependent variable is total annual wage and salary earnings in 1969 for the head of household. Undiscounted lifetime earnings is the integral under the age-earnings curve from the last year of schooling to age 65.

*Significant at the 5 percent level (two-tailed test).

**Significant at the 1 percent level (two-tailed test).

Abbreviations: A, age; N, sample size; R², coefficient of determination.

earnings are then constructed. The first is AE, accumulated earnings, the present value of the stream of earnings from the start of working life to the present. For this, actual statistics on mean labor earnings growth are used in the computation and the ten-year treasury bill rate is used as the discount rate. The second, AE1, is a variant of AE in which the human capital earnings function is adjusted so that it passes through the individual's current earnings. For retirees, AE1 is imputed according to the percentile ranking of retirees in the distribution of Social Security benefits of their age cohort, discounted according to real earnings growth since retirement.[86]

Regressions of wealth on A^2, A^3, and the various measures of lifetime earnings were estimated on the full sample and various demographic subsamples. The most statistically significant results are found for urban whites (see Table 6.6). The results for the unadjusted lifetime earnings forms

Table 6.6. Regressions of wealth on age and lifetime earnings for urban white residents

Lifetime Earnings Estimate	Independent Variables					
	Constant	A^2	A^3	AE(AE1)	R^2	R_a^2
$AE_0 (g = 0.0)$	15,298	−15.23 (0.8)	0.069 (0.4)	0.180** (3.3)	0.014	0.013
$AE_1 (g = 0.01)$	19,792	−25.3 (1.2)	0.207 (1.0)	0.221** (3.7)	0.015	0.014
$AE_2 (g = 0.02)$	20,636	−31.09 (1.5)	0.306 (1.4)	0.256** (3.7)	0.015	0.014
$AE_3 (g = 0.03)$	20,628	−34.64 (1.6)	0.376 (1.6)	0.290** (3.9)	0.015	0.114
$AE_4 (g = 0.04)$	19,970	−36.23 (1.7)	0.419 (1.7)	0.321** (3.9)	0.015	0.015
$AE_5 (g = 0.05)$	18,853	−36.2 (1.7)	0.44 (1.8)	0.348** (4.0)	0.015	0.015
$AE1_0 (g = 0.0)$	18,028	21.92 (1.8)	−0.219 (1.4)	0.485** (4.4)	0.016	0.016
$AE1_1 (g = 0.01)$	19,473	21.56 (1.7)	−0.204 (1.3)	0.526** (4.3)	0.016	0.015
$AE1_2 (g = 0.02)$	11,084	22.77 (1.8)	−0.205 (1.3)	0.522** (4.2)	0.016	0.015
$AE1_3 (g = 0.03)$	818	24.91* (2.0)	−0.22 (1.4)	0.481** (3.9)	0.015	0.014
$AE1_4 (g = 0.04)$	−883	27.37* (2.2)	−0.241 (1.5)	0.413** (3.5)	0.014	0.013
$AE1_5 (g = 0.05)$	−1,637	29.63* (2.4)	−0.262 (1.7)	0.336** (3.0)	0.014	0.013

Source: Author's computations from the 1969 MESP file.

The sample size is 3,134. Heads of household under 65 with no current earnings were assigned an adjustment factor of 1. All household heads 65 and over were implicitly assigned an adjustment factor of 1. Household heads with no recorded occupation were assigned the average lifetime earnings for their schooling group.

t-statistics are shown in parentheses.

*Significant at the 5 percent level (two-tailed test).

**Significant at the one percent level (two-tailed test).

Abbreviations: A, age; AE(AE1), lifetime earnings; R^2, coefficient of determination; R_a^2, adjusted R^2.

(AE_0 to AE_5) are all very similar in coefficient values, significance levels, and R^2 value. The coefficients on A^2 and A^3 are both insignificant and, indeed, the signs are opposite to the predicted direction. The coefficient on AE is in the predicted direction and extremely significant, and the R^2 statistics are all about 0.015, considerably higher than the form without lifetime earnings included (cf. Table 6.4). The regression results for the adjusted lifetime earnings forms (AE1) are almost as uniform as those with the unadjusted estimates. The signs on A^2 and A^3 are all in the predicted direction, and in three cases the coefficient estimates of A^2 are significant at the 5 percent level. The coefficients of AE1 are all in the predicted direction and significant at the 1 percent level. The R^2 statistics are all about 0.015 or about five times the R^2 statistics of the same regression on the urban white sample with the lifetime earnings variable excluded. Thus, the inclusion of the AE1 variable increases the overall explanatory power of the LCM but at the cost of reducing the significance levels of the age variables. These results strongly suggest that the primary reason that wealth follows an inverted U-shaped age profile is not the LCM hypothesis, that households save for retirement and then consume out of their savings after retiring, but that earnings follow an inverted U-shaped profile. Thus, wealth increases with age until about sixty in the cross-sectional profile primarily because earnings increase with age and families save according to what they earn.

Adjusting the Sample for Size of Wealth and Asset Type

A regression of the squared residual on size of wealth yielded an R^2 in excess of 0.80 for each of the equations in Table 6.6. Not surprisingly, this indicates that most of the unexplained variation in wealth holdings is attributable to the failure of the LCM to account for large wealth holdings. One way to adjust for this is to eliminate the top percentiles from the sample.[87] The results of reestimating Equation 6.6 on the bottom 99 percentiles (eliminating the top percentile), the bottom 95 percentiles, and the bottom 90 percentiles are shown in Table 6.7.[88]

The results are quite striking. First, when the top 1 percent is eliminated, the R^2 statistic jumps from 0.015 to 0.065. When the top 5 percent is removed, the R^2 becomes 0.075. And when the top 10 percent is eliminated, the R^2 increases to 0.078. Second, as more and more of the top of the distribution is

Table 6.7. Regressions of wealth on age and lifetime earnings for urban whites on selected subsamples

| Sample | Constant | Independent Variables | | | R^2 | R_a^2 |
		A^2	A^3	AEl_3		
All	818	24.91**	−0.22	0.481**	0.015	0.014
		(2.0)	(1.4)	(3.9)		
Bottom 99 percent	4,174	19.63**	−0.194**	0.190**	0.065	0.064
		(6.4)	(5.0)	(6.1)		
Bottom 95 percent	6,508	13.30**	−0.136**	0.144**	0.075	0.074
		(7.5)	(6.0)	(6.3)		
Bottom 90 percent	6,289	11.67**	−0.130**	0.086**	0.078	0.077
		(9.3)	(8.1)	(6.7)		

Source: Author's computations from the 1969 MESP file.

Total sample size is 3,134. Household heads with no current earnings were assigned an adjustment factor of 1, and those with no recorded occupation were assigned the average lifetime earnings for their schooling group. t-statistics are shown in parentheses.

*Significant at the 5 percent level (two-tailed test).

**Significant at the 1 percent level (two-tailed test).

Abbreviations: A, age; AEl_3, adjusted lifetime earnings; R^2, coefficient of determination; R_a^2, adjusted R^2.

removed, the significance levels of the coefficients on A^2 and A^3 increase, and the life cycle profiles become more and more "plausible." The age at maximum wealth declines from 73 for the whole sample to 69 then to 66 and finally to 61. The LCM thus seems quite inappropriate for accounting for the acquisition of wealth by the very wealthy but works much better for the less wealthy households.

Certain asset holdings, such as stocks, bonds, and business equity, are heavily concentrated in the hands of the rich. Therefore, another way to adjust for size of wealth is to divide the household portfolio into its constituent components and analyze the life cycle accumulation pattern of each. For this, I first segment household net worth into the following parts: owner-occupied housing; consumer durables; cash and demand deposits; savings and time deposits; stocks and bonds; investment real estate and business equity (including farms); and household debt. Each component is then regressed on age for the full sample. Two forms are used: the symmetrical form A, A^2 and the asymmetrical form A^2, A^3. The better fit for each is shown in Table 6.8. The differences are striking. The equations with own home, durables, cash

Table 6.8. Full sample regression of wealth components on age variables

Wealth Component	Constant	A	A^2	A^3	R^2	R_a^2
		Independent Variables				
Own home	−12,051	968.8** (16.5)	−9.46** (16.3)	—	0.041	0.041
Durables	1,344	198.9** (18.7)	−2.28** (21.7)	—	0.099	0.099
Cash and demand deposits	54	53.93** (5.4)	−0.301** (3.1)	—	0.029	0.029
Savings and time deposits	1,110	—	4.13 (1.5)	−0.035 (1.1)	0.001	0.001
Stocks and bonds	−11,677	—	24.09** (2.9)	−0.247 (1.9)	0.001	0.001
Real estate plus business equity (including farms)	−1,927	—	14.55** (3.2)	−0.159** (3.0)	0.002	0.002
Total household debt	−3,333	427.3** (9.3)	−4.50** (10.0)	—	0.017	0.016
Life cycle wealth (W_1)	−8,137	838.9** (19.9)	−7.68** (18.4)	—	0.064	0.064
Capital wealth (W_2)	−124,100	—	41.8** (3.2)	−0.434** (2.8)	0.002	0.002
Total wealth (W)	−7,855	—	50.9** (3.8)	−0.537** (3.4)	0.003	0.003

Source: Author's computations from the 1969 MESP file.
Sample size = 6,316.
t-statistics are shown in parentheses.
*Significant at the 5 percent level (two-tailed test).
**Significant at the 1 percent level (two-tailed test).
Abbreviations: A, age; R^2, coefficient of determination; R_a^2, adjusted R^2; W_1, own home + durables + cash and demand deposits less mortgage debt; W_2, savings and time deposits + stocks and bonds + investment real estate and business equity (including farms) less other debt.

and demand deposits, and household debt as dependent variables have much higher R^2 statistics than the other three components. Indeed, the R^2 for the durables equation is almost 100 times greater than the R^2 for the stocks and bonds equation. Moreover, the best fit for these four components is the symmetrical A, A^2, while the asymmetrical form A^2, A^3 is the best fit for the other three components. In addition, the significance levels of the age coefficients for these four components are much greater than the significance levels of the age coefficients for the other three wealth components.

Because of the differences in regression results, I divided total household wealth into two parts. The first part, which I call "life cycle wealth," is defined as the sum of own home, durables, and cash and demand deposits less mortgage debt. The second part, which I call "capital wealth," is defined as the sum of savings and time deposits, stocks and bonds, and investment real estate and business equity less other debt.[89] Life cycle wealth W_1 was then regressed on the age variables. The R^2 statistic is 0.064, about twenty times as great as that for the total wealth regression. The t-ratios on the age coefficients are both above 18, and the estimates indicate age 55 as the age of maximum life cycle wealth. The regression of capital wealth on age yielded an R^2 of 0.002, much lower t-ratios, and an age of maximum capital wealth of 64. The regression of total wealth on age yields slightly higher R^2 and t-ratios than the capital wealth regression. The age at maximum total wealth is 63, quite close to that for capital wealth. It is apparent that the regression results for total wealth are much more strongly influenced by the capital wealth component than by the life cycle wealth component.[90]

The two wealth components are then each regressed on the age variables within selected demographic groups (see Table 6.9 and Table 6.10). A comparison with Table 6.4 indicates that the W_1 regressions have considerably higher t-statistics on the age variables and R^2 statistics that are approximately ten times as great as the corresponding total wealth (NWB) regressions by demographic group. Moreover, all the coefficients in the W_1 regressions are significant at the 1 percent level (and in the predicted direction). However, the rank order in goodness of fit remains the same for the W_1 regressions as for the W regressions. The life cycle accumulation process of life cycle wealth is still a more appropriate model for whites than for nonwhites, but for the first time, the coefficients on age are significant for nonwhites. The process better describes urban residents than their rural counterparts and fits highly educated groups better than the less educated. Indeed, the R^2 statistic reaches 23 percent for college graduates. The W_2 regressions on the other hand, have uniformly lower R^2 and t-statistics on the age variables (except for the rural group) than the total wealth regressions, but the rank order across demographic group remains the same.[91]

The lifetime earnings variable $AE1_3$ is then added to the regression specification. Results are shown for urban white residents in Table 6.11. The R^2 statistic is extremely high for the W_1 regression at 0.16, more than ten times

Table 6.9. Regression of life cycle wealth (W_1) on age variables by demographic groups

Demographic Group	Independent Variables			R^2	R_a^2	N
	Constant	A	A^2			
Full sample	−8,137	838.9** (19.9)	−7.68** (18.4)	0.064	0.064	6,316
Whites, Asians	−9,253	911.3** (19.9)	−8.38** (18.6)	0.071	0.071	5,617
Other racial groups	1,427	248.2** (3.3)	−2.06** (2.8)	0.026	0.024	702
Urban, suburban residents	−10,247	950.1** (18.5)	−8.67** (17.0)	0.077	0.077	4,633
Rural residents	−1,389	478.3** (6.7)	−4.39** (6.3)	0.029	0.028	1,543
Schooling less than 12 years	−1,964	447.3** (8.5)	−3.75** (7.6)	0.029	0.029	2,866
12 years schooling	−8,612	843.5** (11.5)	−7.47** (9.9)	0.097	0.096	1,791
Schooling 13–15 years	−15,457	1214.0** (8.9)	−10.85** (7.5)	0.150	0.147	788
Schooling 16 years or more	−35,803	2246.5** (13.8)	−20.55** (12.1)	0.231	0.230	868

Source: Author's computations from the 1969 MESP file.
Households are classified according to the demographic characteristics of the head of household.
t-statistics are shown in parentheses.
*Significant at the 5 percent level (two-tailed test).
**Significant at the 1 percent level (two-tailed test).
Abbreviations: A, age; N, sample size; R^2, coefficient of determination; R_a^2, adjusted R^2.

the R^2 statistic for the comparable total wealth regression (Table 6.6), and the t-values on the age coefficients are more than seven times those for the total wealth regression. The R^2 statistic for the W_2 regression, on the other hand, is considerably lower than the total wealth regression, as are the t-values. These results indicate that the accumulation of life cycle wealth is much more strongly influenced by labor earnings than the accumulation of capital wealth.

Conclusions and Speculations

How adequate is the life cycle savings model to account for the observed differences in marketable household wealth? Before answering this question, let me respond to three possible objections that might be made to the results

Table 6.10. Regression of capital wealth (W_2) on age by demographic group

Demographic Group	Constant	A^2	A^3	R^2	R_a^2	N
		Independent Variables				
Full sample	−12,410	41.8**	−0.434**	0.002	0.002	6,316
		(3.2)	(2.8)			
Whites, Asians	−13,965	44.6**	−0.463**	0.002	0.002	5,617
		(3.0)	(2.7)			
Other racial groups	656	19.5	−0.208	0.005	0.002	702
		(1.6)	(1.4)			
Urban, suburban residents	−3,148	27.4**	−0.268**	0.006	0.006	4,633
		(3.5)	(2.9)			
Rural residents	−38,602	83.2	−0.903	0.002	0.001	1,543
		(1.8)	(1.7)			
Schooling less then 12 years	−15,217	43.4	−0.447	0.001	0.001	2,866
		(1.7)	(1.6)			
12 years schooling	−6,091	31.7	−0.332	0.003	0.002	1,791
		(1.7)	(1.5)			
Schooling 13–15 years	−9,987	37.6	−0.369	0.007	0.004	788
		(1.3)	(1.0)			
Schooling 16 years or more	−26,816	69.1*	−0.735*	0.013	0.010	868
		(2.5)	(2.1)			

Source: Author's computations from the 1969 MESP file.
Households are classified according to the demographic characteristics of the head of household.
t-statistics are shown in parentheses.
*Significant at the 5 percent level (two-tailed test).
**Significant at the 1 percent level (two-tailed test).
Abbreviations: A, age; N, sample size R^2, coefficient of determination; R_a^2, adjusted R^2.

presented. The first objection may be that the LCM is a longitudinal model, whereas the empirical results are based on a cross-sectional sample. It is possible to show that under some fairly general conditions the LCM will imply an inverted U-shaped cross-sectional age-wealth profile, *whereas the converse is not true.* Thus, an inverted U-shaped cross-sectional profile becomes a necessary though not sufficient condition to show the existence of an inverted U-shaped longitudinal age-wealth profile.

The second objection may be that the MESP sample is constructed with synthetically matched data sets, which may bias downward the covariance among nonmatching variables with respect to their true (population) covariance. Experiments that estimate regressions on a true sample and one that has been synthetically created show no statistically significant differences in

Table 6.11. Regressions of life cycle wealth and capital wealth on age and lifetime earnings for urban white residents

Dependent Variable	Independent Variables					R^2	R_a^2
	Constant	A	A^2	A^3	$AE1_3$		
W_1	−11,895	1,022**	−9.93**	—	0.126**	0.159	0.158
		(15.1)	(13.9)		(15.2)		
W_2	−2,620	—	13 (1.0)	−0.075	0.363**	0.010	0.009
				(0.5)	(3.0)		

Source: Author's computations from the 1969 MESP file.

Sample size is 3,134. Household heads with no current earnings were assigned an adjustment factor of 1, and those with no recorded occupation were assigned the average lifetime earnings for their schooling group.

t-statistics are shown in parentheses.

*Significant at the 5 percent level (two-tailed test).

**Significant at the 1 percent level (two-tailed test).

Abbreviations: A, age; $AE1_3$, adjusted lifetime earnings; R^2, coefficient of determination; R_a^2, adjusted R^2; W_1, life cycle wealth; W_2, capital wealth.

the estimated coefficients. Moreover, even if such a downward bias exists, the relative success of the LCM *across demographic groups* would remain valid unless there were a systematic relation between this bias and demographic characteristics.

A third objection might address the omission of certain assets from the MESP sample (Appendix 2). One set of omitted assets that consists of household inventories, life insurance reserves, and pension reserves, might be suspected, a priori, of closely following a life cycle accumulation pattern. Thus, the exclusion of these elements would bias downward the explanatory power of the LCM. This group comprised only 13 percent of total household assets, and therefore the bias would be relatively small. The other set, comprising 5 percent of total assets, includes state and local government securities and trust fund equity, assets that one might suspect on a priori grounds to be unrelated to a life cycle wealth accumulation process. Their exclusion would thus likely have the opposite impact.

Even with these qualifications, it is possible to conclude that the LCM is an inadequate model for explaining the distribution of marketable household wealth. Moreover, by implication, the LCM is likewise inadequate as an explanation of aggregate savings. In the simple regression model, the coefficients on the two age variables are significant at the 1 percent level with the predicted signs, whereas the variation in household wealth explained by the model is only 0.3 percent. Even with the inclusion of lifetime income in the regression specification, the goodness of fit of the model increases to only 1.5 percent for urban whites.

The LCM is inappropriate for nonwhites, rural residents, and those who lack a high school education. These groups show insignificant coefficients on the age variables in the regression results. Indeed, the best fit for the LCM is college graduates. The results suggest that the model likewise fails to explain how the wealthy, particularly the top 5 percent, attained their status.[92]

Dividing the household portfolio into two components gives further insight into the validity of the model. If one considers the household accumulation of housing, durables, and cash and demand deposits less mortgage debt, then the model performs much better for the full sample and all demographic groups than for total household wealth. When lifetime earnings are added to the specification, the R^2 reaches 0.16 for the urban white sample. On the other hand, if one considers the household accumulation of savings and time deposits, stocks and bonds, investment real estate and business equity less consumer debt, then the model's explanatory power is extremely small for every demographic group. This makes sense when you consider that these assets are heavily concentrated in the hands of the rich.

The LCM's validity must then be limited to white, urban, educated middle-class accumulation of the standard forms of middle-class wealth—housing, durables, and cash. This is the group that saves out of its labor earnings to accumulate housing, durables, and liquid assets for its retirement years.

Two other distinct groups emerge from this study. The first is the poor, as represented in this study by nonwhites, for whom there is virtually no accumulation of wealth over the life cycle, except perhaps in the form of durables (at least in 1969). The reason is that the poor do not receive sufficient earnings in order to save for accumulation. The other group is the very wealthy—the top 5 percent or so—who do not become wealthy by saving out of their labor earnings. This group acquires a substantial portion of its wealth from capital gains and in the form of stocks, bonds, real estate, and business equity. The growth of this wealth—"capital wealth"—is tied to the overall growth of the total capital stock of the economy. To be generous, one could conclude that the LCM is a reasonable descriptive of the wealth behavior of about the middle two-thirds of the U.S. population. But, because of the tremendous concentration of household wealth in the hands of the rich, the model may account for the acquisition of about a quarter of household wealth.

The results of this investigation have several important implications regarding the proper modeling of the size distribution of household wealth. Most important, a proper model must be a *three-class model,* in which each class has its own generating mechanism. The first class is the capitalist class, whose wealth takes the form of capital wealth, whose motive for accumulation is to build up large estates, and whose mechanism of transmission is through both savings and capital gains. Bequest may also play an important role in this group's wealth accumulation. The actual generating mechanism of the wealth held by this class must be tied into the growth of the real aggregate capital stock of the productive sectors.[93] The wealth of the second class, the middle class, takes the form of "life cycle wealth." The main motivation for accumulation of wealth by this class is for the consumption of the services from housing and durables and for retirement. This class accumulates wealth by saving out of labor earnings, and the distribution of wealth among this class depends on age as well as differences in earnings, savings rates, and rates of return. The lifetime income of the third class, which may be considered "the poor," is too low to permit any significant accumulation, except in the form of durables and perhaps housing.

An Extension of the Life Cycle Model to Incorporate Pension and Social Security Wealth

SSW and DBW can be directly incorporated into the LCM because they are forms of retirement wealth. The question arises as to how their inclusion in household wealth affects the explanatory power of the LCM. Cross-sectional regression analysis incorporating these two forms of retirement wealth will provide an answer.[94] The two most important findings are that (1) the performance of the LCM is improved when SSW and DBW are incorporated in household wealth and (2) the explanatory power of the LCM is substantially greater (in some cases, by a factor of two) on the bottom 95 percent of the wealth distribution than for the full sample.

Age-Wealth Profiles

We begin the analysis with aggregate age-wealth profiles including retire-ment wealth. These have *not* been corrected for the two sources of bias that affect the use of cross-sectional profiles as a test of the longitudinal LCM. First, because real earnings and income typically increase over time, the cross-sectional age-wealth profiles may be hump-shaped even though the longitudinal profiles rise over time. Second, there is typically a positive cor-relation between wealth and longevity, so there is a sample selection bias in the use of cross-sectional profiles as a test of the LCM. In particular, cross-sectional profiles may show an upward trend in wealth among older cohorts, even though the longitudinal profiles are hump-shaped. The two biases offset each other but the net effect of the two is not known.

Table 6.2 shows the raw age-wealth profiles for marketable net worth and augmented wealth in the two sample years (also see Figure 6.3). The first, based on the 1962 SFCC, shows a steady increase in mean marketable net worth across the younger age cohorts, a peak of 1.74 for the overall mean for the 55–59 age group, and a fairly continuous decline among older age groups.[95] The 1983 SCF shows a similar inverted U-shaped pattern, though the peak is higher at 2.29 and occurs for an older age group, ages 65 to 69. These two sets of results suggest rather strongly that the cross-sectional age-wealth profiles have become more hump-shaped over the 1962–1983 period with higher mean wealth at the peak.

The next three columns of Table 6.2 show the effect of adding DBW and SSW to net worth. It should be noted that the construction of SSW reflects conditional mortality rates, so that there is a built-in bias for its mean value to decline after age 70 or so. However, the net effect is a flattening of the age-wealth profile. The younger age cohorts gain relative to the older ones and peak wealth relative to the overall mean declines. Moreover, the greater the assumed future Social Security benefit growth rates (g and g'), the more the younger groups gain and the more the peak flattens. However, the basic hump shape remains among all three measures of augmented wealth.

I also compute the mean ratio of NWB to human capital (HK) and of aug-mented wealth (AWB) to HK by age class, where HK is the estimated human capital of the household.[96] This procedure corrects for the difference in human capital among age cohorts as well as the mortality bias induced by the positive correlation between wealth and life expectancy. The basic hump-shaped profiles remain unchanged, though they are somewhat flatter than the corresponding raw age-wealth profiles because of the elimination of the two biases. This result also suggests that the permanent income bias in the raw profiles is somewhat stronger than the mortality bias.

Econometric Analysis of the LCM with Retirement Wealth

The following econometric analysis, with basic life cycle regressions of household wealth on various functions of age, uses estimations for 1962 and 1983. The unit of observation is the household and the age variable is the age of the head of household in 1962 and the age of the respondent in 1983. The regressions are cross-sectional in nature. Cohort effects are controlled for by the addition of the human capital variable.

Various specifications were estimated in regard to the basic LCM, including quadratic, cubic, and fourth power functions of age, as well as piecewise linear functions.[97] The best fit in terms of the adjusted R^2 is the cubic form (Table 6.12). The coefficients of the two age variables have the predicted signs and are significant at the 1 percent level. However, the R^2 statistic is very low, with a value of 0.005. Regression results are also shown for AWB. Results for AWB are quite similar to those for NWB in the two years, even though they differ substantially in magnitude, and SSW is constructed so that its value declines with life expectancy. The R^2 values for the three forms of AWB vary from 0.0051 to 0.0066 for the 1962 data and from 0.0147 to 0.0159 for the 1983 data.

Lifetime Earnings and the Cohort Effect

The use of cross-sectional data tends to produce a biased test of the (longitudinal) LCM if real earnings rise over time. The introduction of measures of lifetime earnings should control for this effect. Moreover, differences in lifetime earnings should also explain a substantial portion of intra-cohort variation in household wealth.[98]

As in the estimation of AE and AE1, cohort-specific earnings functions are estimated separately for each race, gender, and schooling group in order to compute HK, defined as the present value of lifetime earnings from the

Table 6.12. Life cycle regressions of marketable wealth and augmented wealth on the full sample, 1962 and 1983

Dependent Variable	Constant	Independent Variables		R^2	R_a^2	F-Test	Sample Size
		A^2	A^3				
1962 SFCC							
NWB	−11,170* (2.02)	39.86** (6.57)	−0.392** (5.47)	0.0053	0.0052	45.14**	2,557
AWB (g = g' = .01)	−478 (0.08)	45.46** (6.66)	−0.449** (5.72)	0.0066	0.0064	47.28**	2,557
AWB (g = g' = .02)	−3,421 (0.56)	44.32** (5.63)	−0.442** (5.63)	0.0059	0.0058	42.49**	2,557
AWB (g = g' = .03)	−8,311 (1.37)	42.66** (6.40)	−0.431** (5.48)	0.0051	0.0050	36.76**	2,557
1983 SCF							
NWB	−49,287 (1.91)	190.6** (6.20)	−2.048** (5.57)	0.0120	0.0116	25.93**	4,262
AWB (g = g' = .01)	−27,381 (1.00)	216.8** (6.66)	−2.272** (5.87)	0.0159	0.0154	34.38**	4,262
AWB (g = g' = .02)	−19,036 (0.69)	214.5** (6.58)	−2.257** (5.83)	0.0151	0.0147	32.72**	4,262
AWB (g = g' = .03)	−8,485 (0.31)	211.0** (6.46)	−2.232** (5.76)	0.0142	0.0137	30.60**	4,262

Source: Author's calculations from the 1962 Survey of Financial Characteristics of Consumers and the 1983 Survey of Consumer Finances.

The statistics are for household wealth. Households are classified into age group by age of the head of household in 1962 and age of respondent in 1983.

g' is the assumed rate of growth of Social Security benefits over time for current beneficiaries.

g is the assumed rate of growth of Social Security benefits over time for future beneficiaries.

k is the assumed rate of growth of labor earnings, set at 0.01 per year.

t-statistics are shown in parentheses.

*Significant at the 5 percent level (two-tailed test for coefficients; one-tail test for F value).

**Significant at the 1 percent level (two-tailed test for coefficients; one-tail test for F value).

Abbreviations: A, age; R^2, coefficient of determination; R_a^2, adjusted R^2.

start of working life *to retirement* (see Table 6.5). For this computation, various values are assumed for average real earnings growth (k) over the future work life. As with AE1, HK is imputed to retirees according to their percentile ranking in the distribution of Social Security benefits and years since retirement.[99]

In the first set of regressions, shown in Table 6.13, HK is included as an independent variable along with the square and the cube of age. HK is highly significant, with a t-statistic of 21.1 for the 1962 NWB regression and 24.1 for the 1962 NWB regression, and with values of 13.2 and 15.9 for the corresponding 1983 forms.[100] In the 1962 regressions, the inclusion of HK causes the R^2 statistic to increase by a factor of 15. In the 1983 regressions, the inclusion of HK triples the fit of the model. With the 1962 data, the addition of HK to the model causes a drop in the t-ratios of the age variables, but they remain statistically significant. In the 1983 data, the addition of HK causes the t-ratios of the age variables to fall slightly, yet they again remain statistically significant. The likely reason for this is that HK, by construction, captures cohort effects on lifetime earnings (from the growth of real earnings over time) and is thus correlated with the age variables.[101]

The same equations are then estimated on two subsets of the original sample. In the first of these, I exclude the upper 1 percent of the wealth distribution.[102] The significance level of all the independent variables, particularly lifetime earnings, increases, as does the fit of the equation (results not shown). In the NWB equation on the 1962 data, the t-ratio for HK increases from 21.7 to 23.1 and the R^2 statistic from 0.079 to 0.091. Moreover, the t-ratios of the age variables increase and both are now significant at the 1 percent level in the NWB equation. In the second sample, I exclude the upper five percentiles of the wealth distribution. The significance level of each of the independent variables increases, particularly that of lifetime earnings, and the explanatory power of the model again increases substantially. For the NWB equation on the 1962 data, the R^2 statistic rises from 0.079 to 0.101; for AWB on the 1962 data, the R^2 reaches 0.17 (see Table 6.13). For the 1983 data, the R^2 statistic increases to 0.12 for the NWB equation and to 0.20 for the AWB equation.

Corresponding logarithmic forms are also estimated on the two sets of data. For this, the bottom 1 percent of each sample is eliminated in order to avoid observations with zero or negative net worth. As expected, the goodness of fit rises substantially, since the residuals resulting from very large wealth holdings are more than proportionately reduced. The R^2 for log(AWB) reaches 0.30 on the 1962 full sample (less the bottom 1 percent) and 0.37 on the 1983 full sample. On the sample that excludes the top 5 percent and the bottom percentile, the R^2 jumps to 0.38 on the 1962 data and 0.41 on the 1983 data. The t-statistics on the independent variables also increase substantially.

The regression forms used in Table 6.13 are not quite in accord with the LCM, since it assumes that household wealth rises proportionately (and directly) with lifetime earnings. A more appropriate form may be:

$$R \equiv NWB / HK = h(Age) + \varepsilon \qquad (6.7)$$

where h indicates a functional form and ε is a stochastic error term.[103] This form represents a rather strict interpretation of the LCM and assumes, in particular, no independent effect exerted on R from the level of lifetime earnings. In order to allow for a nonproportional effect of lifetime earnings on household wealth accumulation, the following specification is used:

$$NWB = b_0 + b_1 HK + b_2 AGE^2 \cdot HK + b_3 AGE^3 \cdot HK + \varepsilon \qquad (6.8)$$

Results are shown in Table 6.14. The t-ratio of the interactive human capital-age variables is about double the corresponding t-values of the age variables in Table 6.13 for the 1962 data. For the 1983 data, the t-ratios are smaller for the full sample but about the same magnitude for the bottom 95 percent of the distribution. In the NWB regressions, the HK variable is negative and significant, indicating a nonproportional effect of lifetime earnings on traditional wealth accumulation. This result is consistent with that of King and Dicks-Mireaux, but Hubbard and Diamond and Hausman find strong positive effects of lifetime earnings on R.[104] The reason for my negative result is now apparent in contrast with the AWB regression results, in which the HK variable is statistically insignificant. The strong negative effect of HK on R is thus due to the omitted variable effect—in particular, to the strong positive correlation between lifetime earnings and retirement wealth (King and Dicks-Mireaux obtained a similar result). Also of interest is that excluding the top 5 percent of the sample doubles the R^2 value for both the NWB and AWB regression equations.

In the last set of regressions, shown in Table 6.15, DBW and SSW are included as independent variables to analyze the substitution between traditional wealth, NWB, and retirement wealth. For the 1962 full sample regressions, the substitution effect between NWB and DBW is negative though statistically weak. The substitution effect between NWB and SSW, on the other hand, is negative and statistically significant, although the coefficient of SSW is considerably less than one. After the top five percentiles are excluded

Table 6.13. Life cycle regressions with human capital on the full sample and the bottom 95 percentiles, 1962 and 1983

Dependent Variable	Constant (thousands)	A^2	A^3	HK (k = .01)	Log HK (k = .01)	R^2	R_a^2	F-Test	Sample Size
				Independent Variables					
1962 SFCC: Full Sample									
NWB	−112.0**	68.41**	−0.5952*	0.2359**		0.0790	0.0785	161.95**	2,557
	(8.30)	(3.41)	(2.07)	(21.17)					
AWB (g=g' =.02)	−141.1**	133.03**	−1.4276**	0.2439**		0.0995	0.0990	208.69**	2,557
	(20.36)	(6.58)	(4.93)	(24.10)					
Log (AWB) (g=g' =.02)	4.04**	.00128**	−.143E-4**		0.937**	0.2985	0.2976	304.58**	2,532
	(9.02)	(9.09)	(8.58)		(20.33)				
1962 SFCC: Excluding Top 5%									
NWB	−146.8**	31.37**	−0.2503**	0.1888**		0.1006	0.1000	168.36**	2,429
	(10.48)	(5.45)	(3.75)	(26.63)					
AWB (g=g' =.02)	−143.4**	35.41**	−0.3000**	0.1980**		0.1673	0.1668	298.71**	2,429
	(12.75)	(7.66)	(5.60)	(34.72)					
Log (AWB) (g=g' =.02)	−5.45**	0.713E-3**	−0.908E-5**		0.718**	0.3814	0.3803	328.68**	2,404
	(9.21)	(9.00)	(9.63)		(23.92)				
1983 SCF: Full Sample									
NWB	−37.8	157.6*	−1.635**	0.1947**		0.0371	0.0364	54.64**	4,262
	(1.43)	(5.03)	(4.40)	(13.21)					

						R^2	R_a^2	F	N
AWB (g = g' = .02)	-4.9	176.0**	-1.681**	0.2074**		0.0509	0.0502	75.14**	4,262
	(0.18)	(5.48)	(4.73)	(15.91)					
Log (AWB) (g = g' = .02)	1.59**	0.137E-2**	-0.139E-4**		1.153**	0.3715	0.3692	426.26**	4,219
	(7.93)	(11.81)	(9.38)		(29.35)				
1983 SCF: Excluding Top 5%									
NWB	-20.7	55.40**	-0.582*	0.2486**		0.1217	0.1201	426.26**	4,049
	(1.81)	(9.72)	(7.82)	(18.36)					
AWB (g = g' = .02)	-66.0*	144.48**	-1.784**	0.3393**		0.1978	0.1923	235.84**	4,049
	(2.03)	(11.04)	(10.45)	(27.04)					
Log (AWB) (g = g' = .02)	4.00**	0.728E-3**	-0.910E-5**		0.991**	0.4110	0.4094	324.29**	4,009
	(6.91)	(8.57)	(8.26)		(33.60)				

Source: Author's calculations from the 1962 Survey of Financial Characteristics of Consumers and the 1983 Survey of Consumer Finances.

The statistics are for household wealth. Households are classified into age group by age of the head of household in 1962 and age of respondent in 1983.

g' is the assumed rate of growth of Social Security benefits over time for current beneficiaries.

g is the assumed rate of growth of Social Security benefits over time for future beneficiaries.

k is the assumed rate of growth of labor earnings, set at 0.01 per year.

For the logarithm form, the bottom 1 percent of the sample is excluded.

t-statistics are shown in parentheses.

*Significant at the 5 percent level (two-tailed test for coefficients; one-tail test for F value).

**Significant at the 1 percent level (two-tailed test for coefficients; one-tail test for F value).

Abbreviations: A, age; HK, (lifetime) human capital; R^2, coefficient of determination; R_a^2, adjusted R^2.

Table 6.14. Life cycle regressions with interactive forms of human capital on the full sample, and the bottom 95 percentiles, 1962 and 1983

| Dependent Variable | Independent Variables | | | | | | | Sample Size |
	Constant (thousands)	HK	HK·A² (1,000s)	HK·A³ (100,000s)	R^2	R_a^2	F-Test	
1962 SFCC: Full Sample								
NWB	−79.4** (4.69)	−0.2321* (2.26)	0.5921** (6.85)	−0.697** (7.87)	0.0685	0.0679	111.83**	2,557
AWB (g=g' = .02)	−78.5** (4.61)	−0.0287* (0.26)	0.5109** (5.68)	−0.643** (6.96)	0.0873	0.0867	145.27**	2,557
1962 SFCC: Excluding Top 5%								
NWB	−72.2** (6.70)	−0.3126* (4.65)	0.5847** (10.14)	−0.687** (11.25)	0.1122	0.1116	190.35**	2,429
AWB (g=g' = .02)	−62.4** (7.26)	−0.0689 (1.22)	0.4132** (9.11)	−0.513** (10.86)	0.1909	0.1903	350.61**	2,429
1983 SCF: Full Sample								
NWB	−240.5** (4.44)	0.1947* (3.43)	−0.3946* (2.12)	−0.361* (1.98)	0.0643	0.0632	58.45**	4,262
AWB (g=g' = .02)	−255.6** (4.65)	0.1268 (1.26)	−0.4137** (2.96)	−0.247** (3.10)	0.0957	0.0946	90.05**	4,262
1983 SCF: Excluding Top 5%								
NWB	26.6** (4.19)	−0.5822* (2.01)	0.3481** (11.14)	−0.373** (10.12)	0.1714	0.1698	180.16**	4,049
AWB (g=g' = .02)	31.7** (5.89)	0.0314 0.98	0.7574** (10.64)	−0.927** (11.02)	0.2101	0.2086	224.21**	4,049

Source: Author's calculations from the 1962 Survey of Financial Characteristics of Consumers and the 1983 Survey of Consumer Finances.

The statistics are for household wealth. Households are classified into age group by age of the head of household in 1962 and age of respondent in 1983.

g' is the assumed rate of growth of Social Security benefits over time for current beneficiaries.

g is the assumed rate of growth of Social Security benefits over time for future beneficiaries.

k is the assumed rate of growth of labor earnings, set at 0.01 per year.

t-statistics are shown in parentheses.

*Significant at the 5 percent level (two-tailed test for coefficients; one-tail test for F value).

**Significant at the 1 percent level (two-tailed test for coefficients; one-tail test for F value).

Abbreviations: A, age; HK, (lifetime) human capital; R^2, coefficient of determination; R_a^2, adjusted R^2.

from the sample, the coefficients on DBW and SSW are both negative and highly statistically significant. The substitution effect between DBW and NWB is about half, while that between NWB and SSW is very close to one. For the 1983 regressions, no statistically significant substitution effect is found between NWB and DB pension wealth. The substitution effect between SSW and NWB is marginally significant for both the full sample and the bottom 95 percentiles, and the coefficient is less than half in both cases. This result contrasts rather strongly with that of Avery, Elliehausen, and Gustafson, who found no substitution between fungible wealth and SSW but substantial substitution between pension and fungible wealth.[105] Finally, it is important to note that in regressions with interactive HK-age variables, HK is statistically insignificant once retirement wealth has been included.

Summary and Concluding Remarks on the Life Cycle Model

The explanatory power of the LCM in accounting for differences in wealth holdings among U.S. households has been analyzed in this chapter using regression analysis. The regressions are cross-sectional in nature, with observations on households of different ages at a given point in time. However, cohort effects were controlled for by the addition of a lifetime earnings variable. Various specifications were tried, including quadratic, cubic, and fourth power functions of age, as well as piece-wise linear functions. The best fit in terms of the adjusted R^2 is the cubic form. On the basis of data from the 1983 SCF, with marketable wealth (NWB) as the dependent variable, the coefficients of the two age variables had the predicted signs (the coefficient of AGE^2 was positive and that of AGE^3 was negative) and both were significant at the 1 percent level. However, the R^2 (the measure of the goodness of fit or the explanatory power of the equation) was very low, with a value of 0.012 (only about 1 percent of the variation of household wealth could be explained by age). Regression results were also shown for augmented household wealth (AWB). The R^2 for this regression form was about 0.015.

The use of cross-sectional data tends to produce a biased test of the (longitudinal) LCM if real earnings are rising over time. The introduction of measures of lifetime earnings should control for this effect. Moreover, differences in lifetime earnings should also explain a substantial portion of the

Table 6.15. Tests of the substitution hypothesis between marketable wealth (NWB) and retirement wealth, 1962 and 1983

Dependent Variable	Constant	A^2	A^3	HK	HK·A^2 (thousands)	HK·A^3 (hundred thousands)	DBW	SSW	R^2	R^2_a	F-Test	Sample Size
I. 1962 SFCC												
A. Full Sample												
NWB	-37.0* (2.19)			-0.123 (0.98)	0.524** (5.41)	-0.0662** (6.47)	-0.307 (1.53)	-0.570** (3.64)	0.100	0.099	120.1**	2,555
NWB	-102.0** 4.88	15.36 (1.71)	-0.091 (0.87)	0.161** (14.36)			-0.429* (2.16)	-0.458** (2.27)	0.086	0.085	102.2**	2,555
B. Bottom 95%												
NWB	-32.7** (3.12)			-0.145 (1.58)	0.524** (8.68)	-0.0622** (9.77)	-0.577** (5.01)	-1.201** (0.39)	0.181	0.180	237.6**	2,429
NWB	-93.0** (7.17)	17.85** (3.21)	-0.139** (2.85)	0.118** (19.02)			-0.581** (6.43)	-0.921** (7.86)	0.169	0.168	28.7**	2,429
II. 1983 SCF												
A. Full Sample												
NWB	-206.7** (3.84)			0.114 (1.81)	0.315** (3.34)	-0.0291** (3.52)	-0.178 (1.26)	-0.314* (2.21)	0.081	0.079	53.4**	4,262

NWB	−435.2** (6.94)	140.4** (4.57)	−1.407** (3.86)	0.124** (6.36)		−0.202 (0.96)	−0.278* (2.30)	0.082	0.081	102.1**	4,262
3. Bottom 95%											
NWB	−147.9** (3.21)		−0.015 (1.32)	0.422** (7.51)	−0.0396** (5.39)	−0.292 (1.54)	−0.416* (2.38)	0.213	0.210	182.3**	4,049
NWB	−257.7** (4.74)	29.41** (9.69)	−0.295** (5.92)	0.151* (4.88)		−0.338 (1.67)	−0.442* (2.42)	0.242	0.240	201.4**	4,049

Source: Author's calculations from the 1962 Survey of Financial Characteristics of Consumers and the 1983 Survey of Consumer Finances.

The statistics are for household wealth. Households are classified into age group by age of the head of household in 1962 and age of respondent in 1983.

k is the assumed rate of growth of labor earnings, set at 0.01 per year.

t-statistics are shown in parentheses.

*Significant at the 5 percent level (two-tailed test for coefficients; one-tail test for F value).

**Significant at the 1 percent level (two-tailed test for coefficients; one-tail test for F value).

Abbreviations: A, age; DBW, defined benefit pension wealth; HK, (lifetime) human capital; R^2, coefficient of determination; R^2_a, adjusted R^2; SSW, Social Security wealth (the rate of growth of future Social Security benefits is set at 2 percent per year).

intra-cohort variation (differences among households of the same age) in household wealth. When human capital (HK) is included in the specification for the 1983 data, HK is highly significant. The inclusion of HK triples the goodness of fit of the model. Even so, the extended model explains only 4 to 5 percent of the variation of wealth holdings among households.

The same equations were then estimated on a subset of the original sample, in which the upper 5 percent of the wealth distribution was excluded. The significance level of all the independent variables—the age terms and lifetime earnings—increased markedly. Moreover, the explanatory power of the model rose substantially, with the R^2 increasing from 0.037 to 0.122 for NWB and from 0.051 to 0.198 for AWB.

These results suggest that the power of the LCM to explain the variation of marketable wealth among all households is quite weak. This remains true even when differences in lifetime earnings among households are controlled for. When the concept of household wealth is expanded to include both SSW and DBW, the goodness of fit of the regression improves. The inclusion of retirement wealth in household wealth is more consistent with the LCM than the use of marketable household wealth alone. However, the explanatory power of the model is still very low (at most 5 percent of the variation of wealth explained), even when lifetime earnings are introduced into the model.

Perhaps the most telling result is that the explanatory power of the LCM (particularly with lifetime earnings) is substantially greater (by a factor of three or four) when the sample is restricted to the bottom 95 percent of the wealth distribution. This holds for all measures of household wealth and suggests that, although the LCM predicts household savings behavior well for the vast majority of households, it is not successful in explaining the wealth accumulation motives of the top wealth classes, who also happen to hold the majority of household wealth. On the surface, it does not appear likely that the difference in behavior between the top 5 percent and the rest of the population is due to the uncertainty effect, unless one believes that top wealth holders have much greater uncertainty or much greater risk aversion about their date of death. It may be that it is due to differences in the strength of the bequest motive. One inference from these results is that the top wealth classes likely form a distinct social class in the sense that their motivation for wealth accumulation is for political and economic power and social status. It also appears that this class is interested in the expansion of family wealth over generations.

These results also suggest that tests of the LCM depend very heavily on the sample used—particularly on how much of the upper tail of the distribution is captured in the sample. Analysis using data sources, such as the PSID, RHS, and SIPP, which focus almost exclusively on middle-income families, will give very different results than surveys like the SCF, which has a good representation of the very wealthy.

7

Inheritances and the Distribution of Wealth

Inheritances and inter vivos gifts, collectively referred to as wealth transfers, play an important role in the household accumulation of wealth. They come into play in two ways. First, they influence time trends in median and mean household wealth. Second, they also impact the household distribution of wealth and overall wealth inequality. It is therefore important to investigate time trends in wealth transfers and to determine their effect on overall wealth inequality. Time trends in wealth transfers are also an interesting issue in their own right.

Direct survey evidence is available from the Federal Reserve Board's Survey of Consumer Finances (SCF) on the receipt of inheritances and gifts, as well as the amount given in the form of gifts. Though retrospective bequest data are problematic, because they require recall of events that may have often occurred a decade or more earlier, and tend to underestimate the value of such wealth transfers, the survey evidence does show that bequests and gifts play a major role in wealth accumulation.

Previous work based on the SCF showed that on average over the period from 1989 to 2007, about one-fifth of American households at a given point in time reported a wealth transfer and these accounted for quite a sizable figure, about a quarter of their net worth. Over their lifetimes, about 30 percent of households could expect to receive a wealth transfer and these would account for close to 40 percent of their net worth near time of death. However, there was little evidence of an inheritance "boom." In fact, from 1989 to 2007, the share of households reporting a wealth transfer fell by 2.5 percentage points, a time trend statistically significant at the 1 percent level. The average value of inheritances received among *all* households increased at a slow pace, by 10 percent; the time trend was not statistically significant. On the other hand, wealth transfers as a proportion of current net worth fell sharply over this period, from 29 to 19 percent, though the time trend once again was not statistically significant. It was also found that inheritances and other wealth transfers tended to be equalizing in terms of the distribution of household wealth.[1]

This chapter will update these results to the year 2013. It also includes calculations of *net* wealth transfers—the difference between inheritances and gifts received and gifts made to others. Net wealth transfers are more relevant to trends in median wealth and wealth inequality than gross wealth transfers received.[2]

This chapter's focus is to examine trends in inheritances and other wealth transfers and their effect on overall wealth inequality over the period from 1989 to 2013. The basic data are drawn from the SCF. Three main issues are addressed. The first is whether wealth transfers (the sum of inheritances and gifts) increased or decreased in importance from 1989 to 2013. Before addressing this issue, we must specify what we mean by "important." There are two common metrics: the level of wealth transfers (in constant dollars) and the ratio of wealth transfers to current net worth. This topic is of interest because it grows out of an extensive literature on the *relative* importance of savings and transfers as a source of household wealth accumulation. If wealth transfers turn out to be the major factor in accounting for household wealth, the implication may be that intergenerational mobility is low. On the other hand, if savings is the dominant factor, then the results suggest that families can accumulate wealth over their lifetimes on the basis of their own income and savings.

There is reason to believe that the share of wealth transfers in net worth has been rising over time because the current generation of elderly people is now the richest in history.[3] Moreover, the baby-boom generation has now reached the prime inheritance age group of 50 to 59.[4] For both reasons, the baby boomers may be the first generation to inherit a considerable amount of money both in terms of the percentage of families inheriting as well as the amount inherited. Indeed, more than twenty years ago, Avery and Rendall forecasted that an inheritance boom would occur for baby boomers over the decade 2000–2010.[5] Later, Schervish and Havens predicted that over the fifty-five-year period from 1998 to 2052, a minimum of $41 trillion (in 1998 dollars) would pass from the older generation to the younger one. More recently,

Munnell et al. projected that the baby boom generation (those born between 1946 and 1964) will inherit $84 trillion (in 2009 dollars) over its lifetime.[6]

However, not much evidence supports a rising role of wealth transfers in household wealth accumulation. Instead, if anything, as a proportion of household net worth they declined over these years (though the change is not statistically significant).

The second topic is whether wealth transfers help contribute to an increase in household wealth inequality, as common wisdom suggests. It is true that richer households receive more in the way of wealth transfers than poorer ones. However, poorer households receive a *higher share* of their wealth from such transfers than richer ones. As a result, I find that wealth transfers actually tend to decrease wealth inequality rather than increasing it. The third issue is whether the inequality of wealth transfers themselves has increased over time. Here, too the evidence suggests otherwise and there appears to be no indication that the inequality of wealth transfers trended either upward or downward between years 1989 and 2013.

This chapter also investigates the level of inheritances and gifts and related time trends for different socioeconomic groups, which are determined by income class, wealth group, race and ethnicity, age, and educational attainment. The results show which groups relied on wealth transfers more over time and which relied on them less. In addition, the chapter examines types of wealth transfers (inheritances, gifts, trust fund, and others), sources of wealth transfers (parents, grandparents, other relatives, and friends), and the nature of these transfers (for example, money, family business, real estate). Finally, gifts and charitable donations are analyzed from the standpoint of the donor.

The advantage of the data sources (1989 and 2013 SCF) is that they provide detailed information on holdings of assets and liabilities as well as on inheritances and gifts received and gifts and donations made. Interviewees were asked to record both the amount of the transfer and the year of receipt. In addition, they were asked to indicate for selected asset holdings (real estate and businesses) whether the original source of the holding was from an inheritance or gift. This information enables us to calculate the mean and median value of wealth transfers and to determine whether wealth transfers are, on net, equalizing or disequalizing with respect to overall wealth.

The new results are quite similar to the earlier ones. With regard to the importance of wealth transfers, the proportion of households reporting a wealth transfer over their lifetime fell by 2 percentage points from 1989 to 2013, a time trend that is statistically significant at the 1 percent level. The average value of inheritances received by recipients increased by 31 percent, but the time trend is not statistically significant. On the other hand, the median value in constant dollars among recipients grew by 58 percent and this trend is significant at the 1 percent level. Among *all* households, the mean value of wealth transfers in 2013 dollars was up by 20 percent, but the trend is not significant.[7] Perhaps, most importantly, the ratio of wealth transfers to current net worth declined over these years by 4.8 percentage points, but the time trend is once again not statistically significant. I also find that wealth transfers tend to be equalizing in terms of the distribution of household wealth.

The next section of the chapter provides a brief literature review, which is followed by a description of the data source. The chapter then presents an analysis of inheritance and gift patterns in the United States over the period 1989 to 2013; overall trends in both the recipiency rate and value of wealth transfers; statistics by socioeconomic group; time trends in the inequality of wealth transfers and the effect of wealth transfers on overall wealth inequality; and wealth transfers received in the recent past (five-year and ten-year retrospectives).

Background Literature

A preponderance of studies on this subject has tried to assess the relative roles of inheritances and other wealth transfers versus savings on the household accumulation of wealth.[8] Among the early studies on the subject, Projector and Weiss, using the 1963 Survey of Financial Characteristics of Consumers, reported that only 17 percent of families had ever received any inheritance.[9] This compares with a figure of 18 percent reported by Morgan, David, Cohen, and Brazer.[10] The Projector and Weiss study also reported that only 5 percent of households had received a "substantial" proportion of their wealth from inheritance. They found that this latter proportion rose with household wealth: 34 percent of families with net worth exceeding half a million dollars indicated receiving a substantial bequest. Barlow, Brazer, and Morgan found from a 1964 Brookings Survey on the Economic Behavior of the Affluent that covered families with incomes of $10,000 or more, that only 7 percent mentioned gifts and inheritance as the source of most of their current wealth.[11] Barlow et al. also estimated that about one-seventh of the total wealth of this group came from inheritance.

Menchik and David, using probate records of men who died in Wisconsin between 1947 and 1978, obtained an estimate of $7,500 (in 1967 dollars) for the average intergenerational bequest, which amounted to less than 20 percent of average household wealth in 1967 and about 10 percent of the average wealth of families with a household head age 65 or older.[12] Hurd and Mundaca analyzed data from both the 1964 Survey on the Economic Behavior of the Affluent and the 1983 SCF.[13] They found from the former that only 12 percent of households in the top 10 percent of the income distribution received more than half their wealth from gifts or inheritances. The corresponding figure from the 1983 data was 9 percent. They inferred from these results that intergenerational transfers were not a major source of wealth, even for rich families.

Gale and Scholz, using the 1983–1986 panel of the SCF, estimated that at least 51 percent of household wealth was accounted for by inheritances and other "intentional" wealth transfers.[14] Their method is a hybrid of direct survey data and simulation. They estimated that inter vivos transfers were the source of at least 20 percent of aggregate wealth, and bequests, whether intended or not, accounted for an additional 31 percent. The rather high estimate for inter vivos transfers was estimated from the donor side rather than the donee (recipient) side, and included life insurance and trusts in addition to inter vivos gifts. Moreover, the inheritance estimate was based on accumulating inheritances received at a rather high real rate of return of 4.5 percent per year (3 percent is the benchmark rate used in this chapter) and projecting forward over time a rate of growth for inheritances equal to that of income (3.5 percent per year).

Brown and Weisbenner, using the 1998 SCF, estimated that 19 percent of households received a wealth transfer, which is very close to my own estimate, and that one-fifth to one-fourth of aggregate household wealth was traceable to wealth transfers, depending on the interest rate used to capitalize past inheritances.[15]

Kessler and Masson performed a similar analysis on French data.[16] A 1975 survey of two thousand French families asked whether they had received any significant inheritance (above $4,000) or gifts (above $2,000). Of all the households in the sample, 36 percent reported that they had already received a wealth transfer. Kessler and Masson then estimated that about 35 percent of total personal wealth originated from inheritances and gifts. Among those who had reported receiving an intergenerational transfer (who were about two-and-a-half times richer than the average household), the corresponding proportion was 40 percent. Klevmarken computed that 34 percent of Swedish households reported receiving a gift or inheritance in the 1998 Household Market and Non-Market Activities Survey (HUS).[17] On the basis of a 3 percent capitalization rate for inheritances and gifts, Klevmarken computed that 19 percent of total household wealth in 1998 originated from wealth transfers.

Laitner and Sonnega provided some more recent evidence on this subject on the basis of the 1992–2008 Health and Retirement Survey (HRS).[18] The HRS is a panel survey that began in 1992 with a sample of respondents between ages 51 and 61. It has an extensive battery of questions about inheritances and gifts received. The authors estimated that 30 to 40 percent of households would eventually receive an inheritance (by time of death). This figure is a little higher than my estimate of around 30 percent. They also surmised that inheritances reflect a mixture of intentional and accidental bequests, with the latter twice as prevalent.

Karagiannaki examined time trends in inherited wealth in the United Kingdom and its effects on the overall distribution of wealth.[19] She examined the trend in the *annual flow* of inheritances over the period 1984 to 2005 and found that it increased markedly, from £22 billion (2005 GBP) in 1984 to £56 billion in 2005. In addition, the mean value of estates more than doubled, from £81,000 to £204,100. Total annual inheritances rose from 3 percent of GDP in 1984 to 4.3 percent in 2005. The proportion of households receiving inheritances increased as well, from 0.8 percent in the 1986–1990 period to 1.4 percent in 2001–2005.

Karagiannaki reported that the inequality of inheritances among recipients was very large, and was comparable to inequality of total household wealth. In fact, inheritances were fairly small for the majority of recipients and large inheritances were limited to a very small share of the population.

Karagiannaki found that the inequality of inheritances among recipients increased over this period, an effect that was counter-balanced by a rise in the share of the population that received an inheritance. As a result, the inequality of inheritances among the whole population declined slightly between 1996 and 2005.

Karagiannaki investigated the effects of inheritances over the lifetime on the distribution of wealth among the whole population in 1995, 2000, and 2005.[20] She found that inheritances over these years accounted for between 10 and 15 percent of household wealth accumulation (depending on the capitalization rate) and between 26 and 30 percent of the accumulation of inheriting households. These figures are lower than those calculated for the United States.

Piketty tracked annual wealth transfers (inheritance and gifts) in France from 1820 to 2010.[21] His main finding was that annual inheritances as a share of national income was about 20 to 25 percent between 1820 and 1910, fell to less than 5 percent in 1950, and then rebounded to 15 percent in 2010. For the period under consideration here, the share rose from about 6 percent in 1980 to about 13 percent in 2010. This analysis differs from others in that only annual wealth transfers flows were calculated, rather than the capitalized value of current and past wealth transfers, and they were computed as a fraction of national income instead of total household wealth.

The media made much of this finding, asserting that inheritances are rising in importance in France (and other Organisation for Economic Cooperation and Development member countries, such as the United States). The ratio of inheritances to national income, however, is not the appropriate metric of the relative importance of wealth transfers. Rather, wealth transfers should be measured as a share of personal wealth. Indeed, Piketty also reported that the ratio of private wealth to national income rose from about 300 percent in 1980 to about 550 percent in 2005. As a result, the ratio of annual wealth transfers to private wealth remained fairly constant at about 2 percent from 1980 to 2010.

Atkinson used similar methodology in his case for the United Kingdom and reported very similar findings.[22] He examined estate duty (tax) records back to 1896 and found that before World War I, total inherited wealth represented about 20 percent of national income. In the interwar years, this ratio fell to 15 percent and then fell to about 10 percent after World War II and only 5 percent in the late 1970s. The ratio then rose from 4.8 percent in 1977 to 8.2 percent in 2006. Atkinson also found that the ratio of personal wealth to national income increased starting in the 1970s, with the former growing twice as fast as the latter in real terms. As a result, the ratio of inherited wealth to total personal wealth was about the same in 2006 as in 1976.

Crawford and Hood investigated the effect of lifetime inheritances and gifts received on the distribution of wealth.[23] Their data source was the English Longitudinal Study of Ageing, which contains information on the lifetime receipt of inheritances and gifts of older individuals. This group was unlikely to expect any further wealth transfers. Whereas previous work has looked only at marketable wealth, Crawford and Hood considered broader measures of wealth, including state and private pensions. They found that once pension wealth was included, inheritances and gifts no longer had an equalizing impact on the distribution of wealth. Without pension wealth, including wealth transfers reduced the Gini coefficient for wealth from 0.57 to 0.52. With pension wealth, the impact was negligible. They argued that the latter effect gave a better indication of the impact of inheritances on the distribution of lifetime income.

Generally speaking, analysis of the importance of inheritances and other wealth transfers in household wealth accumulation is quite varied. Based on the studies reviewed here, about 20 to 30 percent of household wealth emanates from inheritances and other forms of wealth transfers.

Data Sources and Methods

In my analysis, I use data from the SCF, covering the years 1989 to 2013.[24] One major advantage of the SCF is that it provides detailed information on inheritances and gifts received. Data collection is based on recall. Respondents are asked to record both the amount of the transfer received and the year of receipt. In addition, for selected asset holdings (real estate, businesses, and trust funds) they are asked to indicate whether the original source of the holding comes from an inheritance or gift.

Information gathered for the SCF about wealth transfers is categorized as "general wealth transfers" (i.e., any type of gift or inheritance) or inheritances and gifts related to real estate and businesses. In principle, the questions on general wealth transfers should also capture the specific transfers indicated in the questions on real estate and business. However, in my data analysis, I did find a few discrepancies between the responses to the two sets of questions.[25] To be on the conservative side, I therefore included the value of the specific wealth transfer for a particular household only in cases where no general wealth transfer was reported.

The recall method is likely to have under-reporting problems, which causes estimates of inheritances and gifts to be biased downward. It is difficult to ascertain whether there is a systematic bias in under-reporting according to wealth level, income level, or demographic characteristics of the respondent.

The present value of all wealth transfers received by a household up to the survey year can be computed on the basis of the date and reported value of each wealth transfer.[26] The value of the wealth transfer is first converted to 2013 dollars. Then, for household i, the present value of all wealth transfers received up to the survey year y, $PVWT_{yi}$, is given by

$$PVWT_{yi} = \sum_{t=t_0}^{y} WT_{ti} \cdot e^{r(y-t)} \tag{7.1}$$

where WT_{ti} is the wealth transfer in 2013 dollars received in year t by household i, t_0 is the earliest year that wealth transfers are recorded (about sixty years prior to the survey year), and r is the capitalization rate. For the purpose of this chapter, I use a 3 percent real rate of return r. This is the approximate rate of return on household wealth for the period under consideration.[27]

Bear in mind that there is considerable sample variation from year to year. This is expected because inheritances and other wealth transfers are received by a small fraction of the population and their distribution is very skewed.

Overall Trends in Inheritances and Gifts, 1989–2013

Table 7.1 provides general statistics on wealth transfers by type and source. Depending on the year, between 80 and 90 percent of households who received some type of wealth transfer received an inheritance (see Panel A). Over the full twenty-four-year period, the share averaged 84 percent. On average,

14 percent of households who received a wealth transfer received a gift and 6 percent a trust fund or other type of transfer. Among households receiving a transfer, 78 percent of the value of these transfers on average came from inheritances, 7 percent from gifts, and 15 percent from trusts or other transfers (Panel B). The importance of gifts rose sharply over time from 1.7 percent in 1989 to 13.8 percent in 2013 of total transfers, while that of trusts generally declined (though there was an uptick in 2013). Indeed, it is noteworthy that the share of *all* households reporting receipt of an inter vivos transfer climbed from 0.8 percent in 1989 to 3 percent in 2007 before falling off to 2.5 percent in 2013, and the mean value of gifts (in 2013 dollars) among recipients increased more than eightfold between 1989 and 2013. There is no noticeable time trend for inheritances.[28] The large rise in gifts, particularly relative to inheritances, may reflect, in part, the increasing life expectancy of donors, as well as the rising wealth of older persons relative to younger ones. On the other hand, the steep decline in gifts from 2007 to 2010 is probably traceable to the Great Recession and the sizable decline in household wealth at that time.

On average, two-thirds of all wealth transfers (in dollar terms) came from parents, 16 percent from grandparents, 14 percent from other relatives, and 3 percent from friends and other sources (see Panel D). The contribution from parents alone rose from 56 percent of the total value of wealth transfers in 1989 to 78 percent in 2013 and that from parents and grandparents together increased from 74 to 88, while the share from other relatives, friends, and other sources slipped.

Panel E of Table 7.1 also tabulates responses to the general wealth transfer questions versus questions on specific types of transfers (i.e., real estate and businesses). On average, over the 1989–2007 period, 20.7 percent responded "yes" to the questions on general wealth transfers, 2.9 percent indicated receiving their own home as a gift or inheritance, 3.3 percent said "yes" for other real estate, 0.5 percent responded "yes" for their own business, and 6.5 percent for either real estate or a business.

Only about half (52 percent) of wealth transfers in dollar terms, on average, took the traditional form of an inheritance from parent to child. The remainder was made up of gifts and other types of transfers, as well as inheritances received from grandparents, other relatives, and friends. This is an important finding in light of the theoretical literature on the subject,

Table 7.1. Distribution of wealth transfer received by type and source of transfer, 1989–2013

	1989	1992	1995	1998	2001	2004	2007	2010	2013	Average
A. Percent of All Recipients Receiving Indicated Transfer[a]										
1. Inheritances	88.7	91.4	79.2	79.7	82.4	85.8	82.3	85.8	83.8	84.3
2. Gifts	4.2	7.3	17.2	19.4	17.8	15.4	18.2	13.6	15.2	14.2
3. Trust funds or other transfers	10.7	5.0	8.0	4.4	4.6	4.3	4.5	4.9	6.4	5.9
B. Present Value of Transfer Received by Type as a Percent of Total Wealth Transfers[b]										
1. Inheritances	76.9	78.6	87.4	79.7	83.6	66.4	78.8	83.7	66.7	78.0
2. Gifts	1.7	2.5	5.6	10.8	7.2	5.5	10.3	6.4	13.8	7.1
3. Trust funds or other transfers	21.4	19.0	7.0	9.5	9.2	28.1	10.9	9.9	19.5	14.9
Total	100.0	100.0	100.0	100.0	100.0	100.0	100.0	100.0	100.0	100.0
C. Percent of Wealth Transfer Recipients Receiving Transfer by Donor[a]										
1. Parents	71.3	61.7	68.2	71.3	70.2	66.3	72.6	76.3	73.4	70.2
2. Grandparents	17.4	21.1	16.8	17.4	19.0	19.4	19.6	18.0	18.1	18.5
3. Other relatives	19.6	30.0	23.8	19.6	16.9	22.9	17.6	13.9	18.7	20.3
4. Friends and others	4.7	5.4	5.0	4.7	3.5	3.3	2.7	2.1	3.3	3.9

D. Present Value of Transfer Received by Donor as a Percent of Total Wealth Transfers[b]

1. Parents	56.3	61.9	57.8	64.3	73.0	55.0	76.5	80.4	78.3	67.1
2. Grandparents	17.5	11.5	6.8	23.0	15.3	35.3	13.3	10.5	9.8	15.9
3. Other relatives	16.1	22.0	33.9	9.7	9.9	8.2	9.8	8.5	9.6	14.2
4. Friends and others	10.1	4.6	1.5	3.0	1.7	1.5	0.5	0.5	2.3	2.8
Total	100.0	100.0	100.0	100.0	100.0	100.0	100.0	100.0	100.0	100.0

E. Percent of Households Receiving Wealth Transfer by Source

1. General wealth transfer	23.1	20.5	21.3	20.3	17.8	20.3	21.0	20.4	21.5	20.7
2. Homes	2.8	2.2	3.2	3.1	3.0	2.7	2.8	3.1	3.7	2.9
3. Other real estate	4.1	2.3	4.4	3.1	2.7	3.2	3.5	3.1	3.2	3.3
4. Business	0.6	0.3	0.5	0.4	0.3	0.3	0.7	0.4	0.6	0.5
5. Real estate or business	7.6	5.0	7.8	6.5	5.9	6.1	6.5	6.3	7.2	6.5

Source: Author's computations from the 1989, 1992, 1995, 1998, 2001, 2004, 2007, 2010, and 2013 Survey of Consumer Finances. Tabulations are only for general wealth transfer questions except for Panel E.

a. The column sum may be greater than unity since a household may receive more than one type of transfer.

b. The figures are based on the present value of all transfers as of the survey year that were received up to the time of the survey and accumulated at a real interest rate of 3 percent.

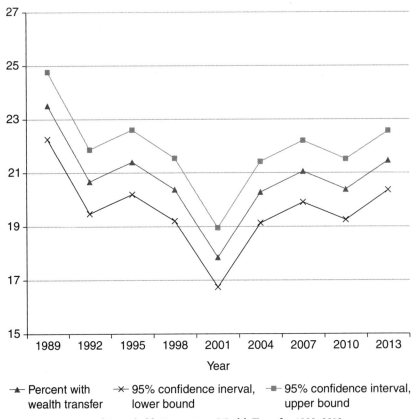

Figure 7.1. Percent of Households Reporting a Wealth Transfer, 1989–2013

which has focused almost exclusively on the traditional form of inheritance, from parent to child. However, such models miss almost half of all wealth transfers.

On average, 21 percent of all households reported receiving a wealth transfer over years 1989 to 2013 (also see Figure 7.1). This figure is comparable to those from previous U.S. surveys but lower than the corresponding figures from French and Swedish household surveys. The fraction of households receiving a wealth transfer declined from 24 percent in 1989 to a low point of 18 percent in 2001 but then rose to 22 percent in 2012. The difference between 1989 and 2013 is a negative 2 percentage points, a difference that is statistically significant at the 1 percent level. A logit regression of a dummy variable with a value of 1 if the household received an inheritance and zero if it did not on a constant and a time trend variable yields a coefficient of −3.66 on time, significant at the 1 percent level.[29] The results indicate that over the full twenty-four-year period there is a statistically significant decline in the share of households receiving wealth transfers.

The second row of Table 7.2 shows the mean value of wealth transfers among recipients only (also see Figure 7.2). Its average value over the nine years was $489,300 (in 2013 dollars). The results also indicate a sharp decline in the mean value of transfers among recipients between 1989 and 1998—over 16 percent. However, from 1998 to 2013, the situation reversed and the mean value of wealth transfers among recipients climbed by 57 percent. Over the full twenty-four-year period, the mean value rose by 31 percent. However, the change between 1989 and 2013 is not statistically significant, though the time trend coefficient is positive and significant at the 5 percent level. The median value among recipients only showed a 58 percent increase from 1989 to 2013 (also see Figure 7.4). The difference between the two years is statistically significant at the 1 percent level, and a regression of median values on time over the nine years also yields a positive coefficient, which is significant at the 1 percent level.

Row 4 (also see Figure 7.4) puts together trends in mean wealth transfers among recipients with trends in the share of households receiving transfers to yield average transfers among all households. Overall mean transfers were down by 28 percent from 1989 to 1998 and then up by 66 percent from 1998 to 2013, for a net gain of 20 percent. This compares to a 31 percent increase of mean transfers among recipients alone. However, here, the difference between 1989 and 2013 is not statistically significant; nor is the time trend coefficient.

Row 5 (also see Figure 7.5) shows the present value of wealth transfers received as a percent of the current net worth of households. This ratio provides a rough gauge of the importance of wealth transfers in household wealth accumulation and is the most crucial variable. The unweighted average over the entire 1989 to 2013 period was 23 percent. This figure is comparable to previous estimates for U.S. households and for Swedish households (19 percent in 1998) but lower than the figure of 35 percent for French households in 1975. However, since net worth rose during the 1990s in the United States and the mean value of wealth transfers dipped, this proportion also fell rather sharply from 1989 to 2001 (29 to 15 percent). From 2001 to

Table 7.2. Time trends in wealth transfers among all households, 1989–2013 (figures are in thousands, 2013 dollars)

Variable	1989	1992	1995	1998	2001	2004	2007	2010	2013	Unweighted Average, 1989–2013	Two-tailed z-test 1989 = 2013?	Time Trend Coefficient[d]
1. Percent of households reporting a transfer[a]	23.5 (0.72)	20.7 (0.68)	21.4 (0.69)	20.4 (0.67)	17.9 (0.63)	20.3 (0.66)	21.1 (0.66)	20.4 (0.65)	21.5 (0.63)	20.8	−3.66**	−0.197** (7.17)
2. Mean present value of transfers, recipients only[b]	434.9 (57.0)	452.6 (106.8)	456.9 (97.8)	363.5 (75.6)	425.4 (39.5)	545.3 (139.3)	533.7 (59.5)	620.0 (118.4)	571.5 (91.9)	489.3	1.71	71.5* (1.98)
3. Median present value of transfers, recipients only[b]	74.3 (7.03)	71.5 (5.35)	73.1 (6.79)	79.7 (7.05)	96.9 (7.60)	82.7 (7.86)	100.8 (9.57)	100.7 (7.86)	117.7 (7.23)	88.6	2.61**	5.32** (5.75)
4. Mean present value of transfers, all households[b]	102.3 (19.2)	93.6 (32.6)	97.5 (30.8)	74.0 (23.0)	75.9 (11.1)	110.6 (42.2)	112.4 (18.8)	126.4 (36.1)	122.7 (27.3)	101.7	0.72	12.7 (1.37)
5. Mean present value of transfers as a percent of net worth, all households[c]	28.9 (11.4)	26.0 (5.4)	31.2 (5.2)	19.1 (26.3)	15.2 (15.9)	22.1 (17.8)	18.7 (6.5)	25.5 (8.3)	24.1 (7.8)	23.4	−0.25	−0.716 (1.09)
Sample size	3,143	3,906	4,299	4,305	4,442	4,519	4,418	6,482	6,015			41,529

Source: Author's computations from the 1989, 1992, 1995, 1998, 2001, 2004, 2007, 2010, and 2013 Survey of Consumer Finances. Standard errors are shown in parentheses.

a. The figures record the proportion of households that indicate receiving a wealth transfer at any time before the time of the survey.

b. The figures show the present value of all transfers as of the survey year that were received up to the time of the survey and accumulated at a real interest rate of 3 percent.

c. The figures show the present value of all wealth transfers as of the survey year that were received up to the time of the survey and accumulated at a real interest rate of 3 percent as a ratio to net worth.

d. The time trend coefficient is estimated from a pooled sample, from years 1989, 1992, 1995, 1998, 2001, 2004, 2007, 2010, and 2013. The regression uses a constant and time trend as independent variables.

The exceptions are the median (number 3) and the ratio of transfers to net worth (number 5). The regression estimates are based on a time series of annual averages (9 data points).

t-ratios are shown in parentheses below the coefficient estimate.

Significance levels: # 10%; * 5%; ** 1%.

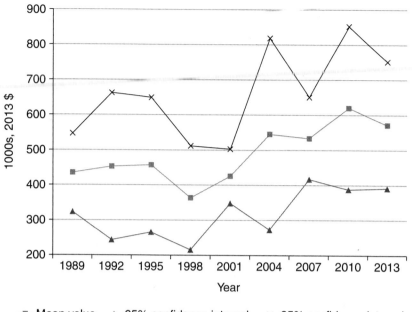

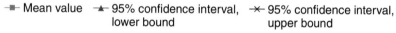

Figure 7.2. Mean Value of Wealth Transfers, Recipients Only, 1989–2013

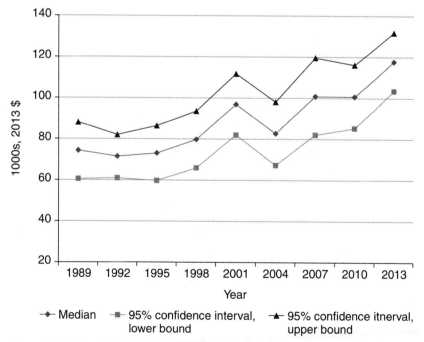

Figure 7.3. Median Value of Wealth Transfers, Recipients Only, 1989–2013

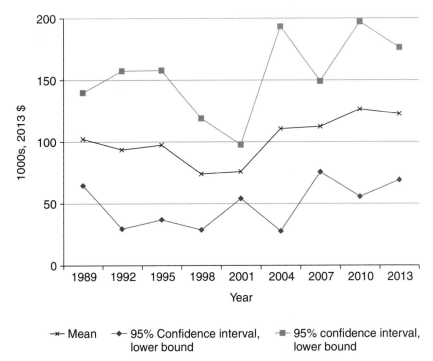

Figure 7.4. Mean Value of Wealth Transfers, All Households, 1989–2013

2013, the mean value of wealth transfers rose by 62 percent while mean net worth was up by only 2 percent, so that the ratio climbed to 24 percent. This ratio appears to be much more sensitive to movements in net worth than in wealth transfers, rising during recessionary periods and falling during upturns. Over the full twenty-four-year period, wealth transfers as a share of net worth fell from 29 to 24 percent, but the difference is not statistically significant (nor is the time trend coefficient).[30]

Wealth Transfer Trends by Income, Wealth, and Demographic Group

The recpiency rate shows significant variation by income, wealth, and demographic class (see Table 7.3). As expected, the share of recipients rises very strongly with income and wealth level. On average, over the nine survey

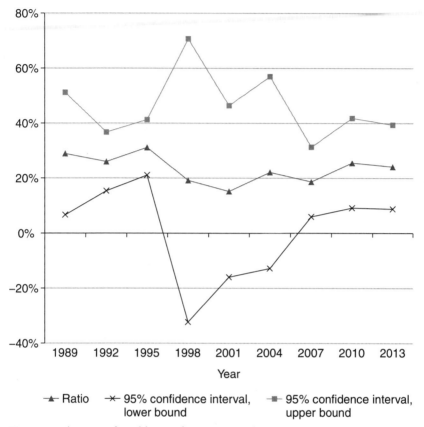

Figure 7.5. The Ratio of Wealth Transfers to Net Worth, 1989–2013

years, 38 percent were transfer recipients in the highest income bracket in comparison to 15 percent in the lowest income bracket. Likewise, 45 percent in the highest wealth bracket received a transfer, compared to 9 percent in the lowest. The figure was also 45 percent for the top 1 percent of wealth holders.[31]

The share of non-Hispanic whites ("whites") reporting a wealth transfer was, on average, more than twice as great as the proportion of non-Hispanic African Americans ("blacks"). Only 6 percent of Hispanic households reported a transfer, while the figure was 12 percent for Asian and other races.

As expected, the recipiency rate rises with age. On average, 12 percent of households under age 35 received a transfer, in comparison to 31 percent in age bracket 65–74. However, the share in age group 75 and older was slightly lower, at 29 percent. This pattern reflects both life cycle effects (the parents

Table 7.3. Percentage of households receiving wealth transfers, 1989–2013

Category	Period Average	(Std. err.)	Two-tailed z-test with Respect to Omitted Category	Change, 1989–2013	Time Trend Coefficient[c]	Pooled Sample Size
All Households	20.8	(0.22)		-2.1	-0.197**	41,529
A. Income Level (1998$)						
Under $15,000	15.0	(0.28)	26.9**	0.9	-0.056	6,895
$15,000–$24,999	18.2	(0.34)	21.9**	-4.3	-0.413**	5,220
$25,000–$49,999	20.3	(0.30)	20.7**	-1.7	-0.169*	9,579
$50,000–$74,999	23.4	(0.37)	16.5**	-5.9	-0.121	5,439
$75,000–$99,999	25.9	(0.47)	12.6**	-4.0	-0.461**	2,859
$100,000–$249,999	31.2	(0.48)	7.43**	2.2	-0.522**	4,837
$250,000 or more	38.0	(0.74)	[omitted]	-8.4	-0.269**	6,700
B. Wealth Level (1998$)						
Under $25,000	9.2	(0.20)	52.4**	1.6	-0.040	13,183
$25,000–$49,999	20.3	(0.40)	31.5**	-2.6	-0.113	2,623
$50,000–$99,999	21.0	(0.37)	31.1**	-5.3	-0.070	3,612
$100,000–$249,999	26.2	(0.37)	24.6**	-5.1	-0.322**	5,399
$250,000–$499,999	33.4	(0.47)	13.4**	-6.6	-0.425**	3,756
$500,000–$999,999	41.5	(0.55)	3.47**	-3.0	-0.330*	2,942
$1,000,000 or over	45.1	(0.58)	[omitted]	-0.2	-0.264**	10,014
Top 1% of wealth	44.5	(0.86)	—	-9.8	-0.348**	5,766

C. Race

Non-Hispanic whites	24.8	(0.26)	[omitted]	-0.9	-0.199**	32,566
Non-Hispanic African Americans	10.5	(0.28)	34.6**	0.0	-0.013	4,352
Hispanics[a]	5.6	(0.23)	50.2**	0.2	-0.144*	2,942
Asian and other races	12.4	(0.41)	23.5**	-2.7	-0.465**	1,668

D. Age Class[b]

Under 35	12.2	(0.26)	29.5**	-3.0	-0.233**	7,553
35–44	15.9	(0.30)	21.5**	-3.3	-0.443**	8,198
45–54	21.1	(0.34)	12.5**	-4.1	-0.381**	9,223
55–64	27.7	(0.40)	2.63**	1.4	-0.109	7,734
65–74	30.8	(0.44)	(3.67)	-0.3	-0.211*	5,226
75 & over	28.5	(0.44)	[omitted]	-10.4	-0.289*	3,594

E. Education[b]

Less than 12 years	13.2	(0.28)	31.2**	-5.6	-0.335**	5,523
12 years	18.0	(0.29)	22.1**	-1.0	-0.180**	10,288
13–15 years	20.6	(0.32)	15.9**	-1.5	-0.268**	8,449
16 years or more	28.5	(0.34)	[omitted]	-6.5	-0.413**	17,269

Source: Author's computations from the 1989, 1992, 1995, 1998, 2001, 2004, 2007, 2010, and 2013 Survey of Consumer Finances. Each year is given equal weight. The figures record the proportion of households that indicated receiving a wealth transfer at any time up to the time of the survey.

a. Hispanics can be of any race.

b. Households are classified according to the age and education of the head of household.

c. The time trend coefficient is estimated from a pooled sample from years 1989, 1992, 1995, 1998, 2001, 2004, 2007, 2010, and 2013. The regression uses a constant and time trend as independent variables.

Significance levels: # 10%; * 5%; ** 1%.

of older individuals are more likely to have died than those of younger ones), as well as cohort effects (parents of persons 75 and older were more likely to have been poorer than parents of younger people). If the 75 and older age group is considered to represent the "end of lifetime," it appears that about 29 percent of households will on average receive a wealth transfer over their lifetime. The likelihood of a wealth transfer also rises with education—from 13 percent for the lowest schooling group to 29 percent for college graduates. This result is consistent with the pattern found by income class.

The recipiency rate generally fell for all income, wealth, and demographic groups from 1989 to 2013, with a few exceptions.[32] The decline was particularly steep for the top income class (8.4 percentage points), the top 1 percent of wealth holders (9.8 percentage points), and the oldest age group (10.4 percentage points).

Table 7.4 and Table 7.5 show the mean and median value of wealth transfers among recipients only. On average, the mean value of wealth transfers among recipients was $489,300 and the median was $88,600 (both in 2013 dollars). It is of note that the large difference between mean and median is of the same order of magnitude as that between mean and median household wealth, and indicates considerable skewness in the distribution of wealth transfers.

Results for mean and median values by income, wealth, and demographic group have a pattern similar to that for recipiency rates. The values generally rise with both household income and wealth, and there is a substantial jump for the highest income and wealth class. On average, the mean value of wealth transfers for the top income class was 8.9 times greater than for the lowest, and the median transfer was 6.4 times larger. The mean value of wealth transfers for the highest wealth class was 29 times greater than for the lowest, and the median transfer was 19 times larger. Indeed, the ratio was 70 for mean values and 40 for median values between the top 1 percent of wealth holders and the bottom wealth class.[33]

Wealth transfers are also higher for whites than for African Americans, by 84 percent on average for the mean value and 27 percent for median values. Hispanics ranked third and Asians first in terms of mean wealth transfers. Not surprisingly, the value of wealth transfers rises with age. On average, the mean transfer for households aged 75 and older was 4.8 times greater as that for the youngest age group, while the median transfer was 4.2

times larger. The value of wealth transfers also rises with education and is particularly high for college graduates. On average, the mean transfer of college graduates was 3.1 times greater than for households with the least education, and the median value was 2.5 times larger.

Over years 1989 to 2013, the bottom four income classes and the sixth registered gains in mean wealth transfers, while the other two suffered declines.[34] All wealth classes except the top saw gains in mean transfers. The top 1 percent saw their transfers more than double in value. Median values increased for all income classes and all but two wealth classes. Both mean and median wealth transfers increased among all racial, age, and educational groups except among the least educated.

Table 7.6 presents trends in mean wealth transfers among recipients and trends in the recipiency rate to yield mean transfers among all households within each group. We now see a much greater spread than among recipients alone, which reflects the positive correlation between the recipiency rate and the mean value of wealth transfers.

On average, over the nine years, the ratio of mean transfers between the top and bottom income classes was 80, compared to an 8.9 ratio among recipients only. The ratio in mean transfers between the top and bottom wealth class was 149, compared to 29 among recipients alone. The ratio in mean transfers between white and black households was 5.6, in comparison to 1.8 among recipients only. While the spread between the oldest and youngest age classes in mean transfers was about the same now as that among recipients, that between college graduates and the least educated was 7 among all households, compared to 3.1 among recipients.[35]

Changes in mean transfers between 1989 and 2013 show a mixed pattern by income class but were positive by wealth class except in two instances. Average transfers rose among white and Asian households but were down among black and Hispanic households. Mean transfers were generally up by age and education but fell for the youngest group and for age group 65 to 74, as well as for college graduates.[36]

Table 7.7 is crucial to this discussion. It shows wealth transfers as a percent of current net worth by socioeconomic category. The most notable finding is that while both the percentage of households receiving a wealth transfer and the value of those transfers rise almost monotonically with income and

Table 7.4. Mean value of wealth transfers, recipients only, 1989–2013 (figures are in thousands, 2013 dollars)

Category	Period average	(Std. err.)	Two-tailed z-test with Respect to Omitted Category[c]	% Change, 1989–2013	Time Trend Coefficient[c]	Pooled Sample Size
All Households	489.3	(33.0)		31.4	71.5*	10,225
A. Income Level (1998$)						
Under $15,000	360.3	(25.0)	8.99**	33.5	87.3*	1,004
$15,000–$24,999	267.1	(11.2)	9.23**	7.6	10.7**	907
$25,000–$49,999	323.4	(15.3)	9.04**	14.7	16.1#	1,984
$50,000–$74,999	363.8	(21.8)	8.86**	83.4	-8.1	1,326
$75,000–$99,999	510.0	(26.7)	8.42**	-2.2	-22.3	825
$100,000–$249,999	800.4	(41.7)	7.62**	34.7	-6.7	1,654
$250,000 or more	3203.3	(381.4)	[omitted]	-23.3	123.9	2,526
B. Wealth Level (1998$)						
Under $25,000	76.1	(3.4)	14.74**	16.6	0.2	1,193
$25,000–$49,999	137.8	(6.3)	14.21**	5.7	4.1	519
$50,000–$99,999	176.8	(7.6)	13.89**	54.1	5.6#	749
$100,000–$249,999	259.9	(10.1)	13.47**	28.4	10.9**	1,400
$250,000–$499,999	401.6	(21.8)	12.66**	28.9	28.3*	1,195
$500,000–$999,999	721.2	(32.4)	9.66**	17.0	-14.4	1,117
$1,000,000 or over	2200.6	(166.3)	[omitted]	-2.3	107.1	4,051
Top 1% of wealth	5335.4	(500.9)	—	109.6	322.1#	2,296

C. Race						
Non-Hispanic whites	499.7	(35.4)	[omitted]	55.4	56.2	9,401
Non-Hispanic African Americans	271.7	(13.1)	6.30**	-12.4	14.7	432
Hispanics[a]	350.9	(24.1)	2.25*	-92.7	6.9#	166
Asian and other races	566.9	(47.1)	-1.02	43.8	81.3	226
D. Age Class[b]						
Under 35	177.5	(9.5)	8.91**	-8.9	1.1	917
35–44	321.0	(20.8)	5.75**	26.6	-27.3	1,466
45–54	506.3	(50.4)	3.09**	115.3	4.1	2,223
55–64	501.8	(40.1)	2.54*	80.5	-27.1	2,579
65–74	594.7	(48.2)	1.91#	-34.6	86.0	1,892
75 & over	790.2	(75.7)	[omitted]	116.8	31.1	1,148
E. Education[b]						
Less than 12 years	237.5	(9.1)	9.22**	-24.7	0.6	705
12 years	328.4	(23.6)	7.83**	68.0	51.5*	1,876
13–15 years	364.7	(25.0)	6.56**	35.9	-31.3	1,892
16 years or more	737.3	(59.0)	[omitted]	8.0	79.1	5,752

Source: Author's computations from the 1989, 1992, 1995, 1998, 2001, 2004, 2007, 2010, and 2013 Survey of Consumer Finances. Each year is given equal weight. The figures are only for households that indicated receiving a wealth transfer up to the time of the survey and are accumulated at a real interest rate of 3 percent.

a. Hispanics can be of any race.

b. Households are classified according to the age and education of the head of household.

c. The time trend coefficient is estimated from a pooled sample from years 1989, 1992, 1995, 1998, 2001, 2004, 2007, 2010, and 2013. The regression uses a constant and time trend as independent variables.

Significance levels: # 10%; * 5%; ** 1%.

Table 7.5. Median value of wealth transfers, recipients only, 1989–2013 (figures are in thousands, 2013 dollars)

Category	Period Average	(Std. err.)	Two-tailed z-test with Respect to Omitted Category[c]	% Change, 1989–2013	Two-tailed z-test 1989 = 2013[c]	Pooled Sample Size
All households	88.6	7.4	2.61**	35.5		10,225
A. Income Level (1998$)						
Under $15,000	62.3	15.8	2.99**	55.9	1.38	1,004
$15,000–$24,999	66.5	13.1	2.99**	21.0	0.99	907
$25,000–$49,999	80.8	11.8	2.86**	31.2	1.36	1,984
$50,000–$74,999	87.5	16.1	2.78**	38.0	0.99	1,326
$75,000–$99,999	108.4	27.8	2.56*	36.5	0.70	825
$100,000–$249,999	174.7	37.5	1.92#	14.7	0.38	1,654
$250,000 or more	397.1	106.6	[omitted]	13.4	0.25	2,526
B. Wealth Level (1998$)						
Under $25,000	24.6	4.2	5.22**	29.2	0.95	1,193
$25,000–$49,999	50.1	10.9	4.90**	43.3	1.18	519
$50,000–$99,999	63.7	15.0	4.70**	27.6	0.51	749
$100,000–$249,999	88.7	12.5	4.44**	105.3	3.21**	1,400
$250,000–$499,999	138.9	22.5	3.76**	66.4	1.87#	1,195
$500,000–$999,999	230.7	38.2	2.55*	−28.9	−0.93	1,117
$1,000,000 or over	477.0	84.1	[omitted]	20.1	0.63	4,051
Top 1% of wealth	986.0	252.5	—	−46.0	−1.14	2,296

C. Race

Non-Hispanic whites	91.7	8.1	[omitted]	2.43*	9,401
Non-Hispanic African Americans	72.4	21.5	-0.84	2.89**	432
Hispanics[a]	56.3	33.1	1.04	0.66	166
Asian and other races	101.5	56.7	-0.17	0.58	226

D. Age Class[b]

Under 35	35.5	8.7	2.87**	0.55	917
35–44	55.5	11.2	2.38*	0.09	1,466
45–54	87.5	14.0	1.52	0.83	2,223
55–64	114.5	16.9	0.82	1.62	2,579
65–74	138.3	21.6	0.22	2.05*	1,892
75 & over	147.5	36.9	[omitted]	1.07	1,148

E. Education[b]

Less than 12 years	54.6	17.7	3.21**	-0.09	705
12 years	66.3	9.0	3.61**	2.52*	1,876
13–15 years	83.5	11.3	2.51*	0.24	1,892
16 years or more	135.3	17.3	[omitted]	1.81#	5,752

Source: Author's computations from the 1989, 1992, 1995, 1998, 2001, 2004, 2007, 2010, and 2013 Survey of Consumer Finances. Each year is given equal weight. The figures are only for households that indicated receiving a wealth transfer up to the time of the survey and are accumulated at a real interest rate of 3 percent.

a. Hispanics can be of any race.

b. Households are classified according to the age and education of the head of household.

c. Significance levels: # 10%; * 5%; ** 1%.

Table 7.6. Mean value of wealth transfers, all households in group, 1989–2013 (figures are in thousands, 2013 dollars)

Category	Period Average	(Std. err.)	Two-tailed z-test with Respect to Omitted Category[c]	% Change, 1989–2013	Time Trend Coefficient[c]	Pooled Sample Size
All households	102.3	(24.3)		19.9	12.7	41,529
A. Income Level (1998$)						
Under $15,000	23.1	(14.7)	7.65**	41.0	13.9*	6,895
$15,000–$24,999	56.7	(7.3)	7.68**	−14.2	1.5*	5,220
$25,000–$49,999	52.3	(11.4)	7.58**	5.8	2.4	9,579
$50,000–$74,999	67.5	(17.5)	7.44**	44.6	−2.3	5,439
$75,000–$99,999	179.9	(24.9)	7.08**	−15.1	−11.1*	2,859
$100,000–$249,999	301.7	(42.8)	6.45**	43.9	−7.3	4,837
$250,000 or more	1855.1	(437.1)	[omitted]	−36.9	34.7	6,700
B. Wealth Level (1998$)						
Under $25,000	7.9	(1.4)	12.42**	38.5	0.4	13,183
$25,000–$49,999	25.5	(4.5)	12.14**	−5.3	0.7	2,623
$50,000–$99,999	24.2	(5.9)	11.99**	22.8	1.5#	3,612
$100,000–$249,999	60.1	(8.7)	11.70**	8.8	2.9*	5,399
$250,000–$499,999	113.7	(23.2)	10.97**	6.3	8.1#	3,756
$500,000–$999,999	278.7	(42.8)	8.07**	9.3	−7.0	2,942
$1,000,000 or over	1176.4	(217.9)	[omitted]	−2.7	13.2	10,014
Top 1% of wealth	1587.7	(633.9)	—	73.7	88.2	5,766

C. Race

Non-Hispanic whites	110.5	(29.7)	[omitted]	50.1	11.2	32,566
Non-Hispanic African Americans	19.7	(6.3)	8.24**	-12.3	1.9	4,352
Hispanics[a]	110.3	(7.1)	8.77**	-92.4	0.3	2,942
Asian and other races	53.2	(25.0)	5.70**	20.4	1.4	1,668

D. Age Class[b]

Under 35	34.5	(4.8)	7.65**	-26.5	-1.5	7,553
35–44	55.9	(12.8)	6.03**	4.5	-9.2*	8,198
45–54	71.4	(37.3)	3.75**	79.0	-8.1	9,223
55–64	82.6	(36.8)	2.13*	90.3	11.9	7,734
65–74	343.9	(48.1)	0.99	-35.2	25.4	5,226
75 & over	149.0	(70.7)	[omitted]	51.1	98.3	3,594

E. Education[b]

Less than 12 years	39.5	(5.1)	8.72**	0.0	-0.5	5,523
12 years	37.2	(15.6)	7.58**	59.6	8.9*	10,288
13–15 years	68.4	(18.2)	6.50**	26.8	-12.2#	8,449
16 years or more	277.6	(54.4)	[omitted]	-12.5	10.9	17,269

Note: author's computations from the 1989, 1992, 1995, 1998, 2001, 2004, 2007, 2010, and 2013 Survey of Consumer Finances. Each year is given equal weight. The figures show the present value of all transfers as of the survey year that were received up to the time of the survey and accumulated at a real interest rate of 3 percent.
a. Hispanics can be of any race.
b. Households are classified according to the age and education of the head of household.
c. The time trend coefficient is estimated from a pooled sample from years 1989, 1992, 1995, 1998, 2001, 2004, 2007, 2010, and 2013. The regression uses a constant and time trend as independent variables.
Significance levels: # 10%; * 5%; ** 1%.

Table 7.7. Wealth transfers as a percentage of net worth, 1989–2013

Category	Period Average	(Std. Err.)	Two-tailed z-test with Respect to Omitted Category	Change, 1989–2013	Time Trend Coefficient[c]	Pooled Sample Size
All households	23.4	(4.4)		−4.8	−0.72	41,529
A. Income Level (1998$)						
Under $15,000	65.8	(8.7)	4.50**	−8.1	3.32**	6,895
$15,000–$24,999	38.0	(8.0)	2.59	7.5	0.87	5,220
$25,000–$49,999	34.0	(4.2)	2.43**	6.2	1.39#	9,579
$50,000–$74,999	24.8	(4.0)	1.83	4.6	0.55	5,439
$75,000–$99,999	25.6	(1.7)	2.92**	−9.8	−1.07	2,859
$100,000–$249,999	19.1	(1.3)	1.03	8.9	−0.73**	4,837
$250,000 or more	16.6	(2.0)	[omitted]	−18.2	−0.67**	6,700
B. Wealth Level (1998$)						
Under $25,000	—	—	—	—	—	13,183
$25,000–$49,999	51.7	(4.0)	6.57**	−2.0	0.19	2,623
$50,000–$99,999	35.5	(2.1)	6.67**	5.0	0.59	3,612
$100,000–$249,999	28.6	(1.7)	3.64**	2.0	0.51	5,399
$250,000–$499,999	25.9	(1.5)	2.59**	0.9	0.37	3,756
$500,000–$999,999	31.1	(1.7)	6.61**	1.7	−1.63**	2,942
$1,000,000 or over	18.8	(1.3)	[omitted]	−3.1	−0.59**	10,014
Top 1% of wealth	16.9	(1.5)	—	−7.9	1.05**	5,766

C. Race

Non-Hispanic whites	23.7	(4.8)	[omitted]	-0.1	0.8*	32,566
Non-Hispanic African Americans	33.1	(5.3)	1.31	-6.4	1.15	4,352
Hispanics[a]	20.6	(2.0)	-0.58	-124.2	0.22	2,942
Asian and other races	16.2	(6.5)	0.92	-4.0	1.23	1,668

D. Age Class[b]

Under 35	30.4	(5.7)	1.23	4.3	0.03	7,553
35–44	19.8	(3.9)	1.82#	-8.5	1.49*	8,198
45–54	20.4	(4.1)	2.01*	11.8	1.11	9,223
55–64	17.8	(5.1)	2.06*	7.1	1.34	7,734
65–74	25.8	(8.7)	1.42	-36.6	0.02	5,226
75 & over	42.0	(7.5)	[omitted]	8.0	-0.04	3,594

E. Education[b]

Less than 12 years	25.9	(7.1)	-0.31	-7.8	1.73#	5,523
12 years	28.0	(5.2)	0.77	15.9	2.11**	10,288
13–15 years	25.0	(7.1)	-0.18	10.1	1.16	8,449
16 years or more	23.6	(2.6)	[omitted]	-13.9	-0.53#	17,269

Source: Author's computations from the 1989, 1992, 1995, 1998, 2001, 2004, 2007, 2010, and 2013 Survey of Consumer Finances. Each year is given equal weight. The figures show the present value of all transfers as of the survey year that were received up to the time of the survey and accumulated at a real interest rate of 3 percent as a share of current net worth.

a. Hispanics can be of any race.

b. Households are classified according to the age and education of the head of household.

c. The time trend coefficient is estimated from a pooled sample from years 1989, 1992, 1995, 1998, 2001, 2004, 2007, and 2010. The regression uses a constant and time trend as independent variables.

Significance levels: # 10%; * 5%; ** 1%.

wealth class, wealth transfers as a share of household net worth monotoni-cally *declines* with both income and wealth (with one exception in each case). On average, wealth transfers amounted to 66 percent of the net worth of the lowest income class and only 17 percent for the highest income class and 52 percent of the wealth of the second lowest wealth class,[37] compared to 19 percent for the top wealth class and 17 percent for the top one percent.[38] The rationale for the results is as follows: while the dollar value of wealth transfers is greater for wealthier groups, small gifts and bequests comprise a higher *share* of the net worth of poorer families. This relation supports the finding that wealth transfers tend to *lower* wealth inequality.

The inverse relation between the ratio of transfers to net worth and both income and wealth level generally became more pronounced over years 1989 to 2013. While the ratio increased by 7.5 percentage points for the second income class, it fell by 18.2 percentage points for the top. Likewise, while the ratio was down by 2 percentage points for the second wealth class, it dropped by 8 percentage points for the top 1 percent.[39]

It is also of note that wealth transfers amounted to a greater proportion of the wealth of black households than of white households in 1998 (33 versus 24 percent on average). Wealth transfers also made up a smaller share of the wealth holdings of Hispanics and Asian Americans. However, the share is not statistically different between whites and the other three groups. This share declined over time among all four groups.[40]

Though the total value of wealth transfers tends to rise with age, transfers as a share of wealth has a U-shaped pattern. The share is high for young households because of their low savings, and for older households because of the high absolute value of such transfers. It is low for middle-aged households, because of the relatively small amount of wealth transfers that they have received and because of their large savings. The shares are statisti-cally different between the oldest age group and the three middle age groups. This pattern remains fairly robust over time.[41]

The ratio of wealth transfers to net worth is relatively constant across educational groups. The shares are not statistically different between the highest educational group and the other three educational groups. How-ever, this pattern is not very robust over time, with considerable year-to-year fluctuation.[42]

The Inequality of Wealth Transfers and the Overall Inequality of Wealth

I next look at whether the inequality of wealth transfers themselves changed over time. Table 7.8 (Panels I and II) uses two different measures of inequality, the Gini coefficient and the coefficient of variation (CV). The Gini coefficient of wealth transfers among all households is incredibly high, 0.96 on average over the nine survey years. Even limiting the sample to recipients alone lowers the Gini coefficient to only 0.82 on average. This compares to an average Gini coefficient for net worth of 0.83. Likewise, the average CV of wealth transfers over the nine years is 19.5 among all households and 8.1 among recipient households only, in comparison to a value of 6.4 for net worth. Overall, there is no clear indication that the inequality of wealth transfers had any notable upward or downward time trend between 1989 and 2013 (the pattern is very irregular over time).

It is beyond the scope of this chapter to fully simulate the effects of eliminating wealth transfers on the size distribution of wealth. Such an exercise would require a full behavioral model of household savings, and, in particular, a fully estimated response function of savings to the receipt of a wealth transfer. It would also be necessary to estimate this response function for different income and wealth classes and for different demographic groups.

A full model would be extremely complicated. First, in a world without transfers, the savings behavior of those potentially leaving inheritances would be affected. This is especially so if a family is accumulating wealth in order to give a gift or leave an inheritance to heirs. If such wealth transfers are no longer allowed, a family is likely to accumulate less wealth. Second, household savings would also respond to *anticipated* wealth transfers. In particular, a household that expects to receive an inheritance or gift is likely to save less, ceteris paribus. This effect should be much weaker than actually receiving a wealth transfer. In the case of an inheritance, it is uncertain when the parent will die. It is also unclear how much wealth will be left in the benefactor's estate, especially if he or she must pay for medical expenses and personal care in old age. And a benefactor's intent is rarely known in regard to how the estate will be split among possible heirs.

Table 7.8. Inequality of wealth transfers, 1989–2013

Category	1989	1992	1995	1998	2001	2004	2007	2010	2013	Unweighted Average, 1989–2013
I. Gini Coefficient										
A. Wealth transfers: all households	0.959	0.968	0.967	0.959	0.962	0.968	0.961	0.966	0.960	0.963
B. Wealth transfers: recipients only	0.824	0.843	0.844	0.799	0.787	0.840	0.814	0.833	0.814	0.822
C. Net worth	0.828	0.823	0.828	0.822	0.826	0.829	0.834	0.866	0.871	0.847
II. Coefficient of Variation										
A. Wealth transfers: all households	13.3	23.4	21.8	22.5	9.9	37.1	11.8	19.9	15.7	19.5
B. Wealth transfers: recipients only	6.0	10.5	9.7	9.4	4.1	11.8	5.2	8.9	7.2	8.1
C. Net worth	6.6	6.4	7.0	6.6	5.4	6.2	6.2	6.6	7.0	6.4
III. Coefficient of Variation Decomposition										
A. Coefficient of Variation										
1) NW	6.6	6.4	7.0	6.6	5.4	6.2	6.2	6.6	7.0	6.4
2) NWX	9.1	13.0	12.8	9.1	6.4	13.4	7.6	10.5	9.8	10.2
3) WT	13.3	23.4	21.8	22.5	9.9	37.1	11.8	19.9	15.7	19.5

B. Decomposition of CV²(NW)

1) $\bar{p}_1^2$ CV²(NWX)	45.5	80.5	77.3	54.2	29.1	104.7	37.9	60.9	55.0	60.6
2) $\bar{p}_2^2$ CV²(WT)	12.0	52.9	46.9	18.9	2.3	76.1	4.9	25.7	14.3	28.2
3) 2CC(NWX,WT)	−14.2	−92.6	−75.9	−29.9	−1.8	−142.6	−4.6	−42.8	−20.1	−47.2
4) CV²(NW)	43.3	40.8	48.4	43.2	29.6	38.1	38.2	43.8	49.1	41.6
Memo: Correl(NWX,WT)	−0.30	−0.71	−0.63	−0.47	−0.11	−0.80	−0.17	−0.54	−0.36	−0.45

C. Percentage Decomposition of CV²(NW)

1) $\bar{p}_1^2$ CV²(NWX)	105.1	197.4	159.8	125.4	98.5	274.6	99.2	139.0	111.9	145.7
2) $\bar{p}_2^2$ CV²(WT)	27.6	129.8	97.1	43.7	7.7	199.6	12.8	58.8	29.1	67.3
3) 2CC(NWX,WT)	−32.7	−227.2	−156.9	−69.1	−6.2	−374.2	−12.0	−97.8	−41.0	−113.0
4) CV²(NW)	100.0	100.0	100.0	100.0	100.0	100.0	100.0	100.0	100.0	100.0

IV. Gini Decomposition

1) Gini (NWX)	1.153	1.297	1.330	1.017	0.972	1.122	1.019	1.214	1.148	1.141
2) Percentage difference between Gini (NW) and Gini (NWX)	−28.2	−36.6	−37.7	−19.1	−15.0	−26.1	−18.2	−28.7	−24.2	−26.0

Source: Author's computations from the 1989, 1992, 1995, 1998, 2001, 2004, 2007, 2010, and 2013 Survey of Consumer Finances.

Abbreviations: CC, coefficient of covariation; CV, coefficient of variation; NW, total net worth (NWX + WT); NWX, total net worth excluding wealth transfers; WT, wealth transfers.

$p_1 = E(\text{NWX})/E(\text{NW})$; $p_2 = E(\text{WT})/E(\text{NW})$

I address the question by using two decomposition analyses, implicitly assuming in both cases that savings do not respond to wealth transfers.[43] The first is based on the coefficient of variation. For any variable $X = X_1 + X_2$,

$$CV^2(X) = p_1{}^2 CV^2(X_1) + p_2{}^2 CV^2(X_2) + 2CC(X_1, X_2),$$

where CV is the coefficient of variation (the ratio of the standard deviation to the mean), CC is the coefficient of covariation, defined as $COV(X_1, X_2) / E(X)^2$, $p_1 = E(X_1) / E(X)$, and $p_2 = E(X_2) / E(X)$. In this case, X equals net worth (NW), X_1 equals net worth minus transfers (NWX) and X_2 equals wealth transfers (WT). Results are shown in Panel III of Table 7.8.

It is of interest that the correlation between wealth transfers (WT) and current wealth excluding transfers (NWX) is negative in all nine years. This result indicates that on average households with lower wealth excluding transfers receive higher wealth transfers. The value of the correlation coefficient varies over time, but not in a way that suggests any particular time trend. For 1998, the value is –0.47. For 2001 and 2007, the correlation is quite low in absolute value (–0.11 and –0.17, respectively) but for 2004 it is at its highest point, –0.80. The average correlation over the nine years is –0.45.

In all nine years, the (negative) correlation between WT and NWX serves to reduce overall wealth inequality (the third line in Table 7.8, Panels B and C). The distribution of wealth transfers WT is much more skewed than the distribution of NWX. This is true for all nine years. For 1998, for example, CV(NWX) is 9.1, compared to 22.5 for CV(WT). The average value of CV(NWX) over the nine years is 10.2, compared to an average value of 19.5 for CV(WT).

Empirically, it does turn out that CV(NW) is less than CV(NWX) in every year. In 1998, CV(NWX) is 9.1, while CV(NW) is 6.6. Thus, adding wealth transfers to NWX results in a 28 percent reduction of wealth inequality in that year. The CV also declines by 28 percent in 1989, 51 percent in 1992, and 46 percent in 1995. The percentage decline is 15 percent in 2001, 54 percent in 2004, 18 percent in 2007, 37 percent in 2010, and 28 percent in 2013. On average, the CV declines by 37 percent. From this standpoint, the net effect of wealth transfers is to equalize the overall distribution of wealth.

The second decomposition is based on the Gini coefficient. In this case, I look at how much the Gini coefficient for NWX changes when WT is added to create NW. As shown in Panel IV, the Gini index declines by on average of 26 percent over the nine years. Percentage changes are negative in all nine years and vary from a low of −15 percent in 2001 to a high of −38 percent in 1995. Once again, the net effect of adding wealth transfers to wealth excluding transfers (NWS) is to equalize the overall distribution of wealth.

In this decomposition it is assumed that the saving behavior of the donors and that of those receiving transfers is not affected. Let us consider gifts and inheritances separately. For gifts, while wealth is measured post-transfer, we do not have information on who in the sample provided the gifts to a particular household. However, gifts invariably flow from a more wealthy to a less wealthy household, as the vast majority of such transfers are from an older (and likely richer) to a younger (and likely poorer) person—in particular, from parent to child. Such inter vivos transfers will very likely reduce measured wealth inequality.

With inheritances, the key point is that, unlike with gifts, we no longer observe the wealth of the donor in the sample since the donor is no longer alive. In other words, with death, one observation in the sample disappears, while with gifts both observations remain. We saw earlier that wealth transfers are greater in absolute terms for richer households than for poorer ones, yet they raise the wealth of poorer households by a *greater percentage* than that of the rich. This effectively raises the share of wealth of the poor more than that of the rich, thus lowering wealth inequality.

Recent Wealth Transfers

Another cut of the data is provided in Table 7.9. Here I look at wealth transfers received in the five and ten years preceding the survey year.[44] These figures are likely to be more reliable than those on wealth transfers received over the whole lifetime, since recall is better for more recent events. There is a lot of bouncing around from year to year in the share of households reporting a wealth transfer over the prior five years, from 7.7 percent in 1989 to 4.6 percent in 2010 and then up to 7.8 percent in 2013 (line 1), as well as over the prior ten years, from 12.1 in 1989 to 10.2 percent in 2010 and then up to 12.6 percent in 2013 (line 4). The time trend coefficient is negative and significant at the 1 percent level in the case of the former. The effect of the Great Recession is particularly notable (2007–2010), with a sharp drop in the recipiency rate over the previous five years.

Table 7.9. Time trends in recent wealth transfers among all households, 1989–2013 (figures are in thousands, 2013 dollars)

Variable	1989	1992	1995	1998	2001	2004	2007	2010	2013	Unweighted Average, 1989–2013	Two-tailed z-test 1989=2013?	Time Trend Coefficient[a]
1. Percent of households reporting a transfer in the previous five years	7.7 (0.41)	7.6 (0.40)	6.2 (0.36)	8.1 (0.41)	6.9 (0.37)	7.5 (0.38)	8.4 (0.40)	4.6 (0.30)	7.8 (0.38)	7.2	0.15	−0.126**
2. Mean value of transfers received over previous five years, recipients only	202.3 (35.3)	147.5 (17.4)	228.0 (100.9)	153.3 (19.2)	148.2 (13.9)	218.0 (26.5)	185.7 (17.2)	171.7 (14.9)	198.3 (18.5)	183.7	−0.10	−1.43
3. Mean value of transfers received over previous five years, all households	15.6 (5.2)	11.2 (2.6)	14.2 (12.6)	12.4 (3.0)	10.2 (1.9)	16.3 (3.9)	15.6 (2.8)	7.9 (1.6)	15.6 (2.9)	13.2	0.00	−0.70
4. Percent of households reporting a transfer in the previous ten years	12.1 (0.93)	13.1 (0.58)	12.2 (0.64)	12.3 (0.80)	11.1 (0.61)	11.5 (0.68)	13.3 (0.57)	10.2 (0.39)	12.6 (0.47)	12.0	0.39	

5. Mean value of transfers received over previous ten years, all households	25.4 (5.6)	22.5 (2.9)	25.2 (15.4)	22.3 (3.4)	20.4 (2.6)	32.7 (5.4)	31.8 (3.4)	21.3 (1.9)	28.4 (3.7)	25.6	0.45
6. Mean value of gifts only received over previous five years, all households	0.39 (0.05)	0.12 (0.37)	0.82 (0.34)	1.41 (1.28)	0.65 (0.70)	1.58 (0.22)	2.04 (0.36)	1.34 (0.70)	1.43 (0.46)	1.09	2.02*
7. Mean value of gifts given, over preceding year, all households	1.00 (0.08)	0.88 (0.12)	0.96 (0.10)	0.89 (0.13)	1.24 (0.14)	1.33 (0.15)	1.67 (0.94)	1.33 (0.14)	1.39 (0.22)	1.19	1.69#
8. Mean value of donations made over preceding year, all households	1.62 (0.26)	1.28 (0.90)	1.32 (0.36)	1.57 (0.37)	2.23 (0.49)	1.95 (0.48)	2.01 (0.43)	1.73 (0.49)	1.89 (0.47)	1.73	0.20
Sample size	3,143	3,906	4,299	4,305	4,442	4,519	4,418	6,482	6,015		41,529

Source: Author's computations from the 1989, 1992, 1995, 1998, 2001, 2004, 2007, 2010, and 2013 Survey of Consumer Finances. In the 2007 SCF data, the prior five years would be for the period 2003–2007. The prior ten years would be the period 1998–2007.

Standard errors are shown in parentheses.

a. The time trend coefficient is estimated from a pooled sample from years 1989, 1992, 1995, 1998, 2001, 2004, 2007, 2010, and 2013. The regression uses a constant and time trend as independent variables.

Significance levels: # 10%; * 5%; ** 1%.

There is not much trend in the mean value of transfers received over the previous five years among recipients alone (line 2), or of the mean value of transfers among all households received in the preceding five or ten years (lines 3 and 5). Once again, the effect of the Great Recession is evident, with a steep fall-off in mean values over both the previous five and the previous ten years.

Line 6 shows the mean value of inter vivos gifts received over the previous five years only as recorded by the recipient. On average, only 15 percent of wealth transfers took the form of gifts (the remainder being mainly inheritances). In this case, despite a sharp drop over the Great Recession there is a statistically significant (at the 5 percent level) upward trend in gifts between 1989 and 2013.

Lines 7 and 8 show results from the donor side.[45] It is at once apparent that there is an enormous discrepancy between the donor and recipient sides— more than fivefold on an *annualized* basis ($1,190 versus $210, on average, in 2013 dollars). In theory, the two figures should be approximately equal.[46] It is likely that the donor side is more reliable since it is easier to recall gifts that are made than received. Moreover, because of Internal Revenue Service limitations on gift giving, record keeping is probably better on the donor side than the recipient side.[47] In any case, even on the donor side the value of gifts given is fairly trivial—representing about 0.3 percent of household wealth on average. The time pattern for gifts given, however, is very similar to gifts received, with a big drop-off between 2007 and 2010 and a slight recovery in 2013.

Donations made to charities show a similar time pattern as gifts made, with a large decline from 2007 to 2010 and a modest rebound in 2013. On average, donations were 46 percent larger than gifts given.[48]

Table 7.10 presents summary statistics on the share of households that received a wealth transfer over the preceding five years by income, wealth, and demographic group. It should be noted that the data, in principle, overlap between consecutive observations, since there are three years that separate the observations, whereas the wealth transfers cover the preceding five years. The pattern of results is generally similar to that for the recipiency rate of wealth transfers over the lifetime. As in Table 7.3, the recipiency rate rises strongly with income and wealth level. On average over the nine years, 13 percent of households in the highest income bracket reported a wealth transfer over the last five years, compared to 4 percent in the lowest income bracket; and 16 percent in the highest wealth bracket compared to 4 percent in the lowest wealth bracket. The proportion of white households reporting a wealth transfer was on average more than twice as great as the share of African Americans (8.6 versus 3.5 percent) and Hispanics (2.2 percent), and about twice as great as the share of Asians (4.4 percent).

In contrast to Table 7.3, the likelihood of receiving a wealth transfer over the preceding five years has an inverted U-shaped pattern, rising from 6.4 percent on average for the youngest age bracket to 9.7 percent for age bracket 55–64, and then falling off to 5 percent for the oldest age group. This pattern mainly reflects the life expectancies of the parental generation. The period of peak inheritance is between ages 55 and 64. The likelihood of receiving a wealth transfer in the preceding five years also rises with education—from 3.3 percent for those with less than four years of high school to 10.8 percent for college graduates. This result is consistent with the patterns found by income class.[49]

The third column of Table 7.10 shows results on the mean value of transfers received over the last five years among recipients only and the fifth column shows these results for all households. Once again, the pattern of results is generally similar to those for the mean value of transfers received over the lifetime by recipients only (see Table 7.4) and by all households in the group (see Table 7.5).

The mean value tends to rise with household income in both cases, and there is a huge jump at the highest income class. On average, the mean wealth transfers among recipients in the top income class was 7 times greater than that for the lowest, and mean transfers among all households was 21 times greater. Wealth transfers increase monotonically with wealth, and there is a big jump at the top 1 percent. On average, mean wealth transfers among recipients in the highest wealth class was 15 times greater than that for the lowest, and the mean value among all households was 68 times greater. Transfers are also higher for whites than for African Americans. On average, the ratio of means among recipients between the two groups was 1.9, and the ratio among all households in the two groups was 4.5. Asians ranked second and Hispanics last in terms of mean wealth transfers among all households.

Similar to the pattern for the recipiency rate, wealth transfers rise with age from the lowest age group to age group 45–54 and then decline. The mean value of wealth transfers also rises with education and was particularly high for college graduates. On average, the mean value among recipients was 2.9 times greater for college graduates as for high school graduates; among all households, the ratio was 5.2.[50]

Table 7.10. Average wealth transfers received over previous five years and gifts and donations given by group, 1989–2013 (period averages)

Category	Percent of Households Receiving Transfer[a]	(Std. Err.)	Mean Value of Transfers, Recipients Only[b]	(Std. Err.)	Mean Value of Transfers, All HHs in Group[b]	(Std. Err.)	Mean Value of Gifts Made, All HHs in Group[b]	(Std. Err.)	Mean Value of Donations Made, All HHs in Group[b]	(Std. Err.)	Mean Net Wealth Transfers, Aligned, All HHs in Group[b,c]
All Households	7.2	(0.38)	183.7	(29.3)	13.2	(4.0)	1.2	(0.22)	1.7	(0.47)	15.2
A. Income Level (1998$)											
Under $15,000	4.4	(0.44)	102.5	(15.2)	4.7	(1.6)	0.3	(0.06)	0.2	(0.06)	6.0
$15,000–$24,999	5.6	(0.53)	93.6	(9.0)	5.1	(1.1)	0.4	(0.05)	0.4	(0.04)	6.2
$25,000–$49,999	7.0	(0.51)	111.2	(9.2)	7.8	(1.4)	0.7	(0.07)	0.8	(0.05)	9.2
$50,000–$74,999	8.5	(0.65)	267.4	(64.2)	18.9	(8.1)	1.1	(0.12)	1.6	(0.08)	22.8
$75,000–$99,999	10.2	(0.86)	166.3	(13.3)	17.2	(2.8)	1.9	(0.22)	2.3	(0.14)	19.2
$100,000–$249,999	12.4	(0.91)	330.4	(41.2)	41.3	(9.3)	3.4	(0.38)	4.5	(0.36)	48.7
$250,000 or more	13.4	(1.36)	751.7	(205.0)	97.8	(44.0)	13.8	(3.42)	32.4	(9.68)	87.6
B. Wealth Level (1998$)											
Under $25,000	3.6	(0.35)	41.0	(8.8)	1.4	(0.7)	0.3	(0.03)	0.3	(0.02)	1.3
$25,000–$49,999	6.7	(0.67)	59.7	(5.2)	3.7	(0.7)	0.5	(0.07)	0.6	(0.05)	3.0
$50,000–$99,999	6.3	(0.60)	71.1	(5.9)	4.6	(0.9)	0.7	(0.08)	0.9	(0.06)	4.8
$100,000–$249,999	8.9	(0.64)	93.1	(5.8)	8.4	(1.1)	0.9	(0.10)	1.3	(0.07)	9.1
$250,000–$499,999	10.9	(0.82)	167.3	(11.2)	18.3	(2.5)	1.5	(0.17)	2.2	(0.11)	21.1
$500,000–$999,999	14.2	(1.04)	468.7	(94.5)	61.4	(20.1)	2.5	(0.28)	3.1	(0.21)	76.0
$1,000,000 or over	16.2	(1.14)	602.8	(92.1)	98.2	(24.8)	8.4	(1.74)	15.5	(4.42)	110.4
Top 1% of wealth	16.9	(1.70)	1319.3	(249.8)	212.6	(67.3)	20.6	(6.06)	48.3	(14.5)	221.1

C. *Race*

Non-Hispanic whites	8.6	(0.44)	192.6	(31.6)	16.4	(4.9)	1.3	(0.28)	2.1	(0.59)	19.0
Non-Hispanic African Americans	3.5	(0.45)	101.7	(19.7)	3.6	(1.8)	0.7	(0.10)	0.8	(0.12)	3.3
Hispanics[a]	2.2	(0.40)	115.3	(13.0)	2.3	(0.8)	0.6	(0.07)	0.4	(0.06)	2.1
Asian and other races	4.4	(0.67)	184.4	(27.4)	8.4	(3.1)	1.5	(0.22)	1.1	(0.39)	9.2

D. *Age Class*[b]

Under 35	6.4	(0.52)	111.1	(13.9)	7.1	(1.9)	0.4	(0.05)	0.5	(0.05)	8.8
35–44	6.8	(0.54)	163.7	(34.1)	11.2	(4.7)	0.6	(0.09)	1.3	(0.26)	13.3
45–54	7.7	(0.59)	263.5	(59.4)	19.8	(8.5)	1.5	(0.17)	2.1	(0.70)	23.2
55–64	9.7	(0.70)	201.8	(28.0)	19.6	(5.1)	1.9	(0.27)	2.6	(0.58)	22.7
65–74	7.4	(0.65)	204.1	(36.3)	15.1	(4.7)	2.0	(0.39)	2.8	(1.21)	15.9
75 & over	5.0	(0.56)	137.7	(22.6)	7.2	(2.8)	1.6	(0.83)	2.3	(0.98)	5.9

E. *Education*[b]

Less than 12 years	3.3	(0.40)	74.9	(11.2)	2.7	(1.0)	0.5	(0.07)	0.3	(0.05)	2.8
12 years	6.0	(0.47)	95.9	(12.3)	5.7	(1.6)	0.7	(0.09)	0.8	(0.22)	6.4
13–15 years	7.4	(0.55)	142.9	(18.7)	10.8	(2.8)	0.9	(0.13)	1.2	(0.27)	12.6
16 years or more	10.8	(0.62)	275.2	(51.1)	29.5	(9.7)	2.3	(0.51)	4.0	(1.11)	33.9

Source: Author's computations from the 1989, 1992, 1995, 1998, 2001, 2004, and 2007 Survey of Consumer Finances (SCF). Each year is given equal weight. Pooled sample sizes are given in Table 7.6.

a. Hispanics can be of any race.

b. Households are classified according to the age and education of the head of household.

c. Net wealth transfers equal total wealth transfers received over the last five years minus gifts and donations given on a five-year basis. Total gifts received are set equal to total gifts given and individual entries in the SCF microdata are proportionately adjusted.

The seventh column shows the mean value of gifts made in the preceding year from the donor side and the ninth column shows the mean value of donations made. The pattern is very similar to that of column 5, with the exception of the breakdown by age group. There is again a monotonic rise in both gifts and donations made, with an immense jump at the top income and wealth classes. Gifts and donations were about twice as large for whites as for blacks, though Asians made the largest gifts (and Hispanics the smallest). Gifts and donations increased with age, peaked at age group 65–74, and then fell off. Both increased with educational level, with a substantial leap for college graduates.

The last column shows mean *net* wealth transfers by socioeconomic group. Net wealth transfers over the last five years is equal to total wealth transfers received over these years minus annual gifts and donations given converted to a five-year basis. Net wealth transfers are then adjusted so that total gifts received is equal to total gifts given for the full population, which is probably the more reliable of the two variables. The ratio between the two is then used to proportionately adjust gifts received in the SCF microdata.

The pattern of results is, not surprisingly, very similar to that for total wealth transfers received because both gifts and donations given are very small in comparison to wealth transfers received. On average, the mean net wealth transfers in the top income class was 15 times greater than for that for the lowest, compared to a ratio of 21 for (gross) wealth transfers received. Average mean net wealth transfers for the highest wealth class was 83 times greater than for the lowest, compared to a ratio of 68 for wealth transfers received. The ratio of mean net wealth transfers between black and white families was 5.8, compared to a ratio of 4.5 for gross wealth transfers. The ratio of mean net wealth transfers between college and high school graduates was 5.3, compared to a ratio of 5.2 for gross wealth transfers.

Summary and Concluding Remarks

About one-fifth of American households, on average, reported receiving a wealth transfer, and these transfers accounted for about a quarter of their total wealth. These figures are comparable to previous studies of wealth transfers in the United States. For the middle class, the figure is closer to one-third. Over an individual's lifetime, about 30 percent could expect to receive a wealth transfer. The mean value of these transfers would be about $149,000 (in 2013 dollars), which would account for about 42 percent of their net worth near time of death.

Have Wealth Transfers Become More Important over Time?

The evidence is largely (though not completely) negative in this regard. The share of households reporting a wealth transfer fell by 2.1 percentage points between 1989 and 2013, a time trend that is statistically significant. The mean and median value of wealth transfers among recipients alone climbed over the period, by 31 percent for the former and 36 percent for the latter. Both time trends are statistically significant. The average value of wealth transfers received among *all* households increased at a slower pace, by 20 percent, but in this case the trend is not statistically significant. Most notably, transfers as a proportion of net worth fell over this period from 29 to 24 percent, but the trend is not statistically significant.

The share of households reporting wealth transfers in the five years preceding the survey year was the same in 2013 as in 1989, but the time trend coefficient is negative and statistically significant at the 1 percent level. The average value of these recent transfers among recipients alone was slightly lower in 2013 than in 1989 and almost exactly the same in 2013 as in 1989 among all households. The bulk of the evidence suggests that there was no increase in the importance of wealth transfers between 1989 and 2013. Thus, despite the fact that the baby boom generation was reaching "prime" inheritance age (see Table 7.8) and the wealth of their parents was the highest in history for that age group, wealth transfers were actually less important in accounting for current net worth in 2013 than in 1989.

There are several possible explanations. First, life spans increased over these years. Since elderly people are living longer, the number of bequests per year declines. Indeed, wealthier people live longer than poorer ones and recent evidence indicates that the gap in life expectancy has also climbed in recent years. This trend would also lower the size of bequests received per year. One might, of course, think that as people live longer, they would be more inclined to give inter vivos gifts, particularly to their children. A greater volume of gifts might offset the decline in bequests per year. However, it is not likely that a greater value of gifts would fully compensate for a reduction in bequests in dollar terms, since gifts are much smaller in value than inheritances.

Second, since medical expenses rise with age, as people live longer less money is available to transfer to children at time of death. This might also be true for gifts. Indeed, end-of-life medical expenses among the very old may eat up a substantial share of their financial resources. Changes in Medicare co-payments and those from private health insurance policies might have exacerbated this trend. Third, the share of money left in estates for charitable contributions might have risen over time. This trend may have been particularly so for the rich.

Fourth, pensions have deteriorated over time, particularly with the discontinuation of many defined benefit pension plans, which means that older people may have less money to give away at time of death. Though defined benefit pensions are not directly inheritable, they provide income to their beneficiaries while they are alive, which results in more available resources to provide gifts. Defined contribution plans like 401(k)s have also deteriorated over time for many people, resulting in lower wealth at older ages.

Fifth, very low returns on safe financial assets like interest-bearing accounts and bonds may force older people to run down their principal because they are not able to live off the interest generated by these assets. Older people have a higher share of their assets in stocks and mutual funds than on average but they are generally more conservative in their investment strategies than younger people. Older people will accept lower rates of return in exchange for more security in their investments, which also results in relatively low wealth at time of death.

A counteracting effect may have come from the increasing spread in wealth between parent and child over time. It is likely that a parent will be more likely to transfer wealth and give a larger amount (either as a gift or in the form of a bequest) to his or her children if the gap in wealth between parent and child is greater. Since the wealth gap between older and younger households rose over time from 1989 to 2013, we would have expected that the rising wealth gap led to a rise in wealth transfers over this period, not a decline.

Have Wealth Transfers Led to Greater Wealth Inequality?

The answer to this question seems to be decidedly "no." Indeed, if anything, wealth transfers tend to have an equalizing effect on the distribution of household wealth. It is true that the share of households receiving a wealth transfer climbs sharply with both household income and wealth, as do the mean and median values of these transfers. However, transfers as a *share* of wealth decline almost monotonically with both income and wealth levels. As a result, net worth excluding wealth transfers is negatively correlated with wealth transfers themselves.

Indeed, it appears that the addition of wealth transfers to other sources of household wealth has a sizable effect on reducing wealth inequality. On the surface, this result appears to go against common wisdom. Richer households do receive greater inheritances and gifts in money terms than poorer ones. *As a proportion of their wealth holdings,* however, wealth transfers are greater for poorer households than richer ones. That is to say, a small gift to the poor means relatively more than a large gift to the rich.

Since wealth transfers and net worth excluding wealth transfers are negatively correlated, adding transfers to net worth reduces overall wealth inequality. Oddly enough, while wealth inequality in the United States remained largely unchanged between 1989 and 2007, it might have risen if not for the mitigating effects of inheritances and gifts. Moreover, wealth inequality spiked between 2007 and 2010, a period during which recent wealth transfers, particularly gifts, were notably down.

The finding that wealth transfers are equalizing at first appears to be counterintuitive, but further reflection suggests that this result may, in fact, be rather obvious. In the case of gifts, a transfer is typically made by a more wealthy to a less wealthy person, as the vast majority of such transfers are from an older (and typically richer) to a younger (and relatively poorer) person—in particular, from parent to child. Such inter vivos transfers will reduce wealth inequality. Inheritances are similar, generally flowing from a (richer) parent to a (poorer) child, though in this case the wealth of the decedent is no longer observed in the sample.

The result that wealth transfers are equalizing in terms of the distribution of wealth requires several qualifications. In particular, one has to be specific about the counterfactuals that are being assumed to reach this conclusion. Eliminating wealth transfers would affect the behavior of both donors and recipients. My implicit assumption in the decompositions reported in Table 7.8 is that if wealth transfers were eliminated, there would be no effect on the savings behavior of either the recipient or the donor.

The assumption that eliminating bequests would have a relatively small effect on the savings behavior of donors would not be unreasonable if the bequest motive was relatively weak. Consider the following scenario: Suppose the estate tax were to become confiscatory. What would happen to the savings behavior of those who intend to leave a bequest? There is prior work consistent with the assumption of a relatively small effect on saving behavior. For example, Dynan, Skinner, and Zeldes claim "that allowing for uncertainty resolves the controversy over the importance of life-cycle and bequest saving by showing that these motives for saving are overlapping and cannot generally be distinguished. A dollar saved today simultaneously serves both a precautionary life-cycle function, guarding against future contingencies such as health shocks or other emergencies, and a bequest function because—in the likely event that these contingencies do not absorb the dollar—it will be available to bequeath to children or other worthy causes."[51] In their model, if there is a confiscatory estate and gift tax, savings behavior would change very little for all but the very wealthy.

It may be of interest to consider the case of a country that did not allow bequests. All households except the rich (perhaps, the top 1 percent or even the top 0.1 percent) do *not* appear to have a strong bequest motive. Their main motivations for savings are for retirement and for precautionary reasons. What about the rich—would they accumulate less wealth even if bequests were not allowed?

One possibility is that the rich might spend down their wealth over their lifetimes. Of course, if this were the case then the inequality of wealth would be reduced to a (much) greater degree than it would be reduced by wealth transfers themselves. However, there are several reasons why such a response might not be the case. First, as a very wealthy person once confided to me, it is very difficult to spend more than a million dollars a year, except for "big ticket" items like yachts, art, jewelry, and the like. Ironically, if the money were spent on these items, they would enter the balance sheet of the household (they are already included in the category "other assets" in the SCF) and would not reduce the household's wealth.

Second, even with a confiscatory estate tax, it would still be possible for money to be passed on through trust funds. Third, even without a bequest motive, there are other purposes that may explain why the very rich will save

and accumulate vast amounts of wealth—charitable contributions, foundations, and, recently, political contributions.

And finally, social status, respect, and social prestige are associated with
high wealth. Large fortunes may enable an individual to keep his or her name
going, to achieve immortality. Consider, for example, the well-known phil-
anthropic organizations the Ford Foundation, the Sloan Foundation, the
Mellon Foundation, and more recently the Gates Foundation.

Have Wealth Transfers Become Less Equal Over Time?

The inequality of wealth transfers is extremely high, with an average Gini
coefficient of 0.96 among all households and 0.82 among recipients alone as
compared to an average Gini coefficient for net worth of 0.84. However, there
is no indication that the inequality of wealth transfers increased (or decreased) over time, at least between 1989 and 2013.

Other Issues of Interest

Do Wealth Transfers Rise with Age?
The mean and median value of total wealth transfers received rise with age.
The differences between age groups are also generally statistically significant.
In contrast, mean wealth transfers received in only the prior five years has
an inverted U-shaped pattern, rising from the youngest age group, peaking
in middle age (age group 45–54), and then declining with age. This pattern
mainly reflects the life expectancy of the parental generation.

How Important Are Wealth Transfers for the Very Rich?

Contrary to popular belief, the proportion of the net worth of the very rich
attributable to wealth transfers is quite low, at least according to direct survey
evidence. Wealth transfers as a share of net worth averaged 19 percent for
the top wealth class ($1 million or more) and 17 percent for the top 1 percent
of wealth holders over the years 1989 to 2013. These figures compare to a
share of 29 percent for the middle wealth class ($100,000–$249,999). Likewise, the fraction of net worth accountable by wealth transfers averaged

17 percent for the highest income class ($250,000 or more), compared to 25 percent for the middle-income class ($50,000–$74,999).

The share of households receiving a wealth transfer fell very sharply for the top income and wealth classes between 1989 and 2013. Its average value also fell for the top income class, though its median value rose. In contrast, the mean value increased for the top wealth class, while the median declined. Nonetheless, for both the top income and wealth class, wealth transfers as a share of net worth fell between 1989 and 2013. The same trend held true for college graduates. In the case of the top income class, wealth transfers as a proportion of wealth plummeted from 32 percent in 1989 to 14 percent in 2013. For the top 1 percent of wealth holders, the share dropped from 23 to 15 percent, while for college graduates it fell from 36 to 22 percent. The evidence shows that that inheritances and gifts became less important for the rich as a source of wealth accumulation, at least over these years.

How Did the Great Recession Affect Wealth Transfers?

There was a precipitous drop of 44 percent in median wealth between 2007 and 2010 and a more modest decline of 16 percent in mean wealth. One may speculate that it is likely that inter vivos transfers are particularly sensitive to the business cycle and specifically to changes in household wealth. If younger people are becoming poorer because of a business cycle downturn, then the need for a wealth transfer will likely increase. However, if their parents' net worth is also down, then the likelihood and size of an inter vivos transfer may also fall. Inheritances may also be affected in terms of their size because parents' wealth may have fallen during the recession.[52]

The results of this analysis indicate that the net effect of the Great Recession was a sharp downturn in wealth transfers. The percent of households that received a wealth transfer over the preceding five years plummeted from 8.4 percent in 2007 to 4.4 percent in 2010, though there was a rebound to 7.8 percent in 2013. The share receiving a bequest actually increased slightly between 2007 and 2010 but the share receiving a gift fell by more than four percentage points. Overall, the mean value of these transfers (in constant dollars) dropped by 49 percent (even greater than the percentage decline in median net worth over these years). By 2013 the mean value of these transfers was back to where it had been in 2007.

8

The Role of Social Security and Private Pensions

T he publication of Martin Feldstein's article, "Social Security, Individual Retirement and Aggregate Capital Accumulation," instituted the standard practice of including Social Security wealth in the household balance sheet.[1] In this chapter, I address two major issues related to the wealth created by the retirement system.

First, what are the aggregate trends in Social Security wealth (SSW) and, correspondingly, private pension wealth? Have they become more important over time? Since the inception of the Social Security system in 1937, SSW has grown much faster than conventional wealth, so that by 1992 it was just about equal to conventional household wealth. For the sake of consistency, however, it is also necessary to include private pension wealth, defined as the present value of future defined benefit pension wealth (DBW). I find that private pension wealth grew even faster than SSW from the early 1960s through the early 1980s. However, after robust gains in the 1980s and 1990s, pension wealth experienced a marked slowdown in growth from 2001 to 2007 and an absolute decline from 2007 to 2010, though growth picked up again from 2010 to 2013. Median augmented wealth (the sum of net worth [NW], DBW, and SSW) advanced at about the same rate as median NW from 1989 to 2007 for the overall population, as DBW essentially stagnated. However, from 2007 to 2010, while median NW plummeted by 44 percent, median augmented wealth fell by only 27 percent, and from 2010 to 2013, while median NW was almost stagnant, median augmented wealth increased by 6.1 percent. The differences are due to the moderating influence of SSW.

Second, what are the distributional implications of Social Security and DB pension wealth? Including SSW along with conventional wealth in the household balance sheet reduces the degree of measured wealth inequality.

Moreover, given the growth of SSW relative to conventional wealth, the equalizing effect increased over time. However, what is not well known is that pension wealth is much more unequally distributed than SSW (though less so than conventional household wealth). Its inclusion in the household portfolio is also equalizing but much less so than SSW. As a result, the net equalizing effect of the whole retirement system turned out to be relatively modest. From 1989 to 2007, the inequality of augmented wealth for the full population advanced more than that of NW, as DB pension wealth remained essentially unchanged. However, from 2007 to 2010, while the inequality of NW spiked by 0.032 Gini points, the Gini coefficient for augmented wealth rose by 0.021 points, less than that of NW. And from 2010 to 2013, while the former rose by a modest 0.005 points, that of augmented wealth declined by 0.003 points. The difference is once again due to the moderating influence of SSW.

This chapter begins with a review of the pertinent literature on this subject,[2] which is followed by a description of the data sources and the accounting framework used in the analysis. The analysis involves an investigation of changes in pension wealth over these years and time trends in SSW, private augmented wealth, and (total) augmented wealth. A sensitivity analysis of the results includes a discussion of alternative concepts of retirement wealth.[3]

A Brief Literature Review

Several studies have documented changes in pension coverage in the United States, particularly the decline in DB pension coverage among workers over the last few decades. Bloom and Freeman used the 1979 and 1988 Current Population Survey (CPS) for and were among the first to call attention to the drop in DB pension coverage.[4] They reported that the percentage of all workers in age group 25–64 covered by these plans declined from 63 to 57 percent over this period. Gustman and Steinmeier documented the changeover from DB to defined contribution (DC) pension plans.[5] On the basis of IRS 5500 filings, they estimated that only about half of the switch from DB to DC plans between 1977 and 1985 was due a decline in DB coverage conditional on industry, size, and union status and that the other half was due to a shift in employment mix toward firms with industry, size, and union status historically associated with low DB coverage rates. Even and

Macpherson also found a pronounced drop in DB pension coverage among male workers, particularly those with low levels of education.[6]

A U.S. Department of Labor report found that a large proportion of workers were not covered by private pensions.[7] The coverage rate of all private sector wage and salary workers was 44 percent in 1997. Coverage of part-time, temporary, low-wage, and minority workers was especially low. This appeared to be ascribable to the proliferation of 401(k) plans and the frequent requirement of employee contributions to such plans. It also found important ethnic differences, with 47 percent of white workers participating but only 27 percent of Hispanics. Another important finding was that 70 percent of unionized workers were covered by a pension plan, compared to only 41 percent of those who were not unionized. Pension participation was found to be highly correlated with wages. While only 6 percent of workers earning less than $200 per week had a pension plan, 76 percent of workers earning $1,000 per week did have one.

Using data from the CPS, Munnell and Perun reported a sharp drop-off in pension coverage between 1979 and 2004.[8] In 1979, 51 percent of nonagricultural wage and salary workers in the private sector in age group 25–64 participated in a pension plan. By 2004, that figure was down to 46 percent. The authors also found that the decline in pension coverage occurred for all five earnings quintiles, though it was particularly pronounced for the middle quintile. In general, these studies reported an overall increase in pension coverage during the 1980s and 1990s despite the collapse of DB plans because of an offsetting rise in DC plans. However, they also indicated a drop in pension coverage from 2000 to 2004. A rise in overall pension coverage among households has been observed from 1989 to 2001. This was followed by a modest decline from 2001 to 2007, a steep drop from 2007 to 2010, and a slight recovery in 2013.

Poterba found that SSW was more important in the household portfolio of lower wealth families than richer ones, and, correspondingly, DC pension wealth was more important for the latter than for the former.[9] Among all households in 2008, the share of SSW in total wealth was 44 percent at the thirtieth percentile of the wealth distribution but only 21 percent at the ninetieth percentile. In contrast, the share of personal retirement account assets in total wealth was zero percent at the thirtieth percentile and 19 percent at the ninetieth percentile.

With regard to the financial crisis of 2007–2009, Gustman, Steinmeier, and Tabatabai offered a rather sanguine view of the effects of the stock market crash on retirement preparedness.[10] Their findings indicated that although the consequences of the decline in the stock market were serious for those approaching retirement, the average person approaching retirement age was not likely to suffer a life-changing financial loss from the stock market downturn of 2007–2009. Using Health and Retirement Survey (HRS) data, they calculated trends in pensions among three cohorts: those aged 51–56 in 1992, those 51–56 in 1998, and those 51–56 in 2004. Gustman, Steinmeier, and Tabatabai found that pension coverage was much more extensive than was generally recognized. More than three-quarters of households in the third cohort were either currently covered by a pension or had had pension coverage in the past. Pension wealth accounted for 23 percent of the augmented wealth (including SSW) of those on the verge of retirement. For those nearing retirement age, DC plans remained small. As a result, 63 percent of pension wealth held by those aged 51–56 in 2004 was in the form of a DB plan.[11] The figures were even higher for older cohorts—75 percent for the first cohort and 65 percent for the second. The authors argued that the high share of pension wealth in the form of DB pension wealth would cushion the drop in overall pension wealth caused by the stock market crash.

Several authors have investigated whether DC plans substituted for (i.e., crowded out) other assets and whether there was any net savings derived from them. Poterba, Venti, and Wise concluded that the growth of IRAs and 401(k) plans did not substitute for other forms of household wealth and that they actually raised household NW relative to what it would have been without these plans.[12] Their results also suggested that the transition from DB to DC plans increased pension wealth dramatically.

Poterba et al. considered whether the switchover from DB to DC plans helped or hurt workers in terms of expected retirement wealth.[13] The American private pension system, which had been dominated by DB plans, was now divided between DC and DB plans. Wealth accumulation in DC plans depends on a participant's contribution behavior and on financial market returns, while accumulation in DB plans is dependent on a participant's labor market experience and on plan parameters. Using data from the HRS, the authors simulated the distribution of retirement wealth under representative DB and DC plans. In particular, they investigated how asset yields, earnings histories, and retirement plan characteristics contributed to the variation in retirement wealth outcomes. The simulations yielded distributions of both DC and DB wealth at retirement. They found that average retirement wealth accruals under current DC plans exceeded those under private sector DB plans, although DC plans were also more likely to generate very low retirement wealth outcomes. The comparison of current DC plans and public sector DB plans was less definitive, because public sector DB plans were more generous on average than their private sector DB counterparts.

In contrast, Gale and colleagues found very little net savings emanating from DC plans. For example, Engen and Gale used data from the 1987 and 1991 Survey of Income and Program Participation (SIPP) and found that 401(k) plans held by low earners may more likely represent additions to NW than 401(k) plans held by high earners, who held the largest portion of this asset.[14] Overall, only between zero and 30 percent of the value of 401(k) plans represented net additions to private savings.

Kennickell and Sunden found that DB plans and SSW had a significant negative effect on nonpension NW, but they concluded that the effects of DC plans on other assets were statistically insignificant.[15] In contrast, Chernozhukov and Hansen used data from the 1990 SIPP and found a positive and statistically significant effect of 401(k) plan participation on net financial assets over the entire range of the asset distribution.[16] Moreover, the increase in the lower tail of the distribution of 401(k) wealth translated almost completely into an increase in net wealth. The authors concluded that 401(k) accumulations added to the NW of households in general, particularly for those in the lower wealth groups. There was, however, significant evidence of substitution of 401(k) accumulations for other asset types in the upper tail of the distribution.

Engelhardt and Kumar used detailed information on pensions and lifetime earnings in the 1992 wave of the HRS and estimated that each dollar of pension wealth was associated with a 0.53 to 0.67 dollar decline in nonpension wealth.[17] Most of the effect was concentrated in the upper part of the wealth distribution. Finally, I have found strong evidence of a substitution effect between SSW and nonpension NW on the basis of regressions performed on the 1962 Survey of Financial Characteristics of Consumers (SFCC) and the 1983 Survey of Consumer Finances (SCF). I also found a negative and significant relation between DBW and nonpension NW in the 1962 data, but only after excluding the top 5 percent of the NW distribution. No statistically significant relation was found in the 1983 data.

What is the bottom line on the substitution between various forms of retirement wealth and fungible (nonpension) wealth? The results are inconclusive, but I would surmise that SSW and DB pension wealth probably substitute for marketable NW and DC pension wealth probably has a minimal impact on the accumulation of nonpension wealth.

With regard to the distributional effects of retirement wealth, based on data gathered from the 1962 Survey of Financial Characteristics of Consumers, the inclusion of SSW led to a sharp reduction in measured wealth inequality.[18] The Gini coefficient for the sum of NW and SSW among families in age class 35–64 was 0.51, which is significant when compared to a Gini coefficient of 0.72 for NW. Since the publication of Feldstein's 1962 article on this topic, very little research was done prior to my own.

My research first focused on examining the distributional implications of both Social Security and private pension wealth.[19] Using the 1969 Measurement of Economic and Social Performance (MESP) database, I showed that while SSW had a pronounced equalizing effect on the distribution of augmented wealth, pension wealth had by itself a much smaller equalizing effect. In particular, the addition of SSW to NW reduced the overall Gini coefficient from 0.73 to 0.48, but the addition of pension wealth to the sum of NW and SSW raised the Gini coefficient back to 0.66. The sum of Social Security and pension wealth together had an equalizing effect on the distribution of augmented wealth but substantially less than SSW alone.

McGarry and Davenport analyzed the 1992 wave of the HRS and found that pension wealth was only slightly more equally distributed than NW, but adding pension wealth to NW had an equalizing effect (with the wealth share of the top decile declining from 53 to 45 percent with the addition of pension wealth).[20] Kennickell and Sunden used the 1992 SCF and found a net equalizing effect from the inclusion of both private pension and SSW, reducing the share of total wealth held by the top 1 percent of nonelderly households from 31 to 16 percent.[21]

Total (augmented) household wealth is made up of pension wealth, SSW, and standard NW. Gustman et al. used data from the 1992 HRS to determine that pensions, Social Security, and health insurance accounted for about half of the wealth held by all households in age group 51–61.[22] They also found that the proportion of these components varied by wealth level, making up 60 percent of the wealth held by those in the 45 to 55 wealth percentiles but only 48 percent of those in the 90 to 95 percentiles. Gustman et al. concluded that pension wealth and SSW (as well as health insurance) were more important for middle-class households than for the rich. In a follow-up study, Gustman and Steinmeier found that on average pensions accounted for one-quarter of accumulated wealth, Social Security benefits another quarter, and traditional NW the remainder.[23] My findings reported in this chapter are quite similar.

Data Sources and Accounting Framework

This study relies on the 1983, 1989, 2001, 2007, 2010, and 2013 SCF conducted by the Federal Reserve Board.[24] The SCF provides considerable detail on both pension plans and Social Security contributions. It also provides detailed information on expected pension and Social Security benefits for both husband and wife.[25]

The imputation of both DBW and SSW involves many steps.[26] As with the concept of household NW, there are alternative formulations of both DBW and SSW and none of them is necessarily the "correct" measure.[27] I have elected to use the standard gross measure of both pension and SSW as my principal concept. Kennickell and Sunden used *net* SSW, the difference between the gross value of expected Social Security benefits and the discounted value of future Social Security contributions.[28] This formulation is also legitimate. The distributional effect of net SSW is likely to be smaller than that of gross SSW since its average value will be smaller. I prefer to use gross SSW because it is the standard concept and its use will make it easier to compare my results with those of the vast majority of other research on the topic.

It should also be noted that the definitions of DBW and SSW are based on the conventional "on-going concern" treatment. It is assumed that employees continue to work at their place of employment until their expected date of retirement. An alternative is to use the accrual value, in which DBW and SSW are valued as of the current year on the basis of work experience *up to that date only*. The accrual method will produce lower values of both DBW and SSW for current workers. The accrual method and the on-going concern treatment represent two extremes in the valuation of DBW and SSW. The latter treatment, in particular, relies on the assumptions that (1) the firm or organization remains in existence over time and (2) the employee continues working at the enterprise.

In my analysis, I define nonpension wealth (NWX) as marketable household wealth (NW) minus DC wealth (DCW):

$$NWX = NW - DCW. \tag{8.1}$$

Total pension wealth, PW, is given by:

$$PW = DCW + DBW. \tag{8.2}$$

Private augmented wealth PAW is defined as:

$$PAW = NWX + PW. \tag{8.3}$$

The term "private augmented wealth" is used to distinguish contributions to wealth from private savings and employment contracts with both private and government employers from those of social insurance provided by the state—notably, Social Security. Retirement wealth is defined as the sum of pension wealth (PW) and SSW:

$$RW = PW + SSW \tag{8.4}$$

and augmented household wealth, AW, is given by

$$AW = NWX + PW + SSW. \tag{8.5}$$

Pension Wealth

There are three primary concerns in the empirical parts of this chapter. First, how have the three major components of retirement wealth—DBW, DCW, and SSW—changed in relative importance over the years 1983 to 2013?[29] Second, how does the addition of PW and SSW to the household portfolio affect trends in mean and median wealth? I am particularly concerned about how both PW and SSW influenced wealth trends over the Great Recession of 2007–2013.[30] This is particularly important because median (conventional) NW among all households collapsed by 44 percent in real terms from 2007 to 2010. Third, how does the inclusion of these two forms of retirement wealth affect trends in wealth inequality, particularly over the Great Recession? This is again a salient issue since (conventional) NW inequality as measured by the Gini coefficient climbed from 0.834 to 0.866 over years 2007 to 2010.

I also consider three age groups—under 47, 47–64, and 65 and older. Time trends differ among these age classes. I highlight the age group 47–64 because there is complete data available for this group from 1983 to 2013 and this is the age group most affected by the transition of the pension system, which I discuss in detail.[31]

We begin the empirical analysis by looking at pension wealth. One of the most dramatic changes in the retirement income system over the last three decades has been the replacement of many traditional DB pension plans with DC pensions. The first focus of this chapter is to analyze the effects of the changeover in the pension system on the growth of pension wealth and time trends in wealth inequality from 1983 to 2013.

Table 8.1 highlights trends in pension coverage over years 1983 to 2013. In this and subsequent tables, it should be noted that the unit of observation is the household. Households are classified by the age of the household head. The picture that unfolds is a precipitous drop in DB coverage among all households largely compensated by a sizable increase in DC coverage, at least until 2007. Moreover, while mean pension wealth gained rapidly in the 1990s, its growth among all households slowed down considerably in the years 2001 to 2007, showed an absolute decline over years 2007 to 2010, and a recovery by 2013.

The share of households with DC pension accounts skyrocketed over the years 1983 to 2001, from 11 to 52 percent, or by 41 percentage points (see Panel A). Most of the gain occurred after 1989. The picture changed from 2001 to 2007 when there was virtually no change in the DC coverage rate. Trends are different for DB pension wealth. The share of households with a DB pension plan fell by 11 percentage points between 1989 and 2001, from 46 to 34 percent.[32] There was little change from 2001 to 2007. The share of all households covered by either a DC or a DB plan increased from 56 to 66 percent between 1989 and 2001. However, from 2001 to 2007, the share declined by 1.4 percentage points.

The time pattern is even more pronounced for age group 47–64 (the middle-aged). The share of these households with DC pensions jumped by 50 percentage points from 12 percent in 1983 to 62 percent in 2001. Once

Table 8.1. Percent of households with pension wealth, 1983–2013

	1983	1989	2001	2007	2010	2013	Percentage Point Change				
							1983–1989	1989–2001	2001–2007	2007–2010	2010–2013
A. All Households											
1. DC accounts	11.1	24.0	52.2	52.6	51.4	50.3	12.9	28.2	0.4	-1.2	-1.1
2. DB plans	—	45.6	34.4	34.0	35.6	39.0	—	-11.2	-0.5	1.6	3.5
3. Pension wealth	—	56.0	65.6	64.1	62.9	63.6	—	9.6	-1.4	-1.2	0.7
B. Ages 46 and Under											
1. DC accounts	13.7	31.2	53.8	49.9	47.9	47.3	17.5	22.6	-3.9	-2.0	-0.5
2. DB plans	—	37.9	22.8	22.6	11.6	19.5	—	-15.1	-0.2	-11.0	7.9
3. Pension wealth	—	52.2	60.7	54.7	52.0	53.0	—	8.6	-6.1	-2.7	1.1
C. Ages 47–64											
1. DC accounts	12.3	28.3	62.0	63.8	59.6	58.2	16.0	33.7	1.8	-4.2	-1.4
2. DB plans	68.5	56.8	45.3	38.8	29.6	36.5	-11.7	-11.5	-6.5	-9.2	7.0
3. Pension wealth	70.3	67.5	75.9	74.1	69.2	69.5	-2.8	8.4	-1.8	-5.0	0.4
D. Ages 65 and Over											
1. DC accounts	2.0	1.3	35.0	40.8	41.0	39.5	-0.7	33.7	5.8	0.2	-1.5
2. DB plans	67.0	51.3	46.5	50.6	51.5	54.0	-15.7	-4.7	4.1	0.9	2.5
3. Pension wealth	67.8	51.8	62.6	68.5	69.4	69.3	-15.9	10.8	5.9	0.9	-0.1

Source: Author's computations from the 1983, 1989, 2001, 2007, 2010, and 2013 Survey of Consumer Finances.
Households are classified into age groups by the age of the head of household.
Pension Wealth PW = DBW + DCW

again there was little change from 2001 to 2007. The proportion with a DB plan plummeted by 23 percentage points from 69 percent in 1983 to 45 percent in 2001 but then fell by an additional 6.5 percentage points to 39 percent in 2007. All told, the fraction with some form of pension wealth increased by 5.6 percentage points from 70 percent in 1983 to 76 percent in 2001, but then slipped to 74 percent in 2007.

Time trends are similar for the under-47 age group (young households). In this case, the share with a DC or DB pension plan declined rather sharply from 2001 to 2007, by 6.1 percentage points. The pattern is somewhat different for age group 65 and over (seniors). In this case, the fraction with a DC plan climbed by 33 percentage points from almost nothing in 1983 to 35 percent in 2001 but then continued to rise to 41 percent in 2007. This change is largely a cohort effect as the newly entering members of this group were more likely to have DC plans than the older members. The share with a DB plan also fell from 1983 to 2001, from 67 to 47 percent or by 20 percentage points, but then ticked up by 4.1 percentage points to 51 percent in 2007. This is puzzling, as one would have expected a continued decline in 2007 since those entering the ranks of the elderly were less likely to have a DB plan than older members.[33] The proportion of seniors with some form of pension wealth was slightly higher in 2007 than in 1983.

Table 8.2 reflects huge increases in the average holdings of DCW, with the average value among all households increasing by a factor of 13.6 between 1983 and 2001 to $71,000.[34] The rise in DCW slowed down from 2001 to 2007, with the mean increasing by (only) 22 percent. Opposite trends are again evident for DBW. The mean rose by only 2.6 percent between 1989 and 2001. The years 2001 to 2007 again saw a small rise, 5.5 percent. Did the spread of DC pension plans adequately compensate for the decline in traditional DB pension coverage? Average PW (which is the sum of DCW and DBW) climbed by 80 percent from 1989 to 2001.[35] The growth in PW slowed markedly from 2001 to 2007, with mean PW up by 14.2 percent. Median PW among holders did worse than mean PW from 1989 to 2001, rising 39 percent, but gained 19 percent from 2001 to 2007.

Results are similar for middle-aged households. There was again an enormous increase in average DCW, increasing by a factor of 11.7 from 1983 to 2001, to $127,000. Gains in DCW again slowed from 2001 to 2007, with the mean rising by 18 percent. On the other hand, mean DBW increased by only

Table 8.2. Mean and median household pension wealth (PW), 1983–2013 (in thousands, 2013 dollars)

	1983	1989	2001	2007	2010	2013	Percentage Change				
							1983–1989	1989–2001	2001–2007	2007–2010	2010–2013
A. All Households											
1. Mean DC pension wealth	5.2	11.9	70.6	86.3	92.0	99.0	128.6	494.4	22.2	6.5	7.7
2. Mean DB pension wealth	—	63.5	65.2	68.8	53.9	65.6	—	2.6	5.5	-21.7	21.8
3. Mean pension wealth	—	75.4	135.8	155.1	145.8	164.6	—	80.1	14.2	-6.0	12.9
Memo: Median PW among PW holders only	—	63.9	88.6	105.1	78.0	104.0	—	38.7	18.6	-25.8	33.4
B. Ages 46 and Under											
1. Mean DC pension wealth	3.3	10.4	37.2	34.5	32.5	36.8	210.8	258.7	-7.2	-5.8	13.4
2. Mean DB pension wealth	—	28.3	22.9	27.7	10.1	12.8	—	-19.2	21.0	-63.7	27.1
3. Mean pension wealth	—	38.6	60.0	62.2	42.5	49.6	—	55.5	3.6	-31.6	16.6
Memo: Median PW among PW holders only	—	34.7	40.8	47.2	29.8	35.0	—	17.5	15.7	-36.9	17.5
C. Ages 47–64											
1. Mean DC pension wealth	10.9	23.0	127.1	150.4	153.8	140.8	111.3	452.8	18.4	2.3	-8.5
2. Mean DB pension wealth	101.2	112.7	111.1	102.8	73.6	86.2	11.3	-1.4	-7.5	-28.4	17.1
3. Mean pension wealth	112.1	135.6	238.2	253.2	227.4	226.9	21.0	75.6	6.3	-10.2	-0.2
Memo: Median PW among PW holders only	96.0	112.8	148.9	168.6	135.4	173.7	17.4	32.0	13.3	-19.7	28.2
D. Ages 65 and Over											
1. Mean DC pension wealth	2.3	2.6	70.5	95.0	112.6	147.8	11.1	2652.3	34.8	18.5	31.2
2. Mean DB pension wealth	82.7	92.6	100.3	102.5	109.3	129.0	11.9	8.3	2.3	6.6	18.1
3. Mean pension wealth	85.0	95.2	170.7	197.6	221.9	276.8	11.9	79.4	15.7	12.3	24.7
Memo: Median PW among PW holders only	92.9	93.4	142.7	134.9	142.1	175.4	0.6	52.7	-5.5	5.3	23.5

Source: Author's computations from the 1983, 1989, 2001, 2007, 2010, and 2013 Survey of Consumer Finances.
Households are classified into age groups by the age of the head of household.
Pension Wealth PW = DBW + DCW

10 percent between 1983 and 2001, and years 2001 to 2007 witnessed a 7.5 percent loss. Average PW jumped 113 percent among middle-aged households between 1983 and 2001. However, from 2001 to 2007, mean PW inched up by only 6 percent. Median PW rose by 55 percent from 1983 to 2001 among account holders and then 13 percent from 2001 to 2007.

Similar patterns are again evident for young and older households. Among the former, mean DCW rose elevenfold from 1983 to 2001 and fell by 7.2 percent from 2001 to 2007. Mean DBW was down 19 percent over years 1989 to 2001 and then up by 21 percent over the period 2001 to 2007. Mean PW increased 56 percent over the first but only 3.6 percent over the second, while median PW among holders rose 18 percent in the first and 16 percent in the second. Older households saw a thirty-onefold increase in DCW from 1983 to 2001 followed by a 35 percent rise, while mean DBW gained 21 percent from 1983 to 2001 but only 2.3 percent from 2001 to 2007. Overall, mean PW doubled over the first period and then advanced 16 percent from 2001 to 2007. On the other hand, median PW among holders gained 54 percent over the first but fell by 5.5 percent over the second.

What happened over the Great Recession? From 2007 to 2010, the share of all households with a DC account fell off by 1.2 percentage points and then another 1.1 percentage points from 2010 to 2013 as firms discontinued 401(k) plans, start-ups of IRA plans slackened, and, in some cases, workers closed down IRA accounts in response to financial stress (see Table 8.1). By 2013, the ownership share was down to 50.3 percent. In contrast, the DB coverage rate actually rose by 5.1 percentage points, from 34 percent in 2007 to 39 percent in 2013. As a result, the share covered by either a DC or a DB plan remained at 64 percent in 2007 and 2013.

Mean DCW expanded during the Great Recession by a respectable 14.7 percent, to $99,000 in 2013. Mean DBW was down by 4.6 percent from 2007 to 2013, despite the rise in DB coverage. By 2013, mean DBW was $65,600. As a result, mean PW rose by 6.2 percent, to $164,600 in 2013.

The time trend was different for middle-aged households. Their DC coverage rate fell by 5.6 percentage points between 2007 and 2013, down to 58 percent. The DB coverage rate also shrank a bit, to 37 percent in 2013. As a result, the share covered by either a DC or a DB plan declined by 4.6 percentage points to 70 percent in 2013. Mean DCW also dropped over the Great Recession, by 6.4 percent, to $141,000 in 2013, reflecting the sharp decline in the coverage rate. In contrast, there was a precipitous drop in mean DBW by 16.1 percent from 2007 to 2013, reflecting in part the drop in DB coverage. By 2013, mean DBW was $86,000. As a result, mean PW fell in absolute terms, by 10.4 percent to $227,000.

The time pattern is quite similar for young households as for middle-aged ones. By 2013, 53 percent of young households had a pension plan, and their mean pension wealth was down to $49,600. Older households, in contrast, saw a slight increase in their pension coverage rate over the Great Recession, to 69 percent in 2013, and their mean PW rose substantially, by 40 percent to $277,000.

With the transition in the pension system, did the inequality of pension wealth increase or decline? Pension inequality among DC plan holders is considerably greater than that among DB plan holders. As a result, the transition to DC plans raised overall pension inequality. This was true despite a decline in inequality in DC wealth itself.

Table 8.3 records the inequality of pension wealth. Among all households, the inequality of holdings of DC accounts among account holders declined continuously over the years from 1983 to 2007. The drop in the Gini coefficient from 1983 to 2007 was a substantial 0.065. Despite the reduction of inequality in DCW, its level was still very high in 2007. The Gini coefficient among DC pension account holders was 0.728 in 2007. This compares to a Gini coefficient for NW (among all households) of 0.834. However, the period from 2007 to 2010 saw a reversal in this trend, with the Gini coefficient for DCW rising by 0.014 points to 0.741. This change likely reflects the fact that lower paid workers either reduced their contributions to DC accounts or withdrew money from these accounts, particularly IRAs, while higher paid workers continued to contribute money into their DC accounts. From 2010 to 2013, on the other hand, the Gini coefficient came down to 0.732, which was still above its 2007 level. This development is likely due to lower paid workers paying back the loans on their DC plans and starting to contribute again.

The inequality of DBW among plan members also showed a downward trend over years 1989 to 2007 followed by an upward trend to 2013. When we consider total pension wealth among pension holders, we find a sharp increase in inequality from 1989 to 2010, of 0.059 Gini points, despite the decline in DCW and DBW inequality over these years. On the surface, these results may appear to be paradoxical. However, the explanation emanates

from the fact that DCW inequality is considerably higher than DBW inequality. In 2010, for example, the Gini coefficient for DCW among those with
a DC plan was 0.741, compared to 0.593 for DBW among plan holders. The
Gini coefficient for the sum of DBW and DCW is equal to a weighted sum of
the Gini coefficients for DBW and DCW individually (plus an interaction
term), where the weight is equal to the share of that component in total pension wealth. The rising share of DCW in total PW over time, from 16 percent
in 1989 to 63 percent in 2010, thus led to a rise in the Gini coefficient for overall
pension wealth, despite the fact that the Gini coefficient for both DCW and
DBW individually declined over time.[36] From 2010 to 2013, on the other hand,
the Gini coefficient for PW fell by .023 Gini points to 0.677. This decline reflected three factors: the fall in DC inequality, the drop in DB inequality, and
the reduction of the share of DCW in total PW from 63 to 60 percent.

When the sample is extended to *all* households (including nonpension
holders), the increase in PW inequality is less marked, an increase of the Gini
coefficient of 0.016 from 1989 to 2010 compared with 0.059 for pension
holders only. The difference stems mainly from the fact that pension coverage
among all households rose over these years (from 56 to 63 percent). From
2010 to 2013, the Gini coefficient of PW declined about the same degree among
all households as among pension holders alone.

Figure 8.1a provides further details on the change in the distribution of
PW among all households by period. There were large gains in PW over the
1989 to 2001 period at all percentiles, reflecting the increase in the share of
households with a pension plan and the rising value of PW. However, the
overall pattern is U-shaped. The percentage gain declined from 214 percent
at the fiftieth percentile to 71 percent at the ninetieth percentile and then increased to 86 percent at the ninety-ninth percentile.[37] These results illustrate
that the largest growth of PW occurred at both the bottom and the top of
the PW distribution. As a result, overall PW inequality showed a small drop
over these years. From 2001 to 2007, PW showed much more modest gains
at all percentiles (from about 8 to 23 percent). These results accord with the
finding that the Gini coefficient for PW changed very little over this period.
The pattern is very different for the 2007–2013 period, when PW decreased
at all percentiles except the eighty-fifth and above. In this case, percentage
changes were far lower (that is, more negative) at lower PW percentiles—
indeed, percentage changes rose almost monotonically with PW percentile.

Table 8.3. Inequality of pension wealth among pension holders, 1983–2013 (Gini coefficients)

	1983	1989	2001	2007	2010	2013	Change				
							1983–1989	1989–2001	2001–2007	2007–2010	2010–2013
A. All Pension Holders											
1. DC accounts	0.792	0.750	0.741	0.728	0.741	0.732	-0.042	-0.009	-0.014	0.014	-0.010
2. DB plans	—	0.606	0.582	0.549	0.593	0.587	—	-0.024	-0.034	0.044	-0.005
3. Pension wealth	—	0.641	0.676	0.661	0.700	0.677	—	0.035	-0.015	0.039	-0.023
Memo: PW among all households	—	0.799	0.788	0.783	0.815	0.798	—	-0.011	-0.005	0.032	-0.017
B. Pension Holders: Ages 46 and Under											
1. DC accounts	0.778	0.731	0.719	0.693	0.699	0.710	-0.047	-0.012	-0.026	0.007	0.011
2. DB plans	—	0.576	0.552	0.511	0.574	0.534	—	-0.024	-0.041	0.063	-0.039
3. Pension wealth	—	0.635	0.672	0.653	0.681	0.672	—	0.037	-0.020	0.028	-0.039
Memo: PW among all households in age group 46 and under	—	0.810	0.801	0.810	0.834	0.826	—	-0.009	0.009	0.024	-0.008
C. Pension Holders: Ages 47–64											
1. DC accounts	0.732	0.726	0.714	0.681	0.700	0.669	-0.005	-0.012	-0.032	0.018	-0.031
2. DB plans	0.507	0.537	0.571	0.519	0.572	0.526	0.030	0.034	-0.052	0.053	-0.045
3. Pension wealth	0.524	0.577	0.637	0.617	0.659	0.609	0.053	0.060	-0.020	0.042	-0.050
Memo: PW among all households in age group 47–64	0.666	0.715	0.724	0.716	0.764	0.728	0.049	0.010	-0.008	0.048	-0.036
D. Pension Holders: Ages 65 and Over											
1. DC accounts	0.687	0.635	0.703	0.736	0.721	0.726	-0.053	0.068	0.033	-0.014	0.004
2. DB plans	0.458	0.605	0.541	0.556	0.573	0.575	0.147	-0.064	0.015	0.017	0.002
3. Pension wealth	0.466	0.607	0.607	0.642	0.648	0.648	0.141	0.000	0.035	0.006	0.001
Memo: PW among all households in age group	0.638	0.796	0.754	0.755	0.755	0.756	0.158	-0.042	0.001	0.001	0.001

Source: Author's computations from the 1983, 1989, 2001, 2007, 2010, and 2013 Survey of Consumer Finances.
Households are classified into age groups by the age of the head of household.
Pension Wealth PW = DBW + DCW

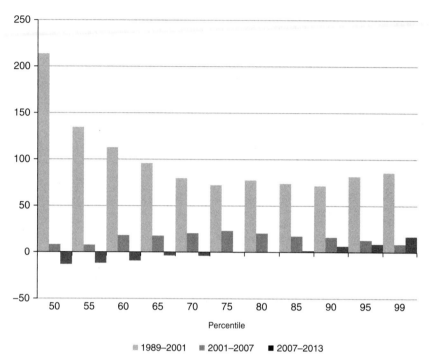

Figure 8.1a. Percentage Change in Pension Wealth (PW) in 2013 Dollars by PW Percentile, All Households, 1989, 2001, 2007, and 2013

These results are consistent with the increase in the Gini coefficient for PW over these six years.

Among middle-aged households, the inequality of DCW among account holders generally declined over the years from 1983 to 2013. The drop in the Gini coefficient was 0.063, about the same as among all households with accounts. The inequality of DB wealth did not show a clear time trend over these years but a fair amount of year-to-year variation. However, the Gini coefficient for total PW among pension holders showed a sharp increase from 1983 to 2010 (0.135 Gini points). This result reflects the rising share of DCW in total PW, from 10 percent in 1983 to 68 percent in 2010. From 2010 to 2013, on the other hand, the Gini coefficient for PW fell sharply as it did for all households—in this case, by .050 Gini points to 0.609. This reduction reflects the same factors as before: the fall in DCW and DBW inequality and the decrease of the proportion of DCW in total PW, in this case from 68 to 62 percent.

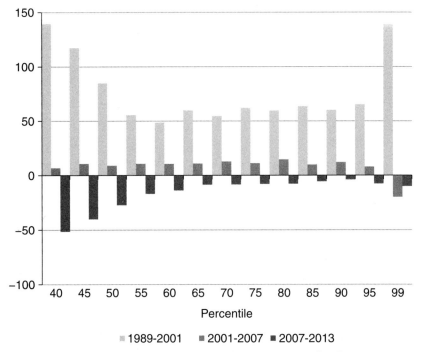

Figure 8.1b. Percentage Change in Pension Wealth (PW) in 2013 Dollars by PW Percentile, Ages 47–64, 1989, 2001, 2007, and 2013

Among all households in age group 47–64 (including nonpension holders), the increase in PW inequality is less marked from 1983 to 2010, an increase of the Gini coefficient of 0.098 compared to 0.135 for pension holders only. The major difference stems from the 1989–2001 period, when PW inequality among all households grew appreciably less than among pension holders (the change in the Gini coefficient was very close between the two during the other periods). The difference for the 1989–2001 period reflects the relatively large increase in the share of households with pension wealth (8.4 percentage points). From 2010 to 2013, the Gini coefficient of PW declined somewhat less among all households than among pension holders.

Figure 8.1b provides additional details on trends in PW among all middle-aged households. The pattern is similar to that among all households. There were large gains in pension wealth over the 1989–2001 period at all percentiles, reflecting the increase in the share of households with a pension plan and the rising value of PW. However, the overall pattern was U-shaped. The percentage gain declined from 139 percent at the fortieth percentile to 49 percent at the sixtieth percentile and then increased to 139 percent at the ninety-ninth percentile.[38] In other words, over these years, the largest gains in PW occurred at both the bottom and the top of the distribution. As a result, overall PW inequality showed only a modest increase over these years. From 2001 to 2007, PW showed modest gains at all percentiles (from about 7 to 15 percent), and the Gini coefficient for PW showed a slight decline. This changed again in the 2007–2013 period, when PW decreased at all percentiles but percentage changes were far lower (that is, more negative) at lower PW percentiles. These results again accord with the increase in the Gini coefficient for PW over these years.

Results are similar for young households. Among young pension holders, the inequality of PW rose between 1989 and 2010 and then showed a modest decline in 2013. The same pattern holds among all young households. Among older households with pensions, PW inequality rose almost continuously from 1983 to 2010 and then showed no change in 2013. Among all older households, there was a sharp increase in PW inequality from 1983 to 1989 followed by a pronounced decline from 1989 to 2001 when it leveled off. This time pattern almost exactly mirrors the time trend in pension coverage in this age group.

Social Security and Augmented Wealth

Social Security Wealth

Augmented wealth (AW) is the sum of NWX, pension wealth, and SSW. AW is the most comprehensive measure of the full set of resources available for retirement, and so its change over time is of considerable interest when considering trends in retirement adequacy. Moreover, an analysis of trends in AW will allow us to determine whether the basic findings with regard to NW are changed when pension and SSW are included in the definition of household wealth. There was rapid growth in mean AW during the 1990s, a slowdown occurred over the 2001–2007 period, and from 2007 to 2013 there was an absolute decline. Moreover, median AW showed slower growth over time than mean AW. In fact, from 2007 to 2013, median AW showed a much larger drop than mean AW. Private augmented wealth (PAW) experienced a similar trend.

Before we proceed to a discussion of AW, it is first useful to look at trends in SSW. Mean SSW among all households rose by 46 percent between 1989 and 2001 (see Table 8.4), compared to an 80 percent gain in mean PW. The percentage increase in median SSW was very close to that of mean SSW, which reflects relative constancy in SSW inequality over time (see Tables 8.5 and 8.6).[39] The rise in SSW over this period largely reflected increasing real wages, particularly in the late 1990s, and rising longevity. This was offset, in part, by the increase in the age at which full Social Security benefits are received from age 65 to age 67 for persons born after 1938 and the rising share of minorities in the labor force, whose life expectancy and average earnings are lower than those of whites.

SSW averaged $186,000 (in 2013 dollars) in 2007 among all households. This compares to a mean NW of $603,000 and mean PW of $155,000. Median SSW in 2007 was $156,000—84 percent of mean SSW. This suggests a normal or close to normal distribution of SSW. Moreover, median SSW ($156,000) was 36 percent higher than median NW. The years 2001 to 2007 witnessed almost no growth in mean and median SSW. This turnaround from earlier years was largely attributable to the wage stagnation of this decade as well as to the increasing age at which full Social Security benefits took effect. Other factors include the increasing share of minorities in the workforce, higher unemployment rates in 2000–2007 than in the previous decade, and the drop in the median retirement age as compared to the 1990s. The latter two factors (high unemployment and the drop in retirement age) led to fewer years of employed work life overall. Moreover, while longevity increased over this period, the rate of increase slowed down relative to the 1990s. The Great Recession (2007–2013) witnessed a small decline in both mean and median SSW, the likely reason for which was increased unemployment.

The inequality of SSW was much lower than that of NW or pensions (see Table 8.6). In 2007, the Gini coefficient for SSW among all households was 0.36, compared to 0.83 for NW and 0.78 for PW. The inequality of SSW was relatively unchanged from 1989 to 2013.

Mean SSW among middle-aged households rose by 36 percent between 1983 and 2001. This compares to a 113 percent gain in their mean PW. The increase in median SSW was again very close to that of mean SSW—also a reflection of stability in SSW inequality for this age group.[40] As for all households, there was almost no advance in SSW from 2001 to 2007. In fact, median SSW fell by 5.2 percent among middle-aged households. As for all households, mean and median SSW fell between 2007 and 2013.

Time trends in mean and median SSW are similar for young and middle-aged households. However, the inequality of SSW showed a more or less steady rise over the years 1989 to 2013. This trend may reflect widening dispersion in the underlying wage distribution among young workers, as well as widening differentials in unemployment spells and Social Security coverage. The picture is a little different for the older age group. For them, mean and particularly median SSW actually showed an increase over the Great Recession years. This result is probably due to a cohort effect whereby newly retired persons likely accumulated more lifetime earnings and therefore higher Social Security benefits than older seniors. Moreover, among seniors, there was a substantial drop in the inequality of SSW, reflecting primarily increased Social Security coverage.[41]

Retirement Wealth

Retirement wealth (RW) is a combination of pension and Social Security wealth. Among all households, mean retirement wealth grew by 59 percent from 1989 to 2001. The percentage gain was lower than that of PW but higher than that of SSW. Median RW was up by 46 percent over these years. Similar to PW and SSW, this was followed by a marked slowdown in growth from 2001 to 2007, and then little change in mean RW but a 6 percent drop in median RW from 2007 to 2013. Similar patterns held for middle-aged and young households except that in both cases there was a relatively sharp drop in mean and median RW from 2007 to 2013. Among age group 65 and over, there were also large gains in RW from 1983 to 2001 and a pronounced slowdown from 2001 to 2007, but in their case, both mean and median RW showed sizable gains from 2007 to 2013 (of 27 and 23 percent, respectively).

Table 8.3 showed a high level of PW inequality. However, SSW exerted a moderating influence so that the inequality of retirement wealth was sub-

Table 8.4. Mean Social Security, private augmented, and augmented wealth, 1983–2013 (in thousands, 2013 dollars)

	1983	1989	2001	2007	2010	2013	Percentage Change				
							1983–1989	1989–2001	2001–2007	2007–2010	2010–2013
A. All Households											
1. Social Security wealth	—	125.8	183.6	185.8	170.8	179.0	—	46.0	1.2	-8.1	4.8
2. Retirement wealth	—	201.2	319.4	340.9	316.7	343.6	—	58.8	6.7	-7.1	8.5
3. Nonpension net worth	298.8	336.3	429.6	516.2	413.9	409.9	12.6	27.7	20.2	-19.8	-1.0
4. Net worth	304.0	348.2	500.2	602.5	505.9	508.9	14.6	43.7	20.4	-16.0	0.6
5. Private augmented wealth	—	411.5	565.6	671.6	559.7	574.5	—	37.4	18.7	-16.7	2.6
6. Augmented wealth	—	537.3	749.2	857.4	730.6	753.5	—	39.4	14.4	-14.8	3.1
B. Ages 46 and Under											
1. Social Security wealth	—	104.4	144.5	141.3	120.2	127.8	—	38.3	-2.2	-15.0	6.3
2. Retirement wealth	—	143.0	204.5	203.5	162.7	177.4	—	43.0	-0.5	-20.0	9.0
3. Nonpension net worth	138.6	182.0	193.2	201.4	123.1	162.1	31.3	6.1	4.2	-38.9	31.7
4. Net worth	142.3	192.4	230.4	235.9	155.6	199.0	35.2	19.7	2.4	-34.0	27.9
5. Private augmented wealth	—	220.7	253.2	263.5	165.6	211.7	—	14.8	4.1	-37.1	27.8
6. Augmented wealth	—	325.1	397.7	404.9	285.8	339.5	—	22.3	1.8	-29.4	18.8
C. Ages 47–64											
1. Social Security wealth	178.2	155.6	242.7	242.4	210.9	214.2	-12.7	56.0	-0.1	-13.0	1.6
2. Retirement wealth	289.8	291.2	480.9	495.6	438.3	441.1	0.5	65.2	3.1	-11.6	0.6

3. Nonpension net worth	479.4	513.2	660.3	752.4	616.0	521.6	7.0	28.7	14.0	−13.1	−15.3
4. Net worth	491.8	536.1	787.3	902.8	769.9	662.3	9.0	46.9	14.7	−14.7	−14.0
5. Private augmented wealth	591.5	648.8	898.5	1005.6	843.4	748.5	9.7	38.5	11.9	−16.1	−11.3
6. Augmented wealth	769.2	804.4	1141.2	1248.0	1054.3	962.7	4.6	41.9	9.4	−13.5	−8.7
D. Ages 55 and Over											
1. Social Security wealth	157.3	143.4	193.0	190.7	208.1	217.9	−8.8	34.6	−1.2	9.1	4.7
2. Retirement wealth	242.4	238.6	363.7	388.2	430.0	494.7	−1.6	52.4	6.7	10.3	15.0
3. Nonpension net worth	483.6	507.8	663.3	814.5	671.0	684.7	5.0	30.6	22.8	−17.6	2.0
4. Net worth	488.0	510.4	733.8	909.5	783.7	832.4	4.6	43.8	23.9	−13.8	6.2
5. Private augmented wealth	568.6	603.0	834.0	1012.0	893.0	961.4	6.0	38.3	21.3	−11.8	7.7
6. Augmented wealth	726.0	746.4	1027.0	1202.7	1101.1	1179.4	2.8	37.6	17.1	−8.4	7.1

Source: Author's computations from the 1983, 1989, 2001, 2007, 2010, and 2013 Survey of Consumer Finances.

Households are classified into age groups by the age of the head of household.

PW = DCW + DBW

RW = PW + SSW

NWX = NW − DCW

PAW = NWX + PW

AW = NWX + PW + SSW

Abbreviations: AW, augmented wealth; DBW, defined benefit pension wealth; DCW, defined contribution pension wealth; NWX, nonpension net worth; PAW, private augmented wealth; PW, pension wealth; RW, retirement wealth; SSW, Social Security wealth.

Table 8.5. Median Social Security, private augmented, and augmented wealth, 1983–2013 (in thousands, 2013 dollars)

	1983	1989	2001	2007	2010	2013	Percentage Change				
							1983–1989	1989–2001	2001–2007	2007–2010	2010–2013
A. All Households											
1. Social Security wealth	—	112.9	158.8	156.4	142.5	149.7	—	40.6	-1.5	-8.9	5.1
2. Retirement wealth	—	141.7	207.4	210.9	182.3	198.2	—	46.4	1.7	-13.6	8.7
3. Nonpension net worth	76.4	79.4	76.3	84.5	44.0	41.6	4.0	-3.9	10.7	-47.9	-5.6
4. Net worth	78.1	83.6	96.7	115.2	64.6	63.9	7.0	15.8	19.1	-43.9	-1.1
5. Private augmented wealth	—	128.2	133.0	160.5	90.1	102.5	—	3.7	20.7	-43.9	13.8
6. Augmented wealth	—	252.9	311.9	347.6	254.1	269.5	—	23.3	11.4	-26.9	6.1
B. Ages 46 and Under											
1. Social Security wealth	—	98.6	134.7	126.5	106.3	113.2	—	36.6	-6.1	-15.9	6.5
2. Retirement wealth	—	112.8	153.3	146.7	118.1	124.3	—	35.9	-4.3	-19.5	5.2
3. Nonpension net worth	32.9	27.0	16.8	13.0	1.9	2.0	-17.9	-37.7	-22.5	-85.6	7.0
4. Net worth	34.2	31.3	27.2	24.5	8.3	7.0	-8.5	-13.0	-10.1	-66.0	-16.0
5. Private augmented wealth	—	45.5	43.3	39.3	11.6	12.2	—	-4.8	-9.2	-70.5	5.2
6. Augmented wealth	—	158.0	185.8	175.2	128.1	131.5	—	17.6	-5.7	-26.9	2.7
C. Ages 47–64											
1. Social Security wealth	167.6	155.3	232.0	220.1	194.5	197.8	-7.3	49.4	-5.2	-11.6	1.7
2. Retirement wealth	231.2	213.0	335.3	339.3	263.9	282.7	-7.9	57.5	1.2	-22.2	7.1

3. Nonpension net worth	141.2	160.2	136.1	161.9	90.1	70.5	13.4	-15.0	18.9	-44.4	-21.7
4. Net worth	142.6	175.3	181.1	232.1	141.3	110.7	23.0	3.3	28.2	-39.1	-21.7
5. Private augmented wealth	242.0	255.0	280.3	319.0	195.8	190.8	5.4	9.9	13.8	-38.5	-2.6
6. Augmented wealth	409.9	419.5	534.4	545.6	394.9	396.2	2.3	27.4	2.1	-27.6	0.3
D. Ages 65 and Over											
1. Social Security wealth	145.1	119.1	167.1	149.1	176.0	189.3	-17.9	40.3	-10.8	18.1	7.6
2. Retirement wealth	207.3	172.6	245.9	238.1	266.2	291.7	-16.7	42.5	-3.2	11.8	9.6
3. Nonpension net worth	137.7	144.0	186.9	214.7	180.0	162.5	4.5	29.8	14.9	-16.1	-9.7
4. Net worth	137.7	144.0	198.4	237.3	208.4	195.0	4.5	37.8	19.6	-12.2	-6.4
5. Private augmented wealth	215.7	210.9	290.6	311.5	295.9	290.0	-2.2	37.8	7.2	-5.0	-2.0
6. Augmented wealth	384.7	349.3	479.3	489.5	505.2	497.5	-9.2	37.2	2.1	3.2	-1.5

Source: Author's computations from the 1983, 1989, 2001, 2007, 2010, and 2013 Survey of Consumer Finances.
Households are classified into age groups by the age of the head of household.
See notes to Table 8.4 for the key.
PW = DCW + DBW
RW = PW + SSW
NWX = NW − DCW
PAW = NWX + PW
AW = NWX + PW + SSW

Abbreviations: AW, augmented wealth; DBW, defined benefit pension wealth; DCW, defined contribution pension wealth; NWX, nonpension net worth; PAW, private augmented wealth; PW, pension wealth; RW, retirement wealth; SSW, Social Security wealth.

Table 8.6. Inequality of Social Security, private augmented, and augmented wealth, 1983–2013 (Gini coefficients)

	1983	1989	2001	2007	2010	2013	Percentage Point Change				
							1983–1989	1989–2001	2001–2007	2007–2010	2010–2013
A. All Households											
1. Social Security wealth	—	0.370	0.344	0.363	0.369	0.369	—	−0.026	0.019	0.006	−0.001
2. Retirement wealth	—	0.485	0.493	0.514	0.538	0.539	—	0.009	0.021	0.024	0.001
3. Nonpension net worth	0.802	0.835	0.845	0.857	0.894	0.902	0.033	0.011	0.011	0.037	0.008
4. Net worth	0.799	0.828	0.826	0.834	0.866	0.871	0.029	−0.002	0.008	0.032	0.005
5. Private augmented wealth	—	0.793	0.796	0.805	0.840	0.836	—	0.003	0.009	0.035	−0.003
6. NWX + SSW	—	0.676	0.665	0.693	0.708	0.708	—	−0.011	0.028	0.014	0.000
7. Augmented wealth	—	0.663	0.661	0.684	0.705	0.701	—	−0.002	0.023	0.021	−0.003
B. Ages 46 and Under											
1. Social Security wealth	—	0.306	0.320	0.327	0.347	0.346	—	0.013	0.008	0.020	−0.001
2. Retirement wealth	—	0.405	0.430	0.440	0.445	0.454	—	0.024	0.010	0.005	0.009
3. Non-Pension worth	0.801	0.903	0.892	0.917	1.050	1.024	0.102	−0.011	0.025	0.133	−0.026
4. Net worth	0.797	0.887	0.859	0.880	0.972	0.964	0.089	−0.027	0.021	0.092	−0.008
5. Private augmented wealth	—	0.851	0.830	0.850	0.945	0.936	—	−0.021	0.019	0.095	−0.009
6. NWX + SSW	—	0.650	0.612	0.636	0.649	0.683	—	−0.038	0.024	0.013	0.034
7. Augmented wealth	—	0.642	0.616	0.636	0.652	0.682	—	−0.025	0.020	0.015	0.030
C. Ages 47–64											
1. Social Security wealth	0.297	0.314	0.297	0.305	0.308	0.304	0.017	−0.017	0.008	0.003	−0.004
2. Retirement wealth	0.378	0.454	0.464	0.470	0.508	0.485	0.075	0.010	0.007	0.037	−0.023

3. Nonpension net worth	0.762	0.780	0.823	0.827	0.858	0.882	0.017	0.043	0.004	0.031	0.024
4. Net worth	0.761	0.775	0.798	0.795	0.825	0.838	0.013	0.024	−0.003	0.030	0.013
5. Private augmented wealth	0.688	0.721	0.756	0.758	0.795	0.794	0.033	0.034	0.003	0.057	−0.001
6. NWX + SSW	0.607	0.644	0.655	0.673	0.691	0.686	0.037	0.011	0.017	0.019	−0.005
7. Augmented wealth	0.574	0.619	0.637	0.650	0.678	0.665	0.045	0.018	0.013	0.028	−0.013
D. Ages 65 and Over											
1. Social Security wealth	0.412	0.463	0.356	0.415	0.380	0.391	0.051	−0.108	0.059	−0.035	0.012
2. Retirement wealth	0.378	0.529	0.486	0.535	0.515	0.545	0.151	−0.043	0.049	−0.020	0.030
3. Nonpension net worth	0.777	0.778	0.766	0.790	0.787	0.806	0.001	−0.013	0.024	−0.003	0.020
4. Net worth	0.778	0.778	0.762	0.784	0.781	0.801	0.000	−0.016	0.022	−0.003	0.021
5. Private augmented wealth	0.708	0.738	0.724	0.748	0.738	0.752	0.029	−0.013	0.024	−0.011	0.014
6. NWX + SSW	0.638	0.670	0.637	0.678	0.647	0.666	0.032	−0.033	0.041	−0.031	0.020
7. Augmented wealth	0.599	0.652	0.626	0.665	0.636	0.656	0.053	−0.026	0.039	−0.028	0.019

Source: Author's computations from the 1983, 1989, 2001, 2007, 2010, and 2013 Survey of Consumer Finances.

Households are classified into age groups by the age of the head of household.

PW = DCW + DBW

RW = PW + SSW

NWX = NW − DCW

PAW = NWX + PW

AW = NWX + PW + SSW

Abbreviations: AW, augmented wealth; DBW, defined benefit pension wealth; DCW, defined contribution pension wealth; NWX, nonpension net worth; PAW, private augmented wealth; PW, pension wealth; RW, retirement wealth; SSW, Social Security wealth.

stantially lower. In fact, the inequality of retirement wealth lay between that of PW and SSW. In 2007, the Gini coefficient for RW among all households was 0.51, compared to 0.36 for SSW and 0.78 for pension wealth.

Unlike SSW, there was a distinct upward trend in the inequality of RW over years 1989 (or 1983) and 2013. It increased by 0.029 Gini points from 1989 to 2007 among all households, despite a reduction in the inequality of both PW and SSW. There are two explanations: First, the share of PW in total RW rose over the period, from 37 to 45 percent (see Table 8.7). Since PW was more unequally distributed than SSW, this change had the effect of raising the inequality of RW (the sum of the two components). Second, the correlation between the two rose from 0.26 to 0.38.[42] In other words, households with large PW holdings tended to have increasing levels of SSW over time, thus leading to greater skewness in the distribution of retirement wealth. From 2007 to 2013, the Gini coefficient of RW increased by another 0.025. The same two factors explain this change—(1) the rise in the ratio of RW to PW (from 0.45 to 0.48) and (2) an increase in the correlation between PW and SSW (from 0.38 to 0.42).

Among young households, the Gini coefficient for RW rose by 0.034 Gini points from 1989 to 2007, largely because of the rising inequality of SSW, and then by another 0.014 from 2007 to 2013, reflecting increases in the inequality of both SSW and PW. Among middle-aged households, there was a sizable increase in the Gini coefficient for RW of 0.106 between 1983 and 2013, despite little change in the inequality of SSW. This can be explained by, first, a sharp increase in PW inequality over these years (from a Gini coefficient of 0.67 to 0.73) and, second, by a rising share of PW in total RW from 39 to 51 percent. Among older households, the inequality of RW also experienced a sharp increase over these years, from a Gini coefficient of 0.38 to 0.55. The same two factors were at play. In addition, there was a sharp rise in the correlation between PW and SSW (from 0.15 to 0.37).

Figures 8.2a and 8.2b give a clearer picture of changes in the distribution of RW. Among all households, percentage gains in RW were positive over the 1989–2001 period and formed a U-shaped pattern. The strong growth in retirement wealth among the lowest percentiles reflected the large increases in SSW at the bottom, while the sharp gains among the top percentiles were due to the substantial gains of PW at the top (primarily DC wealth). The decline in the middle was a reflection of the losses in PW in this part of the distribution.

Table 8.7. The composition of augmented wealth, 1983–2013 (percentages)

	1983	1989	2001	2007	2010	2013
A. All Households						
1. Nonpension net worth	—	62.6	57.3	60.2	56.7	54.4
2. DC wealth	—	2.2	9.4	10.1	12.6	13.1
3. DB wealth	—	11.8	8.7	8.0	7.4	8.7
4. Social Security wealth	—	23.4	24.5	21.7	23.4	23.8
Augmented wealth	—	100.0	100.0	100.0	100.0	100.0
Memo: Ratio PW to RW	—	37.5	42.5	45.5	46.0	47.9
B. Ages 46 and Under						
1. Nonpension net worth	—	56.0	48.6	49.7	43.1	47.7
2. DC wealth	—	3.2	9.3	8.5	11.4	10.9
3. DB wealth	—	8.7	5.7	6.8	3.5	3.8
4. Social Security wealth	—	32.1	36.3	34.9	42.1	37.6
Augmented wealth	—	100.0	100.0	100.0	100.0	100.0
Memo: Ratio of PW to RW	—	27.0	29.3	30.5	26.1	28.0
C. Ages 47–64						
1. Nonpension net worth	62.3	63.8	57.9	60.3	58.4	54.2
2. DC wealth	1.4	2.9	11.1	12.1	14.6	14.6
3. DB wealth	13.2	14.0	9.7	8.2	7.0	8.9
4. Social Security wealth	23.2	19.3	21.3	19.4	20.0	22.2
Augmented wealth	100.0	100.0	100.0	100.0	100.0	100.0
Memo: Ratio of PW to RW	38.7	46.6	49.5	51.1	51.9	51.4
D. Ages 65 and Over						
1. Nonpension net worth	66.6	68.0	64.6	67.7	60.9	58.1
2. DC wealth	0.3	0.3	6.9	7.9	10.2	12.5
3. DB wealth	11.4	12.4	9.8	8.5	9.9	10.9
4. Social Security wealth	21.7	19.2	18.8	15.9	18.9	18.5
Augmented wealth	100.0	100.0	100.0	100.0	100.0	100.0
Memo: Ratio of PW to RW	35.1	39.9	46.9	50.9	51.6	55.9

Source: Author's computations from the 1983, 1989, 2001, 2007, 2010, and 2013 Survey of Consumer Finances.

Households are classified into age groups by the age of the head of household.

PW = DCW + DBW

RW = PW + SSW

NWX = NW − DCW

PAW = NWX + PW

AW = NWX + PW + SSW

Abbreviations: AW, augmented wealth; DBW, defined benefit pension wealth; DCW, defined contribution pension wealth; NWX, nonpension net worth; PAW, private augmented wealth; PW, pension wealth; RW, retirement wealth; SSW, Social Security wealth.

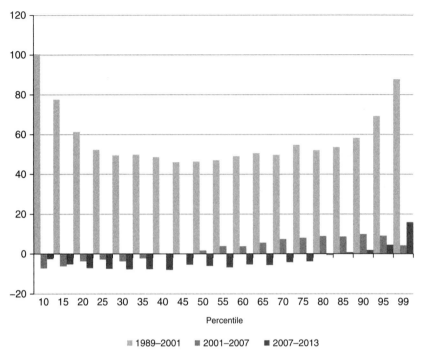

Figure 8.2a. Percentage Change in Retirement Wealth (RW) in 2013 Dollars by RW Percentile, All Households, 1989, 2001, 2007, and 2013

There was a modest gain in inequality over these years as well. However, from 2001 to 2007 changes in RW were much smaller. They were negative up to the fortieth percentile or so and then generally positive above this. These changes reflected declines in SSW in the bottom percentiles and increases of PW in the middle and upper percentiles. This period, not surprisingly, was characterized by an increase in the Gini coefficient for RW. From 2007 to 2013, changes in RW were negative up to the eighty-fifth percentile and then positive and rising with the percentile level. This pattern was mainly due to the drop in PW among the bottom three-quarters or so of the wealth distribution. This period also saw a rise in RW inequality. The pattern of percentage gains was also U-shaped among middle-aged households over the first period. Over the second period, RW recorded losses in the bottom percentiles (up to the fortieth) and then generally positive gains after that. From 2007 to 2013, losses in RW were recorded at all percentile levels, though steeper for lower percentiles of the

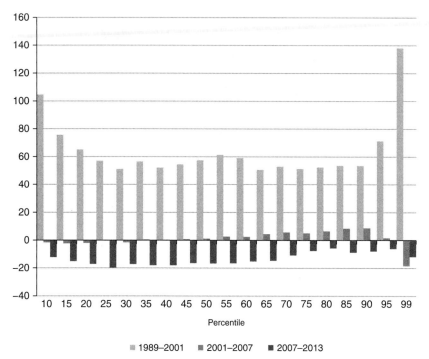

Figure 8.2b. Percentage Change in Retirement Wealth (RW) in 2013 Dollars by RW Percentile, Ages 47 to 64, 1989, 2001, 2007, and 2013

RW distribution. This finding is consistent with the relatively steep fall-off in mean PW for this age group over this period.

Composition of Augmented Wealth

The next part of the analysis investigates how the addition of RW to the household portfolio affects trends in mean and median wealth, the level of wealth inequality, and trends in wealth inequality. This is done by successively adding the components of RW to NWX (NW excluding DCW). First, I will review trends in the composition of AW. The effect of RW on mean and median wealth and the inequality of wealth will reflect, in part, the relative importance of RW in AW.

Among all households, there was an almost continuous decline in the share of nonpension wealth (NWX) in AW, from 63 percent in 1989 to

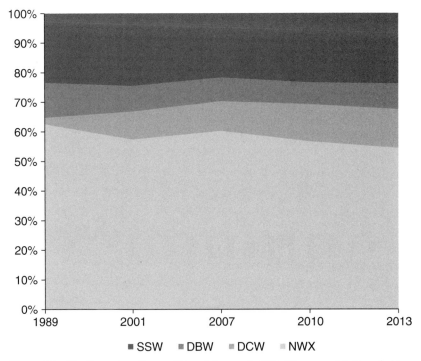

Figure 8.3a. The Percentage Composition of Augmented Wealth among All Households

54 percent in 2013 (see Table 8.7 and Figure 8.3a).[43] Correspondingly, the share of retirement wealth in AW rose from 37 to 46 percent. The large up-surge in RW came from DCW, which mushroomed from 2.2 percent in AW in 1989 to 13.1 percent in 2013. DBW, in contrast, fell from 11.8 to 8.7 percent, while SSW remained more or less constant as a proportion of AW—around 23 to 24 percent.

Time trends for the different components of AW were similar by age group, but their relative importance differed. Among young households, SSW amounted to a higher share of AW, between 32 and 42 percent. Middle-aged households saw a steeper rise in the share of DCW in AW—from 1.4 percent in 1983 to 14.6 percent in 2013—and a sharper fall-off in DBW—from 13.2 to 8.9 percent (see Figure 8.3b). SSW formed a slightly lower pro-portion of AW, approximately one-fifth. Older households also saw a sharp drop in the share of NWX in AW. DCW showed a very sharp rise, from

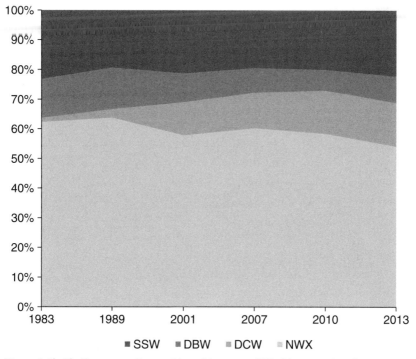

Figure 8.3b. The Percentage Composition of Augmented Wealth among Age Group 47 to 64

0.3 percent in 1983 to 12.5 percent in 2013 because entering cohorts had greater DCW than older ones. Interestingly, the proportion of DBW in AW was about the same in 2013 as in 1983 (11 percent). On the other hand, SSW experienced a downward trajectory, from 22 to 19 percent, as PW rose in importance.

Time Trends in Augmented Wealth

As shown in Table 8.4, mean NWX among all households climbed 54 percent between 1989 and 2007 but dropped 21 percent from 2007 to 2013. When DCW is added to obtain NW, we find that NW advanced faster than NWX from 1989 to 2007 (73 percent) and declined less from 2007 to 2013 (only 16 percent). The reason for the difference is the rising share of DCW in total wealth over these years. Medians tell a similar story (Table 8.5). Whereas median NWX increased by 6.4 percent in the first period, median NW rose 38 percent. In the second period, median NWX dropped 51 percent compared to a 45 percent decline in median NW.

PAW, the sum of NW and DBW, represents the resources available to households for retirement from private sources—their own wealth accumulations and private (including government DB plans but not public plans like Social Security) pension funds. The use of this variable also allows us to isolate the effects of pensions, particularly DB plans, on wealth trends before introducing SSW into the concept of wealth.

The results indicate that with the dismantling of the DB pension system, mean PAW among all households grew slower than household NW from 1989 to 2007 (63 versus 73 percent) but declined to about the same degree over the Great Recession (about 15 percent). Median PAW also advanced slower than median NW from 1989 to 2007 (25 versus 38 percent) but declined less from 2007 to 2013 (36 versus 45 percent).

Differences between the two measures reflect the much lower gains in DBW than in NW from 1989 to 2007. Generally speaking, households fared worse in terms of PAW than conventional NW between 1989 and 2007. This finding indicates that the explosive growth of DC plans after 1989 did not fully compensate for the collapse of DB plans at least in terms of the growth of household wealth. However, from 2007 to 2013 the share of DBW in AW actually increased a bit, accounting for the fact that mean PAW declined at about the same rate as mean NW. Moreover, since DB wealth was more concentrated in the middle of the wealth distribution than NWX, median PAW declined less over these years than median NW.

Another notable finding is that median PAW grew much slower than mean PAW from 1989 to 2007 and declined more in percentage terms from 2007 to 2013. Insofar as the median is more reflective of the welfare of the average household than the mean, these results indicate lower growth in welfare for the average household than indicated by the change in mean values. They are also indicative of rising PAW inequality.

The 1980s and 1990s saw strong growth in overall NW, as did the 2001–2007 period. But a collapse occurred from 2007 to 2013. The pattern is similar for age group 47–64. In addition, mean NWX rose by 57 percent from 1983 to 2007, but NW increased 84 percent. Median NWX was up by only 15 percent over this period, compared to 63 percent for median NW. This result is similar for all households. This shows how important DC plans were for the growth of NW. This is not to say that households would not have accumulated wealth in alternative instruments in the absence of DC plans. However, the accumulations were likely to have been less because savings in DC plans are tax-sheltered, which means that they accumulate at a higher rate in DC plans, ceteris paribus, than in taxable investments. And the value of employer-provided DC plans like 401(k)s also incorporates the contributions made by employers.

From 2007 to 2013, mean NW among middle-aged households fell by 27 percent and the median by a whopping 52 percent (both figures are much higher than for all households combined). Mean NWX actually fell even more than NW (31 percent), as did median NWX (56 percent). This difference reflects the rising proportion of DCW in AW among middle-aged households over these years. Mean PAW was up by 70 percent between 1983 and 2007, lower than that of NW (84 percent), while its median value increased by 32 percent, in this case much slower than that of NW (63 percent). From 2007 to 2013, mean PAW declined by 26 percent, about the same as that of NW, while median PAW plunged by 40 percent but less than median NW for this group (52 percent). Here, too, median PAW among age group 47–64 grew much slower than mean PAW from 1983 to 2007 and declined more in percentage terms than mean PAW from 2007 to 2013.

Among young households (under age 47), the story is somewhat different. Mean PAW rose by 19 percent from 1989 to 2007, compared to a 23 percent increase in NW. This result is similar to the other age groups. However, median PAW was actually down by 14 percent, compared to a 22 percent drop in median NW. Over the Great Recession years, 2007–2013, mean PAW dropped more in percentage terms than mean NW—20 versus 16 percent—whereas median PAW fell to about the same degree as median NW—an astonishing 70 percent. Indeed, by 2013, median net worth had plummeted to $7,000 among young households and median PAW to $12,200. This illustrates that the fortunes of young households deteriorated during the 1990s and 2000s.

The pattern is similar among age group 65 and over as among middle-aged and all households. Mean PAW advanced 78 percent from 1983 to 2007, less than the 86 percent gain in mean NW, and median PAW grew by 44 percent, again less than the 72 percent increase in median NW. From 2007 to 2013, mean PAW declined by 5.0 percent, less than the 8.5 percent reduction in mean NW, and median PAW fell by 7 percent, again less than the 18 percent fall in median NW.

Generally speaking, households fared worse in terms of PAW than in conventional NW between 1989 (or 1983) and 2007 (except for young households for whom median PAW declined less in percentage terms than did median NW). This finding indicates that the explosive growth of DC plans after 1989 did not fully compensate for the collapse of DB plans, at least in terms of the growth of household wealth through 2007. However, over the Great Recession, from 2007 to 2013, mean and median PAW dropped somewhat less in percentage terms than mean and median NW (except for young households).

I now turn to an appraisal of what happened to AW, the sum of NWX, PW, and SSW. Augmented wealth is the most comprehensive measure of the set of resources available for retirement, and so its change over time is of interest when considering trends in retirement adequacy. There was rapid growth in AW during the 1990s but a marked slowdown occurred during the period 2001–2007. Indeed, median AW barely advanced at all for the older age groups and actually fell in absolute terms among young households. Over the Great Recession, from 2007 to 2013, both mean and median AW declined in absolute terms, with the sole exception of age group 65 and over for whom median AW remained steady.

Mean NW among all households rose by 44 percent between 1989 and 2001, while median NW increased by 16 percent. Adding in DBW, we find that mean PAW was up by 37 percent and median PAW by 4 percent. If we include SSW, mean AW rose by 39 percent and median AW by 23 percent. The rapid growth of SSW over the 1990s made up, in part, for the slower growth of PW in the middle of the distribution, thus explaining the more rapid increase in AW than PAW.

Patterns vary by age group. Among young households, mean AW increased by 22 percent, compared to a 20 percent rise in NW, and median AW rose by 18 percent, compared to a 13 percent drop in NW. Among middle-aged households, mean AW grew by 42 percent, compared to a 47 percent increase in NW, and median AW gained 27 percent, compared to a 3 percent rise for NW. Older households experienced a 38 percent gain in mean AW, compared to a 44 percent growth in mean NW, and median AW advanced by 37 percent, about the same as median NW.

The years 2001 to 2007 were different. The growth in mean AW slowed down, registering a 14 percent gain among all households compared to a 39 percent increase in 1989–2001. This translates into an annual growth rate of 2.77 percent in the first period and 2.25 percent in the second. On the other hand, median AW advanced slightly faster in the second period, an annual rate of 1.8 percent in comparison to an annual rate of 1.75 percent in 1989–2001. However, there is evidence of a slowdown for each of the three age groups. Mean AW remained virtually unchanged and median AW declined in absolute terms for young households in the 2001–2007 period, whereas both rose by about 20 percent during the 1990s. Mean AW grew by only 9 percent for middle-aged households in the later period, whereas it increased by 42 percent in the 1989–2001 period, and median AW showed almost no change in the 2000s compared to a 27 percent growth in the 1990s. For older households, median AW remained virtually unchanged in the later period though it gained 37 percent in the earlier period, but mean AW advanced at about the same annual rate in 2001–2007 as it had in the 1990s.

Over the period 1989–2007, mean AW grew 60 percent among all households, slower than PAW (63 percent) or NW (73 percent). On the other hand, median AW grew at about the same rate as median NW among all households (about 37 percent) and faster than median PAW (25 percent). The relatively slower growth in mean AW versus mean PAW (and mean NW) is due to the fact that mean SSW increased less rapidly than mean NW over these years. But the higher growth in median AW versus median PAW (and median NW) reflects the fact that SSW is heavily concentrated in the middle of the wealth distribution, and that median SSW advanced at the same rate as median NW over these years.

The same pattern held for middle-aged households over these years (and over the period 1983–2007). Among young households mean AW rose faster than mean NW or mean PAW, whereas median AW showed positive growth and gains were negative for median PAW and median NW. Among seniors, mean and median NW increased faster than PAW, which in turn showed a higher percentage gain than AW. It is also the case that median AW grew slower than mean AW among all households—60 percent for mean AW from 1989 to 2007 and only 37 percent for median AW. Results are similar by age group. These results are indicative of rising inequality in augmented wealth over these years.

The picture once again changed over the Great Recession. From 2007 to 2013, mean AW among all households fell by 12 percent, but this decline was less in percentage terms than that of PAW (14 percent) and NW (16 percent). More notably, median AW dropped by 22 percent, though this was considerably less than PAW (36 percent) and NW (45 percent). Results are quite similar by age group. Among young households, median AW dropped by 25 percent whereas median NW fell by a stunning 71 percent; among the middle-aged, the former slipped by 27 percent while the latter went down by 52 percent; and among seniors median AW actually went up by 1.6 percent, compared to an 18 percent fall in median NW. These comparisons highlight the moderating influence of SSW on middle-class wealth over the Great Recession when median SSW was down a lot less than median NW and median PW, particularly DBW. Indeed, the Social Security system acted as a cushion for household wealth, softening the blows from the Great Recession.

Inequality of Augmented Wealth

I next look at what happened to the inequality of AW from 1983 to 2013. It is first useful to look at the relative levels of inequality of its components. In 2007, SSW was the most equal component, with a Gini coefficient of 0.363 among all households. PW registered a value of 0.783 and NWX a value of 0.857. Adding DCW lowered the Gini coefficient to 0.834, indicating that despite its high degree of inequality, on net it had an equalizing effect on household wealth. Next, adding DBW to obtain PAW lowered the Gini coefficient to 0.805. Thus, DBW also had an equalizing effect on household wealth. This result reflects the fact that DBW is distributed much more equally than NW. Altogether, the addition of PW to NWX lessened inequality by 0.052 points. However, a much larger impact came from SSW, which when added to NWX reduced the Gini coefficient by 0.163 points. This effect is due to the much lower inequality of SSW than of NW, as well as its relatively low (though positive) correlation with NW. Finally, adding both PW and SSW to NWX led to a 0.173 decline in the Gini coefficient. As a consequence, it is apparent that the main equalizing effect of retirement wealth comes from Social Security, not private pensions. Results are similar for the three individual age groups.

The inequality of NW among all households increased from 1983 to 1989 (0.029 Gini points), stayed fairly steady from 1989 to 2007, and experienced another sharp spike from 2007 to 2010 (0.032 Gini points) and a very modest increase from 2010 to 2013 (0.005 Gini points). How does the addition of PW and SSW affect trends in wealth inequality?

The attrition of DB plans from 1983 to 2007 led to a rise in wealth inequality. DB wealth is fairly equalizing, so when it is diminished, it helps to fuel a rise in inequality. In addition, the equalizing effect of DBW has lessened with the passage of time. Whereas the Gini coefficient for NW among all households increased by a very modest 0.006 points over the years 1989 to 2007, the Gini coefficient for PAW advanced by 0.012 points. Alternatively, adding DBW to NW resulted in a 0.035 decline in the Gini coefficient in 1989 but only a 0.029 decrease in 2007. However, from 2007 to 2013, DB wealth ameliorated the rise in inequality. Over these years, the Gini coefficient for PAW rose by 0.032 whereas that for NW was up by 0.037. In other words, adding DB wealth to NW produced a 0.029 drop in the Gini coefficient in 2007 but a 0.035 decrease in 2013. This difference reflected a rise in DBW over these years.

The results are even stronger for middle-aged households and over a longer time span, 1983 to 2007. For this group, the Gini coefficient for NW increased by 0.033 points while that for PAW ballooned by 0.070 points. Here we see even stronger evidence that the equalizing effect of DBW wore off over time. Adding DBW caused the Gini coefficient to decline by 0.073 in 1983 and 0.036 in 2007. From 2007 to 2013, on the other hand, the Gini coefficient went up by 0.043 for NW but only 0.036 for PAW. The addition of DBW to NW lessened the Gini coefficient by 0.036 in 2007 but by 0.044 in 2013.

Results for older households are similar. Among them PAW inequality increased by 0.040 Gini points from 1983 to 2007, whereas NW inequality remained virtually unchanged. From 2007 to 2013, the Gini coefficient was up by 0.003 for PAW but by 0.018 for NW. However, the pattern is different for young households. Among them, the Gini coefficient for PAW changed by −0.001 from 1989 to 2007, slightly more than the −0.007 change in the Gini coefficient for NW. From 2007 to 2013, the Gini coefficient rose by 0.086 points for PAW, slightly more than the 0.084-point rise for NW.

Figure 8.4a provides an alternative picture of the change in the size distribution of PAW among all households between 1989 and 2013. Over the 1989–2001 period, major gains were made by households at the high end of the PAW distribution while households at the bottom of the distribution experienced an absolute decline. Between these two extremes, relative gains showed

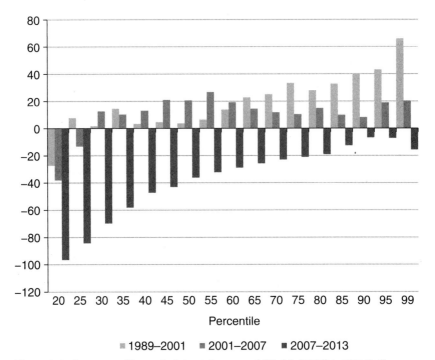

Figure 8.4a. Percentage Change in Private Augmented Wealth (PAW) in 2013 Dollars by PAW Percentile, All Households, 1989, 2001, 2007, and 2013

no discernable pattern, which is consistent with the finding of a slight increase in the Gini coefficient over these years. From 2001 to 2007, the highest growth in PAW occurred roughly in the middle of the PAW distribution, with sharp declines at the bottom end. This pattern is also consistent with the modest increase in the Gini coefficient for PAW over these years. In contrast, from 2007 to 2013, the percentage change in PAW was negative at all percentiles. However, there was an almost positive monotonic relationship between percentile and the percentage change in PAW, which is consistent with the finding of rising inequality in PAW over these years.

Among middle-aged households, the percentage change in PAW was negative up to the forty-fifth percentile and then positive after that over years 1989 to 2001 (see Figure 8.4b). Over the second period, the percentage growth in PAW was positive at all percentiles but with no distinct pattern. These results are consistent with a rising Gini coefficient over the earlier period and

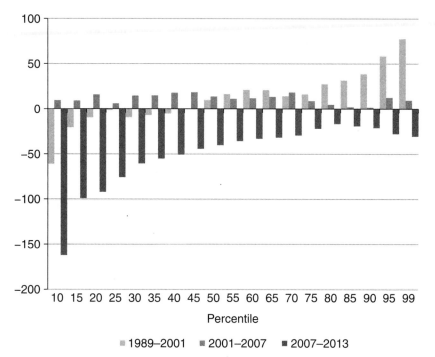

Figure 8.4b. Percentage Change in Private Augmented Wealth (PAW) in 2013 Dollars by PAW Percentile, Ages 47 to 64, 1989, 2001, 2007, and 2013

little change over the second. As was the case for all households, from 2007 to 2013 the percentage change in PAW was negative at all percentiles and there was an almost positive monotonic relationship between percentile and percentage change, which is again consistent with the finding of rising inequality in PAW over these years.

We saw that adding DBW to NW to create PAW resulted in a modest reduction in measured inequality. Here, it will become apparent that including SSW resulted in a fairly sizable decrease in measured inequality.

The inequality of NW among all households was essentially unchanged over the years 1989 to 2007. In contrast, the inequality of AW showed a sizable increase, rising by 0.021 Gini points. This is tantamount to saying that the equalizing effect of retirement wealth mitigated over the 1989–2007 period. While the addition of RW to NW reduced the Gini coefficient by 0.165 points in 1989, the difference was only 0.15 in 2007. Thus, the inequality reduction resulting from the addition of RW to NW fell over years 1989 to 2007. In contrast, from 2007 to 2013, the inequality of AW increased by only 0.017, while that for NW went up by 0.037. In other words, the effect increased over these years in contrast to the 1989–2007 period.

Among young households, the inequality of both NW and AW declined slightly from 1989 to 2007, but from 2007 to 2013 the Gini coefficient for NW was up 0.084 while that for AW rose only about half as much, 0.046. Among middle-aged households the Gini coefficient for NW increased by 0.02 from 1989 to 2007 whereas for AW it advanced by 0.031 points. Indeed, over the full 1983–2007 period, while the Gini coefficient of NW was up by 0.033 points, for AW it gained 0.076 points. Over the Great Recession, the former rose much more than the latter—0.043 versus 0.015. Among older households the Gini coefficient for NW was almost unchanged, while that for AW climbed by 0.066 points between 1983 and 2007. From 2007 to 2013, in contrast, inequality in AW actually declined a bit while it rose for NW. Thus, for both middle-aged and older households, the same pattern occurred as for all households, namely that the inequality of AW rose more than for NW between 1983(1989) and 2007. From 2007 to 2013, inequality increased less for AW than for NW in all households and all age groups individually.

The inequality of AW increased while that of NW remained unchanged from 1989 to 2007 because of the increased inequality of RW. This result held for the sample of all households, that of young households, and that of middle-aged ones (though not for the sample of older households). In addition, the correlation coefficient between nonpension wealth NWX and RW advanced from 0.18 to 0.25 among all households and from 0.16 to 0.22 among middle-aged ones.[44] Yet, the inequality of AW rose less than that of NW from 2007 to 2013 because the share of RW in AW went up over these years, while that of NWX declined. Since RW inequality was much lower than NWX inequality, this shift lowered overall AW inequality. This shift occurred for all the sample of all households and those of each of the three age groups individually. An additional factor is that the correlation coefficient between NWX and RW declined slightly, from 0.25 in 2007 to 0.23 in 2013 among all households and from 0.22 to 0.20 among age group 47–64.

Figure 8.5a gives a graphical depiction of changes in the distribution of AW among all households over the period 1989–2013. Among all households, percentage changes in AW over the 1989–2001 period were positive and formed a U-shaped pattern, bottoming out at the fiftieth percentile. In con-

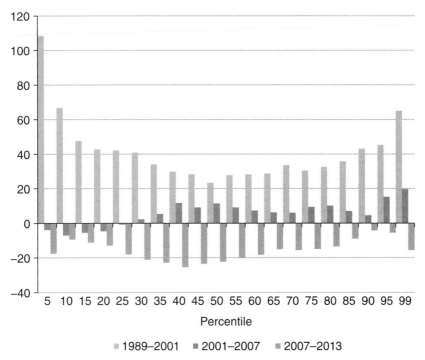

Figure 8.5a. Percentage Change in Augmented Wealth (AW) in 2013 Dollars by AW Percentile, All Households, 1989, 2001, 2007, and 2013

trast, from 2001 to 2007, changes in AW were negative at the bottom of the distribution (up through the thirtieth percentile) and generally positive above this. Moreover, percentage gains were positively correlated with the initial AW level. These results are consistent with the finding of little change in the inequality of AW from 1989 to 2001 and an increase in inequality from 2001 to 2007. In contrast, percentage changes in AW over years 2007 to 2013 were uniformly negative and were largest in the middle of the distribution (the twentieth to seventy-fifth percentiles), which explains the very small increase in AW inequality over these years.

Among middle-aged households, percentage changes in AW over the 1989–2001 period were positive and formed a U-shaped pattern, bottoming out at the thirtieth percentile (see Figure 8.5b). This was a period when AW saw a moderate increase in inequality, reflecting the fact that percentage gains were somewhat more heavily concentrated in the upper 70 percent of

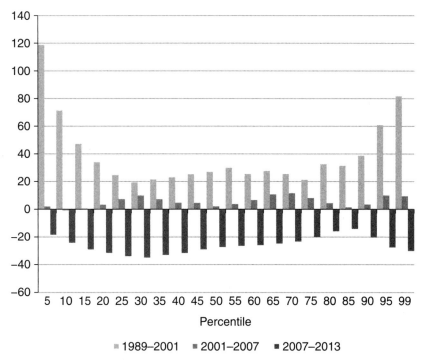

Figure 8.5b. Percentage Change in Augmented Wealth (AW) in 2013 Dollars by AW Percentile, Ages 47 to 64, 1989, 2001, 2007, and 2013

the distribution. From 2001 to 2007, changes in AW were generally positive and small but the pattern was uneven. However, once again, positive gains were somewhat more heavily concentrated in the upper tail of the distribution, accounting for the moderate increase in AW inequality. In contrast, percentage changes in AW over the period 2007–2013 were uniformly negative and were largest in the middle of the distribution (the twentieth to seventieth percentiles), which explains the relatively small increase in AW inequality over these years.

Alternative Concepts of Retirement Wealth

There is no one "correct" concept of retirement wealth.[45] This chapter has used the standard measure of pension wealth and SSW. The following sensitivity analysis introduces four alternative concepts of retirement wealth to determine whether the basic results still hold up, particularly for the years of the Great Recession.

Employer Contributions to DC Pension Plans

The analysis so far has treated DC and DB pension wealth (as well as SSW) the same. There is, however, an important difference between DCW and the other two elements. DBW is defined as the discounted future stream of DB pension benefits and assumes that the employee remains at his or her firm of employment until the expected retirement date (i.e., the "ongoing concern" assumption). The computation of SSW makes the same assumption. The valuation of DCW, on the other hand, is based solely on the current market value of the DC plan. The length of the individual's employment does not add value to the calculation of DCW.

Adding a projection of the future stream of *employer* contributions to DC accounts puts DCW on comparable footing with DBW. In most cases, the employer contribution is a fixed percentage of the employee's salary. On the basis of estimated human capital earnings functions and the ongoing concern assumption, it is possible to calculate the present value of the annual stream of future employer contributions to the DC plan until retirement (referred to as DCEMP).[46] Adding DCEMP to DCW makes DCW comparable to DBW, as both now reflect the available retirement wealth at an individual's time of retirement due to *employer* contributions to retirement plans.

Even with the addition of DCEMP to DCW, however, there are still some differences between the two types of pension wealth. In particular, there is greater risk associated with DCW. The benefit levels in DB plans are set by the plan terms. DBW depends only on future labor force participation in the company and future earnings. The establishment of the Pension Benefit Guaranty Corporation in 1974 insured pension benefits up to a fixed amount in the event of company bankruptcy. In comparison, DCW depends not only on future labor force participation and future earnings but also on future employee contributions, future employer contributions, and future rates of return. Indeed, the stock market experience of the 2000 to 2003 period and of the 2007 to 2010 period shows how difficult it would have been to project the future value of DCW even over these short periods. DB benefits are more certain than DC benefits. The shifting of the risk from employer to employee is one of the reasons behind the increase of DC plans.

The basic accounting framework can then be modified as follows:

$$DCEMP = DCEMP_a + DCEMP_b. \qquad (8.6)$$

$$DCW^* = DCW + DCEMP. \qquad (8.7)$$

$$PW^* = DBW + DCW^*. \qquad (8.8)$$

$$PAW^* = NWX + PW^*. \qquad (8.9)$$

$$RW^* = PW^* + SSW \qquad (8.10)$$

$$AW^* = NWX + PW^* + SSW \qquad (8.11)$$

Gains generally look stronger when DCEMP is included (see Table 8.8).[47] In 2001, the average value of DCEMP among age group 47–64 was $39,600 (in 2013 dollars), or 31 percent of DCW. In 1989, the corresponding ratio was greater, at 60 percent. The higher ratio in 1989 reflects the lower accumulations of DCW in that year compared to 2001 (the absolute value in DCEMP was much greater in 2001 than in 1989). In 2007, the mean value of DCEMP was $41,500, slightly larger than in 2001. The change from 2001 to 2007 reflects lower contributions to DC plans by employers and, for some firms, the termination of employer contributions. By 2007, the ratio of DCEMP to DCW had fallen to 28 percent. Somewhat surprisingly, the ratio then jumped to 36 percent in 2010. Part of this change reflected the fall-off in DCW over this period from the stock market tumble but it also reflected a sizable increase in mean DCEMP, from $41,500 to $55,400. In contrast, from 2010 to 2013, the mean value of DCEMP fell to $31,200. This reduction probably reflects the fact that many firms discontinued 401(k) and other DC plans or reduced contributions over these years.[48]

The addition of DCEMP increased the mean value of PW by 17 percent in 2001. The corresponding figure in 1989 was 10 percent. The addition of DCEMP, not surprisingly, generally enhanced the growth of mean pension wealth between 1983 and 2001. Mean PW* increased by 148 percent over the 1983–2001 period, compared to a 113 percent gain in PW. The situation was different in 2001–2007. In 2007, the inclusion of DCEMP enhanced the mean value of PW by 16 percent, almost exactly the same as in 2001. As a result, mean PW* gained 6.1 percent from 2001 to 2007, slightly lower than the growth of mean PW. From 2007 to 2013, mean PW* dropped by 8.8 percent while mean PW remained largely unchanged.

Evidence of the slowdown in the growth of AW is also evident for AW* (see Table 8.8 and Figure 8.6). Median AW* gained 37 percent from 1983 to 2001, compared to 30 percent for median AW, but only 2 percent from 2001 to 2007, about the same as median AW. From 2007 to 2013, median AW* plummeted by 27 percent, also about the same as median AW. As with AW, median AW* grew slower than mean AW*—40 percent versus 68 percent from 1983 to 2007 and −27 percent versus −23 percent for 2007–2013. However, notably, as with median AW, median AW* grew at a higher rate than median NW over years 1983 to 2007 but diminished less in percentage terms over the 2007 to 2013 period than median NW.

Trends in inequality are also very similar between AW* and AW. The Gini coefficient for AW* climbed by 0.073 from 1983 to 2007, about the same as AW, and in both cases more than that of NW. It then increased by 0.014 from 2007 to 2013, about the same as AW, and less than that of NW. As was the case for RW, the inequality reducing effect of RW* lessened over years 1989 to 2007 and then enlarged over years 2007 to 2013.

Employee Contributions to DC Pension Plans

The next consideration is the addition of the discounted value of future *employee* contributions to DC plans (DCEMPW).[49] The inclusion of this variable is a logical extension of the addition of DCEMP. In fact, for the vast majority of firms, the provision of an employer contribution to a DC plan is *contingent* on payments made by an employee into a company-sponsored pension plan.

The new accounting framework becomes:

$$DCW^{**} = DCW + DCEMP + DCEMPW \qquad (8.12)$$

$$PW^{**} = DBW + DCW^{**} \qquad (8.13)$$

$$PAW^{**} = NWX + PW^{**} \qquad (8.14)$$

$$RW^{**} = PW^{**} + SSW \qquad (8.15)$$

$$AW^{**} = NWX + PW^{**} + SSW \qquad (8.16)$$

Table 8.8. Time trends in alternative measures of augmented wealth, age group 47–64, 1983–2013 (dollar figures are in thousands, 2013 dollars)

	1983	1989	2001	2007	2010	2013	Percentage Change[a]				
							1983–1989	1989–2001	2001–2007	2007–2010	2010–2013
A. *Mean Values*											
1. Pension wealth	112.1	135.6	238.2	253.2	227.4	226.9	21.0	75.6	6.3	-10.2	-0.2
2. Pension wealth*	112.1	149.5	277.9	294.7	282.9	258.1	33.4	85.8	6.1	-4.0	-8.8
3. Pension wealth**	—	165.2	290.3	319.6	363.0	319.7	—	75.7	10.1	13.6	-11.9
4. Pension wealth accrued	—	—	—	204.7	219.7	207.7					
5. Social Security wealth	178.2	155.6	242.7	242.4	210.9	214.2					
6. Social Security wealth accrued	—	—	—	228.8	206.0	198.0					
B. *Mean Values*											
1. Net worth	491.8	536.1	787.3	902.8	769.9	662.3	9.0	46.9	14.7	-14.7	-14.0
2. Augmented wealth	769.2	804.4	1141.2	1248.0	1054.3	962.7	4.6	41.9	9.4	-15.5	-8.7
3. Augmented wealth*	769.2	818.3	1180.9	1289.5	1109.8	993.8	6.4	44.3	9.2	-13.9	-10.4
4. Augmented wealth**	—	834.0	1193.3	1314.4	1189.9	1055.5	—	43.1	10.1	-9.5	-11.3
5. Projected augmented wealth	—	1011.8	1267.8	1372.3	1310.8	1116.6	—	25.3	8.2	-4.5	-14.8
6. Accrued augmented wealth	—	—	—	1034.9	887.7	786.5	—	—	—	-14.2	-11.4
C. *Median Values*											
1. Net worth	142.6	175.3	181.1	232.1	141.3	110.7	23.0	3.3	28.2	-39.1	-21.7
2. Augmented wealth	409.9	419.5	534.4	545.6	394.9	396.2	2.3	27.4	2.1	-27.6	0.3
3. Augmented wealth*	410.6	420.9	561.9	573.7	417.7	418.1	2.5	33.5	2.1	-27.2	0.1

4. Augmented wealth**	—	427.8	570.7	588.4	451.7	439.7	—	33.4	3.1	−23.2	−2.7
5. Projected augmented wealth	—	487.0	591.6	607.7	480.1	458.2	—	21.5	2.7	−21.0	−4.6
6. Accrued augmented wealth				417.7	333.5	309.3	—	—	—	−20.2	−7.2
D. Gini Coefficients											
1. Net worth	0.761	0.775	0.798	0.795	0.825	0.838	0.013	0.024	−0.003	0.030	0.013
2. Augmented wealth	0.574	0.619	0.637	0.650	0.678	0.665	0.045	0.018	0.013	0.028	−0.013
3. Augmented wealth*	0.574	0.618	0.633	0.647	0.679	0.661	0.044	0.016	0.013	0.032	−0.018
4. Augmented wealth**	—	0.617	0.632	0.643	0.677	0.659		0.015	0.011	0.033	−0.018
5. Projected augmented wealth	—	0.644	0.640	0.648	0.688	0.667		−0.004	0.008	0.040	−0.021
6. Accrued augmented wealth				0.668	0.681	0.681				0.013	−0.001

Source: Author's computations from the 1983, 1989, 2001, 2007, 2010, and 2013 Survey of Consumer Finances. Households are classified into age groups by the age of the head of household.

AW = NWX + PW + SSW.

AW* = NWX + PW* + SSW.

AWP = NWP + DBW + SSW, where NWP is projected net worth at year of retirement in 2010 dollars.

AWACC = NW + DBACC + SSWACC.

*, augmented wealth including future employer contributions to defined contributions plans; **, augmented wealth including future employer and employee contributions to defined contributions plans;

a. Percentage point change in Panel D.

Abbreviations: AW, augmented wealth; AWACC, augmented wealth accrued; AWP, projected augmented wealth; DBACC, defined benefits accrued; DBW, defined benefit pension wealth; NW, net worth; NWP, projected net worth; NWX, nonpension wealth; PW, pension wealth; SSW, Social Security wealth; SSWACC, Social Security wealth accrued.

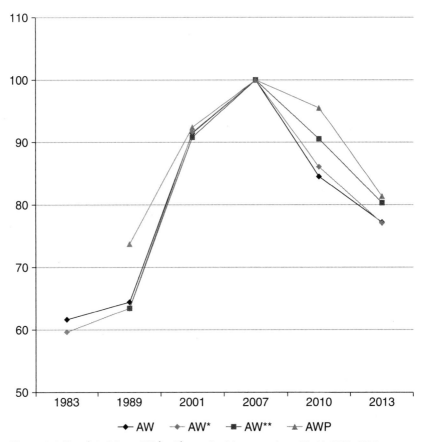

Figure 8.6. Trends in Mean AW for Alternative Measures, Ages 47–64, 1983–2013 (Index, 2007 = 100)

DCEMPW was a little higher than DCEMP in 1989, quite a bit lower in 2001 and 2007, and higher in 2010 and 2013. There was also a sizable increase in mean DCEMPW, as there was in DCEMP, from 2007 to 2010. In this case the mean value increased from $24,900 to $80,100. The likely reason is that workers were trying to make up for the lost value in their DC balances, which resulted from the stock market decline over those years. As with DCEMP, DCEMPW fell between 2010 and 2013 as firms discontinued plans and reduced their contributions. PW** grew slightly slower than PW* from 1989 to 2007 (93 versus 97 percent) and remained almost constant from 2007 to 2013, while PW* lost 12.4 percent.[50]

However, the time trend for AW** is almost the same as those for AW and AW* (see Table 8.8 and Figure 8.6). Mean AW** advanced by 43 percent from 1989 to 2001, almost exactly the same as mean AW and mean AW*; mean AW** then grew by 10 percent from 2001 to 2007, also almost the same as AW and AW*; and mean AW** declined by 20 percent from 2007 to 2013, somewhat less than AW and AW*. Median AW** gained 33 percent from 1989 to 2001, almost identical to AW* but more than AW, and then only 3 percent from 2001 to 2007, about the same as AW* and AW. From 2007 to 2013, median AW** fell by 20 percent, compared to 23 percent for median AW and median AW*. As with AW and AW*, median AW** declined less in percentage terms than NW. Trends in inequality are also similar between AW** and both AW* and AW (in fact, the Gini coefficients are almost exactly the same for all three). Of note is the fact that once again, the inequality of AW**, like that of AW and AW*, increased more from 1989 to 2007 than that of NW and rose less than that of NW from 2007 to 2013.

Projected Wealth at Retirement

The third concept is based on a projection of total household wealth up to the year of retirement (in most cases, age 65). Both DBW and SSW are valued as of age of retirement. DCEMP and DCEMPW show the discounted value of projected employer and employee contributions to DC plans from current age to age of retirement. At first glance, the sensible procedure might be to project nonpension wealth (NWX) to year of retirement and add that to DBW, SSW, DCEMP, and DCEMPW.

However, this procedure implicitly assumes that there is *no* substitution between DC contributions and savings in nonpension wealth. Employees who contribute to a DC plan are likely to save less in other forms of wealth, ceteris paribus, than workers who do not contribute. Moreover, if the employer also makes a contribution to a DC plan, other savings might be reduced even more. It is not possible to accurately estimate the elasticity of substitution between DCW and other forms of wealth and, as a result, not feasible to independently project nonpension wealth to age of retirement.

Another possibility is to project household NW on the basis of the household's portfolio composition and historical rates of return by asset type. The downside of this approach is that while it is feasible to project future capital gains on this basis, it is very hard to project future savings rates.[51] Therefore, this approach will give only a partial answer to estimating future NW.

An alternative method is the straightforward projection of NW (including DCW, DCEMP, and DCEMPW) based on historical changes in the NW of age group 47–64. Moreover, these computations are made for seven income classes (results are very similar using wealth classes as well). For example, using data from the SCF for age group 47–64 over the period from 1983 to 2007, I calculate an annual average real growth rate in NW of 2.54 percent for this age group. This approach also avoids the difficulty of determining whether there is substitution between DC contributions and other forms of savings.

In the projection, I use the actual growth rates by income class for each of five periods: 1983–1989, 1989–2001, 2001–2007, 2007–2010, and 2010–2013. For the period after 2013, I use the 1983–2013 average annual growth rate for NW to project NW after this year.

Results in Table 8.8 are shown for projected augmented wealth (AWP), where

$$AWP = NWP + DBW + SSW + DCEMP + DCEMPW \qquad (8.17)$$

and NWP equals projected NW at year of retirement (also see Figure 8.6).[52] The percentage difference between mean AWP and mean AW** was quite small in 2001, 2007, 2010, and 2013—varying from 4 to 10 percent. These modest differences reflect the fact that a large proportion of middle-aged households were close to retirement, so that their current NW was close to what it would be at retirement. The difference was much larger in 1989, at 21 percent, because the average growth in NW for this age group was much higher than in subsequent periods (3.2 percent per year from 1989 to 2001).

As a consequence, AWP grew slower than AW** from 1989 to 2007. While mean AW** increased by 58 percent, AWP grew by only 36 percent, and while median AW** rose by 38 percent, median AWP gained only 35 percent. The Gini coefficients for AWP were higher than those for AW**, especially in 1989, reflecting the faster growth in NW for higher income households. As a result, whereas the Gini coefficient for AW** rose by 0.026 points from 1989 to 2007, that for AWP increased by only 0.004. Likewise, while the Gini coefficient for AW** advanced by 0.016 points from 2007 to 2013, that for

AWP rose by 0.019. The rise in the Gini coefficient between 2007 and 2013 for both AW** and AWP, however, was less than that of NW (0.043 points).

The Accrual Value of Retirement Wealth

The fourth alternative measure is based on the accrual value of DBW and SSW. This shows the value of each plan based on the individual's work history *to date.* In the case of DBW, the value is based on the answer to the following question in the SCF questionnaire: "If you left this job now, what would you be eligible to receive from this plan—a lump sum distribution or settlement to keep or to roll over or would you receive regular payments now or later?" The computation of the accrual value of DBW is exactly the same as that for DBW except that the accrual benefit replaces the expected benefit at retirement. The total accrual value of DB pension wealth, DBACC, is then the sum of the present value of future accrual DB benefits from current jobs plus the present value of future DB benefits from previous jobs, including DB benefits currently being received.

In the case of SSW, the accrual value (SSWACC) is based on the individual's average indexed monthly earnings computed on the basis of the individual's work history *to date* and the corresponding value of the primary insurance amount (PIA).[53] DBACC and SSWACC thus put retirement wealth on an equal footing with NW, since all three are valued as of the current date. This is similar to the relation among NWP and DBW and SSW, which in this case are all valued as of the date of retirement. Then, the accrual value of AW is given by:

$$AWACC = NW + DBACC + SSWACC. \qquad (8.18)$$

Whereas DBW fell by 16 percent between 2007 and 2013 as many plans were halted and benefit levels frozen, the accrual value of DB plans (DBACC) actually rose by 23 percent. The difference is likely due to the fact that by law DB accruals (in the United States at least) cannot be eliminated or even reduced even if a plan is terminated. As a result, the ratio of DBACC to DBW rose from 53 to 78 percent over these years. The ratio of PWACC to PW was quite high, from 81 to 97 percent in these years—a reflection of the predominance of DCW in PW.

Like SSW, the mean value of SSWACC fell over years 2007 to 2013. The percentage declines were very similar. Indeed, mean SSWACC was quite close to mean SSW—ratios ranging from 92 percent to 98 percent over the three years. Many workers in this age group were nearing the end of their work life, so further accumulations into the Social Security system were relatively small. Indeed, the ratio of accrual PIA to full PIA was 0.79 for male workers and 0.75 for female workers in 2013 for this age group. In addition, the Social Security benefit formula is progressive, giving a larger benefit (PIA) relative to contributions for lower-income workers.

Time trends for AWACC are also remarkably similar to those for AW, at least over years 2007 to 2013 (see Table 8.8). Mean AW and mean AWACC fell from 23 to 24 percent from 2007 to 2013, and the median values dropped by 26 to 27 percent. In both cases, the median fell far less than median NW. With regard to inequality trends, it is first of note that the Gini coefficient for AWACC was higher than that for AW. The difference reflected the lower weight of DB wealth, which tends to be equalizing, in AWACC than in AW. The Gini coefficient for AW increased by 0.015 between 2007 and 2013, whereas that for AWACC was up by 0.012. In both cases, the Gini coefficient rose substantially less for AW than for NW.

Conclusion

The picture that unfolded over the three decades from 1983 to 2013 revolves around the four components of AW—nonpension wealth (NWX), traditional DBW, DCW, and SSW. DBW and SSW played the role of "equalizers," reducing inequality and pulling up the median. In contrast, NWX and DC were the "disequalizers," increasing inequality and lowering the median. As DB plans fell off and were replaced by DC plans, the growth of median wealth slowed and wealth inequality rose. SSW was a stable presence throughout these years but grew in relative terms during the Great Recession, helping to moderate the precipitous decline in median wealth and the sharp rise in wealth inequality.

The years from 1983 to 2013 witnessed the transformation of the traditional DB pension system in favor of DC pension coverage, with the share of households covered by DB plans falling sharply and those covered by a DC plan increasing sharply. DCW was also up dramatically as DBW fell.

By conventional wealth measures, the period from 1983 to 2007 was one of robust growth, with mean NW surging by 84 percent among middle-aged households.[54] However, for PAW, the gains were a bit more modest, only 70 percent. Mean SSW grew at a slower rate, 36 percent over the period, and, all told, mean AW gained 62 percent.

The story is not quite as robust when we look at median values. Median NW advanced by 63 percent, median PAW was up by 32 percent, and median AW rose by 33 percent. The difference in trends between mean and median reflected the relative decline in DBW and the corresponding relative increase in DCW. Moreover, both median PAW and median AW increased only about half as much as median NW, again reflecting the relative decline in DBW.

Even these relatively healthy trends over years 1983 to 2007 hide important differences by subperiod. Indeed, one of the key findings of this chapter is that there was a marked slowdown in the growth of PW, PAW, and AW in the years 2001 to 2007 as compared to the 1980s and 1990s. Indeed, the DC pension system looked very successful in the 1980s and 1990s, while the stock market was booming, but then fell flat from 2001 to 2007 even before the financial meltdown. Among middle-aged households, in particular, the annual growth rate of average PW fell by more than three-quarters, from 4.2 percent over the 1983 to 2001 period to 1 percent over the 2001 to 2007 period.

Likewise, the annual growth rate of mean AW fell off from 2.2 percent over the 1983–2001 period to 1.5 percent over the 2001–2007 period, while that of median AW showed an even steeper decline, from 1.5 percent to 0.3 percent per year. The slow growth in median AW from 2001 to 2007 once again reflected the relative decline in DBW and corresponding rise in DCW.

The years of the Great Recession saw a 10 percent decrease in mean PW, a 27 percent decline in mean NW, and a staggering 52 percent decline in median NW. Mean and median PAW each declined about the same degree as NW. However, median AW was down by "only" 27 percent because of the relative increase in SSW over these years and its concentration in the middle of the wealth distribution.

Retirement wealth does have a marked effect on inequality. Adding RW to NW substantially lowers the Gini coefficient. Most of the equalizing effect came from the addition of SSW. However, the equalizing effects of retirement wealth lessened from 1983 to 2007. From 1983 to 2007, while the Gini coefficient for NW among middle-aged households rose by 0.033 points, and that for AW climbed by 0.076. In other words, the addition of RW to NW reduced the overall Gini coefficient by 0.187 in 1983 but by only 0.145 in 2007. This was the result of the relative decline of DBW and the corresponding rise of DCW.

In contrast, from 2007 to 2013, while the Gini coefficient for NW among middle-aged households jumped by 0.043, that for AW went up by only 0.015 points. The explanation for this is both the rising share of SSW in AW and the declining share of NWX. Since SSW has much lower inequality than NWX, its relative increase acted as a moderating influence on the increase in AW inequality over these years.

One important proviso to these results is that there now appears to be a very large (and growing) gap in life expectancies between upper- and lower-income households.[55] As a consequence, the use of mortality rates conditional on income (or wealth) level will lower the estimated equalizing effects of DBW and SSW. As the gap in longevity grows over time, the redistributional effects of these two components of augmented wealth would also lessen over time.

III

Who Are the Rich
and the Poor?

9

Wealth Differences among Socioeconomic Groups

I t is well known that there are important differences in income among different demographic groups. This chapter documents similar differences in wealth holdings and analyzes basic trends in and sources of these differences. The decomposition analysis herein is based on differences in capital revaluation, savings, and net intergenerational transfers between selected groups. Another approach used in this chapter is to standardize the composition of households by their average share in the population in consecutive years to analyze trends in overall mean wealth and wealth inequality.

Income class is paramount among socioeconomic variables. Though income and wealth are highly correlated, the correlation is far from unity. It is therefore of interest to examine wealth trends by income class. Earlier works have noted a sharp decline in the wealth of *middle-income* families from 2007 to 2013.[1] In this chapter, I use decomposition analysis to show that differences in capital appreciation, savings, and net wealth transfers can explain time trends in wealth holdings by income class. I then standardize wealth trends using a constant income distribution to see how the change in the income distribution affects overall mean wealth.

A related division is by educational group. It is true that education and income are closely related but once again the correlation is far from perfect. It is therefore of interest to examine wealth trends by years of schooling. Using decomposition analysis, I show that differences in the same three factors can account for time trends in wealth holdings by educational group. I then standardize wealth trends using a constant educational distribution to see how the change in the schooling distribution affects these time trends.

The standard Modigliani-Blumberg life cycle model predicts that wealth will rise with age until retirement age and then decline.[2] Cross-sectional age-wealth profiles for various years verify this general pattern. However, what is especially striking is that these profiles are not invariant over time. In particular, there was a steady shift in relative wealth holdings toward older Americans over the postwar period. Using decomposition analysis, I show again that the three factors cited here can explain time trends in wealth holdings by age group. I then standardize wealth trends using a constant age distribution to see how the change in the age distribution affects time trends in overall mean wealth.[3]

While black and Hispanic families have steadily gained on white families since 1983 in terms of relative income, relative wealth holdings, and the relative homeownership rate, by 2013 the gap in wealth between minorities and whites was still considerably greater than the gap in income. The analysis in this chapter shows that differences in capital revaluation, savings, and wealth transfers explain most of the racial/ethnic wealth gap. I also standardize wealth trends using a constant racial/ethnic mix to see how changes in race/ethnicity composition affects overall time trends.[4]

I divide the population into three basic household types: married couples, single males, and single females. Most analyses show that part of the rise in income inequality during the 1980s, particularly the drop in the share of income accruing to the bottom quintile, can be attributed to the increase in the proportion of female-headed families in the population. A similar analysis on wealth holdings, based on standardizing the composition of households by household type in consecutive years, shows that only a small part of the change in wealth inequality over time was due to changes in the composition of families over time. Most of the increase in inequality was within group.

Another dimension concerns the relative well-being of families with children. Families with children have seen their economic fortunes slip relative to childless families over the last forty years. Between 1974 and 1992, for example, the median income of the former fell by 2 percent in real terms, whereas the median income of the latter increased by 16 percent. Relative losses occurred among both married couples and female-headed households. Families with children also had lower wealth holdings than those without children. In 1992, the net worth of married couples with children was, on average, 64 percent of the net worth of nonelderly married couples without children and 63 percent of elderly families' new worth. Poverty rates have also increased for families with children both in absolute terms and relative to families without children.[5]

Another important socioeconomic division is between homeowners and renters. Whereas homeowner status is not independent of wealth holdings (wealthier households are more likely to own their own homes), it is important to distinguish the fortunes of these two groups. The fortunes of homeowners have advanced much more than those of renters over the last three decades.

The major finding of this chapter is the almost compete evaporation of financial resources among poor, lower middle-class, and even middle-class households over the Great Recession. Similar findings are reported for younger households, minorities, the less educated, single females with children, and renters.

There is a huge spread in wealth holdings by income class, with wealth rising almost monotonically with income levels. In 2013, the ratio of mean net worth between the top 1 percent and bottom quintile of income recipients was 156 to 1. Wealth disparities fanned out over time from 1983 to 2013. Moreover, racial and ethnic disparities in wealth holdings widened considerably in the years between 2007 and 2010. In terms of net worth and net equity in their homes, Hispanics were hit particularly hard by the Great Recession. Young households (under age 45) also got pummeled by the Great Recession, as their relative and absolute wealth declined sharply from 2007 to 2010. From 2010 to 2013 the racial and ethnic wealth gap also remained largely unchanged, though there was some recovery of the net worth of young households.

In 2013, the mean net worth of individuals with college degrees was ten times greater than the wealth of those with less than four years of high school, six times that of high school graduates, and almost four times that of people with one to three years of college. Between 1983 and 2013 the wealth of college graduates grew much more than that of the other three schooling groups. In 2013 married couples as a group had the highest mean wealth, 1.4 times that of married couples with children, 4.2 times that of single females as a group, and 14 times that of single females with children. The spread generally widened over years 1983 to 2013, with single mothers experiencing a sizable drop (22 percent) in their net worth. The gap in mean net worth between homeowners and renters was also very large—about a ten to one ratio—while median net worth and financial resources among renters were virtually zero throughout the thirty-year period.

Wealth Splays Out across Income Classes

The first part of this analysis looks at wealth holdings by income class. Income and wealth are not independent since part of wealth (like financial assets) generates income. However, it is of interest to determine how the wealth of different income percentiles evolved over time.

The ranking of wealth holdings in 2013 corresponded almost exactly to income class (see Table 9.1). The differences were huge. The top 1 percent of households *as ranked by income* held 156 times the mean wealth of the bottom quintile, 135 times that of the second quintile, 89 times that of the third quintile, and 44 times that of the fourth quintile. Mean net worth (NW) showed positive gains for all quantiles from 1983 to 2007 and then losses from 2007 to 2013.[6] Over the full thirty-year stretch from 1983 to 2013, the relative growth in mean NW was positively associated with income ranking, with the exception of the bottom quintile and top percentile (also see Figure 9.1). The percentage growth ranged from a low of −6 for the second quintile (this was the only group to lose in terms of mean NW over the thirty years) to a high of 98 percent for the top 5 percent. Mean NW by income class splayed out over time like a peacock opening its tail, with the ratio in mean NW between the top 1 percent and the second quintile rising from 79 to 135 and that between the top 1 percent and the middle quintile from 64 to 89.

Results are quite similar for median NW. The ranking of median NW in 2013 once again lined up almost exactly with income class. The differences were again enormous, with the top income percentile holding 7,300 times the median wealth of the bottom quintile, 583 times that of the second quintile, 162 times that of the third quintile, and 55 times that of the fourth quintile. Median NW increased for all quantiles from 1983 to 2007 except the bottom two quintiles and then decreased from 2007 to 2013. From 1983 to 2013, the percentage growth in median NW was positively related income ranking, with the exception of the top 1 percent. However, in this case, the bottom three quintiles showed absolute losses over these years, with the median NW of the bottom quintile down 85 percent to $1,000, the second quintile declining

Table 9.1. Household wealth and homeownership rates by income class, 1983–2013 (in thousands, 2013 dollars)

Income Quantile	1983	1989	2001	2007	2010	2013	% Change[a] 1983–2013
A. Mean Net Worth							
Bottom quintile	57.5	42.7	64.0	109.9	117.0	88.1	53.3
Second quintile	109.0	143.6	141.8	144.0	129.9	102.3	−6.2
Middle Quintile	135.2	191.5	202.8	217.1	197.0	155.4	14.9
Fourth quintile	209.8	240.0	363.8	401.2	290.4	312.8	49.1
Top quintile	1,008	1,134	1,798	2,153	1,817	1,904	88.8
Top 10 percent	1,631	1,859	2,914	3,636	3,009	3,174	94.6
Top 5 percent	2,682	2,948	4,686	5,900	4,970	5,315	98.2
Top 1 percent	8,639	8,627	11,141	16,094	12,293	13,775	59.4
Ratio to Top Quintile							
Bottom quintile	0.06	0.04	0.04	0.05	0.06	0.05	−0.01
Second quintile	0.11	0.13	0.08	0.07	0.07	0.05	−0.05
Middle quintile	0.13	0.17	0.11	0.10	0.11	0.08	−0.05
Fourth quintile	0.21	0.21	0.20	0.19	0.16	0.16	−0.04
Top quintile	1.00	1.00	1.00	1.00	1.00	1.00	0.00
Top 10 percent	1.62	1.64	1.62	1.69	1.66	1.67	0.05
Top 5 percent	2.66	2.60	2.61	2.74	2.73	2.79	0.13
Top 1 percent	8.57	7.61	6.20	7.47	6.76	7.23	−1.33
B. Median Net Worth							
Bottom quintile	6.8	1.3	2.9	3.4	1.0	1.0	−85.3
Second quintile	34.3	53.7	38.2	32.2	20.2	12.5	−63.5
Middle quintile	60.7	77.7	71.9	80.3	55.1	45.0	−25.8
Fourth quintile	106.6	120.0	165.7	212.1	108.8	132.2	24.0
Top quintile	321.7	372.6	540.8	631.3	543.8	569.5	77.0
Top 10 percent	516.1	626.4	1,053	1,214	1,214	1,091	111.4
Top 5 percent	871.5	1036.3	1,849	2,725	2,366	2,400	175.4
Top 1 percent	4,751	3,539	7,070	9,174	6,581	7,299	53.6
Ratio to Top Quintile							
Bottom quintile	0.02	0.00	0.01	0.01	0.00	0.00	−0.02
Second quintile	0.11	0.14	0.07	0.05	0.04	0.02	−0.08
Middle quintile	0.19	0.21	0.13	0.13	0.10	0.08	−0.11
Fourth quintile	0.33	0.32	0.31	0.34	0.20	0.23	−0.10
Top quintile	1.00	1.00	1.00	1.00	1.00	1.00	0.00
Top 10 percent	1.60	1.68	1.95	1.92	2.23	1.92	0.31
Top 5 percent	2.71	2.78	3.42	4.32	4.35	4.21	1.51
Top 1 percent	14.77	9.50	13.07	14.53	12.10	12.82	−1.95
C. Mean Financial Resources							
Bottom quintile	27.4	20.5	30.3	56.7	74.9	49.7	81.5
Second quintile	58.5	86.1	75.0	68.6	61.8	49.9	−14.7
Middle quintile	77.8	118.3	133.0	124.7	120.5	97.1	24.8
Fourth quintile	122.9	152.9	253.0	252.8	192.8	217.4	76.9
Top quintile	816.6	929.1	1,533	1,760	1,496	1,627	99.2
Top 10 percent	1,381	1,580	2,540	3,080	2,547	2,762	100.0
Top 5 percent	2,335	2,592	4,160	5,135	4,305	4,685	100.7
Top 1 percent	7,913	7,967	10,148	14,664	11,052	12,549	58.6

(*continued*)

Table 9.1. (continued)

Income Quantile	1983	1989	2001	2007	2010	2013	% Change[a] 1983–2013
Ratio to Top Quintile							
Bottom quintile	0.03	0.02	0.02	0.03	0.05	0.03	0.00
Second quintile	0.07	0.09	0.05	0.04	0.04	0.03	−0.04
Middle quintile	0.10	0.13	0.09	0.07	0.08	0.06	−0.04
Fourth quintile	0.15	0.16	0.17	0.14	0.13	0.13	−0.02
Top quintile	1.00	1.00	1.00	1.00	1.00	1.00	0.00
Top 10 percent	1.69	1.70	1.66	1.75	1.70	1.70	0.01
Top 5 percent	2.86	2.79	2.71	2.92	2.88	2.88	0.02
Top 1 percent	9.69	8.58	6.62	8.33	7.39	7.71	−1.98
D. Median Financial Resources							
Bottom quintile	0.9	0.0	0.1	0.2	0.0	0.1	−89.3
Second quintile	6.7	7.7	5.7	2.7	1.1	1.1	−83.5
Middle quintile	12.4	22.4	22.2	17.4	9.3	10.9	−12.3
Fourth quintile	32.0	39.4	79.6	84.5	40.1	57.0	78.1
Top quintile	170.2	208.0	378.8	355.5	333.2	391.6	130.0
Top 10 percent	312.3	448.7	765.6	844.9	878.0	819.0	162.3
Top 5 percent	653.9	736.1	1,530	1,994	1,770	1,930	195.2
Top 1 percent	4,206	2,934	5,755	8,058	5,361	6,550	55.7
Ratio to Top Quintile							
Bottom quintile	0.01	0.00	0.00	0.00	0.00	0.00	−0.01
Second quintile	0.04	0.04	0.01	0.01	0.00	0.00	−0.04
Middle quintile	0.07	0.11	0.06	0.05	0.03	0.03	−0.05
Fourth quintile	0.19	0.19	0.21	0.24	0.12	0.15	−0.04
Top quintile	1.00	1.00	1.00	1.00	1.00	1.00	0.00
Top 10 percent	1.83	2.16	2.02	2.38	2.64	2.09	0.26
Top 5 percent	3.84	3.54	4.04	5.61	5.31	4.93	1.09
Top 1 percent	24.70	14.11	15.19	22.67	16.09	16.73	−7.97
E. Homeownership Rate (in Percentage)							
Bottom quintile	40.2	33.2	40.5	41.5	37.3	37.6	−2.6
Second quintile	52.3	56.8	57.7	56.1	56.5	54.3	1.9
Middle quintile	60.3	63.4	66.8	68.9	71.1	63.2	2.9
Fourth quintile	75.3	74.8	82.2	84.5	81.0	80.8	5.5
Top quintile	88.9	87.8	92.7	93.4	91.5	91.0	2.1
Top 10 percent	89.1	92.0	94.4	94.3	92.0	93.7	4.5
Top 5 percent	90.5	92.8	96.3	95.2	94.6	96.1	5.6
Top 1 percent	95.2	88.4	95.5	97.5	96.8	95.2	−0.1
Ratio to Top Quintile							
Bottom quintile	0.45	0.38	0.44	0.44	0.41	0.41	−0.04
Second quintile	0.59	0.65	0.62	0.60	0.62	0.60	0.01
Middle quintile	0.68	0.72	0.72	0.74	0.78	0.69	0.02
Fourth quintile	0.85	0.85	0.89	0.90	0.89	0.89	0.04
Top quintile	1.00	1.00	1.00	1.00	1.00	1.00	0.00
Top 10 percent	1.00	1.05	1.02	1.01	1.01	1.03	0.03
Top 5 percent	1.02	1.06	1.04	1.02	1.03	1.06	0.04
Top 1 percent	1.07	1.01	1.03	1.04	1.06	1.05	−0.03

Source: Author's computations from the 1983, 1989 2001, 2007, 2010, and 2013 Survey of Consumer Finances.

a. Percentage point change for homeownership rates and for ratios.

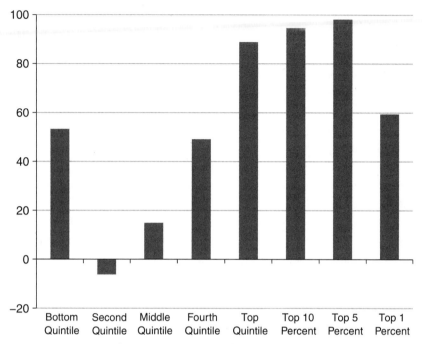

Figure 9.1. Percentage Change in Mean Net Worth by Income Class, 1983–2013

by 64 percent to $12,500, and that of the middle quintile falling by 26 percent to $45,000 and by 44 percent over the Great Recession alone.

Patterns are again similar for mean and median financial resources (FR). The ranking corresponded exactly with income class and again with extreme differences. Mean FR showed positive gains between 1983 and 2007 for all income classes and losses from 2007 to 2013, while median FR increased from 1983 to 2007 for all income levels except the bottom two quintiles and declined from 2007 to 2013 except for the top quintile. Percentage changes in mean and median FR from 1983 to 2013 were directly correlated with income level except for the bottom quintile and top percentile in the case of mean FR. The bottom three quintiles once again showed absolute losses in median FR, with the bottom quintile down 89 percent to virtually zero, the second quintile by 84 percent to $1,100, and that of the middle quintile falling by 12 percent to $10,900 and by 38 percent over the Great Recession alone.

Differences in homeownership rates by income class were less marked than those in NW or FR. In 2013, homeownership rates were still directly associated with income level but the range was smaller, from 38 percent for the bottom quintile to 95 percent for the top 1 percent—a factor of 2.5. The homeownership rate increased at all income levels between 1983 and 2007 and then declined from 2007 to 2013 with a single exception. Over the Great Recession the homeownership rate dropped by 4 percentage points for the bottom quintile and by 5.7 percentage points for the middle quintile. Over the thirty-year stretch, it increased for all income classes except the bottom 20 percent, which saw a 2.6 percentage point decline.

Changes in the wealth of different income classes over time in large measure reflect relative asset price movements and differences in wealth composition, as shown in Table 9.2 for 2007. Houses made up about half the value of total assets for the bottom four income quintiles, a quarter for the top quintile, 17 percent for the top five percent, and only 11 percent for the top percentile. Liquid assets as a share of total assets tended to fall with income level, while pension accounts as a share rose from the bottom quintile through the fourth quintile and then diminished. Corporate stock and financial securities remained flat with respect to income level up to the fourth quintile and then rose steadily with income, reaching over one-fourth for the top 1 percent. The pattern was similar for total stocks as a percentage of all assets. The share of unincorporated business equity and nonhome real estate in assets was fairly high for the bottom income quintile, dropped for the second quintile, remained steady through the fourth quintile, and then increased again with income, attaining 46 percent for the top 1 percent.

Relative indebtedness showed a U-shaped pattern with respect to income level. The debt to NW ratio rose from 17 percent for the bottom quintile, peaked at 36 percent for the fourth quintile, and then fell off to 4 percent for the top 1 percent. Similarly, the debt-income ratio rose from 138 percent for the bottom income quintile to a peak of 171 percent for the fourth quintile and then diminished to 32 percent for the top percentile. The assets of lower and middle income households were thus more concentrated in homes and their relative debt was higher than upper-income households, whereas the portfolio of upper-income households was more concentrated in financial assets and business equity. As a result, the former benefited relatively when housing prices rose and inflation was strong while the latter benefited relatively from rising stock prices.

Table 9.2. Composition of household wealth by income class, 2007 (percent of gross assets)

Asset	All	Bottom Quintile	Second Quintile	Middle Quintile	Fourth Quintile	Top Quintile	Top 10 Percent	Top 5 Percent	Top 1 Percent
Principal residence	32.8	49.7	55.5	51.6	47.2	24.7	20.2	15.9	11.2
Liquid assets (bank deposits, money market funds, and cash surrender value of life insurance)	6.6	8.0	10.7	8.2	7.0	5.9	5.8	5.7	5.6
Pension accounts	12.1	1.8	8.6	11.7	16.2	12.1	11.2	10.6	7.3
Corporate stock, financial securities, mutual funds, and personal trusts	15.5	10.3	9.5	8.2	10.9	18.2	20.3	22.8	27.6
Unincorporated business equity other real estate	31.3	29.0	14.1	18.4	17.5	37.4	40.5	42.1	46.3
Miscellaneous assets	1.7	1.2	1.5	1.8	1.2	1.8	1.9	1.9	2.0
Total assets	100.0	100.0	100.0	100.0	100.0	100.0	100.0	100.0	100.0
Memo (selected ratios in percent)									
Debt / equity ratio	18.1	17.4	23.9	35.6	35.9	12.7	9.4	7.2	3.9
Debt / income ratio	118.7	137.7	109.6	148.7	170.9	97.6	78.6	63.0	32.4
Net home equity / total assets[a]	21.4	41.2	42.3	31.4	27.2	16.2	14.0	12.1	8.6
Principal residence debt / house value	34.9	17.0	23.9	39.1	42.3	34.4	30.8	28.2	23.8
All stocks / total assets[b]	16.8	7.5	10.3	10.1	16.0	18.8	20.2	21.5	23.6
Annual Rate of Return on Net Worth (in percentage)[c]									
2001–2007	4.04	4.24	3.97	4.47	4.26	3.94	3.88	3.81	3.74
2007–2010	−7.28	−8.30	−8.19	−8.57	−8.34	−6.83	−6.65	−6.56	−6.43
2010–2013	6.20	5.46	5.26	6.09	6.53	6.22	6.18	6.17	6.22

Source: Author's computations from the 2007 Survey of Consumer Finances.

a. Ratio of gross value of principal residence less mortgage debt on principal residence to total assets.

b. Includes direct ownership of stock shares and indirect ownership through mutual funds, trusts, and IRAs, Keogh plans, 401(k) plans, and other retirement accounts

c. Based on average portfolio composition and rates of return by asset type over the period.

Consequently, the rate of return on NW was generally higher for the lower- and middle-income classes over years 2001 to 2007 than for the top 10 percent, though the variation was not as dramatic as by wealth class.[7] The highest rate recorded was for the middle-income quintile at 4.47 percent per year and the lowest for the top 1 percent at 3.74 percent per year. These differentials in rates of return reflect the steeper rise in house prices than in stock prices over these years, the higher concentration of homes among the lower- and middle-income groups and that of stocks among the upper-income classes, and the higher relative indebtedness of the middle-income groups.

From 2007 to 2010, rates of return were about two percentage points lower for the lower- and middle-income groups than for the high-income groups. There were several reasons for this: the lower- and middle-income groups were much more heavily invested in homes than the upper-income classes; and the former had a much higher degree of relative indebtedness; and the steep decline in house prices from 2007 to 2010 led to a relatively steeper loss in home equity for middle-income homeowners, about 30 percent, than other homeowners, about 20 percent.[8] Differences were again much smaller than those between wealth classes, particularly the top 1 percent and the three middle wealth quintiles. From 2010 to 2013 rates of return were higher for the upper three income quintiles than the bottom two, though again the variation was relatively small. This pattern reflected the higher share of stocks in the portfolios of higher-income households and the sharp rise in stock prices over those years.

Table 9.3 shows the results of the decomposition of the change in mean NW by income class into capital appreciation, savings, and net wealth transfer components. The spread in rates of return across income classes was relatively minor, so differences in returns played a relatively small role in explaining movements in wealth differences across income classes.

Looking first at the 2001–2007 period, we find that the simulated mean wealth of the bottom income quintile climbed by 95 percent (the actual increase was 72 percent). Of this, capital gains accounted for about one-third, implied savings for a little over half, and net wealth transfers about 15 percent. The figure for capital gains is much lower than that for all households (78 percent). The implied annual savings rate was an extremely high 39 percent.

Table 9.3. Decomposing wealth trends by income class, 2001–2013

	Period			FFA
Income Class	2001–2007	2007–2010	2010–2013	2010–2013
I. Contribution by Component to Percentage Growth in Simulated Mean NW over Period (percentage)				
A. Bottom Income Quintile				
Percentage growth in simulated mean NW	94.6	10.6	−18.1	−2.1
Contribution of capital gains (losses)	31.1	−23.1	17.0	17.0
Contribution of net wealth transfers	14.0	2.0	8.6	10.3
Contribution of Savings (implied)	49.5	31.7	−43.7	−29.3
Memo: Annual Savings Rate (implied)[a]	38.9	83.2	−124.8	−70.0
B. Second Income Quintile				
Percentage growth in simulated mean NW	20.1	−0.1	−12.9	4.2
Contribution of capital gains (losses)	32.5	−22.0	19.0	19.0
Contribution of net wealth transfers	−2.7	−1.1	−2.6	−3.1
Contribution of savings (implied)	−9.7	22.9	−29.3	−11.7
Memo: Annual savings rate (implied)[a]	−7.3	36.1	−43.5	−14.5
C. Third Income Quintile				
Percentage growth in simulated mean NW	29.3	−7.5	−15.8	0.8
Contribution of capital gains (losses)	31.8	−21.5	20.1	20.1
Contribution of net wealth transfers	1.3	−1.0	0.2	0.2
Contribution of savings (implied)	−3.9	15.0	−36.1	−19.6
Memo: Annual savings rate (implied)[a]	−2.5	21.5	−49.3	−22.4
D. Top One Percent of Income Distribution				
Percentage growth in simulated mean NW	52.5	−7.5	26.1	50.8
Contribution of capital gains (losses)	25.5	−18.7	20.7	20.7
Contribution of net wealth transfers	−0.5	−0.4	−0.2	−0.2
Contribution of savings (implied)	27.6	11.6	5.5	30.3
Memo: Annual savings rate (implied)[a]	27.6	36.7	13.3	60.8
II. Percentage Change in the Simulated Ratio of Mean NW between Top 1% and Quintile 1				
A. Actual ratio	−15.9	−28.3	48.9	48.9
B. Simulated ratio	−21.6	−16.3	54.0	54.0
C. Contribution to the Percentage Change in the Simulated Top 1%/Quintile 1 Ratio of NW (in percentage points)[b]				
1. Differences in rates of return	−2.5	3.4	6.6	5.2
2. Differences in the ratio of net wealth transfers to NW	−6.4	−1.9	−17.5	−17.6
3. Differences in the ratio of savings to NW	−7.7	−17.7	61.4	58.2
Total	−16.6	−16.2	50.5	45.8
D. Percent of Actual Percentage Change in the Simulated Top 1%/Quintile 1 NW Ratio[c]				
1. Differences in rates of return	−11.7	20.6	12.3	9.6
2. Differences in the ratio of net wealth transfers to NW	−29.4	−11.3	−32.5	−32.5
3. Differences in the ratio of savings to NW	−35.8	−108.3	113.7	107.8
Residual	−23.1	−0.9	6.4	15.2

Table 9.3. (continued)

	Period			FFA
Income Class	2001–2007	2007–2010	2010–2013	2010–2013
III. Percentage Change in the Simulated Ratio of Mean NW between Top 1% and Quintile 2				
A. Actual ratio	42.2	−15.3	42.3	42.3
B. Simulated ratio	27.0	−7.4	44.7	44.7
C. Contribution to the Percentage Change in the Simulated Top 1% / Quintile 2 Ratio of NW (in percentage points)[b]				
1. Differences in rates of return	−7.3	3.0	2.7	2.3
2. Differences in the ratio of net wealth transfers to NW	2.5	0.6	4.2	4.1
3. Differences in the ratio of savings to NW	30.0	−11.6	43.5	40.0
Total	25.3	−7.9	50.4	46.4
D. Percent of Actual Percentage Change in the Simulated Top 1% / Quintile 2 NW Ratio[c]				
1. Differences in rates of return	−26.9	41.2	6.1	5.1
2. Differences in the ratio of net wealth transfers to NW	9.3	8.1	9.3	9.3
3. Differences in the ratio of savings to NW	111.4	−156.6	97.4	89.5
Residual	6.3	7.3	−12.8	−3.9
IV. Percentage Change in the Simulated Ratio of Mean NW between Top 1% and Quintile 3				
A. Actual ratio	34.9	−15.8	42.1	42.1
B. Simulated ratio	18.0	0.0	49.7	49.7
C. Contribution to the Percentage Change in the Simulated Top 1% / Quintile 3 Ratio of NW (in percentage points)[b]				
1. Differences in rates of return	−5.7	3.0	0.9	0.8
2. Differences in the ratio of net wealth transfers to NW	−1.5	0.6	−0.2	−0.2
3. Differences in the ratio of savings to NW	23.5	−4.0	52.4	48.7
Total	16.3	−0.3	53.1	49.3
D. Percent of Actual Percentage Change in the Simulated Top 1% / Quintile 3 NW Ratio[c]				
1. Differences in rates of return	−31.9	9138.5	1.8	1.7
2. Differences in the ratio of net wealth transfers to NW	−8.2	1988.9	−0.4	−0.5
3. Differences in the ratio of savings to NW	131.0	−12197.6	105.5	98.0
Residual	9.1	970.2	−6.9	0.8

Households are classified into groups according to the income of the household. Decompositions are then based on the change in the mean wealth of the group over the period. The method is to "age" households over the period. Thus households in age group 25–29 in 2001 are aged to age group 31–35 in 2007. I also assume that the age distribution of the first year (e.g., 2001) remains unchanged over the period (e.g., 2001–2007). Overall simulated mean wealth in 2007 is then equal to the mean wealth by age group in 2007 (e.g., age group 31–35) weighted by the share of households in the corresponding age group in 2001 (in this case, age group 25–29).

a. The savings rate is the ratio of total savings to the average of the mean income of the first year and the simulated mean income of the second year.

b. A positive entry indicates that the component increases the mean NW ratio while a negative entry indicates that the component reduces the mean NW ratio.

c. The components (including the residual) sum to 100 percent if the percentage change in simulated NW is positive and to −100 percent if the percentage change in simulated NW is negative.

Abbreviations: FFA, Financial Accounts of the United States; NW, net worth.

In previous work, I have suggested that this extraordinary gain might be explainable by unreported wealth transfers (principally, unreported inter vivos gifts) received by these families.[9] In other words, it is likely that the actual savings of this income group were much smaller and that net wealth transfers were much larger. In any case, it is not possible to confirm this supposition from the data at hand.

The simulated growth in NW for the second income quintile was 20 percentage points. Capital appreciation by itself would have led to growth in mean wealth of about 33 percentage points. Net wealth transfers were negative, leading to a 2.7 percentage point decline. As a result, implied savings led to a 9.7 percentage point fall in mean wealth, and the implicit annual savings rate was –7.3 percent. Among the third income quintile, capital gains accounted for a little more than 100 percent of their simulated mean wealth gains, net wealth transfers were positive (but minor), and, as a result, implied savings had a small negative effect. The implicit savings rate was –2.5 percent. In contrast, among the top income percentile, simulated wealth growth was 53 percentage points. Of this, capital appreciation and implied savings each contributed about half, and the implied savings rate was a rather high 28 percent.

From 2007 to 2010, the simulated growth in mean wealth of the bottom quintile was 11 percentage points, much smaller than in the previous period. Capital losses by themselves would have caused a reduction of 23 percentage points and net wealth transfers were positive but minor, so that implicit savings in this case made a positive 32 percentage point contribution and the implied savings rate was an enormous 83 percent. Here, again, it is likely that the simulated high savings component reflected unreported wealth transfers. There was almost no change in mean wealth for the second income quintile because of offsetting effects from capital losses and implicit savings. For both the third income quintile and the top 1 percent, simulated mean wealth declined by 7.5 percentage points. In both cases, capital losses by themselves more than exceeded the percentage decline in mean wealth, so that implicit savings made a strong positive contribution.

The results for years 2010 to 2013 based on the adjusted Financial Accounts of the United States (FFA) data indicate a slight 2.1 percent fall in simulated mean wealth for the bottom quintile. In this case, capital gains would have caused a 17 percentage point increase and net wealth transfers a 10 percentage point advance, so that implicit savings resulted in a 29 percentage point decline. For the second quintile, simulated wealth growth was 4.2 percent, with capital appreciation making a positive contribution but being offset by a large negative contribution from dissavings.[10] Simulated wealth for the middle quintile was close to zero, with offsetting effects coming from capital gains and dissavings. Among the top income quintile, in contrast, there was enormous growth of 51 percentage points.[11] About 40 percent of this growth was due to capital gains and the other 60 percent or so to implied savings.

The ratio of simulated mean wealth between the top income percentile and the bottom income quintile plummeted by 22 percent (16 percent in actuality) between 2001 and 2007 as the simulated mean wealth of the former climbed by 53 percent and that of the latter by 95 percent (Panel II). The major factor was the higher (implied) savings rate of the bottom group, which explained 36 percent of the fall. Their higher rate of return accounted for another 12 percent and their higher ratio of net wealth transfers to wealth an additional 29 percent (with 23 percent unexplained). Over the period from 2007 to 2010, the simulated mean wealth of the top group dropped by 7.5 percent while that of the bottom quintile was up by 10.6 percent, so that the simulated ratio dropped by 16 percent (the actual ratio was down by 28 percent). This pattern closely reflected changes in the mean real incomes of these groups, that is, the top group declined by 28 percent whereas the bottom was largely unchanged. By far the biggest contributor to the trend in the ratio of simulated mean wealth is the difference in implicit savings rates, which strongly favored the bottom quintile. This effect was partially offset by the higher return on wealth among the top 1 percent of the income distribution (a 1.87 percentage point difference).

Between 2010 and 2013, the mean income of the top group shot up by 19 percent while that of the bottom group dipped by 3.3 percent. As a consequence, the simulated mean wealth of the former rose by 51 percent (on the basis of the FFA data), the latter dipped by 2.1 percent, and the simulated ratio skyrocketed by 54 percent (the actual ratio was up by 49 percent). Once again, differences in savings rates—this time in favor of the top group— explained somewhat more than 100 percent of the change. The higher rate of return of the top group added to this trend but was offset in part by the higher ratio of net wealth transfers to wealth of the bottom group.

The time trend in the ratio of simulated mean NW between the top 1 percent and the second income quintile showed a 27 percentage point advance over years 2001 to 2007 (Panel III). The difference in implicit savings rates, which favored the top group, explained more than 100 percent of this trend. This effect was partially offset by the higher returns received by the second quintile. Time trends in the top 1 percent to second quintile ratio for the 2007–2010 and 2010–2013 periods were similar to those for the ratio between the top 1 percent and bottom quintile. Once again, differentials in savings rates explained the lion's share of movements in the ratios over time.

The time trend in the ratio of simulated mean wealth between the top 1 percent and the middle income quintile was quite similar to that between the top group and the second quintile, increasing between 2001 and 2007, flattening out between 2007 and 2010, and then surging from 2010 to 2013 (Panel IV). Once again differences in savings rates accounted almost completely for the time trend in the 2001–2007 and 2010–2013 periods. For years 2007 to 2010, the rate of return was greater (less negative) for the top group (a 2.14 percentage point differential), which increased the wealth gap. The effect was almost exactly offset by the impact of the higher ratio of savings to net worth of the middle group.

As noted earlier, income and wealth are not independent. Still, it might be of interest to consider the counterfactual question of what would have happened if the distribution of income had remained constant over time but mean NW by income class had changed as it did in actuality. To answer this, I standardize on the basis of the 2001 income distribution by fixed dollar income classes, since 2001 is close to the midpoint of the time period under consideration.[12] I then reweight NW in each year by the corresponding 2001 share of households in each income group and recompute mean and median NW and the Gini coefficient.[13] (Results are shown in Table 9.4, Panel B.) Not surprisingly, since income was rising over time, reweighting increased median and mean NW in years before 2001 and decreased them in years after 2001 since higher income households hold higher wealth. The reweighted results still indicate strong gains in wealth from 1983 to 2007 and a substantial decline from 2007 to 2013.

The rate of change of both median and mean NW, especially the latter, is almost uniformly lower with standardization by income class than in actuality. Standardized mean NW grew by only 12 percent between 1983 and

Table 9.4. Trends in net worth: Actual and standardized by 2001 sociodemographic characteristics, 1983–2013 (in thousands, 2013 dollars)

Variable	1983	1989	2001	2007	2010	2013	Percentage Change[a]		
							1983–2007	2007–2013	1983–2013
A. Actual Net Worth									
1. Median	78.0	83.5	96.7	115.1	64.6	63.8	47.5	−44.6	−18.2
2. Mean	303.8	348.1	500.0	602.3	505.7	508.7	98.2	−15.5	67.4
3. Gini Coeff.	0.799	0.832	0.826	0.834	0.866	0.871	0.035	0.034	0.072
B. Net Worth Standardized by the 2001 Income Distribution									
1. Median	93.5	98.2	96.7	112.4	69.7	69.6	20.2	−38.0	−25.5
2. Mean	458.3	433.6	500.0	574.1	515.3	510.9	25.3	−11.0	11.5
3. Gini Coeff.	0.828	0.840	0.826	0.833	0.861	0.864	0.005	0.020	0.036
C. Net Worth Standardized by the 2001 Age Distribution									
1. Median	89.5	91.7	96.7	106.3	54.5	52.5	18.9	−50.7	−41.4
2. Mean	322.5	361.5	500.0	573.3	462.6	462.0	77.8	−19.4	43.3
3. Gini Coeff.	0.789	0.824	0.826	0.837	0.874	0.879	0.048	0.049	0.091
D. Net Worth Standardized by 2001 Racial / Ethnic Composition									
1. Median	70.6	85.5	96.7	117.6	70.9	72.6	66.6	−38.2	2.8
2. Mean	289.8	345.9	500.0	609.0	527.5	534.6	110.1	−12.2	84.5
3. Gini Coeff.	0.803	0.827	0.826	0.834	0.862	0.866	0.031	0.035	0.063
E. Net Worth Standardized by the 2001 Distribution of Educational Attainment									
1. Median	89.4	108.8	96.7	112.1	58.8	56.0	25.4	−50.1	−37.4
2. Mean	359.5	452.8	500.0	589.6	477.2	466.9	64.0	−20.8	29.9
3. Gini Coeff.	0.803	0.825	0.826	0.836	0.869	0.875	0.033	0.044	0.073
F. Net Worth Standardized by the 2001 Distribution of Family Types and Parental Status									
1. Median	64.7	79.5	96.7	105.6	58.5	58.6	63.3	−44.6	−9.4
2. Mean	285.2	348.7	500.0	576.5	480.5	491.2	102.1	−14.8	72.2
3. Gini Coeff.	0.812	0.830	0.826	0.836	0.870	0.875	0.024	0.040	0.063

Source: Author's computations from the 1983, 1989, 2001, 2007, 2010, and 2013 Survey of Consumer Finances.

a. Change for the Gini coefficient.

2013, compared to a 67 percent gain in actual mean NW, and standardized median NW dropped by 26 percent, compared to an 18 percent fall in actual median NW. Part of the gain in actual net worth over this time period was related to rising incomes. The resulting advance is smaller when the income effect is controlled for. Over the full thirty-year stretch, 74 percent of the growth in actual mean NW is attributable to rising incomes (1 − 52.6 / 204.9).

However, standardizing the population weights on the basis of the 2001 income distribution made only a small difference in estimated Gini coefficients— half of one Gini point or less. Standardization gives lower weight to lower income and therefore to less wealthy households before 2001 but greater weight to higher income and therefore to wealthier households. The latter effect seems to dominate in the estimated Gini coefficients before 2001. Conversely, standardization lowers estimated Gini coefficients after 2001 since it gives smaller weight to higher income and therefore to wealthier households. Over the full thirty-year period, the Gini coefficient standardized for changes in the income distribution increased by only 0.036, compared to the actual increase of 0.072. As a result, changes in the distribution of income over this time period accounted for almost exactly half of the rise in wealth inequality.

Wealth Shifts from the Young to the Old

As shown in Table 9.5, cross-sectional age-wealth profiles between 1983 and 2013 generally follow the predicted hump-shaped pattern of the life cycle model. Mean wealth increases with age until age 65 or so and then falls off. FR has an almost identical profile, though the peak is generally somewhat higher than that for NW. Homeownership rates also have a similar profile, though the fall-off after the peak age is much more attenuated than for the wealth numbers (and in 2004 they actually show a steady rise with age). In 2013, the wealth of elderly households (age 65 and over) was 2 times as high as that of the nonelderly and their homeownership rate was 24 percentage points higher.

Despite the apparent similarity in age-wealth profiles, there were notable shifts in the relative wealth holdings of age groups between 1983 and 2007 (also see Figures 9.2 and 9.3). The relative wealth of the youngest age group, under 35 years of age, expanded from 21 percent of the overall mean in 1983 to 29 percent in 1989 but then collapsed to 17 percent in 2007. In 2007, the

Table 9.5. Age-wealth profiles and homeownership rates by age, 1983–2013

Age	1983	1989	1992	1995	1998	2001	2004	2007	2010	2013
A. Mean Net Worth (Ratio to Overall Mean)										
Overall	1.00	1.00	1.00	1.00	1.00	1.00	1.00	1.00	1.00	1.00
Under 35	0.21	0.29	0.20	0.16	0.22	0.19	0.14	0.17	0.11	0.12
35–44	0.71	0.72	0.71	0.65	0.68	0.64	0.65	0.58	0.42	0.64
45–54	1.53	1.50	1.42	1.39	1.27	1.25	1.21	1.19	1.14	0.99
55–64	1.67	1.58	1.82	1.81	1.91	1.86	1.91	1.69	1.80	1.52
65–74	1.93	1.61	1.59	1.71	1.68	1.72	1.57	1.86	1.73	2.01
75 and over	1.05	1.26	1.20	1.32	1.12	1.20	1.19	1.16	1.35	1.17
B. Mean Financial Resources (Ratio to Overall Mean)										
Overall	1.00	1.00	1.00	1.00	1.00	1.00	1.00	1.00	1.00	1.00
Under 35	0.17	0.28	0.18	0.14	0.21	0.19	0.12	0.15	0.10	0.10
35–44	0.59	0.68	0.69	0.62	0.67	0.61	0.64	0.54	0.40	0.63
45–54	1.53	1.48	1.45	1.43	1.31	1.27	1.24	1.19	1.15	1.00
55–64	1.72	1.60	1.89	1.86	1.99	1.94	1.97	1.80	1.87	1.55
65–74	2.12	1.69	1.60	1.75	1.66	1.74	1.61	1.86	1.74	2.04
75 and over	1.10	1.27	1.14	1.26	1.00	1.11	1.08	1.10	1.27	1.10
C. Homeownership Rate (in Percent)										
Overall	63.4	62.8	64.1	64.7	66.3	67.7	69.1	68.6	67.2	65.1
Under 35	38.7	36.3	36.8	37.9	39.2	40.2	41.5	40.8	37.5	35.6
35–44	68.4	64.1	64.4	64.7	66.7	67.6	68.6	66.1	63.8	61.7
45–54	78.2	75.1	75.5	75.4	74.5	76.1	77.3	77.3	75.2	69.1
55–64	77.0	79.2	77.9	82.3	80.6	83.2	79.1	80.9	78.1	74.2
65–74	78.3	78.1	78.8	79.4	81.7	82.5	81.2	85.5	82.5	85.8
75 and over	69.4	70.2	78.1	72.5	76.9	76.2	85.1	77.0	81.3	80.1

Source: Author's computations from the 1983, 1989 1992, 1995, 1998, 2001, 2004, 2007, 2010, and 2013 Survey of Consumer Finances.
Households are classified according to the age of the householder.

mean wealth of the youngest age group was $102,400 (in 2013 dollars), which was only slightly more than the mean wealth of this age group in 1989 ($99,500). Educational loans expanded markedly over the 2000s, but 74 percent of the total debt of this age group in 2007 was mortgage debt and only 9.5 percent took the form of student loans.[14]

The mean NW of the next youngest age group, 35–44, relative to the overall mean tumbled from 0.71 in 1983 to 0.58 in 2007, with most of the decline oc-

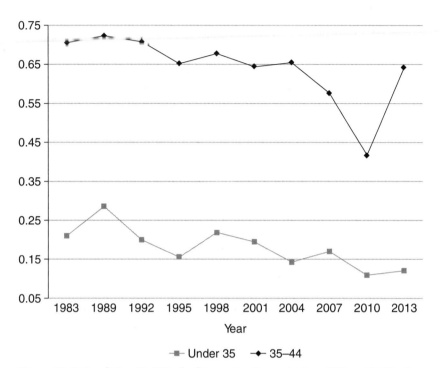

Figure 9.2. Ratio of Mean Net Worth of Young Age Groups to Overall Mean Net Worth, 1983–2013

curring between 2004 and 2007. The relative wealth of the next youngest age group, 45–54, also declined rather steadily over time, from 1.53 in 1983 to 1.19 in 2007, while that of age group 55–64 grew from 1.67 in 1983 to 1.91 in 2004 but then fell to 1.69 in 2007. The relative NW of age group 65–74 dipped somewhat from 1.93 in 1983 to 1.86 in 2007, while that of the oldest age group went from 5 percent above the mean in 1983 to 16 percent above in 2007.

Results for FR are very similar. The average FR of the youngest age group climbed from 17 to 28 percent of the overall mean from 1983 to 1989 and then plummeted to only 15 percent in 2007. A similar pattern is evident for age group 35–44. The relative average FR of age groups 45–54 and 65–74 also fell over the 1983–2007 period, whereas that of age group 55–64 rose and that of the oldest age group was the same in 2007 as in 1983 (10 percent above the mean).

Changes in homeownership rates tend to mirror NW trends. While the overall ownership rate increased by 5.2 percentage points between 1983 and

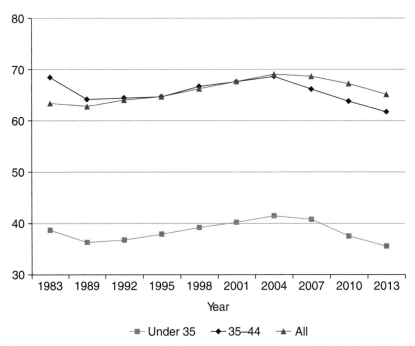

Figure 9.3. Homeownership Rates for Young Age Groups and All Households, 1983–2013 (Percentage)

2007 (from 63.4 to 68.6 percent), the share of households in the youngest age group owning their own homes increased by only 2.1 percentage points. The homeownership rate of households between 35 and 44 of age actually fell by 2.3 percentage points, and that of age group 45–54 declined by 0.9 percentage points. Big gains in homeownership were recorded by the older age groups: 3.9 percentage points for age group 55–64, 7.1 percentage points for age group 65–74, and 7.6 percentage points for the oldest age group.[15] By 2007, home-ownership rates rose monotonically with age up to age group 65–74 and then dropped for the oldest age group. The statistics point to a relative shifting of homeownership away from younger toward older households between 1983 and 2007.

Changes in relative wealth were even more dramatic from 2007 to 2010. The relative wealth of the under 35 age group plummeted from 0.17 to 0.11 and that of age group 35–44 from 0.58 to 0.42, while that of age group 45–54 fell somewhat from 1.19 to 1.14. In actual (2013 dollar) terms, the average wealth of the youngest age group collapsed almost in half, from $102,400 in 2007 to $55,400 in 2010, its second lowest point over the thirty-year period (the lowest occurred in 1995),[16] while the relative wealth of age group 35–44 shrank from $346,900 to $211,200, its lowest point over the whole 1983–2010 period. One possible reason for these steep declines in wealth is that younger households were more likely to have purchased their homes near the peak of the housing cycle.

In contrast, the relative NW of age group 55–64 increased sharply from 1.69 to 1.80 (though it shrank in actual 2013 dollar terms from $1,015,300 to $910,900) and that of the oldest age group from 1.16 to 1.36 (though once again it was down in absolute terms from $698,400 to $684,700), while the relative wealth of age group 65–74 declined from 1.86 to 1.73 (and fell in absolute dollars as well, from $1,120,200 to $873,500). The pattern of change was very similar for FR. Homeownership rates fell for all age groups from 2007 to 2010 (except the very oldest) but the percentage point decline (3.3 percentage points) was greatest for the youngest age group.

Changes in the relative wealth position of different age groups depend in large measure on relative asset price movements and differences in asset composition. The latter are highlighted in Table 9.6 for the year 2007. Homes comprised over half the value of total assets for age group 35 and under, and its share of total assets fell off with age to about a quarter for age group 55–64 and then rose to 30 percent for age group 75 and over. Liquid assets as a share of total assets remained relatively flat with age group at around 6 percent except for the oldest group for whom it was 11 percent, perhaps reflecting the relative financial conservativeness of older people. Pension accounts as a share of total assets rose from 4 percent for the youngest group to 16 percent for age group 55–64 and then fell off to 5 percent for the oldest age group. This pattern likely reflects the build-up of retirement assets until retirement age and then a decline as these retirement assets are liquidated.[17] Corporate stock and financial securities show a steady rise with age, from a 4 percent share for the youngest group to a 26 percent share for the oldest. A similar pattern is evident for total stocks as a percentage of all assets. Unincorporated business equity and nonhome real estate are relatively flat as a share of total assets with age, about 30 percent.

There is a pronounced fall-off of debt with age. The debt to NW ratio declined from 93 percent for the youngest group to 2 percent for the oldest, the

Table 9.6. Composition of household wealth by age class, 2007 (percent of gross assets)

Asset	All	Under 35	35–44	45–54	55–64	65–74	75 and over
Principal residence	32.8	54.3	43.7	33.8	25.6	28.2	30.2
Liquid assets (bank deposits, money market funds, and cash surrender value of life insurance)	6.6	5.7	5.4	6.4	6.3	6.1	10.5
Pension accounts	12.1	6.0	10.7	13.0	15.8	12.9	5.0
Corporate stock, financial securities, mutual funds, and personal trusts	15.5	4.2	8.6	13.1	16.4	20.5	25.6
Unincorporated business equity other real estate	31.3	28.7	30.1	32.0	34.4	30.2	27.1
Miscellaneous assets	1.7	1.2	1.5	1.7	1.5	2.1	1.6
Total assets	100.0	100.0	100.0	100.0	100.0	100.0	100.0
Memo (selected ratios in percent):							
Debt/equity ratio	18.1	92.7	41.3	20.2	11.9	7.1	2.1
Debt/income ratio	118.7	167.5	156.5	118.2	100.0	79.7	29.9
Net home equity/total assets[a]	21.4	18.8	21.3	20.9	18.1	23.4	28.7
Principal residence debt/ house value	34.9	65.4	51.4	38.3	29.2	16.9	4.9
All stocks/total assets[b]	16.8	5.9	11.2	15.1	19.4	21.5	20.0
Annual Rate of Return on Net Worth (in percentage)[c]							
2001–2007	4.04	7.90	5.63	4.25	3.68	3.38	2.53
2007–2010	−7.28	−13.49	−9.56	−7.54	−6.64	−6.50	−6.47
2010–2013	6.20	10.70	7.50	6.51	5.92	5.71	5.32

Source: Author's computations from the 2007 Surveys of Consumer Finances. Households are classified into age class according to the age of the household head.

a. Ratio of gross value of principal residence less mortgage debt on principal residence to total assets.

b. Includes direct ownership of stock shares and indirect ownership through mutual funds, trusts, and IRAs, Keogh plans, 401(k) plans, and other retirement accounts.

c. Based on average portfolio composition and rates of return by asset type over the period.

debt-income ratio from 168 percent to 30 percent, and principal residence debt as a share of house value from 65 to 5 percent. As a result of the latter, net home equity as a proportion of total assets rose from 19 to 29 percent from the youngest to oldest age group.

Younger households are thus more heavily invested in homes and more heavily in debt whereas the portfolio of older households is more heavily skewed to financial assets, particularly corporate stock. As a result, younger households benefit relatively when housing prices rise and inflation is strong, whereas older households benefit relatively from rising stock prices. Changes in the relative NW position of age groups over the 1983–2007 period are to a large extent due to differences in portfolio composition and relative asset price movements. Conversely, the higher leverage of younger age groups makes them vulnerable when asset prices, particularly housing prices, decline.

Consequently, the steep decline in house prices from 2007 to 2010 led to a relatively steeper loss in home equity for the youngest homeowners, 53 percent, than all homeowners, 29 percent,[18] and this factor in turn led to a much steeper fall in NW. Indeed, in terms of the annual rate of return on their wealth portfolios, this group, which had the highest over the 2001–2007 period, 7.9 percent, had the lowest over the 2007–2010 period, –13.5 percent! Moreover, the very high leverage of the youngest age group and the general decline in asset prices also led to much steeper losses in FR.

The story is very similar for age group 35–44. Their debt-equity ratio was 0.41 in 2007, their ratio of mortgage debt to house value was 0.51, and their share of housing in gross assets was 44 percent, all much higher than overall. As with the youngest age group, the drop in home prices from 2007 to 2010 caused a large fall in home equity of 48 percent among homeowners, which in turn caused a steep fall-off in their relative NW, and their higher-than-average overall leverage led to the relative deterioration of FR as well. In terms of the annual rate of return on their wealth portfolio, this group went from being the second highest in years 2001–2007, 5.6 percent, to the second lowest in years 2007 to 2010, –9.6 percent.

Years 2010 to 2013 saw an increase in NW of 11 percent (real) for the youngest age group as well as a slight rise in relative terms.[19] On the surface, one might have expected an even steeper rise since the rate of return on the portfolio of this age group was a robust 10.7 percent per year—the highest of any age group. However, further investigation indicates that the main reason this group's NW did not increase more was the continued decline in its homeownership rate, which fell by almost two percentage points. Results are similar for FR.

Age group 35–44 made a big comeback in terms of NW, which rose an astonishing 54 percent (in real terms) from 2010 to 2013. The average net home equity among homeowners in this age group jumped by 36 percent, and though the homeownership rate did fall by two percentage points, average home equity among all households in this age group expanded by 32 percent. This age group had a 7.5 annual average return on its portfolio over these years, and, partly as a result, the mean value of other real estate was up by 39 percent, that of business equity by 137 percent,[20] mean pension accounts by 42 percent, and mean corporate stock and mutual funds by 40 percent. There was also a big recovery in FR for this age group from 2010 to 2013.

The pattern is mixed for the older age groups. Age group 45–54 shows relative losses in NW from 2010 to 2013, as do age groups 55–64 and 75 and over but age group 65–74 experienced a large gain in its relative NW position. Results are similar for FR.

Once again we turn to a decomposition of the change in mean NW into a capital appreciation, a savings, and a net wealth transfer component (see Table 9.7).[21] As noted earlier, the spread in rates of return across age groups was quite large, so that differences in returns are likely to play an important role in explaining relative movements in wealth by age group.

Looking first at the 2001–2007 period, we find that simulated mean wealth of the youngest age group (under age 35) more than doubled. The percentage gain in the actual mean NW of the youngest *age group* was only 5.6 percentage points. The size of the discrepancy is the result of the simulation effectively *aging* the group over the simulation period. As a result, an age group effectively moves up to an older (and wealthier) age group over the period. The jump in wealth is particularly great for the youngest age group and even more so over a long period like 2001–2007. Of this simulated growth, capital gains accounted for 56 percent (the rate of return over this period was quite high, 7.9 percent per year), net wealth transfers for 15 percent, and implied savings for the remaining 28 percent. The figure for capital gains was much lower than that for all households (78 percent). The implied annual savings rate was a rather high 17 percent. It is possible that this estimated large gain from savings might be explained by unreported inter vivos gifts received by the families in this age group.

The simulated growth in NW for the next age group, 35–44, was lower at 71 percentage points. In fact looking across age groups, we can see that the simulated growth tailed off across age classes, down to 50 percentage points for age class 45–54, 23 percentage points for age group 55–64, and −0.2 percentage

Table 9.7. Decomposing wealth trends by age group, 2001–2013

Age Group	Period			FFA
	2001–2007	2007–2010	2010–2013	2010–2013
I. Contribution by Component to Percentage Growth in Simulated Mean NW over Period (percentage)				
A. Ages Under 35				
Percentage growth in simulated mean NW	107.4	–34.7	88.0	124.9
Contribution of capital gains (losses)	60.6	–33.3	37.9	37.9
Contribution of net wealth transfers	16.3	–0.8	2.1	2.6
Contribution of savings (implied)	30.5	–0.6	48.0	84.5
Memo: Annual savings rate (implied)[a]	17.4	–0.8	32.4	21.6
B. Ages 35–44				
Percentage growth in simulated mean NW	71.1	–3.8	86.7	123.3
Contribution of capital gains (losses)	40.1	–24.9	25.2	25.2
Contribution of net wealth transfers	5.8	–0.3	3.1	3.7
Contribution of savings (implied)	25.2	21.4	58.4	94.4
Memo: Annual savings rate (implied)[a]	13.1	26.9	42.7	57.8
C. Ages 45–54				
Percentage growth in simulated mean NW	50.3	–10.0	13.9	36.3
Contribution of capital gains (losses)	29.0	–20.2	21.6	21.6
Contribution of net wealth transfers	3.3	0.3	1.9	2.2
Contribution of savings (implied)	17.9	9.9	–9.5	12.5
Memo: Annual savings rate (implied)[a]	14.5	20.3	–16.5	18.0
D. Ages 55–64				
Percentage growth in simulated mean NW	22.6	–1.8	–10.6	6.9
Contribution of capital gains (losses)	24.7	–18.1	19.4	19.4
Contribution of net wealth transfers	1.8	0.4	1.8	2.2
Contribution of savings (implied)	–3.9	15.8	–31.9	–14.7
Memo: Annual savings rate (implied)[a]	–5.3	46.8	–89.7	–34.6
E. Ages 65–74				
Percentage growth in simulated mean NW	–0.2	–29.3	8.8	30.2
Contribution of capital gains (losses)	22.5	–17.7	18.7	18.7
Contribution of net wealth transfers	–0.5	–0.1	0.6	0.7
Contribution of savings (implied)	–22.1	–11.5	–10.5	10.8
Memo: Annual savings rate (implied)[a]	–44.8	–52.3	–38.1	32.8
F. Ages 75 and Over				
Percentage growth in simulated mean NW	16.4	–1.8	–11.9	5.1
Contribution of capital gains (losses)	16.4	–17.6	17.3	17.3
Contribution of net wealth transfers	–0.3	–0.8	0.0	0.0
Contribution of savings (implied)	0.3	16.7	–29.2	–12.2
Memo: Annual savings rate (implied)[a]	0.7	81.7	–137.8	–48.1
II. Percentage Change in the Ratio of Mean NW between Ages 55–64 and Under 35				
A. Actual ratio	3.0	76.6	48.7	–48.7
B. Simulated ratio	–40.9	50.4	–52.5	–52.5

(*continued*)

Table 9.7. (continued)

Age Group	Period			FFA
	2001–2007	2007–2010	2010–2013	2010–2013

C. Contribution to the Percentage Change in the Simulated Ages 55–64 and Under 35
Ratio of NW (in percentage points)[b]

1. Differences in rates of return	−12.8	28.0	−5.4	−9.8
2. Differences in the ratio of net wealth transfers to NW	−4.3	2.4	0.2	0.2
3. Differences in the ratio of savings to NW	−33.7	27.2	−129.2	−37.9
Total	−50.8	57.5	−134.4	−47.5

D. Percent of Actual Percentage Change in the Simulated Ages 55–64/Under 35 NW Ratio[c]

1. Differences in rates of return	−31.3	55.6	−10.4	−18.7
2. Differences in the ratio of net wealth transfers to NW	−10.5	4.7	0.4	0.5
3. Differences in the ratio of savings to NW	−82.4	53.9	−246.3	−72.3
Residual	24.1	−14.2	156.2	−9.5

III. Percentage Change in the Ratio of Mean NW between Ages 55–64 and 35–44

A. Actual ratio	1.0	46.1	−51.5	−51.5
B. Simulated ratio	−28.3	2.1	−52.1	−52.1

C. Contribution to the Percentage Change in the Simulated Ages 55–64 and 35–44
Ratio of NW (in percentage points)[b]

1. Differences in rates of return	−7.5	6.9	−1.8	−2.9
2. Differences in the ratio of net wealth transfers to NW	−1.6	0.7	0.0	0.0
3. Differences in the ratio of savings to NW	−14.8	−7.0	−52.4	−44.8
Total	−23.9	0.6	−54.2	−47.7

D. Percent of Actual Percentage Change in the Simulated Ages 55–64/35–44 NW Ratio[c]

1. Differences in rates of return	−26.4	332.4	−3.5	−5.6
2. Differences in the ratio of net wealth transfers to NW	−5.6	34.5	0.0	0.0
3. Differences in the ratio of savings to NW	−52.4	−339.4	−100.4	−86.0
Residual	−15.7	72.4	3.9	−8.4

Source: Author's computations from the 2001, 2007, 2010, and 2013 Survey of Consumer Finances.

Households are classified into groups according to the age of the household head. Decompositions are then based on the change in the mean wealth of the group over the period. The method is to "age" households over the period. Thus households in age group 25–29 in 2001 are aged to age group 31–35 in 2007. I also assume that the age distribution of the first year (e.g., 2001) remains unchanged over the period (e.g., 2001–2007). Overall simulated mean wealth in 2007 is then equal to the mean wealth by age group in 2007 (e.g., age group 31–35) weighted by the share of households in the corresponding age group in 2001 (in this case, age group 25–29).

a. The savings rate is the ratio of total savings to the average of the mean income of the first year and the simulated mean income of the second year.

b. A positive entry indicates that the component increases the mean NW ratio while a negative entry indicates that the component reduces the mean NW ratio.

c. The components (including the residual) sum to 100 percent if the percentage change in simulated NW is positive and to −100 percent if the percentage change in simulated NW is negative.

Abbreviations: FFA, Financial Accounts of the United States; NW, net worth.

points for ages 65 to 74, but then increased to 16 percentage points for the oldest age bracket. In contrast, actual percentage point gains in mean NW rose from 5.6 for the youngest group to 15.6 for ages 45–54, dipped to 8.8 for age bracket 55–64, climbed to 28.9 for age group 65–74, and then dropped to 18.1 for the oldest group. The importance of asset revaluation also increased with age, from 56 percent of the total change for the two youngest groups to 58 percent for age class 45–54, and then to 100 percent or more for the three oldest. In contrast, the contribution of net wealth transfers fell off with age, from 16.3 percentage points for the youngest group to negative for the two oldest. The rationale is that gifts typically flow from older to younger households (particularly, from parent to child).

As a consequence, the contribution of simulated savings likewise declined with age, from 30.5 percentage points for age group 35 and under to –22.5 percentage points for age group 65–74, though it did rise to slightly positive for the oldest group of households. The implicit annual savings rate likewise tailed off with age, from 17.4 percent for the youngest to –44.8 percent for age group 65–74. Net implicit savings were positive for the three youngest age groups (and the oldest) and negative for age groups 55–64 and 65–74.

Simulated wealth growth turned negative for all age groups from 2007 to 2010. The figures ranged from –34.7 percentage points for the youngest age group to –1.8 percentage points for age groups 55–64 and 75 and over. Capital gains were negative for all age groups. For age group 35 and under, capital losses explained almost the whole reduction in simulated mean wealth (the annual rate of return for this group was –13.5 percent). For age group 35 to 44, capital losses by themselves would have caused their simulated NW to plummet by 24.9 percentage points, but this was offset by a 21.4 percentage point contribution from implicit savings. For the next two age groups and the oldest one as well, capital losses also exceeded the drop in their wealth and simulated savings once again made a positive contribution. However, in the case of age group 65–74, negative capital gains explained 60 percent of the loss in their wealth and dissavings the other 40 percent.

The situation turned around over the 2010–2013 period with positive gains in simulated mean NW for all age classes. As in the 2001–2007 period, simulated percentage wealth gains, based on the aligned FFA data, fell with age, from 125 percent for age group 35 and under and 123 percent for age group 35 to 44 to 5.1 percent for the oldest group. Though rates of return were strongly positive over these years for the two youngest groups, at 10.7 and 7.5 percent per year, respectively, capital appreciation accounted for only 43 percent of the wealth gain for the former and 29 percent for the latter, with simulated savings largely making up the difference. For age group 45–54, capital gains accounted for 60 percent of simulated wealth growth and savings 34 percent (with 6 percent from net wealth transfers), and for age group 65–74, the former explained 62 percent and the latter 36 percent (with a small contribution from net wealth transfers). For age groups 55–64 and 75 and older, capital gains exceeded the simulated wealth growth and implied savings were negative.

The ratio of simulated mean wealth between age groups 55–64 and under 35 plummeted by 41 percent between 2001 and 2007 as the simulated mean wealth of the former climbed by 107 percent and that of the latter by 23 percent (see Panel II of Table 9.7).[22] The actual ratio, in contrast, showed a slight increase. The difference was due to the much higher rate of simulated wealth growth for the youngest age bracket over these years than the corresponding rate of actual mean wealth growth for the *under 35 age group*. The major factor was the higher (implied) savings rate of the younger group, which explained 82 percent of the decline. Their higher rate of return accounted for another 31 percent and their higher ratio of net wealth transfers to wealth an additional 11 percent (with 24 percent unexplained). Over the 2007–2010 period, the simulated mean wealth of the older group was basically unchanged while that of the younger one plummeted by 35 percent, so that the simulated ratio climbed 50 percent (the actual ratio was up by 77 percent).[23] The much higher (less negative) return of the older group (a 6.85 percentage point difference) and their higher implicit savings rate contributed about equally to the sharp rise in the NW ratio.

Between 2010 and 2013, the simulated mean wealth of age group 35 and under on the basis of the FFA-aligned data skyrocketed by 125 percent while that of age group 55–64 was up only 6.9 percent, so the simulated ratio plunged by 53 percent (the actual ratio by 49 percent). The differential in savings rates—this time in favor of the younger group—explained the lion's share (72 percent), while the higher annual return on the wealth of the younger group (a 4.78 percentage point gap) accounted for an additional 19 percent.

The time trend in the ratio of simulated mean NW between age group 55–64 and age group 35–44 was similar (Table 9.7, Panel III). For the 2001–2007 period, the simulated ratio fell by 28 percent, with differences in savings rates contributing 52 percent and differentials in rates of return another 26 percent. Over years 2007 to 2010, the simulated ratio rose by only 2.1 percent (in contrast to 50 percent for the simulated ratio between ages 55–64 and under age 35). In this case, the higher rate of return received by the older group would have added 6.9 percentage points to the change in the ratio over the period but this was almost exactly offset by the higher ratio of savings to *net worth* of the younger age class. Over the period from 2010 to 2013, the ratio of simulated mean wealth between the age groups dropped by 52 percent (almost exactly the same as between age groups 55–64 and under 35). Once again, the vast bulk (86 percent) of this time trend based on the FFA-aligned data can be explained by the higher implicit savings of the younger age class.

What role did the shift in age distribution play in accounting for trends in household wealth? A way to answer this question is to standardize the age distribution for a selected year (2001 is a good choice because it is near the midpoint of the period) as done earlier for income class. I use five-year age intervals and reweight NW in each year by the corresponding 2001 share of households in each age interval. I then recompute mean and median NW and the Gini coefficient.[24] Results are shown in Table 9.4, Panel C. Not surprisingly, since the average age of the population was rising over the years 1983 to 2013, reweighting increases median and mean NW in the years before 2001 and decreases them in years after 2001 since older households have greater wealth. The results show precisely this. The reweighted results still indicate fairly robust growth in wealth from 1983 to 2007, a substantial collapse from 2007 to 2010, and little change from 2010 to 2013.

Despite the fact that the age distribution shifts relatively slowly over time, the effects on growth rates are quite large. In particular, the rate of change of both median and mean NW, especially the former, is uniformly lower with age standardization. The annual growth rate of median wealth was about one percentage point lower and that of mean wealth about half a percentage point lower. Part of the increase in actual NW over time is simply due to the aging of the population and the accompanying life cycle accumulation of wealth. Once controlling for the age effect, one finds that the resultant gains are considerably smaller. From 1983 to 2007, actual mean NW grew 98 percent but standardized NW increased only 78 percent. This result implies that 21 percent $(1 - 77.8/98.2)$ of the advance of mean NW was caused by the increased age of the population over those years (the "aging effect"). Between 2007 and 2013, actual mean NW fell by 15.5 percent but standardized NW was down 19.4 percent, so that the aging effect once again helped to raise mean NW. Over the full thirty-year stretch, 36 percent of the gain in actual mean NW (1 − 43.3 / 67.4) is attributable to the aging effect. Over these years, likewise, actual median NW fell by 18.2 percent while standardized median NW dropped by 41.4 percent, so that here too the aging effect partially offset the decline in median NW.[25]

Standardizing the population weights on the basis of the 2001 age distribution makes only a minor difference in estimated Gini coefficients—one Gini point or less. Standardization gives lower weight to younger poorer households before 2001 but higher weights to richer older households. The former effect seems to dominate since estimated Gini coefficients are lower before 2001. Conversely, standardization raises the Gini coefficients after 2001 since it gives greater weight to younger households but also lower weight to older households. Once again, the former effect appears to dominate. Over the full thirty-year period, the Gini coefficient standardized for changes in the age distribution advanced by 0.091, compared to its actual increase of 0.072.

The Racial Divide Widens over the Great Recession

Striking differences are found in the wealth holdings of different racial and ethnic groups. In Table 9.8, households are divided into three groups: non-Hispanic whites, non-Hispanic African Americans, and Hispanics.[26] In 2006, while the ratio of mean incomes between non-Hispanic white ("white") and non-Hispanic black ("black") households was an already low 0.48 and the ratio of median incomes was 0.60, the ratios of mean and median wealth holdings in 2007 were even lower, at 0.19 and 0.06, respectively, and those of FR still lower, at 0.14 and 0.01, respectively (also see Figure 9.4).[27] The home-ownership rate for black households was 49 percent in 2007, a little less than two-thirds the rate among whites, and the percentage of black households with zero or negative NW stood at 33.4, more than double the corresponding percentage among whites.

Between 1982 and 2006, while the average real income of white households increased by 42 percent and the median by 10 percent, the former rose by only 28 percent for blacks and the latter by 18 percent. As a result, the ratio of mean income slipped from 0.54 in 1982 to 0.48 in 2006, while the ratio of median income rose from 0.56 to 0.60.[28] The contrast in the time trends for the ratio of means and that of medians reflects the fact that a relatively small number of white households increased their incomes by a huge amount over these years—a result of rising income inequality among white households.

Between 1983 and 2001, average net worth (in constant dollars) climbed by 73 percent for whites but rose by only 31 percent for black households, so that the NW ratio fell from 0.19 to 0.14. Most of the slippage occurred between 1998 and 2001, when white NW surged by a spectacular 34 percent and black NW advanced by only 5 percent. Indeed, mean NW growth among black households was slightly higher in the years 1998–2001, at 1.55 percent per year, than in the preceding 15 years, at 1.47 percent per year. The difference in the 1998–2001 period was the huge increase in household wealth among white households. However, between 2001 and 2007, mean NW among black households gained an astounding 58 percent while white wealth advanced only 29 percent, so that by 2007 the NW ratio was back to 0.19, the same level as in 1983.

It is not clear how much of the sharp drop in the racial wealth gap between 1998 and 2001 and the turnaround between 2001 and 2007 was due to actual wealth changes in the African-American community and how much was due to sampling variability.[29] One salient difference between the two groups was the much higher share of stocks in the white portfolio and the much higher share of homes in the portfolio of black households. In 2001, homes formed 46 percent of the total assets of black households, compared to 27 percent among whites, while (total) stocks were 25 percent of the total assets of whites and only 15 percent that of black households.[30] Moreover, while the debt ratio was much higher for black than white households in 2001 (debt to asset ratios of 0.324 and 0.115, respectively), the ratio declined among black households to 0.297 in 2004 but then bounced back to 0.356 in 2007. For whites the debt to asset ratio first rose to 0.140 in 2004 but then fell slightly to 0.134 in 2007. In the case of median wealth, the black-white ratio increased from 7 percent in 1983 to 10 percent in 2001 but then dipped to 6 percent in 2007, a little less than the ratio in 1983. In this case, median wealth among white households grew by 37 percent between 1983 and 2001 but more than doubled among black households. However, between 2001 and 2007, median NW among black households actually dropped by 26 percent, reflecting in part the rising share of black households with zero or negative NW.

Table 9.8. Household income and wealth by race and ethnicity, 1983–2013 (in thousands, 2013 dollars)

Component	1983	1989	1992	1995	1998	2001	2004	2007	2010	2013
A. Mean Income										
Whites	72.8	79.8	79.3	72.8	82.7	99.8	96.0	103.7	92.7	99.9
Blacks	39.2	35.5	39.7	35.2	40.6	48.3	47.0	50.1	44.3	41.5
Hispanics	44.1	36.4	37.4	47.2	44.5	49.5	47.4	52.1	52.4	44.8
Ratio:										
Blacks/Whites	0.54	0.45	0.50	0.48	0.49	0.48	0.49	0.48	0.48	0.42
Hispanics/Whites	0.60	0.46	0.47	0.65	0.54	0.50	0.49	0.50	0.57	0.45
B. Median Income										
Whites	51.2	53.1	48.8	48.9	52.9	57.9	59.2	56.2	54.5	54.0
Blacks	28.5	20.2	27.7	26.0	28.6	32.9	34.5	33.7	32.1	30.0
Hispanics	34.0	25.5	26.0	33.6	32.9	31.6	32.1	39.3	36.3	32.0
Ratio:										
Blacks/Whites	0.56	0.38	0.57	0.53	0.54	0.57	0.58	0.60	0.59	0.56
Hispanics/Whites	0.66	0.48	0.53	0.69	0.62	0.55	0.54	0.70	0.67	0.59
C. Mean Net Worth										
Whites	355.0	420.1	406.5	370.5	458.7	612.7	658.5	732.7	646.4	656.2
Blacks	66.8	70.4	75.6	62.3	83.3	87.3	125.1	137.8	92.8	84.5
Hispanics	57.7	69.1	90.4	78.4	113.2	105.4	141.1	191.4	99.4	98.2
Ratio:										
Blacks/Whites	0.19	0.17	0.19	0.17	0.18	0.14	0.19	0.19	0.14	0.13
Hispanics/Whites	0.16	0.16	0.22	0.21	0.25	0.17	0.21	0.26	0.15	0.15
D. Median Net Worth										
Whites	102.2	121.4	101.9	93.2	116.7	140.0	145.9	161.4	110.5	116.8
Blacks	6.8	3.1	17.1	11.2	14.3	14.0	14.6	10.4	6.7	1.7
Hispanics	4.0	2.5	6.1	7.6	4.3	3.9	6.8	10.2	2.9	2.0
Ratio:										
Blacks/Whites	0.07	0.03	0.17	0.12	0.12	0.10	0.10	0.06	0.06	0.01
Hispanics/Whites	0.04	0.02	0.06	0.08	0.04	0.03	0.05	0.06	0.03	0.02

E. Mean Financial Resources

	1983	1989	1992	1995	1998	2001	2004	2007	2010	2013
Whites	261.6	317.5	313.0	288.0	364.1	486.3	496.4	556.5	513.2	530.1
Blacks	33.7	34.5	43.0	32.4	53.7	56.9	75.9	79.4	50.7	53.3
Hispanics	17.1	33.8	58.0	44.7	72.0	67.7	82.6	108.2	57.0	58.2
Ratio:										
Blacks/Whites	0.13	0.11	0.14	0.11	0.15	0.12	0.15	0.14	0.10	0.10
Hispanics/Whites	0.07	0.11	0.19	0.16	0.20	0.14	0.17	0.19	0.11	0.11

F. Median Financial Resources

	1983	1989	1992	1995	1998	2001	2004	2007	2010	2013
Whites	28.4	38.4	31.3	27.6	53.7	55.4	44.5	49.0	35.6	40.8
Blacks	0.0	0.0	0.2	0.3	1.7	1.4	0.3	0.6	0.3	0.2
Hispanics	0.0	0.0	0.0	0.0	0.0	0.3	0.1	0.4	0.1	0.2
Ratio:										
Blacks/Whites	0.00	0.00	0.01	0.01	0.03	0.03	0.01	0.01	0.01	0.00
Hispanics/Whites	0.00	0.00	0.00	0.00	0.00	0.01	0.00	0.01	0.00	0.00

F. Homeownership Rate (in Percent)

	1983	1989	1992	1995	1998	2001	2004	2007	2010	2013
Whites	68.1	69.3	69.0	69.4	71.8	74.1	75.8	74.8	74.6	72.1
Blacks	44.3	41.7	48.5	46.8	46.3	47.4	50.1	48.6	47.7	44.0
Hispanics	32.6	39.8	43.1	44.4	44.2	44.3	47.7	49.2	47.3	43.9
Ratio:										
Blacks/Whites	0.65	0.60	0.70	0.67	0.64	0.64	0.66	0.65	0.64	0.60
Hispanics/Whites	0.48	0.57	0.62	0.64	0.61	0.60	0.63	0.66	0.63	0.60

G. Percentage of Households with Zero or Negative Net Worth

	1983	1989	1992	1995	1998	2001	2004	2007	2010	2013
Whites	11.3	12.1	13.8	15.0	14.8	13.1	13.0	14.5	17.9	16.3
Blacks	34.1	40.7	31.5	31.3	27.4	30.9	29.4	33.4	32.9	40.0
Hispanics	40.3	39.9	41.2	38.3	36.2	35.3	31.3	33.5	34.6	33.9
Ratio:										
Blacks/Whites	3.01	3.38	2.28	2.09	1.85	2.35	2.27	2.30	1.84	2.16
Hispanics/Whites	3.55	3.31	2.98	2.56	2.45	2.69	2.41	2.30	1.93	2.09

Source: Author's computations from the 1983, 1989 1992, 1995, 1998, 2001, 2004, 2007, 2010, and 2013 Survey of Consumer Finances.

Households are divided into four racial/ethnic groups: (1) non-Hispanic whites; (2) non-Hispanic blacks; (3) Hispanics; and (4) American Indians, Asians, and others. For 1995, 1998, and 2001, the classification scheme does not explicitly indicate non-Hispanic whites and non-Hispanic blacks for the first two categories so that some Hispanics may have classified themselves as either whites or blacks.

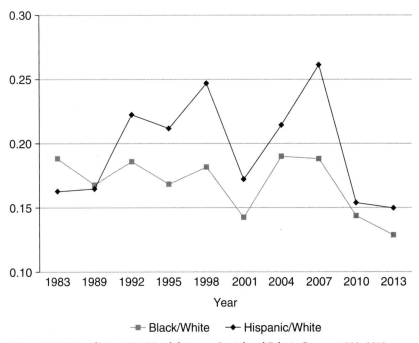

Figure 9.4. Ratio of Mean Net Worth between Racial and Ethnic Groups, 1983–2013

Average FR also increased about the same for black and white households between 1983 and 2001, so that the ratio remained basically unchanged. Between 2001 and 2007, it increased somewhat faster for blacks so that the ratio increased to 0.14. The main reason was the larger share of home value in total assets for black households and the surge in home prices over these years.

The median FR of black households also increased, from virtually zero in 1983 to a positive $1,400 in 2001, and the corresponding ratio also grew, from zero to 3 percent. However, from 2001 to 2004, median FR among blacks toppled to only $300 and the corresponding ratio fell to only 1 percent. The reason for the decline was the faster growth of debt among black middle-class households than among whites, and this, in turn, was predominantly the result of a run-up of mortgage debt. There followed a slight recovery in median FR among blacks to $600 in 2007 but the racial ratio remained at 0.01.

The homeownership rate of black households grew from 44 to 47 percent between 1983 and 2001 but relative to white households, the homeownership ratio slipped slightly to 0.64 in 2001. The change over the 1998–2001 period primarily reflected a big jump in the white homeownership rate, of 2.3 percentage points. However, from 2001 to 2004, the black homeownership rate surged to a little over half, while the white homeownership rate moved up to 75.8 percent. The large increase in the black home ownership rate was most likely due to the lending practices of mortgage companies and banks— particularly, selling subprime mortgages to black families in order to make a profit on higher interest rates charged and mortgage origination and other fees. As a result, the homeownership ratio recovered a bit to 0.66 by 2004. The homeownership rates dropped a bit for both black and white households between 2004 and 2007, and the ratio of homeownership rates fell slightly, to 0.65.

In contrast, the percentage of black households reporting zero or negative NW fell from 34.1 percent in 1983 to 30.9 percent in 2001 (and also fell relative to the corresponding rate for white households).[31] However, by 2007, the share was up to 33.4 percent (though a bit lower relative to whites). The share of households with zero or negative wealth very likely reflects the boom / bust cycle in the housing market. For example, if a family bought a home in 2001, its home value increased substantially as home prices surged, but then tanked as home prices collapsed, which led to a sharp decline in NW.

The picture is somewhat different for Hispanics. The ratio of mean income between Hispanics and (non-Hispanic) whites in 2007 was 0.50, almost the same as that between blacks and whites. However, the ratio of median income was 0.70, much higher than the ratio between black and white households. The ratio of mean NW was 0.26 compared to a ratio of 0.19 between blacks and whites and the ratio of mean FR was 0.19, compared to 0.14. However, the ratios of medians were 0.06 and 0.01, respectively, almost identical to those between blacks and whites. The Hispanic homeownership rate was 49 percent, almost identical to that of black households, and 34 percent of Hispanic households reported zero or negative wealth, almost the same as among African Americans.

Progress among Hispanic households over the period from 1983 to 2007 is generally a positive story. Mean household income for Hispanics grew by 18 percent and median household income by 16 percent, so that the ratio of mean income slid from 60 to 50 percent while that of median income advanced from 66 to 70 percent. In fact, from 2004 to 2007 median income for Hispanics apparently surged by 23 percent while that for whites declined by 5 percent.[32]

Between 1983 and 1998, mean wealth almost doubled for Hispanic households and mean FR grew more than fourfold, but between 1989 and 2001 both declined in absolute terms. As a result, the ratio of mean NW between Hispanic and white households climbed from 16 percent in 1983 to 25 percent in 1998 and then tumbled to 17 percent in 2001, and the ratio of mean FR jumped from 7 to 20 percent between 1983 and 1998 then fell off to 14 percent in 2001. However, both recovered in 2004. Mean NW among Hispanics climbed by 32 percent between 2001 and 2004 and mean FR by 22 percent, and the corresponding ratios advanced to 21 percent and 17 percent, respectively. Another wealth surge occurred from 2004 to 2007 for Hispanics. Mean NW among Hispanics gained 36 percent and mean FR advanced by 31 percent and the corresponding ratios climbed to 26 and 19 percent, respectively, quite a bit higher than those between black and white households. The upturn in Hispanic wealth from 2001 to 2007 can be traced to a jump of five percentage points in the Hispanic home ownership rate.

From 1983 to 2007, median wealth among Hispanics remained largely unchanged, as did median FR (at virtually zero!), so that the ratio of both median wealth and median FR between Hispanics and whites stayed virtually the same. In contrast, the homeownership rate among Hispanic households climbed from 33 to 44 percent between 1983 and 1998 and the ratio of homeownership rates between the two groups grew from 0.65 to 0.67. No progress was made among Hispanics in homeownership between 1998 and 2001, so that the homeownership ratio fell back to 0.60. However, between 2001 and 2007, the Hispanic homeownership rose once again, to 49 percent, about the same as black households, and the homeownership ratio recovered to 0.66.

The percentage of Hispanic households with zero or negative NW fell rather steadily over time, from 40 percent in 1983 to 31 percent in 2004, and the share relative to white household tumbled from a ratio of 3.55 to 2.41. Here, too, the ratio first spiked upward from 2.4 in 1998 to 2.7 in 2001 before recovering partway to 2.4 in 2004. However, from 2004 to 2007, the share of Hispanics with nonpositive wealth rose to 34 percent, almost the same as among black households, though the ratio relative to white households fell to 2.3.

Despite some progress from 2001 to 2007, the respective wealth gaps between African Americans and Hispanics on the one hand and non-Hispanic whites on the other were still much greater than the corresponding income gaps in 2007. While mean income ratios were on the order of 50 percent, mean wealth ratios were on the order of 20 to 25 percent. Median FR among black and Hispanic households was still virtually zero in 2007 and the percent with zero or negative NW was around a third, in contrast to 15 percent among white households (a difference that appeared to mirror the gap in poverty rates). While blacks and Hispanics were left out of the wealth surge of the years 1998 to 2001 because of relatively low stock ownership, they actually benefited from this (and the relatively high share of houses in their portfolio) in the 2001–2007 period. However, all three racial/ethnic groups saw an increase in their debt to asset ratio from 2001 to 2007.[33]

The racial/ethnic picture with regard to wealth changed radically by 2010. While the ratio of both mean and median income between black and white households changed very little between 2007 and 2010 (mean income, in particular, declined for both groups), the ratio of mean NW dropped from 0.19 to 0.14 and that of mean FR from 0.14 to 0.10. The proximate causes were the higher leverage of black households and their higher share of housing wealth in gross assets (see Table 9.9). In 2007, the ratio of debt to NW among African-American households was an astounding 0.553, compared to 0.154 among whites, while housing as a share of gross assets was 54 percent for the former compared to 31 percent for the latter. The ratio of mortgage debt to home value was also much higher for blacks, 0.49, than for whites, 0.32. The sharp drop in home prices from 2007 to 2010 thus led to a relatively steeper loss in home equity for black homeowners, 26 percent, than for white homeowners, 24 percent. This factor in turn led to a much steeper fall in mean NW for black households than white households.[34] In fact, the annual rate of return on the NW of black families over years 2007 to 2010 was a staggering −9.9 percent, compared to −7.1 percent for white households. Moreover, the higher leverage of African-American households relative to white households and the broad decline in asset prices led to greater relative losses in mean FR for the former than for the latter.[35]

The early part of the Great Recession actually hit Hispanic households much harder than black households in terms of household wealth. Mean income among Hispanic households rose a bit from 2007 to 2010 and the ratio with respect to white households increased from 0.50 to 0.57. On the other hand, the median income of Hispanics fell, as did the ratio of median income between Hispanic and white households. However, the mean NW in constant

Table 9.9. Composition of household wealth by race and ethnicity, 2007 (percent of gross assets)

Asset	All	Non-Hispanic Whites	African Americans	Hispanics
Principal residence	32.8	30.8	54.0	52.5
Liquid assets (bank deposits, money market funds, and cash surrender value of life insurance)	6.6	6.6	7.6	3.9
Pension accounts	12.1	12.5	12.3	7.7
Corporate stock, financial securities, mutual funds, and personal trusts	15.5	17.1	3.4	2.5
Unincorporated business equity other real estate	31.3	31.3	20.9	32.9
Miscellaneous assets	1.7	1.7	1.8	0.4
Total assets	100.0	100.0	100.0	100.0
Memo (selected ratios in percent)				
Debt/equity ratio	18.1	15.4	55.3	51.1
Debt/income ratio	118.7	109.0	152.2	187.9
Net home equity/total assets[a]	21.4	20.8	27.3	28.8
Principal residence debt/house value	34.9	32.4	49.4	45.2
All stocks/total assets[b]	16.8	18.3	5.0	5.1
Annual Rate of Return on Net Worth (in percent)[c]				
2001–2007	4.04	3.87	6.00	6.51
2007–2010	−7.28	−7.07	−9.92	−10.76
2010–2013	6.20	6.12	7.14	7.48

a. Ratio of gross value of principal residence less mortgage debt on principal residence to total assets

b. Includes direct ownership of stock shares and indirect ownership through mutual funds, trusts, and IRAs, Keogh plans, 401(k) plans, and other retirement accounts.

c. Based on average portfolio composition and rates of return by asset type over the period.

dollars of Hispanics fell almost by half, and the ratio of this to the mean NW of white households plummeted from 0.26 to 0.15. The same factors were responsible as in the case of black households. In 2007, the debt-equity ratio for Hispanics was 0.51, compared to 0.15 among whites, while housing as a share of gross assets was 53 percent for the former compared to 31 percent for the latter (see Table 9.9). The ratio of mortgage debt to home value was also higher for Hispanics, 0.452, than for whites, 0.324. As a result, net home equity dropped by 47 percent among Hispanic homeowners, compared to 24 percent among white homeowners, and this factor in turn was largely responsible for the huge decline in Hispanic NW, in both absolute and relative terms. Indeed, the annual rate of return on the NW of Hispanic families over these years was an astonishing –10.8 percent, compared to –7.1 percent for white households. The high overall leverage among Hispanic households was also mainly responsible for the nearly 50 percent decline in their mean FR in real terms and the fall in the ratio of this to that of white households from 0.19 to 0.11.

There are two reasons that might explain the extreme drop in Hispanic NW. First, a large proportion of Hispanic homeowners bought their homes in the interval from 2001 to 2007, when home prices were peaking. This is reflected in the sharp increase in their homeownership rate over this period. As a result, they suffered a disproportionately large percentage drop in their home equity. Second, it is likely that Hispanic homeowners were more heavily concentrated than whites in parts of the country like Arizona, California, Florida, Arizona, and Nevada, where home prices plummeted the most.

There was also a steep drop in the homeownership rate among Hispanic households of 1.9 percentage points from 2007 to 2010. Indeed, after catching up to white households in this dimension from 1983 to 2007, Hispanic households fell back in 2010 to the same level as in 2004. Hispanics had by far the highest percentage of any group who were delinquent in their mortgage payments in 2009.

Was there any relative improvement over the second half of the Great Recession, 2010–2013? Black households continued to suffer moderate losses in both mean and median household income in absolute terms and relative to whites. The mean NW of black households also continued to fall, in this case by 9 percent, and the ratio of mean NW between black and white households dipped further to 0.13 from 0.14. Their median NW actually fell from $6,700 to $1,700, and the ratio relative to white households plunged from 0.06 to 0.01. Mean FR for black households increased slightly but the ratio relative to white households remained the same, while their median FR declined slightly and also relative to whites.

One of the most notable developments was a sharp fall in the black homeownership rate from 47.7 to 44 percent, which followed a more modest 0.9 percentage point decrease from 2007 to 2010, and a decline in the homeownership rate relative to white households from 0.64 in 2010 to 0.60 in 2013. Equally striking was the steep uptick in the share of black households with no NW, from 33 percent in 2010 to 40 percent in 2013. Thus, by almost all indicators, the absolute and relative position of black households deteriorated even further from 2010 to 2013.

The absolute and relative decline in the NW of black households over these years actually seems surprising in light of the fact that the annual yield on the portfolio of black households was 7.14 percent, compared to 6.12 percent for white households. The key is the sharp decline in their homeownership rate. Indeed, this led to a considerable loss in home equity in the black portfolio, which fell by 26 percent overall and 20 percent among black homeowners.

Income developments were very similar for Hispanics but wealth developments were different. Mean incomes of Hispanics were down 15 percent from 2010 to 2013, and the ratio relative to white households plunged from 0.57 to 0.45. The story was similar for median income. On the other hand, the mean NW of Hispanic households remained stable from 2010 to 2013, as did their position relative to white households, though their median wealth fell from $2,900 to $2,000. Their mean FR remained unchanged from 2010 to 2013, as did their relative position, and their median FR increased slightly.

However, like black families, their homeownership rate continued to fall, in this case from 47.3 percent to 43.9 percent (back to where it was in 1992), and their homeownership rate relative to white households slipped from 0.63 to 0.60. The percent of Hispanics with nonpositive wealth actually fell slightly from 2010 to 2013. Overall, Hispanic households had an average annual rate of return on their portfolios of 7.48 percent, compared to 7.14 percent for black households. The main difference with respect to black households was a much smaller decline in home equity—only 5 percent overall—and an actual 1.6 percent increase among Hispanic homeowners.

Table 9.10 shows the results of a decomposition of the change in mean NW by race and ethnicity into a capital appreciation (revaluation), savings, and net wealth transfer component.[36] Considering each of the three groups in order, we find that over the 2001–2007 period for white households capital gains accounted for the bulk of the 30 percent simulated growth in mean household wealth (88 percent of the total growth). This figure is somewhat more than that for all households (78 percent). Implied savings made a minimal contribution (3 percent), as did net wealth transfers (9 percent), and the implied annual savings rate was only 0.9 percent. From 2007 to 2010, the simulated mean wealth of white households declined by 6.4 percentage points. Capital losses by themselves would have caused their mean wealth to decline

Table 9.10. Decomposing wealth trends by race/ethnicity, 2001–2013

Race/Ethnicity	Period			FFA
	2001–2007	2007–2010	2010–2013	2010–2013

I. Contribution by Component to Percentage Growth in Simulated Mean NW over Period (percentage)

A. White Households

Percentage growth in simulated mean NW	29.8	−6.4	5.6	26.3
Contribution of capital gains (losses)	26.1	−19.1	20.2	20.2
Contribution of net wealth transfers	2.8	0.1	1.5	1.8
Contribution of savings (implied)	0.9	12.6	−16.1	4.3
Memo: Annual savings rate (implied)[a]	0.9	31.1	−35.8	8.0

B. Black Households

Percentage growth in simulated mean NW	64.8	−40.0	−1.7	17.6
Contribution of capital gains (losses)	43.3	−25.8	23.9	23.9
Contribution of net wealth transfers	−4.5	−1.8	−2.8	−3.4
Contribution of savings (implied)	26.0	−12.4	−22.8	−2.9
Memo: Annual savings rate (implied)[a]	8.2	−13.9	−16.3	−1.7

C. Hispanic Households

Percentage growth in simulated mean NW	136.8	−42.4	8.8	30.2
Contribution of capital gains (losses)	47.8	−27.6	25.1	25.1
Contribution of net wealth transfers	3.5	−1.3	0.6	0.7
Contribution of savings (implied)	85.5	−13.5	−16.9	4.3
Memo: Annual savings rate (implied)[a]	28.3	−16.5	−11.3	2.4

II. Percentage Change in the White to Black Ratio of Mean NW

A. Actual ratio	−30.0	52.8	11.6	11.6
B. Simulated ratio	−21.2	56.0	7.4	7.4

C. Contribution to the Percentage Change in the Simulated White to Black Ratio of NW (in percentage points)[b]

1. Differences in rates of return	−9.3	15.2	−4.2	−3.8
2. Differences in the ratio of net wealth transfers to NW	3.6	4.9	4.5	4.5
3. Differences in the ratio of savings to NW	−13.9	43.2	7.3	6.1
Total	−19.6	63.3	7.6	6.7

D. Percent of Actual Percentage Change in the Simulated White/Black NW Ratio[c]

1. Differences in rates of return	−43.7	27.2	−57.2	−52.3
2. Differences in the ratio of net wealth transfers to NW	16.8	8.7	60.8	60.7
3. Differences in the ratio of savings to NW	−65.3	77.2	99.4	82.3
Residual	−7.7	−13.1	−3.0	9.3

(continued)

Table 9.10. (continued)

Race/Ethnicity	Period			FFA
	2001–2007	2007–2010	2010–2013	2010–2013
III. Percentage Change in the White to Hispanic Ratio of Mean NW				
A. Actual ratio	−34.2	69.9	2.8	2.8
B. Simulated ratio	−45.2	62.7	−3.0	−3.0
C. Contribution to the Percentage Change in the White to Hispanic Ratio of NW (in percentage points)[b]				
1. Differences in rates of return	−5.8	20.6	−4.7	−4.6
2. Differences in the ratio of net wealth transfers to NW	0.2	3.9	0.8	0.8
3. Differences in the ratio of savings to NW	−29.5	47.9	0.5	0.0
Total	−35.2	72.3	−3.3	−3.7
D. Percent of Actual Percentage Change in the Simulated White/Hispanic NW Ratio[c]				
1. Differences in rates of return	−12.8	32.8	−155.4	−153.7
2. Differences in the ratio of net wealth transfers to NW	0.3	6.2	27.9	27.9
3. Differences in the ratio of savings to NW	−65.4	76.4	16.0	1.3
Residual	−22.2	−15.3	11.5	24.4

Source: Author's computations from the 2001, 2007, 2010, and 2013 Survey of Consumer Finances.

Households are classified into groups according to the race/ethnicity of the household head. Decompositions are then based on the change in the mean wealth of the group over the period. The method is to "age" households over the period. Thus households in age group 25–29 in 2001 are aged to age group 31–35 in 2007. I also assume that the age distribution of the first year (e.g., 2001) remains unchanged over the period (e.g., 2001–2007). Overall simulated mean wealth in 2007 is then equal to the mean wealth by age group in 2007 (e.g., age group 31–35) weighted by the share of households in the corresponding age group in 2001 (in this case, age group 25–29).

a. The savings rate is the ratio of total savings to the average of the mean income of the first year and the simulated mean income of the second year.

b. A positive entry indicates that the component increases the mean NW ratio while a negative entry indicates that the component reduces the mean NW ratio.

c. The components (including the residual) sum to 100 percent if the percentage change in simulated NW is positive and to −100 percent if the percentage change in simulated NW is negative.

Abbreviation: FFA, Financial Accounts of the United States; NW, net worth.

by 19 percentage points, so that implied savings over this period made a positive 12.6 percentage point contribution to the growth in mean wealth and the implied savings rate was 31 percent (compared to 21 percent for all households). Net wealth transfers had a negligible effect. The results for 2010 to 2013 based on the unadjusted data from the Survey of Consumer Finances

(SCF) indicate a 5.6 percentage point increase in mean wealth, a 20 percentage point rise due to capital gains and very high dissavings, causing a 16 percentage point fall in mean wealth over these years (very similar to that of all households) and a –36 percent savings rate. The FFA-aligned data paint a different picture for the 2010–2013 period, with a 26 percentage point gain in mean wealth, a positive 4.3 percentage point contribution from implied savings, and a 8.0 percent savings rate. The latter findings again seem more reasonable for the 2010–2013 period.

Results for the two minority groups are quite different. Simulated wealth growth among black households was 65 percentage points for years 2001 to 2007 (the actual growth was 71 percentage point). Of the simulated growth, capital gains made up 67 percent and imputed savings 40 percent (with –7 percent from negative net wealth transfers). The implied savings rate was 8.2 percent. It is of interest that despite the high rate of return on the portfolio of black households (6.0 percent per year), capital appreciation was not sufficient to explain the large leap in their wealth. As a result, the implied savings rate was very high. Once again, this very high gain might be explainable by unreported wealth transfers (principally, unreported inter vivos gifts) received by these families.

Years 2007 to 2010 saw a decline in simulated mean wealth of 40 percentage points (the actual figure was –42 percent). Capital losses accounted for 64 percent of the collapse and dissavings for 31 percent (with the other 5 percent from negative net wealth transfers). The imputed savings rate was –13.9 percent. Here, too, the very large negative rate of return on the wealth holdings of black families (–9.9 percent per year) was not sufficient to account for the full drop in their wealth. As a result, the implied savings rate was extremely negative (in contrast to white household among whom the implied savings rate was a *positive* 31 percent). Over years 2010 to 2013, the simulated mean wealth of black households grew by 18 percentage points on the basis of the aggregate FFA-aligned figures. Capital gains would have caused an increase of 24 percentage points but this was offset by a –2.9 percentage point contribution from imputed savings and a –3.4 percentage point contribution from net wealth transfers. It is also of interest that net wealth transfers were negative for black households in all three periods. The apparent reason was the low level of inheritances reported by them. Gifts given and received were of the same order of magnitude as those of white households.

As shown in Panel II of Table 9.10, the ratio of simulated mean wealth between whites and blacks dropped by 21 percentage points between 2001 and 2007 (the actual ratio declined by 30 percentage points). The higher rate of return received by black households relative to white households (2.1 percentage point gap) explained 44 percent of the decline, while the higher imputed savings rate among black households accounted for 65 percent of the decline (these were offset by the higher net wealth transfer ratio among white households). Over years 2007 to 2010 the simulated ratio of mean wealth between whites and blacks reversed and rose by 56 percentage points (53 percentage points in actuality). In this case, the rate of return was 2.9 percentage points higher (that is, less negative) for white families and this factor accounted for 27 percent of the rise. However, though the gap in returns was quite high, the principal factor accounting for the large jump in the racial wealth gap was the discrepancy in savings rates, which explained 77 percent of the change (the remainder was due to differences in the net wealth transfer ratio and the residual). The simulated racial wealth ratio continued to rise from 2010 to 2013 (by 7.4 percentage points). In this case, the gap in savings rates and the ratio of net wealth transfers to net worth made about equal contributions, while the gap in rates of return (in favor of black households) partially offset these effects.

Results for Hispanics were similar to those for blacks. Simulated wealth growth among Hispanic households was a stunning 137 percent from 2001 to 2007 (the actual growth was 82 percent, as shown in Panel IC). Of the simulated growth, capital gains made up only 35 percent (despite the very high 6.5 percent per year rate of return) and imputed savings the majority 62 percent (with 3 percent from net wealth transfers). The implied savings rate was a huge 28 percent. Here, too, the high savings rate might be due to unreported inter vivos gifts received by these households.

Hispanic simulated mean wealth collapsed by 42 percentage points from 2007 to 2010 (the actual figure was 48 percent). Capital losses in this case accounted for the bulk of the drop (65 percent) and dissavings for 32 percent (with the other 3 percent from negative net wealth transfers). The implied savings rate was −16.5 percent. Here, too, the very large negative rate of return on the wealth holdings of Hispanics (−10.8 percent per year) was not enough to explain the full decline in their wealth. As a result, the implied savings rate was highly negative, as it was for black households. Over the years 2010 to 2013, the simulated mean wealth of Hispanic households grew by 30 percentage points on the basis of the FFA-aligned data. In this case, capital gains made up 83 percent of the surge in mean wealth, imputed savings 14 percent, and net wealth transfers 2 percent.

The ratio of simulated mean wealth between whites and Hispanics fell by 45 percentage points (compared to 34 percentage points for the actual ratio) from 2001 to 2007 (see Panel III). The higher rate of return for Hispanic households (2.6 percentage point gap) explained 13 percent of the decrease, while the higher imputed savings rate among Hispanic households accounted for the majority—65 percent (with a very small offsetting contribution from the higher net wealth transfer ratio among whites). Between 2007 and 2010 the simulated mean worth ratio again reversed, as it did for black households, and surged by 63 percentage points (70 percentage points in actuality). In this case, the return was 3.7 percentage points less negative among whites and this factor explained one-third of the jump. However, once again, the primary factor was the difference in savings rates, which accounted for 76 percent of the change (the remainder was again due to differences in the net wealth transfer ratio and the residual). The simulated wealth ratio, as well as the actual, was basically unchanged from 2010 to 2013.

How does the changing racial and ethnic composition of the U.S. population affect trends in household wealth? To answer this question, I standardize the racial/ethnic distribution for year 2001 as I did for income and age class. I then reweight NW in each year by the corresponding 2001 share of households in each group and recompute mean and median NW and the Gini coefficient. Results are shown in Table 9.4, Panel D. Since the share of Hispanics rose sharply over the years 1983 to 2013, from 3.5 to 10.6 percent of all households, and the share of black households increased moderately, from 12.7 to 14.6 percent, reweighting decreases median and mean NW in the years before 2001 and increases them in the years after 2001 since Hispanic and black households hold less wealth than whites. The reweighted results still indicate strong growth in wealth from 1983 to 2007 and a substantial collapse from 2007 to 2013 for all groups.

Unlike age standardization, the rate of change of both median and mean NW is higher with standardization by race and ethnicity than in actuality. Standardized mean NW gained 85 percentage points between 1983 and 2013, compared to a 67 percentage point rise in actual mean NW, and standardized median NW showed a slight gain, compared to an 18 percentage point fall in actual median NW. The reason is that a rising share of minorities in the total population lowers the growth in mean and median wealth, ceteris paribus, since these groups hold lower wealth than white households. If the racial / ethnic composition had remained constant over time, both mean and median NW would have grown faster than in actuality.

Standardizing the population weights on the basis of the 2001 racial and ethnic composition once again makes a very small difference in estimated Gini coefficients. Standardization gives greater weight to minority and hence poorer households before 2001 and lesser weight to white and hence richer households. The former effect seems to dominate for the Gini coefficient calculation in 1983 but the latter effect seems to dominate for 2001. After 2001, standardization gives greater weight to richer white households and lower weight to minorities. In this case, the former effect appears to dominate in 2010 and 2013, lowering the Gini coefficient. Over the full thirty-year period, the Gini coefficient standardized for changes in the racial / ethnic composition advances by 0.063, less than the actual increase of 0.072.

College Graduates Pull Away from the Rest of the Pack

In 2013, the mean NW of individuals with a college degrees or more ("college graduates") was far ahead of the NW of people with less schooling—ten times the wealth of those with less than four years of high school, six times that of high school graduates, and almost four times that of those with one to three years of college (see Table 9.11). Mean NW increased between 1983 and 2007 and then declined between 2007 and 2013 for all four schooling groups, mirroring the pattern for overall mean NW. The mean NW of high school graduates, in particular, plummeted by a third over the later period. Over the full thirty-year stretch, the NW of college graduates advanced by 52 percent, much more than that of the other three groups (also see Figure 9.5). Indeed, high school dropouts saw their mean NW drop by 12 percent and high school graduates by 7 percent, while those with some college saw a very modest gain of 3 percent.

A similar pattern unfolds for median NW. However, in this case median NW fell continuously over time for high school dropouts, tumbling to $6,800 in 2013. In the case of high school graduates, median NW was down by about

Table 9.11. Household wealth and homeownership rates by educational attainment, 1983–2013 (in thousands, 2013 dollars)

Schooling	1983	1989	2001	2007	2010	2013	% Change[a] 1983–2013
A. Mean Net Worth							
Less than high school 4	120.7	153.9	126.1	142.1	92.4	106.8	−11.6
High school 4	197.5	254.8	226.3	274.4	224.4	183.1	−7.3
College 1–3	278.1	371.0	330.0	355.8	271.8	285.1	2.5
College 4 or more	729.7	897.2	1132.7	1357.7	1122.6	1110.3	52.2
Ratio to college 4+							
Less than high school 4	0.17	0.17	0.11	0.10	0.08	0.10	−0.07
High school 4	0.27	0.28	0.20	0.20	0.20	0.16	−0.11
College 1–3	0.38	0.41	0.29	0.26	0.24	0.26	−0.12
B. Median Net Worth							
Less than high school 4	43.7	40.8	23.8	20.2	7.4	6.8	−84.4
High school 4	73.8	83.9	60.8	80.3	44.1	41.0	−44.4
College 1–3	73.2	97.5	86.3	87.9	44.0	33.0	−54.9
College 4 or more	195.8	272.5	278.0	324.6	226.3	233.0	19.0
Ratio to college 4+							
Less than high school 4	0.22	0.15	0.09	0.06	0.03	0.03	−0.19
High school 4	0.38	0.31	0.22	0.25	0.20	0.18	−0.20
College 1–3	0.37	0.36	0.31	0.27	0.19	0.14	−0.23
C. Mean Financial Resources							
Less than high school 4	64.4	93.5	70.9	67.7	41.8	57.1	−11.4
High school 4	125.6	175.1	154.5	173.2	146.6	119.8	−4.6
College 1–3	196.1	282.4	246.3	243.6	191.2	217.4	10.9
College 4 or more	591.9	733.3	939.7	1084.7	902.9	924.2	56.1
Ratio to college 4+							
Less than high school 4	0.11	0.13	0.08	0.06	0.05	0.06	−0.05
High school 4	0.21	0.24	0.16	0.16	0.16	0.13	−0.08
College 1–3	0.33	0.39	0.26	0.22	0.21	0.24	−0.10
D. Median Financial Resources							
Less than high school 4	4.0	5.2	1.2	0.3	0.0	0.2	−96.2
High school 4	15.6	21.8	11.6	13.9	3.7	3.9	−75.0
College 1–3	19.0	32.0	31.2	19.1	6.2	8.8	−54.0
College 4 or more	88.2	130.4	155.7	165.3	108.9	124.1	40.8
Ratio to college 4+							
Less than high school 4	0.04	0.04	0.01	0.00	0.00	0.00	−0.04
High school 4	0.18	0.17	0.07	0.08	0.03	0.03	−0.15
College 1–3	0.22	0.25	0.20	0.12	0.06	0.07	−0.15
E. Homeownership Rate (in Percentage)							
Less than high school 4	61.3	54.1	58.8	52.4	54.2	51.6	−9.7
High school 4	64.8	66.7	65.8	70.1	65.1	64.6	−0.2
College 1–3	58.2	66.5	63.7	64.7	64.5	58.8	0.6
College 4 or more	69.1	76.7	78.0	78.4	76.7	75.2	6.1
Ratio to college 4+							
Less than high school 4	0.89	0.71	0.75	0.67	0.71	0.69	−0.20
High school 4	0.94	0.87	0.84	0.89	0.85	0.86	−0.08
College 1–3	0.84	0.87	0.82	0.82	0.84	0.78	−0.06

Source: Author's computations from the 1983, 1989 2001, 2007, 2010, and 2013 Survey of Consumer Finances.

Households are classified according to the education of the householder.

a. Percentage point change for homeownership rates and for ratios

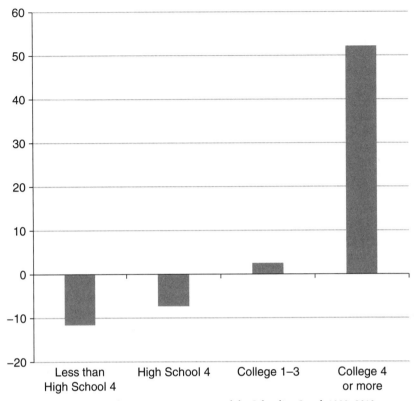

Figure 9.5. Percentage Change in Mean Net Worth by Schooling Level, 1983–2013

half between 2007 and 2013. Over the full thirty-year period, median NW sank by 84 percent for high school dropouts, by 44 percent for high school graduates, and by 55 percent for those with some college, while it was up by 19 percent for college graduates.

The patterns for mean and median FR were similar to those for NW. Median FR fell almost continuously over time for high school dropouts as well as graduates, reaching virtually zero in the case of the former and $3,900 for the latter. The homeownership rate showed a different pattern. In 1983 homeownership rates were similar across the four schooling groups. The rate was over 60 percent for both high school dropouts and graduates, compared to 69 percent for college graduates. Over time, however, from 1983 to 2013, the homeownership rate fell almost continuously for the high school dropout group. For high school graduates, it rose from 65 percent in 1983 to 70 percent in 2007 but then dropped back to 65 percent in 2013. Likewise, for those with one to three years of college it increased from 58 percent in 1983 to 65 percent in 2007 but then fell off to 59 percent in 2013. The same time pattern holds for college graduates, with the homeownership rate expanding from 69 percent in 1983 to 78 percent in 2007 and then slackening to 75 percent in 2013. Only college graduates saw a higher homeownership rate in 2013 than in 1983 (a 6 percentage point increase).

There were some notable differences in wealth composition among educational groups (shown in Table 9.12 for 2007). Houses comprised 55 percent of total assets for the lowest educational group, 46 percent for high school graduates, 38 percent for those with some college, and 28 percent for college graduates. The share of pension accounts in total assets rose from 7 percent for the lowest schooling group to 13 percent for college graduates, as did the share of stock and financial securities (from 8 to 18 percent), businesses and nonhome real estate (from 23 to 32 percent), and total stocks (from 7 to 20 percent). The debt to NW ratio was relatively flat among the first three educational groups (about a quarter) but much lower for college graduates (15 percent). The assets of the lowest three schooling groups were thus more heavily concentrated in homes and their debt-equity ratio was higher than for college graduates, whereas the assets of college graduates were more concentrated in financial assets and business equity.

As a result, the return on NW over years 2001 to 2007 was generally larger for the lower three schooling groups than for college graduates, though the range was relatively narrow (about one percentage point). From 2007 to 2010, returns increased with schooling levels, from −8.8 percent for those with less than a high school degree to −6.9 percent for college graduates. Differences were about the same magnitude as those between income classes. Over years 2010 to 2013 rates of return increased with educational level, with a spread of about one percentage point between lowest and highest—a reflection mainly of the higher share of stocks in the portfolios of more educated households.

Table 9.13 shows the results of a decomposition of the change in mean NW by educational group into a capital appreciation, savings, and net wealth transfer component.[37] Looking first at the 2001–2007 period, we find that capital gains accounted for 72 percent of the 43 percentage point growth in simulated mean wealth among households with less than four years of high school. This figure was about the same as that for all households (78 percent).

Table 9.12. Composition of household wealth by educational attainment, 2007
(percent of gross assets)

Asset	All	Less Than High School 4	High School 4	College 1–3	College 4 or More
Principal residence	32.8	54.5	45.9	38.0	27.7
Liquid assets (bank deposits, money market funds, and cash surrender value of life insurance)	6.6	7.0	7.2	6.4	6.4
Pension accounts	12.1	6.9	9.6	10.7	13.2
Corporate stock, financial securities, mutual funds, and personal trusts	15.5	7.8	9.1	10.0	18.4
Unincorporated business equity other real estate	31.3	22.5	26.9	33.8	32.4
Miscellaneous assets	1.7	1.2	1.3	1.1	1.8
Total assets	100.0	100.0	100.0	100.0	100.0
Memo (selected ratios in percent):					
Debt/equity ratio	18.1	24.0	27.5	24.9	14.8
Debt/income ratio	118.7	104.0	130.3	130.7	113.1
Net home equity/total assets[a]	21.4	41.3	29.4	23.3	18.1
Principal residence debt/house value	34.9	24.2	36.0	38.6	34.6
All stocks/total assets[b]	16.8	7.3	10.2	10.9	19.9
Annual rate of return on net worth (in percentage)[c]					
2001–2007	4.04	4.52	4.69	4.61	3.78
2007–2010	–7.28	–8.76	–8.28	–8.08	–6.91
2010–2013	6.20	5.22	5.79	6.11	6.28

Source: Author's computations from the 2007 Survey of Consumer Finances.
Households are classified according to the education of the householder.
a. Ratio of gross value of principal residence less mortgage debt on principal residence to total assets.
b. Includes direct ownership of stock shares and indirect ownership through mutual funds, trusts, and IRAs, Keogh plans, 401(k) plans, and other retirement accounts.
c. Based on average portfolio composition and rates of return by asset type over the period.

Implied savings contributed another 37 percent but net wealth transfers were negative and reduced growth by 4.1 percentage points. The implied annual savings rate was a robust 10 percent.[38] Among those with four years of high school, capital appreciation explained a bit more than 100 percent of their simulated mean wealth growth, implied savings made a small negative contribution, and net wealth transfers a small positive one. The implicit annual savings rate was –2.3 percent. Among those with one to three years of college, capital gains accounted for 92 percent of their simulated mean wealth gains, savings again had a small negative effect, but in this case net wealth transfers were positive (but minor). Among college graduates, capital appreciation contributed 66 percent to their simulated wealth growth and savings another 27 percent, with again a small positive contribution from net wealth transfers. In this case, the implied savings rate was a rather large 11.4 percent.

From 2007 to 2010, the simulated mean wealth of those with less than a high school degree decreased by 27 percentage points. Capital losses by themselves would have caused a 23 percentage point reduction, so the implicit savings in this case made a negative 2.9 percentage point contribution and the implied savings rate was −4.0 percent. Net wealth transfers were negative but had a very small effect. For high school graduates, simulated mean wealth fell by 11 percentage points. Capital losses would have led to a 22 percentage point fall so that implicit savings made a strong positive 11.4 percentage point contribution. Results are similar for the other two educational groups. Capital losses exceeded the decline in simulated wealth and implied savings made a positive contribution.

The results for 2010 to 2013 based on the aligned FFA data indicate a 48 percentage point increase in mean wealth for those with less than a high school degree, a 17 percentage point rise due to capital gains and a very high contribution from implicit savings, causing a 31 percentage point rise. The implied annual savings rate was also very high at 24 percent. For high school graduates, the simulated wealth growth was a rather paltry 1.8 percentage points, with capital appreciation making a positive contribution but being offset by an almost equal negative contribution from dissavings.[39] Among those with one to three years of college, simulated wealth growth was 33 percentage points, with about two-thirds coming from capital gains and one-third from savings. Results were similar for college graduates.[40]

As shown in Table 9.13, Panel II, the ratio of simulated mean wealth between college graduates and those with less than four years of high school was largely unchanged over years 2001 to 2007 even though the annual rate of return on the latter's wealth was somewhat higher than that of the former (a 0.74 percentage points difference). Over the 2007–2010 period, the ratio of simulated wealth between the two groups climbed by 23 percentage points (the actual ratio was up by 27 percentage points). The rate of return was higher for college graduates (less negative) over these years—a 1.85 percentage point

Table 9.13. Decomposing wealth trends by educational attainment, 2001–2013

Educational Group	Period			FFA
	2001–2007	2007–2010	2010–2013	2010–2013
I. Contribution by Component to Percentage Growth in Simulated Mean NW over Period (percentage)				
A. Less than High School 4				
Percentage growth in simulated mean NW	43.1	–27.2	23.7	48.0
Contribution of capital gains (losses)	31.1	–23.1	17.0	17.0
Contribution of net wealth transfers	–4.1	–1.1	0.3	0.4
Contribution of savings (implied)	16.1	–2.9	6.5	30.7
Memo: Annual savings rate (implied)[a]	10.0	–4.0	6.0	23.7
B. High School 4				
Percentage growth in simulated mean NW	31.2	–10.9	–14.9	1.8
Contribution of capital gains (losses)	32.5	–22.0	19.0	19.0
Contribution of net wealth transfers	2.2	–0.2	0.9	1.1
Contribution of savings (implied)	–3.5	11.4	–34.8	–18.3
Memo: Annual savings rate (implied)[a]	–2.3	19.2	–51.0	–22.4
C. College 1–3				
Percentage growth in simulated mean NW	34.6	–17.1	11.4	33.2
Contribution of capital gains (losses)	31.8	–21.5	20.1	20.1
Contribution of net wealth transfers	3.8	0.4	1.5	1.8
Contribution of savings (implied)	–1.1	4.0	–10.2	11.4
Memo: Annual savings rate (implied)[a]	–0.8	7.0	–14.4	13.4
C. College 4 or more				
Percentage growth in simulated mean NW	38.8	–10.6	9.2	30.6
Contribution of capital gains (losses)	25.5	–18.7	20.7	20.7
Contribution of net wealth transfers	2.8	0.0	1.5	1.8
Contribution of savings (implied)	10.5	8.1	–13.0	8.1
Memo: Annual savings rate (implied)[a]	11.4	22.5	–30.9	16.1
II. Percentage Change in the Ratio of Mean NW between College 4+ and Less than High School 4				
A. Actual ratio	6.3	27.2	–14.4	–14.4
B. Simulated ratio	–3.0	22.7	–11.7	–11.7
C. Contribution to the Percentage Change in the College 4+/ Less than HS 4 Ratio of NW (in percentage points)[b]				
1. Differences in rates of return	–4.0	6.8	2.7	3.0
2. Differences in the ratio of net wealth transfers to NW	4.5	1.9	0.9	0.9
3. Differences in the ratio of savings to NW	–3.9	15.2	–17.8	–15.6
Total	–3.4	23.9	–14.2	–11.7

Table 9.13. (continued)

Educational Group	Period			FFA
	2001–2007	2007–2010	2010–2013	2010–2013
D. Percent of Actual Percentage Change in the Simulated College 4+/ Less than HS 4 NW Ratio[c]				
1. Differences in rates of return	−130.6	30.0	22.7	25.7
2. Differences in the ratio of net wealth transfers to NW	147.6	8.3	7.7	7.7
3. Differences in the ratio of savings to NW	−128.3	66.8	−151.3	−133.3
Residual	11.3	−5.1	20.9	−0.2
III. Percentage Change in the Ratio of Mean NW between College 4+ and High School 4				
A. Actual ratio	−1.2	1.1	21.2	21.2
B. Simulated ratio	5.8	0.3	28.2	28.2
C. Contribution to the Percentage Change in the College 4+/High School 4 Ratio of NW (in percentage points)[b]				
1. Differences in rates of return	−5.8	3.6	2.5	2.1
2. Differences in the ratio of net wealth transfers to NW	0.4	0.3	0.5	0.5
3. Differences in the ratio of savings to NW	10.3	−3.8	27.8	25.8
Total	4.9	0.1	30.8	28.4
D. Percent of Actual Percentage Change in the Simulated College 4+/High School 4 NW Ratio[c]				
1. Differences in rates of return	−99.6	1307.8	8.9	7.5
2. Differences in the ratio of net wealth transfers to NW	6.5	97.3	1.8	1.8
3. Differences in the ratio of savings to NW	177.1	−1381.0	98.4	91.4
Residual	16.0	75.9	−9.1	−0.6

Source: Author's computations from the 2001, 2007, 2010, and 2013 Survey of Consumer Finances.

Households are classified into groups according to the education of the household head. Decompositions are then based on the change in the mean wealth of the group over the period. The method is to "age" households over the period. Thus households in age group 25–29 in 2001 are aged to age group 31–35 in 2007. I also assume that the age distribution of the first year (e.g., 2001) remains unchanged over the period (e.g., 2001–2007). Overall simulated mean wealth in 2007 is then equal to the mean wealth by age group in 2007 (e.g., age group 31–35) weighted by the share of households in the corresponding age group in 2001 (in this case, age group 25–29).

a. The savings rate is the ratio of total savings to the average of the mean income of the first year and the simulated mean income of the second year.

b. A positive entry indicates that the component increases the mean NW ratio while a negative entry indicates that the component reduces the mean NW ratio.

c. The components (including the residual) sum to 100 percent if the percentage change in simulated NW is positive and to −100 percent if the percentage change in simulated NW is negative.

Abbreviations: FFA, Financial Accounts of the United States; NW, net worth.

gap—which explained 30 percent of the gain. The higher savings rate of college graduates accounted for another 67 percent, with a minor contribution (of 8 percent) from their higher net transfer ratio. Over years 2010 to 2013 the simulated ratio fell by 12 percentage points (the actual ratio by 14 percentage points). More than 100 percent of this change was explained by the higher implicit savings rate of the less educated group, but this was offset in part by the higher rate of return on the portfolio of college graduates.

There was very little change in the ratio of simulated mean wealth between college graduates and high school graduates over years 2001 to 2007 and 2007 to 2010 (see Panel III). However, years 2010 to 2013 showed a sharp spike in the simulated ratio of 28 percent (the actual ratio rose by 21 percentage points). Despite the fact that the rate of return was somewhat higher for college graduates over these years (a 0.49 percentage point difference), the bulk of this increase (91 percent) was due to the higher savings rate of college graduates on the basis of the FFA-aligned data.

To determine the effect of the shift in educational distribution when accounting for trends in household wealth, I once again standardize on the basis of the 2001 educational distribution. I then reweight NW in each year by the corresponding 2001 share of households in each schooling group and recompute mean and median NW and the Gini coefficient. Results are shown in Panel E of Table 9.4. Not surprisingly, since the population was becoming more educated over years 1983 to 2013, reweighting increases median and mean NW in years before 2001 and decreases them in years after 2001 since more educated households hold higher wealth. The results again show precisely this. The reweighted results still indicate strong gains in wealth from 1983 to 2007 and a substantial decline from 2007 to 2013.

As with age standardization, the rate of change of both median and mean NW, especially the former, is uniformly lower with standardization by educational attainment than in actuality. Standardized mean NW grew by only 30 percent between 1983 and 2013, compared to a 67 percent gain in actual mean NW, and standardized median NW dropped by 37 percent, compared to an 18 percent fall in actual median NW. The reason is that a portion of the advance in actual NW over this time period was due to the rising educational attainment of the population. The resultant gains are considerably smaller when the education effect is controlled for. Over the full thirty-year stretch, 56 percent $(1 - 29.9 / 67.4)$ of the gain in actual mean NW was attributable to rising educational levels.

Standardizing the population weights on the basis of the 2001 educational distribution makes a very small difference in estimated Gini coefficients—half of one Gini point or less. Standardization gives lower weight to less-educated and therefore poorer households before 2001 but greater weight to better-educated and therefore richer households. The latter effect seems to dominate in estimating the Gini coefficient in 1983 but the former effect appears dominant for 2001. Conversely, standardization raises the Gini coefficients after 2001since it gives greater weight to the less-educated households but also lower weight to households with more education. In this case, the former effect appears to dominate in all three years. Over the full thirty-year period, the Gini coefficient standardized for changes in the educational distribution increases by 0.073—about the same as the actual increase of 0.072.

Single Mothers Fall Behind

In 2013 married couples as a group recorded the highest mean NW, followed by married couples with children, single males, single females as a group, and then single females with children (see Table 9.14). The NW of the last group was only 7 percent of that of married couples.[41] As with overall mean NW, all groups saw their mean NW rise from 1983 to 2007 and then fall off from 2007 to 2013. Single males saw the largest percentage increase from 1983 to 2013 at 195 percent, followed by married couples with children, all married couples, and then all single females (also see Figure 9.6). Single females with children, on the other hand, experienced a sizable drop in their NW of 22 percent. Between 1983 and 2013, married couples with children and single males as a group gained in relative terms on married couples while single females as a group and single females with children fell further behind (the last dropping from 17 to 7 percent of the NW of married couples).

Time trends in median NW were similar except for single females with children, whose median NW fell almost continuously from 1983 to 2013. Over the thirty years, median NW more than doubled for single males and rose a modest 9 percent for all married couples but declined sharply, by 37 percent, for married couples with children, by 42 percent for all single females, and by a startling 93 percent for single females with children, reaching only $500 in 2013 in the last case.[42]

Table 9.14. Household wealth and homeownership rates by family type and parental status, 1983–2013 (in thousands, 2013 dollars)

Family Type	1983	1989	2001	2007	2010	2013	% Change[a] 1983–2013
A. Mean Net Worth							
Married couples (all)	407.2	477.3	746.8	823.6	709.1	725.5	78.2
Married couples with children	252.9	306.5	548.5	574.1	488.3	507.6	100.7
Single males (all)	104.7	226.2	281.0	360.6	272.5	308.5	194.5
Single females (all)	152.8	143.0	176.8	249.0	196.4	171.5	12.2
Single females with children	68.5	55.6	82.5	111.2	72.8	53.6	−21.8
Ratio to all married couples							
Married couples with children	0.62	0.64	0.73	0.70	0.69	0.70	0.08
Single males (all)	0.26	0.47	0.38	0.44	0.38	0.43	0.17
Single females (all)	0.38	0.30	0.24	0.30	0.28	0.24	−0.14
Single females with children	0.17	0.12	0.11	0.13	0.10	0.07	−0.09
B. Median Net Worth							
Married couples (all)	115.0	139.0	189.8	176.4	111.7	124.7	8.5
Married couples with children	84.9	95.4	123.3	107.2	45.5	53.1	−37.4
Single males (all)	11.5	24.6	35.1	48.5	30.2	25.2	118.5
Single females (all)	35.1	22.5	27.6	46.6	24.3	20.2	−42.3
Single females with children	7.3	0.4	0.9	1.2	0.3	0.5	−93.2
Ratio to all married couples							
Married couples with children	0.74	0.69	0.65	0.61	0.41	0.43	−0.31
Single males (all)	0.10	0.18	0.19	0.28	0.27	0.20	0.10
Single females (all)	0.31	0.16	0.15	0.26	0.22	0.16	−0.14
Single females with children	0.06	0.00	0.00	0.01	0.00	0.00	−0.06
C. Mean Financial Resources							
Married couples (all)	300.2	363.0	595.7	632.4	554.4	590.0	96.5
Married couples with children	161.8	216.0	430.5	427.5	376.3	411.3	154.2
Single males (all)	74.8	182.5	220.1	275.3	204.4	246.2	229.2
Single females (all)	102.2	86.8	120.4	147.8	121.0	110.2	7.8
Single females with children	32.0	30.7	55.2	51.0	36.4	25.4	−20.7

Table 9.14. (continued)

Family Type	1983	1989	2001	2007	2010	2013	% Change[a] 1983–2013
Ratio to all married couples							
Married couples with children	0.54	0.60	0.72	0.68	0.68	0.70	0.16
Single males (all)	0.25	0.50	0.37	0.44	0.37	0.42	0.17
Single females (all)	0.34	0.24	0.20	0.23	0.22	0.19	−0.15
Single females with children	0.11	0.08	0.09	0.08	0.07	0.04	−0.06
D. Median Financial Resources							
Married couples (all)	31.3	42.2	84.4	52.6	29.8	42.5	35.8
Married couples with children	14.3	25.5	53.5	20.7	6.6	16.1	12.2
Single males (all)	5.0	11.0	9.0	12.8	3.2	4.1	−17.5
Single females (all)	6.1	2.5	4.6	5.8	1.0	1.9	−68.3
Single females with children	0.1	0.0	0.0	0.0	0.0	0.0	−100.0
Ratio to all married couples							
Married couples with children	0.46	0.60	0.63	0.39	0.22	0.38	−0.08
Single males (all)	0.16	0.26	0.11	0.24	0.11	0.10	−0.06
Single females (all)	0.19	0.06	0.05	0.11	0.03	0.05	−0.15
Single females with children	0.00	0.00	0.00	0.00	0.00	0.00	0.00
E. Homeownership Rate (in Percentage)							
Married couples (all)	64.8	66.7	65.8	70.1	65.1	64.6	−0.2
Married couples with children	75.7	77.1	82.5	79.0	77.5	75.5	−0.1
Single males (all)	58.2	66.5	63.7	64.7	64.5	58.8	0.6
Single females (all)	69.1	76.7	78.0	78.4	76.7	75.2	6.1
Single females with children	28.9	38.4	51.7	51.4	48.9	46.8	17.9
Ratio to all married couples							
Married couples with children	1.17	1.16	1.25	1.13	1.19	1.17	0.00
Single males (all)	0.90	1.00	0.97	0.92	0.99	0.91	0.01
Single females (all)	1.07	1.15	1.19	1.12	1.18	1.16	0.10
Single females with children	0.45	0.58	0.79	0.73	0.75	0.72	0.28

Source: Author's computations from the 1983, 1989 2001, 2007, 2010, and 2013 Survey of Consumer Finances.

a. Percentage point change for homeownership rates and for ratios.

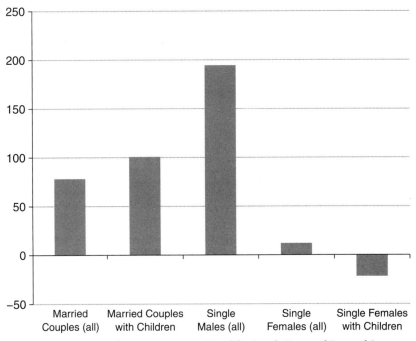

Figure 9.6. Percentage Change in Mean Net Worth by Family Type and Parental Status, 1983–2013

Mean financial resources followed the same time trend as mean NW, rising from 1983 to 2007 and then declining from 2007 to 2013. Over the thirty years mean FR was up strongly for all married couples, married couples with children, and especially single males. It rose 8 percent for all single females but fell by 21 percent for single females with children, reaching $25,400 in 2013. Median FR trended the same way over time for the first three groups, rising from 1983 to 2007 and then falling. It fell over time for single females as a group and remained virtually at zero over the whole time span for single women with children. In this case, all married couples showed the highest percentage gain from 1983 to 2013, at 36 percent, followed by couples with children, at 12 percent. Median FR declined by 18 percent for single males and plummeted by 68 percent for all single females (for women with children it remained steady at zero).

Families with children did much better in terms of homeownership. In 2013, couples with children had the highest homeownership rate at 76 percent, followed closely by single females as a group at 75 percent, all married couples at 65 percent, and single males at 59 percent. Females with children were not too far behind, at 47 percent. The homeownership rate among couples as a group, couples with children, and single males was about the same in 2013 as in 1983. Among single females as a group, it rose by 6 percentage points over the thirty years and among women with children by a substantial 18 percentage points.

The share of couples without children, the highest wealth group, among all households rose a bit between 1983 and 2013, from 29 to 31 percent, that of couples with children, the second highest wealth group, fell from 31 to 26 percent, and that of single males, the third highest wealth group, increased from 8 to 15 percent (see Table 9.4, Panel F). The proportion of single women without children, the second lowest wealth group, fell from 23 to 19 percent, while that of single women with children remained steady at 8 percent. The net effect was a slight dampening of the percentage growth of mean NW over the thirty years, from 72 to 64 percent, but a larger fall in median NW, from 9 to 18 percent. These demographic shifts also led to a slightly greater rise in wealth inequality of 0.072 Gini points, compared to 0.063 Gini points with the demographic composition of the population standardized at its 2001 composition.

Of the five family groups, single females had the highest share of assets in owner-occupied housing; couples without children and single males the largest percentage in financial assets and total stocks; and couples (both with and without children) in business equity and other real estate (see Table 9.15). The debt to NW ratio was highest by far among single mothers with children (0.36), followed by couples with children (0.28). Consequently, over years 2001 to 2007, returns on NW were highest for couples with children and single females with children because of their high debt-equity ratio, lowest (that is, most negative) for the same two groups over the period from 2007 to 2010, and highest for the same two groups over years 2010 to 2013.

Renters Take a Beating

According to the SCF data the overall homeownership rate advanced from 63.4 percent in 1983 to 68.6 percent in 2007 and fell to 65.1 percent in 2013 (see Table 9.16).[43] The actual number of homes owned climbed from 53.2 million in 1983 to 79.7 million in 2007 and then inched up to only 79.8 million in 2013. What happened over the Great Recession? If the homeownership rate had re-

Table 9.15. Composition of household wealth by family type and parental status, 2007 (percent of gross assets)

Asset	All	Couples: No Children	Couples with Children	Single Males	Single Females No Children	Single Females with Children
Principal residence	32.8	26.5	36.6	30.7	43.0	54.1
Liquid assets (bank deposits, money market funds, and cash surrender value of life insurance)	6.6	6.3	6.1	8.3	8.3	6.4
Pension accounts	12.1	13.1	11.1	13.6	11.3	8.7
Corporate stock, financial securities, mutual funds, and personal trusts	15.5	18.7	11.4	18.6	15.4	11.5
Unincorporated business equity other real estate	31.3	33.6	33.4	26.7	20.6	16.6
Miscellaneous assets	1.7	1.8	1.4	2.0	1.3	2.6
Total assets	100.0	100.0	100.0	100.0	100.0	100.0
Memo (selected ratios in percent)						
Debt/equity ratio	18.1	11.2	27.7	17.0	13.0	35.8
Debt/income ratio	118.7	92.2	144.1	104.1	103.3	148.9
Net home equity/total assets[a]	21.4	19.4	19.9	20.2	34.5	33.3
Principal residence debt/house value	34.9	26.7	45.5	34.2	19.8	38.4
All stocks/total assets[b]	16.8	19.7	13.5	21.0	14.6	11.5
Annual Rate of Return on Net Worth (in percentage)[c]						
2001–2007	4.04	3.58	4.93	3.62	3.16	4.89
2007–2010	−7.28	−6.70	−7.98	−7.03	−7.25	−9.32
2010–2013	6.20	5.54	6.55	6.18	5.80	6.87

Source: Author's computations from the 2007 Survey of Consumer Finances.

a. Ratio of gross value of principal residence less mortgage debt on principal residence to total assets.

b. Includes direct ownership of stock shares and indirect ownership through mutual funds, trusts, and IRAs, Keogh plans, 401(k) plans, and other retirement accounts.

c. Based on average portfolio composition and rates of return by asset type over the period.

Table 9.16. Household wealth by homeownership status, 1983–2013 (in thousands, 2013 dollars)

	1983	1989	2001	2007	2010	2013	% Change[a] 1983–2013
A. Overall Trends							
Homeownership rate	63.4	62.8	67.7	68.6	67.2	65.1	1.74
Number of homes owned (in millions)	53.2	58.5	72.1	79.7	79.1	79.8	50.0
Mean house value (homeowners only)	166.1	196.8	238.5	339.9	279.0	262.6	58.1
Mean home equity (homeowners only)	131.4	141.4	158.7	221.3	163.9	159.4	21.3
Median house value (homeowners only)	125.4	131.5	161.8	224.7	181.6	170.0	35.6
Median home equity (homeowners only)	93.6	93.9	92.1	118.0	80.1	80.0	−14.5
B. Mean Net Worth							
Homeowners	447.9	498.1	709.3	846.2	727.3	745.9	66.5
Renters	54.0	94.3	62.8	69.3	51.7	65.9	22.1
Ratio	0.12	0.19	0.09	0.08	0.07	0.09	−0.03
C. Median Net Worth							
Homeowners	154.2	177.8	199.3	238.4	166.0	172.5	11.8
Renters	1.9	0.9	0.3	0.0	0.1	0.1	−94.7
Ratio	0.01	0.01	0.00	0.00	0.00	0.00	−0.01
D. Mean Financial Resources							
Homeowners	316.5	356.7	550.5	624.9	550.0	586.5	85.3
Renters	54.0	95.9	62.8	69.3	48.4	65.9	22.1
Ratio	0.17	0.27	0.11	0.11	0.09	0.11	−0.06
E. Median Financial Resources							
Homeowners	43.2	53.9	80.2	78.7	49.0	61.3	41.9
Renters	1.9	0.9	0.3	0.0	0.0	0.1	−94.7
Ratio	0.04	0.02	0.00	0.00	0.00	0.00	−0.04

Source: Author's computations from the 1983, 1989 2001, 2007, 2010, and 2013 Survey of Consumer Finances.

a. Percentage point change for homeownership rates and for ratios.

mained constant from 2007 to 2013, then the number of homes owned should have reached 84.1 million. What happened to the missing 4.4 million units? According to CoreLogic, it seems that some 4.4 million homes were lost to foreclosure from the start of the financial crisis in September 2008 through 2013, which would explain the bulk of what happened to the "lost" homes.[44]

In terms of dollar values (in 2013 dollars), the mean house value among homeowners more than doubled between 1983 and 2007 but lost 23 percent from 2007 to 2013. Mean home equity among homeowners showed a smaller gain from 1983 to 2007 of 68 percent because of the rising ratio of mortgage debt to home value and then declined even more than house value from 2007 to 2013, by 28 percent, for the same reason. Time trends in medians show a similar pattern.

Mean NW, not surprisingly, was much higher among homeowners than renters—about a ten to one ratio over years 1983 to 2013. The gap in median NW between the two groups was even more substantial—about 100 to 1. In fact, the median NW of renters was about zero throughout these years. FR is defined as NW minus home equity. As a result, FR is equal to NW for renters. What is surprising is that the ratio of mean FR between renters and homeowners was only slightly greater than the ratio of mean NW, 0.11 versus 0.09 in 2013 (the ratio of median FR was about the same as that of median NW—zero). In other words, homeowners tended to accumulate much more in the way of nonhome assets than renters. There are several possible explanations. First, prospective homeowners develop the habit of saving for the down payment on their home (at least, when down payments were required). Second, the need to pay the monthly mortgage and possible repair and maintenance work means that homeowners have to provide ample financial resources in order to meet these obligations. Third, homeowners are likely to have greater financial "literacy" and knowledge than renters, which makes it more likely that they will invest.

It is also possible that the greater NW and FR among homeowners is due to the fact that they have higher incomes, are older, are more likely to be white, or are better educated than renters. Table 9.17 standardizes ratio of mean NW and FR between renters and homeowners for these characteristics. First, with regard to income differences, homeowners had greater NW and FR than renters at every income level, but the higher the income level, the smaller the gap. Indeed, for the highest income class the FR was about equal for renters and homeowners. These results suggest that higher-income families also have a strong savings incentive even if they do not own their own homes.

Second, homeowners tend to be, on average, older than renters. In this regard, homeowners had higher NW and FR than renters for every age group. The ratios did not show much variation across age groups except for the oldest

Table 9.17. Mean wealth for homeowners versus renters by income class and demographic characteristic, 2013 (figures are in thousands, 2013 dollars)

Category	Net Worth			Net Worth Excluding Home Equity (FR)		
	Owners	Renters	Ratio	Owners	Renters	Ratio
All Households	745.9	65.9	0.088	586.5	65.9	0.112
A. Income Level						
Under $15,000	291.5	1.9	0.006	182.6	1.9	0.010
$15,000–$24,999	183.4	11.3	0.062	78.7	11.3	0.143
$25,000–$49,999	178.7	16.1	0.090	88.1	16.1	0.183
$50,000–$74,999	281.1	67.4	0.240	179.2	67.4	0.376
$75,000–$99,999	420.4	116.0	0.276	295.7	116.0	0.392
$100,000–$249,999	843.8	339.9	0.403	661.3	339.9	0.514
$250,000 or more	6010.3	4938.1	0.822	5284.5	4938.1	0.934
B. Age Class						
Under 35	141.3	18.2	0.129	88.0	18.2	0.207
35–44	495.6	58.4	0.118	383.4	58.4	0.152
45–54	688.3	102.4	0.149	546.5	102.4	0.187
55–64	1007.2	77.7	0.077	813.2	77.7	0.096
65–74	1178.2	124.6	0.106	946.0	124.6	0.132
75 and over	695.2	205.8	0.296	506.5	205.8	0.406
C. Race/Ethnicity						
Whites (non-Hispanic)	860.5	101.4	0.118	688.1	101.4	0.147
Blacks (non-Hispanic)	178.8	10.5	0.059	108.0	10.5	0.097
Hispanics	214.7	6.8	0.032	123.6	6.8	0.055
D. Education						
Less than high school 4	195.3	12.2	0.062	99.1	12.2	0.123
High school 4	270.6	23.4	0.086	172.6	23.4	0.135
College 1–3	451.4	48.1	0.107	336.1	48.1	0.143
College 4 or more	1416.3	180.5	0.127	1168.9	180.5	0.154

Source: Author's computations from the 2013 Survey of Consumer Finances.
Households are classified according to the age and education of the head of household.

one (age 75 and over), among whom the gap was significantly smaller. Renters in this age group likely accumulated sufficient financial savings to provide for their retirement years. Third, the ratios in both NW and FR between renters and homeowners were quite small across racial/ethnic groupings. Interestingly, the ratio of FR was higher for whites than blacks or Hispanics, suggesting that even among renters white families had a stronger savings propensity than minorities. Fourth, even controlling for educational attainment, homeowners had much higher FR than renters. The variation across educational levels was quite limited, though the gap was smaller among college graduates.[45]

Summary and Concluding Remarks

The Great Recession witnessed the virtual disappearance of financial resources among poor, lower-middle-class, and even middle-class households. The same was true for younger households, minorities, the less educated, single females with children, and renters.

Chapter 5 emphasized the role of differential leverage and the resulting differences in rates of return on NW in explaining the wealth gap between the rich and the middle class. In this chapter, these two factors play a particularly important role in accounting for the relative collapse of the wealth of young households (under age 35 and ages 35–44) and minorities.[46] Capital losses almost fully accounted for the decline in simulated mean NW between 2007 and 2010 for the under-35 age group, and more than accounted for the fall for those in the 35–44 age group. Differences in returns explained about half the slide in the NW of the under-35 age group relative to age group 55–64 from 2007 to 2010, and all (actually more than 100 percent) of the drop in the wealth of age group 35–44 relative to age group 55–64.

Capital revaluation also explained two-thirds of the advance of simulated mean NW among black households from 2001 to 2007 and 64 percent of the ensuing collapse from 2007 to 2010. Among Hispanics, the corresponding figures were 35 percent for the earlier period and 65 percent for the later one. Differentials in rates of return accounted for 44 percent of the 21 percentage point gain in the simulated NW of black households relative to whites over years 2001 to 2007 and 27 percent of the 56 percentage point decline in the wealth ratio over years 2007 to 2010. Disparities in returns played a smaller role in explaining changes in the ratio of mean wealth between Hispanics and whites. Over years 2001 to 2007, they accounted for 13 percent of the 45 percentage point relative gain in mean NW of Hispanics and over years 2007 to 2010 for 33 percent of the 63 percentage point collapse in the relative wealth of Hispanic households.

Not surprisingly, both mean and median NW and financial resources rose monotonically with income level. The differences were huge: 99 to 1 in mean NW between the top 1 percent and middle-income quintile, 162 to 1 in median NW, 129 to 1 in mean FR, and 602 to 1 in median FR. The percentage growth in mean and median NW and FR between 1983 and 2013 also climbed almost monotonically with income level, indicating a fanning out of wealth differences over time. Between 1983 and 2013 mean NW and FR were up in absolute terms except for the second income quintile. Median NW and FR, on the other hand, fell in absolute terms for the bottom three income quintiles between 1983 and 2013. In fact, by 2013 median FR was close to zero for the bottom two income quintiles and only $11,000 for the middle quintile. There was relatively little variation in rates of return across income class, so that relative movements in NW by income class were largely explained by differentials in savings rates.

The Great Recession pummeled young households. The ratio of NW between households under age 35 and all households fell from 0.21 in 1983 to 0.17 in 2007 and then plunged to 0.11 in 2010. In (real) dollar terms, their mean NW declined by 46 percent from 2007 to 2010. Among age group 35–44, the ratio of their NW to the overall figure fell from 0.71 in 1983 to 0.58 in 2007 and then declined further to 0.42 in 2010. In dollar terms, their wealth fell by 39 percent over the latter three years. Similar trends were evident for FR.

Two factors that explained the losses suffered by young households over years 2007 to 2010 are the higher share of homes in their wealth portfolio and their very high leverage. In terms of rates of return, the youngest age group had an annual return of −13.49 percent and age group 35–44 had a return of −9.56 percent compared to −7.28 percent for all households. The relative NW of the under-35 age group recovered slightly to 0.12 in 2013 while that of age group 35–44 rebounded to 0.64. These trends reflected in part the high annual rate of return on their wealth portfolios—10.7 percent for the under-35 age group and 7.5 percent for age group 35–44 compared to 6.2 percent overall.

The simulated ratio of mean wealth between age groups 55–64 and under 35 dropped by 41 percentage points between 2001 and 2007. This trend was mainly due to differences in savings rates. Over the years 2007 to 2010, the simulated ratio jumped 50 percentage points. About equal contributions were made by the higher (that is, less negative) return of the older group and their higher implied savings rate. From 2010 to 2013, the simulated ratio plummeted by 53 percentage points, due primarily to savings rate disparities.

For the 2001–2007 period, the simulated ratio in NW between ages 55–64 and 35–44 declined by 28 percentage points, with the differential in savings rates explaining 52 percent and that in rates of return another 26 percent. From 2007 to 2010, the simulated ratio basically remained unchanged because the higher returns received by the older group were almost exactly offset by the higher implicit savings of the younger age class. Over years 2010 to 2013, the ratio of simulated mean wealth between the age groups nosedived by 52 percentage points, with 86 percent of the change related to differences in savings rates.

The racial disparity in wealth holdings, after fluctuating over the years from 1983 to 2007, was almost exactly the same in 2007 as in 1983. However, the Great Recession hit African-American households much harder than white households and the ratio of mean wealth between the two groups plunged from 0.19 in 2007 to 0.14 in 2010, reflecting a 33 percent decline (in real terms) in black wealth. The relative (and absolute) losses suffered by black households from 2007 to 2010 are ascribable to the fact that blacks had a higher share of homes in their portfolio than did whites and much higher leverage than whites (a debt to NW ratio of 0.55 versus 0.15). These factors led to a wide discrepancy in rates of return on their respective portfolios (–9.92 versus –7.07 percent per year). From 2010 to 2013, the wealth ratio slipped to 0.13, despite the fact that the rate of return on the portfolio of black families was greater than that of white families (7.14 versus 6.12 percent per year). The trend reflects the substantially higher dissavings rate among black families than white families over these years.

Hispanic households made sizable gains on (non-Hispanic) white households from 1983 to 2007. The ratio of mean NW grew from 0.16 to 0.26, the homeownership rate among Hispanic households climbed from 33 to 49 percent, and the ratio of homeownership rates with white households advanced from 48 to 66 percent. However, in a reversal of fortunes, Hispanic households suffered in years 2007 to 2010, with their mean NW plunging by half, the ratio of mean NW with white households falling from 0.26 to 0.15, their homeownership rate down by 1.9 percentage points, and their net home equity plummeting by 47 percent. The relative (and absolute) losses suffered by Hispanic households over these three years were also mainly due to the much larger share of homes in their wealth portfolios and their much higher leverage (a debt-equity ratio of 0.51 versus 0.15). These factors led to a wide disparity in returns on their respective portfolios over years 2007 to 2010 (–10.76 versus –7.07 percent per year). From 2010 to 2013, their relative NW remained unchanged despite the fact that they had a higher rate of return on their wealth portfolios than did whites (7.48 versus 6.12 percent per year). This result reflects the fact that Hispanics had higher dissavings than did whites.

In 2013, the mean NW of college graduates was ten times the wealth of those with less than four years of high school, six times that of high school graduates, and almost four times that of those with one to three years of college. These wealth gradients, while large, were much smaller than those by income class. Between 1983 and 2013, the NW of college graduates gained 52 percent, while that of households with less than four years of high school was down by 12 percent and that of high school graduates by 7 percent. Median NW plummeted by 84 percent for high school dropouts between 1983 and 2013, by 44 percent for high school graduates, and by 55 percent for those with one to three years of college, while it was up by 19 percent for college graduates. Homeownership rates showed a much smaller spread across schooling groups. However, only college graduates had a higher homeownership rate in 2013 than in 1983 (a 6 percentage point increase). The variation in rates of return across educational groups was relatively small, so that differentials in savings rates explain most of the movement in relative NW over time.

There was also a clear ranking in wealth levels by family type and parental status. In 2013 married couples as a group possessed the highest mean NW, followed by married couples with children, single males, single females as a group, and then single females with children. The spread was very large, with a ratio of mean NW between the first and last group of almost fourteen to one. Single females with children experienced a sizable drop in their NW of 22 percent over these years. Over the same period, median NW dropped by a huge 93 percent for single females with children, down to only $500 in 2013.

Mean NW was (not surprisingly) much greater among homeowners than renters—about ten to one. The gap in median NW between the two groups was even larger. In fact, the median NW of renters was about zero throughout years 1983 to 2013. Even after controlling for income, age, race, and education, the gap in wealth between renters and homeowners remained very large.

10

Who Are the Rich? A Demographic Profile of High-Income and High-Wealth Americans

This chapter investigates the demographic characteristics of the rich. Who are they? Do they tend to be elderly or middle-aged? What is their racial makeup? Are they all highly educated? Do they work for others or do they own their own businesses? What occupations and industries employ them? Have these patterns changed over time? In particular, has there been a shift from "rentier" wealth to entrepreneurial wealth? How do their demographics compare to the general population? In this chapter empirical analysis will cover selected years between 1983 and 2013.

Several questions are of particular interest. First, with the substantial increase of inequality over this period and especially with the record-high salaries recorded on Wall Street and among professional workers in general, has there been a shift in the composition of the rich away from the classic "coupon-clippers" toward entrepreneurs? Second, along with this trend, has there been a shift toward finance and professional services as the main sources of employment of the rich? Third, with the high-tech boom of the 1990s and 2000s and the emergence of young software developers as represented by Amazon, Facebook, Google, and the like, has there been a corresponding change in the composition of the rich toward younger families and away from middle-aged and older groups? Fourth, with the large incomes recorded in the entertainment and sports industries, do we find an increasing proportion of black Americans in the ranks of the rich? Fifth, given the rising premium to education observed since the decade of the 1980s, has there been a notable shift in the composition of the rich toward college-educated workers? Sixth, with the strong correlation observed between health and wealth, has the health of the rich improved over time?

The composition of the wealthy class, defined here as both the top percentile of the wealth distribution and the top percentile of the income distribution, underwent significant change during the years from 1983 to 1992.[1] The number of households under the age of 45 that joined the ranks of the rich grew from 9.9 to 15 percent. Moreover, the percentage of the top 1 percent, as ranked by income, under the age of 35 increased from 1.6 to 5.7 and the percentage in age group 35–44 climbed very sharply, from 16.3 to 25.5.

In regard to education, despite significant growth in the overall educational attainment of the population during this time period, there was no corresponding increase in the educational attainment of the top 1 percent as ranked by wealth. In fact, the fraction of this group that had college degrees actually declined. The same result was found for the top 1 percent of households as ranked by household income.

The proportion of non-Hispanic black households among the top wealth percentile actually fell over this period, while the proportion of Hispanics increased from virtually zero to almost 1 percent and the proportion of Asians and other races from 1.6 to 4.8 percent. Results were similar with regard to the top 1 percent of income. In fact, the fraction of non-Hispanic black families in their ranks fell from 1.2 to 0.1 percent over this period, while the fraction of Hispanics remained at zero in both years.

There is also evidence that entrepreneurial activity played much more of a role in gaining entry to the ranks of the rich. Among the richest 1 percent of households ranked in terms of wealth, the share of proprietary income, including self-employment, partnerships, and unincorporated business ownership, in total income rose sharply, from 27 to 40 percent. Many of the new rich were also more apt to rely on wages and salaries as a source of income. Its share of their total income rose from 24 to 30 percent. In contrast, property income of all forms, such as dividends and capital gains, declined sharply, from 46 to 27 percent of total income.

When ranked in terms of income, the top 1 percent of households again showed a large increase in their reliance on wage and salary income, from 35 to 44 percent of total income. It is notable that this finding was reported several years before that of Piketty and Saez, who reported an increase in the share of labor earnings in the total income of the top 1 percent of the income distribution.[2] Proprietary income fell somewhat as a share of total income, from 26 to 24 percent. Property income, including interest, dividends, capital gains, and rental, royalty, and trust income declined as a proportion of total proceeds, from 36 to 30 percent.

There is corroborating evidence from the change in household portfolios of the rich. While the proportion of the total wealth of the top 1 percent as ranked by wealth held in the form of business equity remained unchanged between 1983 and 1992, their share of the total value of business equity among all households grew sharply, from 52 to 62 percent. Moreover, among the richest 1 percent of households as ranked by income, the proportion of their wealth held in the form of business equity increased from 28 to 32 percent and their share of the total value of business equity surged from 39 to 48 percent. Conversely, the proportion of the total wealth of the rich, classified by both dimensions, held in the form of stocks and mutual funds and trust funds fell sharply over this period, as did their share of the total outstanding value of these assets. This was in part compensated by sharply increased holdings of financial securities, both as a percent of the total assets of the top 1 percent and as a share of the total amount of financial securities held by all households.

The main focus of this chapter is to determine whether these trends continued through 2013. The years 2001 and 2013 are included in the analysis so that the four years are about a decade apart (and also correspond to the Survey of Consumer Finances [SCF]). The analysis reviews characteristics of high-wealth households as well as high-income households over the four years in question.

Characteristics of the Richest 1 Percent of Households, as Ranked by Wealth

Are the rich really different from the rest of us? Table 10.1 provides information on the demographic characteristics of the top 1 percent of households as ranked by net worth, in comparison to that of all households in 1983, 1992, 2001, and 2013. Panel A shows the age distribution in the four years (see also Figures 10.1a and 10.1b). In 1983, the rich were considerably older, on average, than members of other households. Whereas the mean age of household heads in the top 1 percent was 57.3 and their median age was 56, the mean age of all household heads in that year was 46.8 and the median was 44. While 8 percent of all households were under the age of 25, 23 percent were in the age range 25–34, and 20 percent were in the age range 35–44, none of the rich were under 25. Only 0.7 percent of the rich were in the age group 25–34, and 9 percent were in the range 35–44. In contrast, while 43 percent of all households were in the age range 45–74, 84 percent of the rich were in this age group. The fraction of the rich that were aged 75 and older was slightly lower than for all households—5.9 versus 7.1 percent.

Between 1983 and 1992, the general population aged somewhat, with the mean age of household heads rising from 46.8 to 48.4 and the median age from 44 to 45. However, despite this trend, the proportion of the top 1 percent under age 35 increased from 0.7 to 2 percent, and the proportion in the age range 35–44 from 9.2 to 12.8 percent. This result is consistent with the observation that the huge salaries generated on Wall Street, in the entertainment business, and in other professions created a whole new class of young wealthy individuals.

The proportion of the top 1 percent in age group 45–54 fell sharply, from 33 to 25 percent, and the percentage aged 65–74 declined substantially relative to the overall demographic trends. The percentage of the rich in age range 55–64 increased somewhat, from 29.4 to 31.3, though this seems to be a cohort effect since that group was highly represented in the top 1 percent in 1983 (then in age range 45–54). This group consists of individuals born during the Great Depression (1928 to 1937). The age group 75 and older also gained as a share, from 5.9 to 9.8 percent, and relative to overall demographic trends.

From 1992 to 2013 the mean age of all household heads rose from 48.4 to 51.1 and the median age from 45 to 51. The mean and median age of the top 1 percent also continued to rise, from 58.1 to 61.3 for the former and from 58 to 63 for the latter. Whereas the share of the top 1 percent under age 35 remained about the same between 1992 and 2013, it did increase relative to overall population trends (the differential between the top 1 percent and the overall proportion increased from −18.4 to −13.6). The share in age group 35–44 fell but remained about the same relative to overall population trends, whereas the proportion of the top percentile in age group 45–54 declined by almost half and waned relative to population trends. The biggest gain among the top 1 percent was recorded by age group 65–74, which rose from

Table 10.1. Demographic and work-related characteristics of the top 1 percent of wealth holders and all households, 1983, 1992, 2001, and 2013 (percentage distribution except for mean and median values)

	1983			1992			2001			2013		
	Top 1%	All	Diff.	Top 1%	All	Diff.	Top 1%	All	Diff.	Top 1%	All	Diff.
A. Age of Head												
Less than 25	0.0	8.0	-8.0	0.2	5.2	-5.0	1.4	5.6	-4.2	0.0	5.0	-5.0
25–34	0.7	22.6	-21.8	2.0	20.4	-18.4	2.0	17.2	-15.2	2.2	15.8	-13.6
35–44	9.2	19.5	-10.3	12.8	22.7	-9.9	11.6	22.1	-10.5	8.3	17.3	-9.0
45–54	32.9	15.6	17.2	24.6	16.4	8.2	28.6	20.7	7.9	13.9	19.6	-5.8
55–64	29.4	15.1	14.4	31.3	13.4	17.9	30.5	13.2	17.3	34.3	18.7	15.6
65–74	21.8	12.1	9.7	19.3	12.7	6.6	19.3	10.7	8.6	30.6	12.9	17.3
75 and over	5.9	7.1	-1.2	9.8	9.2	0.6	6.6	10.4	-3.8	10.7	10.7	0.0
All age groups	100.0	100.0	0.0	100.0	100.0	0.0	100.0	100.0	0.0	100.0	100.0	0.0
Mean age	57.3	46.8	10.5	58.1	48.4	9.8	56.9	49.0	8.0	61.3	51.1	10.1
Median age	56.0	44.0	12.0	58.0	45.0	13.0	57.0	47.0	10.0	63.0	51.0	12.0
B. Education of Head												
0–11 years	2.7	29.0	-26.3	1.8	21.1	-19.3	2.2	18.1	-15.9	1.1	12.4	-11.3
High school graduate	10.0	30.2	-20.1	9.2	28.9	-19.7	7.6	29.6	-22.0	4.7	29.9	-25.2
College 1–3	11.6	19.6	-8.1	15.6	21.0	-5.4	8.4	22.6	-14.2	11.4	24.2	-12.8
College graduate	40.0	10.6	29.4	32.9	16.5	16.3	39.7	17.6	22.1	33.7	20.0	13.6
Some graduate school	35.7	10.6	25.1	40.6	12.5	28.1	42.1	12.0	30.1	49.2	13.5	35.7
All educational groups	100.0	100.0	0.0	100.0	100.0	0.0	100.0	100.0	0.0	100.0	100.0	0.0
Mean education	15.5	12.2	3.3	15.6	12.9	2.7	15.7	13.1	2.6	16.0	13.5	2.5
Median education	16.0	12.0	4.0	16.0	13.0	3.0	16.0	13.0	3.0	16.0	14.0	2.0

C. Race												
White (non-Hispanic)	97.9	80.9	17.0	94.2	75.3	18.9	95.7	76.2	19.5	93.9	70.1	23.8
Black (non-Hispanic)	0.5	12.7	-12.2	0.1	12.6	-12.5	0.0	13.0	-13.0	1.7	14.6	-12.9
Hispanic	0.0	3.5	-3.5	0.9	7.6	-6.6	2.2	8.0	-5.8	1.0	10.6	-9.6
Asian and others	1.6	2.8	-1.2	4.8	4.6	0.2	2.1	2.8	-0.7	3.4	4.7	-1.2
All racial groups	100.0	100.0	0.0	100.0	100.0	0.0	100.0	100.0	0.0	100.0	100.0	0.0
D. Marital Status												
Married, spouse present[a]	88.1	60.8	27.3	83.4	57.6	25.7	89.0	60.3	28.7	88.1	57.2	31.0
Male, separated, divorced or widowed	3.2	6.8	-3.6	7.0	8.6	-1.5	6.2	7.5	-1.3	7.3	7.7	-0.3
Male, never married	1.3	6.3	-5.0	2.3	6.5	-4.2	2.5	6.1	-3.6	1.1	7.5	-6.4
Female, separated, divorced, or widowed	7.4	19.9	-12.5	7.3	19.4	-12.1	2.3	17.5	-15.2	3.4	13.7	-15.3
Female, never married	0.0	6.2	-6.2	0.0	7.9	-7.9	0.0	8.6	-8.6	0.0	3.9	-8.9
All marital groups	100.0	100.0	0.0	100.0	100.0	0.0	100.0	100.0	0.0	100.0	100.0	0.0
E. Employment Status of Head (age less than 65 only)												
Full-time	86.4	75.8	10.6	76.7	74.9	1.9	76.2	79.1	-2.9	77.8	70.7	7.1
Part-time	4.6	4.0	0.6	8.6	4.5	4.1	7.5	6.2	1.2	9.5	8.0	1.5
Unemployed or temporarily laid off	0.0	8.8	-8.8	1.4	7.1	-5.7	0.1	4.3	-4.2	0.0	6.2	-6.2
Retired	3.6	7.3	-3.7	9.7	3.8	5.9	11.6	3.2	8.4	8.0	4.7	3.4
Not in labor force	5.4	4.1	1.3	3.6	9.8	-6.1	4.6	7.2	-2.6	4.7	0.4	-5.7
All under age 65	100.0	100.0	0.0	100.0	100.0	0.0	100.0	100.0	0.0	100.0	100.0	0.0
F. Industry of Employment of Head (working and age less than 65)												
Agriculture	9.2	3.9	5.3	1.4	2.7	-1.3	1.8	1.9	-0.1	2.7	2.6	0.1
Mining and construction	11.5	8.9	2.6	4.7	7.4	-2.7	9.9	10.5	-0.6	7.0	11.1	-4.1
Manufacturing	19.5	23.7	-4.2	21.8	28.3	-6.5	17.2	18.7	-1.5	12.6	13.1	-0.5

(*continued*)

Table 10.1. (continued)

	1983			1992			2001			2013		
	Top 1%	All	Diff.	Top 1%	All	Diff.	Top 1%	All	Diff.	Top 1%	All	Diff.
Transportation, communications, utilities, personal services, and professional services	23.4	32.0	−8.6	22.5	25.5	−3.0	28.7	32.4	−3.7	46.2	40.3	5.9
Trade (wholesale and retail)	11.3	15.5	−4.2	13.3	14.9	−1.5	14.6	15.6	−1.0	10.3	15.2	−4.9
Finance, insurance, real estate, and business and repair services	25.0	8.7	16.3	35.8	13.8	22.0	27.8	16.0	11.8	21.2	11.5	9.7
Public administration	0.0	7.2	−7.2	0.4	7.4	−7.0	0.0	5.0	−4.9	0.0	6.2	−6.2
All employed persons	100.0	100.0	0.0	100.0	100.0	0.0	100.0	100.0	0.0	100.0	100.0	0.0
G. Occupation of Head (working and age less than 65)												
Self-employed[b]	37.5	15.4	22.1	68.9	17.2	51.7	71.9	16.7	55.2	84.4	15.3	69.1
Professionals[c]	6.4	15.0	−8.6	26.5	25.5	0.9	27.7	27.1	0.6	13.4	34.3	−20.9
Managers and administrators	55.2	13.9	41.3									
Sales and clerical workers[d]	1.0	13.0	−12.1	2.8	22.4	−19.6	0.1	18.5	−18.4	2.2	14.9	−12.7
Craft workers[e]	0.0	16.9	−16.9	1.8	10.6	−8.8	0.0	12.8	−12.8	0.0	14.1	−14.1
Other blue-collar workers[f]	0.0	25.8	−25.8	0.0	18.1	−24.3	0.1	15.0	−14.9	0.0	9.4	−9.4
Service workers				0.0	6.2	−6.2	0.2	9.8	−9.6	0.0	11.9	−11.9
All employed persons	100.0	100.0	0.0	100.0	100.0	0.0	100.0	100.0	0.0	100.0	100.0	0.0

H. Health of Household

H. Health of Head of Household												
Excellent	61.2	37.9	23.3	55.9	34.6	21.3	60.5	29.1	31.4	45.1	23.9	21.3
Good	32.1	39.6	-7.5	31.8	40.9	-9.1	30.7	46.1	-15.3	44.8	48.8	-4.0
Fair	5.9	15.4	-9.6	7.8	17.5	-9.7	4.5	19.0	-14.6	9.0	21.0	-12.1
Poor	0.8	7.1	-6.2	4.5	7.0	-2.5	4.3	5.8	-1.5	1.1	6.3	-5.2
All	100.0	100.0	0.0	100.0	100.0	0.0	100.0	100.0	0.0	100.0	100.0	0.0
I. Inheritances Received												
Percent receiving a wealth transfer	47.6			20.7		26.9	43.9	17.9	26.1	47.4	21.5	26.0
Average value of wealth transfer[g]	5,356			453		4,903	2,259	425	1,834	5,812	571	5,240

Source: Author's computations from the 1983, 1992, 2001, and 2013 Survey of Consumer Finances.

Lower bounds for the top 1 percent (in current dollars) are as follows:

1983—$1,550,000
1992—$2,420,000
2001—$5,840,000
2013—$7,770,000

All computations are for the head of household unless otherwise indicated.

a. Includes "partners" in 1992, 2001, and 2013.

b. Self-employed of any occupation are classified separately in this category.

c. Includes technical workers in 1983.

d. Includes technical workers in 1992, 2001, and 2013.

e. Includes protective service workers in 1983.

f. Includes operatives (both machine and transportation equipment), laborers, and farm workers.

g. Recipients only. Present value as of 2013 in thousands, using a 3 percent real interest rate.

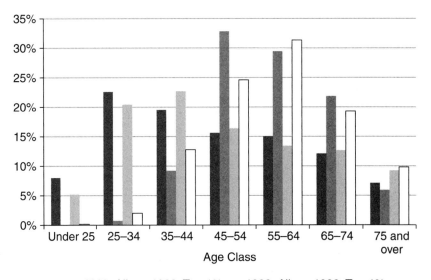

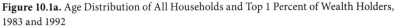

■ 1983, All   ■ 1983, Top 1%   ■ 1992, All   □ 1992, Top 1%

Figure 10.1a. Age Distribution of All Households and Top 1 Percent of Wealth Holders, 1983 and 1992

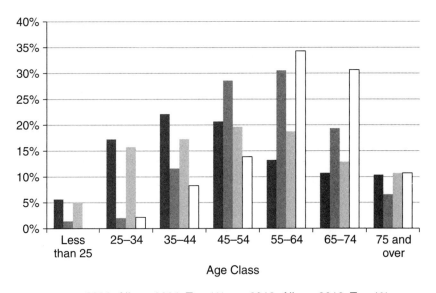

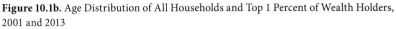

■ 2001, All   ■ 2001, Top 1%   ■ 2013, All   □ 2013, Top 1%

Figure 10.1b. Age Distribution of All Households and Top 1 Percent of Wealth Holders, 2001 and 2013

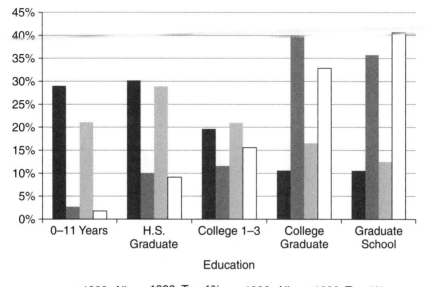

Figure 10.2a. Educational Distribution of All Households and Top 1 Percent of Wealth Holders, 1983 and 1992

19 percent in 1992 to 31 percent in 2013 and also increased relative to overall population trends. Thus, if anything, the rich became notably older between 1992 and 2013.

The rich are also much more highly educated than the overall population (Table 10.1, Panel B, and Figures 10.2a and 10.2b). In 1983, while 21 percent of household heads were college graduates (or had advanced degrees), 76 percent of the top 1 percent had graduated college (or attended graduate school). While 29 percent of household heads overall had failed to graduate high school in 1983, less than 3 percent of the rich fell into this category.

Between 1983 and 1992, overall educational attainment increased in the general population. The percent of household heads who had graduated high school increased from 71 to 79, the percent who had graduated college from 21 to 29, mean educational attainment rose from 12.2 to 12.9 years, and median education from 12 to 13 years. However, somewhat surprisingly, the proportion of the rich who had graduated college actually fell from 76 to 73 percent, though of this group the proportion that had completed some

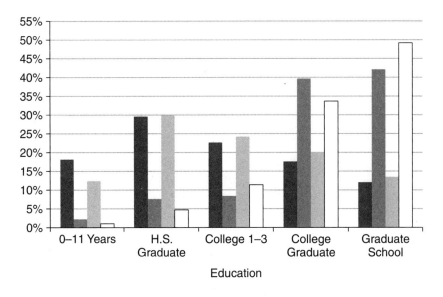

Figure 10.2b. Educational Distribution of All Households and Top 1 Percent of Wealth Holders, 2001 and 2013

graduate work increased. There was a particularly large increase in the percentage of college "dropouts" (one to three years of college) among the rich, from 11.6 in 1983 to 15.6 percent in 1992—perhaps, the "Bill Gates" phenomenon. In any case, there is no clear evidence that more education paid off in terms of entry into the ranks of the top 1 percent of wealth holders over the period 1983 to 1992.

From 1992 to 2013, the general population continued to become more educated, with mean years of schooling rising from 12.9 to 13.5 and median years from 13 to 14. The rich remained better educated than the overall population and expanded their lead, particularly at the graduate school level. Over these years, the share of the top 1 percent who had attended graduate school leaped from 41 percent to 49 percent and the proportion with a college degree or more from 74 to 83 percent.

The racial composition of the rich also differs significantly from that of the general population (Table 10.1, Panel C and Figures 10.3a and 10.3b). Whereas 81 percent of households in 1983 were non-Hispanic whites, 98 percent of the rich fell into this category. While 16.2 percent of households classified

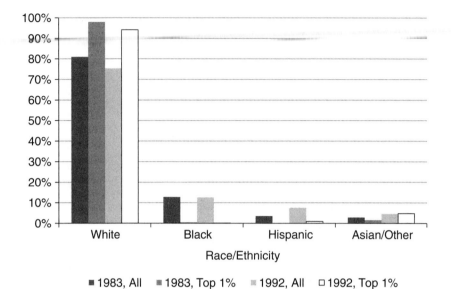

■ 1983, All   ■ 1983, Top 1%   ▪ 1992, All   □ 1992, Top 1%

Figure 10.3a. Racial Composition of All Households and Top 1% of Wealth Holders, 1983 and 1992

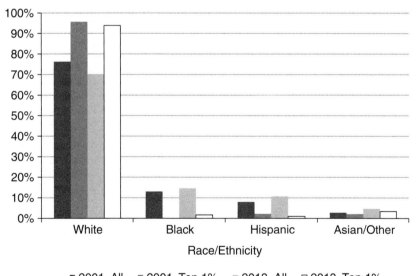

■ 2001, All   ■ 2001, Top 1%   ▪ 2013, All   □ 2013, Top 1%

Figure 10.3b. Racial Composition of All Households and Top 1 Percent of Wealth Holders, 2001 and 2013

themselves as black or Hispanic, only 0.5 percent of the top 1 percent was in this group.

Between 1983 and 1992, the overall racial composition of households shifted rather significantly, with non-Hispanic whites falling from 81 to 75 percent, blacks remaining at about 12.5 percent, Hispanics increasing from 3.5 to 7.6 percent, and Asians and others from 2.8 to 4.6 percent. The proportion of white households among the top 1 percent did fall somewhat over this period, from 97.9 to 94.2 percent. However, the proportion of blacks also fell from 0.5 to 0.1 percent, while the proportion of Hispanics increased somewhat from zero to 0.9 percent. The most significant growth was in the share of Asians and other races among the top 1 percent of wealth holders, from 1.6 to 4.6 percent.

By 2013, the share of whites among the top 1 percent remained about the same as in 1992, though the overall share of whites in the general population fell from 75.3 to 70.1 percent. The proportion of blacks in the top percentile did increase somewhat, to 1.7 percent, while the share of Hispanics in this group remained about the same, despite an increase in their overall population share to 10.6 percent, and that of Asians and others fell somewhat.

Panel D shows the marital status of the two groups. In 1983, the wealthy were much more likely to be married than the general population (88 versus 61 percent). Unmarried males made up 4.5 percent of this group (in contrast to a population share of 13.1 percent); formerly married women (separated, divorced, or widowed) constituted 7.4 percent of the group (in comparison to a population share of 19.9 percent); and there were no women who had never married in the ranks of the top 1 percent (compared to an overall proportion of 6.2 percent).

Between 1983 and 1992, the proportion of married families in the top 1 percent of wealth holders fell from 88 to 83 percent and this change was almost exactly offset by the increase in the percentage of unmarried males in this group, from 4.5 to 9.3 percent. The share of formerly married women in the top percentile remained almost unchanged, and there were again no women who had not married among the rich.

From 1992 to 2013, the share of married families among the top percentile was back to where it was in 1983, at 88 percent, though the overall share of married couples in the general population fell somewhat. The share of single males remained about the same, that of formerly married women fell to 3.4 percent, and that of never married women stayed at zero.

The next three panels in Table 10.1 provide employment statistics. Tabulations are made for individuals younger than 65 in Panel E and for those younger than 65 and with a job in Panels F and G. As shown in Panel E, the percentage of nonelderly household heads who worked full time in 1983 was much higher among the rich than in the general population (86 versus 76). In contrast, none of the wealthy reported that they were unemployed or on temporary layoff, compared to 8.8 percent of all nonelderly households. Only 3.6 percent of the nonelderly wealthy reported that they were retired in 1983, in contrast to 7.3 percent of the general population.

Between 1983 and 1992, the proportion of full-time workers in the ranks of the nonelderly wealthy fell precipitously, from 86 to 77 percent. This change was offset by big increases in the share of part-time workers in this group, from 4.6 to 8.6 percent, and in the share of retirees, from 3.6 to 9.7 percent. These results indicate that the top wealth percentile cut back rather dramatically on their work effort over this period. There was relatively little change from 1992 to 2013.

In 1983, 25 percent of rich families reported working in finance, insurance, real estate, and business and repair services, compared to only 9 percent of all workers (Panel F and Figures 10.4a and 10.4b).[3] Farmers, mining, and construction workers were also over-represented in the ranks of the rich (20.7 compared to 12.8 percent of all workers). In contrast, workers in manufacturing; transportation, communications, utilities, and personal and professional services; and wholesale and retail trade were under-represented. Moreover, there were no government employees in the top percentile in 1983 (compared to 7.2 percent of all workers).

The most notable change between 1983 and 1992 was, as speculated, a huge gain in the share of finance, insurance, and real estate (as well as business) employees in the ranks of the rich, from 25 to 36 percent (and also a large increase relative to the employment share of all workers, from a difference of 16.3 to 22 percentage points). The proportion of farmers in their ranks fell precipitously, from 9.2 to 1.4 percent, as did the proportion employed in mining and construction, from 11.5 to 4.7 percent. The proportion

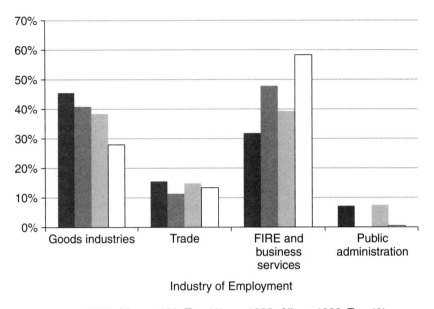

Figure 10.4a. Industry of Employment of All Households and Top 1 Percent of Wealth Holders, 1983 and 1992

of the rich working in the conglomerate category of transportation, communications, utilities, and personal and professional services remained relatively unchanged, as did the share in trade and in public administration (essentially zero for the latter).

Panel G reports the occupational composition of household heads who are at work and under age 65 (also see Figures 10.5a and 10.5b). In this case, I separate out all self-employed workers into a single category. So, for example, a lawyer who is also self-employed is classified only as self-employed, not in the professional worker category. In terms of occupational composition, the results show that the self-employed were substantially over-represented in the ranks of the rich in 1983—38 percent versus 15 percent of all workers. The same was true for managers and administrators—55 percent compared to 14 percent of all persons in the labor force. In contrast, only 6.4 percent of the rich classified themselves as professional workers, compared to a 15 percent share of all workers. Moreover, there were virtually no sales, clerical, craft, or

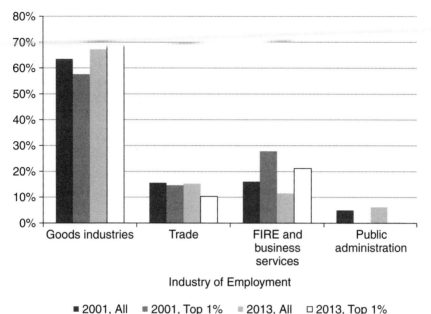

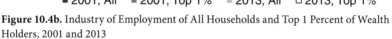

■ 2001, All   ■ 2001, Top 1%   ▪ 2013, All   □ 2013, Top 1%

Figure 10.4b. Industry of Employment of All Households and Top 1 Percent of Wealth Holders, 2001 and 2013

other blue-collar workers found among the top 1 percent of wealth holders in 1983.

Between 1983 and 1992, the most notable change was a huge increase in the share of the self-employed among the top 1 percent—almost doubling from 38 to 69 percent—in contrast to a modest gain among all workers, from 15.4 to 17.2 percent.[4] This result tends to confirm our speculation about increased entrepreneurial activity in the ranks of the rich. Correspondingly, the proportion of professional, managerial, and administrative workers declined sharply, from 62 to 27 percent.[5] There were modest gains among sales, clerical, and craft workers, from 1 to 4.6 percent of the top 1 percent.

The share of self-employed among the ranks of working persons (actually, household heads) in the top wealth percentile continued to expand, first to 72 percent in 2001 and then to an astounding 84 percent in 2013. Among all workers, the self-employment share actually fell from 17.2 percent in 1992 to

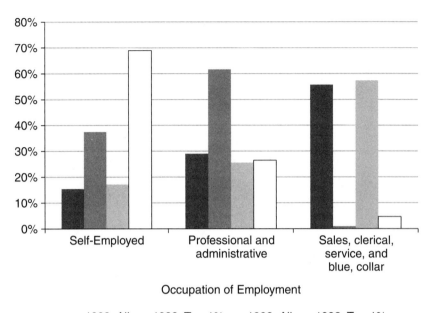

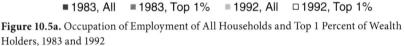

Figure 10.5a. Occupation of Employment of All Households and Top 1 Percent of Wealth Holders, 1983 and 1992

15.3 percent in 2013. Consequently, the share of all other occupational groups among the top percent fell from 1992 to 2013 (in the case of service workers it remained at zero).

Panel H shows statistics on health (also see Figures 10.6a and 10.6b). This is a self-reported category, so that there is a large subjective element involved in the classification. Despite this, the results suggest rather strongly that the rich are healthier than the average population. In 1983, 61 percent of the rich classified themselves as having excellent health, compared to 38 percent of the general population. Only 6.7 percent of the top 1 percent indicated that there health was fair or poor, in comparison to 22.5 percent of all respondents.

Between 1983 and 1992 there appeared to be a slight deterioration in the health of the rich and the overall population. In the general population, the proportion reporting excellent health fell from 37.9 to 34.6 percent, while the percentage reporting fair or poor health increased from 22.5 to

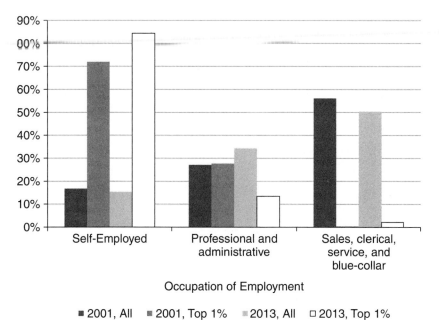

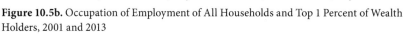

Figure 10.5b. Occupation of Employment of All Households and Top 1 Percent of Wealth Holders, 2001 and 2013

24.5 percent. Among the wealthy, the share with excellent health fell from 61 to 56 percent whereas the share with fair health grew from 5.9 to 7.8 percent and the share with poor health from 0.8 to 4.5 percent.

The share of the rich reporting excellent health picked up to 61 percent in 2001, about the same as in 1983. However, the share with fair or poor health also rose from 6.7 percent in 1983 to 8.8 percent in 2001. This was followed by a huge change between 2001 and 2013, with only 45 percent of the rich reporting excellent health and 10.1 percent reporting fair or poor health. It is not clear whether this worsening of reported health among the top percentile was due to a true decline in health between 2001 and 2013 or a change in response patterns. However, one pertinent factor is the significant aging of the top 1 percent over these years, with mean age rising by 4.4 years and median age by a full six years. Interestingly, among the general population there appears to have been a steady deterioration in health between 1983 and 2013, with the "excellent" proportion dropping from 38 to 24 percent and the

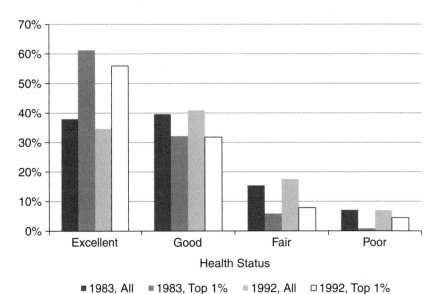

Figure 10.6a. Health Status of All Households and Top 1 Percent of Wealth Holders, 1983 and 1992

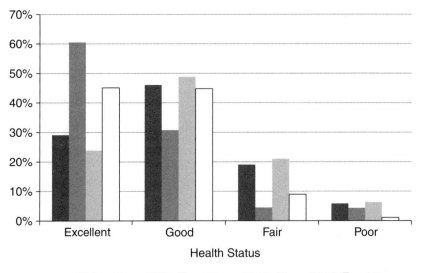

Figure 10.6b. Health Status of All Households and Top 1 Percent of Wealth Holders, 2001 and 2013

"fair" or "poor" proportion rising from 22.6 to 27.3 percent. As a result, the health differential between the top 1 percent and the overall population was about the same in 2013 as in 1983.

The last panel in Table 10.1 shows some statistics on wealth transfers (both inheritances and inter vivos gifts) received in 1992, 2001, and 2013.[6] These results are based on respondent recall; that is, the individual is asked to indicate both the amount and the date that any wealth transfer was received at any time up to the time of the survey. The value of these wealth transfers are then accumulated over time at a real interest rate of 3 percent to obtain the present value of wealth transfers as of the survey year. The present value is then converted to 2013 dollars.

Despite the difficulties with "recall" variables, the results clearly indicate that in 1992 the wealthy were more apt to receive a wealth transfer than the general population (48 versus 21 percent) and that the mean value of the wealth transfers received (among recipients only) was much greater—almost twelve times as great among the very wealthy as in the general population. The overall mean value of wealth transfers (among all households) was therefore 27 times as large. The greater value of wealth transfers among the very wealthy as opposed to general population can be explained, in part, by the age of the parties: the rich are considerably older and wealth transfers increase with age. This factor explains only a small fraction of the difference between the two groups. In addition, although the rich receive greater wealth transfers than the poor, they are greater as a *proportion* of net worth among the poor than among the rich. Between 1992 and 2013, mean wealth transfers increased by 8 percent among the top wealth percentile and by 31 percent among the general population, so that the ratio between the two groups fell from 27.3 to 22.5.

Table 10.2 shows the composition of the gross assets for the top 1 percent of households as ranked by net worth, in comparison to that of all households in 1983 (also see Figures 10.7a and 10.7b). The results shown in Table 10.2 indicate that the rich hold their wealth in very different forms than other households. Compared to the average portfolio of all households, the top percentile had a higher proportion of their gross assets in the form of non-home real estate (19.6 versus 14.9 percent), stocks and mutual funds (17.1 versus 9.0 percent), business equity (32.2 versus 18.8 percent), and trust funds (6.9 versus 2.6 percent); and lower proportions in their principal residence

Table 10.2. Portfolio composition of the top 1 percent of wealth holders and all households, 1983, 1992, 2001, and 2013 (percentage of gross assets)

Wealth Component	1983			1992			2001			2013		
	Top 1%: Percent of Gross Assets	All HH: Percent of Gross Assets	Ratio: Top 1% to Total Value	Top 1%: Percent of Gross Assets	All HH: Percent of Gross Assets	Ratio: Top 1% to Total Value	Top 1%: Percent of Gross Assets	All HH: Percent of Gross Assets	Ratio: Top 1% to Total Value	Top 1%: Percent of Gross Assets	All HH: Percent of Gross Assets	Ratio: Top 1% to Total Value
Principal residence	8.1	30.1	8.2	7.6	29.8	8.4	8.4	28.2	8.5	8.7	28.5	9.8
Other real estate[a]	19.6	14.9	40.0	20.0	14.7	45.7	11.4	9.8	33.1	10.8	10.2	33.7
Unincorporated business equity[b]	32.2	18.8	52.1	32.8	17.7	62.0	32.9	17.2	54.4	36.1	18.3	62.8
Liquid assets[c]	8.5	17.4	14.9	6.9	12.2	18.9	5.7	8.8	18.3	6.1	7.6	25.6
Pension accounts[d]	0.9	1.5	17.9	3.0	7.2	14.1	5.5	12.3	12.7	9.2	16.5	17.8
Financial securities[e]	5.7	4.2	41.9	10.0	5.1	65.5	4.4	2.3	55.1	2.5	1.5	54.7
Corporate stock and mutual funds	17.1	9.0	57.5	12.2	8.1	50.1	21.7	14.8	41.9	19.8	12.7	49.8
Net equity in personal trusts	6.9	2.6	80.0	4.6	2.7	56.5	7.4	4.8	44.0	5.0	3.2	49.5
Miscellaneous assets[f]	1.0	1.3	22.7	2.8	2.5	38.1	2.6	1.8	39.4	1.9	1.5	39.4
Total Gross Assets	100.0	100.0	29.6	100.0	100.0	32.5	100.0	100.0	28.4	100.0	100.0	31.9

Debt on principal residence	0.7	6.3	3.2	1.2	9.8	4.3	1.5	9.4	4.4	1.4	11.2	4.1
All other debt[g]	4.7	6.8	21.4	5.1	6.0	28.7	1.0	3.1	9.1	1.1	4.0	8.9
Total Debt	5.4	13.1	12.7	6.3	15.7	13.6	2.4	12.5	5.6	2.6	15.2	5.4
Net home equity[h]	7.4	23.8	9.6	6.2	20.1	10.5	7.0	18.8	10.6	7.3	17.3	13.4
Investment-type assets[i]	81.4	49.6	50.1	79.7	48.3	55.1	77.8	48.8	45.4	74.2	45.9	51.6
Life-cycle assets[j]	17.6	49.0	5.1	17.5	49.3	5.2	19.6	49.4	11.3	24.0	52.6	14.6
Memo:												
Debt/net worth ratio (percent)	5.7	15.1		6.8	18.7		2.5	14.3		2.6	17.9	

Source: Authors' computations from the 1983, 1992, 2001, and 2013 Survey of Consumer Finances.

a. In 2001 and 2013, this equals the gross value of other residential real estate plus the *net equity* in nonresidential real estate.

b. Net equity in unincorporated farm and nonfarm businesses and closely held corporations.

c. Checking accounts, savings accounts, time deposits, money market funds, certificates of deposit, and the cash surrender value of life insurance.

d. IRAs, Keogh plans, 401(k) plans, the accumulated value of defined contribution pension plans, and other retirement accounts.

e. Corporate bonds, government bonds (including savings bonds), open-market paper, and notes.

f. Gold and other precious metals, royalties, jewelry, antiques, furs, loans to friends and relatives, future contracts, and miscellaneous assets.

g. Mortgage debt on all real property except principal residence; credit card, installment, and other debt.

h. Gross value of principal residence less mortgage debt on principal residence.

i. Defined as the sum of nonhome real estate, business equity, financial securities, stocks, mutual funds, and personal trusts.

j. Defined as the sum of principal residence, liquid assets, and pension accounts.

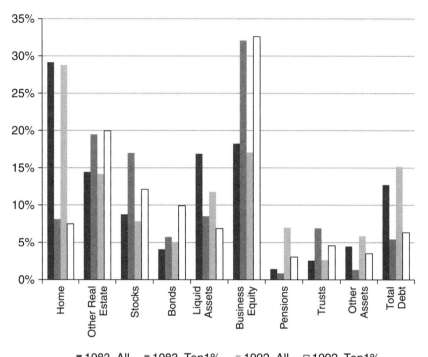

Figure 10.7a. Portfolio Composition of All Households and Top 1 Percent of Wealth Holders, 1983 and 1992
(Share of gross assets)

(8.1 versus 30.1 percent) and liquid assets (8.5 versus 17.4 percent). The richest 1 percent also had a lower debt-net worth ratio—5.7 versus 15.1 percent. Moreover, whereas the top percentile accounted for 33.8 percent of total net worth, they held 40 percent of nonhome real estate, 57.5 percent of stocks and mutual funds, 41.9 percent of financial securities, 52.1 percent of business equity, and 80 percent of trust fund equity.

The next three columns of Table 10.2 show the corresponding statistics for 1992. The most notable shift in the overall portfolio was a sharp drop in the share of liquid assets in total assets (from 17.4 to 12.2 percent) and a corresponding rise in the share held in the form of pension accounts (from 1.5 to 7.2 percent). This is a clear indication of the substitution of nontaxable for taxable assets. The ratio of debt to net worth also rose, from 15.1 to 18.7 percent.

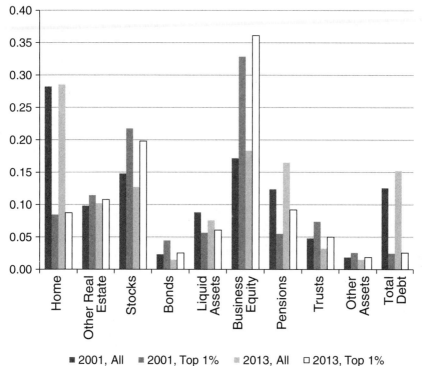

Figure 10.7b. Portfolio Composition of All Households and Top 1 Percent of Wealth Holders, 2001 and 2013 (Share of gross assets)

Among the richest 1 percent of households (who may be different in the two years), the major change was a fall in the share of gross assets held in the form of stocks and mutual funds (from 17.1 to 12.2 percent) and in trust funds (from 6.9 to 4.6 percent), and corresponding increases in the share held in financial securities (from 5.7 to 10.0 percent) and pension accounts (0.9 to 3.0 percent). The substitution of financial securities for stocks is a bit of a surprise, given the robust performance of the stock market over these years, while the switch to pension accounts is likely due to their preferred tax status. Interestingly, the share of total assets held in both investment real estate and business equity remained virtually unchanged over this period, suggesting a minimal increase of entrepreneurship among the rich, at least according to this dimension. While the share of total net worth held by the top 1 percent increased from 33.8 to 37.2 percent between 1983 and 1992, their share of nonhome real estate increased from 40 to 45.7 percent, their share of financial securities from 41.9 to 65.5 percent, and their share of net business equity from 52.1 to 62 percent. In contrast, their share of total stocks and mutual funds fell from 57.5 to 50.1 percent and their share of trust fund equity from 80 to 56.5 percent.

The last three columns of Table 10.2 show the corresponding statistics for 2013. Among all households, the most notable portfolio changes between 1992 and 2013 were declines in the share of total assets held in the form of nonhome real estate (from 14.7 to 10.2 percent), liquid assets (from 12.2 to 7.6 percent), and financial securities (from 5.1 to 1.5 percent), and corresponding increases in the proportions held in pension accounts (from 7.2 to 16.5 percent) and in corporate stock and mutual funds (from 8.1 to 12.7 percent). There was a slight decline in the ratio of debt to net worth, from 18.7 to 17.9 percent.

Among the top 1 percent, there were substantial declines in the share of gross assets held in nonhome real estate (from 20 to 10.8 percent) and in financial securities (from 10 to 2.5 percent) and offsetting increases in the proportion held in business equity (from 32.8 to 36.1 percent), pension accounts (from 3 to 9.2 percent), and stock and mutual funds (from 12.2 to 19.8 percent). The debt-net worth ratio also fell off, from 6.8 to 2.6 percent. Whereas the share of total net worth held by the top 1 percent declined a bit from 37.2 percent in 1992 to 36.7 percent in 2013, their share of liquid assets rose from 18.9 to 25.6 percent, as did their share of pension accounts (from 14.1 to 17.8 percent). In contrast, their share of nonhome real estate was down substantially from 45.7 to 33.7 percent, as was their share of financial securities (from 65.5 to 54.7 percent).

If we divide the wealth portfolio into "investment-type" assets, including nonhome real estate, business equity, financial securities, corporate stock, mutual funds, and personal trusts, and "life-cycle assets," including owner-occupied housing, liquid assets, and pension accounts, we can see how skewed the portfolio of the rich is toward the former. In 1983, 81.4 percent of the assets of the top percentile were invested in investment-type assets and only 17.6 percent in life-cycle assets.[7] Half of all investment-type assets were held by the top 1 percent, compared to only 5 percent of life-cycle assets. By 2013, the share of investment-type assets in total assets of the top percentile fell off a bit, to 74.2 percent, while that of life-cycle assets rose to 24.0 percent, as the rich put more money into pensions accounts. The top percentile still held half of all investment-type assets but their share of life-cycle assets increased to 14.6 percent.

Table 10.3 shows the composition of total household income in 1983 of all households and of the richest 1 percent of households ranked in terms of *net worth* (also see Figures 10.8a and 10.8b). Among all households, the primary source of income was wages and salaries, which made up 63 percent of total income. Self-employment or proprietary income, including partnership and net profit from unincorporated businesses, ranked second, constituting 12 percent. Together, these two forms of labor income constituted three-quarters of all income. Retirement income, including Social Security and pension benefits, comprised 8.2 percent. The only other significant entry was interest income, 5.3 percent of total income.

Among the richest 1 percent of households, the primary source of income was proprietary income, which amounted to 27.4 percent of the total. This was followed by wages and salaries at 23.6 percent. Interest income made up 12.7 percent, dividends another 12 percent, capital gains 13.2 percent, and rental, royalty, and trust income 7.8 percent. The amount of other components was very small. All told, the top 1 percent of households earned over half of all dividends and capital gains, 22 percent of proprietary income, 25 percent of interest, and 31 percent of rental, royalty, and trust income.

Between 1983 and 1992, the biggest change in the overall composition of personal income was that the share of wages and salaries fell from 62.9 to 58.5 percent. This was compensated to some extent by self-employment income, which rose from 12.4 to 13.8 percent. Retirement income also fell, from 8.2 to 6.6 percent, though this was offset by a huge increase in the "other income" category, from 0.3 to 8 percent.[8] The changes in the other components of personal income were relatively small.

Among the richest 1 percent of households, the most significant development was that proprietary income rose from 27.4 percent of their total income in 1983 to 39.5 percent in 1992. This change accords with the results of Table 10.1, which show a huge increase of the self-employed in the ranks of the top wealth percentile. Moreover, wages and salaries increased from 23.6 to 29.6 percent. Altogether, labor earnings rose from 51 to 69 percent. Property

Table 10.3. Income composition of top 1 percent of wealth holders and all households, 1983, 1992, 2001, and 2013 (percentage)

Component	1983 Top 1%	1983 All HHs	1983 Top 1% Share of All Income	1992 Top 1%	1992 All HHs	1992 Top 1% Share of All Income	2001 Top 1%	2001 All HHs	2001 Top 1% Share of All Income	2013 Top 1%	2013 All HHs	2013 Top 1% Share of All Income
Total income[a]	100.0	100.0	10.1	100.0	100.0	12.6	100.0	100.0	15.5	100.0	100.0	14.7
Wages and salaries	23.6	62.9	3.8	29.6	58.5	6.4	31.6	68.3	7.2	29.3	63.3	6.9
Self-employment income[b]	27.4	12.4	22.4	39.5	13.8	36.2	25.8	11.7	34.2	35.6	13.5	39.7
Rental, royalty, and trust income	7.8	2.6	30.8	7.0	3.4	26.0						
Total interest	12.7	5.3	24.5	8.2	4.1	25.6	6.2	2.7	35.7	4.8	1.5	48.6
Dividends	12.0	2.3	53.9	4.3	1.7	31.7	3.1	1.5	32.3	6.2	2.0	47.3
Capital gains	13.2	2.6	50.9	7.4	2.4	38.7	30.3	6.7	69.6	21.2	4.6	68.8
Unemployment and workers' compensation	0.0	0.9	0.0	0.0	0.5	0.0	0.0	0.2	0.0	0.0	0.6	0.3
Alimony payments[c]	0.3	1.5	1.9	0.0	0.4	0.0	0.0	0.4	0.2	0.1	0.4	3.1
Public assistance[d]	0.0	1.0	0.0	0.0	0.6	0.1	0.0	0.3	0.0	0.0	0.7	0.1
Retirement income[e]	2.5	8.2	3.0	1.1	6.6	2.2	1.8	7.6	3.7	2.2	11.4	2.9
Other income	0.4	0.3	15.0	2.8	8.0	4.5	1.2	0.7	25.4	0.5	1.9	4.2

Source: Author's computations from the 1983, 1992, 2001, and 2013 Survey of Consumer Finances.
a. Defined as the sum of income components.
b. Includes partnership and net profit from unincorporated businesses.
c. Includes child support payments.
d. Includes Aid to Families with Dependent Children, food stamps, supplemental security income, and other welfare benefits.
e. Includes Social Security and pension benefits, annuities, disability payments, and other forms of retirement income.

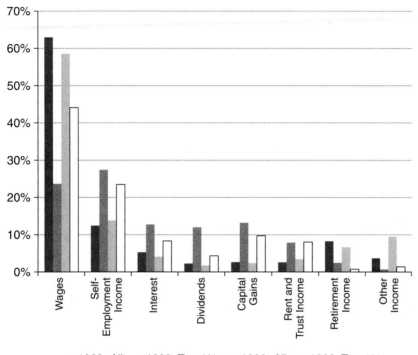

Figure 10.8a. Composition of Income of All Households and Top 1 Percent of Wealth Holders, 1983 and 1992
(Share of total income)

income, particularly interest, dividends, and capital gains, declined as a proportion of total proceeds (altogether, from 46 percent to 27 percent). In 1992, the richest 1 percent earned 6.4 percent of all wage and salary income (up from 3.8 percent in 1983), 36.2 percent of all self-employment income (up from 22.4 percent), and 26 percent of all interest income (about the same share as in 1983). However, their share of total dividends and capital gains fell sharply, and their share of total rental, royalty, and trust income was also down. On the surface, at least, the evidence does seem to support the presumption that the rich in 1992 were more entrepreneurial and less apt to depend on property wealth for their support.[9] Moreover, they were also more apt to depend on wage and salary earnings than on property income.

Between 1992 and 2013, the share of wages and salaries in total personal income rebounded to its 1983 level, 63 percent. Interest fell as a share of

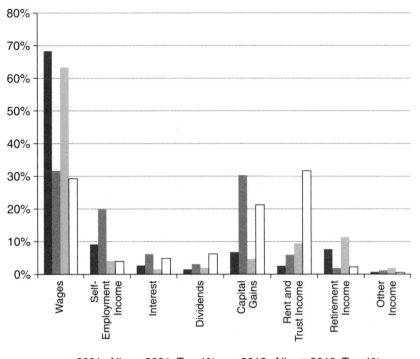

Figure 10.8b. Composition of Income of All Households and Top 1 Percent of Wealth Holders, 2001 and 2013
(Share of total income)

total income but capital gains were up somewhat and retirement income surged from 6.6 to 11.4 percent. Other income also fell sharply as a proportion of total income. Among the top percentile, there was little change in the share of wages and salaries in total income. Interest was down but dividends were up. Capital gains surged from 7.4 to 21.4 percent. There was a change in income definitions in 2001 so that self-employment and proprietor's income were now classified with rental, royalty, and trust income. The combined category fell steeply between 1992 and 2001, from 46.5 percent to 25.8 percent, but then rebounded to 35.6 percent in 2013, about the same level as in 1983. The shift in the share of this combined category in total income may on the surface seem surprising since as we saw in Table 10.1 the share of self-employed among *employed* members of the top percentile continued to rise after 1992. There was also a marked increase in the share of employed members in this group who were over age 65 between 1992 and 2013, and a substantial percentage of these were retired. The sharp rise in capital gains received by the top percentile also would have contributed to this result.

There were also large increases in the share of total capital income (among all households) accounted for by the top 1 percent of wealth holders. Their share of total interest income rose from 26 percent in 1992 to 49 percent in 2013, their share of dividends from 32 to 47 percent, their share of capital gains from 39 to 69 percent, and the share of the combined category of proprietor's and rental, royalty, and trust income from 34 to 40 percent.

Characteristics of the Richest 1 Percent of Households as Ranked by Income

The next group of tables shows a similar set of statistics, except that the rich here are defined as households in the top 1 percent of the income distribution. One important difference between this definition and status based on wealth holdings is that there are fewer elderly in this grouping. The vast majority of the elderly are retired and therefore have little or no labor income, but in general members of this group have amassed a considerable amount of wealth holdings.

Table 10.4 illustrates these differences by presenting the joint distribution of income and wealth in the four years. The joint distribution is surprisingly diffuse. For example, households in the sixth decile of the income distribution (centiles 50–60) are found in all wealth centiles except the top wealth percentile in all years, and the distribution appears almost uniform from wealth deciles one through nine. There was concentration of households at the top of both distributions. For example, households in the top percentile of the income distribution were found exclusively in the top five percentiles of the wealth distribution in both 1983 and 1992 and in the top ten percentiles in 2001 and 2013, and households in the top percentile of the wealth distribution were found only in the top decile of the income distribution in 1983 and 2001 and in the top two deciles in 1992 and 2013. However, the overall correlation between household income and wealth (computed from the orig-

Table 10.4. The joint distribution of income and wealth by centile, 1983, 1992, 2001, and 2013 (percentage)

Income Centile	Wealth Centile												Total
	0–10	10–20	20–30	30–40	40–50	50–60	60–70	70–80	80–90	90–95	95–99	99–100	
A. 1983													
0–10	3.2	2.0	1.3	1.2	0.8	0.7	0.3	0.3	0.1	0.1	0.0	0.0	10.0
10–20	2.3	1.8	1.4	1.2	0.8	0.8	0.8	0.5	0.2	0.1	0.0	0.0	10.0
20–30	1.4	1.9	1.3	1.0	1.0	0.9	1.1	0.6	0.6	0.1	0.1	0.0	10.0
30–40	1.3	1.3	1.2	1.2	0.9	1.0	1.1	0.9	0.8	0.3	0.1	0.0	10.0
40–50	0.7	1.0	1.5	1.4	1.3	1.3	0.9	0.8	0.7	0.3	0.1	0.0	10.0
50–60	0.6	1.1	1.1	1.2	1.1	1.5	1.1	0.7	1.0	0.4	0.2	0.0	10.0
60–70	0.2	0.5	1.1	1.2	1.4	1.2	1.4	1.2	1.0	0.5	0.3	0.0	10.0
70–80	0.2	0.2	0.6	1.1	1.4	1.5	1.3	1.5	1.5	0.5	0.4	0.0	10.0
80–90	0.0	0.2	0.4	0.3	1.1	0.8	1.4	2.2	1.9	1.2	0.6	0.0	10.0
90–95	0.1	0.0	0.0	0.1	0.2	0.3	0.6	0.8	1.2	0.9	0.7	0.1	5.0
95–99	0.0	0.0	0.0	0.0	0.1	0.1	0.1	0.5	1.1	0.6	1.2	0.2	4.0
99–100	0.0	0.0	0.0	0.0	0.0	0.0	0.0	0.0	0.0	0.0	0.3	0.6	1.0
Total	10.0	10.0	10.0	10.0	10.0	10.0	10.0	10.0	10.0	5.0	4.0	1.0	100.0

Note: Overall Correlation Coefficient: 0.610

B. 1992													
0–10	3.1	2.3	1.1	1.1	1.2	0.7	0.3	0.2	0.1	0.1	0.0	0.0	10.0
10–20	2.2	2.0	1.3	1.0	1.0	0.9	0.7	0.6	0.3	0.1	0.0	0.0	10.0
20–30	1.2	1.7	1.3	1.0	1.1	1.1	0.9	0.9	0.6	0.1	0.0	0.0	10.0
30–40	0.8	1.4	1.4	1.1	1.0	1.1	1.3	0.8	0.8	0.2	0.0	0.0	10.0

40–50	0.9	1.2	1.7	1.0	1.2	1.0	0.9	0.7	1.1	0.3	0.1	0.0	10.0
50–60	0.6	0.6	1.3	1.3	1.0	1.1	1.1	1.1	1.2	0.4	0.2	0.0	10.0
60–70	0.7	0.4	0.9	1.5	1.2	1.2	1.4	0.8	1.1	0.6	0.2	0.0	10.0
70–80	0.3	0.2	0.5	1.1	1.2	1.6	1.4	1.6	1.4	0.6	0.2	0.0	10.0
80–90	0.1	0.1	0.3	0.7	1.0	1.0	1.5	2.1	1.5	1.0	0.6	0.1	10.0
90–95	0.1	0.0	0.1	0.0	0.2	0.4	0.5	0.9	1.0	0.9	0.8	0.1	5.0
95–99	0.0	0.0	0.0	0.1	0.0	0.0	0.2	0.2	0.9	0.8	1.5	0.3	4.0
99–100	0.0	0.0	0.0	0.0	0.0	0.0	0.0	0.1	0.0	0.0	0.4	0.5	1.0
Total	10.0	10.0	10.0	10.0	10.0	10.0	10.0	10.0	10.0	5.0	4.0	1.0	100.0

Note: Overall Correlation Coefficient: 0.639

C. 2001

0–10	0.9	4.0	1.4	1.1	1.0	0.9	0.3	0.1	0.2	—	0.0	0.0	10.0
10–20	1.2	2.3	1.5	1.0	0.8	0.9	0.7	0.4	0.1	0.0	0.0	—	10.0
20–30	1.5	1.3	1.6	1.4	1.3	1.0	1.2	0.9	0.4	0.1	0.0	—	10.0
30–40	1.2	0.9	1.3	1.1	1.0	0.8	0.7	0.6	0.6	0.2	0.0	0.0	10.0
40–50	1.9	0.7	1.7	1.7	1.2	1.1	1.0	1.0	1.0	0.3	0.0	0.0	10.0
50–60	1.2	0.4	1.0	1.3	1.1	1.1	1.0	1.0	0.9	0.3	0.1	0.0	10.0
60–70	1.0	0.2	0.8	1.1	1.6	1.3	1.1	1.3	1.1	0.5	0.3	0.0	10.0
70–80	0.7	0.1	0.4	0.7	1.0	1.3	1.6	1.4	1.8	0.6	0.3	0.0	10.0
80–90	0.4	0.0	0.3	0.5	0.7	1.2	1.5	2.1	2.1	1.0	0.6	0.0	10.0
90–95	0.0	0.0	0.0	0.2	0.1	0.4	0.7	0.8	1.0	1.0	0.7	0.1	5.0
95–99	0.0	—	—	0.0	0.0	0.1	0.2	0.2	0.7	0.9	1.5	0.4	4.0
99–100	0.0	—	0.0	—	—	0.0	—	0.0	—	0.1	0.4	0.5	1.0
Total	10.0	10.0	10.0	10.0	10.0	10.0	10.0	10.0	10.0	5.0	4.0	1.0	100.0

Note: Overall Correlation Coefficient: 0.496

(continued)

Table 10.4. (continued)

	Wealth Centile												
Income Centile	0–10	10–20	20–30	30–40	40–50	50–60	60–70	70–80	80–90	90–95	95–99	99–100	Total
C. 2001
0–10	1.2	2.1	3.6	1.3	1.3	0.7	0.5	0.4	0.2	0.0	0.0	0.0	10.0
10–20	1.0	1.6	2.6	1.3	1.1	1.1	0.6	0.5	0.3	0.1	0.0	—	10.0
20–30	1.2	2.0	2.5	1.5	1.3	1.1	0.8	1.2	0.4	0.2	0.0	—	10.0
30–40	1.7	1.4	1.3	1.7	1.4	1.3	1.0	0.8	0.7	0.1	0.0	0.0	10.0
40–50	1.5	1.0	1.1	1.7	1.5	1.4	1.5	1.3	0.9	0.1	0.0	—	10.0
50–60	1.8	1.1	0.5	1.4	1.3	1.5	1.3	1.2	0.9	0.4	0.1	0.0	10.0
60–70	1.1	0.9	0.2	1.2	1.2	1.5	1.5	1.5	1.3	0.4	0.1	0.0	10.0
70–80	1.1	0.4	0.2	0.7	1.2	1.5	1.9	1.7	1.8	0.7	0.5	0.0	10.0
80–90	0.7	0.3	0.0	0.6	0.9	1.1	1.8	1.9	2.6	1.3	0.7	0.1	10.0
90–95	0.1	0.1	0.0	0.0	0.2	0.3	0.4	1.0	1.7	1.3	0.7	0.1	5.0
95–99	0.1	—	—	0.0	0.0	0.1	0.2	0.2	0.7	1.1	1.8	0.5	4.0
99–100	—	—	—	—	—	—	—	—	0.0	0.1	0.6	0.5	1.0
Total	10.0	10.0	10.0	10.0	10.0	10.0	10.0	10.0	10.0	5.0	4.0	1.0	100.0

Note: Overall Correlation Coefficient: 0.571

Source: Author's computations from the 1983, 1992, 2001, and 2013 Survey of Consumer Finances.

inal microdata) was surprisingly low—0.61 in 1983 and 0.64 in 1992. The correlation coefficient then fell to 0.50 in 2001 but rebounded somewhat to 0.57 in 2013. The lower correlations in the later years are probably due to a higher concentration of retirees in the ranks of the top wealth percentile and their correspondingly lower incomes.

Despite these relatively low correlations, results based on the top income recipients are qualitatively very similar to those based on the top 1 percent of wealth holders. Table 10.5 shows the demographic characteristics of the richest 1 percent of households as ranked by income. As shown in Panel A, only 1.6 percent of all households ranked in the top 1 percent by income in 1983 were under age 35, compared to 30.6 percent of all households in that age range (also see Figures 10.9a and 10.9b). Moreover, while 19.5 percent of all households fell in the age range 35–44, only 16.3 percent of the top 1 percent were in that age group. In contrast, age groups 45–54, 65–74, and especially 55–64 were over-represented in the ranks of the top income percentile. The mean age of the top 1 percent was 55.3, compared to 46.8 overall, and the median age was 56, compared to 44 overall.

Between 1983 and 1992, the share of rich households in the top 1 percent under the age of 35 increased from 1.6 to 5.7 percent, even as their share of the total population fell. The proportion in age group 35–44 also increased very sharply, from 16.3 to 25.5 percent (and increased relative to the size of their overall population share). The percentage of the top 1 percent in the next three older age groups all fell, both as a fraction of all households in the top 1 percent and relative to changes in overall population shares by age group. On net, the mean age of the top percentile declined by 3.4 years, as the overall population aged, and their median age declined by five years.[10]

This trend reversed after 1992, particularly after 2001. The mean age of the rich advanced to 55.1 by 2013, about where it was in 1983, and the median age to 53, though below its 1983 value. The overall population also aged over these years, so that relative to the full population there was little change between 1992 and 2013. The share of the income rich under age 35 fell to about its 1983 level (1.3 percent), though relative to overall population trends there was little change between 1992 and 2013. The biggest change was for age group 65–74, which accounted for 21.2 percent of the rich in 2013, compared to 10.1 percent in 1992, and their share also increased relative to the population as a whole.

Table 10.5. Demographic and work-related characteristics of the top 1 percent of households as ranked by income and all households, 1983–2013 (percentage distribution except for mean and median values)

	1983			1992			2001			2013		
	Top 1%	All	Diff.	Top 1%	All	Diff.	Top 1%	All	Diff.	Top 1%	All	Diff.
A. Age of Head												
Less than 25	0.0	8.0	-8.0	0.5	5.2	-4.7	0.0	5.6	-5.6	0.0	5.0	-5.0
25–34	1.6	22.6	-21.0	5.2	20.4	-15.2	2.2	17.2	-15.1	1.3	15.8	-14.5
35–44	16.3	19.5	-3.2	25.5	22.7	2.8	26.4	22.1	4.3	20.7	17.3	3.4
45–54	28.6	15.6	13.0	25.8	16.4	9.4	35.9	20.7	15.3	29.6	19.6	10.0
55–64	33.8	15.1	18.8	29.1	13.4	15.7	24.4	13.2	11.2	22.8	18.7	4.0
65–74	16.8	12.1	4.6	10.1	12.7	-2.5	9.1	10.7	-1.6	21.2	12.9	8.4
75 and over	2.9	7.1	-4.3	3.7	9.2	-5.5	2.0	10.4	-8.4	4.4	10.7	-6.3
All age groups	100.0	100.0	0.0	100.0	100.0	0.0	100.0	100.0	0.0	100.0	100.0	0.0
Mean age	55.3	46.8	8.5	51.9	48.4	3.5	51.8	49.0	2.9	55.1	51.1	4.0
Median age	56.0	44.0	12.0	51.0	45.0	6.0	52.0	47.0	5.0	53.0	51.0	2.0
B. Education of Head												
0–11 years	0.1	29.0	-28.9	0.7	21.1	-20.4	0.6	18.1	-17.5	0.3	12.4	-12.1
High school graduate	3.8	30.2	-26.4	4.6	28.9	-24.3	7.0	29.6	-22.6	2.8	29.9	-27.1
College 1–3	10.4	19.6	-9.3	11.5	21.0	-9.5	5.6	22.6	-17.1	11.1	24.2	-13.1
College graduate	33.6	10.6	22.9	32.7	16.5	16.2	33.3	17.6	15.7	30.9	20.0	10.9
Some graduate school	52.1	10.6	41.5	50.5	12.5	38.0	53.5	12.0	41.5	55.0	13.5	41.5
All educational groups	100.0	100.0	0.0	100.0	100.0	0.0	100.0	100.0	0.0	100.0	100.0	0.0
Mean education	16.1	12.2	3.9	16.0	12.9	3.1	16.1	13.1	3.0	16.2	13.5	2.7
Median education	16.0	12.0	4.0	16.0	13.0	3.0	17.0	13.0	4.0	17.0	14.0	3.0

C. Race												
White (non-Hispanic)	97.0	80.9	16.1	94.1	75.3	18.8	95.4	76.2	19.1	95.8	70.1	25.7
Black (non-Hispanic)	1.2	12.7	-11.5	0.1	12.6	-12.5	2.1	13.0	-10.9	0.3	14.6	-14.3
Hispanic	0.0	3.5	-3.5	0.0	7.6	-7.6	2.0	8.0	-6.0	0.9	10.6	-9.7
Asian and others	1.8	2.8	-1.0	5.8	4.6	1.2	0.6	2.8	-2.2	3.0	4.7	-1.6
All racial groups	100.0	100.0	0.0	100.0	100.0	0.0	100.0	100.0	0.0	100.0	100.0	0.0
D. Marital Status												
Married, spouse present[a]	91.9	60.8	31.1	87.6	57.6	30.0	90.9	60.3	30.6	84.1	57.2	27.0
Male, separated, divorced or widowed	6.1	6.8	-0.7	6.7	8.6	-1.9	6.3	7.5	-1.2	10.2	7.7	2.6
Male, never married	2.0	6.3	-4.3	1.5	6.5	-5.0	0.3	6.1	-5.8	3.8	7.5	-3.7
Female, separated, divorced, or widowed	0.1	19.9	-19.8	2.1	19.4	-17.3	2.5	17.5	-15.0	1.6	18.7	-17.1
Female, never married	0.0	6.2	-6.2	2.1	7.9	-5.8	0.0	8.6	-8.6	0.2	8.9	-8.7
All marital groups	100.0	100.0	0.0	100.0	100.0	0.0	100.0	100.0	0.0	100.0	100.0	0.0
E. Employment Status of Head (age less than 65 only)												
Full-time	92.1	75.8	16.3	87.4	74.9	12.6	85.0	79.1	5.9	92.0	70.7	21.3
Part-time	3.1	4.0	-1.0	7.4	4.5	2.9	3.9	6.2	-2.4	6.4	8.0	-1.6
Unemployed or temporarily laid off	0.0	8.8	-8.8	2.2	7.1	-5.0	1.2	4.3	-3.1	0.0	6.2	-6.2
Retired	4.8	7.3	-2.4	1.8	3.8	-2.0	4.9	3.2	1.7	1.5	4.7	-3.2
Not in labor force	0.0	4.1	-4.1	1.3	9.8	-8.4	5.1	7.2	-2.1	0.1	10.4	-10.3
All under age 65	100.0	100.0	0.0	100.0	100.0	0.0	100.0	100.0	0.0	100.0	100.0	0.0
F. Industry of Employment of Head (working and age less than 65)												
Agriculture	0.6	3.9	-3.3	1.1	2.7	-1.7	0.5	1.9	-1.4	0.3	2.6	-2.3
Mining and construction	9.1	8.9	0.2	5.8	7.4	-1.5	3.3	10.5	-7.1	3.5	11.1	-7.6

(continued)

Table 10.5. (continued)

	1983			1992			2001			2013		
	Top 1%	All	Diff.	Top 1%	All	Diff.	Top 1%	All	Diff.	Top 1%	All	Diff.
Manufacturing	20.0	23.7	-3.7	13.3	28.3	-15.1	9.8	18.7	-8.9	8.6	13.1	-4.5
Transportation, communications, utilities, personal services, and professional services	29.5	32.0	-2.5	47.4	25.5	21.9	36.5	32.4	4.2	41.9	40.3	1.6
Trade (wholesale and retail)	8.3	15.5	-7.2	5.3	14.9	-9.6	12.7	15.6	-2.9	8.4	15.2	-6.8
Finance, insurance, real estate, and business and repair services	32.4	8.7	23.7	26.5	13.8	12.7	36.9	16.0	20.9	37.3	11.5	25.8
Public administration	0.0	7.2	-7.2	0.6	7.4	-6.8	0.2	5.0	-4.8	0.0	6.2	-6.2
All employed persons	99.9	99.9	0.0	100.0	100.0	0.0	100.0	100.0	0.0	100.0	100.0	0.0
G. Occupation of Head (working and age less than 65)												
Self-employed[b]	26.6	15.4	11.3	63.7	17.2	46.5	59.2	16.7	42.5	55.8	15.3	40.4
Professionals[c]	12.0	15.0	-3.0	34.1	25.5	8.6	38.1	27.1	11.0	38.9	34.3	4.6
Managers and administrators	58.1	13.9	44.1	2.2	22.4	-20.1	2.7	18.5	-15.8	5.3	14.9	-9.6
Sales and clerical workers[d]	3.2	13.0	-9.8	0.0	10.6	-10.6	0.0	12.8	-12.8	0.0	14.1	-14.1
Craft workers[e]	0.0	16.9	-16.9	0.0	18.1	-24.3	0.0	15.0	-15.0	0.0	9.4	-9.4
Other blue-collar workers[f]	0.0	25.8	-25.8									
Service workers				0.0	6.2	-6.2	0.0	9.8	-9.8	0.0	11.9	-11.9
All employed persons	100.0	100.0	0.0	100.0	100.0	0.0	100.0	100.0	0.0	100.0	100.0	0.0

H. Health of Head of Household

Excellent	63.1	37.9	25.2	64.3	34.6	29.7	54.1	29.1	25.0	52.3	23.9	28.4
Good	33.1	39.6	−6.5	32.5	40.9	−8.4	40.0	46.1	−6.1	43.1	48.8	−5.7
Fair	2.9	15.4	−12.5	3.1	17.5	−14.4	3.9	19.0	−15.2	3.8	21.0	−17.3
Poor	0.8	7.1	−6.3	0.1	7.0	−6.9	2.1	5.8	−3.7	0.8	6.3	−5.5
All	100.0	100.0	0.0	100.0	100.0	0.0	100.0	100.0	0.0	100.0	100.0	0.0

I. Inheritances Received

Percent receiving inheritances				39.2	20.7	18.5	30.0	17.9	12.2	28.9	21.5	7.4
Average value of inheritances[g]				4,940	453	4,487	2,238	425	1,812	7,303	571	6,731

Source: Author's computations from the 1983, 1992, 2001, and 2013 Survey of Consumer Finances.

Lower bounds for the top 1 percent (in current dollars) are as follows:

1983—$170,000
1992—$285,000
2001—$500,000
2013—$682,000

All computations are for the head of household unless otherwise indicated.

a. Includes "partners" in 1992.

b. Self-employed of any occupation are classified separately in this category.

c. Includes technical workers in 1983.

d. Includes technical workers in 1992.

e. Includes protective service workers in 1983.

f. Includes operatives (both machine and transportation equipment), laborers, and farm workers.

g. Recipients only. Present value as of 2013 in thousands, using a 3 percent real interest rate.

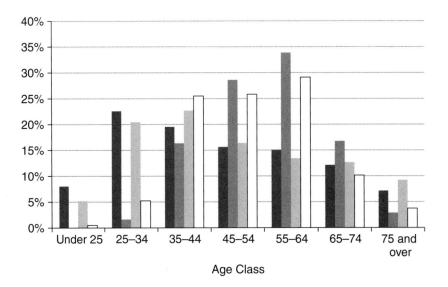

Figure 10.9a. Age Distribution of All Households and Top 1 Percent as Ranked by Income, 1983 and 1992

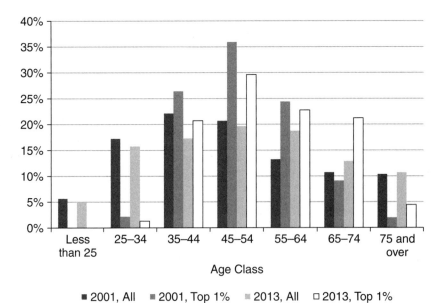

Figure 10.9b. Age Distribution of All Households and Top 1Percent as Ranked by Income, 2001 and 2013

A comparison of Tables 10.1 and 10.5 shows that households who were rich in terms of income tend to be younger than those who are rich in terms of wealth. This was true in all four years. In 1992, whereas 15 percent of the top percentile in terms of wealth was under the age of 45, 31 percent of the top income percentile was in this age group. Conversely, while 29 percent of households in the top wealth percentile was age 65 and over, only 14 percent of the top income percentile was in this age bracket. In 2013, the median age of the wealthiest 1 percent was 63, while the median age of the top 1 percent in terms of income was only 53, and the mean age of the former was 61.3, compared to 55.1 for the latter.

In 1983, over half of the top 1 percent of income earners had engaged in graduate work and 86 percent of this group were college graduates or better, compared to 21 percent of the general population (see Table 10.5, Panel B, and Figures 10.10a and 10.10b). Indeed, only 4 percent of this group had not attended college, compared to 59 percent of all household heads. However, here too, despite the general rise in educational attainment in population between 1983 and 1992, there was a slight decline in the educational attainment

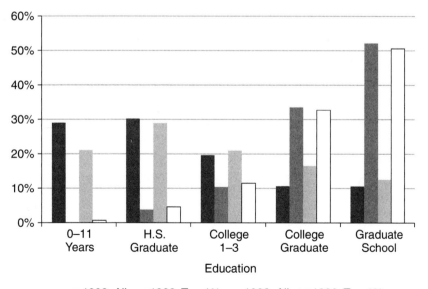

Figure 10.10a. Educational Distribution of All Households and Top 1 Percent as Ranked by Income, 1983 and 1992

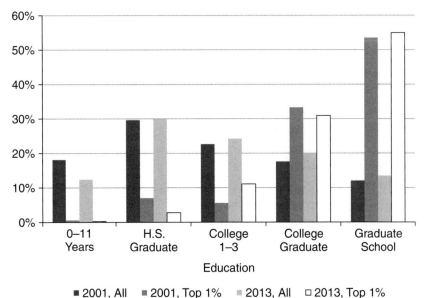

Figure 10.10b. Educational Distribution of All Households and Top 1 Percent as Ranked by Income, 2001 and 2013

of the top 1 percent. The fraction with some graduate school fell from 52.1 to 50.5 percent, the fraction with college degrees or better fell from 86 to 83 percent, and the fraction who had never attended college rose from 3.9 to 5.3 percent. There was also a moderate increase in the fraction of the rich who were college dropouts.

Between 1992 and 2013, the income rich became better educated. By 2013, 55 percent had attended graduate school, compared to 51 percent in 1992, and 86 percent had graduated college, compared to 83 percent in 1992. This group was also somewhat better educated than the rich in terms of wealth. For example, whereas over half the top income percentile had attended graduate school in both 1983 and 1992, the corresponding percentages for the top wealth percentile were 36 and 41 percent, respectively. In 2013, the median education of the richest 1 percent in terms of income was seventeen years, compared to sixteen years for the top 1 percent in terms of wealth.

In 1983, 97 percent of the households in the top 1 percent according to income were non-Hispanic whites, compared to a population share of 81 percent (see Table 10.5, Panel C, and Figures 10.11a and 10.11b). Non-Hispanic

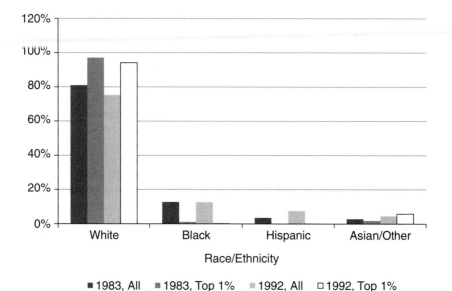

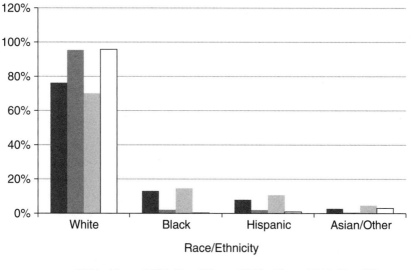

■ 1983, All   ■ 1983, Top 1%   ■ 1992, All   □ 1992, Top 1%

Figure 10.11a. Racial Composition of All Households and Top 1 Percent as Ranked by Income, 1983 and 1992

■ 2001, All   ■ 2001, Top 1%   ■ 2013, All   □ 2013, Top 1%

Figure 10.11b. Racial Composition of All Households and Top 1 Percent as Ranked by Income, 2001 and 2013

blacks made up only 1.2 percent of the top 1 percent of households (compared to a 12.7 percent population share), Hispanics zero percent (compared to a 3.5 percent population share), and Asians and other races 1.8 percent. Between 1983 and 1992, while the share of white households in the general population fell by 5.6 percentage points, their proportion of the top 1 percent fell by only 2.9 percentage points. Black families constituted only 0.1 percent of the top 1 percent, down from 1.2 percent in 1983, while Hispanic families remained at zero percent of the top 1 percent, despite the fact that their population share more than doubled. However, Asians and other races increased as a share of the top 1 percent from 1.8 to 5.8 percent.

Between 1992 and 2013, the share of whites in the top income percentile rose to 96 percent, slightly below its 1983 proportion, but, relative to the overall population, the differential was up sharply, from 18.8 to 25.7 percentage points. The share of black families in the top percentile was down to 0.3 percent, that of Hispanics was up slightly to 0.9 percent, and that of Asians and others fell to 3 percent. The racial composition of the top income percentile was almost identical to that of the top wealth percentile in each of the four years.

As shown in Panel D of Table 10.5, 92 percent of the top income percentile were married couples in 1983 (compared to 61 percent of the general population), 8 percent were headed by unmarried men, and virtually none by unmarried women (compared to 26 percent of the overall population). Between 1983 and 1992, while the proportion of married families among the top 1 percent of income earners fell from 92 to 88 percent, the proportion of households headed by an unmarried women increased from 0.1 to 4.2 percent and the share of households headed by an unmarried male remained almost unchanged.

From 1992 to 2013, the share of married couples in the ranks of the top income percentile slipped a bit, to 84 percent, while the share of unmarried men rose to 14 percent, and that of unmarried women fell to 1.8 percent. However, relative to overall population trends, there was little change in the marital composition of the income rich. The major difference between the top percentile of income earners and wealth holders was the greater presence of separated, divorced, or widowed women in the ranks of the latter, particularly in 1983 and 1992.

In 1983, 86 percent of nonelderly rich households were headed by a full-time worker (compared to 76 percent of all nonelderly households), 4.6 percent by a part-time worker, and 3.6 percent by a retiree (see Table 10.5, Panel E). The most striking change between 1983 and 1992 is that the proportion of rich households headed by a full-time worker declined from 92 to 87 percent, and this was almost exactly offset by a corresponding rise in the percentage headed by a part-time worker, from 3.1 to 7.4 percent. The share of retirees in the ranks of the top percentile also fell, from 4.8 to 1.8 percent, but this was compensated by a corresponding rise in the proportion who were either unemployed, from zero to 2.2 percent, or not in the labor force, from zero to 1.3 percent.

This trend reversed itself between 1992 and 2013, by which time the share of full-time workers among the nonelderly top 1 percent rebounded to 92 percent, about the same as in 1983, that of part-time workers fell slightly to 6.4 percent, and that of nonworkers (unemployed, retired, or not in the labor force) fell to 1.6 percent. These trends contrast with those for the top 1 percent of wealth holders, among whom the share of full-time workers fell by 8.6 percentage points between 1983 and 2013 and the share of retirees rose by 4.4 percentage points. There was also a greater percentage of full-time workers in the ranks of the top income percentile than the top wealth percentile (for household heads under age 65) and a smaller percentage of retirees (except for 1983).

In 1983, 32 percent of the top percentile headed by someone at work reported working in finance, insurance, real estate, or business services, compared to only 9 percent of all workers (Panel F). In contrast, 8 percent of the these rich workers were found in trade, compared to 16 percent of all workers, and zero percent in public administration, compared to 7 percent overall. The most dramatic change between 1983 and 1992 was a substantial increase in the share of workers employed in transportation, communications, utilities, personal services, and professional services in the ranks of the top percentile, from 30 to 47 percent (and also a large increase relative to the employment share of all workers, from a difference of –2.5 to 21.9 percent). The share in finance, insurance, real estate, and business services fell by 6 percentage points (and declined relative to overall trends). Together, these two aggregated sectors accounted for almost three-quarters of all rich households headed by someone at work in 1992. In contrast, the shares of workers in the top percentile employed in mining and construction, manufacturing, and trade fell in both absolute and relative terms.

These trends generally continued from 1992 to 2013. While the share in the top percentile in transportation, communications, utilities, personal services, and professional services fell off a bit to 42 percent, the share in finance, insurance, real estate, and business services rose to 37 percent, and together these two groups made up 79 percent of all workers among the income rich. The proportion of workers in the other industry groups continued to fall, with the exception of trade.

A comparison of the industry composition of the top income and wealth percentiles indicates that whereas a larger proportion of the former were employed in transportation, communications, utilities, personal services, and professional services in 1983, the opposite was the case in 2013. The share of the top income percentile in finance, insurance, real estate, and business services was higher than that of the top wealth percentile in all years except 1992.[11] Agriculture, mining and construction, and manufacturing were all more important as a source of employment among the wealthiest than among the income rich. One potential explanation for these differences rests on the fact that current wealth reflects, to a large extent, incomes in the past. Thus, the results suggest that these three sectors were a major source of high incomes in the early postwar period but diminished over time (probably since the 1960s) as major sources of large incomes, whereas finance and business and professional services increased in importance. This hypothesis might also explain the diminution of the importance of these three sectors as a source of both high income and high wealth since 1983.

Self-employed workers were substantially over-represented in the ranks of the top percentile of households in terms of income in 1983—27 percent versus 15 percent of all workers—as were managers and administrators—58 versus 14 percent (see Table 10.5, Panel G). However, only 12 percent of the rich classified themselves as professionals, in contrast to 15 percent of all workers. These results are similar to those of Table 10.1, wherein the rich are classified according to wealth. Moreover, as we saw in Table 10.1, there was a striking growth in the share of the self-employed among the top 1 percent—in this case, from 27 to 64 percent among the top income group from 1983 to 1992. In contrast, the proportion of professional, managerial, and administrative workers who were not self-employed fell precipitously, from 70 to 34 percent of the top income percentile.

These trends reversed between 1992 and 2013. The share of self-employed among the income rich fell rather substantially, from 64 to 56 percent. This contrasts with the trend among the top 1 percent of wealth holders, among whom the self-employed share grew to 84 percent. On the other hand, the share of professional and managerial workers among the top 1 percent in terms of income rose from 34 to 39 percent, whereas it fell from 28 to 13 percent among the top wealth group.

As we also saw in Table 10.1, the rich (in terms of income here) appear to be much healthier than the average population. In 1983, 63 percent of the rich said that their health was excellent, compared to 38 percent of the overall population (see Table 10.5, Panel H). Only 3.7 percent of the top 1 percent indicated that their health was fair or poor, in comparison to 22.5 percent of all respondents. Between 1983 and 1992, while the overall health of the population appears to have deteriorated somewhat, the health of the top income percentile seems to have improved slightly, with the proportion reporting excellent health rising by 1.2 percentage points and the proportion reporting fair or poor health falling by 0.6 percentage points. Between 1992 and 2013 the proportion of the top income percentile reporting excellent health fell from 64 to 52 percent, but overall health was also down among the population at large so that relative to the general population the health of the rich remained unchanged. These trends are very similar to those among the top 1 percent of wealth holders.

The households in the top income percentile were more apt to receive a wealth transfer than the general population in 1992—39 versus 21 percent (see Table 10.5, Panel I). Moreover, the average value of wealth transfers of the top percentile was much greater than in the general population (a 21-fold difference). The proportion of the top income percentile that had received a wealth transfer was, however, smaller than that of the top wealth percentile (39 versus 48 percent), and the average value of the transfers was smaller among the top income percentile than the top wealth percentile. The share of the top income percentile receiving a wealth transfer fell off from 39 percent in 1992 to 29 percent in 2013 but its average value was up by 9 percent (in real terms). In comparison, the share of the top wealth percentile receiving a wealth transfer was almost exactly the same in 2013 as in 1992 and its average value grew by 8 percent.

As shown in Table 10.6 (also see Figure 10.12a and 10.12b), in 1983 the top 1 percent of households as ranked in terms of income had a higher share of their wealth in the form of nonhome real estate than the general population (19.2 versus 14.9 percent), stocks and mutual funds (18.0 versus 9.0 percent),

Table 10.6. Portfolio composition of the top 1 percent of households as ranked by income and all households, 1983, 1992, 2001, and 2013 (Percentage of gross assets)

Wealth component	1983			1992			2001			2013		
	Top 1%: Percent of Gross Assets	All HH: Percent of Gross Assets	Ratio of Top 1% to Total Value	Top 1%: Percent of Gross Assets	All HH: Percent of Gross Assets	Ratio of Top 1% to Total Value	Top 1%: Percent of Gross Assets	All HH: Percent of Gross Assets	Ratio of Top 1% to Total Value	Top 1%: Percent of Gross Assets	All HH: Percent of Gross Assets	Ratio of Top 1% to Total Value
Principal residence	8.9	30.1	7.9	8.4	29.8	7.4	11.3	28.1	8.4	11.0	28.4	9.3
Other real estate	19.2	14.9	33.9	16.4	14.7	29.2	9.7	9.8	20.8	9.3	10.1	21.9
Unincorporated business equity	27.9	18.8	39.2	32.5	17.7	48.0	31.0	17.5	37.0	34.1	18.7	43.5
Liquid assets	9.4	17.4	14.3	7.4	12.2	15.9	6.9	8.8	16.5	6.9	7.5	21.8
Pension accounts	1.3	1.5	23.2	4.5	7.2	16.2	8.2	12.3	13.9	9.0	16.4	13.1
Financial securities	6.1	4.2	38.7	10.4	5.1	53.4	4.7	2.3	42.9	2.8	1.5	45.4
Corporate stock and mutual funds	18.0	9.0	52.6	12.7	8.1	40.8	20.0	14.7	28.6	20.6	12.6	38.9
Net equity in personal trusts	7.8	2.6	78.2	4.4	2.7	42.8	5.4	4.7	23.9	4.4	3.2	33.2
Miscellaneous assets	1.3	1.3	26.3	3.2	2.5	33.7	2.8	1.8	31.8	1.9	1.5	30.6
Total Gross Assets	100.0	100.0	25.7	100.0	100.0	25.5	100.0	100.0	20.9	100.0	100.0	23.9
Debt on principal residence	1.1	6.3	4.6	2.2	9.8	5.9	2.8	9.4	6.2	2.5	11.2	5.4
All other debt	5.3	6.8	20.6	6.0	6.0	26.2	1.5	3.1	10.3	1.5	4.0	9.2
Total Debt	6.4	13.1	12.9	8.2	15.7	13.6	4.3	12.5	7.2	4.0	15.1	6.4
Net home equity	7.8	23.8	8.7	6.2	20.1	8.1	8.5	18.7	9.6	8.5	17.2	11.8
Investment-type assets	79.0	49.6	42.1	76.5	48.3	41.4	70.8	49.0	27.8	71.2	46.1	36.8
Life-cycle assets	19.7	49.0	4.9	20.3	49.3	4.5	26.4	49.1	10.3	26.9	52.4	12.3
Memo:												
Debt/net worth ratio (percent)	6.8	15.1		8.8	18.7		4.5	14.3		4.2	17.8	

Source: Authors' computations from the 1983, 1992, 2001, and 2013 Survey of Consumer Finances.
See footnotes to Table 10.2 for technical details on asset definitions.

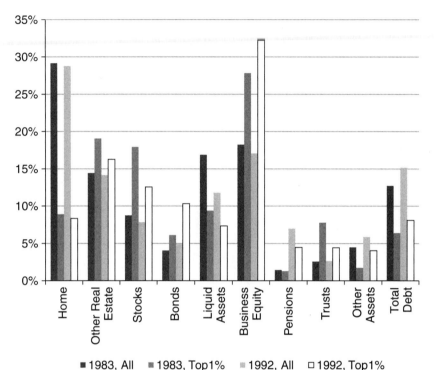

Figure 10.12a. Portfolio Composition of All Households and Top 1 Percent as Ranked by Income, 1983 and 1992
(Share of gross assets)

business equity (27.9 versus 18.8 percent), and trust funds (7.8 versus 2.6 percent); and lower proportions in their principal residence (8.9 versus 30.1 percent) and liquid assets (9.4 versus 17.4 percent). Collectively, the top 1 percent had 79 percent of its wealth in investment-type assets, compared to 49.6 percent overall, and only 19.7 percent in life-cycle assets, compared to 49.0 percent overall. The richest 1 percent in terms of income also had a lower debt / equity ratio—6.8 versus 15.1 percent. Moreover, whereas the top income percentile accounted for 27.6 percent of total net worth, they owned 33.9 percent of nonhome real estate, 52.6 percent of stocks and mutual funds, 38.7 percent of financial securities, 39.2 percent of business equity, and 78.2 percent of trust fund equity. These results closely resemble those of Table 10.2, which is based on the top wealth percentile.

Major changes between 1983 and 1992 among the top income percentile were declines in the share of assets held in stocks and mutual funds (from

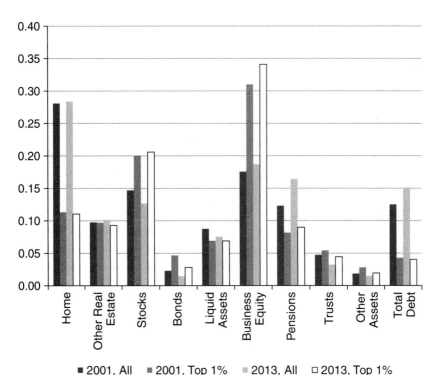

■ 2001, All   ■ 2001, Top 1%   ■ 2013, All   □ 2013, Top 1%

Figure 10.12b. Portfolio Composition of All Households and Top 1 Percent as Ranked by Income, 2001 and 2013
(Share of gross assets)

18.0 to 12.7 percent), in investment real estate (from 19.2 to 16.4 percent), and in trust funds (from 7.8 to 4.4 percent) and corresponding increases in the share held in business equity (from 27.9 to 32.5 percent), in financial securities (from 6.1 to 10.4 percent), and in pension accounts (1.3 to 4.5 percent). While the share of total net worth held by the top 1 percent of income recipients remained unchanged at 27.6 percent between 1983 and 1992, their share of total business equity increased sharply from 39.2 to 48 percent and their share of total financial securities from 38.7 to 53.4 percent. In contrast, their share of total stocks and mutual funds dropped from 52.6 to 40.8 percent, their share of trust fund equity from 78.2 to 42.8 percent, and their share of pension assets from 23.2 to 16.2 percent.

Between 1992 and 2013, other real estate held by the richest 1 percent fell from 16.4 to 9.3 percent of gross assets and that of financial securities from 10.4 to 2.8 percent, while corporate stock and mutual funds increased from 12.7 to

20.6 percent of total assets and that of pension accounts rose from 4.5 to 9 percent. The share of investment-type assets held in their portfolio declined from 76.5 to 71.2 percent, while the proportion in life-cycle assets rose from 20.3 to 26.9 percent. The debt to net worth ratio was also down from 8.8 to 4.2 percent. The share of total net worth held by the top 1 percent of income recipients fell slightly to 27.1 percent between 1992 and 2013, and the shares of all asset classes also fell with the exception of liquid assets and life-cycle assets.

These results suggest increased entrepreneurial activity among the rich, with the share of business equity in the wealth portfolio of the top income percentile rising from 28 percent in 1983 to 34 percent in 2013 and that of the top wealth percentile from 32 to 36 percent. Moreover, the value of business equity held by both the top 1 percent of wealth holders and the top 1 percent of income recipients also increased as a share of the total value of business equity among all households.

In 1983, the primary source of income among the richest 1 percent of households ranked by income was wages and salaries, at 35 percent of their total income (see Table 10.7 and Figures 10.13a and 10.13b). Proprietary (self-employment) income was second, at 26 percent, followed by capital gains at 12 percent, interest at 10 percent, and dividends at 9 percent. The top percentile accounted for over half of all dividends and capital gains, about one-quarter of proprietary income, interest, and rental, royalty, and trust income. (They also accounted for 11.5 percent of all alimony payments!)

Between 1983 and 1992, the most substantial change is that wages and salaries increased from 35 to 44 percent of the total income of the top 1 percent. However, proprietary income fell somewhat, from 25.9 to 23.5, though, altogether, labor earnings rose from 60 to 68 percent. Property income, including interest, dividends, capital gains, rents, royalties, and trust income declined as a proportion of their total proceeds, from 36 to 30 percent.

In 1992, the richest 1 percent earned 11.8 percent of all wage and salary income (up from 7 percent in 1983), 26.7 percent of all self-employment income (the same as in 1983), and 32 percent of all interest income (up from 25 percent in 1983). However, while their share of total dividends fell sharply, their share of capital gains actually increased somewhat and their share of total rental, royalty, and trust income was also up sharply.

From 1992 to 2013, the share of wages and salaries in the total income of the richest 1 percent fell from 44 to 39 percent, though still above its 1983 level. The sum of self-employment, rental, royalty, and trust income as a proportion

Table 10.7. Income composition of top 1 percent of households as ranked by income and all households, 1983, 1992, 2001, and 2013 (percentage)

Component	1983 Top 1%	1983 All HHs	1983 Top 1% Share of All Income	1992 Top 1%	1992 All HHs	1992 Top 1% Share of All Income	2001 Top 1%	2001 All HHs	2001 Top 1% Share of All Income	2013 Top 1%	2013 All HHs	2013 Top 1% Share of All Income
Total income	100.0	100.0	12.8	100.0	100.0	15.7	100.0	100.0	20.4	100.0	100.0	19.8
Wages and salaries	34.5	62.9	7.0	44.1	58.5	11.8	45.2	68.3	13.5	38.9	63.3	12.2
Self-employment income	25.9	12.4	26.7	23.5	13.8	26.7	24.4	11.7	42.6	33.1	13.5	48.5
Rental, royalty, and trust income	5.0	2.6	25.1	8.0	3.4	36.8	⎣		⎦	⎣		⎦
Total interest	10.2	5.3	24.8	8.3	4.1	32.1	3.5	2.7	27.0	3.1	1.5	40.8
Dividends	9.4	2.3	53.7	4.3	1.7	39.1	2.0	1.5	27.8	4.8	2.0	47.5
Capital gains	11.7	2.6	57.3	9.7	2.4	63.4	23.2	6.7	70.2	17.1	4.6	72.9
Unemployment and workers' compensation	0.0	0.9	0.1	0.0	0.5	0.5	0.0	0.2	0.3	0.0	0.6	1.0
Alimony payments	1.4	1.5	11.5	0.1	0.4	2.0	1.0	0.4	2.6	0.9	0.4	1.6
Public assistance	0.0	1.0	0.0	0.0	0.6	0.1	0.7	0.3	20.6	2.0	0.7	20.9
Retirement income	1.7	8.2	2.6	0.7	6.6	1.8	0.0	7.6	0.0	0.0	11.4	0.0
Other income	0.1	0.3	6.3	1.3	8.0	2.6	0.0	0.7	15.5	0.0	1.9	14.7

Source: Author's computations from the 1983, 1992, 2001, and 2013 Survey of Consumer Finances.
See footnotes to Table 10.3 for technical details on income definitions.

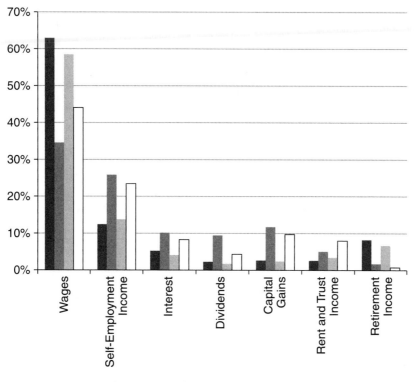

Figure 10.13a. Composition of Income of All Households and Top 1 Percent as Ranked by Income, 1983 and 1992
(Share of total income)

of their total income was up slightly, from 31.5 to 33.1 percent.[12] Interest was down as a percentage of their total income but capital gains were way up. The richest 1 percent also accounted for a higher portion of overall total interest, dividends, and capital gains in 2013 than in 1992.

Over the full 1983 to 2013 period, the rich showed a substitution of earned income for property income. Among the top income percentile, wages and salaries grew from 35 to 39 percent and that of self-employment, rental, royalty, and trust income from 30.9 to 33.1 percent. Among the top percentile of wealth holders, the share of total income received in the form of wages and salaries advanced from 24 to 29 percent, while that in the form of self-employment, rental, royalty, and trust income remained unchanged. The

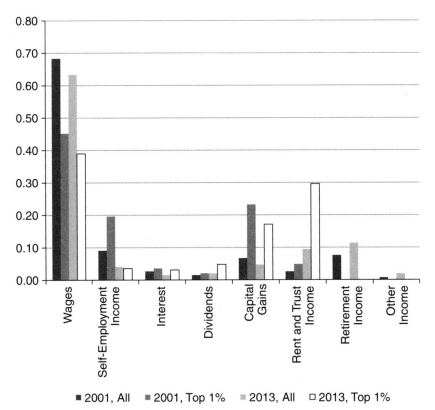

Figure 10.13b. Composition of Income of All Households and Top 1 Percent as Ranked by Income, 2001 and 2013
(Share of total income)

sum of interest, dividends, and capital gains, in contrast, declined from 31.3 to 25 percent among the richest 1 percent as ranked by income and from 37.9 to 32.2 percent among the top 1 percent of wealth holders.

Concluding Remarks

The results show some striking differences between the characteristics of the rich and those of the general population and some important changes in the composition of the rich over time from 1983 to 2013. First, the rich were, on average, older than the population at large, though there was a notable increase in the share of young families in the ranks of the top wealth and income percentile between 1983 and 1992. Despite the hype about "dot.com millionaires," the rich became decidedly older between 1992 and 2013.

Second, the rich were much better educated than the overall population. Despite significant growth in the overall educational attainment of the population between 1983 and 1992, however, there was no corresponding increase in the educational attainment of the top percentile as ranked by both wealth and income. From 1992 to 2013, this trend reversed and the rich became better educated. Third, the rich remained an almost exclusively white enclave, though by 2013 there was some representation of blacks in the top wealth percentile (1.7 percent). Asian Americans (and other races) did show gains relative to their population share into the ranks of the rich over this period.

The rich, both in terms of income and wealth, were composed predominantly of married couples, particularly in comparison to the population at large. In 1983, men (both married and unmarried) headed 99.9 percent of households in the top percentile of income earners, though by 2013 this figure had slipped slightly to 98.2 percent. Moreover, among the top income percentile, the proportion of married couples fell almost continuously from 1983 to 2013.

There were some important changes in both the labor force participation and employment patterns of the rich. While the vast majority of household heads under 65 years of age in both the top wealth and top income percentile were full-time workers, their share in the ranks of the top wealth holders declined between 1983 and 2013. Among the top income percentile, however, the share of full-time workers was the same in 2013 as in 1983.

In addition, despite this apparent reduction in labor force effort, at least among the top wealth percentile, between 1983 and 2013, the income statistics show a greater reliance on labor income than other forms of income among both the wealth and income rich. Over these years, labor earnings (both wages and salary and self-employment income) as share of the total income of the top wealth percentile jumped upward, as did that of the top income percentile. A substantial increase in the number of working wives among rich households contributed to this trend.

There is also evidence that entrepreneurial activity played a larger role in gaining entry into the ranks of the rich. Between 1983 and 2013, there were substantial increases recorded in the share of self-employed persons in their ranks, both in terms of income and wealth. Their share in the top wealth percentile more than doubled between 1983 and 2013, from 38 to 84 percent, as did the corresponding proportion in the top income percentile, from 27 to 56 percent. In contrast, among workers in the general population, the self-employed share was the same in 2013 as in 1983, 15 percent.

There is also some corroborating evidence from the balance sheets of the wealthy. Among the richest 1 percent of households ranked in terms of wealth, the share of total assets held in the form of business equity rose from 32 percent in 1983 to 36 percent in 2013, and their portion of the total value of business equity held by all households increased from 52 to 63 percent. Among the richest 1 percent of households as ranked by income, the proportion of their wealth held in the form of business equity advanced from 28 to 34 percent and their share of the total value of business equity held by all households grew from 39 to 44 percent. As noted in Chapter 2, fully 77 percent of the households in the top wealth percentile reported owning their own businesses in 2013 (compared to 10 percent of the general population).

The apparent rise in entrepreneurial activity among the rich might be one factor accounting for increasing wealth inequality over the last thirty years. It also has tax implications since taxing rentiers and taxing entrepreneurs could have quite different effects on investment, risk-taking, and the like.

These results should be interpreted with some caution. Changes in the tax laws from the 1986 Tax Reform Act led to a strong incentive for regular corporations to convert to Sub-Chapter S corporations and partnerships, which are categorized as unincorporated business enterprises (and the corresponding income as self-employment income).[13] These conversions might also be responsible for the rising importance of business equity in the portfolios of the rich and the corresponding decline in corporate stock holdings.

Whatever the rationale behind the increased importance of self-employment income and unincorporated business equity among the rich, this group appears to be relying less and less on property income. In particular, property income in the form of interest, dividends, and capital gains declined sharply, from 38 to 32 percent of the income of the top wealth percentile between 1983 and 2013, and from 31 to 25 percent for the top income percentile.[14]

The traditional sources of large fortunes in this country—notably agriculture, mining, construction, manufacturing, and trade—appear to have diminished in importance over time and to have been supplanted by the financial sector, as well as business and professional services. The former group accounted for 52 percent of employment in the top wealth percentile in 1983 and only 33 percent in 2013, whereas the share employed in finance and business and professional services (as well as transportation, communications, utilities, and personal services) rose from 48 to 67 percent. The results are even more dramatic for the top income percentile, among which the share of total employment in these traditional industries fell from 38 to 21 percent and correspondingly rose from 62 to 79 percent in the latter group.

In sum, this study indicates that the wealthy are apt to be healthier and wiser (at least, better educated) and older than the general population. Moreover, the rich are more likely to work in finance and business and professional services than the overall population, and over this period have relied increasingly on labor income and correspondingly less on property income as sources of their fortunes. Finally, and most notably, the rich are much more likely to be self-employed than the general population, and this differential has widened over the years 1983 to 2013. Thus, despite the fact that CEOs and star athletes and entertainers get most of the attention in the press, the most notable finding is the incredible rise of the self-employed in the ranks of the rich, particularly in terms of wealth. These self-employed workers are likely to own their own businesses, including partnerships like those found among doctors, lawyers, and investment bankers. Moreover, as we know from recent initial public offerings, the value of many of these small, unincorporated businesses can be extremely high.

11

The Persistence of Asset Poverty

O ur focus now moves from the very high end of the wealth (and income) distribution to the low end. This chapter investigates the wealth
holdings of the poor over the years 1962 through 2013. For the purpose of
this chapter, poverty is defined according to the U.S. Census Bureau.[1] The
analysis of wealth is followed by a discussion of so-called asset poverty, which
examines trends over the years 1983 through 2013.

Previous research has shown that families below the poverty line were
better off in terms of wealth than income.[2] In 1962, the ratio of mean income
between families below and above the poverty line was 0.19 while the ratio of
mean wealth was 0.29. The corresponding ratios for 1983 were 0.16 and 0.19.
On average, the elderly poor were better off in terms of wealth than the
younger poor, particularly relative to their own income. However, the poor
became worse off in terms of wealth between 1962 and 1983, when their real
income grew by 6 percent and their real wealth declined by 11 percent. The
inclusion of pension wealth and Social Security wealth in the household
portfolio narrowed the wealth gap between the poor and nonpoor, particularly for families under 65 years of age. Alternative poverty rates were also
calculated based on the inclusion of annuity flows from wealth into household
income. The reduction in the measured poverty rate in 1962 and 1983 with
these alternative definitions varied from 15 to 21 percent relative to the poverty rate calculated from income alone.

Asset poverty can be defined in several ways. One definition, for example,
is the availability of financial resources to provide for normal consumption
over a period of three months. Asset poverty has been remarkably persistent
over the last three decades despite a sharp increase in median household net

worth (at least until 2007). Asset poverty rates then spiked during the Great Recession.

Despite massive growth in overall assets in the United States, the level of asset poverty actually rose between 1983 and 1998, when the overall rate was 37 percent.[3] This high overall level of asset poverty for the entire population disguised even higher rates for various groups. Asset poverty rates in 1998 for some of the most disadvantaged groups were 61 percent for blacks and Hispanics; 73 percent for families whose head of household was younger than 25; 60 percent for those in the 25–34 age group; 59 percent for those with less than a high school degree; 63 percent for renters; and 64 percent for nonelderly female heads with children.

The Wealth of the Poor

Some early work on poverty focused on its persistence among families. Bane and Ellwood estimated the dynamics of poverty spells among families.[4] Beach and Thornton, Agnello, and Link looked at income distribution and the poverty rate over the business cycle.[5] Ruggles and Williams estimated the duration of poverty spells using monthly data.[6] The findings of Bane and Ellwood and those of Ruggles and Williams indicated that most families who entered poverty had only retained that status for a short time. On the other hand, the majority of families that were poor at a given point in time had a protracted spell of poverty before they escaped.

One implication of such studies is that current income may not be the best indicator of poverty status. A better measure of poverty status, and also a more comprehensive measure of family well-being, may be a joint index of family income and wealth, since wealth reflects accumulated lifetime income (to the present age). Thus, some families who are below the poverty line on the basis of current income may have enjoyed relatively prosperous periods in previous years. For these families, poverty may be a transitory phenomenon, based on a temporary period of unemployment, illness, or the like, or a recent change in family status, such as divorce. These families may have relatively high wealth. For others, poverty may be a more or less persistent feature of their life history. Such families may consist of a single nonworking parent with several children and no previous labor force participation, and they may have had a long history of low-income years. As a result, their wealth holdings may be low even relative to current income. One goal of research into the wealth holdings of the poor is to assess the persistence of poverty in this group.

This chapter delves into the issues of how relative wealth holdings of families below and above the poverty line compare to income and how the composition of wealth varies between the two groups. In particular, are the poor able to accumulate liquid and investment wealth or does their wealth largely go toward satisfying immediate consumption needs and thus take the form of housing and consumer durables? And do poor families face severe credit constraints on borrowing and thus have a lower debt-net worth ratio than families above living the poverty line?

The relative wealth holdings of the poor, both in terms of level and composition, vary with age. This chapter investigates whether the disparity between relative wealth holdings and relative income between families below and above the poverty line are greater for elderly families than for younger ones. Another factor is pension and Social Security wealth. Does it widen or narrow the gap in relative wealth holdings between the poor and nonpoor?

I also propose several new measures of poverty status based on combined indices of income and wealth. In one set of calculations, household wealth is converted into an annuity flow, which is included as part of family income. In a second set, imputed rent to owner-occupied housing is also included as part of household income.[7] In a third set, a joint criterion of low income and low wealth is used to determine poverty status. The results show that calculations of the poverty rate can be quite sensitive to the definition used.

The analysis in this chapter covers the period from 1962 to 2013. It compares family income by source for the populations above and below the poverty line for 1982 and presents results on the relative wealth holdings of the poor and the nonpoor populations. In addition, we extend the household balance sheet to include both pension and Social Security wealth and develop alternative calculations of the poverty rate based on both family income and wealth.

Comparative Income Statistics

Before the analysis is begun, it is useful to compare results from the Survey of Consumer Finances (SCF) with data from the Current Population Survey Reports (CPS) on poverty rates and mean family income (see Table 11.1).[8] The official poverty statistics for 1982 indicate that 12.2 percent of all *families* had income below the official (U.S.) poverty line. Calculations from the SCF indicate a poverty rate of 14.2 percent for *households*.[9] On the other hand, the official poverty rate for individuals is 15 percent, compared to a 14.9 percent rate calculated by the SCF.

Table 11.1, Panels 2 and 3, show a comparison of mean income by component for the full population and the poor, as calculated from the CPS and the SCF. Mean income was almost identical in the two samples, and most individual components were quite close. Wage and salary income and self-employment income differed between the two sources, but total labor income (the sum of the two) was comparable. However, property income was higher in the SCF, a result that was likely due to the stratified sample used in the SCF (the CPS is a representative sample). However, all in all, the SCF lined up with the CPS in regard to income data and poverty rates.

Table 11.2 provides comparative income statistics for households below and above the poverty line. In 1982, the first year with complete data, average overall income among the poor was only 16 percent of that among households above the poverty line. This ratio was the same for the sample of households including only those under 65 years of age and for the sample including only those households who were age 65 and over. The ratio in median household income between households below and above the poverty line was almost the same as that of mean income in the sample including all households as well as the sample of those under 65 years of age. However, for households 65 and over, the ratio was 0.36. This considerably higher fraction was due to the relatively low median income among elderly households above the poverty line, rather than to a relatively high median income of poor elderly households.

For households under 65, the discrepancy was due mainly to differences in labor earnings. Only 57 percent of poor households reported receiving wage and salary income, compared to 89 percent of households above the

Table 11.1. Comparison of income data between the Current Population Survey and the Survey of Consumer Finances, 1982

Component	CPS[a] (families)	SCF (households)	Ratio: SCF/CPS
1. Poverty Rate			
a. Persons	0.150	0.149	0.99
b. Families (households)	0.122	0.142	1.16
2. Mean Family (household) Income by Type, All Households			
a. Wages and salaries	$20,543	$17,451	0.85
b. Self-employment income[a]	1,643	3,442	2.10
c. Dividends, interest, and rent[b]	1,753	2,800	1.60
d. Social Security[c], pensions, annuities, alimony, and other income	2,739	2,779	1.02
e. Other transfer income[d]	685	524	0.77
f. Total income	27,390	27,039	0.99
3. Mean Family (household) Income by Type, Households below the Poverty Line			
a. Wages and salaries	$2,329	$1,799	0.77
b. Self-employment income[a]	65	154	2.37
c. Dividends, interest, and rent[b]	105	85	0.81
d. Social Security[c], pensions, annuities, alimony, and other income	1,059	1,447	1.37
e. Other transfer income[d]	1,591	1,473	0.93
f. Total income	5,019	4,958	0.99

Sources: U.S. Bureau of the Census, *Characteristics of the Population Below the Poverty Level: 1982,* Current Population Reports, Series P-60, No. 144 (Washington DC: U.S. Government Printing Office, 1984). Income data are for 1982.

a. In the Survey of Consumer Finances (SCF), this entry also includes partnership and net profit from unincorporated businesses.

b. In the SCF, this entry also includes trust income.

c. Social Security income includes retirement and survivors' benefits, permanent disability insurance payments, and railroad retirement benefits.

d. In the CPS, this entry is defined as the sum of Aid to Families with Dependent Children (AFDC), Supplemental Security Income (SSI), unemployment insurance, workers' compensation, veterans' payments, and other (cash) public assistance; in the SCF, this entry is defined as the sum of Aid to Dependent Children (ADC), AFDC, food stamps, SSI, and other public assistance.

poverty line. Among those who worked, the ratio in mean wage and salary earnings between those below and those above the poverty line was 0.16. Seven percent of poor households received self-employment earnings, compared to 17 percent for nonpoor households under 65. The ratio in average self-employment income among the self-employed was 0.12. Only

14 percent of poor households received property income, compared to 55 percent of households above the poverty line. Households above the poverty line with property income earned ten times as much in dividends, interest, and rent as poor households that reported some form of property income.

The discrepancy in property income was even more pronounced among the elderly. Twenty percent of poor elderly households received some form of property income, in contrast to 75 percent of nonpoor elderly households. Among property income recipients, the ratio in earnings between the two groups was 0.08. Over 90 percent of the elderly poor received some form of Social Security or pension income. However, elderly households over the poverty line who received retirement income averaged almost twice as much retirement income as recipients below the poverty line.

In 1962, average income among poor households was 19 percent of that among the nonpoor. This ratio was somewhat higher than in 1983. The ratio in median family income was 0.17, the same as the 1983 ratio. The ratio in mean income was somewhat lower for families 65 and over than for those under 65. However, as in 1983, the ratio of median income was significantly higher among the elderly, and, as in 1983, this was due to the relatively low median income among elderly families above the poverty line.

By 2000 the ratio in mean overall income between the poor and nonpoor slipped to 0.12 compared to 0.16 in 1982, though the ratio of median income remained at 0.17. The main reasons for the decline in the ratio of mean income were sharp falls in the share of the poor who reported self-employment income and those who reported property income. Among the nonelderly, the ratio in average income between the poor and nonpoor also dropped, from 0.16 in 1982 to 0.11 in 2000, while the ratio of median income remained largely unchanged. Once again, the main reason was a slippage in the percentage of the poor with self-employment and property income. Among the elderly, the ratio of mean income fell somewhat from 0.16 to 0.14, while the ratio of median income dropped sharply from 0.36 to 0.26. The latter was due to much higher growth in the median income of the nonpoor than the poor.

The year 2012 saw some relative recovery in the fortunes of the poor, despite the aftermath of the Great Recession. The ratio of overall mean income between the poor and nonpoor increased from 0.12 in 2000 to 0.13 in 2012,

Table 11.2. Household income by type, poverty status, and age group, 1961, 1982, 2000, and 2012

	Recipiency Rate				Recipiency Rate			
	1961				1982			
Component	Below Poverty Line	Above Poverty Line	Ratio	Ratio of Mean Value by Component, Recipients Only	Below Poverty Line	Above Poverty Line	Ratio	Ratio of Mean Value by Component, Recipients Only
1. All Ages								
Wages and salaries					0.442	0.779	0.57	0.16
Self-employment income[a]					0.051	0.159	0.32	0.12
Dividends, interest, and rent					0.151	0.582	0.26	0.10
Retirement income[b]					0.351	0.283	1.24	0.39
Total income[c]	1.000	1.000	1.00	0.19	1.000	1.000	1.00	0.16
Memo: Median income				0.17				0.17
2. Under Age 65								
Wages and salaries					0.572	0.892	0.64	0.16
Self-employment income[a]					0.067	0.172	0.39	0.12
Dividends, interest, and rent					0.135	0.546	0.25	0.10
Retirement income[b]					0.161	0.132	1.22	0.44
Total income[c]	1.000	1.000	1.00	0.21	1.000	1.000	1.00	0.16
Memo: Median income				0.21				0.17
3. Age 65 and over								
Wages and salaries					0.056	0.272	0.21	0.08
Self-employment income[a]					0.005	0.099	0.05	0.02
Dividends, interest, and rent					0.198	0.747	0.27	0.08
Retirement income[b]					0.910	0.961	0.95	0.54
Total income[c]	1.000	1.000	1.00	0.18	1.000	1.000	1.00	0.16
Memo: Median income				0.35				0.36

	2000				2012			
1. All Ages								
Wages and salaries[a]	0.525	0.811	0.65	0.16	0.518	0.752	0.69	0.14
Self-employment income[a]	0.019	0.089	0.21	0.15	0.038	0.091	0.42	0.16
Dividends, interest, and rent	0.093	0.396	0.23	0.13	0.056	0.305	0.18	0.29
Retirement income[b]	0.383	0.294	1.30	0.37	0.337	0.360	0.94	0.32
Total income[c]	1.000	1.000	1.00	0.12	1.000	1.000	1.00	0.13
Memo: Median income				0.17				0.20
2. Under Age 65								
Wages and salaries[a]	0.659	0.948	0.69	0.16	0.621	0.893	0.70	0.14
Self-employment income[a]	0.020	0.092	0.21	0.05	0.041	0.100	0.40	0.10
Dividends, interest, and rent	0.070	0.355	0.20	0.05	0.049	0.270	0.18	0.07
Retirement income[b]	0.232	0.112	2.08	1.35	0.198	0.165	1.20	0.71
Total income[c]	1.000	1.000	1.00	0.11	1.000	1.000	1.00	0.13
Memo: Median income				0.16				0.20
3. Age 65 and over								
Wages and salaries[a]	0.044	0.296	0.15	0.11	0.032	0.321	0.10	0.04
Self-employment income[a]	0.015	0.079	0.19	0.03	0.027	0.064	0.43	0.15
Dividends, interest, and rent	0.176	0.551	0.32	0.08	0.089	0.413	0.22	0.35
Retirement income[b]	0.930	0.980	0.95	0.35	0.995	0.960	1.04	0.29
Total income[c]	1.000	1.000	1.00	0.14	1.000	1.000	1.00	0.14
Memo: Median income				0.26				0.28

Source: Author's computations from the 1983, 2001, and 2013 Survey of Consumer Finances and the 1962 Survey of Financial Characteristics of Consumers.

Age classification is based on the head of household.

a. Includes partnership and net profit from unincorporated businesses.

b. Includes Social Security and pension benefits, annuities, disability payments, and other forms of retirement income.

c. Defined as the sum of income components.

and the ratio of median income expanded from 0.17 to 0.20; that of mean income among the nonelderly from 0.11 to 0.13 and that of median income from 0.16 to 0.20 (primarily from a higher share of the nonelderly poor reporting self-employment income); and while the ratio of mean income among the elderly remained unchanged, the ratio of median income was up from 0.26 to 0.28 (mainly due to a higher share of the elderly poor with retirement income).

Relative Wealth Holdings of the Poor and Nonpoor

A comparison of wealth-holding patterns between households below and above the poverty line beginning with the year 1983 follows. One of the more surprising findings of this chapter was the high homeownership rate among the poor (see Table 11.3), which was 38 percent.[10] Among households above the poverty line, the homeownership rate was 68 percent, almost double that of poor households. Moreover, the mean value of homes owned by households above the poverty line was double that of poor homeowners. Over half of poor households owned an automobile, compared to 90 percent of the nonpoor, and its average value among poor car owners was half that of nonpoor households.

Almost 36 percent of poor households held at least one form of liquid asset, compared to 81 percent of households above the poverty line. The average value of liquid assets among nonpoor depositors was almost eight times that of poor households. The share of poor households with a pension account was 15 percent, compared to 44 percent among the nonpoor, and its average value among pension holders below the poverty line was half that of those above the poverty line.

The percentage of poor households owning their own businesses was less than a third that of nonpoor households, as was the percentage owning investment real estate. The average value of unincorporated business equity among poor households that owned their own businesses was a little over half that of business owners above the poverty line. Only 6 percent of poor households owned some form of financial asset (securities, stocks, mutual funds, and trust funds). Moreover, the average holdings of these assets among owners was less than 10 percent that of households above the poverty line.

Table 11.3. Household wealth by component and poverty status, 1983, 2001, and 2013

Wealth Component	1983				2001				2013			
	Ownership Rate			Ratio of Mean Value, Holders Only	Ownership Rate			Ratio of Mean Value, Holders Only	Ownership Rate			Ratio of Mean Value, Holders Only
	Below Poverty Line	Above Poverty Line	Ratio		Below Poverty Line	Above Poverty Line	Ratio		Below Poverty Line	Above Poverty Line	Ratio	
Owner-occupied housing	0.383	0.676	0.57	0.57	0.331	0.729	0.45	0.38	0.322	0.704	0.46	0.49
Vehicles	0.519	0.898	0.58	0.48	0.536	0.895	0.60	0.42	0.624	0.901	0.69	0.43
Liquid assets[a]	0.355	0.806	0.44	0.13	0.650	0.960	0.68	0.16	0.755	0.964	0.78	0.21
Pension accounts[b]	0.151	0.443	0.34	0.50	0.108	0.585	0.19	0.23	0.061	0.561	0.11	0.30
Unincorporated business	0.049	0.157	0.31	0.53	0.026	0.133	0.20	0.28	0.038	0.114	0.33	0.85
Investment real estate	0.063	0.210	0.30	0.27	0.038	0.187	0.20	0.24	0.033	0.197	0.17	0.37
Securities, stocks, mutual funds, and trusts	0.062	0.295	0.21	0.09	0.070	0.465	0.15	0.33	0.080	0.307	0.26	0.28
Mortgage debt	0.118	0.414	0.29	0.59	0.138	0.493	0.28	0.44	0.141	0.475	0.30	0.51
All other debt[c]	0.430	0.671	0.64	0.22	0.477	0.680	0.70	0.38	0.476	0.671	0.71	0.63

Source: Authors' computations from the 1983, 2001, and 2013 Survey of Consumer Finances.

a. Checking accounts, savings accounts, time deposits, money market funds, certificates of deposits, and the cash surrender value of life insurance.

b. IRAs, Keogh plans, 401(k) plans, the accumulated value of defined contribution pension plans, and other retirement accounts.

c. Mortgage debt on all real property except principal residence; credit card, installment, and other debt.

On the liability side, 12 percent of poor households, or 31 percent of poor homeowners, held mortgage debt, in contrast to 41 percent of households above the poverty line or 61 percent of nonpoor home owners. The ratio in the average value of outstanding mortgages between mortgagees below and above the poverty line was almost three-fifths. Forty-three percent of poor households held some form of other debt, compared to 67 percent of households above the poverty line. However, the average value of other debt for poor households with debt was only a fifth of that of nonpoor households.

The average value of gross assets held by households below the poverty line was 18 percent that of households above the poverty line in 1983 (see Table 11.4). The ratio of total debt between the two groups was slightly lower, at 0.15, so that the ratio of mean NWB (net worth including all durables and household inventories) was slightly higher, at 0.19. This ratio was higher than that of mean incomes (0.16).[11] The ratio in median NWB was almost the same as that of mean NWB. The picture is different when consumer durables and household inventories are excluded to obtain net worth, which is a better measure of disposable wealth than NWB. The ratio in mean net worth between the two groups was 0.14, lower than that of NWB or income. Median net worth among the poor was almost zero, so that the ratio in median net worth between the two groups was only 0.02.

The wealth (NWB) of poor households consisted primarily of three components: owner-occupied housing, consumer durables, and inventories. The mean value of housing among (all) poor households was 27 percent that of nonpoor households, and the mean value of durables and inventories among poor households was 52 percent that of the nonpoor. The ratio of average net equity in owner-occupied housing was 0.28, slightly higher than the ratio of gross housing value, because of the relatively lower ratio of mortgage debt to home value among the poor. Together, owner-occupied housing, durables, and inventories amounted to two-thirds of the gross assets of poor households, compared to a little more than a third for households above the poverty line. The only other asset of appreciable magnitude held by the poor was unincorporated business equity, which amounted to 16 percent of their gross assets.

All other assets combined amounted to only 16 percent of the gross assets of the poor. Average balances of demand deposits, savings deposits, and other liquid assets among poor families totaled only 9 percent that of families above the poverty line. The ratio in average holdings of financial securities, stocks, and other assets between the two groups was only 0.02. This compares to a ratio of property income of 0.03.

Wealth by Age Group

Wealth-holding patterns by age group differ considerably between families below and above the poverty line. Among both groups average wealth was lowest for young families. However, among poor families, wealth was higher for middle-aged families than elderly ones, whereas the opposite was the case for families above the poverty line. As a consequence, the disparity in average wealth holdings between families living below and above the poverty line increased sharply with age. In 1983, the ratio in average net worth NWB between the two groups fell from 0.32 for young families to 0.22 for middle-aged ones and then to 0.12 for the elderly. The pattern for average net worth NW was slightly different, with the ratio between the two groups the same for young and middle-aged families and substantially lower among the elderly. The medians also tell a different story. The ratio in median NWB between the poor and nonpoor was substantially lower for middle-aged families than younger ones, but slightly higher among the elderly than the middle-aged. In contrast, the ratio of median net worth NW increased across the three age groups. The differences can be traced to the fact that mean net worth NW and NWB are actually lower among the elderly poor than among the middle-aged poor, whereas median NWB and net worth NW are greater for the latter than for the former.

The breakdown of wealth by asset type is also revealing. Whereas the ratio of wealth (both NWB and NW) between families below and above the poverty line was decidedly lower for the elderly than for younger families, this was not true for either the gross or net value of owner-occupied housing. The ratio in unincorporated business equity was considerably higher among middle-aged families than among the young or elderly. However, the relative holdings of liquid assets, investment real estate, and stocks and financial securities between the two groups fell sharply with age, and these assets primarily account for the overall pattern of wealth with age.[12]

Relative Wealth Holdings for Other Years

Income-poor households were better off in terms of wealth in 1962 than in 1983. The ratio of mean NWB between poor and nonpoor households was

Table 11.4. Mean household wealth by component, poverty status, and age, 1962, 1983, 2001, and 2013 (ratio between households below and above poverty line)

Wealth Component	1962				1983			
	All Ages	Under 35	Ages 35–64	65 and over	All Ages	Under 35	Ages 35–64	65 and over
Owner-occupied housing	0.29	0.30	0.22	0.39	0.27	0.20	0.31	0.31
Durables and inventories	0.50	0.55	0.51	0.56	0.52	0.58	0.52	0.53
Liquid assets[a]	0.24	0.08	0.18	0.22	0.09	0.14	0.11	0.06
Unincorporated businesses	0.42	0.40	0.58	0.14	0.17	0.11	0.25	0.05
Investment real estate	0.18	0.00	0.11	0.20	0.08	0.21	0.10	0.03
Financial securities, stocks, mutual funds, and trusts	0.16	0.06	0.16	0.10	0.02	0.11	0.01	0.02
Total debt	0.18	0.20	0.20	0.27	0.15	0.17	0.17	0.20
Net home equity[b]	0.33	0.60	0.24	0.38	0.28	0.26	0.32	0.30
Gross assets	0.28	0.28	0.28	0.20	0.18	0.27	0.22	0.12
Net worth NWB[c]	0.29	0.31	0.29	0.20	0.19	0.32	0.22	0.12
Net worth NW	0.26	0.17	0.26	0.18	0.14	0.18	0.19	0.09
Memo:								
Median net worth NWB	0.20	0.42	0.23	0.29	0.20	0.36	0.16	0.19
Median net worth NW	0.03	0.07	0.08	0.24	0.02	0.01	0.05	0.11
	2001				2013			
Owner-occupied housing	0.17	0.19	0.17	0.24	0.22	0.17	0.23	0.40
Vehicles	0.25	0.22	0.30	0.21	0.30	0.33	0.33	0.24

Liquid assets[a]	0.11	0.12	0.13	0.10	0.16	0.21	0.20	0.19
Pension accounts[d]	0.04	0.03	0.04	0.08	0.03	0.02	0.04	0.05
Unincorporated businesses	0.06	0.36	0.05	0.00	0.28	0.30	0.32	0.42
Investment real estate	0.05	0.13	0.05	0.04	0.06	0.03	0.12	0.02
Financial securities, stocks, mutual funds, and trusts	0.05	0.21	0.05	0.03	0.07	0.17	0.10	0.07
Total debt	0.16	0.21	0.15	0.12	0.23	0.21	0.25	0.20
Net home equity[b]	0.20	0.25	0.20	0.25	0.27	0.37	0.27	0.44
Gross assets	0.09	0.20	0.09	0.09	0.15	0.18	0.18	0.20
Net worth NWA[e]	0.09	0.20	0.09	0.10	0.15	0.17	0.18	0.20
Net worth NW	0.09	0.20	0.08	0.09	0.14	0.14	0.17	0.20
Memo:								
Median net worth NWA	0.09	0.02	0.04	0.12	0.15	0.15	0.04	0.20
Median net worth NW	0.00	0.00	0.01	0.11	0.00	0.00	0.00	0.21

Source: Authors' computations from the 1983, 2001, and 2013 Survey of Consumer Finances and the 1962 Survey of Financial Characteristics of Consumers.

a. Checking accounts, savings accounts, time deposits, money market funds, certificates of deposits, and the cash surrender value of life insurance. In 1962 and 1983, the category also includes IRA and Keogh accounts.

b. For the computation of net equity in owner-occupied housing, total mortgage debt is allocated proportionately between the gross value of owner-occupied housing and other real estate in both 1962 and 1983. In 2001 and 2013, mortgage debt on owner-occupied is computed directly from the survey data.

c. NWB is equal to net worth (NW) + consumer durables + household inventories.

d. IRAs, Keogh plans, 401(k) plans, the accumulated value of defined contribution pension plans, and other retirement accounts for 2001 and 2013 only.

e. NWA is equal to NW + vehicles.

0.29 in 1962 compared to 0.19 in 1983, and the ratio of net worth NW was 0.26 compared to 0.14 in 1983 (see Table 11.4). However, the ratio of median NWB and median net worth was about the same in the two years. Whereas the ratio of mean values between the poor and nonpoor was quite close in the two years for homes and durables plus inventories, the ratio was notably higher in 1962 for liquid assets (0.24 versus 0.09), unincorporated businesses (0.42 versus 0.17), investment real estate (0.18 versus 0.08), and financial assets (0.16 versus 0.02). The ratio of mean total debt was similar in the two years.

The homeownership rate among poor households dropped from 38 percent in 1983 to 33 percent in 2001, and the mean value of homes owned by home-owners below the poverty line relative to those above the poverty line fell from 57 to 38 percent (see Table 11.3). The share of poor households owning some form of liquid asset almost doubled over these years, and the average value of these accounts among account holders below the poverty line increased slightly from 0.13 to 0.16 relative to account holders above the poverty line. The proportion of poor households with a pension account declined from 15 to 11 percent over this period, and the average value among pension holders below the poverty line fell from 0.50 to 0.23 relative to those above the poverty line.

The percentage of the poor with a business and with investment real estate also dropped over these years, as did the mean value of these assets relative to the nonpoor, but the share of poor households with a financial asset rose some-what, as did its relative mean value. The share of poor households with mort-gage debt and other debt also rose between 1983 and 2001, despite the fall-off in the homeownership rate, but the mean value of mortgage debt among mort-gagees below the poverty line relative to those above the poverty line declined.

All in all, there was a relative decline in the mean net worth of poor households relative to nonpoor ones, from 0.14 in 1983 to 0.09 in 2001 (see Table 11.4). Declines in the relative value of owner-occupied housing and un-incorporated businesses were largely responsible for the overall drop in rela-tive net worth. The fall-off in relative net worth was particularly notable among middle-aged households. This also was largely due to relative declines in the value of homes and businesses.

As with income, there was a recovery in the relative net worth of poor households by 2013. The ratio of net worth between poor and nonpoor households increased to 0.14 in 2013, the same level as in 1983 (see Table 11.4).

This rebound was largely due to a rise in the relative value of net home equity, from 0.20 in 2001 to 0.27 in 2013, about the same value as in 1983. This was the case despite a small drop in the homeownership rate of the poor (there was a slightly larger decline among the nonpoor). The mean value of unincorporated businesses among poor households also showed a sharp rise relative to the nonpoor, from 0.06 in 2001 to 0.28 in 2013, and the ratio in liquid assets between the two groups also increased, from 0.11 to 0.16. Relative gains in mean net worth were particularly strong among the middle-aged (from 0.08 in 2001 to 0.17 in 2013) and among the elderly (from 0.09 to 0.20), due mainly to gains in the relative value of homes (particularly among the elderly), liquid assets, businesses, and financial assets. In contrast, the ratio in mean net worth declined among young households (from 0.20 to 0.14), due mainly to relative fall-offs in the value of homes, businesses, non-home real estate, and financial assets.[13]

Adding Pension and Social Security Wealth

The next two other forms of wealth added to the household portfolio in this analysis are defined benefit (DB) pension wealth and Social Security wealth.[14] These two forms differ from components of wealth shown in Table 11.3, since they have neither a market value nor a cash surrender value.

The valuation of defined benefit pension wealth and Social Security wealth is based on the present value of the expected income flows emanating from these sources.[15] Five percent of the poverty sample in 1983 reported receiving benefits from DB pension plans (both private and government pensions), compared to 12 percent of the nonpoor (see Table 11.5). Since 36 percent of poor households had at least one family member 65 or over, in contrast to 41 percent of the nonpoor, this result means that 15 percent of elderly poor families received some form of DB pension, in contrast to 28 percent of the nonpoor elderly. Only 7 percent of poor households reported that they expected some form of pension benefit when they retired, in comparison to 26 percent of families above the poverty line. Altogether, 11 percent of poor households were currently receiving or expected to receive DB pension benefits, in comparison to 37 percent of nonpoor households.[16] Thus, over three times the relative number of households above the poverty line reported some form of DB pension wealth.

Table 11.5. Pension and Social Security wealth by poverty status, 1983, 2001, and 2013 (all dollar figures are in current dollars)

	1983 Beneficiaries			2001 Beneficiaries			2013 Beneficiaries		
	Current	Future	All	Current	Future	All	Current	Future	All
I. Families below the Poverty Line									
A. DB pension wealth									
1. Proportion of total households with DB pension wealth	0.053	0.066	0.112	0.030	0.082	0.112	0.018	0.045	0.062
2. Mean value of DBWA (beneficiaries only)									
(a) r = 0.01	24,350	43,808	37,900						
(a) r = 0.02	21,785	31,772	29,485						
(a) r = 0.03	19,637	23,143	21,582						
3. Mean value of DBW (beneficiaries only)				24,061	57,858	48,755	43,442	59,803	55,220
B. Social Security Wealth									
1. Proportion of total households with Social Security wealth	0.189	0.635	0.812	0.174	0.667	0.842	0.155	0.718	0.874
2. Mean value of SSWA (beneficiaries only)									
(a) r = 0.01	66,908	54,811	65,584						
(a) r = 0.02	60,876	38,804	56,204						
(a) r = 0.03	55,687	28,006	49,067						
3. Mean value of SSW (beneficiaries only)				89,998	80,980	82,850	104,194	92,152	94,293

II. Families at or above the Poverty Line

A. DB pension wealth

	(1)	(2)	(3)	(4)	(5)	(6)	(7)	(8)	(9)
1. Proportion of total households with DB pension wealth	0.115	0.258	0.367	0.109	0.271	0.380	0.145	0.234	0.379
2. Mean value of DBWA (beneficiaries only)									
(a) $r = 0.01$	125,182	157,785	149,859						
(a) $r = 0.02$	114,418	127,401	123,783						
(a) $r = 0.03$	105,097	101,723	103,727						
3. Mean value of DBW (beneficiaries only)				169,635	139,465	148,099	242,445	172,573	199,262

B. Social Security Wealth

	(1)	(2)	(3)	(4)	(5)	(6)	(7)	(8)	(9)
1. Proportion of total households with Social Security wealth	0.144	0.848	0.958	0.199	0.776	0.976	0.237	0.739	0.976
2. Mean value of SSWA (beneficiaries only)									
(a) $r = 0.01$	87,304	81,436	87,463						
(a) $r = 0.02$	81,263	64,153	74,550						
(a) $r = 0.03$	75,853	51,404	64,593						
3. Mean value of SSW (beneficiaries only)				166,904	150,547	153,891	240,085	185,874	199,031

Source: Author's computations from the 1983, 2001, and 2013 Survey of Consumer Finances.

Age classification is based on the head of household.

The variable r indicates the discount rate used to compute DBWA and SSWA.

For 1983, separate computations of DBWA and SSWA are made for current and future beneficiaries. The column may not necessarily equal the sum of the first two because a single household may have both a current and future beneficiary.

In 2001 and 2013, DBW and SSW are computed on a household basis and the classification of the household by beneficiary status is based on the beneficiary status of the head of household.

Abbreviations: DBW and DBWA, defined benefit pension wealth; SSW and SSWA, Social Security wealth.

There was also a very large difference in the mean value of pension wealth between the poor and nonpoor. Among current beneficiaries only, the mean value of DB pension wealth at a 1 percent discount rate (r) was $24,000, compared to $125,000 among the nonpoor. Among future recipients, there was more than a threefold difference in mean pension wealth. Altogether, average pension wealth among both current and future beneficiaries was about four times greater among nonpoor than among poor households.

As the discount rate rises, the mean value of pension wealth declines for all groups. The depreciation of pension wealth with higher discount rates is far greater for pension wealth among future beneficiaries than among current beneficiaries because of the greater number of years to wait. Among poor families who expected pension benefits, the average value of their pension wealth declines by 47 percent as the discount rate increases from 1 to 3 percent. The overall ratio of mean pension wealth between all poor and all nonpoor pension wealth holders declines from 0.25 to 0.21 as the discount rate rises from 1 to 3 percent.

Social Security wealth was much more widely held among both poor and nonpoor families than was DB pension wealth. In 1983, 19 percent of poor households were currently receiving Social Security benefits. Moreover, in 64 percent of poor households, the husband or wife expected to receive Social Security benefits when retired. Altogether, 81 percent of the poor were either currently receiving or expected to receive Social Security benefits. Among families above the poverty line, 14 percent were currently receiving benefits, 85 percent were expecting benefits in the future, and 96 percent were either currently receiving or were expecting benefits. The ratio in Social Security coverage rates between the poverty sample and the nonpoverty sample was 0.85, considerably higher than the corresponding ratio in DB pension coverage rates.

The ratio of mean average Social Security wealth among beneficiaries below the poverty line to those above was also considerably higher than the corresponding ratio in DB pension wealth. Among current recipients, the ratio was 0.77 at a 1 percent discount rate, and among future beneficiaries it was 0.67. The ratio among both current and future beneficiaries together between the two samples was 0.75, and this ratio was relatively constant across discount rates.

Results for years 2001 and 2013 are also shown in Table 11.5.[17] In 2001, 11 percent of poor households were receiving or expected to receive DB pension benefits, the same as in 1983, and 38 percent of the nonpoor were current or future DB beneficiaries, about the same as in 1983. However, the ratio in mean DB pension wealth among all beneficiaries between the two groups was higher in 2001, 0.33, compared to a range of 0.21 to 0.25 in 1983. The Social Security coverage rate among poor households was 0.84 in 2001, in comparison to 0.81 in 1983, and that among the nonpoor was 0.98, compared to 0.96 in 1983. The ratio in mean Social Security wealth among both current and future beneficiaries between poor and nonpoor households was lower at 0.54 in 2001, in contrast to about 0.75 in 1983.

By 2013, only 6 percent of poor households were receiving or expected to receive DB pension benefits, much lower than in 2013. This result is mainly a reflection of the gradual disappearance of DB plans over these years for lower earning workers.[18] In contrast, 38 percent of nonpoor households were current or future DB beneficiaries, almost exactly the same as in 2001. The ratio in mean DB pension wealth among all beneficiaries between the poor and nonpoor groups was 0.28, lower than in 2001. The Social Security coverage rate among poor households was 87 percent in 2013, compared to 84 percent in 2001, and the coverage rate among the nonpoor was 98 percent, exactly the same as in 2001. The ratio in mean Social Security wealth among all beneficiaries between poor and nonpoor households slipped to 0.47 in 2013 from 0.54 in 2001.

Table 11.6 calculates augmented wealth for both poor and nonpoor households, where augmented wealth is defined as the sum of marketable wealth, DB pension wealth, and Social Security wealth. The ratio in mean DB pension wealth between all families (including both beneficiaries and nonbeneficiaries) below and above the poverty line varied between 0.07 and 0.08 in 1983, depending on the discount rate. The ratio in average Social Security wealth between the two groups varied between 0.63 and 0.64, considerably higher than the ratio of pension or marketable wealth. The addition of average pension wealth to the household portfolio reduced the ratio of mean wealth between the poor and the nonpoor population from 0.19 to about 0.16. The addition of Social Security wealth had the opposite effect, raising the ratio of average wealth between the two groups to about 0.29. The total

Table 11.6. Mean wealth holdings by poverty status and age, with pension and Social Security wealth included, 1983, 2001, and 2013 (all dollar figures are in current dollars)

| | All Ages | | Ratio: Below / Above Poverty Line | | |
Component	Below Poverty Line	Above Poverty Line	All Ages	Under 65	65 and over
I. 1983					
1. Marketable net worth (NWB)	30,302	163,062	0.19	0.25	0.12
2. Discount rate r – 0.01					
(a) Pension wealth (DBWA)	5,517	69,208	0.08	0.09	0.03
(b) Social Security wealth (SSWA)	63,501	100,151	0.63	0.66	0.43
(c) NWB + DBWA	35,719	232,270	0.15	0.17	0.10
(d) Augmented wealth AWB = NWB + DBWA + SSWA	99,220	332,421	0.30	0.34	0.17
3. Discount rate r – 0.02					
(a) Pension wealth (DBWA)	4,245	54,998	0.08	0.09	0.03
(b) Social Security wealth (SSWA)	53,254	83,790	0.64	0.69	0.44
(c) NWB + DBWA	34,447	218,060	0.16	0.18	0.10
(d) AWB = NWB + DBWA + SSWA	87,701	301,850	0.29	0.34	0.17
4. Discount rate r – 0.03					
(a) Pension wealth (DBWA)	3,302	45,428	0.07	0.09	0.03
(b) Social Security wealth (SSWA)	45,638	71,419	0.64	0.71	0.44
(c) NWB + DBWA	33,504	208,490	0.16	0.18	0.10
(d) AWB = NWB + DBWA + SSWA	79,142	279,909	0.28	0.33	0.17
II. 2001					
1. Marketable net worth (NW)	36,787	432,460	0.09	0.08	0.09
(a) Pension wealth (DBW)	5,478	56,217	0.10	0.13	0.04
(b) Social Security wealth (SSW)	69,724	150,148	0.46	0.46	0.47
(c) NW + DBW	42,265	488,677	0.09	0.08	0.09
(d) AW = NW + DBW + SSW	111,989	638,825	0.18	0.17	0.11
III. 2013					
1. Marketable net worth (NW)	81,975	576,391	0.14	0.13	0.20
(a) Pension wealth (DBW)	3,450	75,471	0.05	0.07	0.02
(b) Social Security wealth (SSW)	82,395	194,325	0.42	0.48	0.28
(c) NW + DBW	85,425	651,862	0.13	0.13	0.19
(d) AW = NW + DBW + SSW	167,819	846,187	0.20	0.20	0.20

Source: Author's computations from the 1983, 1992, 2001, and 2013 Survey of Consumer Finances. Age classification is based on the head of household.

effect of adding both types of wealth to the household portfolio was thus equalizing.

The disparity in DB wealth and Social Security wealth between poor households and those above the poverty line was considerably less for households under age 65 than for the elderly. Among households under age 65, the addition of these two components to the household portfolio narrowed the gap in relative wealth between the two groups from 0.25 to a range of 0.32 to 0.34. Among the elderly, the gap was narrowed from 0.12 to only 0.16 or 0.17. Thus, the equalizing effect of retirement wealth was greater among younger households than among elderly ones.

In 2001, the poor to nonpoor ratio in mean net worth among all age groups was 0.09, compared to 0.19 for NWB in 1983. However, the difference was primarily due to the exclusion of consumer durables and inventories from net worth. The ratio in pension wealth was slightly higher in 2001, 0.10 compared to 0.07 or 0.08 in 1983, but the ratio of Social Security wealth was considerably lower, 0.46 versus 0.64. Adding pension wealth to net worth had very little effect on the poor to nonpoor ratio, whereas it reduced the ratio in 1983. The addition of Social Security wealth raised the ratio of average wealth between the two groups from 0.09 to 0.18, about the same extent as in 1983.

As in 1983, the gap in DB wealth between the poor and nonpoor was smaller among the nonelderly than among the elderly, while, unlike 1983, the differential was about the same for the nonelderly and elderly. Among households under age 65, the addition of DB and Social Security wealth to the household portfolio increased the ratio in relative wealth between the two groups from 0.08 to 0.17, about the same degree as in 1983. However, among the elderly, the ratio rose by only 0.02, much less than in 1983. As in 1983, the equalizing effect of adding pension and Social Security wealth was larger among younger than elderly households.

By 2013 the ratio in net worth between the poor and nonpoor ratio rose to 0.14 from 0.09 in 2001. On the other hand, the ratio in pension wealth dropped in half, from 0.10 to 0.05, and the ratio of Social Security wealth also fell, from 0.46 to 0.42. Adding DB wealth to net worth, as in 2001, did little to alter the poor to nonpoor ratio. The addition of Social Security, on the other hand, raised the wealth ratio from 0.14 to 0.20, about the same degree as in 2001.

Alternative Poverty Rate Calculations

Alternative definitions of the poverty threshold can affect estimates of the poverty rate. The official poverty rate measure is based exclusively on household income. Yet, poverty as a concept should ideally reflect deprivation in the total economic resources required for a minimal level of well-being. This analysis proposes alternative measures of poverty based on both the income and wealth at a family's disposal. This joint criterion gives a better gauge of available resources than one based exclusively on income.

Two techniques are used to compute alternative poverty rates. The first is to convert wealth holdings into an annuity, or income flow, at a given interest rate. For this purpose, it makes sense to use only financial resources, defined as net worth less home equity, since other components of wealth directly serve consumption needs. Moreover, it is assumed that the annuity is paid out like a bond coupon, so that the capital value of net worth remains unchanged. Three alternative interest rates are used in the calculation: 0.03, 0.05, and 0.07.

In Table 11.7, the first line of Panels A, B, and C shows what the poverty rate would be if an annuity computed from financial resources was added to family income as calculated by the census bureau (if the official poverty threshold remained unaltered). This procedure raises measured income and therefore lowers the measured poverty rate. However, there is some double-counting involved since financial resources already produce income in the form of rent, interest, dividends, and unincorporated business profits. Therefore, in line 2, property income is subtracted from the "gross" annuity value. Another source of income not captured by money income is imputed rent to owner-occupied housing. The rationale is that owners of homes often pay less than tenants for comparable housing because of the equity they have accumulated and the capital gains from owning their own homes, and this difference should be included as part of the homeowner's income. Gross imputed rent is estimated as an annuity flow from the gross value of owner-occupied housing (see line 3). Net imputed rent in the 1983 calculations is defined as gross imputed rent less actual payments for mortgage interest, homeowner insurance, and property taxes (line 4).[19] For 2001 and 2013, the return on net home equity is instead used to measure net imputed rent. In line 5, the poverty rate calculation is based on the sum of family income, the gross annuity from financial resources, and gross imputed rent, while in line 6 the corresponding net values are used.

The calculations are quite revealing. At a 3 percent interest rate, overall poverty rates for 1983 were relatively unaffected by expanding the definition of income. The average annuity from financial resources amounted to 10 percent of the average family income of the poor in 1983, and the poverty rate based on the sum of family income and the gross annuity was 94 percent of the rate based on family income alone (line A.1). Average (gross) imputed rent to owner-occupied housing equaled 7 percent of average family income in 1983, and the adjusted poverty based on the sum of family income and gross imputed rent was 94 percent of the income-based rate (line A.3). Expanding income to include both the gross annuity and gross imputed rent resulted in a 10 percent reduction in the poverty rate from the baseline rate (line A.5). However, the reduction in measured poverty rates was considerably greater for elderly families because of their high homeownership rate and a relatively high number with sizable net worth. Expanding income to include both the gross annuity and gross imputed rent resulted in a 19 percent reduction in the measured poverty rate among elderly families. However, when the net annuity from financial resources and net imputed rent were used instead of their gross values, the measured poverty rate among the elderly declined by only 11 percent (line A.6).

At a 5 percent interest rate, the average annuity from financial resources amounted to 16 percent of average family income among the poor in 1983, and average gross imputed rent to 11 percent. Including both gross annuities and gross imputed rent caused a 16 percent reduction in measured poverty, while including the corresponding net values resulted in a 10 percent reduction. Among the elderly population, the reduction in measured poverty was even more substantial, at 41 percent and 22 percent, respectively. At a 7 percent interest rate, the gross annuity from financial resources equaled 23 percent and gross imputed rent 16 percent of family income among the poor. The reduction in the measured poverty rate from including gross annuities and gross imputed rent was 18 percent, and the reduction from including their net counterparts was 13 percent. For the elderly, the corresponding reductions were 44 percent and 33 percent.[20]

Results for 1962 are even more telling. At a 3 percent interest rate, expanding income to include gross annuity flows resulted in a 13 percent reduction in

Table 11.7. Alternative poverty rate calculations based on family income and wealth, 1962, 1983, 2001, and 2013 (poverty rates relative to the income poverty rate)

Component	1962 All Ages	1983 Under 65	1983 65 and Over	1983 All Ages	2001 Under 65	2001 65 and Over	2001 All Ages	2013 Under 65	2013 65 and Over	2013 All Ages
I. Family Income (Y)	1.000	1.000	1.000	1.000	1.000	1.000	1.000	1.000	1.000	1.000
II. Family Income (Y) + annuitized wealth										
A. Interest rate of 0.03										
1. Y + gross annuity from FR	0.872	0.967	0.840	0.941	0.980	0.880	0.958	0.988	0.912	0.975
2. Y + net annuity from FR	0.909	0.975	0.885	0.957	0.992	1.019	0.997	1.021	0.954	1.010
3. Y + gross imputed rent	0.941	0.945	0.908	0.937	0.957	0.792	0.921	0.950	0.709	0.908
4. Y + net imputed rent[a]		0.993	0.961	0.986	0.967	0.798	0.930	0.975	0.717	0.930
5. Y + gross annuity from FR + gross rent	0.814	0.928	0.809	0.904	0.923	0.692	0.873	0.949	0.657	0.898
6. Y + net annuity from FR + net rent		0.969	0.885	0.952	0.945	0.819	0.918	0.995	0.694	0.943
B. Interest rate of 0.05										
1. Y + gross annuity from FR	0.805	0.941	0.824	0.916	0.969	0.843	0.942	1.002	0.890	0.982
2. Y + net annuity from FR	0.827	0.940	0.822	0.917	0.979	0.958	0.975	1.025	0.927	1.007
3. Y + gross imputed rent	0.909	0.917	0.798	0.890	0.924	0.684	0.872	0.919	0.622	0.867
4. Y + net imputed rent[a]		0.970	0.943	0.964	0.947	0.689	0.891	0.954	0.645	0.900
5. Y + gross annuity from FR + gross rent	0.736	0.902	0.592	0.838	0.899	0.607	0.836	0.936	0.600	0.877
6. Y + net annuity from FR + net rent		0.935	0.779	0.903	0.927	0.671	0.871	0.982	0.651	0.925

C. Interest rate of 0.07

1. Y + gross annuity from FR	0.768	0.919	0.738	0.882	0.958	0.812	0.927	1.005	0.874	0.982
2. Y + net annuity from FR	0.786	0.919	0.747	0.884	0.967	0.897	0.952	1.022	0.905	1.002
3. Y + gross imputed rent	0.872	0.892	0.745	0.859	0.902	0.639	0.845	0.894	0.545	0.833
4. Y + net imputed rent[a]		0.951	0.886	0.936	0.933	0.648	0.871	0.944	0.588	0.882
5. Y + gross annuity from FR+ gross rent	0.691	0.886	0.561	0.819	0.865	0.555	0.798	0.912	0.526	0.845
6. Y + net annuity from FR + net rent		0.915	0.674	0.865	0.899	0.603	0.835	0.979	0.591	0.911

III. Joint income and wealth criterion

1. $Y < Y_P$ and $NW < NW_{.5}$		0.871	0.768	0.850	0.894	0.731	0.859	0.900	0.601	0.848
2. $Y < Y_P$ and $NW < NW_{.25}$		0.662	0.504	0.629	0.663	0.407	0.607	0.544	0.240	0.491
3. $Y < Y_P$ and $NW < NW_{.20}$		0.604	0.473	0.577	0.568	0.306	0.512	0.362	0.092	0.315

Source: Author's computations from the 1983, 1992, 2001, and 2013 Survey of Consumer Finances.

Age classification is based on the head of household.

Financial resources (FR) = NW (net worth) – home equity.

$\bar{Y}_P$ = (official) income poverty line.

$NW_{.5}$ = median net worth.

$NW_{.25}$ = 25th percentile of net worth.

$NW_{.20}$ = 20th percentile of net worth.

a. For 2001 and 2013, I use net home equity in the calculation instead of gross home value.

the measured poverty rate among all households whereas including net annuity flows caused a 9 percent decline, both of which were greater than in
1983. Adding gross annuity flows and gross imputed rent reduced the measured poverty rate by 19 percent, also considerably greater than in 1983. The
reduction in the poverty rate from including gross annuity flows and gross
imputed rent was 26 percent at a 5 percent interest rate and 31 percent at a
7 percent interest rate.

The 2001 results were roughly comparable to those for 1983. At a 5 percent
interest rate, the reduction in the poverty rate among the nonelderly from
including gross annuities and gross rent was 10 percent, the same as in 1983,
and the decline from including net annuities and net rent was 7 percent,
about the same as in 1983. Among the elderly, the reduction in measured
poverty was 39 percent from including gross flows in 2001, compared to
41 percent in 1983, and 33 percent when net flows are added in comparison to
22 percent in 1983. The 2013 results, in contrast, show a much smaller reduction in measured poverty among the nonelderly, which reflects the financial
collapse of the Great Recession. At a 5 percent interest rate, the inclusion of
gross flows yielded only a 6 percent decrease, compared to 10 percent in
2001, and the addition of net flows caused a 2 percent decline, compared
to 7 percent in 2001. Among elderly households, results were very similar in
2013 and 2001, because the elderly were more immune from the deleterious
effects of the financial meltdown.

The second technique used to compute an alternative poverty rate was
based on a joint threshold of family income and family net worth. The three
thresholds used for household wealth in this analysis were the median of the
overall distribution of wealth; the twenty-fifth percentile; and the twentieth
percentile. Poverty is defined as inadequate income *and* wealth. Alternative
poverty rates calculated on the basis of the joint threshold were considerably
lower than those based on the census bureau's definition of family income
alone (see Table 11.7, Panel III). A joint criterion based on income and median household wealth resulted in a 15 percent reduction in the measured
poverty rate in 1983; one based on the twenty-fifth percentile of household
wealth caused a 37 percent reduction; and one based on the twentieth wealth
percentile decreased the poverty rate by 42 percent. The reduction in measured poverty was considerably greater for elderly households than nonelderly ones because of the former's greater relative wealth.

Who Are the Asset Poor? Levels, Trends, and Composition, 1983–2013

The robust growth in household wealth from 1983 to 2007 created the impression that American households did well, particularly in terms of wealth acquisition. This was decidedly not the case for many households. Moreover, asset poverty worsened even further over the Great Recession. Table 11.7 introduced a joint income and wealth criterion to measure the poverty rate. This section develops the concept of "asset poverty" as a measure of economic hardship, distinct from and complementary to the more commonly used concept of "income poverty."

Asset poverty measures the extent to which American households lack a stock of assets that is sufficient to sustain a basic needs level of consumption during temporary hard times. I should emphasize that this concept of poverty, based on only the extent of asset holdings, does not take into account the income level of the household. The central question is whether the assets held by the household enable it to survive at a minimum level of consumption for a temporary period should other sources of income—particularly, earnings—be unavailable during this period. As such, this measure complements standard measures of income poverty. Income poverty measures identify poor households as those whose annual income fails to support some socially determined minimum level of consumption, abstracting from the household's assets; the asset poverty measure analogously identifies the poor as households whose wealth or assets are insufficient to enable them to survive at this same minimum level, abstracting from the income available to the family.

After a discussion of poverty measurement in general, this chapter focuses on the official U.S. income poverty indicator that serves as the basis for assessing the status of the nation's least well-off citizens. Four alternative asset poverty measures employ alternative concepts of wealth, but use the same poverty cutoff thresholds. This analysis also measures asset poverty by employing an absolute dollar cutoff, irrespective of family size. These measures reveal that in the face of the large growth in overall assets in the United States, at least from 1983 to 2007, the level of asset poverty was actually rising. And during the Great Recession period asset poverty spiked sharply upward.

The analysis in this chapter provides details on asset poverty in 2001 for the entire population, as well as for subgroups of the population distinguished by race, age, education, tenure status, and family type. These details support an investigation into trends in asset poverty over the entire 1983 to 2013 period. Trends in asset poverty are compared to those of income poverty, differences in the prevalence and composition of asset poverty and income poverty are explored, and a joint measure of income and asset poverty is developed.

The Concept of Poverty: Resources and Needs

Although poverty reduction is a universal goal for nations and international organizations, there is no commonly accepted way of identifying who is poor. Some argue for a multidimensional poverty concept that reflects the many aspects of well-being. In this context, people deprived of social contact (with friends and families) are described as being socially isolated, and hence poor in this dimension. Similarly, people living in squalid housing are viewed as "housing poor," and people with health deficits as "health poor." Economists tend to prefer a concept of hardship that reflects the resources available to families, or their "economic position" or "economic well-being," somehow measured. Income is typically taken as the measure of available resources, which is then compared to the income needs of the family. This economic concept underlies the official U.S. poverty measure and the proposed revision of it based on the National Research Council (NRC) Panel Report.[21]

Virtually all measures of economic poverty identify poor families as those whose economic position (defined in terms of command over resources) falls below some minimally acceptable level. There are two requirements for such a measure—a precise definition of "economic resources" and a measure of the minimum acceptable level of well-being (or "needs") in terms that are commensurate with the concept of "resources."[22] Such a measure does not impose any norm on people's preferences among goods and services (such as for necessities versus luxuries) or between work and leisure. Moreover, it allows for differentiation according to household size and composition, and it enables intertemporal variability in access to these resources and (in principle, at least) one's ability to "enjoy" the fruits of the resources (given, for example, one's health status). It does, however, link "access to resources" to "economic position" or "well-being," hence excluding many factors that may affect "utility" but are not captured by "command over resources."

Within this economic perspective, there are substantial differences regarding the specific economic well-being indicators believed to best identify those whose economic position lies below some minimally acceptable level. For example, the official U.S. poverty measure relies on the *annual cash income* of a family, and compares this to some minimum annual income standard or "poverty line." An alternative—and equally legitimate—position is that the level of annual consumption better reflects a family's access to resources, or that a measure of a family's income-generating capacity is a more comprehensive indicator.[23]

Official U.S. Poverty and Median Incomes, 1983–2013

The official definition of poverty in the United States has played a special role in the development of the nation's social policy. A case can be made that one of the most important contributions of the 1960s-era War on Poverty was the establishment of an official national "poverty line." This official measure (including the NRC proposed revision of it) has several distinct characteristics. First, it is a measure of "income" poverty, the purpose of which is to identify families that do not have sufficient annual cash income (in some cases, including close substitutes to cash income such as food stamps) to meet what is judged to be their annual basic need. As such, it compares two numbers for each living unit—the level of annual income and the level of income that a unit of its size and composition requires in order to secure a minimum level of consumption. By relying solely on annual income as the indicator of resources, this measure ignores many potential sources of utility or welfare (such as social inclusion, or "security") that may be weakly tied to annual income flows. Second, distinct from the measures of relative poverty so common in Europe (that is, poverty lines defined relative to median income), the U.S. indicator is an absolute poverty measure. As a result, decreases in inequality are reflected in reductions in poverty only if families with incomes below the absolute income cutoff are raised above it. A growing gap between families with the least money income and the rest of society need not affect the official poverty rate.

Table 11.8. Official income poverty rates for families and median family income, 1983–2013

Year	Official Poverty Rate for Families (percent)	Median Family Income[a] (in thousands, 2013 dollars)
1983	12.3	54.6
1989	10.3	62.1
1992	11.9	59.5
1995	10.8	61.6
1998	10.0	66.7
2001	9.2	67.6
2004	10.2	66.7
2007	9.8	68.9
2010	11.8	64.4
2013	11.2	63.8

Source: U.S. Census Bureau, available at https://www2.census.gov/programs-surveys/cps/tables/time-series/historical-poverty-people/hstpov4.xls and https://www2.census.gov/programs-surveys/cps/tables/time-series/historical-income-families/f05.xls , accessed April 12, 2017.

a. Based on the Consumer Price Index CPI-U-RS deflator.

The economic resource concept on which the U.S. measure rests (annual cash income) has been subject to criticism. Similarly, the arbitrary nature of the denominator of the poverty ratio—the minimum income needs indicator—has also been criticized.[24] Given its conceptual basis and the crude empirical evidence on which the dollar cutoffs rest, the U.S. official poverty line is essentially an arbitrary construct. Finally, adjustments in the poverty line to account for differences in family size and composition also rest on weak conceptual and empirical foundations.[25]

In spite of the criticism, the official U.S. poverty measure provides a baseline against which to judge estimates of asset poverty. Table 11.8 presents official figures on the percent of U.S. *families* who were poor over the 1983–2013 period for the years corresponding to the asset poverty measure used here, together with official figures on median family income in constant dollars for those years.

Both the poverty and median income indicators of well-being closely followed macroeconomic conditions since the beginning of the 1980s. The income poverty rate for families stood at over 12 percent at the end of the severe recession of the early 1980s.[26] During the several years of economic growth following that recession, poverty fell steadily, reaching a level of 10.3 percent by 1989. By 1992, family poverty had again risen as the recession early in that decade took its toll. However, in the prolonged expansion of the 1990s, income poverty again fell, to 10.8 percent in 1995, 10 percent in 1998, and to its lowest level since the 1970s—9.2 percent—in 2001. The poverty rate remained low in 2007, at 9.8 percent, but then shot up over the Great Recession to 11.8 percent in 2010. By 2013 it had declined a bit, to 11.2 percent.

This pattern parallels changes in median family income over this period, which grew from $54,600 (in 2013 dollars) in 1983 to $62,100 in 1989 before falling to $59,500 during the recession of the early 1990s. Persistent growth during the 1990s and early and the first decade of the twenty-first century led to growth in median family income to $67,600 in 2001 and then to $68,900 in 2007. The Great Recession caused median family income to fall, descending to $64,400 in 2010 and $63,800 in 2013.

Asset Poverty: Concepts

The definition and measurement of asset poverty used here views families lacking a "safety-net" composed of asset holdings to be in a vulnerable economic position.[27] If alternative sources of income support such as the labor market or public transfers are not available, only assets are left to avoid destitution. A household with insufficient assets to enable it to meet basic needs for a period of time (three months) is asset poor. This measure does not consider the annual income position of the person, and hence serves to complement indicators of poverty based on income flows alone.

A more demanding measure than either an income or an asset poverty measure would consider both income and assets in defining poverty (see Table 11.7). Such a joint income / asset measure might label as poor households with *neither* income *nor* assets sufficient to sustain a minimum level of consumption for a given period of time.[28] Using this measure, households are considered poor if they have neither annual income in excess of the poverty line nor assets in excess of 0.25 of the poverty line.[29]

A household or a person is defined as being asset poor if access to *wealth-type resources* is insufficient to meet *basic needs* for some limited *period of time*. Clearly, this definition leaves open a number of issues on which judgments are required.

With regard to "basic needs," I begin with the assumption that household needs can be met by access to financial resources, such as income or real assets (for example, homes), that can be valued in monetary units. Clearly, there is no commonly accepted standard for measuring basic needs, as the variety of poverty thresholds used across countries and research analyses varies widely. As indicated earlier, some measure the level of minimum adequacy by referring to norms existing within a nation at a point in time, such as median income. Others use professionally established minimum consumption standards. My definition of asset poverty requires one to make a choice of a standard for minimally acceptable needs.

With regard to time period, the poverty thresholds indicate the level of basic resource needs for households of various sizes measured over the course of a year; it is an annual "need-for-resources" concept. When this standard is compared to the income flow over the course of a year, an income poverty measure is obtained. For the purpose here, the questions are: How can these annual thresholds be used to indicate the adequacy of a stock of wealth-type resources? How much of an asset stock should a household have in order to meet this annual level of basic needs, were other resources not available. Over what period should asset holdings be expected to provide a safety net?

The third issue concerns the concept of wealth that is employed in measuring asset poverty. The following require consideration: Should housing equity be included in the definition of assets? Should families be expected to sell their homes in order to obtain resources that are sufficient to provide a protective cushion for periods of inadequate income? How should assets in the form of expected pensions or other forms of retirement saving be handled? Should families be expected to sacrifice these provisions for future security in order to support current needs? And finally, in measuring available asset holdings, how should indebtedness be treated? Are net asset stocks the appropriate measure?

Measures of Asset Poverty

On the basis of these considerations, I propose and apply two primary measures of asset poverty[30] based on the following choices.

First, although there is no commonly accepted standard for the minimum amount of financial resources that are required to meet needs, I use the family-size conditioned poverty thresholds proposed by a National Academy of Science panel.[31] The panel recommended that the thresholds should represent a dollar amount for food, clothing, shelter (including utilities), and a small additional amount to allow for other common, everyday needs (such as household supplies, personal care, and nonwork-related transportation). I employ a threshold developed for a reference family consisting of two adults and two children using data from the U.S. Consumer Expenditure Survey, and then adjust this threshold to reflect the needs of different family sizes and geographic differences in the cost of living. These thresholds are based on the three-parameter equivalence scale for reflecting the needs of families of various sizes and structures.[32] The 2001 threshold for a reference family of two adults with two children was \$17,653, which compares with the 2001 official income threshold of \$17,960.

Second, it is necessary to stipulate a period of time over which assets should be expected to cushion income losses. I propose the following standard: a family should have an asset cushion that would allow its members to meet their basic needs—the threshold poverty line—for three months (25 percent of a year), should all other sources of support fail. Consistent with this standard, I compare the stock of asset holdings at a point in time to 25 percent of the annual family-size specific poverty threshold. Hence, a four-person family would have asset needs equal to \$4,413 (0.25 × \$17,653). With this standard, a family of four that held net assets of less than \$4,413 in 2001 would be declared "asset poor." Similarly, a one-person family with assets below \$2,303 or a six-person family with assets below \$6,229 would likewise fall below the basic needs threshold. Again, note that no other sources of resource support, such as earnings from work or other forms of income, are considered in measuring asset poverty.

Finally, it is necessary to stipulate the definition of "wealth" that is used to construct the asset poverty measure. The primary measure of assets used here is *net worth*, defined as the current value of all marketable or fungible assets less the current value of debts.[33] I take this net worth concept as the primary measure of wealth as it reflects wealth as a store of value that can be liquidated in a short period of time, and therefore is a source of potential consumption. This concept best reflects the level of well-being associated with a family's holdings; thus it includes only assets that can be readily monetized.

This asset poverty measure is viewed as an indicator of the long-run economic security of families. A portfolio of assets as complete as net worth is a point-in-time stock that reflects prior saving and other asset accumulation decisions taken over a long period of time. The issue here is whether these prior decisions have provided a sufficient cushion to enable a family to support itself should alternative sources of support, such as earnings, fail. Relative to standard measures of income poverty that compare a single year's flow of income to a basic needs standard, this measure of asset poverty reflects the long-term ability of a family to meet a minimum consumption standard.

The second main measure of wealth is based on a more restrictive definition of assets, namely *liquid resources,* defined as cash or financial assets that can be easily monetized, excluding IRAs and pension assets.[34] This measure strips away from net worth the equity position in housing and real estate, the cash surrender value of defined contribution pension plans, net equity in unincorporated businesses, and equity in trust funds. It also ignores all forms of debt, including mortgage and consumer debt. This measure is appropriately thought of as an "emergency fund availability" indicator of a family's ability to "get by."[35]

Given these assumptions, the two main standards of asset poverty are (1) A family is asset poor if its net worth is less than 25 percent of the poverty line for families of their size and composition—that is, *net worth < 0.25 family-specific poverty line;* (2) A family is asset poor if its liquid resources are less than 25 percent of the poverty line for families of their size and composition—that is, *liquid resources < 0.25 family-specific poverty line.*

I also use two other definitions of asset poverty in Table 11.9 for comparison. The first of these is financial resources *(net worth less home equity)* less than 25 percent of the poverty line for families of their size and composition. In this definition, it is presumed that it would be untoward to require a household to sell its home in order to secure the financial resources necessary to tide them over a period without income sources. The second of these is an "absolute" standard, defined as liquid resources less than $5,000. This index is, in a sense, an emergency threshold to meet immediate consumption needs.

As discussed earlier, evidence is also presented on the level of poverty when households are both income poor and asset poor, a measure of joint income / asset poverty. In this measure, the income poverty measure is combined with the asset poverty measure based on net worth. By this definition,

Table 11.9. Asset poverty rates by definition and year for households, 1983–2013 (figures are in percentage)

Year	Net Worth < .25 Poverty Line	Financial Resources < .25 Poverty Line	Liquid Resources < .25 Poverty Line	Liquid Resources < $5,000
1983	22.4	36.9	33.2	40.1
1989	24.7	37.3	36.4	39.2
1992	24.0	37.9	37.5	40.5
1995	25.3	40.0	43.8	51.5
1998	25.5	36.8	39.7	45.3
2001	24.5	40.9	37.5	42.8
2004	24.7	43.6	42.9	47.5
2007	25.2	41.7	42.9	45.7
2010	30.4	46.3	47.9	50.2
2013	31.2	46.8	47.1	48.7

Source: Author's calculations from the 1983, 1989, 1992, 1995, 1998, 2001, 2004, 2007, 2010, and 2013 Survey of Consumer Finances.

a family is joint income / asset poor if it has neither the income necessary to meet the income poverty standard nor the assets necessary to meet the net worth asset poverty standard.

Asset Poverty Trends, 1983–2013

The overall estimates of the level of asset poverty are shown in Table 11.9 for selected years over the period 1983 to 2013 (also see Figure 11.1). As expected, the most inclusive measure of assets yields the lowest poverty rates. The values range from a low of 22.4 percent in 1983 to 31.2 percent in 2013. Subsequent to the recession of the early 1980s, net worth poverty rose by about 2 percentage points by 1989, then fell slightly during the recession of the early 1990s, and again rose during the prolonged period of growth during the late 1990s. By this standard, the level of asset poverty in 1998 was the highest level recorded over the 1983–2001 period. By 2001, net worth poverty fell to 24.5 percent. Then, despite the strong growth in median net worth, asset poverty actually inched up to 25.2 percent in 2007. Then the Great Recession hit and asset poverty spiked to 30.4 percent in 2010. It increased a bit more after that and reached 31.2 percent in 2013, its high point over the thirty-year period.

When the liquid assets concept is used as the definition of resources, the asset poverty rate increases substantially. By this measure, asset poverty was

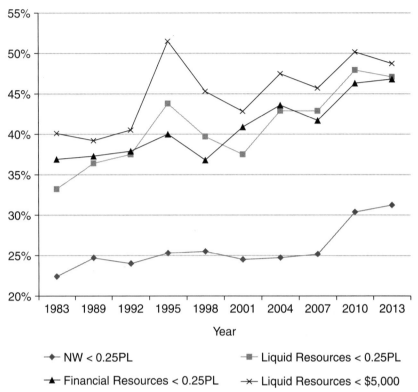

Figure 11.1. Asset Poverty Rates by Definition and Year for Households, 1983–2013

lowest in 1983 at 33 percent, and reached nearly 44 percent in 1995. From the low levels during the 1980s, liquid asset poverty increased substantially in the 1990s. Even at the end of the 1990s growth period, liquid asset poverty stood at nearly 40 percent. The rate fell slightly to 38 percent by 2001. However, once again it rose during the early and mid-2000s, to 43 percent in 2007, and then increased sharply to 48 percent in 2010, though in this case it remitted a bit to 47 percent in 2013. The other two measures show roughly the same time trends.

For all four measures, asset poverty in 2007 exceeded both its 1983 level and its level during the recession of the early 1990s. Moreover, all four measures show a sharp jump in asset poverty between 2007 and 2010. Interestingly, the time pattern of asset poverty rates does not closely reflect macroeconomic conditions, and does not parallel that of income poverty or median family income.

The Prevalence of Asset Poverty by Demographic Group

Table 11.10 presents descriptive statistics on asset poverty for different demographic and labor market groups in 1983, 1992, 2001, and the final year for which data are available, 2013. The population groupings that are discussed include divisions by race / ethnicity, age of family head, education of family head, housing tenure status, and marital status and presence of children.

The racial disparities in poverty rates indicated in the table are enormous, with the asset poverty rates for minorities (blacks / Hispanics) more than twice those for whites.[36] On the basis of the net worth measure of assets together with the three-month cushion criterion, asset poverty rates for whites ranged from 17 percent to 19 percent over the 1983–2001 period, while the range for blacks / Hispanics was from 43 to 47 percent (also see Figure 11.2). In 2013, the asset poverty rate for whites was 23 percent compared to 55 percent for minorities. Using the liquid asset measure of assets, from 1983 to 2001 about 30 percent of white households were in asset poverty, while about 62 percent of black / Hispanic households had inadequate liquid financial reserves to tide them over a three-month period at a level of living equal to the poverty line. In 2013 the respective figures were 38 and 72 percent.

On the basis of the life cycle model of saving behavior, young people borrow to support consumption while investing in human capital, while those in their years of high earnings save for retirement years.[37] Consistent with this framework, we would expect high asset poverty rates for families headed by a young person and low asset poverty rates for those at or beyond their peak earnings years. As shown in Table 11.10, the pattern seen here is consistent with the life cycle framework (also see Figure 11.3). Irrespective of the measure used, households headed by people younger than 25 had remarkably high asset poverty rates—for example, in 2001 more than 72 percent did not have net worth or liquid assets sufficient to support poverty line consumption for a three-month period. Both of these asset poverty rates fell monotonically with age. For households headed by a person aged

Table 11.10. Asset poverty rates for households by demographic group, 1983–2013 (figures are in percentage)

Grouping	Category	Net Worth < .25 Poverty Line					Liquid Resources < .25 Poverty Line				
		1983	1992	2001	2013	Change, 1983–2013	1983	1992	2001	2013	Change, 1983–2013
	All households	22.4	24.0	24.5	31.2	8.8	33.2	37.5	37.5	47.1	13.9
Race	Whites	17.1	19.1	18.0	22.9	5.8	26.9	29.8	30.4	38.2	11.3
	Blacks / Hispanics	47.4	43.2	46.7	54.7	7.3	63.8	66.8	62.1	72.4	8.6
Age	Less than 25	55.6	66.9	72.1	73.5	17.9	56.1	70.3	72.3	72.8	16.7
	25–34	36.3	41.8	44.3	54.8	18.5	44.8	49.4	51.5	58.2	13.4
	35–49	17.7	21.7	22.5	35.0	17.3	30.9	39.2	39.3	52.8	21.9
	50–61	13.8	13.9	13.7	23.6	9.8	26.2	26.2	28.7	45.8	19.6
	62 or older	9.9	10.6	10.8	13.7	3.8	22.5	26.7	24.0	32.3	9.8
Education	Less than HS graduate	29.8	37.6	40.1	47.8	18.0	50.0	62.8	60.1	76.5	26.5
	HS graduate	20.9	26.4	27.8	35.2	14.3	33.6	40.9	45.8	58.5	24.9
	College 1–3	25.5	20.8	25.4	36.3	10.8	31.1	33.7	36.8	51.0	19.9
	College graduate	11.3	14.0	11.0	17.9	6.6	11.8	18.5	15.8	23.2	11.4
Tenure	Homeowner	3.6	4.7	5.8	10.7	7.1	22.6	25.4	24.7	34.3	11.7
	Renter	54.8	58.4	63.6	69.6	14.8	51.7	58.9	64.2	71.0	19.3
Family Type	LT 65 years, married, with children	21.6	21.6	22.3	34.2	12.6	37.6	37.9	42.2	52.2	14.6
	LT 65 years, married, no children	12.9	20.4	18.9	24.8	11.9	19.9	27.6	26.7	36.3	16.4
	LT 65 years, female head with children	48.1	49.7	55.8	64.6	16.5	63.4	66.5	71.2	84.5	21.1
	LT 65 years, male head	37.8	33.5	35.4	42.9	5.1	38.5	43.3	41.6	57.0	18.5
	65 or older, married	5.5	4.9	4.8	6.2	0.7	17.4	16.0	15.6	21.0	3.6
	65 or older, female head	15.3	13.8	18.3	16.9	1.6	29.0	32.8	33.5	40.2	11.2
	65 or older, male head	21.1	21.2	14.6	15.3	–5.8	40.2	36.1	30.2	34.1	–6.1
Memo:	Percent of asset poor with zero or negative net worth	69.1	75.0	71.7	69.9	0.9	46.6	48.0	46.8	46.4	–0.2

Source: Author's calculations from the 1983, 1992, 2001, and 2013 Survey of Consumer Finances.
Abbreviation: LT, less than.

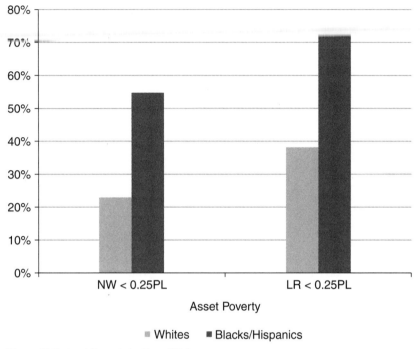

Figure 11.2. Asset Poverty by Race, 2013

35 to 49, net worth poverty rates were about one-third of the rates for the young households, and liquid asset poverty rates for the prime age group were about one-half of those for the youngest group. Those aged 62 or more had the lowest asset poverty rates using either criterion—an average of about 11 percent over the entire period for the net worth measure and 26 percent for the liquid asset measure.

As with age, the asset poverty rates fell monotonically by the education of the head (also see Figure 11.4). Asset poverty rates for households headed by a person with four or more years of college were about one-fourth of those of families with a head who had not completed a high school degree. For example, while 60 percent of families headed by a person with less than a high school degree were in liquid asset poverty in 2001, 16 percent of the college graduates in that year had insufficient liquid assets to enable them to meet the three months of poverty line consumption standard.

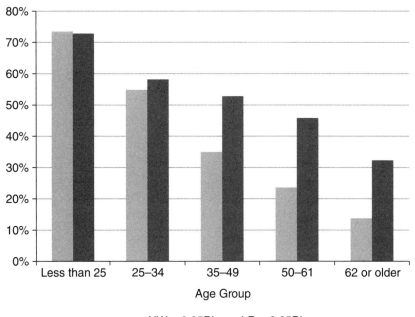

Figure 11.3. Asset Poverty by Age Group, 2013

The pattern of 2001 asset poverty rates by housing tenure is also revealing (also see Figure 11.5). For homeowners, the net worth asset measure that includes the value of home equity indicated an asset poverty rate of
6 percent, compared to 64 percent for renters. While the rates between these
tenure categories became closer when the liquid asset measure that excludes
home equity is used, the asset poverty rates of renters remained more than
double those of homeowners. Indeed, nearly two-thirds of renters had insufficient liquid assets to provide them the three-month cushion of poverty line
consumption in 2001. It seems clear that homeownership implies more
than home equity, and is associated with the ownership of a wide range of
financial assets.

Table 11.10 also indicates that asset poverty rates vary substantially by
family type (also see Figure 11.6). The lowest asset poverty rates were observed among married couple families aged 65 years or older. Using the three-
month cushion standard, asset poverty rates for elderly married couples

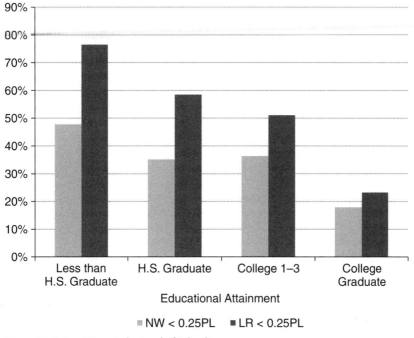

Figure 11.4. Asset Poverty by Level of Schooling

ranged from 5 percent when home equity was included in the asset definition to 21 percent using the liquid asset definition. The rates for two-parent families with children ranged from about 22 percent to 52 percent across the two asset poverty measures, while those for married couples without children had a spread from 13 to 36 percent. The asset poverty rates for female single-parent households were the highest of any family group, averaging 55 percent for the net worth criterion over the four years and 71 percent for the liquid resources criterion.

The share of the asset poor with zero or negative net worth was also extremely high (bottom line of Table 11.10). On average, over the four years 71 percent of the asset poor defined using the net worth criterion fell into this category. For these households, no asset cushion existed to provide support should income from the labor market or the public sector fail. Of the households who were asset poor by the liquid resources measure, 47 percent

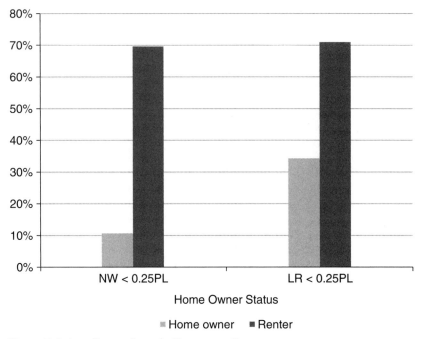

Figure 11.5. Asset Poverty Status by Homeowner Status

on average had no net worth cushion. Those households with no asset cushion at all experienced the most severe levels of asset poverty.

Time Trends in Asset Poverty by Demographic Group
Table 11.10 also shows the percentage point change in asset poverty rates between 1983 and 2013. Note that the first year was a recession year, while 2013 was a recovery year.[38] Given these different macroeconomic conditions, it is expected that the rates of asset poverty would have fallen over this period. For both the net worth and liquid resources poverty measures, the time pattern of change failed to meet these expectations. Increases in asset poverty of 8.8 percentage points (39 percent) and 13.9 percentage points (42 percent) were recorded for these definitions. In 2013, 31 percent of the nation remained in net worth poverty and 47 percent were in liquid resource poverty.

All demographic groups with a single exception saw an increase in their rate of both net worth and liquid resources poverty over this thirty-year

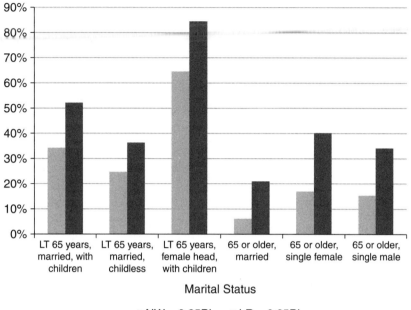

Figure 11.6. Asset Poverty by Age and Marital Status

stretch. It is also noteworthy that those demographic groups with the highest level of asset poverty in 2013 generally experienced the greatest percentage point increase in asset poverty between 1983 and 2013, and those with the lowest asset poverty in 1983 the smallest growth. Minorities recorded a slightly greater gain in asset poverty using the net worth measure over the thirty years than whites though the converse was true based on the liquid resources criterion. Younger households generally showed sharper rises in asset poverty than older ones. The youngest age group (under age 25) saw its net worth poverty rate spike by 18 percentage points and its liquid resources poverty rate by 17 percentage points. In contrast, the respective gains for age group 62 and older were only 4 percentage points and 10 percentage points.

Less-educated households experienced a much greater rise in asset poverty than those with higher education. The net worth poverty rate climbed by 18 percentage points and the liquid resources poverty rate by 27 percentage points between 1983 and 2013, whereas the corresponding figures were 7 and 11 percentage points for college graduates.

Renters experienced about twice the percentage point rise in asset poverty than homeowners. Asset poverty for renters grew substantially over the period on the basis of both measures. Net worth poverty rose by 15 percentage points (27 percent), and liquid resources poverty increased from 52 percent in 1983 to 71 percent in 2013, or by 37 percent over the period. In contrast, asset poverty for homeowners rose by 7.1 percentage points, almost tripling, albeit from a very low base of 3.6 percent in 1983. The ostensible reason was the very high growth in mortgage debt as a percent of house value, which almost doubled over the thirty-year period. When the net asset value of the own home is excluded from the asset base (the liquid resources poverty measure), the rate of asset poverty for homeowners increased by 12 percentage points—or by 52 percent.

Female-headed families, who had the highest incidence of asset poverty in all years, showed the highest percentage point growth in asset poverty over the thirty-year period of any family group, 16.5 percentage points for net worth poverty and 21.1 percentage points for liquid resources poverty. Nonelderly married couples with and without children generally had the second highest percentage point increases. Those with children recorded a 12.6 percentage point rise in net worth poverty and a 14.6 percentage point increase in liquid resources poverty, and those without children an 11.9 and 16.4 percentage point rise, respectively. Married couples aged 65 and over, who had the lowest level of asset poverty in all years, showed the second lowest percentage point increase between 1983 and 2013, of 0.7 and 3.6 percentage points, respectively. Asset poverty actually declined among elderly single males (–5.8 percentage points for net worth poverty and –6.1 percentage points for liquid resources poverty). Female-headed families aged 65 and over—primarily widows—experienced modest increases in asset poverty.

In sum, overall asset poverty grew significantly over the thirty-year period. Among population subgroups, however, the patterns of changing poverty prevalence varied substantially. Large increases in the rate of asset poverty were recorded for the following groups: younger versus older households, less educated versus more educated ones; renters versus homeowners; and female-headed households with children relative to others, particularly elderly ones.

Probit Analysis

This cross-tabulation of poverty rates by family type does not indicate the independent relationship of the racial, age, education, homeowner, and family type characteristics to the probability of being in poverty by either of these measures. To estimate the independent effect of these socioeconomic characteristics on the probability of being poor by any measure, a probit model is fitted to the observations in each year. The dependent variable is defined as being in poverty (using several poverty measures, including income poverty, asset poverty, joint income / asset poverty), and the characteristics of the families serve as explanatory variables.

Table 11.11 shows the probit model fit to net worth poverty status in 1983, 2001, and 2013. It uses the individual characteristics in Table 11.10 as variables.[39] The excluded characteristics are generally those with the lowest asset poverty rate (for example, being a homeowner in the case of housing tenure status). The probit results are remarkably consistent across the three years except for family type. They indicate that being black or Hispanic (relative to being white or other) has a statistically significant positive independent effect on the probability of being net worth poor. In addition, the coefficients by age group are positive and generally decline with age (relative to the oldest age group, which is excluded). They are significant for all age groups in 2001 and for all except age group 50–61 in 1983 and 2013. The coefficients on educational attainment are positive and significant at the 1 percent level but decline with level of education (relative to the excluded group, college graduates) except for college 1–3 in 1983. All of the coefficients are significant at the 1 percent level. The coefficient for being a renter (relative to being a homeowner) is very high in the three years and significant at the 1 percent level.

Finally, in the case of family type, there were some notable changes between 1983 and 2001.[40] In 1983, the coefficients for all family types were positive and statistically significant relative to single males under the age of 65. In both years, the largest coefficient was for female-headed families with children, under age 65. While married couples had significantly higher asset poverty rates than single males in 1983, by 2001 this difference disappeared. Apparently married couples reduced their indebtedness or increased their savings more than single males over the 1983–2001 period. Interestingly, the coefficients on households that were married and aged 65 or over and those headed by older single females were positive and significant in 1983, but by

Table 11.11. Probit B-estimates for net worth poverty, 1983, 2001, and 2013
(standard errors are in parentheses)

Variable	Year 1983		Year 2001		Year 2013	
Intercept	−3.501	***	−2.690	***	−2.091	***
	(0.237)		(0.092)		(0.053)	
Black or Hispanic	0.658	***	0.316	***	0.444	***
	(0.073)		(0.032)		(0.023)	
Age less than 25	0.588	***	1.067	***	0.753	***
	(0.215)		(0.095)		(0.064)	
Ages 25–34	0.807	***	0.879	***	0.589	***
	(0.210)		(0.086)		(0.050)	
Ages 35–49	0.362	*	0.404	***	0.158	***
	(0.210)		(0.085)		(0.048)	
Ages 50–61	0.230		0.147	*	−0.065	
	(0.210)		(0.086)		(0.047)	
Less than HS graduate	0.623	***	1.208	***	0.982	***
	(0.093)		(0.043)		(0.034)	
HS graduate	0.409	***	0.664	***	0.705	***
	(0.091)		(0.037)		(0.026)	
College 1–3	0.421	***	0.476	***	0.519	***
	(0.097)		(0.039)		(0.027)	
Renter	1.794	***	1.713	***	1.507	***
	(0.068)		(0.029)		(0.022)	
Married with children, under 65	0.921	***	0.042		0.174	***
	(0.106)		(0.044)		(0.033)	
Married and childless, under 65	0.660	***	0.003		0.032	
	(0.116)		(0.046)		(0.034)	
Female head with children, under 65	1.084	***	0.330	***	0.554	***
	(0.125)		(0.054)		(0.043)	
Female head, childless, under 65	0.742	***	0.083	*	0.335	***
	(0.111)		(0.051)		(0.038)	
Married, 65 or over	0.517	**	−0.452	***	−0.512	***
	(0.258)		(0.109)		(0.067)	
Female head, 65 or over	0.784	***	−0.068		−0.321	***
	(0.241)		(0.101)		(0.064)	
Male head, 65 or over	1.039	**	0.026		−0.279	***
	(0.509)		(0.125)		(0.086)	
Number of observations	4262		22210		30075	
Wald	1715.1	***	6452.9	***	10291.3	***
Chi square	1090.5	***	10783.4	***	15449.2	***

Source: Author's calculations from the 1983, 2001, and 2013 Survey of Consumer Finances.
Asset poverty is based on: Net Worth < .25 Poverty Line. Excluded groups: whites and other races; age group 62 and over; college graduates; homeowners; and male heads under age 65.
*** Significant at 1% level. ** Significant at 5% level. * Significant at 10% level

2001 these coefficients became negative. In the case of older married couples it became both negative and statistically significant. Between 2001 and 2013, the notable changes were that the coefficient of being married with children was now positive and significant at the 1 percent level in 2013 and those of being a single female and a single male age 65 and over were negative and significant at the 1 percent level in 2013.

Trends in Asset Poverty versus Income Poverty

An interesting question concerns the difference in the trends of asset poverty relative to the official income poverty measure. Table 11.12 presents the pattern of income poverty in the United States for the years 1983, 1992, 2001, and 2013. While the overall asset poverty rose by around 40 percent from 1983 to 2013 according to both measures, the rate of income poverty fell from 14.7 percent to 13.6 percent, or by 7.5 percent.

For nearly all of the groups shown in Table 11.12, income poverty rose between 1983 and 1992, and in some cases substantially. The primary exceptions were those living in families headed by a person aged 50–61, intact nonelderly families with children, elderly married couples, and single males. Much the same pattern held for both of the asset poverty measures, with only a few subgroups recording decreases. The trends in asset and income poverty during this early period were very similar.

During the second period, 1992–2001, substantial differences between the income and asset poverty measures appeared. During this period, overall asset poverty increased slightly, while income poverty fell substantially from 16 percent to 13.2 percent, or by 18 percent. Of the nineteen subgroups shown in Tables 11.10 and 11.12, net worth poverty rose for fourteen of them over this period and liquid asset poverty rose for twelve. However, over this same time period, income poverty fell for sixteen of the nineteen subgroups. Apparently, the gains in income experienced by the income poor during the economic growth period of the 1990s did not find its way into the holding of assets by the asset poor. This pattern was consistent with evidence on the low rates of saving by the poor, even when income was increasing.

Over the third period, 2001 to 2013, the overall income poverty rate increased only slightly despite the deep recession of 2007 to 2009, while overall net worth poverty climbed by 28 percent and liquid resources poverty by

Table 11.12. Income poverty rates for households by demographic group, 1983–2013 (figures are in percentage)

Grouping	Category	1983	1992	2001	2013	Change, 1983–2013
	All households	14.7	16.0	13.2	13.6	−1.1
Race	Whites	10.9	11.0	8.6	9.3	−1.6
	Blacks / Hispanics	32.8	34.6	27.5	25.1	−7.8
Age	Less than 25	26.7	43.1	33.6	45.6	19.0
	25–34	13.1	16.8	13.6	16.9	3.8
	35–49	11.8	12.3	10.5	12.0	0.2
	50–61	12.0	9.8	10.9	10.7	−1.3
	62 and over	17.8	18.1	13.5	10.2	−7.6
Education	Less than HS graduate	29.5	36.9	35.6	32.5	3.0
	HS graduate	11.8	15.3	12.1	15.5	3.7
	College 1–3	10.0	12.4	9.6	12.0	2.0
	College graduate	3.1	4.0	3.2	6.2	3.1
Tenure	Homeowner	9.1	9.3	6.7	7.2	−2.0
	Renter	24.5	27.8	26.8	25.8	1.3
Family Type	LT 65 years, married, with children	9.7	9.1	10.0	10.7	1.0
	LT 65 years, married, no children	4.9	6.7	4.8	5.3	0.5
	LT 65 years, female head with children	39.8	42.8	38.2	36.7	−3.1
	65 or older, married	11.6	6.8	7.1	5.7	−6.0
	65 or older, female head	28.4	29.5	24.4	14.3	−14.1
	65 or older, male head	31.0	15.0	11.7	11.2	−19.7
Memo:	Percent of income poor with zero or negative net worth	37.9	43.2	42.5	42.1	4.2

Source: Authors' calculations from the 1983, 1992, 2001, and 2013 Survey of Consumer Finances. Income poverty is based on the National Academy of Sciences three-parameter scale (see Constance F. Citro and Robert T. Michael, eds., *Measuring Poverty: A New Approach* [Washington, DC: National Academy Press, 1995]). Abbreviation: LT, less than.

26 percent. Over these years, net worth poverty went up for all but one of the subgroups (the exception was elderly female heads) and liquid poverty also for eighteen of the subgroups (the only exception in this case was households under age 25). In contrast, income poverty rose for only eleven groups and declined for eight groups.

I next turn to the development of a joint income / asset poverty indicator. Given the two resource criteria that have been used to analyze the prevalence of poverty—annual income and assets—it is possible to join the two measures and estimate the share of families that is both income poor and asset poor, and their composition. Table 11.13 presents this comparison for years 1983, 2001, and 2013 on the basis of the revised poverty lines and the net worth poverty measure of assets.

In 1983, when 14.7 percent of U.S. families had income below the poverty line and 22.4 percent were asset poor, 7.6 percent were both asset and income poor. These joint poverty families included 52 percent of the families who were income poor, and 34 percent of the families who were asset poor. Thirty percent of families were either income or asset poor. Between 1983 and 2001, the joint poverty rate increased from 7.6 to 7.9 percent, or by about 4 percent, suggesting that the upward trend in the asset poverty rate over time dominated the downward trend in the income poverty rate over these years. In 2001, 60 percent of the families that were income poor were in joint poverty, and 32 percent of asset poor families were poor by the joint asset / income poverty measure. The share of families either asset or income poor remained at 30 percent. Over the eighteen years, an increasing share of the income poor families was also asset poor, whereas among the asset poor a smaller proportion was also income poor.

Between 2001 and 2013 the joint poverty rate increased once again, from 7.9 to 8.7 percent, or by 10 percent. In 2013, 64 percent of the families that were income poor were in joint poverty, as were 28 percent of asset poor families—both figures up from 2001. The share of families either asset or income poor was 36 percent, compared to 30 percent in 2001. Between 2001 and 2013, an increasing share of the income-poor families was also asset poor, and a larger proportion of the asset poor was also income poor.

Certain groups of the population had especially high rates of joint asset / income poverty, including minorities, households under age 25, those in a family headed by a person with less than a high school degree, renters, and female-headed families with children. All of these groups had a rate of joint poverty in excess of 15 percent in 1983, 2001, and 2013. With the exception of minorities and single unmarried mothers, all of these groups experienced large increases in the rate of joint poverty between 1983 and 2013. By 2013, the share of families that were *either* income *or* asset poor was

Table 11.13. Asset and income poverty rates for households by demographic group, 1983, 2001, and 2013 (figures are in percent)

Grouping	Category	1983				2001				2013			
		Asset Poor and Income Poor	Asset Poor Only	Income Poor Only	Asset Poor or Income Poor	Asset Poor and Income Poor	Asset Poor Only	Income Poor Only	Asset Poor or Income Poor	Asset Poor and Income Poor	Asset Poor Only	Income Poor Only	Asset Poor or Income Poor
	All households	7.6	14.8	7.2	29.5	7.9	16.6	5.3	29.8	8.7	22.5	5.0	36.2
Race	Whites	4.5	12.6	6.5	23.6	4.0	14.0	4.6	22.6	5.0	17.9	4.4	27.3
	Blacks / Hispanics	21.7	25.6	11.1	58.5	20.3	26.4	7.2	53.9	18.8	35.9	6.2	61.0
Age	Less than 25	18.7	36.9	7.9	63.6	26.9	45.2	6.6	78.7	36.2	37.3	9.4	82.9
	25–34	9.5	26.7	3.6	39.9	10.5	33.8	3.1	47.4	13.9	40.9	3.0	57.3
	35–49	5.8	11.8	6.0	23.7	7.0	15.5	3.5	26.0	8.5	26.5	3.5	38.5
	50–61	6.0	7.8	6.0	19.8	4.9	8.8	5.9	19.7	6.0	17.6	4.6	28.2
	62 or older	5.2	4.6	12.6	22.4	5.1	5.7	8.4	19.2	3.3	10.4	6.9	20.6
Education	Less than HS graduate	15.1	14.7	14.4	44.2	22.2	17.9	13.4	53.6	20.2	27.6	12.3	60.1
	HS graduate	6.0	15.0	5.9	26.8	7.2	20.6	4.9	32.7	10.4	24.7	5.1	40.2
	College 1–3	5.3	20.3	4.7	30.3	5.1	20.3	4.5	29.9	8.3	28.0	3.6	40.0
	College graduate	1.8	9.6	1.4	12.7	1.9	9.1	1.3	12.3	3.1	14.8	3.1	21.0

Tenure	Homeowner	0.4	3.2	8.7	12.3	0.6	5.2	6.0	11.8	0.9	9.≡	6.2	16.≝
	Renter	20.0	34.8	4.5	59.3	23.0	40.6	3.8	67.3	23.2	46.≝	2.6	72.≝
Family Type	LT 65, married, with children	5.1	16.5	4.6	26.3	6.5	15.8	3.5	25.8	7.9	26.≝	2.8	37.1
	LT 65, married, no children	2.0	10.9	2.9	15.8	2.8	16.1	2.0	20.9	3.3	21.≡	2.1	26.8
	LT 65, female head with children	28.7	19.4	11.0	59.2	27.9	27.9	10.2	66.1	27.8	36.≝	8.9	73.5
	65 or older, married	2.0	3.6	9.6	15.2	2.6	2.2	4.5	9.3	1.4	4.8	4.2	10.4
	65 or older, female head	9.8	5.5	18.6	33.9	9.6	8.7	14.8	33.1	3.7	13.3	10.7	27.6
	65 or older, male head	11.8	9.2	19.2	40.2	6.5	8.2	5.3	19.9	3.6	11.7	7.6	23.0

Source: Author's calculations from the 1983, 2001, and 2013 Survey of Consumer Finances. Income poverty is based on the National Academy of Sciences three-parameter scale. Asset poverty is based on: Net Worth < .25 Poverty Line

especially high for minorities (61 percent), under age 25 (83 percent), age group 25–34 (58 percent), those with less than a high school degree (60 percent), renters (72 percent), and female-headed families (74 percent). All six groups with the exception of minorities showed a marked increase in the probability of being either income or asset poor from 1983 to 2013.

These patterns of joint income / asset poverty prevalence are also reflected in the composition of the poor population by the various measures (see Table 11.14). In 1983, when minorities comprised 16 percent of all families, they made up about 35 percent of all income or asset poor families but 47 percent of families in joint poverty. In 2001, minorities made up 54 percent of families classified as both income and asset poor but by 2013 the figure fell back down to 46 percent, despite an increase in their share of the total population. In 1983, households under the age of 35 constituted 31 percent of the total population but 57 percent of the asset poor, 35 percent of the income poor, and 48 percent of those in joint poverty. In 2001, their share of total households fell to 23 percent while their share of families in joint poverty remained high, at 42 percent. In 2013, while their share of total households fell again, their proportion of families in joint poverty climbed to *more than half* (51 percent).

In 1983, families headed by someone with less than a high school degree comprised 29 percent of all families but 58 percent of those in joint poverty. Between 1983 and 2001, their share of total households declined by 11 percentage points, to 18 percent, while their proportion of families in joint poverty fell by only 7 percentage points, to 51 percent. By 2013, while their proportion of total families fell further to 12 percent, their share of families in joint poverty decreased less in relative terms, to 42 percent. Renters made up about a third of all families in all three years but close to *95 percent* of those who were both asset and income poor in 1983 and 2001 and 86 percent in 2013.

Those living in a family headed by a nonelderly female with children made up 9 percent of all households in both 1983 and 2001 but one-third of those in joint poverty in 1983 and 30 percent in 2001. By 2013 this group made up 8 percent of all households but 27 percent of the joint income / asset poor. Clearly, the composition of the poor as determined by this joint poverty criterion is more heavily weighted toward these vulnerable groups than either the income or asset poverty measures.

Summary and Conclusions

Several interesting findings have emerged from the analysis in this chapter, which is based on the official U.S. Census poverty thresholds for family income.

The wealth holdings of families below the poverty line relative to those above it declined from 1962 to 1983 and then to 2001 but recovered in 2013. The ratio of net worth (excluding durables and household inventories) between the poor and nonpoor fell sharply, from 0.26 in 1962 to 0.14 in 1983, and then dropped to 0.09 in 2001. However, in 2013 the ratio rebounded to 0.14, the same level as in 1983.

In 1983 the addition of DB pension wealth to the household portfolio reduced the ratio of mean wealth between the poor and the nonpoor population from 0.19 to about 0.16, but in 2001 and 2013 this addition did not affect the ratio of mean wealth between the two groups. The addition of Social Security wealth to the household portfolio, on the other hand, raised the ratio of average wealth between the two groups from about 0.16 (depending on the discount rate) to about 0.29 in 1983, from 0.09 to 0.18 in 2001, and from 0.13 to 0.20 in 2013. All in all, the net effect of adding both DB pension and Social Security wealth to the household portfolio was equalizing.

Alternative poverty rate calculations in this chapter revealed that including annuity flows from net worth and the imputed rent on owner-occupied housing in household income reduced the measured poverty rate, based on the official poverty thresholds, by about 10 percent for the full population in 1983. When annuity flows and imputed rent were included in the 2001 data, the reduction in the measured overall poverty rate was 13 percent, greater than in 1983. However, in 2013, the overall poverty rate was reduced by 10 percent, about the same as in 1983.

A final point of interest is the implications of these findings for the persistence of poverty. On the basis of the 1983 data, only 10 to 15 percent of income-poor families had significant wealth holdings. Of these, approximately 4 to 5 percent owned large holdings in real estate or unincorporated business equity, and their "poverty income" was based on large income losses associated with these properties. The remaining families in this group were likely to be recent entrants into the poor population, due to a sudden loss of income. However, the vast majority of families below the income poverty line

Table 11.14. Composition of asset and income poor for households by demographic group 1983, 2001, and 2013 (figures are in percentage)

Grouping	Category	Percent of all Households	Asset and Income Poor	Asset Poor Only	Income Poor Only	All Asset Poor	All Income Poor
I. 1983	All households	100.0	100.0	100.0	100.0	100.0	100.0
Race	Whites	80.9	47.7	69.2	73.1	61.9	60.0
	Blacks/Hispanics	16.3	46.6	28.2	25.2	34.4	36.2
Age	Less than 25	8.0	19.8	20.0	8.9	19.9	14.5
	25–34	22.6	28.4	40.8	11.3	36.6	20.1
	35–49	27.6	21.1	22.1	23.2	21.8	22.1
	50–61	18.4	14.5	9.7	15.3	11.3	14.9
	62 or older	23.5	16.2	7.3	41.2	10.3	28.4
Education	Less than HS graduate	29.0	57.7	28.8	58.3	38.6	58.0
	HS graduate	30.2	23.7	30.6	24.7	28.2	24.2
	College 1–3	19.6	13.7	26.9	13.0	22.4	13.3
	College graduate	21.2	4.9	13.7	4.1	10.7	4.5
Tenure	Homeowner	63.4	3.5	13.7	77.1	10.3	39.2
	Renter	36.6	96.5	86.3	22.9	89.7	60.8
Family Type	LT 65 years, married, with children	31.0	20.9	34.6	20.0	30.0	20.5
	LT 65 years, married, no children	20.0	5.4	14.8	8.0	11.6	6.6
	LT 65 years, female head with children	8.7	32.9	11.4	13.4	18.7	23.4
	65 or older, married	9.8	2.5	2.4	13.1	2.4	7.7
	65 or older, female head	9.1	11.8	3.4	23.6	6.2	17.5
	65 or older, male head	0.4	0.6	0.2	1.0	0.3	0.8

II. 2001	All households	100.0	100.0	100.0	100.0	100.0	100.0
Race	Whites	76.2	38.9	64.1	66.4	56.0	49.9
	Blacks/Hispanics	21.0	54.1	33.3	28.7	40.0	43.9
Age	Less than 25	5.6	19.3	15.3	7.1	16.6	14.4
	25–34	17.2	22.9	35.1	10.2	31.2	17.8
	35–49	33.6	29.9	31.3	22.3	30.8	26.8
	50–61	19.0	11.9	10.0	21.3	10.6	15.7
	62 or older	24.6	16.0	8.4	39.1	10.8	25.3
Education	Less than HS graduate	18.1	51.0	19.6	46.1	29.7	45.0
	HS graduate	29.6	27.1	36.7	27.5	33.6	27.2
	College 1–3	22.6	14.6	27.6	19.2	23.4	16.5
	College graduate	29.6	7.3	16.2	7.2	13.3	7.2
Tenure	Homeowner	67.7	5.6	21.1	76.9	16.1	34.2
	Renter	32.3	94.4	78.9	23.1	83.9	65.8
Family Type	LT 65 years, married, with children	26.9	22.1	25.6	18.0	24.4	20.4
	LT 65 years, married, no children	22.3	7.8	21.6	8.5	17.2	8.1
	LT 65 years, female head with children	8.5	30.2	14.3	16.5	19.4	24.7
	65 or older, married	11.2	3.6	1.5	9.6	4.2	6.0
	65 or older, female head	7.2	8.8	3.8	20.1	9.7	13.3
	65 or older, male head	2.7	2.3	1.3	2.7	2.2	2.5
III. 2013	All households	100.0	100.0	100.0	100.0	100.0	100.0
Race	Whites	70.1	43.8	60.5	67.0	55.9	52.2
	Blacks/Hispanics	25.3	45.5	33.4	26.4	36.8	38.6

(continued)

Table 11.14. (continued)

Grouping	Category	Percent of all Households	Asset and Income Poor	Asset Poor Only	Income Poor Only	All Asset Poor	All Income Poor
Age	Less than 25	5.0	23.5	9.3	10.7	13.3	18.8
	25–34	15.8	27.6	31.3	10.4	30.3	21.4
	35–49	26.7	33.0	39.4	23.6	37.6	29.5
	50–61	23.7	13.1	14.8	17.7	14.3	14.8
	62 or older	28.8	9.5	11.3	34.1	10.8	18.4
Education	Less than HS graduate	12.4	42.1	22.2	44.9	27.7	43.1
	HS graduate	29.9	35.5	32.5	30.3	33.3	33.6
	College 1–3	24.2	21.7	28.1	16.5	26.3	19.9
	College graduate	33.5	10.7	19.4	18.6	17.0	13.6
Tenure	Homeowner	65.1	7.3	29.3	84.8	23.2	35.5
	Renter	34.9	86.3	66.7	17.0	72.1	61.1
Family Type	LT 65 years, married, with children	25.3	24.4	31.4	15.4	29.5	21.1
	LT 65 years, married, no children	20.3	8.5	21.2	9.2	17.7	8.7
	LT 65 years, female head with children	7.8	27.3	13.9	15.3	17.6	22.9
	65 or older, married	11.5	1.8	2.4	9.5	2.2	4.6
	65 or older, female head	9.0	3.0	4.2	15.5	3.9	7.6
	65 or older, male head	3.1	1.1	1.4	4.2	1.3	2.3

Source: Author's calculations from the 1983, 2001, and 2013 Survey of Consumer Finances. Income poverty is based on the National Academy of Sciences three-parameter scale. Asset poverty is based on: Net Worth < .25 Poverty Line. The categories do not necessarily sum to 100 because of the exclusion of certain categories.

had low levels of wealth and were likely to have been below the poverty line or at low income levels for a considerable period of time.

American prosperity in the second half of the 1980s together with the booming economy of the 1990s and early 2000s created the impression that American households had done well, particularly in terms of wealth acquisition. This chapter developed the concept of asset poverty as a measure of economic hardship, distinct from and complementary to the more commonly used concept of income poverty. The results revealed that in the face of the large growth in overall assets in the United States and a fall in standard income poverty over the period from 1983 to 2007, the level of asset poverty increased from 22.4 to 25.2 percent. Over the Great Recession asset poverty spiked even more, reaching 31.2 percent in 2013. Liquid resources poverty also grew over these years, from 33 percent in 1983 to 43 percent in 2007 and then to 47 percent in 2013.

Asset poverty rates for blacks and Hispanics were found to be more than double those for whites. Asset poverty rates fell monotonically with both age and education; were much higher for renters than homeowners; and among family types ranged from a low of about 5 percent for elderly couples to 50 to 65 percent for female single parents, depending on the year.

Results on asset poverty are discouraging in that very high rates of asset poverty for the U.S. population are revealed, irrespective of the measure used. In 2007, even before the onset of the Great Recession, one-fourth of American families had insufficient net worth to enable them to get by for three months at a poverty line level of living, and over two-fifths had insufficient liquid assets to support poverty level living for a three-month period.

These high levels of asset poverty for the entire population disguise even higher rates for various groups. Using the net worth poverty standard, the following indicates asset poverty rates in 2013 for some of the groups most disadvantaged in terms of wealth holdings: blacks and Hispanics (55 percent); heads aged less than 25 years (74 percent); heads aged 25 to 34 (55 percent); household heads with less than a high school degree (48 percent); renters (70 percent); and nonelderly female heads with children (65 percent).

A similar concentration of the most extreme form of poverty, joint income/asset poverty, is also found in these groups. Whereas the overall rate of joint income/asset poverty was 8.7 percent in 2013, it was 19 percent for black and Hispanic households, 36 percent of those with heads aged less than 25 years, 14 percent for heads aged 25 to 34, 20 percent for those with less than a high school degree, 23 percent of renters, and 28 percent for female headed families with children.

Appendix 11.1
Definition of Asset Concepts

Net worth	=	the gross value of owner-occupied housing
	+	other real estate owned by the household
	+	cash and demand deposits
	+	time and savings deposits
	+	certificates of deposit and money market accounts
	+	government, corporate, and foreign bonds, and other financial securities
	+	the cash surrender value of life insurance plans
	+	the cash surrender value of defined contribution pension plans, including IRAs, Keogh, 401(k)s
	+	corporate stock and mutual funds
	+	net equity in unincorporated businesses
	+	equity in trust funds
	−	mortgage debt
	−	consumer debt, including auto loans and credit card balances
	−	other debt.
Liquid resources	=	cash and demand deposits
	+	time and savings deposits
	+	certificates of deposit, and money market accounts
	+	government, corporate, and foreign bonds, and other financial securities
	+	the cash surrender value of life insurance plans
	+	corporate stock and mutual funds.

IV

Wealth over the Long Term

12

Long-Term Trends in Aggregate Household Wealth

The primary objective of this chapter is to present estimates of aggregate household wealth for the United States covering selected years in the period from 1900 to 2013.[1] Since there is no single set of data available for the entire period, a major contribution of this work is to develop consistent estimates for the entire period based on sources that used various accounting frameworks and data sources. I also present figures on the growth in per capita and per household wealth over the period, as well as trends in the aggregate portfolio composition.

Marketable wealth per household grew at an average rate of 1.26 percent per year in real terms during this period, which amounted to a more than fourfold increase in average household wealth in real terms over the 113 years. Indeed, real per capita wealth mushroomed by a factor of 7.5, but the growth rate was not uniform. In particular, real wealth per household grew quickly during the 1949–1969 and 1989–2007 periods, more slowly over the 1900–1929 and 1969–1989 periods, and showed an absolute decline over years 1929–1949 and 2007–2013. Moreover, real per capita wealth actually increased somewhat faster than real per capita disposable income and real per capita GDP over the 113 years. This chapter also investigates the relevance of such estimates for household well-being.

This period was one of dramatic changes in the composition of household wealth. Gross owner-occupied housing increased only moderately as a proportion of marketable assets, from 17 percent in 1900 to 22 percent in 1979, but then fell off to 15 percent in 2013. Liquid assets (including defined contribution retirement accounts) rose rather steadily as a share of total assets from 8 percent in 1900 to 23 percent in 2013. Financial securities, on the other hand, slid from 8 to 5 percent. Stock holdings as a proportion of total assets were volatile over time, growing from 15 percent of total assets in 1900 to 31 percent in 1929, falling to 21 percent in 1933 and then to 14 percent in 1949, rising to 27 percent in 1965, falling to 12 percent in 1979, the low point, and then rising to 32 percent in 2013. These shares tended to follow movements in the stock market.

Perhaps the most dramatic change was in the importance of unincorporated business equity, which comprised over a third of total assets in 1900 but fell steadily over the century, reaching 6 percent of total assets in 2013. Debt as a proportion of total assets rose rather steadily from 5 percent in 1900 to 18 percent in 2013 and finally, both pension reserves and Social Security wealth increased relative to marketable assets over the period. By 2013, pension reserves had assumed about the same magnitude as business equity and consumer durables, while Social Security wealth exceeded total tangible assets. The analysis in this chapter provides some explanations for these trends.

This chapter details alternative concepts of household wealth. The standard concept of household wealth includes only assets (and liabilities) that are fungible and that have a readily available market value. I broaden the concept of wealth to include not only standard components but also claims against future income streams. Such claims include pension and Social Security entitlements as well as trust income. I also argue that, because of data limitations, empirical measures of household wealth often do not correspond precisely to those implied by theoretical models of household wealth. I discuss the correspondence between such empirical measures and those implied from behavioral models, such as the life cycle or liquidity constraint model.

The rest of the chapter presents estimates of aggregate household balance sheet data covering the period from 1900 to 2013[2] and of net worth and gross assets based on alternative wealth definitions.[3]

Alternative Definitions of Household Wealth

As with other economic concepts, there is no single measure of household wealth that can fulfill all possible uses of the concept. This section develops four alternative operational measures of household wealth. Table 12.1 provides a summary of these measures.

The first of measure (W1) is defined as the cash surrender value of tangible and financial assets (less liabilities). The second measure (W2), a slightly broader concept, is defined as W1 less the cash surrender or actuarial value of trusts plus the full reserve value of trusts. As is apparent, the difference between W1 and W2 is in the treatment of trusts. W1 measures trusts at their actuarial or cash surrender value, while W2 assigns the full value of trusts to their beneficiaries. In the case of trusts over which the beneficiary has complete control, the cash surrender value is identical to the full equity value of the trust. However, in the case of second- or third-party trusts, in which the beneficiary and owner are different, the trust has no cash surrender value to the beneficiary. In this case, the beneficiary is assigned the so-called actuarial value of the trust, which is defined as its full value discounted over the expected lifetime of the second and/or third parties. The actuarial value is included in W1, while the full trust equity is included in W2.[4]

Both W1 and W2 measure pensions at their cash surrender value, which has historically been very small. The third measure (W3) is defined as W2 less the cash surrender value of pensions plus the total value of pension reserves. In W3, pension reserves are imputed to both current and future beneficiaries, and thus pension reserves are treated similarly to trust equity. The fourth measure (W4) is defined as W3 plus the expected present value of future Social Security benefits. Though there are several difficult problems associated with the concept and measurement of Social Security wealth, I include this concept because it has attained considerable currency in the literature on household wealth.[5]

Measures W1, W2, and W3 are all based on actual accumulations of wealth. The difference among them is in the alternative treatment of accumulated assets over which individuals do not have full control. Aggregate household balance sheet data differ in their treatment of these assets. The Financial Accounts of the United States (formerly the "flow of funds") data and Goldsmith's estimates include the full value of both trusts and pension funds, as in W3.[6] On the other hand, Ruggles and Ruggles include only the cash surrender value of pensions but the full value of household trusts, as in W2.[7] W4 differs from the first three measures by imputing to households retirement wealth that does not correspond to any accumulated reserves. This

Table 12.1. Primary definitions of wealth

W1	W1 is defined as the cash surrender value (CSV) of total assets less liabilities and is a measure of the wealth currently available to the household or individual. The assets include owner-occupied housing, other real estate, all consumer durables, demand deposits and currency, time and savings deposits, bonds and other financial securities, corporate stock, unincorporated business equity, trust fund equity, the CSV of insurance, and the CSV of pensions. Liabilities include mortgage debt, consumer debt, and other debt. Trusts are measured at their actuarial value, which represents between 40 and 60 percent of the total reserves of trusts, depending on the year. (For an explanation of "actuarial value," see the main text of this chapter under "Alternative Definitions of Household Wealth.") Pensions are measured at their CSV, which represents a very small percentage, around 5 percent, of their total reserves. All other tangible and financial assets and liabilities are measured at full value.
W2	W2 is a broader measure of wealth than WI and is defined as W1 plus the full reserves of trust funds less their actuarial value included in W1.
W3	W3 incorporates an extended concept of pension wealth and is defined as W2 plus the total value of pension reserves less the CSV of pensions (which is included in W1 and W2).
W4	W4 is equal to W3 plus the present value of expected future Social Security benefits.

measure may be useful insofar as household behavior may be affected by perceived Social Security or pension wealth.

All four measures of household wealth are operational in that they can be estimated from available data. However, the relationship of these measures to the wealth concepts implied by the behavioral models is not always clearly delineated. A cash surrender wealth concept, such as W1 or W2, is the appropriate one for analyzing behavior if significant liquidity constraints are present or if households have a very short planning horizon. There is no behavioral model of which I am aware that corresponds to the W3 measure. If pension reserves are included, then some form of expected Social Security payments should be as well, even though Social Security does not represent a stock of savings as do pensions. The W3 measure has been introduced in order to separate out the effects of pensions on total household wealth. Several researchers have used W4 in behavioral models under the belief that households consider future pension and Social Security benefits as a form of wealth, which affects current savings and labor force participation decisions.

Trends in Per Capita and Per Household Wealth

Table 12.2 shows total household assets and net worth for wealth measures W1, W2, W3, and W4 for selected years over the period from 1900 to 2013.[8] The figures are in current dollars. Let us first compare the four series. W1 and W2 remained very close throughout the whole 1900–2013 period, since the difference between the two is the difference between the full equity value of trusts and their actuarial value, which was quite small relative to total household assets. W2 and W3 remained almost identical until 1921. The two series then diverged at an increasing rate over the remainder of the period, reflecting the growing relative importance of pension reserves as a form of household wealth. By 1983, pension reserves had grown to 10.9 percent of total W2 assets and 13.1 percent of W2 net worth. As the defined benefit (DB) system retrenched, beginning around 1989 the ratio of pension reserves to W2 dwindled, reaching 5.7 percent in 2013.[9]

W2 and W4 remained quite close until the mid-1930s, with the creation of the Social Security system. By 1939 Social Security wealth had already amounted to 12 percent of traditional marketable assets (W2) and by 1945 to 30 percent. Between 1945 and 1983, Social Security wealth continued to increase relative to W2, though at a slower rate than during the first half of the period. By 1983, Social Security wealth had grown to 48 percent of total W2 assets and 57 percent of W2 net worth. As the Social Security system matured, the growth in Social Security wealth slowed down even more, while net worth growth picked up. As a result, by 2013, the ratio of Social Security wealth to W2 had fallen off to 21 percent.

Another perspective is afforded by computing annual growth rates of the various wealth series. Over the full 1900–2013 period, net worth W2 (in nominal terms) grew at an annual average rate of 6 percent, W3 also at 6 percent, and W4 at 6.2 percent. However, there was a distinct break in the rate of growth that occurred in the late 1950s and early 1960s. I have used the year 1962 to partition the series. Between 1900 and 1962, W2 (and W1) grew at 5 percent per year, W3 at 5.1 percent, and W4 at 5.6 percent. From 1962 to 1983, in contrast, the annual rate of growth of W1 and W2 accelerated to 8.2 percent, that of W3 to 8.5 percent, and that of W4 to 8.8 percent.

Much of the acceleration in the growth of total household wealth was due to an increase in the inflation rate. To correct for this, I convert these nominal

Table 12.2. Household balance sheet totals for assets and net worth using wealth definitions W1, W2, W3, and W4, 1900–2013 (billions, current dollars)

Year	W1	W2	W3	W4	Percentage Difference W3–W2	Percentage Difference W4–W2
I. Total Assets						
1900	80.5	81.5	81.5	81.5	0.0	0.0
1912	157.3	159.7	159.7	159.7	0.0	0.0
1921	280.6	286.3	286.3	286.3	0.0	0.0
1922	309.5	315.6	315.9	315.9	0.1	0.1
1929	465.5	475.7	477.2	477.2	0.3	0.3
1933	316.0	323.0	325.6	325.6	0.8	0.8
1939	370.3	382.2	387.6	434.0	1.4	13.6
1945	637.2	652.6	663.3	856.5	1.6	31.2
1949	854.4	866.8	886.1	1,125.5	2.2	29.8
1953	1,141.0	1,159.4	1,195.0	1,601.0	3.1	38.1
1958	1,632.9	1,662.6	1,731.7	2,317.8	4.2	39.4
1962	1,927.6	1,967.6	2,071.4	2,811.3	5.3	42.9
1965	2,381.3	2,428.7	2,575.8	3,250.1	6.1	33.8
1969	3,104.2	3,158.9	3,366.3	4,727.2	6.6	49.6
1972	3,907.8	3,983.2	4,293.3	6,055.6	7.8	52.0
1976	5,550.1	5,629.5	6,073.3	8,748.8	7.9	55.4
1979	8,161.1	8,255.7	8,920.3	12,995.0	8.1	57.4
1981	9,996.3	10,118.1	11,012.4	15,873.2	8.8	56.9
1983	11,251.6	11,425.7	12,676.3	18,118.1	10.9	58.6
1989	—	20,535.9	21,951.8	30,924.3	6.9	50.6
1992	—	23,879.1	25,605.7	—	7.2	—
1995	—	29,185.4	31,193.0	—	6.9	—
1998	—	39,194.9	41,477.9	—	5.8	—
2001	—	44,983.6	47,683.6	63,017.6	6.0	40.1
2004	—	57,645.6	60,883.4	—	5.6	—
2007	—	70,525.5	74,160.2	90,741.5	5.2	28.7
2010	—	64,868.9	69,209.0	84,865.7	6.7	30.8
2013	—	81,118.9	85,702.9	102,655.3	5.7	26.5
Annual Rate of Growth (in percent)						
1900–1962	5.12	5.14	5.22	5.71		
1962–1983	8.40	8.38	8.63	8.87		
1983–2007	—	7.58	7.36	6.71		
2007–2013	—	2.33	2.41	2.06		
1900–2013	—	6.11	6.16	6.32		
III. Net Worth						
1900	76.4	77.4	77.4	77.4	0.0	0.0
1912	149.6	152.0	152.0	152.0	0.0	0.0
1921	NA	NA	NA	NA	NA	NA

Table 12.2. (continued)

Year	W1	W2	W3	W4	Percentage Difference	
					W3–W2	W4–W2
1922	292.7	298.8	299.1	299.1	0.1	0.1
1929	425.7	435.9	437.4	437.4	0.3	0.3
1933	288.7	295.7	298.3	298.3	0.9	0.9
1939	342.2	354.1	359.5	405.9	1.5	14.6
1945	608.3	623.7	634.4	827.6	1.7	32.7
1949	793.0	805.4	824.7	1,064.1	2.4	32.1
1953	1,033.9	1,052.3	1,087.9	1,493.9	3.4	42.0
1958	1,454.3	1,484.0	1,553.1	2,139.2	4.7	44.2
1962	1,671.6	1,711.6	1,815.4	2,555.3	6.1	49.3
1965	2,039.3	2,086.7	2,233.8	2,908.1	7.0	39.4
1969	2,649.3	2,704.0	2,911.4	4,272.3	7.7	58.0
1972	3,314.9	3,390.3	3,700.4	5,462.7	9.1	61.1
1976	4,687.8	4,767.2	5,211.0	7,886.5	9.3	65.4
1979	6,824.8	6,919.4	7,584.0	11,658.7	9.6	68.5
1981	8,422.5	8,544.3	9,438.6	14,299.4	10.5	67.4
1983	9,402.1	9,576.2	10,826.8	16,268.6	13.1	69.9
1989	—	16,925.1	18,341.0	27,313.5	8.4	61.4
1992	—	19,559.4	21,286.1	—	8.8	—
1995	—	23,879.5	25,887.1	—	8.4	—
1998	—	32,715.6	34,998.7	—	7.0	—
2001	—	36,593.5	39,293.5	54,627.6	7.4	49.3
2004	—	45,973.4	49,211.1	—	7.0	—
2007	—	55,189.1	58,823.8	75,405.1	6.6	36.6
2010	—	50,178.1	54,518.3	70,175.0	8.6	39.9
2013	—	66,488.6	71,072.5	88,024.9	6.9	32.4
Annual Rate of Growth (in percent)						
1900–1962	4.99	4.99	5.09	5.64		
1962–1983	8.22	8.22	8.50	8.81		
1983–2007	—	7.30	7.05	6.39		
2007–2013	—	3.10	3.15	2.58		
1900–2013	—	5.98	6.04	6.23		

Source: Author's computations.

values into constant-dollar series using the consumer price index (CPI) as the deflator for household wealth. This deflator provides the best welfare measure for the household sector, since it allows one to interpret real wealth figures in terms of the amount of consumption goods for which they could be exchanged. Thus, if housing prices rose relative to the CPI, one could interpret this as an increase in real wealth, since the household could now buy more consumption goods in exchange for the house.[10]

Since I am interested in wealth as a welfare measure, I also provide measures of real wealth per capita and per household. Here, again, the choice of unit depends on one's evaluation of how wealth is distributed within the family unit. Insofar as wealth is a "public good" within the household, the household measure may provide the better indicator of welfare. On the other hand, insofar as wealth is a private good within the family, the per capita measure may be preferable. Tangible assets, particularly owner-occupied housing and consumer durables such as automobiles, are probably public goods within the household, since all members benefit fully from the asset. However, financial assets and equities are more in the nature of private goods, since the benefit accruing to family members is inversely related to the size of the family unit.[11] Also, for the sake of comparison, I provide data on real GDP per capita and real family disposable income per capita.

Table 12.3 and Figure 12.1 show results for the wealth measures, as well as real GDP and real family disposable income over the period 1900–2013. Over the entire period, real W2 per capita grew at an average annual rate of 1.79 percent, but the growth was not uniform. Between 1900 and 1929, real W2 per capita grew at a somewhat higher rate, 1.86 percent per year. The annual growth rate then fell markedly during the Great Depression and World War II (1929 to 1949) to 0.40 percent per year. During the high growth period of the 1950s and 1960s, the growth of real W2 per capita accelerated to 2.37 percent per year. Annual growth then slowed a bit to 2.12 percent per year from 1969 to 1989—a period that included the stagflation of the 1970s. It then picked up again to 2.92 percent from 1989 to 2007, its highest level of the century. However, over the Great Recession, from 2007 to 2013, real W2 per capita fell in absolute terms.

A comparison with other measures reveals some striking differences. The growth of W3 per capita averaged 1.85 percent per year over the century and more, slightly higher than that of W2. However, the difference was particularly marked during the immediate postwar period (1949–1969), when W3 grew 0.25 percentage points per annum faster than W2. Real W4 per capita grew considerably faster than W2 per capita, averaging 2.06 percent per year over the century. The difference was particularly striking during the 1929–1949 period, when the Social Security system was inaugurated. During

Table 12.3. Real wealth per capita and per household using wealth definitions W1, W2, W3, and W4, 1900–2013 (1967 dollars)

Year	W1	W2	W3	W4
I. Net Worth per Capita				
1900	4,016	4,069	4,069	4,069
1912	5,411	5,498	5,498	5,498
1921	5,298	5,409	5,414	5,414
1929	6,815	6,978	7,002	7,002
1933	5,925	6,069	6,122	6,122
1939	6,285	6,504	6,603	7,455
1945	8,065	8,270	8,411	10,973
1949	7,445	7,561	7,742	9,990
1953	8,058	8,201	8,479	11,643
1958	9,603	9,799	10,255	14,125
1962	9,891	10,128	10,742	15,120
1965	11,106	11,364	12,166	15,838
1969	11,905	12,151	13,083	19,198
1972	12,604	12,891	14,070	20,771
1976	12,610	12,824	14,017	21,215
1979	13,949	14,142	15,501	23,829
1981	13,435	13,630	15,056	22,810
1983	13,419	13,668	15,453	23,220
1989	—	18,583	20,243	29,980
1992	—	18,307	20,004	—
1995	—	20,015	21,799	—
1998	—	24,444	26,361	—
2001	—	24,874	26,870	37,333
2004	—	28,952	31,161	—
2007	—	31,421	33,670	43,311
2010	—	26,807	29,146	37,573
2013	—	30,689	33,041	41,607

II. Annual Rate of Growth (in percent)

	W1 per Capita	W2 per Capita	W3 per Capita	W4 per Capita	Disposable Income Per Capita	GDP Per Capita
1900–1929	1.82	1.86	1.87	1.87	2.02	1.75
1929–1949	0.44	0.40	0.50	1.78	0.92	1.22
1949–1969	2.35	2.37	2.62	3.27	2.37	2.38
1969–1989	—	2.12	2.18	2.23	1.84	2.23
1989–2007	—	2.92	2.83	2.04	1.36	1.84
2007–2013	—	−0.39	−0.31	−0.67	0.03	0.00
1900–2013	—	1.79	1.85	2.06	1.66	1.69

(continued)

Table 12.3. (continued)

	W1 per Household	W2 per Household	W3 per Household	W4 per Household	GDP Per Household
1900–1929	1.32	1.36	1.37	1.37	1.25
1929–1949	−0.32	−0.36	−0.26	1.02	0.46
1949–1969	1.88	1.91	2.16	2.80	1.91
1969–1989	—	1.71	1.72	1.74	1.55
1989–2007	—	2.76	2.66	1.88	1.68
2007–2013	—	−0.60	−0.52	−0.88	−0.21
1900–2013	—	1.26	1.32	1.53	1.16

All figures are deflated using the Consumer Price Index (CPI), except gross national product (GNP), which is deflated by the implicit GNP deflator. Sources are as follows:

1900–1969

a. Population: U.S. Bureau of the Census, Historical Statistics of the United States, Colonial Times to 1970, Part 2 (Washington, DC: US. Government Printing Office, 1975), Series A 6–8, available at https://www2.census .gov/library/publications/1975/compendia/hist_stats_colonial-1970/hist_stats_colonial-1970p1-chA.pdf.

b. Households: Ibid., Series A 350–352.

c. Consumer Price Index: Ibid., Series E 135.

d. GNP and GNP Implicit Price Deflator: Ibid., Series F 1–5.

e. Disposable Personal Income: Ibid., Series F 9. Estimates for 1900 and 1912 are based on interpolation.

1969–2013

Population and Number of Households: U.S. Bureau of the Census, Current Population Survey, available at http://www.census.gov/hhes/www/income/data/historical/index.html.

Consumer Price Index: U.S. Bureau of Labor Statistics, available at http://www.usinflationcalculator.com /inflation/consumer-price-index-and-annual-percent-changes-from-1913-to-2015/GDP quantity index, available at: http://www.bea.gov/iTable/index_nipa.cfm.

Disposable Personal Income: Financial Accounts of the United States, Table B.101, available at http://www .federalreserve.gov/releases/Z1/Current/data.htm.

this period, real W4 per capita grew at 1.78 percent per year, while the growth in real W2 per capita averaged only 0.40 percent per year. Over the next twenty years, real W4 grew almost a full percentage point faster than real W2, while over the 1969–1989 period the difference was only 0.11 percentage points per year. In contrast, from 1989 to 2007, W2 increased faster than W4, by 0.87 percentage points per annum, as gains in Social Security wealth slowed and those in marketable wealth accelerated. Over years 2007 to 2013, W4 declined by 0.28 percent per year faster than W2.

Real W2 per capita grew slightly faster than real disposable income per capita and real GDP per capita over the full 1900–2013 period. The former grew at an annual rate of 1.79 percent per year, while the latter two increased

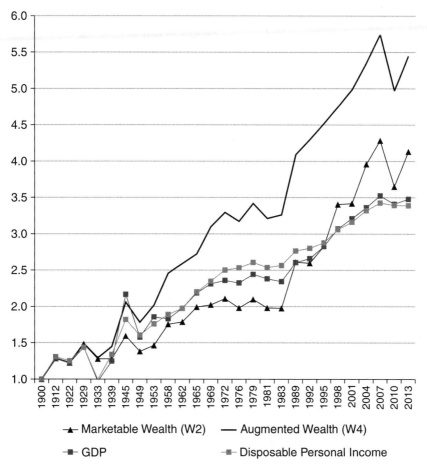

Figure 12.1. Real Marketable and Augmented Wealth, GDP, and Disposable Personal Income per Household, 1900–2013
(Index, 1900 = 1)

at 1.66 and 1.69 percent per year, respectively. Real disposable income per capita grew more rapidly than real W2 per capita from 1900 to 1969 and from 2007 to 2013 but the reverse was true from 1969 to 2007. Indeed, over years 1929 to 1949, real disposable income increased at more than twice the rate as real W2, while during the 1969–1989 period, W2 increased at a quicker pace. Real GDP increased more quickly than W2 during every subperiod except 1900–1929, when W2 grew slightly faster, and 1989–2007, when there was more than a percentage point difference. During the 1929–1949 period, real GDP rose at almost three times the rate of real W2. On the other hand, real W4 per capita rose considerably faster over the full 113-year stretch than either real disposable income or real GDP per capita. W4 grew faster than GDP in every subperiod except 1969–1989, when there was a virtual tie, and 2007 to 2013, when GDP per capita was essentially unchanged and W4 per capita fell. W4 increased at a higher rate than real disposable income in every subperiod except 1900–1929 and 2007–2013.

As shown in Table 12.3, real W2 per household grew considerably slower than real W2 per capita over the full 1900–2013 stretch. It increased at only 1.26 percent per year, a full half point slower than W2 per capita. The difference between the two series reflects the faster growth in the number of households than in population (or, equivalently, the falling average size of the household unit). Indeed, the growth in real wealth per household was lower than that of real wealth per capita in each of the six subperiods as well. As with real wealth per capita, the growth in real wealth per household was highest during the 1989–2007 period, followed by 1949–1969, 1969–1989, and then 1900–1929. In fact, during the 1929–1949 and the 2007–2009 periods, real W2 per household actually fell. During the first of these periods, the reasons are that real marketable wealth was accumulated quite slowly, a consequence of the Great Depression and World War 11, and that the number of households increased more rapidly than the total population (a 0.76 percentage point per year difference). In contrast, real W4 per household increased in each of the subperiods except 2007–2013.

It might also prove helpful to drill down on the period of the Great Recession, 2007 to 2013. The time trends are very different from the SCF results shown in Chapter 2. The annual Financial Accounts of the United States (FFA) balance sheet data indicate a 14.9 percent drop in mean household wealth W2 from 2007 to 2010. This compares to a 16 percent decline in mean net worth NW per household from the SCF data. These results are remarkably close. However, the FFA also shows a *13.3 percent gain* from 2010 to 2013, in contrast to the *0.6 percent rise* from the SCF data. The FFA figures diverge sharply from the SCF data for these three years.

Figure 12.2 shows quarterly FFA results from 2003 to 2014. The figures indicate a peak wealth figure of $576,000 (in 2013 dollars) in the first quarter of 2008. This was followed by a pronounced fall of 24 percent to its lowest

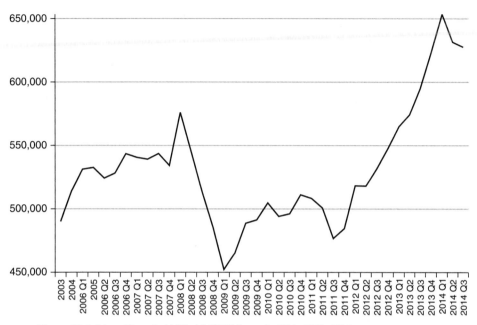

Figure 12.2. Mean Household Wealth (W2) from the FFA, 2003–2014 (2013 dollars)

value of $452,000 in the first quarter of 2009. Mean household wealth then started to increase as asset markets recovered and reached a figure of $574,000 by the second quarter of 2013, just about equal to its previous high point. Indeed, mean FFA household wealth continued to skyrocket after that, attaining a figure of $653,000 in the first quarter of 2014 and then dropping off a bit. These results show the volatility of household wealth figures, particularly because they reflect to a large extent the instability of the stock market. Thus, the actual month of the year in which a survey is carried out affects the SCF survey results. However, what is apparent from the FFA data is that mean wealth in every quarter of 2013 was substantially higher than mean wealth in every quarter of 2010.

A comparison of mean wealth levels is also curious. The annual FFA data shows a mean FFA wealth figure for W2 per household of $541,000 (in 2013 dollars) in 2007. This compares with the SCF figure for mean net worth per household of $602,000. One would have expected a higher figure for the FFA mean for two reasons. First, W2 includes the value of all durables but net worth excludes all durables and second, it was not possible to exclude financial securities, stocks, and pension reserves held by nonprofits from the FFA household sector. This problem would bias upward the FFA mean relative to the SCF mean. However, the SCF showed considerably higher values for owner-occupied housing than the FFA.[12] The wealth of the household and nonprofit sector is estimated as a residual after imputations are made for the other sectors of the economy. It is not clear which way the bias would go in this case. Thus, a surge in the financial assets of nonprofits after 2010 could account for the discrepancy between the SCF results and the FFA results for 2010–2013.

Of the two sources, it is likely that the SCF data are generally superior to the FFA figures, at least until 2013. The SCF generally leads to higher estimates of mean household wealth than the FFA. Since the FFA estimates are biased upward, this recommends the SCF data over the FFA. In addition, home values are underestimated in the FFA relative to the survey data and the SCF figure for mean wealth in 2013 leads to unrealistic decomposition results over years 2010 to 2013. Moreover, the finding of basically no growth in real wealth per household between 2010 and 2013 from the 2013 SCF seems to fly in the face of the evidence that asset prices, particularly stock values, grew robustly over these years. As a result, the FFA data on mean household wealth in 2013 is preferable to the SCF figures.[13]

Changes in Portfolio Composition

There have also been dramatic changes in the composition of household wealth over course of the twentieth century and into the twenty-first. I first divide marketable (W2) assets into three components: tangible assets, fixed-claim assets, and equities (see Figure 12.3).[14] I also include the cash surrender value of life insurance and pension plans in fixed claim assets rather than equities for this analysis. Tangibles remained relatively stable, at about a third of total assets, from 1900 until the mid-1940s, then increased quite sharply to a peak of 49 percent in 1981, but fell off to a third by 2013. Fixed claim assets, in contrast, rose as a proportion of total assets from 16 percent in 1900 to 34 percent in 1945 and then fell to about a quarter in 1962 after which it generally leveled off. Equities comprised almost half of total assets in 1900, then fell rather continuously as a proportion of assets, reaching

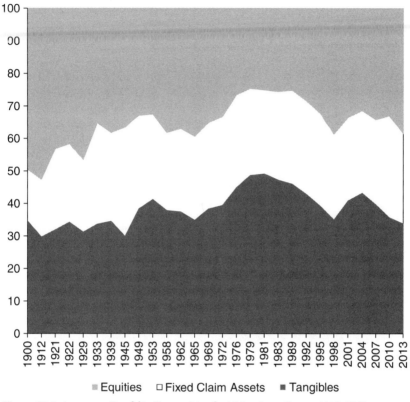

Figure 12.3. Aggregate Portfolio Composition by Major Asset Group, 1900–2013 (Percent of W2 gross assets)

about a quarter in 1983, but reversed course after that, attaining a 38 percent share by 2013.

Between 1900 and 1912, (the gross value of) owner-occupied housing fell from 17 to 13 percent of total assets and then remained relatively stable at this proportion until 1945 (see Figure 12.4 and Table 12.4). During the postwar housing boom, owner-occupied housing rose almost continuously as a proportion of total assets, peaking at 22 percent in 1979. After that, it fell to 15 percent in 1998, rebounded to 19 percent in 2004, and then fell off to 15 percent in 2013. The year-to-year fluctuations tend to reflect cyclical variations in home prices.[15] Total real estate as a share of assets shows a similar time trend, falling from 27 percent in 1900 to 21 percent in 1912, rising

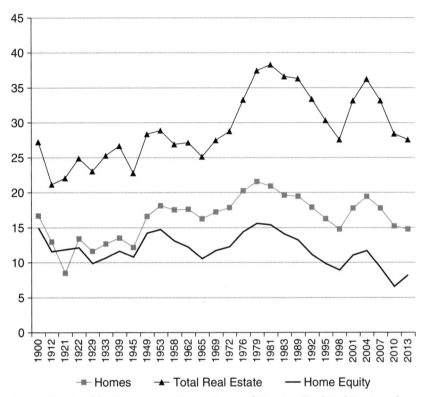

Figure 12.4. Portfolio Composition: Owner-Occupied Housing, Total Real Estate, and Net Home Equity (Percent of W2 gross assets)

from 23 percent in 1945 to 38 percent in 1981, falling to 28 percent in 1998, increasing to 36 percent in 2004, and then dropping to 28 percent in 2013.

The trend in home equity, the difference between the gross value of owner-occupied housing and mortgage debt, was similar though more attenuated.[16] Home equity as a share of total assets fell from 15 percent in 1900 to 10 percent in 1929, rose from 11 percent in 1945 to 15 percent in 1981, fell off to 9 percent in 1998, rebounded to 12 percent in 2004, and then decreased to 8 percent in 2013. However, what is more notable is the widening gap between this series and the share of homes in total assets after 1983. The difference increased from 5.5 percentage points in 1983 to 8.7 percentage points in 2010, though it did dip to 6.6 points in 2013.

Among financial assets, the biggest relative growth occurred in liquid assets, which rose from 8 percent of all assets in 1900 to 21 percent in 1945, fell

Table 12.4. The composition of aggregate marketable household wealth, 1900–2013 (percent of gross assets)

Year	Consumer Durables	Gross House Value	Bank Deposits and Other Liquid Assets	Nonhome Real Estate and Unincorp. Business Equity	Corporate Stock and Financial Securities	Total Debt	Home Equity
1900	7.4	16.7	7.7	45.1	23.1	5.0	15.0
1929	8.2	11.6	11.4	26.8	42.0	8.4	9.9
1949	10.0	16.6	19.0	30.5	23.9	7.1	14.2
1969	10.9	17.2	19.3	30.5	31.3	14.4	11.7
1989	9.6	19.5	21.7	25.0	24.2	17.6	13.2
2007	6.5	17.8	20.3	22.4	33.0	21.7	9.3
2013	6.3	14.8	22.8	19.2	36.9	18.0	8.2

Miscellaneous assets are excluded from the calculation of portfolio shares.

Gross house value: Gross value of owner-occupied housing.

Nonhome real estate and unincorporated business equity: Gross value of nonhome real estate plus net equity in unincorporated farm and nonfarm businesses.

Deposits and other liquid assets: Cash, currency, demand deposits, time deposits, money market funds, cash surrender value of insurance and pension plans, and IRAs.

Corporate stock and financial securities: Corporate stock, including mutual funds; corporate bonds, government bonds, open-market paper, notes, and other fixed-interest financial securities; and net equity in personal trusts and estates.

Total debt: Mortgage, installment, consumer, and other debt.

Home equity: Gross value of owner-occupied housing less apportioned mortgage debt (split proportionally between owner-occupied housing and other real estate).

off to 17 percent in 1958, and then grew rather steadily to 23 percent in 2013 (see Figure 12.5).[17] In contrast, financial securities increased from 8 percent of total assets in 1900 to 14 percent in 1933, fell rather steadily to 5 percent in 1981, rebounded to 8 percent in 1995, fell back to 5 percent in 2001, rose again to 8 percent in 2010, then dropped back to 5 percent in 2013. Corporate stock exhibited an even more volatile behavior. It grew from 15 percent of total assets in 1900 to 31 percent in 1929, as the stock market peaked, fell to 21 percent in 1933 and then to 14 percent in 1949, rose to 27 percent in 1965, fell again to 12 percent in 1979, rebounded to 33 percent in 1998 as the stock market neared another peak, dropped again to 24 percent in 2004, and then surged once more to 32 percent in 2013.

It is of interest that the results on financial assets (the sum of bank deposits, other liquid assets, corporate stock, and financial securities) strongly accord with Goldsmith's long-term analysis covering years 1688 to 1979.[18]

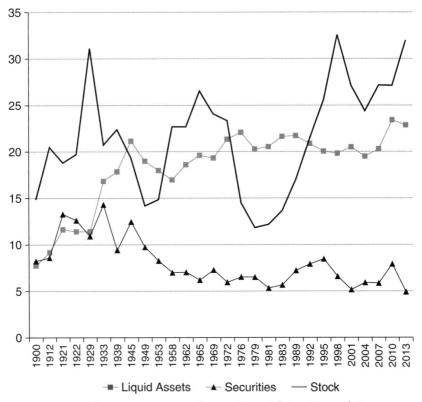

Figure 12.5. Portfolio Composition: Liquid Assets, Financial Securities, and Corporate Stock
(Percent of W2 gross assets)

Goldsmith called the ratio of financial to nonfinancial assets the "financial interrelations ratio." He concluded that this ratio starts out well less than unity in developing countries and then increases toward unity over the course of development. Here, in the case of the U.S., the ratio increased from 0.45 in 1900 to 1.15 in 1929, fell back to 0.75 in 1949, and then generally moved upward to 1.48 in 2013.

Perhaps the most dramatic change in the household portfolio was in the importance of unincorporated business equity (see Figure 12.6). This component comprised over a third of total assets in 1900 but fell almost steadily over the century, reaching 6 percent in 2013. Consumer durables rose from 7 percent of total assets in 1900 to 12 percent in 1953, remained at this level

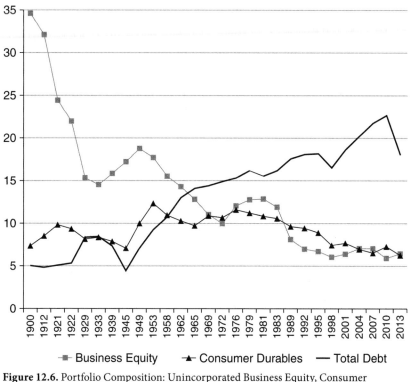

Figure 12.6. Portfolio Composition: Unincorporated Business Equity, Consumer Durables, and Total Household Debt
(Percent of W2 gross assets)

through 1976, but then fell off to 6 percent in 2013. Debt as a proportion of total assets fluctuated during the first half of the century, from 5 percent in 1900 to 9 percent in 1933 and then to 4 percent in 1945. It then rose rather steadily over the postwar period, from 4 percent in 1945 to 23 percent in 2010 but then dropped sharply to 18 percent in 2013.

Finally, both DB pension reserves and Social Security wealth increased relative to marketable (W2) assets until the early 1980s or so and then declined. As a share of augmented wealth (W4), which includes both pensions and Social Security wealth, the former rose almost continuously from zero in 1900 to a peak of 7.3 in percent 1983 and then declined to 4.7 percent in 2013, as the DB pension system unraveled (see Figure 12.7). The latter increased sharply from zero in 1933 to 11 percent in 1939, as the Social Security

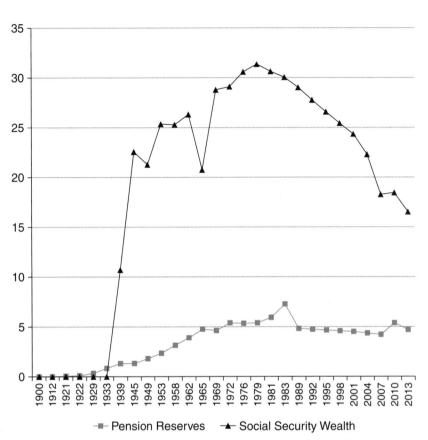

Figure 12.7. Portfolio Composition: Pension Reserves and Social Security Wealth as a Percent of W4 Gross Assets

system became established, peaked at 31 percent in 1979, and then fell off almost continuously to 17 percent in 2013, as the system reached maturity. Social Security wealth increased at a relatively faster rate in the middle years of the last century and pension reserves in later years. By 2013, pension reserves had assumed approximately the same magnitude as business equity and consumer durables, while Social Security wealth was on a par with liquid assets.

A full analysis of the reasons for the changes in the aggregate portfolio composition is beyond the scope of the chapter. However, there are several factors that immediately suggest themselves.

Changes in relative asset prices appear to have a strong bearing on movements in portfolio composition. This factor seems particularly germane to corporate stock, whose share in the aggregate portfolio reached a maximum of 31 percent in 1929, coincident with the peak in the stock market, and then fell to 21 percent in 1933, during the Great Depression. Later peaks in 1965, 1998, and 2013 were also associated with run-ups in stock prices. The sharp rise in the total value of real estate from 1965 to 1979 and the steady rise in both the gross and net values of owner-occupied housing over these years were also related to the sharp increase in real estate prices. Likewise, the downturn from 1979 to 1998, the upswing from 1998 to 2004, and the subsequent fall-off from 2004 to 2013 were each directly associated with movements in house and other real estate prices.

The secular decline in unincorporated business equity as a share of gross assets can be largely explained by two factors. Structural shifts in the economy are the main aspect, particularly the decline in agriculture in the U.S. economy over the twentieth century. For example, the share of unincorporated farm business equity in total assets fell from 27 percent in 1900 to 6 percent in 1983. In addition, small, unincorporated business declined in importance during the postwar period. The share of unincorporated nonfarm business equity in total assets fell from 9.3 percent in 1949 to 3.7 percent in 1972, though it increased to 5.9 percent by 1983.

Changes in household behavior as well as institutional changes also appear to affect portfolio composition. The sharp relative growth of deposits in financial institutions and other liquid assets and the corresponding relative decline of financial securities suggest that household preferences might have switched from risky, nonliquid assets to less risky liquid assets. The rapid relative growth of both pension reserves and Social Security wealth relative to marketable assets, at least until the early 1980s, suggests the importance of institutional changes in the U.S. retirement system.

The rising ratio of liabilities to assets suggests the greater willingness of households to take on debt, as well as the greater availability of credit. To show this, I divided total debt into two components—mortgage debt on owner-occupied housing and other debt, including mortgage debt on other real estate. Home mortgage debt grew from 1.7 percent of total assets in 1900 to 8.7 percent in 2010, though the ratio did come down to 6.6 percent in 2013, and, perhaps more interestingly, from 10.4 percent of the gross value of owner-occupied housing at the beginning of the last century to 57 percent in 2010, though the ratio did slip to 44 percent in 2013. Homeowners have thus appeared more willing and able to secure mortgage debt over the 113-year stretch. The ratio of other debt (including nonhome mortgage debt) to total assets also grew over time, from 3.3 percent in 1900 to 14 percent in 2010, though it fell once again to 11.5 percent in 2013. Thus, both the greater accessibility of mortgages on real property and of consumer credit, as well as greater household willingness to accept debt, appear to account for the sharp increase in household debt.

Concluding Remarks on Aggregate Household Wealth Trends

Average household wealth in real terms grew more than fourfold between 1900 and 2013. Indeed, real per capita wealth increased by a factor of 7.5 over these years. In addition, real marketable wealth (W2) increased at a somewhat faster rate than real disposable income. The ratio of W2 to disposable income, both in real terms, fell from 4.6 in 1900 to 3.6 in 1983 but then reversed course to a value of 5.4 in 2013. Over the full 113 years, the ratio was up quite modestly, by 18 percent, and there were subperiods during which the ratio declined instead. My analysis, however, did not find any evidence to support the well-known findings of Piketty or Saez and Zucman regarding a substantial rise in the wealth to income ratio, at least over this period.[19]

Can we draw any welfare implications from this? Certain assets such as owner-occupied housing and consumer durables confer direct services to households. Indeed, national accounts provide direct estimates of the former in the form of imputed rent to owner-occupied housing. The ratio of the gross value of owner-occupied housing to disposable personal income increased by 21 percent in real terms between 1900 and 2013, and that of durables to disposable income rose by 16 percent. The results suggest a corresponding gain in welfare to households. If so, the growth in personal income may understate the increase in the actual welfare level of the family.

On the other hand, the ratio of total debt to disposable income climbed almost fivefold from 1900 to 2013. This trend is likely to be symptomatic of a declining savings rate (relative to income) among U.S. families over the course of the time period. This result is consistent with those found in many other studies in which household savings are defined as current income (excluding capital gains) less current expenditures. The analysis in this chapter defines household savings as the change in household wealth. I have not separated out real changes in assets (and liabilities) from nominal or revaluation changes (that is, capital gains and losses). However, the evidence strongly suggests a declining propensity to save relative to disposable income. There are two likely reasons for this. First, greater credit accessibility (as reflected in the rising debt to asset ratio) suggests less need for precautionary savings, since loans are readily available in times of need. Second, the growth of institutionalized retirement savings, in the form of pension reserves and Social Security wealth, has to some extent obviated the need for personal retirement savings. Indeed, W3 grew faster than W2, and W4 increased more than W3. Moreover, W4 grew considerably faster than personal income over the 113 years. If W4 is a more appropriate welfare measure for the household than W2, then the growth in personal income may understate the actual increase in family well-being.[20]

In regard to changes in the aggregate portfolio composition, it is clear that several factors were at work. Price changes appear to be important for several assets, particularly corporate stock, whose value is volatile over time. Structural changes in the economy, such as the relative decline in agriculture and the consequent fall in the number of small farms, also had a direct bearing on changes in the composition of wealth. There is also evidence of substitution among various asset types—particularly away from risky, nonliquid assets toward relatively risk-free, liquid assets. Institutional changes, such as the shift from unincorporated to incorporated forms of enterprises, the greater accessibility of credit, both secured and unsecured, and the growth in the retirement system, also played major roles in changes to portfolio composition as did consumer behavioral changes. Consumers became more willing to accept debt and exhibited greater aversion to risky and nonliquid assets. Finally, changes in the composition of household wealth also reflect changes in the distribution of household wealth, particularly the decline in inequality over the first half of the twentieth century and its subsequent rise through the early part of the twenty-first century.

Appendix 12.1 The Construction of Aggregate Household Balance Sheets for Selected Years, 1900–2013

There are several historical time series available on aggregate household wealth, but none covers the entire period from 1900 to 2013. Moreover, the sources available are not entirely consistent with each other, thus necessitating several adjustments to make them comparable. Certain years during this period were selected on the basis of the availability of estate tax data, because in Chapter 13 the aggregate household balance sheet data are used to construct estimates of household wealth concentration.

The construction of the new household balance sheets relied on the following sources: 1900–1958: Full household balance sheet estimates are available in articles by Goldsmith, Brody, and Mendershausen and Goldsmith, Lipsey, and Mendelsen. The figures from these sources will be collectively referred to as the "Goldsmith data." These are the only sources available for nontangible assets for the period from 1900 to 1946.[21] 1925–1985: Musgrave provides estimates of tangible assets for every year in this period.[22] 1946–2013: Complete balance sheet data are contained in the Financial Accounts of the United States of the Board of Governors of the Federal Reserve System.[23] However, the FFA household sector includes not only households but also trusts and nonprofit organizations. For tangible assets this can be corrected, since the FFA's source is Musgrave's series, which reports separate estimates for the more narrowly defined household sector. For nontangible assets, other adjustments must be made. 1946–1980: Ruggles and Ruggles (RR) provide aggregate balance sheet data for the narrowly defined household sector for all assets and liabilities.[24] RR's estimates are based on imputations to the FFA household balance sheet data to separate out nonprofit organizations and trust funds. They also use a wealth concept that includes only the cash surrender value of pensions and insurance and is thus consistent with W2.

The aggregate household balance sheet estimates presented here combine data from these sources. Figures for tangible assets are based on Musgrave for the period from 1925 to 1983. The 1922 figures are estimated from Musgrave's data. The rationale for using Musgrave's data rather than the Goldsmith data for the period prior to 1949 is that Musgrave provided a consistent series over the entire period, from 1925 to 1985, and Musgrave's numbers were based on revised and improved data that were not available to Goldsmith in 1963. Estimates for nontangibles are based on Goldsmith's data for years prior to 1949, on the Ruggles and Ruggles data for most financial assets over the period from 1949 to 1980, and FFA data for all assets in 1981 and 1983, as well as some nontangible assets for the 1949–1980 period. RR's data provide a separate trust category, whereas FFA includes the financial assets, particularly stocks and bonds, held by trusts as part of the household sector. A separate asset category for trust funds is desirable because it differs from other household assets in regard to ownership and control.

In order to create a consistent aggregate balance sheet series, a number of adjustments to these basic data sources were required. Fortunately, for the years between 1946 and 1958, household balance sheet data are available from all four sources: Musgrave, Goldsmith, RR, and the FFA. Major discrepancies were found between Goldsmith and Musgrave for tangible assets (for residential structures, for example, percentage differences ranged between 10 and 32) and between Goldsmith on the one hand and RR and FFA on the other for financial assets (differences of up to 80 percent for some assets). These discrepancies were traced to the following sources: First, there are several differences in the categorization of assets between Goldsmith on the one hand and RR and FFA on the other. These differences do not affect the wealth totals, only the composition among asset categories. Second, there are some differences in the definition of household wealth. Goldsmith's total wealth concept corresponds to W3, which includes total pension reserves, whereas RR's definition corresponds to W2, which includes only the cash surrender value of pensions. Third, there are several methodological differences. For example, Goldsmith attributed all of the agricultural sector's net worth to the household sector, whereas RR assumed that a small percentage of this represents corporate business rather than unincorporated business and its value would be included in the household sector only through corporate stocks. Fourth, a large part of the difference in estimates is attributable to the revisions in the basic data since Goldsmith's study.

The adjustments were done in two stages. In the first, I corrected definitional differences in the asset categories between the various sources and the new classification scheme. In the new scheme, the asset categories are divided into three broad groups: tangibles, financial fixed claims, and equities. Liabilities are separated into mortgage debt, consumer debt, and other debt. This represents only a slight aggregation of the RR classification scheme. However, some substantial realignment of Goldsmith's categories was required.

In the second stage, I adjusted for differences in methodology between Goldsmith on the one hand and RR and FFA on the other, especially with respect to the items to be included in each asset category. Goldsmith differed from the other two in regard to the following assets: farm equity, unincorporated business equity, trusts, insurance, and pensions. Moreover, RR included household inventories, which consist of such items as clothing and food, in their tangible asset category. In 1983, the value of these inventory assets was roughly 253.8 billion dollars, or roughly 2 percent of the total value of household assets of $11.8 trillion. I eliminated the household inventory category from the new balance sheet, since it was not available for the early years. I also added Social Security wealth for wealth concept W4, which is not included in any of the original sources.

Differences in total household net worth between the new estimates and those of Goldsmith and RR varied by year and wealth concept. In regard to Goldsmith's figures, the total net worth figure for W3 differed from RR by between 3 and 6 percent, depending on the year, while for W2 the difference varied between 7 and 8 percent. The total wealth figure for W2 differed from that of RR by between 2 and 6 percent, whereas for W3 the percentage difference ranged from 4 to 12 percent. For W1 and W4, the percentage differences between the new estimates and those of Goldsmith and RR were much larger.

The accuracy of the new aggregate estimates depends on both the reasonableness of the assumptions in realigning Goldsmith's data with RR and the FFA and in the accuracy of the original sources. I assumed, in general, that the techniques and assumptions made in the original aggregate sources were correct. For one important category, owner-occupied housing, it is possible to compare the aggregate household balance sheet estimates with those derived from household survey data (see Appendix Table 12.1). These latter numbers were obtained from the U.S. Census of Housing for years 1950, 1960, 1970, and 1980, and from the 1962 SFCC and the 1983 SCF. Housing values in the census data are recorded in a limited number of groups, with the last consisting of an open-ended interval. An aggregate value of owner-occupied housing for the census data in each year was estimated by first fit-

Appendix Table 12.1. Value of owner-occupied housing and land: A comparison of aggregate values derived from household survey data with aggregate balance sheet estimates

Year	Household Survey Data (billions of dollars)[a]	FFA Balance Sheet Data (billions of dollars)[b]	Percentage Difference
1950	130.8	177.0	35.3
1960	353.4	372.9	5.5
1962	473.9	403.8	−14.8
1970	626.8	689.9	10.1
1980	2,234.3	2,568.9	15.0
1983	3,363.2	3,060.0	−9.0

a. For 1950, 1960, 1970, and 1980, the figures are drawn from the corresponding U.S. Bureau of the Census, Census of Housing (Vol. I, Part 1) for that year: 1950—Table 16; 1960—Table 8; 1970—Table 5; and 1980—Table 5. The 1962 figure is based on author's calculations from the Survey of Financial Characteristics of Consumers and the 1983 figure on author's calculations from the Survey of Consumer Finances.

b. The Flow of Funds (FFA) balance sheet figures are drawn from the FFA household sector. See Board of Governors of the Federal Reserve System, *Balance Sheets for the U.S. Economy, 1946–1985* (Washington, DC: Board of Governors, 1986).

ting a Pareto distribution to the upper tail of the distribution of housing values to obtain the mean for the open-ended category and then by summing across each house value category. For the 1962 SFCC and the 1983 SCF, the total value of owner-occupied housing was calculated directly from the microdata. The estimates from the surveys are compared to the balance sheet figures in Appendix Table 12.1. The difference between the estimated aggregate totals from the household survey data and the FFA varies between −15 and +35 percent. The estimates derived from the census data are always lower than the FFA figures, while the estimates from the 1962 and 1983 surveys are higher.

It is often assumed that for financial assets, such as stocks and bonds, the aggregate estimates are more reliable than survey estimates because of nonreporting and underreporting in the upper tail of the wealth distribution. For real estate, the opposite is often assumed—namely, that the survey estimates are more reliable than the aggregate balance sheet estimates, since households are usually very accurate in their assessment of the current market value of their property. For liquid financial assets, such as bank deposits, there is some controversy over whether the FFA's methodology produces more reliable estimates than those obtained from surveys. Curtin, Juster, and Morgan argued that for such liquid assets the FFA's values overestimated the true value due to its treatment of the household accounts as a residual—that is, what is left over after estimates are made for the other sectors of the economy (such as corporations, the government, and financial institutions).[25] Their evidence was based on the intuition that households should know the value of their bank accounts better than the value of other financial assets, such as stocks and bonds. Thus, if the survey's estimate for stocks was reasonably close to the aggregate balance sheet value, as was the case for the 1983 SCF, but only 30 or 40 percent for liquid assets, then the FFA's household totals for liquid assets were very likely overestimated. While this may be true for surveys that contain a large representation of the wealthy, such as the 1983 SCF, it is not clear that survey estimates are generally better than those from the FFA, particularly when the survey is more subject to underreporting, missing values, and underrepresentation of top wealth holders. In conclusion, comparisons between aggregate household wealth estimates derived from reliable macrodata and microdata sources suggest that the aggregate balance sheet sources used in this chapter may slightly underestimate real estate assets and overestimate liquid assets.[26]

Details follow on the procedures used to adjust the original sources of household balance sheet data to create the new series on household wealth for W1, W2, W3, and W4. The discussion is organized by asset and liability component.

Real Estate

This category includes owner-occupied housing, tenant-occupied housing, and residential land. The estimates for owner-occupied housing and tenant-occupied housing for the 1925–1983 period are based directly on Musgrave's series on the net value of structures. Musgrave's data are also the source for the FFA's tangible assets. The 1922 figures are derived by extrapolating time trends estimated using regression analysis for the 1925–1929 period. Goldsmith's data were used for residential structures only for 1900 and 1912. For the 1922–1959 period, Musgrave's figures were preferred to the Goldsmith data in order to maintain consistency with later years and because the under-lying worksheets were considerably updated and revised since Goldsmith's work. As a result, the 1900 and 1912 estimates are not consistent with the rest of the series for tangible assets. Goldsmith's figures were consistently lower than Musgrave's, between 10 and 32 percent, for every year in which the two series overlap.

There are some definitional differences between my real estate categories and those of Goldsmith, the FFA, and RR. Goldsmith included both residen-tial structures and nonresidential structures in the real estate sector, and his land estimate included both types of property. His figures on the value of nonresidential structures were transferred to the unincorporated business equity category for years 1900–1945. On the other hand, RR and the FFA in-cluded tenant-occupied housing in the unincorporated business category, which I transferred to the real estate category.

The residential land estimate used in the new household balance sheets includes both tenant and owner-occupied land. For the Goldsmith data, nonresidential land was subtracted from his total land estimates and trans-ferred to unincorporated business equity. For the 1949–2013 period, I used the FFA's estimates for owner-occupied land. The FFA total is uniformly higher, with the difference ranging between 5 and 17 percent. For the 1922–1945 period, Goldsmith's estimates of owner-occupied land were incorpo-rated directly into the new balance sheet series, and tenant-occupied land was estimated by assuming that the proportion of tenant-occupied land to owner-occupied land was the same as the ratio of tenant structures to owner-occupied structures in each year.

For the 1949–1983 period, there were substantial differences between RR's estimates and the FFA's estimates for the value of owner-occupied land, with the percentage differences ranging between –1 and +48 percent, though with no systematic trend. There is no apparent explanation for the differences. The FFA data were used in the new balance sheet series. As for the Goldsmith years, tenant-occupied land for the 1949–1983 period was estimated by as-suming that the proportion of tenant-occupied to owner-occupied land was the same as the ratio of tenant- to owner-occupied structures. The estimated value of tenant-occupied land was then subtracted from the total for the un-incorporated business category.

Consumer Durables

The figures for both the motor vehicle and other consumer durables category are based directly on Musgrave's series, which, like the residential structures series, are complete for the period from 1925 to 1984. The 1922 value was derived by extrapolating from the 1925–1929 time trend. Goldsmith's and Musgrave's figures were quite close, with a maximum difference of 9 percent. Musgrave's data were used in the new balance sheet series because they were based on revised and updated data.

Fixed Claim Assets

This category includes demand deposits and currency, deposits in other financial institutions, federal government securities, state and local government securities, corporate and foreign bonds, mortgages, open market paper, and other financial instruments. In the construction of the new balance sheet series for these categories, I used Goldsmith's data for the 1900–1945 period and the RR data for the 1949–80 period. As noted earlier, the FFA's "household sector" also included personal trusts and nonprofit organizations, and their figures could not be directly used. Since the RR series ended in 1980, it was necessary to make imputations for these categories for later years. For each of the three bond and security categories, I first computed the mean of the ratio of the RR figure to the corresponding FFA figure over the 1946–1980 period. This ratio for federal securities and the corporate bond category showed an upward trend approaching one by the end of the period. This implied that trust and nonprofit organization holdings of these two categories were essentially zero in 1980. Since this seemed unlikely, I decided to ignore the trend component in this ratio and relied, instead, on the average value of this ratio over the postwar period. Consequently, I multiplied the FFA figures for 1981 and 1983 by the mean ratio to obtain estimates for the narrowly defined household sector. For the two liquid asset categories (demand deposits and currency and deposits in other financial institutions), I used a trend regression of the ratio between the RR figures and the corresponding FFA figures to estimate the 1981 and 1983 values.

There were no major definitional differences between the Goldsmith and the RR fixed claim asset categories. A small amount of assets was shifted from Goldsmith's farm equity category into the household fixed claim asset categories to maintain consistency with my definition of farm assets held by the household sector. These adjustments are explained in the farm equity section that follows. Despite this adjustment, there were still large percentage differences for state and local government securities between the Goldsmith and RR data. These were usually offset in absolute terms by the discrepancies in the corporate bond category. For the overlapping years (1949,1953, and 1958), Goldsmith's estimates were higher for state and local government securities, from $2 billion to $6 billion. Except for 1958, the RR figures were higher for the corporate bond category. These differences were small relative to total assets, and, since I had no independent information, no correction was made to either series.

Corporate Stock

I used Goldsmith's and RR's corporate stock estimates in my household balance sheets. While there were substantial differences for the overlapping years between Goldsmith's estimates and RR's, there was no discernible trend in the percentage differences. As a result, no correction to either the RR series or the Goldsmith's data was made for this category. As noted earlier, the FFA household balance sheets include the nonprofit sector and personal trusts as well as households. As a result, the FFA values provided an upper bound to corporate stock holdings among households. Both the Goldsmith and the RR figures on household corporate stock were below the FFA values for all years. The 1981 and 1983 values were estimated using a trend regression of the ratio of the RR values to the corresponding FFA figures.

Farm Equity

The new household balance sheet series is based on Goldsmith's data for the 1900–1949 period and the FFA figures for the 1953–1983 period. The RR series and the FFA data were similar once adjustments were made for definitional differences. Before the adjustments, there were large differences for farm equity, both in relationship to total assets and in percentage terms, between Goldsmith on the one hand and both RR and FFA on the other hand. Goldsmith's estimates were approximately 30 percent higher than the RR figures for each of the years.

There are two reasons for this degree of discrepancy. First, on the basis of an examination of the respective farm sector balance sheets, it became apparent that Goldsmith included all of the residential household assets of a farm family in the farm equity category. In contrast, RR included only those assets associated with the farm business, and all others owned by farm families were included in the household sector. The FFA's approach was closer to RR's, except that the FFA included owner-occupied farm housing in farm equity. Second, RR did not attribute all of the farm sector's net worth to households, but instead assigned part of it to the corporate sector, whereas Goldsmith assumed no corporate ownership of farms. In 1958, a year in which farm balance sheets were available from both sources, it became clear that RR transferred 92 percent of total farm equity to the household sector and 8 percent to the corporate sector. I adjusted Goldsmith's farm equity estimates as well as the FFA's data to be consistent with RR's approach. After these adjustments, the differences between the Goldsmith's and RR's figures became quite small, ranging from zero to 8 percent for the overlapping years (1949, 1953, and 1958), in comparison to a range of 28 to 32 percent for the unadjusted data.

Unincorporated Business Equity

For the 1900–1945 period, Goldsmith's data were used for the new household balance sheet series with adjustments for differences in definitions previously discussed. For subsequent years, the new balance sheet figures were based on the FFA series, with the implicit assumption that trust fund and nonprofit organization holdings of this asset were negligible. I decided not to use the RR figures for this category, since even after correcting for differences in concept, RR's numbers were still 13 to 14 percent lower than the FFA's and 6 to 12 percent lower than Goldsmith's estimates for the 1949–1958 period.

Trust Fund Equity

Trust funds were valued differently in Goldsmith's balance sheets than in RR's. Goldsmith distributed trust funds across all financial categories, similar to the FFA approach, although the estimates in his 1956 volume included separate trust estimates for each asset category and his 1963 publication included a separate trust balance sheet for the 1945–1958 period. The FFA balance sheets did not separate out this category from household assets and did not report any estimates for trusts in any year. The RR balance sheets, on the other hand, recorded trust funds as a separate category. I followed the RR approach of recording trust funds as a separate category because it was necessary to distinguish between the actuarial concept of trusts and the full trust value. Goldsmith's balance sheets were thus adjusted by subtracting from Goldsmith's asset categories an amount estimated as belonging to trust funds. The difference between Goldsmith's and RR's estimates of total trust equity was relatively small, ranging from 2 to 14 percent for the years 1949, 1953, and 1958.

For the W1 measure, only the actuarial value of trust funds was included. Based on a comparison of 1965 income tax return data with the FFA data, Smith and Franklin estimated that the actuarial value of trust funds was approximately 54 percent of trust fund equity, and this proportion was used here to estimate the actuarial value of trust funds.[27] The W2 measure includes the total value of trust fund equity as reported in Goldsmith and RR.

Life Insurance Equity

Substantial differences in the concept of insurance equity existed among the three basic sources. Insurance equity refers to the combined value of government employee insurance and private insurance plans. The FFA included the full reserves or equity of life insurance in the category, whereas RR used a cash surrender value (CSV) concept. RR estimated the CSV of life insurance as approximately 95 percent of the FFA's total insurance reserves for every year. Goldsmith, like the FFA, reported the full insurance reserves in his household estimates. In comparing the estimates from the different sources, I found that Goldsmith's estimates of private insurance reserves were substantially higher than the reserve figures of both the government and private insurance systems reported in the FFA. Between 1946 and 1958, the ratio of the FFA's total reserve estimate to Goldsmith's private reserve figure declined from 0.94 to 0.79. Goldsmith's numbers were higher due to his inclusion of both the insurance companies' pension funds and the total net assets of the insurance companies.[28] These items were not included in the FFA or RR estimates. These two additional components in the Goldsmith category increased over time, reaching 45 percent of the FFA's figure on private life insurance reserves in 1958. The narrower FFA definition is used for insurance equity in the new balance sheets, while life insurance pension reserves are included in the pension reserve category. Goldsmith's figures were adjusted by subtracting these two extra components. In addition, I followed RR's convention in including only the cash surrender value (CSV) of life insurance reserves in this category.

Pensions

Goldsmith's balance sheets differed from those of RR and FFA with respect to the definition of the pension category. RR and the FFA included the pension reserves only of the private and government pension systems. Goldsmith's concept was much broader and included such items as the reserves of the unemployment insurance system and those of the Old-Age and Survivors Insurance Trust Fund (OASI) system.[29] As a result, there were significant differences between pension reserve figures calculated by Goldsmith and the FFA, though the percentage difference between the two series fell from 54 to 22 percent between 1949 and 1958. The first adjustment that I made to the Goldsmith figures was the elimination of nonpension reserves from this category.

As with life insurance, RR used a cash surrender concept. The CSV of pensions was estimated to equal about 5 percent of total pension reserves in each year. Goldsmith, in contrast, included the full pension reserves in his household balance sheet. For W1 and W2, I use the CSV of pensions. The W3 and W4 wealth measures incorporate the full pension reserves reported in Goldsmith's data and the FFA. The difference between these pension measures increased in magnitude as pension wealth increased. For example in

1983, total pension reserves were $1,316.4 billion, representing 9.3 percent of net worth, while its CSV was $65.8 billion or less than 1 percent of net worth.

Social Security Wealth

Aggregate estimates of Social Security wealth, defined as the expected value of future Social Security benefits, were not available from any of the balance sheet sources. Feldstein calculated annual aggregate Social Security wealth for his analysis of U.S. savings behavior over the period from 1929 through 1971.[30] Feldstein's estimates were corrected and updated by Leimer and Lesnoy.[31] For the W4 series, it was assumed that Social Security wealth was zero before 1936; from 1936 through 1978, Leimer and Lesnoy's "fixed ratio" estimates was used.[32] The fixed ratio assumption led to the smallest aggregate estimates among the alternative Social Security series calculated by Leimer and Lesnoy.

The 1981 and 1983 Social Security wealth estimates for the W4 series were calculated from two sources: a time trend extrapolation of the Leimer and Lesnoy series and estimates calculated directly from the 1983 SCF. The aggregate Social Security estimates from the 1983 survey varied between $3,467.8 billion and $7,101.4 billion for real growth rates in mean Social Security benefits in a range of zero to 3 percent. The time trend forecasts of Social Security wealth, based on the Leimer and Lesnoy series, are $4,800 billion for 1981 and $6,000 billion for 1953. For the W4 series, 1 use the time trend estimate for 1981 and a value of $5,441.8 billion for 1983 based on direct calculations from the 1983 SCF, with a mean growth rate in real Social Security benefits assumed to be two percent per year.[33]

Liabilities

This category includes mortgage debt, consumer debt, and all other household debt. There were no major differences in the definition of these categories between Goldsmith, RR, and FFA. For the new household balance sheets, Goldsmith's data are used for the 1900–1945 period and the FFA's and RR's estimates for 1949 and subsequent years. For the overlapping years, the difference between Goldsmith's and RR's estimates was quite small, ranging between 1 and 6 percent.

Household Balance Sheets for 1983–2013

The only available source for these years is Table B.101 of the FFA. As noted previously, the sector includes both households and nonprofit organizations. It therefore became necessary to strip away the assets and liabilities of the latter to obtain a "pure" household sector. Some assets and liabilities were easily identifiable as belonging to the nonprofit sector. These included real estate, equipment, and intellectual property products owned by non-profits, other loans and advances, mortgages, and consumer credit on the asset side of the ledger; and debt securities and trade payables on the liability side. Unfortunately, it was not possible to identify (or even estimate) what share of other assets such as deposits, debt securities, corporate equities, mutual fund shares, and pension reserves was owned by the nonprofit sector. On the liability side, it was not possible to separate out loans made to non-profits. As a result, I left these items in the household balance sheet. On net, this will lead to an overstatement of the liabilities of the household sector.

As a result, I benchmarked the 1983 FFA data to balance sheet data for 1983 in a previous work.[34] This was done on a component-by-component basis. Thus, each asset and liability category in the FFA was set equal to the corresponding entry in the earlier data.[35] The 1983 benchmark figures were then updated annually on the basis of the rate of growth of each component derived from the FFA data.

13

Long-Term Trends in the Concentration of Household Wealth

I n this chapter, I construct a reasonably consistent time series on the size distribution of household wealth for the period 1922 to 2013 on the basis of estate tax data and survey data for selected measures of household wealth.[1] The major purpose is to extend and improve this wealth data by reconciling and aligning the different sources on wealth concentration in order to improve comparability. I estimate alternative measures of wealth concentration and inequality on the basis of different sources and different imputation techniques. I also present alternative estimates based on different concepts of household wealth, including retirement wealth.

Analysis of the estate tax data series indicates that wealth concentration is very high. The top 1 percent of wealth holders owned at least one-fourth of total wealth from 1922 to 2013. Wealth concentration fell from 1922 to the mid-1970s and then rose, at least through 2013. The decline in twentieth-century wealth inequality through the mid-1970s is consistent with trends identified by other researchers.[2]

An erratic downward trend in wealth concentration occurred between 1929 and the mid-1970s, after which wealth inequality rose very sharply during the 1980s, leveled off until 2007, and then spiked upward. The downward trend in wealth inequality from the estate data series between 1922 and the mid-1970s remains basically unchanged even after different choices of adjustment procedures and wealth concepts are used. Two factors influence the actual trend in measured inequality. (1) The addition of Social Security wealth, which accelerates the decline in wealth concentration between the early 1920s and the mid-1970s, and (2) the transformation of the estate data series, which is based on the individual as the unit of observation, into corresponding household estimates of wealth concentration. The household-based series shows less of a decline in inequality during and after World War II. The increase in inequality in terms of the proportion of total wealth growth accruing to the top wealth percentiles gives an even more dramatic picture of the rise in inequality since the mid-1970s.

The chapter describes a time series of wealth concentration estimates for the years noted. I compare my adjusted concentration estimates for top wealth holders derived from estate tax data with other sources such as household survey data and synthetic databases. As with the aggregate household balance sheet data, I make several transformations and adjustments to the size distribution data in order to increase consistency within the estate tax data series and to compare estimates from different data sources. I summarize the data adjustments and report different series on the shares of the top percentile of wealth holders.[3] In order to ascertain the sensitivity of estimates of both concentration levels and trends, I analyze the effect of different wealth definitions and imputation procedures on Lampman's and Smith's estimates as well as on the survey data.

Several comparisons are undertaken in this analysis. I compare concentration estimates based on different wealth concepts, such as standard wealth and broader measures that include retirement wealth, for both the estate tax data and the estimates derived from household survey data. I also transform Lampman's estate tax data estimates for the period 1922–1953 to represent the top percentile and half percentile of the population in order to compare the results with Smith's estimates. My adjusted estimates are then compared with the original published estimates and, as a test of the reliability of the reported trends in concentration, I do a preliminary transformation of the estate tax data from an individual base to a household base and compare the resulting household trend with the time trends based on individual data. For these various adjustments and transformations I then compute upper and lower bounds on wealth concentration to test how sensitive the results are to the various assumptions and wealth definitions.

The chapter concludes with consideration of two general issues: the sensitivity of estimated time trends in household wealth inequality to alternative imputation, correction, and adjustment procedures; and how inequality estimates and trends in these estimates differ in regard to different definitions of household wealth, particularly with respect to the inclusion of Social Security and pension wealth.

The Concentration of Wealth, 1922–2013

Information available on household wealth distribution for the twentieth and twenty-first centuries is based mainly on estate data for the very wealthy collected from national estate tax records for selected years between 1922 and 1982 and cross-sectional household surveys for selected years starting in 1953. In addition, there are synthetic databases that were constructed using income tax data merged with census files, estate files, and other sources.[4]

Table 13.1 and Figure 13.1 report Lampman's and Smith's original concentration estimates for the top 0.5 percent of the population from 1922 through 1976.[5] These estimates show a high concentration of wealth throughout the period. Over 20 percent of total wealth was owned by the top 0.5 percent in each of these years except 1949 and 1976. However, the results also indicate a significant decline in wealth concentration over the half century, from a maximum share of 32.4 percent for the top 0.5 percent in 1929 to 14.4 percent in 1976. In particular, there was a substantial decline in the top wealth holders' share during World War I1 and another large fall in the mid-1970s, as indicated in Smith's results.

This section explores the sensitivity of the wealth concentration results in Table 13.1 to the following factors: differences between Smith's and Lampman's imputation assumptions; adjustments to the aggregate balance sheet series; the addition of retirement wealth (W3 and W4); changes in the number of household units and the composition of wealth between household members; and differences in the data and methodology used (in particular,

Table 13.1. Estimates of the share of total household net worth held by the top 0.5 percent of individual wealth holders

	1922	1929	1933	1939	1945	1949	1953
Lampman	29.8	32.4	25.2	28.0	20.9	19.3	22.7
	1958	1962	1965	1969	1972	1976	
Smith	21.4	22.2	25.4	21.8	21.9	14.4	

Sources: 1922–1953: Lampman's so-called basic variant for the wealth holdings of the top 0.5 percent, from Robert J. Lampman, *The Share of Top Wealthholders in National Wealth, 1922–56* (Princeton, NJ: Princeton University Press, 1962), 202; 1958–1976: James D. Smith, "Trends in the Concentration of Personal Wealth in the United States, 1958–1976," *Review of Income and Wealth* 30, no. 4 (1984): 422.

Figure 13.1. Lampman / Smith Combined Series of the Share of Total Wealth Held by the Top 0.5 Percent of Individuals
(Percentage)

a comparison of estate data estimates with those from household surveys and other sources).

Unadjusted Wealth Concentration Estimates from Estate Tax Data

The estate files represent the wealth of the deceased. The wealth estimates for the living population are derived using the estate multiplier method, which divides the population by age and gender and weights the deceased in each group by the reciprocal of the survival probability for that group. The survival probabilities used are higher than those for the population at large, because of the longer expected life span of the wealthy. This method produces a point estimate that can have a very large variance, particularly for the young, since there are very few in the sample. In fact, the multipliers for those under age 50 approach two thousand. Atkinson and Shorrocks have criticized estate estimates as overestimating the decline in inequality.[6] Estate tax estimates are based on individual data rather than the household unit and over time marital customs and relations changed. Married women inherit more wealth than in the past and have higher wealth levels than previously, which reduces individual concentration even if household wealth inequality does not change. For example, between 1929 and 1953, Lampman reported that the percentage of married women among top wealth holders increased from 8.5 to 18 percent.

The estate tax files used by Lampman and Smith did not include all assets, and the authors used different assumptions concerning pensions and trusts. For example, in Smith's estimates, pensions were included only at their cash surrender value (CSV), and a large percentage of trusts—those that were not directly under the control of the deceased—were measured at their actuarial value since that is how they are measured in the estate files. Thus, Smith's wealth definition corresponds to a narrower "available" wealth concept, as in my W1 measure.[7] On the other hand, Lampman used a wealth measure that included the full value of pensions as well as trusts (like W3). Smith's reported concentration estimates are biased downward in relation to Lampman's because he did not include a portion of the value of trusts.

Another asset, life insurance, is overstated in the estate files, a problem that both Lampman and Smith recognized and made adjustments for. Another difference is that Lampman's concentration estimates reported in Table 13.1 are based on Goldsmith's estimates of aggregate household wealth (see Chapter 12 Appendix). In contrast, Smith's estimates are based on Ruggles and Ruggles aggregate data.[8] Also, Lampman used Goldsmith's year-end aggregates, whereas Smith used a midyear aggregate estimate.[9] Finally, neither Smith nor Lampman included expected Social Security benefits in their wealth estimates.

Adjusted Wealth Concentration Estimates from Estate Tax Data

In order to derive a more consistent series on household wealth concentration than the ones presented in Table 13.1 and to include Social Security wealth, I made a series of adjustments to the Lampman and Smith figures. First, I used the adjusted aggregate household balance sheet totals to derive the wealth concentration estimates. Second, imputations were provided for the assets that were excluded from the estate files—trusts, pensions, and

Social Security wealth. For each of them, several alternative assumptions were made, creating upper and lower bounds for the top wealth holders' holdings in each asset category. Tables 13.2 and 13.3 report only selected wealth concentration results from the devised alternative scenarios. Other imputation assumptions yielded estimates that either were not substantially different (less than 2 percent) from those reported in Table 13.1 or fell between the bounds of the other series.

Table 13.2 presents the adjusted wealth concentration shares for top wealth holders from the estate data estimates for W1, W2, W3, and W4, as well as concentration estimates for the top 0.5 and 1 percent of households from household survey data.[10]

In the original Lampman data, for the period 1922–1953, estimates were provided for different proportions of the population in each year. His sample was all wealth holders with total assets above $60,000. Thus, the fraction of population represented in the sample and reported in Table 13.2 varied over the period, from a low of 0.3 percent in 1929 to a high of 1 percent in 1958. In Table 13.2, the percentage of the population represented in the Lampman data is reported in the second column, followed by the corresponding wealth shares for this population percentage for wealth concepts W1, W2, W3, and W4.

Comparisons among the wealth concentration estimates for the different wealth definitions illustrate the sensitivity of the estimated shares of top wealth holders to the different imputation assumptions and to the inclusion of retirement wealth. The difference arising from alternative assumptions in the treatment of trusts is captured by wealth concepts W1 and W2. W2 represents an upper bound for trust holdings since its calculation assumed that the top 1 percent owned 100 percent of total trust assets. W1 represents a reasonable lower bound since it evaluates trusts at their much lower actuarial value and assumes that all the trust holdings of the wealthy were included in the estate file. In contrast, Lampman assumed that only about 10 percent of total trusts were included in the basic estate data, and Smith estimated that the actuarial value represented 54 percent of all trusts.[11] The wealth concentration estimates reported in Table 13.2 for W1 correspond to the wealth definition used by Smith. Those for W2 give the highest concentration ratio because of the assumption that 100 percent of trusts were held by the top 1 percent and the inclusion of the full value of trusts in W2. In addition, W2 excludes retirement wealth, except for pension CSV, which constituted a

Table 13.2. The share of total net worth of top wealth holders based on different wealth definitions: the adjusted series

Year	Share of Top	Wealth Definition			
		W1	W2	W3	W4
A. Estimates from Estate Tax Data[a]					
1922	0.5%	26.8	28.4	28.0	28.0
1929	0.3%	27.3	29.1	28.5	28.5
1939	0.6%	27.2	29.8	28.8	25.9
1945	0.7%	22.3	24.4	23.7	18.9
1949	0.8%	21.9	23.2	22.6	18.4
1953	1.0%	26.6	28.4	27.4	21.3
1958	0.5%	20.8	22.7	21.5	16.4
	1.0%	25.9	27.7	26.6	20.7
1962	0.5%	23.0	25.0	23.4	17.5
	1.0%	29.1	31.1	29.5	22.4
1965	0.5%	25.4	27.7	25.7	18.9
	1.0%	31.3	33.6	31.5	23.6
1969	0.5%	22.5	24.5	22.6	16.4
	1.0%	28.2	30.2	28.3	20.9
1972	0.5%	21.8	24.0	21.9	15.8
	1.0%	27.6	29.8	27.6	20.3
1976	0.5%	12.6	14.6	13.2	9.8
	1.0%	17.3	19.1	17.8	13.4
1981	0.8%	19.7	21.2	19.5	14.0
	2.0%	28.4	29.7	27.8	20.4
B. Estimates from Household Survey Data[b]					
1962	0.5%	22.4	24.8	23.2	16.7
	1.0%	31.0	33.2	31.4	22.7
1983	0.5%	23.2	24.9	22.0	15.1
	1.0%	31.2	27.7	29.2	20.5

Sources: Estate data sources for 1922–1953: Robert J. Lampman, *The Share of Top Wealthholders in National Wealth, 1922–56* (Princeton, NJ: Princeton University Press, 1962); for 1953–1976: James D. Smith, "Trends in the Concentration of Personal Wealth in the United States, 1958–1976," *Review of Income and Wealth* 30, no. 4 (1984): 419–28, and "Recent Trends in the Distribution of Wealth in the U.S.: Data Research Problems and Prospects," in *International Comparisons of the Distribution of Household Wealth*, Edward N. Wolff, ed. (New York: Oxford University Press, 1987), 72–89; for 1981: Marvin Schwartz, "Trends in Personal Wealth, 1976–1981," *Statistics of Income Bulletin* 3 (Summer 1983): 1–26.

The household survey data sources are the 1962 SFCC and the 1983 SCF.

The wealth concentration estimates are from author's calculations.

The adjustments and procedures are explained in the section "The Concentration of Wealth, 1922–2013."

The figures differ slightly from those in the text because of different assumptions concerning trust and pension holdings, which are necessary for consistency between the estate data and the survey data estimates.

a. Data are recorded by year and percentage of population.

b. Data are recorded by year and percentage of households.

negligible fraction of total wealth. The results from Table 13.2 indicate that the share of wealth held by the top wealth holders differs by about 2 percentage points from the upper- and lower-bound assumptions concerning trusts.

The extent to which wealth concentration is lessened when retirement wealth is included in the household balance sheet is indicated by estimates for W3 and W4. W3 includes full pension reserves, which are reported in the aggregate balance sheet data. However, one major difficulty is that there is very little information concerning the percentage of total pensions owned by top wealth holders. I made alternative assumptions about this share, ranging from a minimum of 3 percent to a maximum of 15 percent for the top 1 percent of wealth holders. The different assumptions had little effect on total wealth concentration. In the W3 estimates reported in Table 13.2, it is assumed that the share of total pension wealth held by the top percentile declined over time because of the growth of pensions over the period. The addition of pension wealth had a minor effect on concentration, owing to its relatively small size in relation to total assets. On the other hand, the addition of Social Security wealth (in W4) significantly lowered the degree of inequality because of its relatively large magnitude. The share of net worth of the top percentile dropped between 4 and 8 percentage points from the inclusion of Social Security wealth. This represents a decline of 20 to 33 percent in the share of total net worth held by the top 1 percent.

I next standardized the concentration shares from Lampman and Schwartz shown in Table 13.2 to the top 0.5 and 1 percent of the population using a Pareto distribution. This technique assumes that the Pareto distribution is representative of the wealth distribution of the upper tail in each year. The standardized results are reported in Table 13.3 and are illustrated in Figure 13.1.

The difference in the share of the top 0.5 percent between the original Lampman and Smith estimates and the revised W1 estimates primarily reflects differences between the Goldsmith and Ruggles and Ruggles balance sheet estimates for the household sector.[12] My concentration estimates for W1 (for the top 0.5 percent) are lower than Lampman's figures, while for W2 the shares are higher. The new concentration estimates for W1 based on Smith's data are higher than his original estimates in some years and lower in others. In general, the aggregate adjustments changed the concentration results from 1 to 2 percentage points.

Table 13.3. The share of total assets of the top 0.5 and 1 percent of the population for alternative definitions of wealth, 1922–1981

	Wealth Definition							
	W1		W2		W3		W4	
Year	Top 0.5%	Top 1.0%	Top 0.5%	Top 1.0%	Top 0.5%	Top 1.0%	Top 0.5%	Top 1.0%
1922	28.8	37.1	30.3	38.3	29.9	37.9	29.9	37.9
1929	31.7	35.8	33.2	37.3	27.7	36.7	32.7	36.7
1939	26.7	35.9	29.1	38.1	28.3	37.1	25.6	33.4
1945	20.6	27.0	22.6	28.9	21.9	28.1	17.7	22.4
1949	18.2	23.9	20.2	25.7	19.6	25.0	16.3	20.5
1953	21.2	26.5	22.9	28.1	22.2	27.3	17.9	21.6
1958	20.3	25.4	22.0	27.0	21.0	26.0	16.4	20.7
1962	22.4	28.4	24.2	30.1	22.8	28.8	17.6	22.5
1965	24.2	29.9	26.2	31.9	24.5	30.2	18.7	23.4
1969	21.7	27.3	23.4	29.0	21.8	27.4	16.4	21.0
1972	21.0	26.8	23.0	28.6	21.2	26.8	15.9	20.5
1976	12.8	17.3	14.4	18.9	13.3	17.7	10.1	13.8
1981	16.0	22.0						

Sources: For the Lampman and Schwartz data (years 1922, 1929. 1939, 1945, 1949, 1953, and 1981), I estimated the share of the top 0.5 and 1.0 percent of wealth holders using the Pareto distribution. The 1981 figure is computed for W1 only.

a. Data are recorded by year and percentage of population

Table 13.3, a comparison of the four wealth measures, confirms the previous results. The addition of retirement wealth to conventional wealth reduces measured concentration and the effect of adding pension wealth is relatively small. The addition of Social Security wealth, however, is substantial and relatively constant over time since its introduction in 1935.[13] My adjustments to the estate tax estimates do not account for the underreporting of assets or nonfiling in the estate data. Both omissions bias the reported concentration results downward. The extent of this bias is discussed in the comparisons between estate and survey data (see Table 13.5).

Long-Term Trends in Wealth Inequality: Individuals versus Households

The preceding adjustments to the estate data allowed an examination of the sensitivity of the wealth concentration estimates to different wealth aggregates

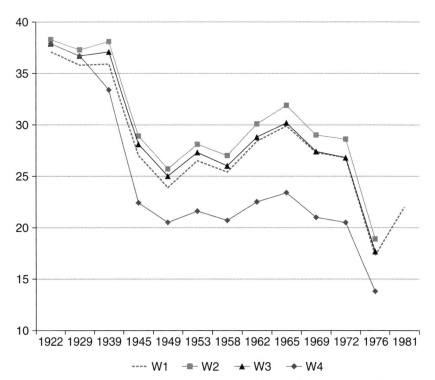

Figure 13.2. Share of Total Wealth Held by the Top 1 Percent of Individual Wealth Holders, 1922 to 1981: Author's Estimates
(Percentage)

and imputations and adjustments. These adjustments did not significantly alter the trend in concentration. The results from Table 13.3 and Figure 13.2 indicate that wealth concentration peaked during the period from 1922 through 1939, declined significantly during World War II, increased between 1949 and 1965, declined slightly in 1972, fell to a record low in 1976, and then partially rebounded by 1981.

A large permanent decline in concentration during the 1970s is not substantiated by the household survey data reported in Table 13.2. A comparison of the 1962 and 1983 survey data for the top 1 percent of households indicates similar concentration levels in the two years. One possible reason for this discrepancy is the difference in the unit of observation between estate and survey data. Estate files record wealth for the individual, while surveys are based on household units. As mentioned earlier, the increased tendency to

Table 13.4. Lower-bound estimates of the share of total assets of the top 1 percent of households from alternative definitions of wealth, 1922–1976

Year	Wealth Definition			
	W1	W2	W3	W4
1922	24.0	25.5	25.2	25.2
1929	29.1	30.7	30.2	30.2
1939	22.7	25.3	24.5	22.2
1945	18.6	20.7	20.1	16.2
1949	16.8	18.8	18.3	15.2
1953	20.0	21.7	21.1	17.0
1958	18.5	20.0	19.1	15.0
1962	20.5	22.1	20.9	16.1
1965	22.1	23.9	22.4	17.1
1969	20.0	21.6	20.7	15.4
1972	18.5	20.2	18.6	14.0
1976	11.3	12.7	11.7	9.0

Source: The household shares are derived from estate tax data on the wealth of individual wealth holders.

divide wealth equally between household members reduces the estate concentration estimates without changing household wealth concentration. In Table 13.4 I perform a preliminary analysis of the sensitivity of the trends in concentration to changes in the unit of observation (also see Figure 13.3). The reported concentration estimates represent the estimated top 1 percent of *households* rather than the top 1 percent of *individuals*.

In order to change the estate data to a household base, certain assumptions must be made about the division of wealth within households. For the values shown in Table 13.4, it was assumed that all married women in the sample of top wealth holders married wealthy men in the sample, while the remaining married men had wives with zero wealth. Married men represented from 55 to 59 percent of the sample, while married woman represented between 9 and 18 percent. This assumption results in the lowest number of households formed from the individuals in the estate tax sample and thus the highest level of household wealth concentration with regard to married women. However, it produces a very low estimate of the total wealth held by the top 1 percent of households because of the assumption that the married men in the sample married women with zero wealth.

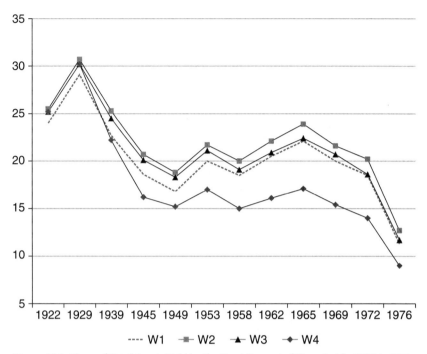

Figure 13.3. Share of Total Assets Held by the Top 1 Percent of Households, 1922 to 1976: Lower–Bound Estimates
(Percentage)

The results from Table 13.4 and Figure 13.3 indicate that a portion of the decline in individual wealth concentration over the period from 1922 to 1953 was due to changes in the wealth of married women. The share of total assets of the top 1 percent of households declined by 4 percentage points over this period, in contrast to a 10 percentage point drop in the share of the wealthiest 1 percent of individuals. The years 1929 and 1949 appear to be outliers, with 1929 a peak and 1949 a trough. During the period from 1958 to 1976, I estimated on the basis of Smith's data that the percentage of married women among the wealthy remained relatively constant at 18 percent.[14] Thus, for Smith's data, there was no significant difference in the concentration estimates between the top 1 percent of households and the top 1 percent of individuals.

While some of the decline in wealth concentration found by Lampman appears to be due to changes in the wealth status of married women, the sharp drop in inequality found in Smith's results cannot be explained by my transformation of the estate data to the household unit. There are several other possible explanations. The 1976 estate estimates could be incorrect, especially with respect to stock holdings. Those results suggested not only a significant drop in the value of stocks but also a substantial fall in the percentage of stock held by the top 1 percent of the population, from 57.4 percent in 1972 to 37.6 percent in 1976. If this drop represented a portfolio shift, then some other asset should have increased. However, this did not happen. A large increase may have occurred in the volume of stocks that were owned primarily by the less wealthy, but there was no evidence of this from other sources. There was also a sharp fall in the price of stock shares relative to that of real estate in the 1970s, but the relative price shift was not substantial enough to account for the magnitude of the fall in wealth concentration between 1972 and 1976. The last possibility is that there was an increase in the degree of underreporting of all assets in the estate data. There is no obvious reason for such an increase in the 1970s, although in the early 1980s this was probably the case, because of the large increase in the gift exclusion in estate tax returns.

Comparison of Inequality Estimates from Various Data Sources

The estate tax data are not corrected for underreporting or the transference of wealth through gifts. In order to examine the extent of any underreporting, a comparison is made between the estate tax estimates and household survey estimates for 1962 and 1983 (see Table 13.5). The concentration estimates for the latter are based on the 1962 Survey of Financial Characteristics of Consumers (SFCC) and the 1983 Survey of Consumer Finances (SCF), both of which have been adjusted to correspond to the aggregate household balance sheet totals for each asset.[15] The household concentration estimates from the 1962 SFCC were significantly higher, by about 7 percentage points, than those derived from estate data. One possible reason for this difference is the conservative assumption used in converting the estate data to a household base. If it had been assumed that all married men in the estate sample of top wealth holders had married women with wealth, the concentration estimates would have been higher, but not enough to account for the difference. Another possible reason for the discrepancy

Table 13.5. A comparison of shares of top wealth holders based on estate tax and household survey data (percentage of total assets)

Wealth Definition	Estate Tax Data				Survey Data	
	1962	1972	1976		1962	1983
A. Top 1 Percent of Households						
W1	20.5	18.5	11.3		27.8	28.2
W2	22.1	20.2	12.7		29.9	29.5
W3	20.9	18.6	11.7		28.5	26.9
W4	16.1	14.0	9.0		22.3	19.7

	Estate Tax Data			
	1962	1972	1976	1981[a]
B. Top 1 Percent of Individuals				
W1	28.4	26.8	17.3	22.0
W2	30.1	28.6	18.9	
W3	28.8	26.8	17.7	
W4	22.5	20.5	13.8	

Sources: For households, estate estimates are taken from Table 13.4 and survey estimates from Table 13.2. For individuals, estate estimates are taken from Table 13.3.

a. The 1981 figure is computed for W1 only.

between the estate and survey estimates is that there was a serious under-reporting problem in the estate data. The results in Tables 13.5 and 13.6 indicate the need for further work on the effect of the unit of observation (household vs. individual) on measures of wealth inequality as well as for further reconciliation between estate tax and household survey estimates of wealth inequality.

Table 13.6 reports wealth concentration estimates from other sources. The results suggest that many surveys do not sufficiently oversample the rich to capture the upper tail of the distribution. For example, the 1979 data from the Income Survey and Development Program (ISDP) captured only 66 percent of net worth, and the 1979 household survey from the President's Commission on Pension Policy estimated an aggregate household wealth that was only 52 percent of my total net worth figure.[16] In comparison, the (unadjusted) 1962 SFCC captured 79 percent and the (unadjusted) 1983 SCF 89 percent of aggregate net worth.[17] The resulting wealth concentration estimates from each survey vary with the degree of underreporting and bias in

Table 13.6. Share of total net worth of richest households: Estimates from other sources, 1969–1984

	1969 MESP Database[a]	1973 Greenwood Database[b]	1979 ISDP Survey[c]	1979 Pension Survey[d]	1984 SIPP Survey[e]
Percentage of richest households	1.0	1.0	1.5	1.0	1.9
Percentage of net worth, based on sample totals	N.A.	32.6	26.0	16.2	26.0
Percentage of net worth, based on national balance sheet totals	30.8	24.0	17.0	8.4	N.A.

Note: N.A. = not available.

a. From Edward N. Wolff, "The Distribution of Household Disposable Wealth in the United States," *The Review of Income and Wealth* 29, no. 2 (June 1983): 125–46, which is based on the MESP file, a synthetic database created by matching income tax return data to the 1970 Census public use sample.

b. From Daphne Greenwood, "Age, Income, and Household Size: Their Relation to Wealth Distribution in the United States," in *International Comparisons of the Distribution of Household Wealth,* ed. Edward N. Wolff (New York: Oxford University Press, 1987), 121–40. The database is derived from a synthetic match of income tax returns with the 1973 Current Population Survey.

c. From Daniel B. Radner and Denton R. Vaughan, "Wealth, Income and the Economic Status of Aged Households," in *International Comparisons of the Distribution of Household Wealth,* ed. Edward N. Wolff (New York: Oxford University Press, 1987), 93–120, which is based on the Income Survey and Development Program. The share of wealth of the top 1.5 percent of households is estimated using a Pareto distribution.

d. From William S. Cartwright and Robert Friedland, "The President's Commission on Pension Policy Household Survey 1979: Net Wealth Distribution by Type and Age for the United States," *Review of Income and Wealth* 31, no. 3 (1985): 285–308.

e. From Enrique J. Lamas and John M. McNeil, "Factors Associated with Household Net Worth" (paper presented at the meeting of the American Economic Association, New Orleans, LA, December 1986), which is based on the Survey of Income and Program Participation (SIPP). The estimates shown were provided by John McNeil.

the sample. The 1979 ISDP sample captured a higher proportion of aggregate wealth and also had a higher proportion of wealthy individuals than the 1979 commission's survey of the same year. Consequently, the reported inequality based on the ISDP was higher. The top 1.5 percent held 26 percent of total wealth in the ISDP, while the top 0.96 percent owned 16.2 percent in the commission's survey. The concentration estimates from the 1984 SIPP and the 1983 SCF (Table 13.6) provide an indication of the extent of the problem of inadequate coverage in some wealth surveys. On the basis of the 1984 Survey of Income and Program Participation (SIPP) file, Lamas and McNeil estimated that the share of wealth held by the top 1.9 percent was 26 percent, compared to 34.5 percent for the top 1 percent from the unadjusted 1983 SCF data.[18]

Inequality estimates from synthetic databases that combine several sources may also be subject to biases, from both the underlying data sources and the methodology employed. Results from two such databases are reported in Table 13.6. The first results are from the 1969 Measurement of Economic and Social Performance (MESP) database, created from a synthetic match of Internal Revenue Service (IRS) tax records to the 1970 Census one in 1,000 public use sample. Selected income flows (such as dividends) were then capitalized to create the corresponding asset value (in this case, the value of stock shares). Asset and liability values were then aligned to the Ruggles and Ruggles national balance sheet totals for the household sector.[19] Various problems arose from the imputation procedures used. Two concerns of particular note are that the tax unit differs from the household unit and a significant fraction of families in the United States were not subject to federal income tax and thus did not file tax returns. Both problems created biases in the matching procedure. From the MESP database, it was estimated that the share of the top 1 percent of households was 30.8 percent of total household net worth, a figure that was slightly greater than the corresponding estimate of 29.3 percent for 1962.

The second source for Table 13.6 is Greenwood's synthetic database, which is based on income tax records that were merged with the 1973 Current Population Survey file. Imputations of asset values were based on an analysis of estate tax records.[20] In this case, there appeared to be some sampling problems. Greenwood's estimated aggregate wealth was 74 percent of the balance sheet figure. Her estimates of total financial securities and stocks, assets held largely by the wealthy, were actually higher than the balance sheet estimates, while the total value of real estate, an asset concentrated in the middle class, was only 80 percent of the aggregate total.[21] Greenwood calculated that the top 1 percent owned 32.6 percent of total wealth in 1973, a share that was probably overestimated as a result of the underestimation of total assets. An alternative estimate of 24 percent is given in row 3 of Table 13.6, calculated by dividing Greenwood's estimated wealth of the top 1 percent by the balance sheet total for the household sector.

Several conclusions are derived from this analysis of twentieth-century wealth concentration trends. The concentration estimates for the early years were slightly reduced when adjusted for inconsistencies in the aggregate data and when pension funds were included. With the exception of Social Security, the effect on the top wealth holders' share of different versions of wealth and / or different asset assumptions is no more than 2 to 3 percentage points. However, the inclusion of Social Security wealth does make a significant difference on the concentration estimates—up to a maximum reduction of 8 percentage points.

Preliminary adjustments for changes in number of households and married women among the top wealth holders indicate that the drop in wealth concentration during and after World War I1 was considerably less than indicated from estimates based on individual shares. In addition, when I include the concentration estimates based on household survey data for 1962 and 1983, I find that the level of wealth inequality in 1983 was about the same as in 1962. The estate data series, on the other hand, shows a large decline in concentration between 1962 and 1976, followed by an increase in 1981, though the inequality level in 1981 was considerably less than it was in 1962. The reason for the apparent difference in results is not clear, though underreporting in the estate data may have increased during the period. A more extensive analysis is required both in comparisons of inequality estimates between survey and estate data and in ascertaining the degree of bias introduced in estate data by gift transfers and unreported trusts. The results reported in Tables 13.5 and 13.6 suggest that inequality estimates are particularly sensitive not only to the inclusion of retirement wealth but also to the quality and representativeness of the data source used.

Putting the Pieces Together and Updating to 2013: The Final Series

Data on the size distribution of household wealth in the United States are available principally from estate tax records and cross-sectional household surveys. A reasonably consistent series of estate tax records for the very wealthy collected from national estate tax records exists for selected years between 1922 and 1981. Comparative estimates of household wealth inequality are available from twelve surveys conducted by the Federal Reserve Board in 1962, 1983, 1986 (a special follow-up of the 1983 survey), 1989, 1992, 1995, 1998, 2001, 2004, 2007, 2010, and 2013. These are based on stratified samples and are reasonably consistent over time. In addition, a figure for 1969 is obtained from the MESP dataset of that year and one for 1979 from the ISDP.

The first column of Table 13.7 shows the estate tax series for the share of total assets held by the top 1 percent of asset owners and the second column for the share of net worth owned by the top 1 percent of wealth holders. The wealth concept used here is W2. Concentration figures are slightly higher based on net worth than total assets, since the relative indebtedness (the debt to net worth ratio) is higher for poorer individuals than richer ones. Column 3 of the table shows the estimates of the share of total assets owned by the top 1 percent of *households*. The series shown in column 3 of Table 13.7 is based on the set of assumptions that yielded the smallest concentration estimates. A comparison of columns 1 and 3 indicates that concentration figures are considerably lower on the basis of the household unit than the individual unit. This is to be expected since a married couple typically mixes a relatively high-wealth spouse with a relatively less wealthy one.

Estimates from nine other sources of wealth data are shown in the next two columns. These are all based on the household as the unit of observation. Seven sources—the 1962 SFCC and the 1983, 1986, 1989, 1992, 1995, and 1998 SCF—were conducted under the auspices of the Federal Reserve Board, and the sample also includes a high-income supplement. Imputations were performed for missing values, and I have aligned each sample to the national balance sheet totals for that year to ensure greater consistency.[22]

The 1969 figure is derived from the MESP file, a synthetic database that is also fully aligned to the national balance sheet totals of that year.[23] The 1979 figure is based on Radner's and Vaughan's calculations from the 1979 ISDP, which I have then benchmarked to my 1969 figure on the basis of a Pareto interpolation.[24] Estimates are also available from the 1986 SCF, which resurveyed the families included in the 1983 SCF sample. Though there was a substantial dropout rate among the survey respondents, Avery and Kennickell have provided some comparative estimates of wealth concentration in the two years.[25] The nine figures shown in column 5 of Table 13.7 are all relatively consistent.

To combine column 5 with the estate tax series, an overlapping year is necessary. Fortunately, two such "Rosetta stones" are provided, for 1962 and 1969. A comparison of columns 3 and 4 for 1962 reveals that the share of total assets owned by the top 1 percent of *households* is estimated to be considerably higher on the basis of the SFCC (29.9 percent) than the estate tax series (22.1 percent). One possible reason for this difference is the conservative assumption used in converting the estate data to a household base. If it was, instead, assumed that all married men in the estate sample of top wealth holders had married women with wealth, the concentration estimates would have been higher, but not enough to account for the difference. Another likely reason for the discrepancy between the estate and survey estimates is that there may be a serious underreporting problem in the estate data.[26]

Column 6 of Table 13.7 shows the new series for the share of net worth owned by the top 1 percent of households from 1922 to 1998. Figure for years 1962, 1969, 1979, 1983, 1986, 1989, 1992, 1995, and 1998 are based on the survey data sources. Other years, with the exception of 1933 and 1981, are calculated as the product of column 3 multiplied by the ratio of the 1962 SFCC figure for the share of household net worth in column 5 (31.8 percent) and the estate tax figure for the share of household assets in column 3 (22.1 percent)—a ratio of 1.44. A similar procedure applied to the 1969 data yields almost the same ratio—1.43—which provides some confidence in this benchmarking procedure. Figures for 1933 and 1981 are interpolated on the basis of column 1. This series is then combined with those from Chapter 2 based on the SCF data to produce the "final series" on net worth, excluding consumer durables, shown in column 8 (also see Figure 13.4).

The estimates of the final series in column 8 for net worth show a high concentration of wealth throughout the period from 1922 to 2013. A quarter or more of total wealth was owned by the top 1 percent in each of these years except 1976 and 1979. A comparison of the two end points reveals a higher concentration figure in 1922 than in 2013: 40.1 versus 36.7. However, this comparison hides important trends over the full period.

Between 1922 and 1929 there was a substantial increase in the wealth share of the top 1 percent, from 40 to 48 percent. Wealth inequality, at least as measured by the top 1 percent share, was at its highest point in 1929 over this period. The Great Depression saw a sizable drop in inequality, with the share of the top percentile falling to 36 percent, but by 1939, the concentration level

Table 13.7. Percentage share of total household wealth held by the richest 1 percent of wealth holders in the United States, 1922–2013

Year	Estate Tax Series[a] Individuals Total Assets (W2)	Estate Tax Series[a] Individuals Net Worth (W2)	Estate Tax Series[a] Households Total Assets (W2)	Other Sources[b] Households Total Assets (W2)	Other Sources[b] Households Net Worth (W2)	Combined Series: Households Net Worth (W2)	Combined Series: Households Augmented Wealth (W4)	Combined Series: Households Net Worth (NW)[c]
1922	38.3		25.5			36.7	34.3	40.1
1929	37.3		30.7			44.2	41.1	48.3
1933	31.3					33.3	28.7	36.4
1939	38.1		25.3			36.4	30.2	39.8
1945	28.9		20.7			29.8	22.0	32.6
1949	25.7		18.8			27.1	20.7	29.6
1953	28.1	28.4	21.7			31.2	23.1	34.1
1958	27.0	27.7	20.0			28.8	20.4	31.5
1962	30.1	31.1	22.1	29.9	31.8	31.8	21.9	33.4
1965	31.9	33.6	23.9			34.4	23.3	34.4
1969	29.0	30.2	21.6		31.1	31.1	20.9	34.0
1972	28.6	29.8	20.2			29.1	19.0	31.8
1976	18.9	19.1	12.7			19.9	13.3	21.8
1979					20.5	20.5	12.9	22.4

1981	23.6				27.2
1983		30.9	24.8	15.5	33.8
1986		31.9	30.9	19.0	34.9
1989		34.2	31.9	19.3	37.4
1992		34.0	34.2	20.3	37.2
1995		35.3	34.0	19.8	38.5
1998		34.9	35.3	20.2	38.1
2001			34.9	19.6	33.4
2004					34.3
2007					34.6
2010					35.1
2013					36.7

Note: The wealth concept used is W2, including consumer durables, unless otherwise indicated.

a. Source: Chapter 8, Tables 8.8 and 8.9. Figures on the share of assets owned by the top 1 percent of households (column 3) are lower bound estimates.

b. Sources: 1962 SFCC, 1979 ISDP from Daniel B. Radner and Denton R. Vaughan, "Wealth, Income and the Economic Status of Aged Households," in *International Comparisons of the Distribution of Household Wealth*, ed. Edward N. Wolff (New York: Oxford University Press, 1987), 93–120, where the share of wealth of the top one percent of households is estimated using a Pareto distribution; and the 1983, 1986, 1989, 1992, 1995, 1998, 2001, 2004, 2007, 2010, and 2013 Survey of Consumer Finances.

c. Source: Chapter 2. Net worth excludes consumer durables.

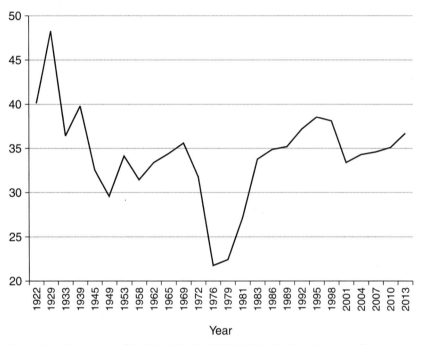

Figure 13.4. Percentage of Total Net Worth (NW) Held by the Top 1 Percent of House-holds, 1922–2013

was almost the same as it was in 1922. There followed a substantial drop in inequality between 1939 and 1945, a result of the leveling effects of World War II, and a more modest decline between 1945 and 1949.

The share of wealth held by the richest one percent of the population showed a gradual upward trend from 30 percent in 1949 to a high point of 34 percent in 1965. Then followed a rather pronounced fall in wealth inequality, lasting until 1979, from 34 to 22 percent.[27] The main reason for the decline in concentration over this four-year period was the sharp drop in the value of corporate stock held by the top wealth holders. The total value of corporate stock owned by the richest 1 percent fell from $491 billion in 1972 to $297 billion in 1976.[28] Moreover, this decline appeared to be attributable to the steep decline in share prices, rather than a divestiture of stock holdings.

Wealth inequality appears to have bottomed out some time during the late 1970s. A sharp increase in wealth concentration occurred between 1979 and 1981, from a 22 to a 27 percent share, again from 1981 to 1983, to a 34 percent share, and then again between 1983 and 1998, to 38 percent.[29] It then took a sharp drop to 33 percent in 2001, and then gradually rose to 37 percent in 2013.[30]

Figure 13.5 shows a comparison of my "final series" on the net worth share of the top 1 percent with those of Saez and Zucman and Kopczuk and Saez.[31] The first of these two series was based on an income capitalization technique applied to U.S. income tax data. Total wealth holdings by asset and liability type were then aligned to national balance sheet totals. The unit of analysis was the tax unit. The second relied on estate tax data for the U.S. over the years 1916 to 2000. They then applied the technique discussed earlier, based on the estate multiplier method, which divides the population by age and gender and weights the deceased in each group by the reciprocal of the survival probability for that group. The unit of analysis was the adult.

Despite the differences in data sources, method, and unit of analysis, the three series track fairly closely from 1913 through 1989 or so. The Wolff series shows a rise in the share of the top percentile from 1989 to 1998, a sharp fall between 1998 and 2001, and then a gradual upturn from 2001 through 2013. The Saez and Zucman series (the "SZ series" in Figure 13.5) shows a continued rise from 1989 to 2001, a slight decline in 2002, and then an almost continuous and quite sharp rise from 2002 through 2012. The Kopczuk and Saez series (the "KS series" in Figure 13.5), in contrast, shows a slight decline in the top percentile share from 1989 through 2000 (the last date of the series). The Wolff and SZ series are not too far off after 1989 but the KS series is quite at variance with the other two. Kopczuk accounted for the discrepancy by noting that the series did not take into account strong increases in the life expectancy of older, very wealthy Americans after 1990 or so.[32] This would imply that the mortality multipliers were biased downward for the very wealthy, understating the wealth share of this group and its increase since 1990 or so.

Retirement Wealth

Column 7 of Table 13.7 shows the combined series for the share of augmented household wealth owned by the top 1 percent of wealth holders. A procedure similar to the one used for marketable wealth was applied here. The original source is the W4 series in Table 13.4, where W4 is defined to include full pension reserves, which are reported in the aggregate data sources, as well

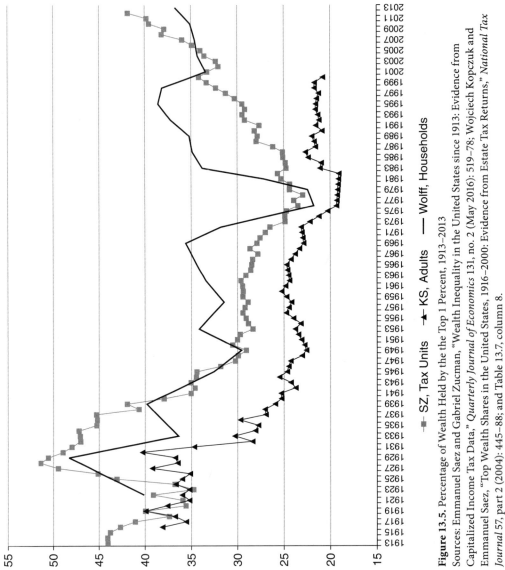

Figure 13.5. Percentage of Wealth Held by the the Top 1 Percent, 1913–2013

Sources: Emmanuel Saez and Gabriel Zucman, "Wealth Inequality in the United States since 1913: Evidence from Capitalized Income Tax Data," *Quarterly Journal of Economics* 131, no. 2 (May 2016): 519–78; Wojciech Kopczuk and Emmanuel Saez, "Top Wealth Shares in the United States, 1916–2000: Evidence from Estate Tax Returns," *National Tax Journal* 57, part 2 (2004): 445–88; and Table 13.7, column 8.

Legend: ▪ SZ, Tax Units   ▲ KS, Adults   — Wolff, Households

as imputations for Social Security wealth. A major difficulty was the dearth of information concerning the percentage of total pensions owned by the top wealth holders. As a result, alternative assumptions were made about this share, ranging from a maximum of 15 percent to a minimum of 3 percent for the top 1 percent of wealth holders. The different assumptions had little effect on total wealth concentration. In the estimates reported for W4 in Table 13.3, it was assumed that the share of total pension wealth held by the top percentile of wealth holders declined over the twentieth century because of the increase of pension coverage over the period.

Direct imputations of pension and Social Security wealth were performed for the 1962 SFCC; the 1969 MESP; and the 1983, 1989, and 1998 SCF.[33] These estimates were used for the combined series for augmented wealth shown in column 7.[34] Figures for W4 from 1922 through 1976 were then benchmarked against the 1962 estimate derived from the SFCC. Other years were filled in by interpolation.

The addition of pension and Social Security wealth had a significant effect on measured wealth inequality. Because of the growth over time in pension and Social Security wealth, particularly the latter, in relation to marketable wealth, the gap between the marketable wealth and the augmented wealth series widened over time, from two percentage points in 1922 to 15 percentage points in 1998. However, the time paths were almost identical. Wealth concentration based on the augmented wealth series showed a sharp increase between 1922 and 1929; a substantial decline from 1929 to 1933 followed by an increase between 1933 and 1939; a significant decrease between 1939 and 1945; a fairly flat trend from 1945 through 1972; a sharp decline from 1972 to 1976; and then a substantial rise between 1979 and 1989. In this case, inequality leveled off in the 1990s. The increase during the 1980s and 1990s (1979 to 1998) was more muted on the basis of augmented wealth, 6.7 percentage points, in comparison to marketable wealth W2, 14.4 percentage points.[35]

Concluding Comments on Long-Term Trends in Wealth Inequality

The long-run record based on original and unadjusted estate data (individual based estimates) shows a decline in wealth concentration in the United States from the late 1920s to the late 1940s, a slight increase in the 1960s, a sharp drop in the 1970s, followed by a minor increase in 1981. These trends generally remain unchanged after corrections for inconsistencies in the national balance sheet data and in wealth definitions and after most other adjustments. There are, however, two factors that do have an effect on the concentration trends. First, including Social Security wealth in the household portfolio augments the decline in inequality over the period 1939–1981. Second, changing the unit of observation in the estate data from individual to household reduces the decline in wealth concentration over the period 1922–1953, although it does not alter the sharp drop-off in the 1970s. The smaller decline in inequality over the period prior to 1953 in the household estimates vis-à-vis the individual series can be explained by changes in wealth-holding patterns among married women.

The decade of the 1970s presents a puzzle. On the basis of estate tax data, there was a precipitous fall in wealth inequality between 1972 and 1976. Unfortunately, there were no household surveys conducted during the 1970s that are comparable in terms of coverage of upper wealth groups to the 1962 SFCC and the 1983 SCF. However, on the basis of the three sources available— Greenwood's synthetic database, with our figures for total household wealth; the 1979 ISDP; and the 1979 pension commission survey—there appeared to be a sizable decline in household wealth inequality between the 1960s and the 1970s. The 1979 results must be interpreted cautiously because the wealthy were thinly sampled. From Schwartz's 1981 estate tax estimates, concentration appears to have risen slightly between 1976 and 1981. Also, the 1983 SCF indicates that wealth inequality in 1983 was as high as it was in 1962. These sources taken together suggest that there was a wealth inequality trough during the 1970s—that is, a period of relatively low wealth inequality—and a reversal during the 1980s. Yet this result must be interpreted cautiously because of the various problems with the data.

Estate tax estimates of wealth concentration were also quite sensitive to the adjustment procedures used. Adjustments in the aggregate balance sheet data and the treatment of trust and pension funds made a difference of 2 to 4 percentage points in the estimated share of the top percentile. The inclusion of Social Security wealth with the estate tax wealth estimates caused a 4 to 8 percentage point drop in the share of the top 1 percent of wealth holders.

Combining the various data sources and updating the series to 2013 to produce the "combined series" for household net worth, I find that between 1922 and 1929 there was a substantial increase in the wealth share of the top percentile, from 40 to 48 percent. There was then a sizable reduction in the share of the richest 1 percent over the Great Depression but by 1939 its share was almost the same as it was in 1922. Wealth inequality then fell sharply from 1939 to 1949, down to 30 percent. However, by 1965 its share was back to 34 percent. This was followed by a substantial decline in wealth inequality, with the share of the top 1 percent falling to 22 percent in 1979. Wealth inequality bottomed out sometime during the late 1970s. A sharp turnaround in wealth inequality occurred, with the top percentile share climbing to 38 percent in 1998. It then dropped sharply to 33 percent in 2001, and then gradually rose back to 37 percent in 2013.

V

Tax Policy and Conclusion

14

Wealth Taxation

B oth the extreme nature of wealth concentration in the United States and its rise in recent years provide some urgency to the consideration of potential policy remedies. If the intergenerational transfer of wealth plays an important role in the process of household wealth accumulation our basic sense of equity might fray even more and lead to increasing political divisiveness.

Personal wealth is currently taxed in two ways on the federal level: realized capital gains (as part of personal income taxes) and estate taxation. Earlier research has suggested that the estate tax collection system may be subject to both tax evasion and tax avoidance. According to my estimates for 1992, total estate tax collections should have been on the order of $44 billion, in comparison to actual tax receipts of $10 billion.[1] Moreover the estate tax system has the unusual feature that capital gains are "forgiven" at time of death—that is, the capital gains that are incorporated in the value of the assets of the deceased are passed to the heirs untaxed. If these gains were taxed like ordinary income, estimates suggest that they would yield another $30 to $40 billion of revenue.

Another consideration is direct taxation of the wealth holdings of households. Almost a dozen European countries have or have had such a system in place, including Denmark, France, Germany, the Netherlands, Sweden, and Switzerland. On the grounds of equity, a combination of annual income and the current stock of wealth provides a better gauge of real living standards and thereby the ability to pay taxes than income alone. Moreover, there is no evidence from other advanced economies that the imposition of a modest direct tax on household wealth had any deleterious effect on personal savings or overall economic growth. Indeed, some argue that such a tax may induce a more efficient allocation of household wealth, that is, toward more productive uses.

In an earlier work, I proposed a very modest tax on wealth (a $100,000 exemption with marginal tax rates running from 0.05 to 0.3 percent).[2] My calculations for year 1989 showed that such a tax structure would yield an average tax rate on household wealth of 0.2 percent, which is less than the loading fee on most mutual funds, and would reduce the average yield on household wealth holdings by only 6 percent. Even the top marginal tax rate of 0.30 percent would reduce the average yield on personal wealth by only 9 percent. These figures suggested that disincentive effects on personal savings would be very modest indeed. Moreover, it is possible that personal savings might actually rise as a result of the imposition of a wealth tax.

I estimated that such a tax could raise $50 billion in additional revenue and have a minimal impact on the tax bills of 90 percent of American families. This represents only about 3 percent of total federal tax receipts but on the margin such additional revenue could be critical. In particular, it could help provide the fiscal latitude to enact more generous social transfers to the poor and provide needed tax relief to the middle class.

The next section reprises my 1995 analysis of direct wealth taxation. This is followed by updated estimates to 2013.

My Earlier Analysis of Direct Wealth Taxation

In my 1995 book, I looked into the issue of how much revenue a direct tax on household wealth would raise and considered what the distributional effects of such a tax would be. Here, I summarize my earlier results.

Systems of Wealth Taxation, Mid-1980s

Given the high and rising degree of wealth inequality in the United States, it seems reasonable to consider the possibility of extending the tax base to include personal wealth holdings. Such a policy not only promotes greater equity in our society—particularly, by targeting those who have a greater ability to pay—but also may provide households with an incentive for switching from less productive (those with a low rate of return) to more productive forms of assets. This section summarizes the forms of wealth taxation in place in the United States and other industrialized countries around 1985 as a preliminary to analyzing some of the potential effects of introducing direct wealth taxation.

The United States

Household wealth was (and is currently) taxed in two ways on the federal level: estate taxes and capital gains taxes. Federal estate taxes were first introduced in 1916, with major revisions in 1976, 1981, and more recently, a big overhaul in 2011. Capital gains were originally included in the personal income tax system, introduced into the country in 1913. Their provisions have been modified over time on a recurrent basis.[3]

The system in 1985 (and currently) provides for the taxation of the value of an estate at the time of death of an individual. The tax is levied on the value of the estate, in contrast to the value of an inheritance received (see below for a discussion of the "inheritance tax"). Moreover, the estate tax system is integrated with the gift tax, which refers to the voluntary transfer of assets from one (living) individual to another. In principle, gifts are aggregated over the lifetime of the individual donor, and the lifetime aggregate of gifts is combined with the value of an estate at death. The estate tax applies to the full value of gifts and estates.[4]

In February 2001, each individual was exempted from estate taxes on net worth up to $675,000. The basic exemption rose to $1 million in 2006. Wealth above that amount was levied at marginal tax rates, which began at 37 percent and reached as high as 55 percent (for estates over $3,675,000). Estates of fewer than forty-eight thousand individuals—about 2 percent of annual deaths—were subject to the estate tax. About half the total was paid out of estates worth $5 million or more—about four thousand people. As of December 2013, the exemption on the estate tax was raised to $5,250,000 for singles and $10,500,000 for couples and the top marginal tax rate was 40 percent, up from 35 percent in 2012. The exemption level is now indexed to the Consumer Price Index.

For gifts, the first $10,000 per recipient ($20,000 in the case of a married couple) was exempt from the combined gift-estate tax. In 2015 the figure was $14,000. There was (and is) also full exemption for transfers (both gifts and estates) between spouses. All forms of wealth are included in the tax base for calculating the gift-estate tax except pension annuities and life insurance. Assets are appraised at market value at time of death, though special rules apply to farm property, closely held business, and unquoted stock and shares. Several states also levy estate taxes, which are generally based on federal rules.

Capital gains refer to the difference between the selling price and purchase price of an asset. There are some adjustments made for the value of capital improvements in the case of real property (such as a home). These are figured in on a cost basis when computing capital gains. In the United States, capital gains are taxed as part of the federal income tax system (and state income tax systems). Only realized capital gains are included (that is, capital gains on actual sales of assets).

In 2001, capital gains on assets held more than five years were subject to a maximum tax of 18 percent (compared to the top marginal tax rate of 39.6 percent). In 2013, the maximum tax rate on capital gains was 20 percent (also compared to the top marginal tax rate of 39.6 percent). Short-term capital gains are treated as ordinary income and do not receive tax preference.[5] However, in the case of owner-occupied housing, there is no tax levied on capital gains in the case when a new primary residence is purchased whose price exceeds the selling price of the old home. There is also a one-time exclusion of $500,000 in capital gains on the primary residence. Tax liability on capital gains on gifts is deferred until the asset is sold. Capital gains on assets that enter an estate at time of death are exempt from taxation.

Other OECD Countries

Other Organization of Economic Cooperation and Development member countries have more extensively taxed household wealth.[6] Besides taxation of estates at death and of capital gains, many countries also imposed taxes on household wealth.

As of 1985, eleven OECD countries had systems in place with direct taxation of household wealth: Austria, Denmark, Finland, Germany, Luxembourg, the Netherlands, Norway, Spain, Sweden, and Switzerland (see Table 14.1). In addition, France had such a system in place from 1982 to 1987 and Ireland from 1975 to 1977.[7] Also, with the exception of Spain, most of these systems had been in place for at least sixty years. In all eleven countries, the wealth tax was administered in conjunction with the personal in-

Table 14.1. Wealth taxation systems among OECD member countries on individual or family wealth holdings, mid-1980s

	Direct Wealth Taxation	Transfer Tax at Death and on Gifts	Capital Gains Taxation	Wealth, Death, and Gift Tax Receipts as Percentage of Total Tax Revenue[a]
Australia	No	None	Income	0.01
Austria	Yes	Inheritance	None	0.51
Belgium	No	Inheritance	None	0.58
Canada	No	None	Income	0.03
Denmark	Yes	Inheritance	Separate	0.92
Finland	Yes	Inheritance	Income	0.50
France	1982–87	Inheritance	Income	0.85
Germany	Yes	Inheritance	None	0.42
Greece	No	Inheritance	None	0.94
Iceland	Yes	Inheritance	Income	—
Ireland	1975–77	Inheritance	Separate	0.30
Italy	No	Estate / Inheritance	None	0.23
Japan	No	Inheritance	Income	1.19
Luxembourg	Yes	Inheritance	Income	0.51
Netherlands	Yes	Inheritance	None	0.94
New Zealand	No	Estate	None	0.19
Norway	Yes	Inheritance	Income	0.61
Portugal	No	Inheritance	None	0.83
Spain	Yes	Inheritance	Income	0.49
Sweden	Yes	Inheritance	Income	0.68
Switzerland	Yes	Estate / Inheritance	Income	3.06
Turkey	No	Inheritance	Income	0.19
United Kingdom	No	Estate	None	0.64
United States	No	Estate	Income	0.77

Source: Organization for Economic Cooperation and Development, Taxation of Net Wealth, Capital Transfers and Capital Gains of Individuals (Paris: OECD, 1988).
a. Figures are for 1985.

come tax. In all cases, except Germany, a joint tax return was filed for both income and wealth. Though actual provisions varied among these eleven countries, the basic structure of the tax was very similar in each.

Countries differed in terms of the level at which the wealth tax took effect. The thresholds for married couples with two children ranged from a low of $9,000 in Luxembourg to a high of $155,000 in Denmark. In Germany, the threshold was $129,000; in the Netherlands, $51,000; and in France, it was (when the tax was in effect) $520,000. These threshold levels did not include the forms of wealth that are entirely excluded from the tax base. Moreover, there were income exclusions in many countries, so that a joint income-wealth threshold had to be passed in order for the wealth tax to become effective.

In several countries (such as Denmark, the Netherlands, and Sweden), there were also ceilings on the total amount payable in both income and wealth taxes combined. These ceilings were usually expressed as a percentage of taxable income (in the Netherlands, for example, it was 80 percent of taxable income).

Tax rates on household wealth tended to be quite low, on the order of a few percent at most. Five countries had a flat rate system: Austria (1 percent), Denmark (2.2 percent), Germany (0.5 percent), Luxembourg (0.5 percent), and the Netherlands (0.8 percent). The other countries had graduated marginal tax rates: Finland (1.5 percent at the threshold, rising to 1.7 percent at $296,000), Norway (0.2 to 1.3 percent, the latter at $47,000), Spain (0.2 to 2 percent, the top rate at $7.1 million), Sweden (1.5 percent initially; reaching 3 percent at $140,000), and Switzerland (0.05 percent, rising to 0.30 percent at $334,000).[8]

Countries also varied in the forms of wealth that were included in the tax base. All the countries except Spain exempted household and personal effects. Most included the value of jewelry above a certain amount. All except Germany included the value of automobiles, and all included boats.

Several countries exempted savings accounts up to a certain level ($4,600 in Germany, for example). All excluded pension rights and pension-type annuities. Other forms of annuities were generally exempt. About half the countries exempted life insurance policies, while the other half included some portion of them in the tax base.

Owner-occupied housing was taxable in all eleven countries. However, in Austria and Finland, a small deduction was allowed, while in the Netherlands and Norway housing was valued at only a small percentage of its actual market value. Other forms of wealth, including bonds, stocks and shares, and unincorporated businesses were included in the tax base in all countries.[9]

Most countries required an annual reassessment of the total value of personal property. However, Austria, Germany, and Luxembourg reassessed every three years and Switzerland every two years. In principle, all eleven countries with a wealth tax system based the valuation of assets on current market value. However, in practice, this procedure was not always easy to enforce. First, some assets were not traded in the open market and hence did not have a readily available market price (small businesses and unquoted shares, for example). Second, housing presented a particular problem, since the usual method, based on the sale of "similar" property, depended in large measure on the definition of the similar class. On the other hand, bonds, quoted shares and stocks, and bank accounts were rather straightforward in their valuation.

Most countries used an "asset basis" to value unincorporated businesses, defined as the sum of the value of the individual assets contained in the business. This would typically understate the true value of the business, since no additional value was given to goodwill. Austria, Finland, and the Netherlands used a market value basis (the value of the business if it were sold immediately). Switzerland used a formula based on the capitalized value of the business's profits over time.

Whereas most countries based their valuation of real property on its open market value, Austria used a formula based on changes in the average costs of construction and changes in land prices. Germany used the assessed valuation for local taxes. Luxembourg used a formula based on the capitalized rental value of property.

Twenty-two of the twenty-four OECD countries had death or gift taxes, or both (see Table 14.1). The only exceptions were Australia and Canada. However, most of the OECD countries had "inheritance taxes" in lieu of the American-style estate tax. The difference between the two is that inheritance taxes are assessed on the recipient, whereas an estate tax is assessed on the estate left by the decedent. With an inheritance tax, the tax schedule is applied to each individual bequest, whereas with an estate tax the assessment is on the total value of the transfer. The inheritance tax has certain advantages over the estate tax. First, it can be adjusted more closely to the ability of an heir to pay the tax. Second, preferential treatment can be accorded to immediate family, as opposed to more distant relatives or friends (so-called consanguinity basis).[10]

Of the four countries with estate taxes—Italy, New Zealand, the United Kingdom, and the United States—the tax threshold varied from $20,000 for Italy to $600,000 for the United States (in 1985). Marginal tax rates ranged from 3 to 31 percent in Italy, 30 to 60 percent in the United Kingdom, and 37 to 55 percent in the United States. In New Zealand there was a flat rate of 40 percent. Spousal transfers were totally exempt in the United Kingdom and the United States but were taxed, with special treatment, in the other two countries. All four countries also had gift taxes. In Italy and the United States, these were aggregated over the person's lifetime and combined with the estate at death to determine the taxable base for the estate tax.

The structure of inheritance taxes was more complicated. Marginal tax rates varied with the relationship of the heir to the decedent, as did the tax thresholds. In France, for example, bequests to spouses had a threshold of $40,000, and the marginal tax rates varied from 5 to 40 percent, whereas bequests to nonrelatives had a threshold of $1,500 with a flat rate of 60 percent applied to the transfer. All nineteen OECD countries with an inheritance tax also had an associated gift tax.

Fifteen of the twenty-four OECD countries also provided for a tax on capital gains (see Table 14.1). All fifteen taxed capital gains as they were realized (that is, at time of sale). In thirteen of the fifteen countries, capital gains were included as part of the personal income tax, whereas in the other two (Denmark and Ireland), a separate tax was collected. Interestingly, in eight countries—Denmark, Finland, Iceland, Luxembourg, Norway, Spain, Sweden, and Switzerland—there was both a direct wealth tax and a tax on capital gains.

There was wide latitude in the tax treatment of these gains across countries. In the United States, long-term capital gains as of 2001 received tax preference, with a maximum tax rate of 18 percent. Short-term gains were treated as ordinary income. In Denmark, there was a flat rate of 50 percent; while in Switzerland, marginal rates ranged from 10 to 40 percent. In both cases, there was no separate treatment of short-term gains.

In Australia, Norway (with some exceptions), and Spain, both short-term and long-term gains were treated as ordinary income and taxed in accordance with the personal income tax schedule. In Canada, three-quarters of capital gains were included as ordinary income. In Japan, half of long-term capital gains were taxed as ordinary income, while short-term gains were treated as ordinary income. In Sweden, a proportion of long-term gains were taxed as ordinary income, with the proportion depending on the nature of the property and the period held, while short-term gains were treated as ordinary income.

In most countries with capital gains taxes, gains on principal residences were exempt from taxation. Exceptions were Switzerland, where such gains were fully taxable; Japan, where the first $178,000 of gains were exempt; Spain, where exemption was subject to the purchase of a new residence; and Sweden and the United States, where only the excess of the sale price over the purchase price of a new residence was subject to taxation.

Though on the books, these wealth taxation mechanisms appear to be a formidable way of collecting revenue, in fact, such levies accounted for only a very small part of total tax revenue in the various OECD countries. The last column of Table 14.1 summarizes the total tax collections from direct wealth and death / gift taxes as a percent of total government revenue in 1985. Unfortunately, these totals do not include capital gains tax, since it was very hard to break out from regular income tax receipts. Among the twenty-three countries shown here, the average percentage was only 0.67. The shares ranged from a low of 0.01 percent in Australia to a high of 3.06 percent in Switzerland. Switzerland was the only country in which the direct wealth tax collected more than 1 percent of total tax revenue—2.25 percent in 1985. The United States was slightly above average, with 0.77 percent of its total tax revenue from estate and gift taxes (of which 0.74 was from estate taxes and 0.03 from gift taxes). In terms of the receipts from death and gift taxes as a share of the total personal tax intake, the United States ranked fifth among OECD countries, after Japan, Greece, Portugal, and Switzerland. In 1998, total federal tax collections from estate and gift taxes in the United States amounted to $24 billion, or 1.4 percent of total tax revenues.[11]

One may wonder why these wealth taxes collected so little revenue, particularly when some of them were in place for more than seventy years, plenty of time for refinement of their efficacy. Three possible reasons suggest themselves. First, particularly in Europe, tax proceeds from the personal income tax and the value-added tax on consumption were already quite substantial, so that relative to total tax revenues wealth tax collections appeared small. This is particularly germane to countries such as Sweden that had a cap on combined income and wealth taxes. Second, there is the strong possibility of evasion or noncriminal avoidance. Unlike labor earnings and interest and dividend payments, which can be recorded at their source, it was much more difficult for a tax collection agency to obtain independent information on the financial securities, stock holdings, unquoted shares, or value of a family business owned by a household. Though real property must be registered with local tax authorities, there was still a possibility that its value was underestimated for tax purposes.

A third and related reason is that it is easy to transfer financial wealth holdings across borders. With the exception of real property and most small businesses, a family normally can purchase assets outside the country of residence with ease. A country that imposes an excessive wealth tax may induce substantial capital flight. As a result, most countries with a wealth tax tried to keep it more or less in line with that of other countries.

Simulations of Direct Wealth Taxation in the United States

This section provides simulation results of the potential revenue effects of three alternative wealth taxation systems as applied to U.S. household economic data in 1989. These were based on the actual tax codes of Germany, Sweden, and Switzerland. The distinctive characteristics of each plan are shown in Table 14.2.[12]

The simulations were performed on the basis of the 1989 U.S. personal income tax schedules and the 1989 Survey of Consumer Finances (SCF).[13] While the data were not perfect, the results were encouraging.[14] Even a very modest wealth tax (like the Swiss system, with marginal tax rates ranging from 0.05 percent to 0.30 percent and an exclusion of about $50,000 in wealth) could have raised $38 billion in 1989. Such a tax would have gone a long way toward providing additional revenue for such programs as expanded welfare (TANF) coverage, Medicaid, food stamps, an expanded prescription drug plan in Medicare, increased unemployment insurance coverage, and the like. Moreover, in the process only 3 percent of families would have seen their federal tax bill rise by more than 10 percent.

Simulations of alternative schemes for wealth taxation also suggested that a combined income-wealth taxation system might indeed be more equitable than the income tax system alone. The wealth tax was, not surprisingly, progressive with respect to wealth. Its incidence also fell more heavily on older households than younger ones (older households were wealthier, on average), on married couples than singles (the former were also richer, on average), and on white individuals than nonwhites (white families were generally much wealthier). Although this approach did not take into account behavioral re-

Table 14.2. Details of direct wealth taxation systems of Germany, Sweden, and Switzerland, mid-1980s

	Germany	Sweden	Switzerland
A. Thresholds			
1. Single persons	$33,000	$56,000	$34,000
2. Married couple, no children	$57,000	$56,000	$56,000
3. Married couple, two children	$129,000	$56,000	$56,000
B. Tax rate schedules	Flat rate of 0.5%	1.5% (to $28,000)	0.05% (to $83,000)
		2.0% (next $28,000)	0.10% (next $139,000)
		2.5% (next $140,000)	0.15% (next $225,000)
		3.0% (over $196,000)	0.20% (next $333,000)
			0.25% (next $333,000)
			0.30% (over $1,110,000)
C. Exclusions	Household effects Automobiles Savings (up to $4,600)	Household effects	Household effects
	Pensions/annuities Life insurance (up to $4,600) Unincorporated business (up to $58,000; excess taxed at 75%)	Pensions/annuities Life insurance	Pensions/annuities
D. Ceiling	None	75 percent up to $50,000 of taxable income; 80 percent on excess	None

Source: Organization for Economic Cooperation and Development (1988).

sponses of families to the imposition of a wealth tax, the calculations nonetheless gave some guidance as to the overall magnitude of likely revenues and redistributional effects.

The actual U.S. personal income tax produced revenues of $445.7 billion, or 11.4 percent of total family income (details are tabulated in Table 14.3). A

Table 14.3. U.S. income tax and new wealth taxes as a percent of family income for alternative wealth taxation systems by income class, wealth class, age group, family type and race, 1989

	U.S. Income Tax	German Wealth Tax		Swedish Wealth Tax		Swiss Wealth Tax	
		Percentage of Income	Ratio to Income Tax	Percentage of Income	Ratio to Income Tax	Percentage of Income	Ratio to Income Tax
All families	11.4	1.7	0.15	8.4	0.74	0.9	0.08
A. Income Class							
Under $5,000	0.0	1.3	—	0.0	—	0.6	—
$5,000–$9,999	1.1	0.9	0.76	0.7	0.57	0.3	0.27
$10,000–$14,999	3.1	1.1	0.35	2.3	0.75	0.5	0.15
$15,000–$24,999	5.2	1.4	0.27	4.2	0.82	0.7	0.13
$25,000–$49,999	8.0	1.1	0.13	5.0	0.62	0.5	0.06
$50,000–$74,999	11.2	0.9	0.08	5.0	0.45	0.4	0.04
$75,000–$99,999	13.5	1.7	0.13	8.8	0.66	0.8	0.06
$100,000 & over	17.1	3.0	0.18	15.7	0.92	1.7	0.10
B. Wealth Class							
Under $25,000	7.2	0.0	0.00	0.0	0.00	0.0	0.00
$25,000–$49,999	8.3	0.0	0.00	0.0	0.00	0.0	0.00
$50,000–$74,999	9.2	0.1	0.02	0.4	0.05	0.2	0.02
$75,000–$99,999	9.4	0.3	0.03	1.4	0.15	0.5	0.05
$100,000–$249,999	10.8	0.7	0.07	4.2	0.39	0.4	0.04
$250,000–$499,999	12.9	1.8	0.14	10.3	0.80	0.4	0.03
$500,000–$999,999	14.4	3.1	0.22	17.8	1.24	1.0	0.07
$1,000,000 & over	17.2	5.7	0.33	25.5	1.48	3.2	0.19
C. Age Class							
Under 35	9.2	0.5	0.05	2.3	0.25	0.3	0.03
35–54	12.3	1.2	0.09	6.6	0.54	0.6	0.05
55–69	11.9	3.2	0.27	14.6	1.22	1.5	0.13
70 and over	10.5	4.1	0.39	16.9	1.60	1.9	0.18
D. Household Type							
Married couple	11.7	1.8	0.15	9.3	0.79	1.0	0.08
Males, unmarried	12.3	1.5	0.12	5.9	0.48	0.7	0.05
Females, unmarried	8.9	1.5	0.17	5.9	0.66	0.6	0.06
E. Race							
White	11.9	1.9	0.16	9.2	0.77	0.9	0.08
Nonwhite	8.7	0.9	0.10	3.9	0.44	0.5	0.05

Source: Author's calculations from the 1989 Survey of Consumer Finances. See text for details on tax calculations.

wealth tax following the German system would have produced total additional tax revenues of $67.5 billion in 1989, or 1.7 percent of total income. Adopting the German-style wealth tax would have increased tax revenues by 15 percent overall. Imposing the Swedish wealth tax, in contrast, would have added an additional $328.7 billion of personal taxes, amounting to 8.4 percent of total income and increasing the total tax intake by 74 percent. The Swiss wealth tax would have raised $38 billion in taxes, representing 0.9 percent of total income and 8 percent of the total income tax proceeds. The Swedish wealth tax would thus have had a massive effect on total tax revenues, while the other two would have had moderate effects. However, even the German- and Swiss-style wealth taxes yielded new revenues considerably in excess of the actual collections from the estate and gift taxes, $8.7 billion in 1989.[15]

The incidence of wealth taxes depends on the joint distribution of income and wealth. If the two were perfectly correlated, then everyone would experience a similar proportional increase in taxes (depending on the wealth tax schedule). However, income and wealth are not perfectly correlated. There are certain groups, such as the elderly, that have large wealth holdings but relatively little income. On the other hand, some young households may have high earnings but relatively little wealth accumulation. This new tax may thus shift the burden away from young households onto elderly ones.

Table 14.3 shows estimates of the new effective tax rates by income class, wealth class, age group, family type, and race.[16] The Swedish wealth tax system, like the graduated income tax in the United States, was highly progressive with respect to income, rising from zero for the lowest income class to 15.7 percent for the highest. Moreover, the proportionate increase in total taxes paid would have been somewhat higher for upper-income families than lower-income ones. In contrast, both the German and Swiss wealth tax systems tended to lay claim to an almost constant percentage of income, except for the highest income class, which would have paid a greater share with respect to its earnings. In both cases, lower-income families would have seen their total tax bill rise proportionately more than higher-income families would. While this may appear unfair, one must remember that the tax did not fall uniformly on lower-income families. Only a household with much wealth, regardless of income, would be liable for taxation. Any household with substantial net worth may legitimately be viewed as capable of contributing to the public good.

The American income tax system was also progressive with respect to household wealth, with tax rates on income rising from 7.2 percent for the lowest wealth class (under $25,000) to 17.2 percent for the richest ($1 million or more). All three European-type wealth tax systems, not surprisingly, were also progressive with respect to wealth. Tax rates measured as a percentage of income would have risen from zero for the lowest wealth class to 5.7 percent for the highest under the German tax system; from zero to 25.5 percent under the Swedish system; and from zero to 3.2 percent under the Swiss system. The proportionate increase in taxes would also have been greater for wealthier families than poorer ones under all three systems.

Referring again to Table 14.3, we see that income tax rates in the United States showed relatively little variation across age groups, rising from 9.2 percent for the youngest families to 12.3 percent for those 35–54, then falling back a bit for older cohorts. In contrast, under all three wealth tax systems, tax rates on income would have risen monotonically with age group, reflecting the fact that wealth-income ratios increased with age. Under the German system, tax rates would have ranged from 0.5 to 4.1 percent; under the Swedish system, from 2.3 to 16.9 percent; and under the Swiss system, from 0.3 to 1.9 percent. Under all three systems, taxes would have increased proportionately more for older Americans than younger ones.

There was also relatively little variation in income tax rates by family type. Unmarried males faced the highest average income tax rates, 12.3 percent, followed by married couples (11.7 percent) and single females (8.9 percent). Under all three wealth tax systems, married couples would have faced the highest tax rates, with unmarried male and female households taxed almost identically. Under the German system, married couples would have paid 1.8 percent of income in wealth taxes, compared to 1.5 percent for unmarried males or females; in the Swedish system, the respective rates were 9.3 and 5.9 percent, and in the Swiss system, 1 and 0.7 percent.

White families in the United States generally paid higher tax rates than nonwhites—11.9 percent compared to 8.7 percent—reflecting the higher relative incomes of whites. Under all three wealth tax systems, white families, on average far better endowed than minority families, would have paid considerably higher taxes than nonwhites. Also, in all three cases, white families would have seen their tax bill rise proportionately more than nonwhite families.

One can measure the effect of wealth taxation on inequality in three steps. (1) Figure out the inequality (based on the Gini coefficient) in the distribution of pretax income. (2) Calculate the Gini coefficient of after-tax income resulting only from the imposition of the personal income tax. (3) Compute the same measure for after-tax income resulting from both the income tax and each of the wealth tax systems. The distributional effect of the wealth tax will depend on its progressivity with respect to income, its magnitude, and the proportionate increase in taxes it generates by income class.

Results are shown in Panel A of Table 14.4. Among all families, the Gini coefficient for pretax income was 0.52 in 1989. The Gini coefficient for income after income taxes was 0.50, indicating that the personal income tax system had a modest equalizing effect on income distribution. Adding the Swedish wealth tax to the personal taxation formula resulted in a further reduction of the Gini coefficient to 0.48. The Swedish wealth tax thus had an equalizing effect on the income distribution similar in magnitude to the personal income tax system. However, neither the German nor the Swiss wealth tax had much effect on measured income inequality, mainly because of the small amount of revenue that they generated and their lack of progressivity with respect to income.

The distributional effect of the wealth tax systems did show some variation by age group, family type, and race. The equalizing effects of the wealth tax exerted greater influence within older age groups than among younger ones. For age group 70 and over, the imposition of the Swedish wealth tax system caused the Gini coefficient to fall from 0.54 to 0.49. The effects were stronger among married couples than unmarried individuals: among married couples, the Gini coefficient declined from 0.45 to 0.42 when Swedish wealth taxes were added to income taxes. The equalizing effect was also larger among white families than among nonwhites.

Panel B of Table 14.4 shows the same set of computations for an alternate measure of income called Income*. Income* is defined as family income plus 3.28 percent of family net worth (3.28 percent is an estimate of the average annual real rate of appreciation on household wealth over the 1962–1989 period). Income* is logically a more inclusive measure of family welfare than normal income. The effects of a wealth tax on this more inclusive measure of income may be considered a better measure of the overall distributional effects of a wealth tax.

Table 14.4. Distributional effects of alternative wealth taxation systems by age group, family type and race, 1989

		Age Group				Family Type			Race	
	All	18–34	35–54	55–69	70+	Married Couple	Unmarried Male	Unmarried Female	White	Nonwhite
A. Gini Coefficients for Income										
Pretax income	0.521	0.441	0.477	0.568	0.568	0.473	0.529	0.451	0.504	0.525
Original posttax income	0.497	0.420	0.454	0.543	0.539	0.446	0.502	0.426	0.479	0.503
New post-income/German wealth tax	0.495	0.421	0.451	0.537	0.534	0.442	0.501	0.424	0.477	0.503
New post-income/Swedish wealth tax	0.476	0.414	0.434	0.505	0.487	0.421	0.487	0.415	0.458	0.490
New post-income/Swiss wealth tax	0.495	0.420	0.452	0.539	0.536	0.444	0.502	0.425	0.477	0.503
B. Gini Coefficients for Income[a]										
Pretax income*	0.544	0.453	0.499	0.599	0.603	0.500	0.549	0.468	0.526	0.542
Original posttax income*	0.527	0.435	0.482	0.583	0.586	0.481	0.528	0.449	0.509	0.524
New post-income*/German wealth tax	0.522	0.433	0.478	0.577	0.578	0.475	0.524	0.445	0.504	0.521
New post-income*/Swedish wealth tax	0.502	0.426	0.460	0.550	0.548	0.453	0.509	0.430	0.483	0.510
New post-income*/Swiss wealth tax	0.524	0.434	0.480	0.580	0.582	0.478	0.526	0.447	0.506	0.522

Source: Author's calculations from the 1989 Survey of Consumer Finances. See text for details on tax calculations.
a. Income* is defined as family income plus 3.28 percent of family net worth.

Results for Income* were quite similar to those for standard family income. Among all families, the Gini coefficient was 0.544 for pretax Income*, 0.527 for Income* after the payment of income taxes, and 0.502 for Income* after both income and Swedish wealth taxes are paid. As before, the German and Swiss wealth tax systems had little distributional impact. The equalizing effects of wealth taxes on the distribution of Income* increased with age, were greater for married couples than for singles, and were stronger among white families than among nonwhites.

Update to 2013

Almost thirty years have elapsed since the publication of the OECD's report on wealth taxation in member nations.[17] The current state of wealth taxation among these nations is summarized in Table 14.5. Of the eleven countries with a direct wealth tax in 1985, only four still had one in 2015—the Netherlands (on the provincial level only), Norway, Spain, and Switzerland (on the canton level). Spain abolished its wealth tax on January 1, 2009, but then reintroduced it in 2012. Austria and Denmark discontinued their wealth tax in 1995, Germany in 1997, Finland and Luxembourg in 2006, and Sweden in 2007. Iceland abrogated its wealth tax in 2006, reintroduced it in 2010 for four years, and then eliminated it in 2015. However, France reintroduced a direct wealth tax in 2011 and it is still in effect.[18] As of 2016, three of the original 24 OECD countries have a national wealth tax and two have a provincial (or canton-level) wealth tax.

With regard to inheritance, gift, and/or estate taxes, of the twenty-two countries with one form of these in 1985, all but four still had one in effect in 2015. New Zealand eliminated its estate duty in 1992. Sweden abolished its inheritance tax in 2005, Austria in 2008, and Norway in 2014.

Why the retrenchment in wealth taxes (both direct and inheritance)? One can think of a backlash on taxes in general beginning with U.S. President Ronald Reagan and British Prime Minister Margaret Thatcher in the 1980s. This was followed by conservative backlash in continental Europe in the 1990s and 2000s. For example, a conservative government was elected to power in Sweden in the mid-2000s, which engineered the elimination of both the direct wealth tax and the inheritance tax.

Table 14.5. Wealth taxation systems among OECD member countries on individual or family wealth holdings, 2015

	Direct Wealth Taxation	Transfer Tax at Death and on Gifts
Australia	No	None
Austria	No	None
Belgium	No	Inheritance
Canada	No	None
Denmark	No	Inheritance
Finland	No	Inheritance
France	Yes	Inheritance
Germany	No	Inheritance
Greece	No	Inheritance
Iceland	No	Inheritance
Ireland	No	Inheritance
Italy	No	Inheritance
Japan	No	Inheritance
Luxembourg	No	Inheritance
Netherlands	Yes[a]	Inheritance
New Zealand	No	None
Norway	Yes	None
Portugal	No	Inheritance
Spain	Yes	Inheritance
Sweden	No	None
Switzerland	Yes[a]	Estate / Inheritance[a]
Turkey	No	Inheritance
United Kingdom	No	Estate
United States	No	Estate

European Commission, *Cross-Country Review of Taxes on Wealth and Transfers of Wealth,* available at https://ec.europa.eu/taxation_customs/sites/taxation/files/docs/body/2014_eu _wealth_tax_project_finale_report.pdf

https://en.wikipedia.org/wiki/Wealth_tax

https://en.wikipedia.org/wiki/Inheritance_tax

http://taxsummaries.pwc.com/ID/Iceland-Individual-Other-taxes

http://www2.deloitte.com/content/dam/Deloitte/global/Documents/Tax/dttl-tax -turkeyguide-2014.pdf

a. Provincial (or canton) tax.

The tax simulations were updated to 2013 on the basis of the 2013 SCF and the 2013 income tax schedules for individuals.[19] In this analysis, I have used only the Swiss wealth tax system since it seems to provide the most reasonable amount of revenue generated. Following the Swiss convention, thresholds and tax brackets are indexed to consumer price changes. Using the

CPI-U, the new exemptions in 2013 were $121,242 for married couples and $73,611 for singles. The top bracket (the 0.30 percent range) now began at $2.4 million. A new restriction is now added such that the sum of income and wealth taxes cannot exceed total income.

The Swiss style wealth tax would have generated $120.8 billion in extra tax revenue in 2013. This is 3.18 times greater than in 1989, considerably more than the 2.17 rise in the CPI. This also represents 1.2 percent of total family income and 9.2 percent of the total income tax revenue, up from 0.9 percent and 8 percent, respectively, in 1989 (see Table 14.6). This figure compares with actual U.S. personal income tax proceeds of $1,316.4 billion in 2013, or 12.7 percent of total income. It also contrasts with total estate and gift taxes of a rather miniscule $18.9 billion in 2013.[20] While 44 percent of families in 2013 would pay an additional wealth tax, only 20 percent of families would see their tax bill rise by more than $200 and only 15.1 percent by more than $500.

As in the 1989 simulations, the Swiss wealth tax system is generally progressive with respect to income, rising from 0.4 percent for the second lowest income class to 2.2 percent for the highest bracket. However, now the percentage increase in total taxes paid would also be generally higher for upper-income families than lower-income ones. Moreover, the fraction of families paying any wealth tax would rise with income level, from 15 percent for the lowest income bracket (under $15,000 of income) to 100 percent for the highest income class ($250,000 of income and over). The wealth tax is again highly progressive with respect to wealth. The only groups that would pay an additional 1 percent or more of income in federal taxes are the millionaires. Upper wealth families would also see a higher proportionate increase in total federal taxes paid. Very few families (only 4 percent) worth less than $100,000 in net wealth would pay any wealth taxes, whereas virtually all families above this amount would wind up paying some wealth tax.

In terms of wealth tax incidence by demographic characteristic, the wealth tax would fall more heavily on older households than younger ones. Wealth tax rates on income would rise monotonically with age group, from 0.2 percent for the youngest age group (age 34 and under) to 2.4 percent for the oldest (age 70 and over), and wealth taxes as a percentage of income taxes would also increase with age, from 3.1 percent for the youngest age group to 24 percent for the oldest. The share of families paying a wealth tax would

Table 14.6. Original income tax and new wealth taxes modeled after the Swiss system by income class, wealth class, age group, family type, and race, 2013

	Ratio of Income Tax to Family Income (percentage)	Swiss Wealth Tax		Percent of Families Paying Wealth Tax
		Percentage of Income	Ratio to Income Tax	
All Families	12.7	1.2	0.09	44.3
A. Income Class				
Under $15,000	−3.1	2.0	—	14.6
$15,000–$24,999	−3.2	0.4	—	23.7
$25,000–$49,999	1.6	0.2	0.14	32.7
$50,000–$74,999	5.9	0.4	0.06	46.3
$75,000–$99,999	7.6	0.5	0.07	58.2
$100,000–$249,999	11.5	0.9	0.07	77.8
$250,000 and over	23.4	2.2	0.10	98.1
B. Wealth Class				
Under $100,000	4.7	0.0	0.00	3.6
$100,000–$249,999	7.6	0.0	0.01	89.6
$250,000–$499,999	9.1	0.2	0.02	100.0
$500,000–$749,999	10.3	0.7	0.07	100.0
$75500,000–$999,999	11.6	0.9	0.08	100.0
$1,000,000–$2,499,999	14.5	1.0	0.07	100.0
$2,500,000–$4,999,999	20.7	2.1	0.10	100.0
$5,000,000 and over	25.1	3.8	0.15	100.0
C. Age Class				
Under 35	5.8	0.2	0.03	13.1
35–54	13.6	0.8	0.06	40.9
55–69	14.7	1.6	0.11	59.4
70 and over	10.0	2.4	0.24	67.7
D. Household Type				
Married couple	13.4	1.2	0.09	50.4
Males, unmarried	13.6	1.1	0.08	36.3
Females, unmarried	6.8	0.6	0.09	36.1
E. Race or Ethnicity				
White	13.8	1.3	0.09	52.9
African American	5.4	0.3	0.05	19.8
Hispanic	5.0	0.3	0.06	20.4
Other	12.4	1.2	0.09	46.8

Source: Author's calculations from the 2013 Survey of Consumer Finances. The figures are based on the Swiss tax schedule as spelled out in Table 14.2 except that the brackets have been updated to 2013 dollars on the basis of the CPI-U (a factor of 2.165)

likewise rise with age, from 13 percent for the youngest to 68 percent for the oldest age group.

Under the Swiss wealth tax system, married couples would face a slightly higher tax rate than unmarried male (1.2 versus 1.1 percent) and female households would be taxed at the lowest rate (0.6 percent). A higher percentage of married couples (50 percent) would pay any wealth tax compared to unmarried male householders (36 percent) and unmarried female householders (36 percent). All three groups would see their overall tax bill grow by about the same percentage (between 8 and 9 percent).

As in the 1989 simulations, (non-Hispanic) white families would pay the highest wealth tax rate—1.3 percent. The "other" racial group (mainly Asian Americans) would face the second highest rate (1.2 percent), followed by Hispanics and (non-Hispanic) African Americans (0.3 percent). Whereas 53 percent of white families would pay some wealth tax, only 47 percent of others and 20 percent of Hispanic and African-American families would be subject to this tax. Whites and others would see about the same proportionate increase in their overall tax bill (9 percent), while Hispanics and African Americans would see their total federal taxes rise by only 5 or 6 percent.

As in the 1989 simulations, the distributional effect of the tax system is measured by the change in the Gini coefficient. Among all families, the Gini coefficient for pretax income was 0.574 in 2013, while the Gini coefficient for income after income taxes was 0.532 (see Table 14.7). Adding the Swiss wealth tax to the personal income tax results in a further reduction of the Gini coefficient to only 0.528 (0.004 Gini point difference). The reason for this rather minimal effect, as in the 1989 simulations, is mainly the small amount of revenue generated by the Swiss-style wealth tax relative to income taxes (9.2 percent). The distributional effects of the Swiss-style wealth tax vary by age group, family type, and race. The equalizing effects of the wealth tax exert greater influence within older age groups than younger ones. The reduction in the Gini coefficient from adding the wealth tax to the income tax rises systematically with age, from 0.001 Gini points for the youngest group to 0.008 points for the oldest. The effects are stronger among married couples than unmarried individuals: among married couples, the Gini coefficient declines by 0.005 Gini points when wealth taxes are added to income taxes, compared to a decline of 0.004 among unmarried men and 0.001 among unmarried women. The equalizing effect is also larger among white

Table 14.7. Distributional effects of the Swiss wealth taxation system by age group, family type and race, 2013 (Gini coefficients)

| | | Age Group | | | | Family Type | | | | Race | |
	All	18–34	35–54	55–69	70+	Married Couple	Unmarried Male	Unmarried Female		Whites and Others	Blacks and Hispanics
Pretax income	0.574	0.439	0.548	0.612	0.574	0.538	0.575	0.438		0.578	0.437
Original posttax income	0.532	0.407	0.504	0.572	0.537	0.491	0.530	0.404		0.537	0.403
New post-income / Swiss wealth tax	0.528	0.406	0.501	0.568	0.528	0.487	0.525	0.403		0.533	0.401

Source: author's calculations from the 2013 SCF. See text for details on tax calculations.

and other (mainly Asian) families (a 0.004 point reduction in the Gini coefficient) than among blacks and Hispanics combined (0.001 Gini points).

I have been assuming that total net worth is the correct base for a wealth tax. It is true that most wealth taxes that have been employed use this (or some small variant) as the base. However, there are other possibilities that might be fairer, or at least more politically palatable. Table 14.8 shows the effects of altering the tax base on wealth tax collections. The base case is net worth (excluding vehicles). It is first of interest to note the concentration of tax collections by socioeconomic characteristic. The top income class, which comprised 4 percent of all households, would account for 66 percent of total wealth taxes, and the top two income classes, which amounted to 20 percent of all households, would pay 86 percent of the total tax bill. The top wealth class, 1.7 percent of all households, would pay 66 percent of all wealth taxes, and the top two, 3.7 percent of households, 80 percent of the total taxes. Age class 55–69, 26 percent of all families, would account for 46 percent of wealth taxes. Married couples, 57 percent of all households, would pay 85 percent of all taxes, and whites, 70 percent of households, would contribute 92 percent of tax revenues.

In this analysis, I alter the tax base in several ways. I exclude principal homes (and the associated mortgage) from the tax base. One rationale for this is that homes are already subject to a local property tax. Total wealth tax revenues now fall by 17 percent. The lower income and wealth cases would get the most benefit (the largest percentage reduction in taxes owed), as would families over age 34, unmarried females, and nonwhites. There is no perceptible effect on the after-income tax and wealth tax Gini coefficient.

Small businesses could be exempted from the wealth tax since they are particularly difficult to value and their inclusion is likely to be opposed by a powerful interest group. This exclusion would cause the total tax bill to fall by 30 percent. The main beneficiaries would be upper income and wealth households (who own most of the businesses), as well as young families and, surprisingly, Hispanics. This restriction would result in a slight increase in the post-tax Gini coefficient (a 0.0014 change). Trust funds might be excluded since they are generally excluded from the estate tax base. The overall reduction in the wealth tax bill would be tiny—3.8 percent. Once again the main beneficiaries would be upper income and wealth households, as well as the youngest and oldest age groups, surprisingly unmarried females, and whites.

Table 14.8. Percentage change in total wealth tax collection on the basis of the Swiss system from changes in the wealth tax base by income class, wealth class, age group, family type and race, 2013

	Baseline Total Wealth Tax Revenue (billions)	Exclude:				Add: Defined Benefit Pension Wealth
		Home Equity on Principal Home	Businesses	Trust Funds	Defined Contribution Pension Plans	
All Families	120.8	-17.0	-29.9	-3.8	-19.1	9.1
A. Income Class						
Under $15,000	2.6	-17.5	-59.0	-0.2	-3.9	1.4
$15,000-$24,999	1.3	-40.8	-20.0	-1.6	-13.7	8.8
$25,000-$49,999	2.7	-47.3	-8.7	-2.3	-22.5	43.6
$50,000-$74,999	4.5	-30.7	-16.4	-3.7	-28.3	35.1
$75,000-$99,999	5.7	-28.9	-16.9	-0.1	-30.8	25.7
$100,000-$249,999	24.6	-22.6	-19.6	-3.8	-30.6	19.7
$250,000 and over	79.3	-12.2	-34.8	-4.3	-14.7	2.2
B. Wealth Class						
Under $100,000	0.0	-68.5	-2.7	0.0	-44.5	—
$100,000-$249,999	0.6	-71.5	-5.9	-0.4	-37.4	223.8
$250,000-$499,999	2.1	-60.5	-5.8	-1.8	-40.9	123.7
$500,000-$749,999	4.4	-57.9	-10.5	-1.9	-47.9	31.7
$75500,000-$999,999	4.4	-40.9	-10.3	-2.4	-42.7	12.6

$1,000,000–$2,499,999	12.3	−23.9	−12.7	−1.7	−32.1	17.2
$2,500,000–$4,999,999	17.5	−25.0	−24.0	−2.1	−28.8	6.0
$5,000,000 and over	79.4	−9.0	−36.9	−4.8	−11.3	1.0
C. Age Class						
Under 35	2.2	−12.3	−54.3	−9.5	−5.7	1.4
35–54	35.0	−17.7	−42.9	−3.0	−15.9	4.3
55–69	55.4	−16.9	−25.5	−2.8	−22.2	11.8
70 and over	28.3	−16.8	−20.7	−6.3	−18.1	10.3
D. Household Type						
Married couple	102.2	−16.2	−30.3	−3.2	−19.8	8.5
Males, unmarried	11.0	−15.4	−38.0	−5.5	−11.8	7.2
Females, unmarried	7.5	−29.8	−12.8	−9.9	−20.6	19.8
E. Race or Ethnicity						
White	111.3	−16.5	−28.8	−4.0	−19.6	8.8
African American	1.9	−19.0	−46.1	−3.0	−18.5	43.4
Hispanic	1.6	−24.1	−58.2	−2.4	−8.1	6.2
Other	6.0	−24.1	−39.0	−0.3	−13.5	4.8
Memo: Post-income and wealth tax Gini coeff. for all households	0.528	0.528	0.529	0.528	0.529	0.528

Source: Author's calculations from the 2013 SCF. The figures are based on the Swiss tax schedule whose brackets have been updated to 2013 dollars on the basis of the CPI-U (a factor of 2.165).

This change, however, would have almost no effect on the posttax Gini coefficient

IRAs, 401(k) plans, and other defined contribution pension plans might be eliminated from the tax base, since they are not taxed for income tax purposes. Overall, total wealth taxes would decline by 19 percent. The groups that would gain the most (that is, experience the greatest reduction in wealth taxes owed) are middle income and middle wealth families, age group 55–69, and whites. This restriction would cause the after-tax Gini coefficient to rise by a very small 0.0006 points. Finally, we might add defined benefit pension wealth to the base since this is an important component of augmented wealth. This would add 9 percent to the wealth tax intake. Middle-income families would be hit hardest, as would lower wealth families, age groups 55 and over, unmarried females, and African Americans (43 percent increase in wealth taxes). Overall, there is almost no effect on the after-tax Gini coefficient.

Concluding Remarks

The pronounced rise in wealth inequality since the early 1980s and particularly over the Great Recession creates some urgency in policy remedies. The most telling statistic is that virtually all the growth in (marketable) wealth between 1983 and 2013 accrued to the top 20 percent of households (see Chapter 2). Indeed, the bottom 40 percent of households saw their wealth decline in absolute terms. This was compounded by the stark reality of a growing proportion of households with zero or negative net worth.

What, if anything, should be done about this? If one policy goal is to moderate the rising inequality of recent years, direct taxation of wealth is one possible remedy. This would compensate for the reduced progressivity of the income tax system. The years since 1980 witnessed falling marginal tax rates on income, particularly for the rich and very rich. The top marginal tax rate fell from 70 percent in 1980 to 35 percent in 2012, and was raised to 39.6 percent under the Obama administration (see Chapter 1, Figure 1.8).

The simulation results in this chapter suggest that a Swiss-style wealth taxation system would have several positive effects. America's current personal income tax system helps mitigate the disparities in earnings, but its overall effects are modest (indeed, they would probably appear even smaller if full information were available on itemized deductions and income adjustments). The Swiss wealth tax system would increase total tax revenues (over and above the personal income tax) by only 9 percent in 2013—too small to have much distributional impact. The wealth tax would have some desirable features from a demographic standpoint. It falls proportionately more on older families than younger ones; more on married couples than singles; and more on whites and Asians than blacks and Hispanics. Moreover, the equalizing effects of the wealth tax would be greater among older families, married couples, and whites.

The rather modest Swiss-style system would have yielded an additional $121 billion of revenue in 2013. In light of the demands on the federal budget, such a tax could be valuable indeed. In spite of the proposed tax's potency as a revenue-raising tool, in 2013 only 11 percent of families would see their federal tax bill rise by more than 10 percent and only 8 percent would have paid an additional $500 or more of taxes. In conclusion, a direct wealth taxation system like Switzerland's could ease the country's budgetary strains and provide greater equity across generational, racial, and familial categories. These characteristics argue in favor of its adoption in the United States.

Two additional arguments have been advanced in support of a wealth tax. First, beyond considerations of overall (vertical) equity, some have argued that a wealth tax can be justified in terms of taxable capacity. Income alone is not a sufficient gauge of well-being or of the ability to pay taxes. The possession of wealth, over and above the income it yields directly, must be figured into the calculation. Two families with identical incomes but different levels of wealth are not equivalent in terms of their well-being, since a wealthier family will have more independence, firmer security in times of economic stress (such as occasioned by unemployment, illness, or family breakup), and readier access to consumer credit. Greater wealth thus confers on the affluent family a larger capacity to pay taxes; in the interests of horizontal equity, wealth and income should both be directly taxed.

A second argument is that an annual wealth tax may induce individuals to transfer their assets from less productive uses to more productive ones. A tax on wealth may provide an incentive to switch from low-yielding to high-yielding investments, in order to offset the additional taxes. For example, a wealth tax based on the market value of property might induce neglectful owners to seek to realize potential returns through development, renovation, or sale. Likewise, a wealth tax might induce individuals to seek more income-generating assets in place of conspicuous consumer durables such as luxury cars and yachts. A direct wealth tax has the added feature that it may inhibit the avoidance of income taxes by encouraging investors to switch assets into income-yielding forms.

The current existing U.S. wealth taxation system works poorly. The estate tax has historically been an extremely porous tax. The thresholds have been raised over time (from $50,000 in 1916, when the estate tax was first instituted, to $60,000 in 1942, then to $175,000 in 1981, to $600,000 in 1987, and to $5,250,000 for singles and $10,500,000 for couples in 2013),[21] so that only a very small percentage of estates (typically on the order of 1 or 2 percent) have been subject to estate tax. The threshold is currently indexed to the CPI-U and will continue to rise over time.

Estate taxes on assets can be avoided altogether by setting up a trust fund with children or other desired "heirs" as beneficiaries (though provisions for such trusts were tightened up in the 1993 federal tax legislation). Moreover, gift exclusions allow a considerable amount of wealth to be passed on before death exempt from taxation. In addition, there are the usual problems of underreporting, valuation of assets, and compliance (for example, how to value a family business?).

Finally, the estate tax system has a provision that capital gains on assets are essentially excluded from consideration. Normally, realized capital gains are counted as part of the taxable base in computing income taxes. However, if an asset is not sold and winds up in an estate, the capital gains are forgiven by the tax authorities. This loophole by itself probably more than equals the total revenue collected by the estate tax system. Given the history of estate taxes in the United States and the vested interest of the wealthy in maintaining the current system (not to speak of the estate planners and lawyers who profit from the system), it may be easier from a political standpoint to institute a new wealth tax than to try to revamp the existing estate tax regime.

Perhaps the strongest argument against direct wealth taxation is that it will inhibit savings and lower capital investment. One unavoidable implication of wealth taxation is that the (after-tax) return to capital will be lowered. By exerting a strong disincentive on the already low U.S. savings rate, it may simply encourage increased consumption. Another possibility is that a wealth tax, by lowering the after-tax rate of return on financial assets, may encourage families to invest in nonfinancial assets, such as certain forms of real estate, collectibles, precious metals, luxury items, and the like. The search for greater opacity to thwart the Internal Revenue Service (IRS) could perversely result in shifting of household portfolios to unproductive uses; though, as suggested previously, one can reasonably argue the opposite case—that taxing both income-yielding and non-income-yielding forms of wealth will induce households to shift to higher-yielding assets.

One simple, though relatively crude, way of addressing this issue is to compare the average savings rates of countries with direct wealth taxes to those without such taxes.[22] On the basis of OECD national accounts data, within both sets of countries there was large variation in average household savings rates over the period 1980 to 1990.[23] Among those with a wealth tax, savings rates ranged from 4 percent in Spain to 10.5 percent in Switzerland. Among those without a wealth tax, figures ranged from 3.6 percent in the United Kingdom to 11.6 percent in Japan. The average savings rate among countries with a wealth tax was 8 percent, and that for countries without a wealth tax was 9.8 percent. Econometric analysis indicated that the absence of a wealth tax is not a statistically significant factor in explaining the cross-country variation in savings rates.

A second potential problem stemming from a wealth tax is capital flight. By inserting a wedge between what an asset earns and what the owner receives, a tax understates the return in the owner's eyes and encourages the owner to look for higher returns elsewhere. This argument applies to every tax, however, and if capital indeed moved like quicksilver, it would render any taxation of capital and wealth all but impossible. The very fact that the wealth tax proposal presented here is based on the Swiss model suggests that capital flight is unlikely to be a serious concern. Like Switzerland, the United States is a safe haven for international wealth, a status unlikely to be threatened by the very low-wealth tax rates suggested in this analysis.[24]

The time is ripe for the introduction of a personal tax on wealth holdings. The statistics point to an enormous degree of inequality in household net worth in the United States today, and an even greater degree in terms of household financial wealth. On the grounds of (horizontal) equity, a combination of annual income and the current stock of wealth provide a better gauge of the ability to pay taxes than income alone. Moreover, there is no evidence from other advanced economies that the imposition of a modest direct tax on household wealth has had a deleterious effect on personal savings or on overall economic growth. In fact, there are arguments to the contrary, that such a tax may induce a more efficient allocation of household wealth, toward more productive uses. Finally, the possibility that such a levy might promote capital flight is not borne out by the evidence.

A wealth tax modeled after the Swiss system might be appropriate for the United States. The basic exclusion could begin at $74,000 for singles and $121,000 for married couples. The marginal tax structure might look as follows: 0.05 percent (applied to household wealth after the exclusion valued from zero to $179,999); 0.10 percent (from $180,000 to $479,999); 0.15 percent (from $480,000 to $967,999); 0.20 percent (from $968,000 to $1,689,999); 0.25 percent (from $1,690,000 to $2,399,999); and 0.30 percent ($2,400,000 and above). As in the Swiss system, all household effects, pensions, and annuities would be excluded.[25] In addition, the rules would provide a $30,000 exemption on automobiles (that is, only expensive cars would be subject to the tax).

The wealth tax would be fully integrated with the personal income tax. The same tax form could be used for both. The family would be required to list the value of all assets and debts on a new subsidiary form (say, "Schedule W"). Verification of most of the assets and debts would be administratively easy to implement. Insofar as banks and other financial institutions provide records to the IRS that list interest payments (Form 1099), such documents could be modified to include also the value of the interest-bearing accounts as of a certain date (December 31, for example). A similar procedure could be applied to dividend forms. Moreover, financial institutions that provide the IRS with information on mortgage payments made by households could now add the value of the outstanding mortgage. Other types of loans (and loan payments) could be similarly recorded by these institutions. Insurance companies could provide the IRS with statements on the value of life insurance equity (they already send these to individuals).

The two main stumbling blocks are the current market value of owner-occupied housing (and other real estate) and the valuation of unincorporated businesses. For the former, there are several possible solutions, some of which are currently in use in other countries. The family could be asked to estimate the current market value (as is now done in household surveys). Alternatively, it could be asked to list the original purchase price and date of purchase, and the IRS could use a regional (or locale-specific) price index based on housing survey data to update the value. Another method would ask residents to provide the figure for assessed valuation of the property, and the IRS could provide a locale-specific adjustment factor, based on periodic survey data, to estimate current market value.

For unincorporated businesses, the simplest technique is to accumulate the value of individual assets invested in the business over time (these figures are already provided in Form C of the personal tax return). Another possibility is to capitalize the net profit figures (also provided on Form C), as the Swiss currently do.

Calculations show that such a tax structure would yield an average tax rate on *household wealth* (as of 2013) of 0.19 percent. Previous work indicates that the annual real rate of return on household wealth over the period from 1983 to 2013 averaged 3.10 percent per year (see Chapter 3). Thus, the new tax regime would reduce the average yield on household assets by only 6.2 percent. Even the top marginal tax rate of 0.3 percent would reduce the average yield on personal wealth by only 9.7 percent. These figures suggest that disincentive effects, if any, on personal savings would be very modest.

Would such a tax be popular? Of course, no additional payment of taxes is likely to be cheered by the American people. But the proposed wealth tax would affect a very small percentage of the population. Only 11 percent of American families would see their overall personal tax bill (combining income and wealth taxes) rise by more than 10 percent. Only 15 percent would pay $500 or more of additional taxes. A full 56 percent would fall below the wealth tax threshold and would therefore be exempt from paying.

A substantial $121 billion would have been raised from levying such a tax in 2013. This is not a large amount, representing 4.4 percent of total federal tax receipts. However, on the margin such additional revenue could be critical. Even at this writing, there are many programs that could benefit from an additional injection of tax revenue—such as expanded welfare (TANF) coverage, Medicaid, food stamps, increased unemployment insurance coverage, higher EITC payouts, additional federal aid to education, and the like. Indeed, 2013 was a low point in the wealth cycle. The additional revenue generated by a wealth tax could be considerably higher in more normal times. A direct annual tax on personal wealth could thus be a valuable addition to the fiscal toolbox available to the federal government.

15

Summary of Principal Findings and Concluding Comments

T his book provided a historical overview of developments in household wealth over the course of a little more than a century in the United States. Particular attention was paid to the years after 1962, which allowed for detailed microdata estimates of the size distribution of household wealth. This book also examined in particular detail the rather devastating effects of the Great Recession on household wealth holdings.

A wide range of topics was addressed in this volume. These included trends in both mean and median household wealth and overall wealth inequality, both in the recent past and the long term; changes in the portfolio composition of wealth over time, with particular attention to household indebtedness; comparisons of wealth levels and wealth inequality in the United States with those of other advanced countries; an analysis of some of the mechanisms behind changing wealth inequality; an empirical examination of the so-called life cycle model, in which it is argued that households accumulate wealth during working years in order to ensure adequate consumption during retirement years; an assessment of the role of inheritances and inter vivos gifts in accounting for disparities in wealth among households; a consideration of the role of Social Security and private pensions in the household accumulation of wealth; wealth differences among socioeconomic groups as demarcated by race, age, family status, and the like; the demographic and workforce characteristics of the rich; the persistence of asset poverty in the United States; and an examination of the redistributional effects of direct wealth taxation in the United States.

We started by examining recent trends in personal wealth. Chapter 1 provided a historical backdrop on trends in the standard of living, the poverty rate, income inequality, labor earnings, and the wage share of national income since 1947. The years since 1973 witnessed slow growth in earnings and income for the middle class, as well as a stagnating poverty rate and rising income inequality. In contrast, the early postwar period, before 1973, saw rapid advances in wages and family income for the middle class, in addition to a sharp decline in poverty and a moderate fall in income inequality. The "booming" 1990s and early 2000s did not bring much help to the middle class, with median family income growing by only 3 percent (in total) between 1989 and 2013. Personal tax rates generally fell since the early 1970s but by much more for the rich than the middle class. In sum, the middle class became squeezed in terms of earnings and income since the early 1970s.

The stagnation of living standards among the middle class over these years can be traced to the slow growth in labor earnings. While average earnings almost doubled between 1947 and 1973, they grew by only 22 percent from 1973 to 2013. There was no growth in real hourly wages according to data from the Bureau of Labor Statistics. As a result, median income in 2013 was still well below its peak in 2007 (by 7.4 percent). In fact in 2013, it was back to where it had been in 1997.

The main reason for the stagnation of labor earnings derived from a clear shift in national income away from labor and toward capital, particularly since the late 1970s. There is a clear connection between rising income inequality and a rising profit share. Over this period, both overall and corporate profitability spiked upward, almost back to postwar highs. The stock market was, in part, fueled by rising profitability. While the owners of capital gained from rising profits, workers experienced almost no progress in terms of wages. On the surface, at least, there appeared to be a trade-off between the advances in the income of the rich and the stagnation of income among the working class.

Strong correlations are evident between inequality and profitability, particularly since 1979. However, the regression analysis shows that only the top income shares (those of the top 1 percent, the top 0.1 percent, and the top 0.01 percent) have a positive and statistically significant relationship to profitability.

Chapter 2 reviewed trends in average wealth holdings and wealth inequality over years 1962 to 2013. Median household net worth showed robust growth between 1962 and 2001, growing 1.43 percent per year. Over the 2001–2007 period the median increased even faster, at 2.91 percent per year.

Mean net worth showed even stronger growth over years 1962 to 2001, gaining 2.26 percent per year, and again from 2001 to 2007, 3.1 percent per year. Median income had a different time trend, rising by 0.92 percent per year from 1962 to 1989, and then by only 7.6 percent (in total) from 1989 to 2007. Mean income, on the other hand, advanced by 1.32 percent per annum from 1962 to 1989 and then by 15 percent from 1989 to 2007.

Then came the Great Recession, which like a tsunami wiped out forty years of wealth gains. From 2007 to 2010, house prices collapsed by 24 percent in real terms, stock prices by 26 percent, and median wealth by a staggering 44 percent. By 2010 median wealth was even below where it had been in 1969. Mean wealth, on the other hand, dropped by a much more modest 16 percent. Median and mean income also dipped but by a more moderate 6.7 and 5.2 percent, respectively.

From 2010 to 2013, asset prices rebounded with stock prices up by 39 percent and house prices by 8 percent. Despite these gains, both median and mean wealth stagnated according to the SCF data. However, during this period mean household wealth increased by 27 percent on the basis of aggregate balance sheet data.

Inequality is measured in four major ways: (1) the Gini coefficient, (2) shares of the top groups, (3) percentile ratios, and (4) the share of total wealth growth accruing to different groups. Results differ according to the measure used. According to the first metric, the Gini coefficient, wealth inequality rose by 0.025 Gini points from 1962 to 1969, returned to its 1962 level in 1983, and then climbed by 0.029 Gini points from 1983 to 1989. It was relatively unchanged from 1989 to 2007 but then surged by 0.032 Gini points over years 2007 to 2010. It was then up slightly form 2010 and 2013. In 2013 the Gini coefficient was at its highest level over the 51 years, at 0.871.

In contrast, the Gini coefficient for income inequality showed an almost continuous rise from 1962 to 2000 (a stunning 0.135 Gini point rise), a slight remission from 2000 to 2003, and then another surge of 0.034 Gini points through 2006. It then dropped substantially from 2006 to 2009 but by 2012 it was back at its 2007 level.

Time trends for top shares show a somewhat different pattern. As with the Gini index, the net worth shares of the top 1 percent shot upward by about two percentage points from 1962 to 1969, returned to its 1962 level by 1983, and then increased sharply from 1983 to 1989. However, unlike the Gini coefficient, which remained relatively flat from 1989 to 2007, the share of the top 1 percent spiked from 1989 to 1995, fell off from 1995 and 2001, and then had a modest rebound through 2007. From 2007 to 2010, when the Gini index showed a sizable upturn, the share of the top 1 percent ticked up by a rather small 0.5 percentage points. In contrast, over years 2010 to 2013, when the Gini coefficient showed a small upturn, the share of the top 1 percent climbed by 1.6 percentage points.

The P99 / P50 ratio (the ratio of wealth at the 90th percentile to that at the 50th percentile) shows a rather different trend. The P99 / P50 ratio tripled from 42.6 in 1962 to 121.6 in 2013. The highest percentage increase was 38 percent, recorded between 2007 and 2010. The ratio then rose by 10 percent from 2010 to 2013. The P95 / P50 ratio rose by a factor of 2.29 from 1962 to 2013. The P50 / P25 ratio followed a different trajectory, declining by 42 percent from 1962 to 1969, up a bit in 1983, almost doubling from 1983 to 1992, leveling off through 2004, rising 41 percent from 2004 to 2007, surging by a factor of four from 2007 to 2010, and then rising 30 percent rise from 2010 to 2013. The spike from 2007 to 2010 reflected the enormous decline in the net worth of the bottom quartile.

The mean wealth of the top 1 percent jumped to 18.6 million dollars in 2013. The percentage increase in net worth from 1983 to 2013 was much greater for the top wealth groups than for those lower in the distribution. All in all, the greatest gains in wealth accrued to the upper 20 percent, particularly the top 1 percent. Between 1983 and 2013, the top 1 percent received 41 percent of the total growth in net worth and the top 20 percent 100 percent. Similar results held for income. Looking at subperiods, we find that two, in particular, were characterized by large inequality spurts—1983–1989 and 2001–2007. Over those years, the top 1 percent received a disproportionate share of the total wealth gain—42.6 and 40.3 percent, respectively.

What can we make of these seemingly disparate trends in wealth inequality? First, there is near universal agreement across the metrics that wealth inequality rose substantially between 1983 and 2013. Over these years, the Gini coefficient climbed by 0.072 Gini points, the net worth share of the top 5 percent was up by 8.8 percentage points, and the net worth share of the top 20 percent by 7.6 percentage points. The wealth share of the top 1 percent showed a more modest increase of 2.9 percentage points. The P99 / P50 ratio shot up by a factor of 2.6, the P95 / P50 ratio by a factor of

2.2, and the P50 / P25 ratio by a factor of 16.3. In addition, 41 percent of the total wealth gains accrued to the top one percent and 100 percent to the top 20 percent.

The main difference among the metrics concerns the timing. According to the Gini coefficient, there were three large upturns in inequality: 1962–1969 (an increase in the Gini coefficient of 0.025); 1983–1989 (0.029 Gini points); and 2007–2010 (0.032 Gini points). With regard to the wealth share of the top 1 percent, there were relatively large increases over the 1962–1969 period (gain of 2.2 percentage points), the 1983–1989 period (1.4 percentage points), and years 2007 to 2013 (2.1 percentage points). The share of the top 5 percent showed large gains in years 1962–1969 (1.6 percentage points), 1983–1989 (1.9 percentage points), 1989–1992 (2.0 percentage points), 2004–2007 (2.9 percentage points), and 2010–2013 (2.3 percentage points), while the share of the top 20 percent showed particularly strong gains over years 1962–1969 (1.5 percentage points), 1983–1989 (1.7 percentage points), and 2007–2010 (3.6 percentage points).

The P99 / P50, the P95 / P50, and the P50 / P25 all indicate a wealth inequality surge from 2007 to 2010—percentage increases of 38 percent, 68 percent, and 408 percent, respectively. However, results differed for other periods. The P50 / P25 ratio rose by 65 percent over years 1983 to 1989 but the P99 / P50 ratio increased by only 12 percent and the P95 / P50 ratio declined slightly. By the P99 / P50 there was an inequality surge from 1995 to 2001—up by 44 percent—while the P99 / P50 ratio rose 20 percent and the P50 / P25 ratio was up only slightly. The share of wealth gains accruing to the top one percent was particularly strong in the 1983–1989 and 2001–2007 periods—42.6 and 40.3 percent, respectively.

Of the measures presented here, the Gini coefficient is probably the most reliable since it reflects the full distribution of wealth. It is also likely that the estimated wealth of the top groups is subject to measurement error. Fortunately, the Gini coefficient is not very sensitive to either the upper or lower tails of the wealth distribution, since the overwhelming mass of the Lorenz curve is found in the middle of the distribution. Based on the Gini coefficient, I would conclude that there were three inequality spurts over the period: 1962–1989, 1983–1989, and 2007–2010. Correspondingly, the P99 / P25 ratio also indicates inequality surges in years 1983–1989 (a 84 percent rise) and, particularly, in years 2007 to 2010 (a sixfold increase!).

Chapter 3 analyzed changes in the portfolio composition of household wealth over years 1983 to 2013 (the period for which consistent data exists) and rates of return on household wealth over the same period, as well as developments in ownership rates for selected assets. In 2013, owner-occupied housing was the most important household asset in the average portfolio breakdown for all households, accounting for 29 percent of total assets. However, net home equity—the value of the house minus any outstanding mortgage—amounted to only 17 percent. Debt as a proportion of gross assets was 15 percent, and the ratio of total household debt to net worth was 0.18.

There were some significant changes in the composition of household wealth over time. The most notable is that relative indebtedness first increased, with the ratio of debt to net worth climbing from 15 percent in 1983 to 21 percent in 2010, and then fell off to 18 percent in 2013. Likewise, the debt-income ratio surged from 68 percent in 1983 to 127 percent in 2010 but then dropped to 107 percent in 2013. A second is that pension accounts rose from 1.5 to 16.5 percent of total assets from 1983 to 2013. This increase largely offset the decline in the share of liquid assets in total assets, from 17.4 to 7.6 percent.

Are the rich really different from the rest of the population? It is evident that there are marked class differences in how middle-income families and the rich save their income. In 2013, about three-fifths of the wealth of the middle class was invested in their own homes—a result that often leads to the misimpression that housing is the major form of family wealth in America. Another 20 percent went into monetary savings of one form or another. Together housing and liquid assets accounted for 87 percent of their wealth. Their debt to net worth ratio was very high, 64 percent, and their ratio of debt to income was 125 percent. In contrast, the rich (the top 1 percent) invested about three-quarters of their savings in investment real estate, unincorporated businesses, corporate stock, and financial securities. Housing accounted for only 9 percent of their wealth, monetary savings another 6 percent, and pension accounts 9 percent. Their debt to net worth ratio was only 2.6 percent and their ratio of debt to income was 38 percent, both substantially lower than for the middle class.

The rather staggering debt level of the middle class in 2013 raises the question of whether this is a recent phenomenon or whether it was going on for some time. There was a sharp rise in the ratio of debt to net worth of the middle class from 37 percent in 1983 to 61 percent in 2007, and the debt to income ratio skyrocketed, more than doubling. In constant dollar terms, the mean debt of the middle class shot up by a factor of 2.6 between 1983 and 2007. The rise in the debt to net worth ratio and the debt-income ratio was much steeper than that for all households. In 1983, for example, the debt to income ratio was about the same for middle class as for all households, but by 2007 the ratio was much larger for the former.

Then, the Great Recession hit. The debt to net worth ratio continued to rise, reaching 69 percent in 2010, but the debt to income ratio actually fell. This was caused by the mean debt of the middle class decreasing by 25 percent in constant dollars. The significant rise in the debt to net worth ratio of the middle class between 2007 and 2010 was due to the steeper drop-off in net worth than in debt, while the decline in the debt-income ratio was exclusively due to the sharp contraction of overall debt. Both the debt to net worth ratio and the debt-income ratios fell from 2010 to 2013. The proximate cause was a decline in overall mean debt, which fell by 8.2 percent in real terms over these years.

There was also a disturbing trend in the financial resources available to the middle class. The average prime working age family in 1989 had accumulated only enough financial wealth to sustain its normal consumption for a period of 3.6 months in case of income loss and to sustain consumption at 125 percent of the poverty standard for only 9 months. Indeed, the next lowest 20 percent of households had only enough savings to keep going for a month at 125 percent of the poverty level in the event of losing their income, while the bottom 20 percent had no financial reserves. By 2013, the average working age family had even lower reserves—enough to sustain its normal consumption by only 0.2 months and consumption at 125 percent of the poverty line by 0.4 months. Both the fraying of the private safety net, as well as the public safety net, may have led to the increasing insecurity of the middle class.

Another way to portray differences between middle-class households and the rich is to compute the share of total assets of different types held by each group. In 2013 the richest 1 percent of households held about half of all outstanding stock, financial securities, trust equity, and business equity, and a third of nonhome real estate. The top 10 percent of families as a group accounted for about 85 to 90 percent of stock shares, bonds, trusts, and business equity, and over three-quarters of nonhome real estate. The richest

10 percent of households also accounted for 81 percent of the total value of directly or indirectly owned stocks.

In contrast, owner-occupied housing, deposits, life insurance, and pension accounts were more evenly distributed among households. The bottom 90 percent of households accounted for 59 percent of the value of owner-occupied housing, 33 percent of deposits, and 35 percent of the value of pension accounts. Debt was the most evenly distributed component of household wealth, with the bottom 90 percent of households responsible for 74 percent of total indebtedness.

Further details are also provided on what happened in the housing market from 2007 to 2013. The overall homeownership rate declined from 68.6 percent in 2007 to 67.2 percent in 2010. This seems pretty modest, given all the media hype about home foreclosures over these years. Percentage point reductions were sharper for Hispanic households (1.9 percentage points) than for white households (almost no change); for high school graduates (4.3 percentage points) than other educational groups; younger age groups in comparison to age group 75 and over (a large net increase); and for households with annual incomes below $25,000 and, surprisingly, those with incomes from $75,000 to $100,000 than for middle income households.

The collapse in home values led to a sharp uptick in the number of families who were under water (that is, with negative home equity). In 2007, only 1.8 percent of homeowners reported that their net home equity was negative. By 2010, 8.2 percent of homeowners were under water. There was also a decline in the average value of home equity among homeowners from 2007 to 2010. For all homeowners, the average decline was 29 percent (in constant dollars). Hispanic homeowners suffered by far the largest percentage decline in home equity—47 percent—of the three racial/ethnic groups. The youngest age group experienced a 53 percent fall in home equity while the oldest age group had "only" a 19 percent decline.

Did the housing situation change by 2013? The overall homeownership rate fell by an additional 2.1 percentage points between 2010 and 2013. Blacks and Hispanics suffered larger declines than whites. There was a modest reduction in the overall share of homeowners under water between 2010 and 2013, from 8.2 to 6.9 percent. The share fell among white households but continued to rise among black and Hispanic households, by 5 and 2.9 percentage points, respectively. By 2013, 14 percent of black homeowners had negative home equity, the largest of the three groups. Overall, mean home equity declined by 3.8 percent in real terms from 2010 to 2013. Among African Americans, it fell by 20 percent, compared to 3.4 percent for whites, and among Hispanics a slight increase was recorded, offsetting the steep fall-off in the previous three years.

Differences in portfolio composition, particularly leverage (indebtedness) between wealth classes translates into large disparities in rates of return on household wealth over time. The overall average annual real rate of return on gross assets rose from 2.3 percent in the 1983–1989 period to 3.3 percent in the 1989–2001 period and then fell slightly to 3.1 percent in 2001–2007 period before plummeting to −6.4 percent over years 2007 to 2010. This was followed by a substantial recovery to 4.8 percent over years 2010 to 2013.

However, because of leverage, the average annual real rate of return on net worth among all households was higher than that of gross assets. It also increased from 3.3 percent in the first period to 4.4 percent in the second, declined somewhat to 4 percent in the third and then fell off sharply to −7.3 percent in the 2007–2010 period. Once again, there was a strong recovery to 6.2 percent in the 2010–2013 period.

When we next consider rates of return by wealth class, we see some striking differences. The highest rates of return were registered by the middle three wealth quintiles when asset prices were rising but in the 2007–2010 period, when asset prices were declining, the middle three quintiles registered the lowest (that is, most negative) rate of return. Differences in returns between the top 1 percent and the middle three quintiles were quite substantial in some years. In the 2001–2007 period, the average annual real rate of return on net worth was 5.6 percent for the latter and 3.9 percent for the former—a difference of 1.7 percentage points. On the other hand, over years 2007 to 2010, when asset prices declined, the real rate of return on net worth was −6.5 percent for the top 1 percent and −10.6 percent for the middle three quintiles—a differential of 4.1 percentage points in favor of the top 1 percent.

A related issue is whether, as some have suggested, there has been growing ownership of stock in this country. In fact, the percentage of families that had an interest in the stock market either directly through direct ownership of stock shares or indirectly through defined contribution (DC) pension accounts and mutual funds increased markedly since 1989. Between 1989 and 2001 it surged from 32 to 52 percent. Much of the increase was fueled by the growth in pension accounts like IRAs, Keogh plans, and 401(k) plans. The next twelve years, 2001–2013, in contrast, saw a retrenchment in stock ownership, with the share dropping to 46 percent in 2013.

One piece of mainly positive news is that among all households there was no deterioration in pension accumulations in DC pension plans over the Great Recession. The share of households with a DC account, after rising from 11 percent in 1983 to 53 percent in 2007, did fall off to 49 percent in 2013. However, average DC pension wealth among all households continued to grow from 2007 to 2010 and from 2010 to 2013. The main reason is a shifting of household portfolios. Pension accounts as a share of total assets, after rising from 1.5 percent in 1983 to 12.1 percent in 2007, jumped to 16.5 percent in 2013. However, while DC pensions were up (in real terms) for younger (ages 46 and under) and elderly households from 2007 to 2013, they fell for middle-aged households.

One hypothesis used to explain the rise of middle-class debt is a consumption "binge" over these years. But the data from the Consumer Expenditure Survey does not bear this out. Indeed, despite the massive increase in debt from 2001 to 2007, the average consumption expenditures of the middle-income quintiles expanded by a mere 1.7 percent in real terms over these years. In addition, the average expenditures in real terms of the middle-income quintile actually tumbled by 7.7 percent from 2007 to 2010 and by another 3.5 percent from 2010 to 2013.

By the mid-1980s, U.S. wealth inequality was considerably greater than in other industrialized countries for which comparable data exist. As indicated in Chapter 4, of the other countries, Australia, Canada, France, Germany, Sweden, and the United Kingdom all seemed to be roughly on par with each other in terms of their level of personal wealth inequality in the 1980s, while Japan was distinctly lower than this group. The situation was the same by 2000 when U.S. wealth inequality ranked considerably higher than Canada, Germany, and Italy. Switzerland ranked the highest, and Denmark and Sweden, despite their low level of income inequality, also had very high wealth inequality. The likely reason for the high level of wealth inequality in Scandinavia is that the extensive welfare system for the elderly obviated the need for substantial precautionary savings.

A comparison of long-term time trends for the United Kingdom and the United States indicates that the very high level of wealth inequality in the latter in the 1980s represented a turnaround from the early part of the twentieth century, and even from the 1950s, when the inequality in personal wealth was much higher in the United Kingdom. Indeed, in 1911, the wealth share of the top 1 percent in Britain was an unbelievable 69 percent! A comparison of long-term trends between Sweden and the United States also shows much higher levels of wealth inequality in Sweden in the early part of the twentieth century. Two crossover points occurred in the U.S.–U.K. comparison. First, during the 1960s and 1970s, wealth inequality became roughly comparable in the two countries, in contrast to the much higher level in Britain earlier on. In the early and mid-1970s U.S. wealth inequality also appeared comparable to that of Canada, France, and Sweden. However, by the early 1980s, U.S. wealth inequality began to exceed that of Canada, France, Sweden, and the United Kingdom, and this pattern held at least through 2010.

Another striking difference is the substantial increase in U.S. wealth inequality between the mid-1970s and the late 1980s. This finding is consistent with the sharp rise in income inequality found over the same period. However, a similar rise in wealth inequality did not occur in Canada, France, the United Kingdom, or Sweden. Moreover, from the early 1980s to 2000, U.S. wealth inequality continued to rise. It also rose in Canada from 1984 to 1999 and in Italy from 1989 to 2000 but fell sharply in Germany between 1983 and 1998.

While the United States ranked highest in terms of mean wealth per adult around the year 2000 among countries for which comparable data are available, it ranked relatively low in terms of *median wealth* per adult. For example, while mean wealth per adult was a third greater in the United States than in Italy, median wealth per adult was only half as great. By 2010, the United States had slipped to third place among eight countries in terms of mean wealth, with Luxembourg by far the highest, but last place in terms of median wealth—a result likely reflective of the very high debt levels among the middle class.

Chapter 5 begins an examination of the mechanisms behind changing wealth inequality and "deconstructs" wealth trends over the period from 1922 to 2013 using two methods: decomposition and regression analysis. First, the change in wealth over a period was decomposed into capital gains (existing wealth multiplied by the rate of return), savings, and net intergenerational transfers for the years 1983 to 2013. For changes in inequality, I examine changes in the ratio of net worth between the top 1 percent and the middle three wealth quintiles.

Capital revaluation explains the bulk of the change in overall simulated mean net worth—80 percent or more over the 1983–1989, 1989–2001, and 2001–2007 periods and 73 percent over years 2010 to 2013. From 2007 to 2010, capital losses would have lowered mean net worth by 20 percent, compared to the 11 percent decline in simulated mean wealth. Savings accounted for 12 percent of the growth in simulated mean wealth from 1983 to 1989, 7 percent over years 1989–2001, 15 percent from 2001 to 2007, and 19 percent over the 2010–2013 period. Over years 2007 to 2010, savings would have caused mean wealth to rise by 9 percent, in contrast to the 11 percent contraction in simulated mean wealth. For years 2010 to 2013, dissavings caused an 8 percent fall in simulated mean wealth.

Results for the top 1 percent were quite similar, with capital appreciation accounting for the bulk of wealth growth in the first three periods and the last period, and savings making a much smaller contribution. Over the 2007–2010 period, capital losses would have reduced simulated mean wealth of this group by 18 percent but savings would have increased it by 7 percent. Among the next 19 percent richest households, capital appreciation accounted for more than 100 percent of wealth growth over the first three and last periods, with dissavings making a negative contribution. Over the years 2007 to 2010, capital losses reduced mean wealth by 18 percent while savings led to a 5 percent advance.

For the middle three wealth quintiles, capital appreciation once again accounted for more than 100 percent of the change in simulated mean wealth over the first three and last periods, and dissavings made a negative contribution. Over the years 2007 to 2010, capital losses caused a decline of 27 percentage points in mean wealth, and dissavings added another –3.1 percentage points.

Trends in inequality as measured by the P99 / P2080 ratio were largely influenced by differences in rates of return and savings rates between the top 1 percent and the middle thee wealth quintiles. The former generally led to lower inequality and the latter to higher inequality.

Over the years 1983 to 1989, the simulated P99 / P2080 ratio rose by 9 percentage points, with differentials in savings rates explaining over 100 percent and those in returns 7 percent. Over the years 1989 to 2001, the simulated ratio rose by 18.5 percentage points. The higher rate of return of the middle group lowered the rise in wealth inequality by 45 percent, while the higher savings rate of the top group made a positive contribution of 137 percent. During the 2001–2007 period, there was very little change in the simulated ratio because the higher rate of return of the middle group offset their lower savings rate.

Between 2007 and 2010, the simulated P99/P2080 ratio spiked by 28.7 percentage points. In this case, both factors contributed positively to this trend—the higher (that is, less negative) rate of return of the top 1 percent, which accounted for about half of the rise, and their higher savings rate, which explained the other half. From 2010 to 2013, the simulated P99/P2080 ratio advanced by 6.7 percentage points. The higher savings rate of the top group added a positive 7.3 percentage points, while the higher returns on wealth of the middle group made a negative 2.9 percentage points contribution.

These results illustrate the importance of leverage for the middle class, particularly for the 2001–2007 and 2007–2010 periods. In the earlier period real home prices gained 3.02 percent per year but because of leverage the annual real return on the net worth of the middle three wealth quintiles averaged 5.58 percent over these years. Capital gains by themselves led to a 39.8 percentage point advance in their mean net worth but this increase was offset by a 16.4 percentage point decline from dissavings, resulting in a net 26.9 percentage point increase in their simulated mean net worth. From 2007 to 2010, homes prices were down by 8.77 percent per year but again because of leverage the annual return on their wealth was even lower at −10.55 percent per year. The simulated net worth of this group plunged by 31.1 percentage points, with capital losses accounting for 27.1 percentage points or 87 percent of the total decline, with an additional 10 percent due to dissavings.

With regard to inequality trends as measured by the simulated P99/P2080 ratio, the higher leverage of the middle group relative to the top 1 percent and the strong advances in housing prices led to a 1.67 percentage point difference in rates of return between the two groups between 2001 and 2007 and this differential lowered the rise in the simulated ratio from 11.6 to 1.4 percentage points or by 88 percent. Between 2007 and 2010, the simulated P99/P2080 ratio climbed by 39 percentage points. In this case, high leverage coupled with the collapse in house prices led to a 4.04 percentage point difference in returns in favor of the top group and explained about half the rise in the simulated ratio over these years.

Implicit savings rates among the three middle wealth quintiles were negative in all five periods used in the present analysis: −1.9 percent in 1983–1989, −5.5 percent in 1989–2001, −6.4 percent in 2001–2007, −3 percent in 2007–2010, and −4.2 percent in 2010–2013. The average expenditures in real terms of the middle-income quintile were up by 2.6 percent from 1984 to 1989, 13.2 percent from 1989 to 2001, and then by 1.7 percent from 2001 to 2007. However, they fell by 7.7 percent from 2007 to 2010, and then declined by another 3.5 percent from 2010 to 2013. Except for years 1989 to 2001, when real median family income climbed by 9 percent, consumer spending was basically stagnant or declining. The implication is that the dissaving of the middle class was generally due to income stagnation (actually, a reduction in median income in the last two periods). It seems to be the case that the middle class was dissaving and going into debt in order to maintain its normal level of consumption and that consumer spending of the middle class rose only when incomes also grew.

The second method, regression analysis on twenty-six data points, covered the years 1922 to 2013. The dependent variable was the share of wealth of the top 1 percent of wealth holders. The results using the Saez-Zuckman top wealth shares data are particularly strong. The estimated coefficient of the income share of the top 1 percent of income recipients is positive and significant at the 1 percent level. The estimated coefficient of the ratio of stock to home prices is also positive and significant at the 10 percent level. The coefficient of the ratio of total debt to net worth is negative and significant at the 1 percent level. The R^2 statistic is quite high, at 0.86.

Chapter 5 also confronted Thomas Piketty's "law" that wealth inequality rises if the rate of return on capital, r, is greater than the rate of real output growth, g—and vice versa. I used my estimate of the average annual rate of return on household wealth for r and the average annual growth of real gross domestic product for g. On the basis of five periods over years 1983 to 2013, the correlation coefficient between the difference (r − g) and the change in the Gini coefficient is actually negative instead of positive. These results raise questions about the validity of Piketty's law. In contrast the simple correlation between the difference in the annual rate of return on the wealth of the top 1 percent and that of the middle three wealth quintiles and the change in the Gini coefficient is positive and quite strong at 0.74. This result suggests a better "law," that is, wealth inequality tends to decline or remain stable when the return on wealth for the middle class is greater than that of the very rich and vice versa.

Chapter 6 provided an econometric analysis of the life cycle model (LCM) and considered its implications for wealth accumulation. The regressions are cross-sectional in nature, with observations on households of different ages for a given year. Cohort effects were controlled for by the addition of a lifetime earnings variable and various specifications were tried. The analysis determined that the best fit in terms of the adjusted R^2 is the cubic form. With marketable wealth as the dependent variable, the coefficients of the two age variables have the predicted signs (the coefficient of AGE^2 is positive and that of AGE^3 is negative) and both are significant at the 1 percent level. However, the R^2 (the measure of the explanatory power of the equation) is very low, with a value of 0.012 (only about 1 percent of the variation of household wealth is explained by the age variables). Regressions were also performed for augmented household wealth, the sum of net worth, defined benefit pension wealth, and Social Security wealth. The R^2 for this regression form is about 0.015. When human capital was included in the specification, the variable was highly significant. In fact, the inclusion of human capital tripled the model's goodness of fit. Even so, the extended model explained only 4 to 5 percent of the variation of wealth holdings.

The same equations were then estimated on a subset of the original sample, excluding the upper 5 percent of the wealth distribution. The significance level of the age terms and lifetime earnings increased markedly as a result. Moreover, the R^2 increased from 0.037 to 0.122 for marketable wealth and from 0.051 to 0.198 for augmented wealth.

These results suggest that the explanatory power of the LCM in accounting for the variation of marketable wealth among all households is quite weak. This remains true even when differences in lifetime earnings among households are controlled for. When the concept of household wealth is expanded to include both Social Security and defined benefit pension wealth, the goodness of fit of the regression improves. The inclusion of retirement wealth in household wealth is more consistent with the LCM than the use of marketable household wealth alone. However, as before, the explanatory power of the model is still very low (at most 5 percent of the variation of wealth explained), even when lifetime earnings are introduced into the model.

Perhaps the most telling finding was that the explanatory power of the LCM (particularly with lifetime earnings) is substantially greater (by a factor of three or four) when the sample is restricted to the bottom 95 percent of the wealth distribution. This result suggests that, though the LCM predicts household savings behavior well for the vast majority of households, it is not successful in explaining the wealth accumulation motives of the top wealth classes, who also happen to hold most of household wealth. It appears likely that the difference in results is due to differences in the strength of the bequest motive. One inference from these results is that the top wealth classes likely form a distinct social class in the sense that their motivation for wealth accumulation is for political and economic power and social status. It also appears that this class is interested in the transmission of family wealth over the generations.

Chapter 7 examined time trends in inheritances and inter vivos gifts received by households over the years 1989 to 2013. About one-fifth of households reported, on average, receiving a wealth transfer and these transfers accounted for about a quarter of their total wealth. These figures are comparable to previous studies of wealth transfers in the United States. For the middle class, the figure was closer to one-third. Over the lifetime, about 30 percent of households could expect to receive a wealth transfer, the mean value of these transfers would be about $149,000 (in 2013 dollars), and they would account for about 42 percent of net worth near the time of death.

While it may seem that wealth transfers became more important over time, the evidence is largely (though not completely) negative. The share of households reporting a wealth transfer over their lifetime up to the time of the survey fell by 2.1 percentage points between 1989 and 2013. The mean and median value of these transfers among recipients alone climbed by 31 percent and 36 percent, respectively. However, the average value of wealth transfers among *all* households rose at a slower pace, by 20 percent, and, most crucially, transfers as a proportion of net worth fell from 29 to 24 percent.

The share of households reporting a wealth transfer in just the five years immediately preceding the survey year was the same in 2013 as in 1989. The average value of these recent transfers was slightly lower in 2013 than in 1989 among recipients only and almost exactly the same among all households. The bulk of the evidence therefore suggests that there was no increase in the importance of wealth transfers between 1989 and 2013, which negates the presence of an "inheritance boom."

Wealth transfers also do not seem to lead to higher wealth inequality. If anything, wealth transfers tend to have an equalizing effect on the distribution of household wealth. It is true that the value of wealth transfers climbs sharply with both household income and wealth, but transfers as a *proportion* of wealth decline almost monotonically with both income and wealth level. As a result, net worth excluding wealth transfers is negatively correlated with wealth transfers themselves. Since the two are negatively correlated, adding wealth transfers to net worth actually reduces overall wealth inequality.

Another consideration is whether wealth transfers themselves have become more unequal over time. The inequality of wealth transfers was extremely high over the period from 1989 to 2013—an average Gini coefficient of 0.96 among all households and 0.82 among transfer recipients. This figure compares to an average Gini coefficient for net worth of 0.84. However, there is no indication that the inequality of wealth transfers increased (or decreased) over these years.

In regard to the importance of wealth transfers for the very rich, their share of net worth was a surprisingly low 19 percent for the top wealth class. On average, it was 17 percent for the top 1 percent of wealth holders and 17 percent for the top income class over years 1989 to 2013. This compares to a share of 29 percent for the middle wealth class and 25 percent for the middle-income class. In addition, over these years wealth transfers as a proportion of wealth dropped from 32 to 14 percent for the top income class and from 23 to 15 percent for the top percentile of wealth holders.

Chapter 8 considered the role of Social Security and defined benefit private pensions in the household accumulation of wealth, which standard measures of wealth generally exclude. The analysis in this chapter investigated whether time trends in mean and median wealth and overall wealth inequality are altered when these two additional components are included in the definition of wealth.

The picture that unfolded over years 1983 to 2013 revolves around the four principal components of augmented wealth: nonpension wealth, defined benefit (DB) pension wealth, defined contribution pension wealth, and Social Security wealth. The main finding was that as DB plans were replaced with DC plans, the growth of median wealth slowed and wealth inequality rose. Social Security wealth was a stable presence throughout years 1983 to 2007 but grew in relative terms over the Great Recession, helping to moderate the sharp decline in median wealth and the steep rise in wealth inequality.

The three decades from 1983 to 2013 saw the gradual elimination of the traditional DB pension system and the offsetting rise of DC pension coverage. I focused on age group 47–64 since it is the one most affected by the transformation of the pension system and complete data are available for this group. The share of households in this age group covered by a DB plan fell from 69 to 37 percent while the proportion with a DC plan climbed from 12 to 58 percent. Mean DB wealth fell by 15 percent, while average DC wealth increased thirteenfold. Mean pension wealth doubled in real terms among this age group, though the share of households covered by either a DB or a DC pension plan was about the same in 2013 as in 1983.

The period from 1983 to 2007 saw robust growth in standard net worth, with the mean value rising by 84 percent in real terms among middle-aged households. However, when we include DB wealth, the percentage gain was a bit smaller, 70 percent. Mean Social Security wealth grew at a slower rate, 36 percent over the period, and all told, mean augmented wealth advanced 62 percent. Results are not quite as strong when we look at median values. Median net worth increased by 63 percent (compared to 84 percent for mean net wealth), and median augmented wealth rose by 33 percent (compared to 62 percent for the mean). The difference in trends between mean and median reflected the relative decrease in DB wealth and the corresponding rise of DC wealth. Moreover, the fact that that median augmented wealth grew only about half as much as median net worth again reflected the relative decline in DB wealth.

Even these strong trends over years 1983 to 2007 hide a marked slowdown in the growth of pension and augmented wealth in the 2001–2007 period compared to the 1980s and 1990s. Among middle-aged households, the annual growth of average pension wealth fell from 4.2 percent over the 1983 to 2001 period to 1 percent over years 2001 to 2007. Social Security wealth also advanced at a slower pace. As a result, the annual growth of mean augmented wealth fell off from 2.2 percent over the 1983–2001 period to 1.5 percent over the 2001–2007 period, while that of median augmented wealth declined from

1.5 percent to 0.3 percent. The slow growth in median augmented wealth over the latter period once again reflected the relative decline in DB wealth.

Years 2007 to 2013 witnessed a 10 percent decline in mean pension wealth, a 27 percent drop in mean net worth and a staggering 52 percent decline in median net worth among age group 47–64. However, median augmented wealth was down by "only" 27 percent because of the relative increase in Social Security wealth over these years and its concentration in the middle of the wealth distribution.

The equalizing effects of retirement wealth lessened between 1983 and 2007. Net worth inequality among age group 47–64 showed an increase of 0.033 Gini points from 1983 to 2007. Adding DB and Social Security wealth to net worth substantially lowered the Gini coefficient (from 0.795 to 0.650 in 2007, for example). Most of the equalizing effect came from the addition of Social Security wealth. However, from 1983 to 2007, the Gini coefficient for augmented wealth jumped by 0.076 Gini points. In other words, the addition of DB and Social Security to net worth reduced the overall Gini coefficient by 0.187 in 1983 but by only 0.145 in 2007, a result of the relative decline of DB wealth, which is more equally distributed than DC wealth.

In contrast, from 2007 to 2013, while the Gini coefficient for net worth climbed by 0.043, that for augmented wealth went up by only 0.015 points as a result of the rising share of Social Security in augmented wealth, which rose from 19.4 to 22.2 percent. Since Social Security wealth was much more equally distributed than net worth, its relative increase acted as a moderating influence on the increase in augmented wealth inequality over these years.

The focus of Part III was the makeup of the various wealth groups. Chapter 9 investigated wealth holdings by socioeconomic group. The major finding of this chapter was the virtual disappearance of financial resources among poor, lower middle-class, and even middle-class households during the Great Recession. We see something very similar in an examination of financial resources among working-age households. The collapse of financial resources was particularly acute among younger households, minorities, the less educated, single females with children, and renters.

Mean net worth increased monotonically with income level. The ratio in mean net worth between the top 1 percent and middle-income quintile was 89.0. The percentage gain in mean net worth between 1983 and 2013 also rose almost monotonically with income level, indicating a fanning out of wealth differences over this period. Between 1983 and 2007 mean net worth rose in absolute terms but then declined from 2007 to 2013 for every income class. Over the years 1983 to 2013, mean net worth was up for every income class except for the second income quintile. Median net worth and financial resources, on the other hand, fell in absolute terms for the bottom three income quintiles over these years. By 2013 median financial resources were close to zero for the bottom two income quintiles and only $11,000 for the middle quintile.

The ratio of net worth between households under age 35 and all households, after rising from 0.21 in 1983 to 0.29 in 1989, fell to 0.17 in 2007 and then to 0.11 in 2010 but recovered slightly to 0.12 in 2013. In constant dollar terms, their mean net worth plunged by 46 percent from 2007 to 2010. Among age group 35–44, the ratio of their net worth to overall net worth dropped from 0.71 in 1983 to 0.58 in 2007 and then to 0.42 in 2010 but rebounded to 0.64 in 2013. In constant dollar terms, their wealth fell by 39 percent from 2007 to 2010. Portfolio revaluation almost fully accounted for the decline in simulated mean net worth between 2007 and 2010 for the under-35 age group, and more than accounted for the fall among age group 35–44.

In terms of rates of return, the under-35 group had the lowest annual return of −13.49 percent over years 2007 to 2010 and age group 35–44 had the second lowest at −9.56 percent compared to −7.28 percent for all households. From 2010 to 2013, the youngest group had an annual return of 10.7 percent and age group 35–44 a 7.5 percent return, compared to 6.2 percent overall.

The racial wealth gap was almost exactly the same in 2007 as in 1983. However, from 2007 to 2010, the ratio of mean wealth between black and white households dropped from 0.19 to 0.14. Blacks were much more leveraged than whites (a debt to net worth ratio of 0.55 versus 0.15) and this discrepancy led to a large spread in rates of return over the 2007–2010 period (−9.92 versus −7.07 percent per year). From 2010 to 2013, the wealth ratio slipped a bit more from 0.14 to 0.13.

The ratio of mean net worth between Hispanic and white households grew from 0.16 to 0.26 between 1983 and 2007 and the homeownership rate among Hispanic households advanced from 33 to 49 percent. However, the mean net worth of Hispanics tumbled in half from 2007 to 2010, the ratio of mean net worth with white households declined from 0.26 to 0.15, and their homeownership rate fell by 1.9 percentage points. Hispanic households like blacks were heavily leveraged (a debt to net worth ratio of 0.51 versus 0.15 for whites). As a result, there was a wide differential in returns over the years 2007 to 2010 (−10.76 versus −7.07 percent per year). From 2010 to 2013, their relative net worth remained unchanged. Capital revaluation accounted for two-thirds of the growth of simulated mean net worth among black households from 2001 to 2007 and 64 percent of the plunge from 2007 to 2010. Among Hispanics, the corresponding figures were 35 percent for the earlier period and 65 percent for the later one.

In 2013, the mean net worth of college graduates was ten times the wealth of those with less than four years of high school, six times that of high school graduates, and almost four times that of those with one to three years of college. Between 1983 and 2013, the net worth of college graduates gained 52 percent, while it was down by 12 percent for those with less than four years of high school and by 7 percent for high school graduates. In 2013, median financial resources were almost zero for high school dropouts and only $3,900 for high school graduates.

The portfolios of the lowest three educational groups were more heavily concentrated in homes and their debt to net worth ratio was higher than college graduates, whereas financial assets and business equity made up the largest part of those with a college degree. However, differentials in rates of return were relatively modest.

In 2013, married couples as a group possessed the highest mean net worth, followed by married couples with children, single males, single females as a group, and then single females with children. The ratio of mean net worth between married couples and single mothers was almost fourteen to one. From 1983 to 2013 single females with children saw a 22 percent drop in their mean net worth and a 93 percent decline in median net worth to only $500 in 2013. Median financial resources stayed basically at zero over the whole time period for single mothers.

The results of the analysis in Chapter 10 show striking differences between the characteristics of both the top wealth percentile and the top income percentile and those of the general population and some important changes in the composition of the rich over time. The rich were found to be on average older than the population at large. However, there was a notable increase in the share of families under age 45 in the ranks of the top wealth holders between 1983 and 1992, from 10 to 15 percent. Likewise, the share under age

45 climbed from 18 to 31 percent of the top income percentile, and their median age fell from 56 to 51. However, despite the hype about the so-called dot com millionaires, the rich became decidedly older between 1992 and 2013, with the share in age group 65 to 74 climbing from 19 to 31 percent of the top wealth percentile, their mean age growing from 58 to 61, and their median age from 58 to 63. Among the top income percentile, the proportion in age group 65 to 74 surged from 10 to 21 percent, and their mean age increased from 52 to 55 and their median age from 51 to 53.

The rich were also much better educated than the overall population. Despite strong growth in overall educational attainment from 1983 to 1992, however, there was no corresponding increase in the educational attainment of the wealth rich or the income rich. From 1992 to 2013, on the other hand, the share of the top wealth percentile that had attended graduate school climbed from 41 percent to 49 percent, and the proportion with a college degree or more from 74 to 83 percent. Correspondingly, the share of the income rich who had attended graduate school went up from 51 to 55 percent and the share who had graduated college rose from 83 to 86 percent.

The rich remained an almost exclusively white enclave, though Asian Americans (and other races) did show gains relative to their population share into the ranks of the rich over the years 1983 to 2013. The rich were composed predominantly of married couples, particularly in comparison to the population at large, and almost all households in the top income percentile were headed by men (either married or unmarried) in 1983. However, there were some modest inroads made by unmarried women into the ranks of the top income percentile between 1983 and 1992. From 1992 to 2013, the share of married families in the top wealth group rebounded to where it was in 1983, 88 percent, though the overall share of married couples in the population as a whole fell somewhat. Among the top income percentile, the proportion of married couples dropped almost continuously between 1983 and 2013.

There were notable changes in both the labor force participation and employment patterns of the rich. For example, in 1983 the vast majority of household heads under age 65 in both the top wealth and income percentiles were full-time workers. However, the share of full-time workers in the ranks of the rich declined between 1983 and 1992. There was relatively little change from 1992 to 2013 among the top wealth percentile, but among the top income percentile the share of full-time workers rebounded after 1992 and by 2013 was back to the same level as in 1983.

Yet, despite this apparent reduction in labor force effort among the rich between 1983 and 1992, the income statistics showed a greater reliance on labor income than other forms. Over these years, labor earnings (both wages and salary and self-employment income) as a share of the total income of the top wealth percentile jumped from 51 to 69 percent and that of the top income percentile from 60 to 68 percent. This apparent contradiction can be explained by the fact that there was a substantial increase in the number of working wives among rich households. The trend reversed between 1992 and 2013. The share of wages and salaries in the total income of the top wealth percentile remained unchanged, while the portion of self-employment, rental, royalty and trust income dropped. Among the top income group, the proportion of both wages and salaries and the sum of self-employment, rental, royalty and trust income in total income declined.

There was also evidence that entrepreneurial activity played much more of a role in gaining entry into the ranks of the rich. Between 1983 and 2013, there were substantial gains recorded in the share of self-employed persons, and a corresponding decline in the proportion of salaried managers and professionals. The number of self-employed workers as a fraction of the total number of employed in the top wealth percentile more than doubled between 1983 and 2013, from 38 to 84 percent, as did the corresponding share in the top income percentile, from 27 to 56 percent. In contrast, among workers in the general population, the self-employed share was the same in 2013 as in 1983, 15 percent.

There is also some corroborating evidence from the balance sheets of the rich. Among the top wealth percentile the fraction of total assets held in the form of business equity rose from 32 percent in 1983 to 36 percent in 2013. Among the top income percentile, this fraction increased from 28 to 34 percent. In addition, 77 percent of households in the top wealth percentile reported owning their own businesses in 2013 (compared to 10 percent of all households).

Whatever the rationale behind the increased importance of self-employment income and unincorporated business equity among the rich, this group appeared to rely less and less on property income. Property income in the form of interest, dividends, and capital gains dropped sharply, from 38 to

32 percent of the income of the top wealth percentile between 1983 and 2013, and from 31 to 25 percent for the top income percentile.

The traditional sources of large fortunes in the United States—notably, agriculture, mining, construction, manufacturing, and trade—lessened in importance over time and were supplanted by the financial sector and business and professional services. The former group accounted for 52 percent of employment among the top wealth percentile in 1983 and only 33 percent in 2013, whereas the share of the latter increased from 48 to 67 percent. The results are even more striking for the top income percentile, among whom the share of employment in the traditional industries fell from 38 to 21 percent and correspondingly rose from 62 to 79 percent in the latter group.

In sum, the analysis in Chapter 10 indicated that the wealthy are apt to be better educated and older than the general population. Moreover, the rich are more likely to work in finance and business and professional services than the overall population, and over the period studied relied increasingly on labor income and correspondingly less on property income sources. Finally, and most notably, the rich are much more likely to be self-employed than the general population, a differential that widened over the years 1983 to 2013. The self-employed are very likely to own their own businesses, including partnerships such as are found among doctors, lawyers, and investment bankers.

Chapter 11 looked at the opposite side of the socioeconomic spectrum—the poor. The analysis began with the wealth holdings of poor families and compared them to the nonpoor. Wealth held by families below the poverty line relative to those above declined from 1962 to 1983 and then to 2001 but recovered in 2013. The ratio of mean net worth, which excludes durables and household inventories, between the poor and nonpoor fell sharply from 0.26 in 1962 to 0.14 in 1983 and then dropped to 0.09 in 2001 but then rebounded to 0.14, the same level as in 1983. The recovery from 2001 to 2013 is due to the fact that mean net worth in constant dollars grew by 69 percent for the poverty population but was unchanged for the nonpoor.

Families below the poverty line were generally equally badly off in terms of net worth in terms of income relative to families above the poverty line. The ratio of mean net worth between the two income groups was slightly lower than that of income in 1962, 1983, and 2001 but about the same in 2013.

The ratio in average net worth between families below and above the official poverty line was considerably lower among the elderly in 1962 and 1983 than among those under age 65. However, the ratio in median net worth between the two groups was considerably greater among the elderly than among younger families. The difference was due to the presence of a relatively large number of wealthy elderly families above the poverty line in the two years. After 1983 the elderly poor became better off in terms of wealth relative to the nonpoor, and in 2013 the elderly poor were better off relative to the nonpoor in terms of both mean and median net worth than in 1983 or 2001.

The addition of DB pension wealth to the household portfolio in 1983 reduced the ratio of mean wealth between the poor and the nonpoor population from 0.19 to about 0.16. In 2001 and 2013, on the other hand, there was no change in the ratio from the addition of DB pension wealth. In contrast, the addition of Social Security wealth to the household portfolio raised the ratio of average wealth between the two groups from about 0.16 (depending on the discount rate) to about 0.29 in 1983, from 0.09 to 0.18 in 2001, and from 0.13 to 0.20 in 2013. The total effect of adding both DB pension and Social Security wealth to the household portfolio was to reduce the wealth gap. However, the equalizing effect of retirement wealth was considerably smaller among elderly households than among younger ones.

Finally, when annuity flows from net worth and imputed rent on owner-occupied housing are included in household income, the measured poverty rate, based on the official poverty thresholds, was reduced by about 10 percent for the full population and 20 percent for elderly families in 1983. The reduction in the measured poverty rate was about 10 percent greater in 1962 because of the greater wealth holdings of the poor in that year. When annuity flows and imputed rent were included in the 2001 data, the reduction in the measured overall poverty rate was 13 percent, greater than in 1983. Among the elderly, the decline was 31 percent, much greater than in 1983, because of the greater wealth of the elderly poor. In 2013, the overall poverty rate was lessened by 10 percent, about the same as in 1983, whereas the elderly poverty rate plummeted by 34 percent, greater than in 1983 or 2001.

The concept of "asset poverty" as a measure of economic hardship is distinct from and complementary to "income poverty." The "asset poor" are those households with insufficient assets to meet basic needs (as measured by the income poverty line) for a period of three months. In the face of the large growth in overall assets and a fall in standard income poverty over the period from 1983 to 2007, the level of asset poverty increased from 22.4 to 25.2 percent. Over the Great Recession asset poverty spiked even more, reaching 31.2 percent in 2013. Liquid resources poverty also rose over these years, from 33 percent in 1983 to 43 percent in 2007 and then to 47 percent in 2013.

Asset poverty rates for blacks and Hispanics are more than two times those for whites. They also fell monotonically with both age and education; were much higher for renters than homeowners; and among family types ranged from a low of about 5 percent for elderly couples to 50 to 65 percent for female single parents, depending on the year.

Results on asset poverty are discouraging in that very high rates of asset poverty for the U.S. population are revealed regardless of the measure used. In 2007, even before the onset of the Great Recession, one-fourth of American families had insufficient net worth to enable them to get by for three months at a poverty line level of living, and over two-fifths had insufficient liquid assets to support poverty-level living for a three-month period.

These high levels of asset poverty for the entire population disguise even higher rates for particular subgroups. Using the net worth poverty definition, asset poverty rates in 2013 for some of the most disadvantaged groups were as follows: blacks and Hispanics (55 percent); heads aged less than 25 years (74 percent); heads aged 25 to 34 (55 percent); household heads with less than a high school degree (48 percent); renters (70 percent); and nonelderly female heads with children (65 percent).

A similar concentration of the most extreme form of poverty, joint income and asset poverty, is also found in these same groups. Whereas the overall rate of joint income / asset poverty was 8.7 percent in 2013, it was 19 percent for black and Hispanic households, 36 percent for those with heads aged less than 25 years, 14 percent for heads aged 25 to 34, 20 percent for those with less than a high school degree, 23 percent for renters, and 28 percent for female headed families with children.

Part IV looked at wealth over the long term in the United States. Chapter 12 considered long-terms trends in average household wealth covering the years 1900 to 2013. Real marketable wealth per household grew at an annual average rate of 1.26 percent over the 113 years, which amounted to a fourfold increase. Indeed, real *per capita* wealth mushroomed by a factor of 7.5 over these years. Augmented wealth per household increased somewhat faster than marketable wealth per household at 1.53 percent per year.

Real marketable wealth increased somewhat more than real disposable income over the 113 years. The ratio of real wealth to real disposable income dropped from 4.6 in 1900 to 3.6 in 1983, but then rebounded to 5.4 in 2013. Over the full 113 years, the ratio rose quite modestly, by 18 percent, and there were subperiods when it fell. In spite of this, there is no strong evidence to support the notion of a substantial increase in the wealth to income ratio.

There are several striking developments in regard to changes in the aggregate portfolio composition. Owner-occupied housing rose from 17 percent of total marketable assets in 1900 to a peak of 22 percent in 1979. After that, it fell off to 15 percent in 2013. There were considerable cyclical fluctuations, which tended to reflect movements in home prices. Home equity as a share of total assets showed a similar though more attenuated pattern, falling from 15 percent in 1900 to 10 percent in 1929, rebounding to 15 percent in 1981, and then falling off to 8 percent in 2013.

Among financial assets, the biggest relative growth occurred in liquid assets, which rose from 8 percent of all marketable assets in 1900 to 23 percent in 2013. Corporate stock exhibited volatile behavior, growing from 15 percent of total assets in 1900 to 31 percent in 1929, as the stock market peaked, declined to 14 percent in 1949, rose to 27 percent in 1965, fell back to 12 percent in 1979, rebounded to 33 percent in 1998 as the stock market neared another high point, dipped again to 24 percent in 2004, and then surged to 32 percent in 2013 as the stock market reached another peak.

Unincorporated business equity made up over a third of total assets in 1900 but declined almost steadily over the century, reaching 6 percent in 2013. Debt as a proportion of total assets fluctuated during the first half of the century but then increased rather steadily from 4 percent in 1945 to 23 percent in 2010 before dropping sharply to 18 percent in 2013. Finally, both DB pension reserves and Social Security wealth increased relative to marketable assets from virtually zero in 1900 to peaks of 7.3 percent of augmented wealth in 1983 for the former and 31 percent in 1979 for the latter. Both DB pension reserves and Social Security then declined in relative terms, as the DB pensions system unraveled and the Social Security system reached maturity.

Chapter 13 presented a "combined series" for the share of total net worth owned by the top wealth percentile. This series combined estate tax and survey data from various sources. Between 1922 and 1929 there was a substantial increase in the wealth share of the top percentile, from 40 to 48 percent. This was followed by a sizable reduction over the Great Depression but by 1939 its share was almost back to where it had been in 1922. The share then fell sharply from 1939 to 1949, down to 30 percent, though by 1965 it was back to 34 percent. This was followed by another rather substantial decline in its wealth share, to 22 percent in 1979. Wealth inequality bottomed out some time during the late 1970s. A sharp turnaround in wealth inequality then ensued, with the top percentile share climbing to 38 percent in 1998. It then dropped sharply to 33 percent in 2001 and gradually rebounded to 37 percent in 2013. The addition of pension and Social Security wealth to the household portfolio substantially lowered measured inequality, but the time trend in the share of total augmented wealth owned by the top 1 percent was basically unchanged.

Part V considered a wealth tax and reviewed the conclusions that resulted from the detailed analysis. Both the extreme nature of wealth concentration in the United States and its rise over the last thirty years or so provide some urgency to a consideration of potential policy remedies. The intergenerational transfer of wealth plays an important role in the process of household wealth accumulation and this could lead to a further disintegration of the concept of equality and increasing political divisiveness. In Chapter 14 I examined the possibility of a direct wealth tax.

Personal wealth is currently taxed on the federal level in two ways: realized capital gains (as part of personal income taxes) and estate taxation. The estate tax collection system appears to be subject to tax evasion and tax avoidance. According to my estimates for 1992, total estate tax collections should have been in the order of $44 billion in comparison to actual tax receipts of $10 billion. Moreover the estate tax system has the feature that capital gains are "forgiven" at time of death—that is, the capital gains that are incorporated in the value of the assets of the deceased are passed to the heirs untaxed. If these gains were taxed like ordinary income, my estimates for 1992 suggest that they would have yielded another $30 billion to $40 billion of tax revenue.

A number of European countries currently have or have had direct tax systems in place. On the grounds of equity, a combination of annual income and the current stock of wealth provides a better gauge of the ability to pay taxes than income alone. Moreover, there is no evidence from other advanced economies that the imposition of a modest direct tax on household wealth has had any deleterious effect on personal savings or overall economic growth. Indeed, there are arguments to the contrary that such a tax might induce a more efficient allocation of household wealth, away from unproductive and toward more productive uses.

In a previous work, I proposed a very modest tax on wealth modeled after the Swiss wealth tax system (a $100,000 exemption with marginal tax rates running from 0.05 to 0.3 percent). My calculations for year 1989 showed that such a tax structure would have yielded an average tax rate on household wealth of 0.2 percent, which is less than the loading fee on most mutual funds, and would have reduced the average yield on household wealth holdings by only 6 percent. Even the top marginal tax rate of 0.30 percent would reduce the average yield on personal wealth by only 9 percent. These figures suggest that disincentive effects on personal savings would be very modest indeed. Moreover, some have concluded that personal savings might actually rise as a result of the imposition of a wealth tax.

A wealth tax could raise $50 billion in additional revenue and have a minimal impact on the tax bills of 90 percent of American families. Fifty billion is not a large amount, representing about 3 percent of total federal tax receipts. However, on the margin such additional revenue could be critical by providing the fiscal latitude to enact more generous social transfers to the poor and provide tax relief to the middle class.

Updated estimates for 2013 provided in Chapter 14 followed the "Swiss-style" tax structure adjusted for inflation. An estimated $121 billion would be raised from levying such a tax in 2013, representing 4.4 percent of total federal tax receipts for that year. Moreover, the average tax rate on household wealth (as of 2013) would be 0.19 percent. The new tax regime would reduce the average yield on household assets by only 6.2 percent. Even the top marginal tax rate of 0.3 percent would reduce the average yield on personal wealth by only 9.7 percent. Only 11 percent of families would see their overall personal tax bill (combining income and wealth taxes) rise by more than 10 percent and only 15 percent would pay $500 or more of additional taxes. A full 56 percent would fall below the wealth tax threshold and would therefore be exempted from paying any wealth tax. These results suggest that disincentive effects on personal savings would be very modest. In addition, although wealth taxes can raise a considerable amount of tax revenue, they make barely a dent in overall wealth inequality.

The Upshot

The thesis of this book could be summarized as the rise and fall of the middle class. Median wealth (in real terms) more than doubled between 1962 and 2007 but then dropped by 45 percent from 2007 to 2013, mainly due to the plunge in housing prices and the high leverage of the middle class. This collapse in median wealth is a principal factor leading to the general malaise of the middle class.

What factors were driving Americans' financial insecurity? The ultimate culprit was wage stagnation, occurring now for over forty years (average real wages peaked in 1973). This translated into income stagnation and a falling share of worker compensation in national income. For a while (until about 1990 or so) families compensated for stagnant wages with the increased participation of wives in the labor force. Once this opportunity was exhausted, real incomes also stagnated. Indeed, according to census data, median family income in 2013 was less than it was in 1997. As a result, over the last twenty years families have been forced to borrow in order to maintain their usual consumption. This process was aided by a generous expansion of credit, particularly through the home mortgage market. Largely abetted by a huge Chinese trade surplus and their consequent purchase of U.S. Treasury bonds, U.S. banks and other financial institutions were awash in cash. Enabled by lax mortgage regulation and rising home prices, financial institutions allowed generous refinancing of existing mortgages, expanded home equity credit lines, and issued a host of new types of mortgages including subprime, with no or little down payment, and even zero-documentation loans.

The result was a huge build-up in household debt, particularly among the middle class (the debt-income ratio more than doubled between 1983 and 2007). This was followed by a catastrophic collapse of the wealth of middle-income and lower-income households. Median net worth plummeted by 44 percent between 2007 and 2013 for middle-income families, 61 percent for lower middle-income families by, and by 70 percent for low-income families. The collapse of wealth was one of the principal factors leading to rising economic insecurity. Both the fraying of the private safety net, as well as the public safety net, may have led to middle class malaise. The recent rise in mortality rates reported among working class whites, particularly from suicide and especially among those with a high school degree or less, might not be unrelated to their growing economic insecurity.[1]

Household leverage and corresponding rates of return explained a large part of the movement in median household wealth, particularly over the 2001–2007 and 2007–2010 periods. The high degree of indebtedness (leverage) of the middle three wealth quintiles translated into a much higher return on net worth than gross assets over the 2001–2007 period, when house prices were rising rapidly. The high leverage coupled with rising house prices led to a sharp increase in median net worth. However, when the housing market crashed from 2007 to 2010, the high leverage translated into a much more negative return on net worth than on gross assets. These two factors caused a very sharp reduction in median net worth.

One hypothesis is that middle-class debt skyrocketed because of a consumption binge over these years. However, available data does not bear out this hypothesis. Indeed, despite the massive increase in debt from 2001 to 2007, the average consumption expenditures of the middle-income quintile inched up a mere 1.7 percent in real terms. It also turns out, based on the same data, that average expenditures in real terms of the middle-income quintile actually tumbled by 7.7 percent from 2007 to 2010 and by another 3.5 percent from 2010 to 2013. So it appears that the middle class was not exactly splurging over these years.

Average expenditures in real terms increased by 2.6 percent from 1984 to 1989 and by 13.2 percent from 1989 to 2001. The period 1989–2001 is interesting as it alone shows a marked increase in consumer expenditures. This period also saw a 9 percent spurt in real median family income. It thus appears that the consumption expenditures of the middle class rise only when incomes also grow.

The wealth simulation results reported in Chapter 5 indicate that implied savings rates (the ratio of savings to the average income over the period) among the three middle wealth quintiles were negative in all five periods used in the analysis: −1.9 percent in 1983–1989, −5.5 percent in 1989–2001, −6.4 percent in 2001–2007, −3 percent in 2007–2010, and −4.2 percent in 2010–2013. This leads to the question of whether the middle class will ever be in a position to save again. This seems possible only if real median family income also increases. However, it is it still possible, and maybe even likely, that rising income would be absorbed by rising consumption.

Middle-class households are not the only ones to feel the effects of economic circumstances. They are joined by the lower class and lower middle-income class, minorities: female-headed households, young (under 35, particularly) households; the less educated; and renters. Over the years 1983 to 2013, median net worth and median financial resources fell in absolute terms for the bottom three income quintiles. By 2013 median financial resources was close to zero for the bottom two income quintiles and only $11,000 for the middle quintile. The median net worth of the under-35 age group slipped to $700 in 2013 and median financial resources to zero. The median net worth of black households fell from a high of $17,100 in 1992 to $1,700 in 2013 and that of Hispanic households from $6,100 to $2,000, while median financial resources was basically zero for the whole time period. The median financial resources of those with less than four years of high school plummeted from a high of $5,200 in 1989 to almost zero in 2013 and that of high school graduates from $21,800 to $3,900. From 1983 to 2013 single females with children saw a 93 percent decline in median net worth to only $500 in 2013, while median financial resources stayed at basically zero over the whole time period. The median net worth of renters fell from $1,900 in 1983 to zero in 2013, as did median financial resources.

Results are similar when considering the financial resources available to prime working age families (ages 25 to 54). In 1989 the middle-income quintile of this group had accumulated enough financial wealth to sustain its normal consumption for a period of 3.6 months in case of income loss and to sustain consumption at 125 percent of the poverty standard for 9 months. The next lowest 20 percent of households had only enough savings to keep going for a month at 125 percent of the poverty level, while the bottom 20 percent had no financial reserves at all. By 2013, the average working age family had even lower reserves—enough to sustain its normal consumption by only 0.2 months and consumption at 125 percent of the poverty line by 0.4 months.

These trends are mirrored in asset poverty rates. In the face of the large growth in overall assets and a fall in standard income poverty over the period from 1983 to 2007, the level of asset poverty increased from 22.4 to 25.2 percent. Over the Great Recession asset poverty spiked even more, reaching 31.2 percent in 2013. Liquid resources poverty also rose over these years, from 33 percent in 1983 to 43 percent in 2007 and then to 47 percent in 2013.

There are even higher rates for particular subgroups. Using the net worth poverty definition, asset poverty rates in 2013 for some of the most disadvantaged groups are as follows: blacks and Hispanics (55 percent); heads aged less than 25 years (74 percent); heads aged 25 to 34 (55 percent); household heads with less than a high school degree (48 percent); renters (70 percent); and nonelderly female heads with children (65 percent).

What about wealth inequality? Since 1962 there have been three big inequality spurts: 1962–1969, 1983–1989, and 2007–2010. According to the Gini coefficient, wealth inequality rose by 0.025 Gini points from 1962 to 1969 but then returned to its 1962 level in 1983. It climbed by 0.029 Gini points from 1983 to 1989, was relatively unchanged from 1989 to 2007, and surged by 0.032 Gini points over years 2007 to 2010. It was then up slightly from 2010 and 2013. Over the full period from 1962 to 2013, the Gini coefficient was up by a hefty 0.068 points, from 0.803 to 0.871, its highest level over the fifty-one years.

Household leverage and corresponding rates of return explained a large part of the movements in wealth inequality, particularly over the 2001–2007 and 2007–2010 periods. The spread in returns between the top 1 percent and the middle three wealth quintiles (1.67 percentage points in favor of the middle) led to very little change in wealth inequality from 2001 to 2007 despite a spike in income inequality. Over the years 2007 to 2010, in contrast, the spread was 4.04 percentage points but this time in favor of the top 1 percent, and this differential helped cause a very sharp upturn in wealth inequality over these years. Needless to say, differential savings rates between the two groups also played a role.

Another important finding is that in the early part of the twentieth century the United States had much lower wealth inequality than the "class-ridden" societies of Europe—particularly the United Kingdom and even Sweden. However, by the 1960s and early 1970s, wealth inequality had fallen considerably in those two countries and the United States was comparable to those two countries as well as Canada, France, Germany, and Australia (countries with comparable data). Then beginning in the late 1970s or early 1980s U.S. wealth inequality took off and by the late 1980s through the present day it became much greater than in other OECD member country (with the exception of Switzerland, which was slightly higher).

Finally, on a policy note I argued in favor of a direct tax on household wealth modeled after a Swiss-type system. A combined income and wealth tax may prove to be more equitable than an income tax alone. Such a tax (with a top marginal rate of 0.3 percent) would yield revenue of 121 billion dollars, representing 4.4 percent of total federal tax receipts for that year. Moreover, the average tax rate on household wealth would be a very low 0.19 percent. However, wealth taxes would barely make a dent in overall wealth inequality.

Adjustments and Imputations Made to the 1962 SFCC and 1983, 1989, 1992, and 1995 SCF Data Files

B ecause the early surveys used in this study were based on different sampling frames and sampling techniques, several adjustments and imputations to the raw survey data were required in order to ensure compatibility. This was particularly the case for the 1962 Survey of Financial Characteristics of Consumers (SFCC) and the 1983 Survey of Consumer Finances (SCF). The 1989 SCF was also based on a somewhat different survey methodology than the 1983 SCF. The 1992 SCF and the 1995 SCF, though ostensibly based on the same survey methods as the 1989 SCF, had some notable anomalies and also required some adjustment to the raw data. After that point, from 1998 onward at least through 2010, the survey data aligned fairly well with the aggregate balance sheet data from the Financial Accounts of the United States (FFA) and no adjustments to the underlying data were required.[1] The 2013 SCF also appears to have some significant anomalies, which are discussed in Chapter 5. Adjustments and imputations to the 1969 MESP file are described in Appendix 2. These procedures are also followed to ensure compatibility with the other surveys used in the study.

This Appendix considers wealth inequality estimates derived from the 1962 SFCC and the 1983 SCF. The main point of interest is the sensitivity of these estimates, particularly the Gini coefficient and the shares of top wealth holders, to adjustments for underreporting and missing assets. I base the underreporting correction on a comparison of asset and liability totals derived from each of the two surveys and the respective aggregate household balance sheet estimates. An asset-by-asset comparison between the survey and the aggregate estimates provides an index of underreporting. However, unlike the SCF files, there are gaps in the asset and liability coverage in the 1962 SFCC. For the 1962 data, corrections for zero entries are based on comparisons between the wealth entries from the survey data and income flows from the Internal Revenue Service's *Statistics of Income* (IRS SOI) that correspond to the wealth entry (such as dividends to corporate stock). For the 1983 data, I use proportional adjustment of each asset and liability in the microdata to correspond to the aggregate balance sheet total. I also consider the effects of including measures of defined benefit (DB) pension and Social Security wealth on measured household wealth inequality. For 1962 and 1983, I provide estimates of the distribution of retirement wealth and augmented household wealth based on the microdata for these years. Alternative estimates of retirement wealth and the distribution of augmented household wealth are devised, according to varying assumptions about the future growth in DB pension and Social Security benefits.

Adjustment procedures applied to the 1989, 1992, and 1995 SCF are discussed, with particular attention paid to the 1992 SCF in which notable problems appeared in the household weighting scheme.

Adjustment Procedures for the 1962 SFCC

In previous work I have presented estimates of the size distribution of household wealth for both 1962 and 1983.[2] Estimates for 1962 are based on the SFCC, and those for 1983 are based on the SCF. Here, I report on adjustments to the underlying survey data for both years. I also investigate the sensitivity of estimates of wealth inequality based on household survey data to adjustments for missing assets, underreporting, and different definitions of household wealth. Several measures of wealth inequality are used, including the Gini coefficient, the shares of the top wealth holders, and quintile shares. Particular attention is paid to the effects on the distribution of household wealth of including measures of DB pension and Social Security wealth in the household portfolio. I find here that estimates of wealth inequality are quite sensitive to imputations for missing assets such as consumer durables and household inventories and to the inclusion of retirement wealth. They are less sensitive to adjustments made for underreporting.

Table A1.1 presents a comparison of household balance sheet totals from the original SFCC data with those from national balance sheet data based on the FFA. The total of all assets in the national balance sheet data for the

Table A1.1. Comparison of national balance sheet and survey data totals for household wealth, 1962 and 1983 (billions, current dollars)

	1962 (end-year)			1983 (mid-year)		
	National Balance Sheet Data	SFCC	Ratio of SFCC to National Balance Sheets	National Balance Sheet Data	SCF	Ratio of SCF to National Balance Sheets
Assets	2,005.7	1,410.1	0.70	11,165.0	11,847.7	1.06
Tangible assets	782.5	643.3	0.82	4,356.0	6,012.2	—
Owner-occupied housing	419.8	473.9	1.13	2,937.6	3,777.8	1.29
Other real estate	104.3	114.4	1.10	—	1,721.4	0.91
Vehicles	74.5	55.0	0.74	413.7	375.5	—
Other consumer durables[a]	127.8	—	—	760.6	137.5	—
Inventories	56.1	—	—	244.1	—	—
Fixed claim assets	415.3	265.0	0.64	2,618.1	1,623.6	0.62
Demand deposits and currency	69.8	23.7	0.34	326.9	122.2	0.37
Time and savings deposits[b]	207.3	104.7	0.51	1,832.3	1,061.8	0.58
Financial securities[c]	138.2	117.4	0.85	458.9	439.6	0.96
Equities	807.9	501.8	0.62	4,190.9	4,211.9	1.01
Corporate stock	361.0	222.8	0.62	1,134.7	1,026.8	0.90
Unincorporated business equity	281.1	224.7	0.80	2,361.8	2,298.3	0.97
Trust fund equity	85.2	54.3	0.64	331.1	461.3	1.39
Insurance (CSV)	75.6	—	—	213.1	273.5	1.28
Pensions (CSV)	5.0	—	—	60.9	121.5	1.99
Miscellaneous assets[d]	—	—	—	89.3	30.5	—
Liabilities	256.0	218.5	0.85	1,749.6	1,509.7	0.86
Mortgage debt	163.8	146.5	0.89	1,116.0	963.4	0.86
Insurance debt	92.2	—	—	633.6	546.3	0.86
Other debt	—	72.0	—			
Net worth	1,749.7	1,191.6	0.68	9,415.4	10,338.0	1.10

Source: For the 1983 SCF tabulations, I used the 1987 Federal Reserve Board tape version of this dataset, which included imputations for missing values from nonresponses (for details, see Avery, Elliehausen, and Kennickell, "Measuring Wealth with Survey Data").

The national balance sheet figures are from the FFA.

a. This includes boats, antiques, precious metals, jewelry, art, and miscellaneous durables in the 1983 SCF.

b. This includes certificates of deposit, individual retirement accounts, Keogh accounts, money-market funds, and U.S. savings bonds in 1983.

c. This includes mortgage assets in both years and U.S. savings bonds in 1962 but excludes U.S. savings bonds in 1983.

d. Miscellaneous assets in the SCF include other investments, consisting of money lent to friends and relatives, and the CSV of company savings plans, including thrift, profit-sharing, stock options, and employee stock option plans. The national balance sheet miscellaneous asset category includes only the FFA miscellaneous financial asset entry, which is not directly comparable to the SCF entry.

Abbreviations: CSV, cash surrender value; FFA, Financial Accounts of the United States; SCF, Survey of Consumer Finances; SFCC, Survey of Financial Characteristics of Consumers.

household sector was $2,005.7 billion. The SFCC database includes all national balance sheet assets except other (that is, nonvehicle) consumer durables, inventories, life insurance cash surrender value (CSV), and pension CSV. The national balance sheet total for only assets included in the SFCC was $1,741.2 billion. The original SFCC asset values totaled to $1,410.1 billion, or 81 percent of the national balance sheet total for corresponding assets. Real estate and unincorporated business equity were quite close between the two sources. The SFCC values were significantly below the corresponding national balance sheet estimates for the following asset categories: Demand deposits and currency were undervalued by two-thirds. (One should note that currency is not included in the SFCC data.) Time and saving deposits were undervalued by almost half. Corporate stock was undervalued by almost 40 percent. Trust fund equity was undervalued by over one-third.

The total of all liabilities in the national balance sheet data for the household sector was $256 billion. This figure probably included the debt on life insurance, which was excluded from the SFCC data tape. The total of all liabilities represented in the SFCC was $218.5 billion. In the SFCC published tables, debt on life insurance was given as $3.6 billion.[3] Adding this to the value of the liabilities found in the SFCC database yielded a figure of $222.1 billion as the SFCC estimate of total liabilities, which was 15 percent lower than the national balance sheet total.

Estimated net worth from the national balance sheet data was $1,485 billion if only comparable assets are included. The SFCC estimate was $1,192 billion. Thus, the national balance sheet estimate was 25 percent greater than the SFCC net worth estimate if only comparable assets are used.

In order to align the SFCC data with the national balance sheet totals, each asset or liability in the SFCC is adjusted either by a constant proportion or in more complex fashion, depending on the degree of error and the availability of outside information.[4] The undervaluation of assets in the survey data could be due to two types of errors—the underreporting of asset ownership and the underreporting of asset values. Moreover, the degree of underreporting of either type could differ by income class. In order to ascertain the type of underreporting present in the SFCC and whether this underreporting varied by income class, I compare SFCC asset information (percentage ownership and mean value) by income class to corresponding income flow information from income data (the percentage of households receiving income from the asset and mean income received).

The income data are obtained from the 1965 SOI. The percentage of households that reported dividends in the SOI figures is compared to the percentage that reported corporate stock holdings in the SFCC. It is then possible to increase the percentage of households holding each asset type in the SFCC by income class if the percentage of units reporting the corresponding income flow was greater in the SOI figures. It is also possible to adjust for underreporting of asset values in the SFCC differentially by income class if average yields, defined as the ratio of the income flow in the SOI to the asset value in the SFCC, differed substantially by income class. These asset comparisons between the SFCC and the SOI along with the adjustment factors are reported in Table A1.2.

For almost all asset types, the percentage of households reporting the asset in the SFCC was greater than or equal to the percentage of units reporting the corresponding income flow in the SOI. Thus, adjustment for nonreporting of assets was not required. The one exception was trust funds. The adjustment for trusts is explained below. For many asset types, average yield figures were fairly uniform across income classes. For these, I used the same adjustment or scaling factor for each income class. The scaling factor was defined as the ratio of the national balance sheet total to the SFCC total for that asset (the reciprocal of the third column of Table A1.2). On the other hand, for stocks, unincorporated business equity, and other financial assets, the average yield figures varied considerably by income class. For these assets, the adjustment factor varied correspondingly by income class. The details of the adjustments for underreporting (if any) and imputations for missing assets are explained by asset category and summarized in Table A1.2.[5]

(1) The owner-occupied housing figures in the SFCC are not adjusted. The SFCC total is a little larger than the national balance sheet figure. The likely reason is that SFCC households report the estimated market value of their homes, while the national balance sheet data, which are based on a perpetual inventory accumulation of the value of residential investment in new construction, are biased downward. Though the balance sheet technique attempts to include price changes, it is possible that it does not fully capture the change in both construction costs and land values.

(2) For the same reason, the other real estate figures in the SFCC are not adjusted.

(3) Automobiles are adjusted through scaling up by a factor of 1.355.

Table A1.2. Reconciliation of SFCC asset categories with corresponding income flows

	Bonds and Bond Interest				Corporate Stock and Dividends			
Income Class	SFCC: Percentage of Households Owning Bonds[a]	SOI: Percentage of Units Reporting Interest[b]	Estimated Yield[c]	Adjustment Factor	SFCC: Percentage of Households Owning Stocks[d]	SOI: Percentage of Units Reporting Dividends[e]	Estimated Yield[f]	Adjustment Factor
Under $3,000	12–16	13.5	0.006	1.83	7	5.1	0.083	1.30
$3,000–$4,999	20–30	17	0.018	1.59	8	6.0	0.121	2.10
$5,000–$7,499	30–41	23.3	0.003	1.83	15	6.9	0.078	1.30
$7,500–$9,999	40–61	32.6	0.001	1.83	19	10.5	0.056	1.50
$10,000–$14,999	51–84	49.2	0.018	1.59	32	20.8	0.079	1.10
$15,000–$24,999	43–88	68.3	0.044	1.43	52	46.7	0.109	1.04
$25,000–$49,999	51–100	78.2	0.060	1.03	83	69.4	0.060	1.10
$50,000–$99,999	69–100	84.9	0.026	1.43	88	85.7	0.078	1.40
$100,000 or more	75–100	88.1	0.109	1.03	97	94.4	0.075	1.60
All units	28–45	23.5	0.010	—	16	9.3	0.078	1.50

	Unincorporated Business Equity and Unincorporated Business Income				Trust Fund Equity and Trust Income			Adjustment Factors	
	SFCC: Percentage of Households Owning Businesses[g]	SOI: Percentage of Units Reporting Bus. Inc.[h]	Estimated Yield[i]	Adjustment Factor	SFCC: Percentage of Households Owning Trust Funds[j]	SOI: Percentage of Units Reporting Trust Inc.	Estimated Yield[k]	% of Units	Value
Under $3,000	12	16.51	0.129	2.10	—	0.4	0.088	—	1.10
$3,000–$4,999	12	16.38	0.311	2.10	1	0.5	0.098	—	1.10

$5,000–$7,499	17	13.38	0.307	2.10	1	0.5	0.004	—	1.10
$7,500–$9,999	18	14.38	0.414	2.10	1	0.6	0.082	—	1.10
$10,000–$14,999	22	19.31	0.404	2.10	3	1.3	0.194	—	1.10
$15,000–$24,999	26	41.44	0.344	2.10	5	3.7	0.042	—	1.10
$25,000–$49,999	64	63.81	0.254	2.10	4	7.1	0.002	+3.19	1.10
$50,000–$99,999	70	68.67	0.112	1.00	5	11.5	0.018	+6.5	1.10
$100,000 or more	35	70.63	0.112	1.00	15	22.3	0.018	+7.3	1.10
All units	17	16.88	0.238	—	1	0.7	0.016	—	—

Note: SOI = Statistics of Income data.

a. This category includes U.S. savings bonds, marketable securities other than stock and state and local bonds, mortgage assets, company savings plans, and loans to individuals. Percentage range indicates lowest and highest possible percentage owning the asset. Mean computed from midpoint of percentage range. See Dorothy Projector and Gertrude Weiss, *Survey of Financial Characteristics of Consumers*, Federal Reserve Board Technical Papers (Washington, DC: Board of Governors of the Federal Reserve System, 1966), Tables A9, A10, A12.

b. Includes interest on time and savings deposits.

c. Interest on bonds is calculated from the SOI and SFCC data under the assumption that interest on time and savings deposits averaged 2.8 percent. The estimated yield is the ratio of mean bond interest to mean bonds by income class.

d. Projector and Weiss, *Survey of Financial Characteristics of Consumers*, Table A10.

e. Dividends after exclusion.

f. Defined as the ratio of SOI dividends to SFCC stock holdings.

g. Projector and Weiss, *Survey of Financial Characteristics of Consumers*, Table A8.

h. Includes partnership income.

i. Defined as ratio of SOI unincorporated business income (excluding losses) to SFCC unincorporated business equity.

j. Projector and Weiss, *Survey of Financial Characteristics of Consumers*, Table A9.

k. Defined as the ratio of SOI trust income to SFCC trust equity.

Abbreviations: SFCC, Survey of Financial Characteristics of Consumers; SOI, Statistics of Income.

(4) Other consumer durables are not included in the SFCC. Their value is imputed to each household on the basis of a regression equation estimated from the 1969 MESP database, which is as follows:

$$OTHRDUR62 = 2871.4 + .08644INC62 - (.3271 \times 10^{-6}) \times (INC62)^2 - 7.1401$$
$$AGEHEAD + 811.32 \text{ MARRIED} - 240.31 \text{ FEMHEAD} + 189.51 \text{ URBANRES}$$

where OTHRDUR62 is the value of other consumer durables in 1962 dollars; INC62 is income of the household unit in 1962 dollars; AGEHEAD is age of head of unit; MARRIED = 1 if head is married, 0 otherwise; FEMHEAD = 1 if head is female, 0 otherwise; and URBANRES = 1 if unit's residence is in an urbanized area.[6] The total value for other consumer durables developed from this equation is then adjusted proportionately to conform to the national balance sheet total.

(5) Inventories such as food and clothing are not included in the SFCC. The ratio of inventory holdings to family income was computed from the 1960–1961 Consumer Expenditure Survey.[7] These ratios were then applied to each household on the basis of family income and adjusted by a scalar to conform to the balance sheet total.

(6) Demand deposits and currency are adjusted by a factor of 2.945.

(7) Time and savings deposits are adjusted by a factor of 1.980.

(8) State and local government bonds are proportionately adjusted by the factor 1.441.

(9) Corporate and U.S. government bonds and instruments and other financial assets are adjusted differentially by income class. The percentage reporting interest income (including interest on both savings and time deposits and financial securities) in the SOI fell either below the range or within the range of households in the SFCC reporting that they owned other financial assets (see Table A1.2). Therefore, it is unlikely that there is an underreporting problem in the SFCC with regard to the number of households who report holding these financial assets. However, the estimated yields, although volatile, seem extremely low. Total interest reported in the SOI ($7.16 billion) divided by total national balance sheet savings deposits plus other financial assets ($329.2 billion) was only 2 percent. Bank rates were about 2.8 percent in 1962, and bond rates were about 5 percent. Thus, it appears that SOI interest was severely underreported. Despite underreporting problems in the SOI data, it appears from comparisons of estimated yields across income levels

that SFCC financial assets were underreported more for lower-income than upper-income groups, and therefore the adjustment factors vary accordingly.

(10) Corporate stock is also adjusted differentially by income class. As shown in Table A1.2, the percentage reporting stock in the SFCC was uniformly greater than the percentage reporting dividends in the SOI. It should be noted that dividends are underreported in the SOI since they are net of the exclusion allowance. Moreover, many stocks pay no dividends. Despite this, the comparison suggests that there was no significant underreporting in percentage of holders in the SFCC. The yield figures showed no clear pattern by income class. However, there were two income classes with yields significantly higher than the average, which suggests greater than average underreporting of asset values in these two income classes. Thus, these income classes were assigned higher than average adjustment factors.

(11) Unincorporated business equity also has different adjustment factors by income class. As shown in Table A1.2, the overall percentage reporting business equity in the SFCC was identical to the percentage reporting business income in the SOI, and the percentages were also similar within income class. However, the estimated yields were particularly high for lower-income groups. All the adjustment was therefore done in the bottom seven income classes.

(12) Trust fund equity is the only asset whose ownership appears to be underreported in the SFCC. The corresponding income category is income from estate and trusts. Since estates were included, the percentage reporting this income item should be higher in the SOI than in the SFCC. However, not all trust funds generate income. In any case, for lower-income groups, the percentage reporting trusts was uniformly greater in the SFCC than in the SOI. For the upper three income groups, the opposite was the case. As a result, for these three income classes, the percentage owning trusts was increased in the SFCC. These additional household units in the top three income classes were assigned the mean asset value of the asset in the SFCC. The yield numbers varied quite erratically, so the adjustment factor assigned to each income class is the same.

(13) The CSV of life insurance and pensions do not appear in the SFCC dataset. Tabulations of both the mean value of each asset and the percentage of households owning each by income class were used to impute these two assets to households in the SFCC tape, and the results are adjusted by a scalar to conform to the national balance sheet totals.[8]

(14) Mortgage debt is proportionately adjusted by a factor of 1.118 to conform with the national balance sheet total.

(15) Life insurance debt is not included in the SFCC dataset, but tabulations of mean value and percentage of households with this liability by income class were used to impute life insurance debt, and the results are proportionately adjusted to conform with the aggregate totals.[9]

(16) Other debt was added to life insurance debt, and the sum is scaled by a factor of 1.07.

(17) The imputation of Social Security and pension wealth in the 1962 SFCC and the 1983 SCF is described in detail in Appendix 3 of this book.

Results for the 1962 SFCC

Table A1.3 presents results on the concentration of different components of household wealth for both the original (unadjusted) data and the data adjusted to align with the national balance sheet totals and other outside information. Each row shows the concentration of that entry based on holdings in that asset or liability alone. Thus, the share of the top 1 percent of stocks is based on the highest holdings of stock shares. The striking result is the differences in the degree of concentration for the different components of wealth. Trust funds, corporate stock, unincorporated business equity, financial securities, and other (mainly investment) real estate were the most highly concentrated; bank deposits were less concentrated; and owner-occupied housing and vehicles were the most equally distributed. In general, the results from Tables A1.1 and A1.2 indicate that highly concentrated assets are also those that were significantly underreported. The last set of columns of Table A1.3 shows concentration estimates for the adjusted data. The adjustment process had almost no effect on the concentration levels of individual assets, with the possible exception of unincorporated business equity, which showed a modest decline in inequality from the adjustment procedure. However, the two assets missing from the SFCC, other consumer durables and household inventories, were much less concentrated than any other asset. Their inclusion in the household portfolio should thus lower estimated wealth inequality.

This implication is confirmed in Table A1.4. The first row indicates that the Gini coefficient for original, unadjusted household wealth was 0.772 and

Table A1.3. Concentration of unadjusted and adjusted household wealth by component, 1962

	Original Data			Adjusted Data	
	Share of Top 1 Percent	Ownership Rate	Gini Coefficient, Holders Only	Share of Top 1 Percent	Gini Coefficient, Holders Only
Assets	28.7	100.0	0.713	26.8	0.675
Owner-occupied housing	8.2	57.0	0.354	8.2	0.354
Other real estate	50.5	11.3	0.658	50.5	0.658
Vehicles	7.4	73.9	0.472	7.4	0.472
Other consumer durables	—	—	—	1.8	0.098
Inventories	—	—	—	4.9	0.284
Demand deposits and currency	34.6	100.0	0.808	34.6	0.808
Time and savings deposits	23.6	58.5	0.729	23.6	0.729
State and local government bonds	100.0	0.4	0.749	100.0	0.749
Other financial securities	50.4	39.5	0.824	52.5	0.832
Corporate stock	71.9	16.1	0.858	69.7	0.853
Unincorporated business equity	53.5	16.2	0.758	46.7	0.725
Trust fund equity	99.7	1.4	0.914	99.7	0.923
Insurance (CSV)	—	—	—	14.8	0.175
Pensions (CSV)	—	—	—	3.8	0.398
Liabilities	15.4	66.1	0.623	16.1	0.521
Mortgage debt	10.2	32.6	0.383	10.2	0.383
Other debt	34.7	58.2	0.694	34.7	0.599
Net worth	32.4	100.0	0.772	29.3	0.715

Source: Results are based on the 1962 SFCC. See the text for details.
Abbreviations: CSV, cash surrender value; SFCC, Survey of Financial Characteristics of Consumers.

Table A1.4. Inequality measures for different concepts of household wealth, based on both unadjusted and adjusted data, 1962

Wealth Concept	Gini Coefficient	Share of Top 1 Percent	Share of Top 5 Percent	Quintile Shares				
				Top	Second	Third	Fourth	Bottom
Unadjusted Estimates								
1. Original wealth components	0.772	32.4	52.5	78.2	14.4	6.2	1.4	−0.3
2. Row 1 plus other durables	0.701	29.5	48.0	72.7	15.0	7.6	3.2	1.5
3. Row 2 plus inventories	0.679	28.4	46.5	70.9	15.2	8.1	3.9	1.9
4. Row 1 less autos	0.798	33.9	54.5	80.3	14.0	5.7	0.6	−0.6
Measures Adjusted to Align with the National Balance Sheets								
5. Original components only	0.793	33.3	54.6	80.9	12.9	5.3	1.2	−0.3
6. Row 5 plus CSV of Insurance and pensions	0.782	32.2	53.2	79.8	13.4	5.7	1.4	−0.3
7. W2 = row 6 plus other durables	0.731	31.8	50.1	75.9	13.8	6.6	2.6	1.0
8. W2* = W2 plus inventories	0.715	29.3	48.9	74.4	14.1	7.1	3.1	1.3
9. W2 less all durables	0.805	33.4	55.0	81.7	12.9	5.2	0.8	−0.5

Augmented Measures of Household Wealth with Retirement Wealth

10. Social Security plus DB pension wealth only[a]

g=0	0.504	8.0	22.7	52.9	22.9	14.3	8.3	1.7
g=-.01	0.482	7.9	21.4	50.6	23.4	15.2	9.0	1.8
g=-.02	0.466	7.8	20.3	48.8	24.1	16.0	9.4	1.8
g=-.03	0.458	7.6	19.4	47.6	24.6	16.5	9.5	1.7

11. W5* = W2* plus Social Security and DB pension wealth

g=0	0.624	23.8	40.8	65.8	16.8	9.5	5.4	2.5
g=-.01	0.607	22.9	39.5	64.3	17.2	9.9	5.9	2.7
g=-.02	0.586	21.9	38.0	62.5	17.6	10.5	6.4	3.1
g=-.03	0.563	20.6	36.1	60.3	18.1	11.2	7.1	3.3

Source: Author's computations from the 1962 SFCC.

a. This panel shows the distribution of retirement wealth only. The quantile shares are based on the size distribution of families ranked by their retirement wealth, not net worth. If ranked by net worth, the top 1 percent would hold about 2 percent of total retirement wealth. Because of data limitations, I am unable to separate DB pension from Social Security wealth. The parameter g is the assumed rate of growth of mean real Social Security benefits.

Abbreviations: CSV, cash surrender value; DB, defined benefit; SFCC, Survey of Financial Characteristics of Consumers.

that the share of the top percentile was 32 percent. The change in inequality that results from adding an asset to the household portfolio is a function of three factors: (1) the degree of concentration of the asset, (2) the relative magnitude of the asset; and (3) its covariance with other components of net worth.[10] The addition of other consumer durables (a category that comprised 6 percent of total balance sheet assets and was distributed relatively equally) to original unadjusted net worth caused the Gini coefficient to decline from 0.77 to 0.70. This decline was primarily due to the increasing wealth shares of the bottom two wealth quintiles. The further addition of household inventories had a similar effect, with the Gini coefficient declining from 0.70 to 0.68.

The adjustment and alignment of the original components of household wealth in the SFCC to the national balance sheet caused an increase in the Gini coefficient from 0.77 to 0.79 (row 5). Most of the increased concentration occurred in the upper quintile, as might be expected, since the most underreported items were those held by the upper part of the wealth distribution. The addition of the CSV of life insurance and pensions to the household portfolio caused relatively little change since these items were quite small. However, the addition of other consumer durables to produce wealth measure W2 caused a sharp reduction in measured inequality, and the further addition of household inventories to create W2* caused another reduction in measured inequality.[11] The net effect of including missing items and aligning with the national balance sheets was a reduction in measured inequality, and the reduction was quite substantial, with the Gini coefficient falling from 0.77 (row 1) to 0.72 (row 8). Most of the change was due to gains by the bottom two quintiles, and, indeed, the share of the top percentile was reduced relatively little. Finally, rows 4 and 9 compare unadjusted and adjusted estimates of what might be called "fungible net worth" (W2 less all consumer durables). The distributional estimates were almost identical, 0.798 compared to 0.805. For fungible wealth, alignment made almost no difference in measured concentration.

Row 10 presents results on the distribution of Social Security and pension wealth. Because of data limitations, I am unable to separate the two components in the 1962 SFCC. Retirement wealth was distributed considerably more equally than marketable wealth. In particular, the shares of the upper percentile and quintile of retirement holdings were substantially lower and the shares of the middle three quintiles considerably higher than the corresponding shares for other types of assets. Moreover, the higher the assumed growth rate in Social Security benefits over time (the parameter g), the greater is measured equality. The reason for this is that raising g increases the equality in Social Security wealth between younger and older age cohorts. Moreover, the higher g is, the greater is the magnitude of retirement wealth since the present value of the future benefit stream is increased. For g = 0.0, total retirement wealth was 23 percent of balance sheet assets, while, for g = 0.03, the ratio became 42 percent.

In row 11, I show results on the distribution of W5*, defined as the sum of W2* plus pension and Social Security wealth.[12] For all values of g, the addition of retirement wealth to marketable wealth causes a marked reduction in measured inequality. Moreover, the higher the value of g, the greater the reduction in measured wealth inequality since the magnitude of retirement wealth increased and its concentration declined. For g = 0.0, the Gini coefficient for W5* was 0.62, and, for g = 0.03, the Gini coefficient was 0.56.

Adjustment Procedures for the 1983 SCF

The 1983 SCF contains richer detail on asset and liability holdings than the 1962 SFCC. As in the SFCC file, there are also a considerable number of missing value problems and inconsistencies in the original survey data. The Federal Reserve Board devoted substantial and careful effort to overcoming the problems of item non-response and internal data inconsistencies, as it did in the case of the 1962 SFCC.[13] For consistency with the 1962 SFCC data, I based all the tabulations and data results reported here on this fully imputed version of the 1983 SCF.

Table A1.1 presents a comparison of balance sheet totals derived from the SCF and the national balance sheet data. The underreporting patterns were very similar to the 1962 SFCC, except for corporate stock, unincorporated business equity, and trust fund equity. Owner-occupied housing and vehicles appeared well covered in the SCF, as did investment real estate and unincorporated business equity. Demand deposits (including currency) and time deposits (including money-market funds, certificates of deposits, and related liquid assets) were significantly underreported—almost to the same extent as in the 1962 SFCC. Financial securities, including bonds and mortgage assets, were well captured in the survey, as they were in the SFCC.

Ninety percent of corporate stock was captured in the SCF, a substantially higher share than in the 1962 survey. The total value of trust funds was considerably higher in the SCF than the balance sheet value. This contrasts with a 64 percent coverage rate in the 1962 data. The total value of life insurance CSV from the survey exceeded the national balance sheet total, though this result may be partly due to a misalignment between insurance savings and time deposit savings. Total pension CSV from the survey was more than double the national balance sheet estimate, though this may be a result of the national balance sheet estimation procedure for this category. Finally, liabilities were well covered in the SCF—almost exactly the same extent as in the 1962 SFCC. On net, the 1983 SCF appeared to have done a better job capturing household wealth than the 1962 SFCC.

There is some debate on the issue of alignment of the 1983 SCF survey results to the national balance sheet totals. For example, Curtin, Juster, and Morgan argued that the 1983 SCF results were more reliable than the FFA data and, as a result, implied that no alignment should be done.[14] For example, they claimed that the apparent low coverage rate of time deposits and savings accounts in the SCF vis-à-vis the FFAs was actually a result of different estimation techniques in the FFA data. A similar argument was also made by Avery, Elliehausen, and Kennickell.[15] Irrespective of the merits of their argument, my interest here is in consistency between the 1962 and the 1983 household surveys. As a result, it seems that the best way to obtain this is to align both surveys to a single source that is, at least, internally consistent—namely, the national balance sheets for the household sector.

For owner-occupied housing, other real estate, vehicles, unincorporated business equity, trust fund equity, and pension CSV, SCF coverage appeared quite adequate, and no alignment was done.[16] For other asset and liability components, alignment to the national balance sheet totals was performed. This was effected by using a proportional adjustment factor for each of the underreported items in the balance sheet, with three exceptions. First, time and savings deposits and insurance CSV were aligned as a single category since the latter was over-reported with respect to the national balance sheet total and the two classifications could be easily confused by the respondent. Second, mortgage debt was constrained to be no greater than the maximum of either its reported value or 80 percent of the gross value of the real estate. Third, nonmortgage debt was constrained to be no greater than the maximum of either its reported value or 50 percent of the total value of gross assets. In the 1983 SCF, there was partial reporting of nonvehicle consumer durables, though the total was less than one-fourth of the balance sheet total. I used the same regression technique to impute the missing portion of the nonvehicle consumer durable category, as I did for the 1962 data, with the total for this category (including the portion reported in the 1983 SCF) aligned to the national balance sheet figure of $760.6 billion. Household inventories were imputed in the same manner as for the 1962 data.[17]

Table A1.5 shows the concentration of each asset and liability after alignment to the corresponding national balance sheet total. The distribution of other consumer durables, household inventories, demand deposits and currency, trust funds, mortgage debt, and other debt remained largely unchanged between 1962 and 1983 (compare Table A1.3). However, there are some important changes between the two years. The percentage of families owning their own homes climbed from 57 to 64, and inequality of home values among homeowners increased from a Gini coefficient of 0.35 to 0.43. However, these two effects were offsetting, so that the overall Gini coefficient for owner-occupied housing (for homeowners and non-homeowners) remained at 0.63 in the two years. The fraction of families owning other real estate grew from 11 to 19 percent, while the Gini coefficient among owners remained unchanged. The percentage of families owning vehicles increased from 74 to 84, and the Gini coefficient among owners fell from 0.47 to 0.44.

In addition, the proportion of families with time deposits rose from 59 to 74 percent and the Gini coefficient for this asset increased slightly, from 0.73 to 0.77. And finally, the percentage of families owning corporate stock increased from 16 to 21, while the Gini coefficient among owners rose from 0.85 to 0.89. The net result was no change in the overall Gini coefficient for corporate stock.[18]

Table A1.6 shows estimates of overall household wealth inequality before and after alignment to the national balance sheet totals. The pattern of results is similar to those derived the 1962 SFCC. On the basis of unadjusted wealth figures, the inclusion of other consumer durables and household inventories in the household portfolio caused a substantial reduction in measured inequality, in this case from a Gini coefficient of 0.79 (row 1) to one of

Table A1.5. Concentration of household wealth by component, based on adjusted data, 1983

Wealth Component	Share of Top 1 Percent	Ownership Rate (%)	Gini Coefficient, Holders Only
Assets	28.6	100.0	0.703
Owner-occupied housing	11.2	63.4	0.427
Other real estate	55.5	18.9	0.750
Vehicles	6.8	84.4	0.442
Other consumer durables	2.2	100.0	0.144
Inventories	7.5	100.0	0.271
Demand deposits and currency	29.6	100.0	0.795
Time and savings deposits	25.8	74.1	0.771
Financial securities	68.9	7.7	0.747
Corporate stock	74.3	20.7	0.891
Unincorporated business equity	63.0	14.2	0.789
Trust fund equity	96.8	4.0	0.933
Insurance (CSV)	30.8	34.1	0.686
Pensions (CSV)	65.7	10.9	0.788
Miscellaneous Assets	63.4	11.2	0.754
Liabilities	23.4	69.8	0.683
Mortgage debt	13.4	37.1	0.455
Other debt	41.9	63.6	0.795
Net worth	30.4	100.0	0.728

Source: Author's computations from the 1987 Federal Reserve Board tape for the 1983 SCF. This version contains imputations for missing values from non-response and corrections of inconsistencies in the data (for details, see Robert B. Avery, Gregory E. Elliehausen, and Arthur B. Kennickell, "Measuring Wealth with Survey Data: An Evaluation of the 1983 Survey of Consumer Finances" (paper presented at the twentieth conference of the International Association for Research in Income and Wealth, Rocca di Papa, Italy, September 1987).

Note: The results are shown after the data are aligned to national balance sheet totals.

0.73 (row 3). As with the 1962 data, alignment to the national balance sheet totals of the original wealth components in the SCF had less of an effect on measured inequality than did adding other consumer durables and inventories. However, the direction of change was different for the 1983 data. In this case, the Gini coefficient declined slightly from 0.79 (row 1) to 0.78 (row 5). The total effect of both the imputation of missing assets and the alignment to the national balance sheet totals was to cause a decline of the Gini coefficient from 0.79 to 0.74 (row 6) and a fall of the share of the top percentile from 35 percent of total wealth to 31 percent.

Row 9 shows results on the distribution of defined benefit (DB) pension wealth, defined as the expected value of the flow of future DB pension benefits, based on the rank ordering of families by the value of pension wealth. The Gini coefficient for pension wealth was 0.84, considerably greater than that for traditional wealth W2* (row 7). However, part of the higher inequality was due to the fact that only 34 percent of families in 1983 held this asset. Among pension wealth holders only, the Gini coefficient was 0.56. As with the 1962 data, Social Security wealth was distributed considerably more equally than W2*. For g (the assumed rate of growth of real Social Security benefits) = 0.02, its Gini coefficient was 0.51 (row 10), compared to 0.73 for W2*. There was a slight increase in the concentration of total retirement wealth between 1962 and 1983. The Gini coefficient for the sum of DB pension and Social Security wealth (for g = 0.02) was 0.47 for the 1962 data (row 10 of Table A1.5), compared to 0.50 for the 1983 data (result not shown). Moreover, the magnitude of retirement wealth relative to traditional wealth grew considerably over the period, from 38 percent of W2* in 1962 to 88 percent in 1983.

As with the 1962 data, the addition of DB pension and Social Security wealth to traditional wealth (W2*) to create W5* caused a marked reduction in estimated inequality. For g = 0.02, the Gini coefficient fell from 0.73 (row 7) to 0.57 (row 11). The decline was greater than in 1962 because of the increased magnitude of retirement wealth relative to traditional wealth.

Table A1.7 summarizes the effects of imputations for missing assets and alignment to the national balance sheet totals on measured wealth inequality (the Gini coefficient). The major effect stems from the inclusion of missing assets in the 1962 and 1983 survey data. The addition of missing consumer durables (and pension and insurance CSV for the 1962 data) to the original components of household wealth to produce W2 resulted in a decline of the Gini coefficient of about 9 percent, and the inclusion of household inventories to create W2* caused a further drop of 2 to 3 percent. The imputation of DB pension and Social Security wealth to produce W5* resulted in another decrease of the Gini coefficient of 0.13 to 0.16 points (for g = 0.02). Alignment, on the other hand, caused only a modest change in measured inequality. The change in the Gini coefficient for the various wealth concepts was in the

Table A1.6. Inequality measures for different concepts of household wealth, based on both unadjusted and adjusted data, 1983

Wealth Concept	Gini Coefficient	Share of Top 1 Percent	Share of Top 5 Percent	Quintile Shares					
				Top	Second	Third	Fourth	Bottom
Unadjusted Estimates								
1. Original wealth components	0.788	34.5	56.2	80.3	12.6	5.6	1.5	0.0
2. Row 1 plus other durables	0.740	32.4	53.0	76.6	13.1	6.5	2.7	1.1
3. Row 2 plus inventories	0.729	31.8	52.0	75.7	13.3	6.8	2.9	1.3
4. Row 1 less vehicles	0.806	35.7	57.9	82.0	12.2	5.1	1.1	-0.3
Measures Adjusted to Align with the National Balance Sheets								
5. Original components only	0.781	32.8	54.6	79.8	12.9	5.7	1.6	0.0
6. W2 = row 5 plus other durables	0.739	30.9	51.8	76.5	13.4	6.5	2.6	1.0
7. W2* = W2 plus inventories	0.728	30.4	51.0	75.6	13.6	6.8	2.9	1.2
8. W2 less all durables	0.800	34.0	56.3	81.5	12.5	5.2	1.1	-0.3
Augmented Measures of Household Wealth with Retirement Wealth								
9. DB pension wealth[a]	0.844	19.8	48.8	90.3	9.7	0	0	0

10. Social Security wealth[b]

g = 0	0.557	7.3	25.2	58.3	21.3	12.8	7.0	0.6
g = .01	0.528	7.5	25.1	55.0	21.9	14.2	8.2	0.7
g = .02	0.509	8.0	25.4	52.9	22.3	15.0	9.1	0.8
g = .03	0.503	8.6	25.7	52.2	22.4	15.2	9.4	0.9

11. W5* = W2* plus Social Security and pension wealth

g = 0	0.607	20.6	39.1	64.2	17.3	10.3	5.8	2.4
g = .01	0.592	20.0	37.9	63.0	17.4	10.5	6.2	2.9
g = .02	0.572	19.0	36.4	61.7	17.4	10.8	6.7	3.3
g = .03	0.550	17.8	34.7	60.2	17.4	11.2	7.4	3.8

Source: Author's computations from the 1987 Federal Reserve Board tape for the 1983 SCF. This version contains imputations for missing values from nonresponse and corrections of inconsistencies in the data.

a. This panel shows the distribution of pension wealth only. The quantile shares are based on the size distribution of families ranked by their pension wealth.

b. This panel shows the distribution of Social Security wealth only. The top percentile and quintile shares are based on the size distribution of families ranked by their Social Security wealth. If ranked by net worth, the top one percent would hold about 3 percent of total Social Security wealth. The parameter g is the assumed rate of growth of mean real Social Security benefits.

Table A1.7. Summary table of the effects of imputations for missing assets and alignment to national balance sheet totals on Gini coefficients for household wealth, 1962 and 1983

	1962		1983	
Wealth Concept	Before Alignment	After Alignment	Before Alignment	After Alignment
Original components only	0.77	0.79	0.79	0.78
W2 components	0.70	0.73	0.74	0.74
W2* components	0.68	0.72	0.73	0.73
W5* components (g=0.02)	—	0.59	—	0.57
WF[a]	0.80	0.81	0.80	0.80

Source: Author's computations from the 1962 SFCC and the 1983 SCF.
a. WF is fungible wealth, defined as W2 less all durables.

range of 0.02–0.04 points for the 1962 data and between 0.0 and 0.01 for the 1983 data. This was also true for fungible wealth, defined as W2 less all consumer durables. In addition, the direction of change was not necessarily the same among different wealth surveys. In the two cases considered here, alignment increased measured wealth inequality when applied to the 1962 SFCC but reduced it slightly for the 1983 SCF.[19]

Results from the 1962 SFCC and 1983 SCF indicate a similar level of wealth inequality in the two years. The original unadjusted survey estimates indicated a small increase in inequality, from a Gini coefficient of 0.77 in 1962 to 0.79 in 1983. Adjustments of the survey data negated this upward trend. Gini coefficients for 1962 and 1983 were quite close, 0.715 and 0.728, respectively, after adjustments for missing assets and alignment to national balance sheet totals. Adding retirement wealth to adjusted marketable net worth to produce W5* resulted in a slight decline in inequality between 1962 and 1983, from a Gini coefficient of 0.59 to 0.57 (for g=0.02). This decline was relatively modest given the rapid growth in Social Security wealth over the period. The apparent reason is that the growth in Social Security was offset by the rapid growth of DB pension wealth, which is distributed less equally.

Adjustments and imputations to the survey data have more effect on the level of inequality than the trend. However, for the 1962 and 1983 surveys, alignment to national balance sheet totals appeared to make relatively little difference, a maximum change in the Gini coefficient of 0.04

by component and 0.02 for overall net worth. On the other hand, imputations for missing assets had a sizable effect on inequality. The inclusion of missing consumer durables caused a 0.05 to 0.07 point change in the Gini coefficient and the inclusion of household inventories an additional 0.01- to 0.02-point decline. The addition of DB pension and Social Security wealth caused an even sharper decrease in the Gini coefficient, of 0.13 to 0.16 points. Finally, if I exclude consumer durables, inventories, and retirement wealth, then inequality measures of "fungible net worth" were quite insensitive to adjustment procedures. Thus, the unadjusted 1962 and 1983 survey data provide reliable concentration estimates of this component of household wealth.

Adjustment Procedures for the 1989, 1992, and 1995 SCF

There were significant discrepancies between survey totals in the 1989, 1992, and 1995 SCF and corresponding national balance sheet (FFA) aggregates for certain assets and liabilities. As a result, proportional adjustment is applied to these components. The adjustment factors by asset type and year are as follows:

	1983 SCF	1989 SCF	1992 SCF	1995 SCF
Checking accounts	1.68			
Savings and time deposits	1.50			
All deposits		1.37	1.32	
Financial securities	1.20			
Stocks and mutual funds	1.06			
Trusts		1.66	1.41	1.45
Stocks and bonds				1.23
Nonmortgage debt	1.16			

No adjustments are made to other asset and debt components, or to subsequent SCF files since the alignment is much closer.

For the 1992 SCF there also appears to be significant problems in the household weighting scheme. It should be noted at the outset that there was a substantial change in the sampling frame used in the 1992 survey in comparison to the 1989 survey. For consistency with the earlier results, I adjust the weights used in the 1992 SCF.

Adjusted gross income or Household income	SCF Distribution Percentage of All Households[a]		SOI Distribution Percentage of All Tax Returns[b]	
[Current $]	1989	1992	1989	1992
Under $100,000	95.7	94.9	97.4	96.7
100,000–199,999	3.107	3.948	1.864	2.474
200,000–499,999	0.895	0.892	0.546	0.657
500,000–999,999	0.187	0.182	0.103	0.124
1,000,000 or more	0.073	0.040	0.051	0.059
Of which:				
1,000,000–3,999,999	0.0550	0.0293		
4,000,000–6,999,999	0.0128	0.0021		
7,000,000 or more	0.0049	0.0002		
Total	100.0	100.0	100.0	100.0

a. Source: Author's computations from the 1989 and 1992 SCF.

b. Sources: "Selected Historical and Other Data," *Statistics of Income Bulletin* 13, no. 4 (Winter 1993–94): 179–80; "Selected Historical and Other Data," *Statistics of Income Bulletin* 15, no. 3 (Winter 1994–95): 180–81.

The problem can be seen most easily in the table above, which provides a comparison of SOI and SCF size distributions:

A comparison of weights used in the 1989 and 1992 SCF shows a very sharp attenuation in the weights at the top of the income distribution. According to these figures, the percentage of households with incomes between $1 million and $4 million declined from 0.055 to 0.029, or by almost half; the percentage in the income range $4 million to $7 million fell from 0.013 to 0.002, or by over 80 percent; and the percentage with incomes of $7 million or more decreased from 0.0049 to 0.0002, or by over 95 percent. These changes were highly implausible—particularly in light of results from the CPS, which showed a slightly rising degree of income inequality over this period (the Gini coefficient increased from 0.427 to 0.428).

The table also compares the size distribution of income computed from the SOI in 1989 and 1992 with that from the two SCF files. The SOI figures are based on actual tax returns filed in the two years. There are three major differences between the two data sources. First, the SOI data use the tax return as the unit of observation, whereas the SCF figures are based on the household unit. Second, individuals who do not file tax returns are excluded from the SOI tabulations. Third, the size distribution for the SOI data is based on adjusted gross income (AGI), whereas the SCF distributions are based on total household income.

Despite the differences in concept and measurement, trends in the size distribution of AGI can give a rough approximation to actual changes in the size distribution of household (census) income. What is most striking is that the SOI figures showed a slight increase in the percent of units in income class $1 million and more, from 0.051 in 1989 to 0.059 percent in 1992, whereas the SCF figures showed a sharp decline, from 0.073 to 0.040 percent.

Results from the SOI data failed to provide any independent corroboration for the sharp decline in the number of households with incomes of $1 million or more between 1989 and 1992. Accordingly, I adjusted the 1992 weights to conform to the 1989 weighting scheme. The adjustment factors for the 1992 weights were given by the inverse of the normalized ratio of weights between 1992 and 1989, shown in the last column of the preceding table:

Income (1989 dollars)	Adjustment Factors for 1992 Weights
Under 200,000	0.992
200,000–999,999	1.459
1,000,000–3,999,999	1.877
4,000,000–6,999,999	4.844
7,000,000 or more	12.258

The resulting size distribution of income for 1989 and 1992 was as follows:

Income Shares (in percent)	1989 SCF Using Original Weights	1992 SCF Using Adjusted Weights
Share of the top 1%	16.4	15.7
Share of the top 5%	29.7	30.5
Share of the top 10%	40.1	41.1
Share of the top 20%	55.3	56.4
Gini Coefficient	0.521	0.528

The calculations show a slight increase in overall income inequality, as measured by the Gini coefficient, a result that is consistent with both the SOI and the CPS data.

Construction of the 1969 MESP Dataset

This appendix presents a description, as well as Gini coefficient estimates, for the size distribution of household wealth for the United States in 1969, from a synthetic database called the Measurement of Economic and Social Performance (MESP).[1] This database was developed at the National Bureau of Economic Research under the direction of Richard Ruggles, from October 1972 to October 1977. The database is the product of three statistical matches and two sets of imputations and contains asset and liability information, as well as detailed demographic data, for a sample of 63,457 households.

Some justification may be required for developing a new (and synthetic) database for estimating household wealth distributions. There are four major sources of household wealth data. The first consists of administrative records, in particular tax returns required of wealth holders for paying wealth taxes. Unfortunately (or fortunately), the United States has not imposed a wealth tax, and such a data source is not available. However, Sweden and several other Western European countries do (or did) have a general wealth tax (see Chapter 14). This type of data is probably the best for wealth distribution analysis. Even so, there are three major problems in using it. First, there is usually a minimum level of wealth required for filing the return; thus the coverage of the population is incomplete. Second, not all assets are included in these tax returns (particularly, consumer durables are excluded), and for those assets that are, there are usually problems of underreporting (both from ignorance of current market value and for tax avoidance). Thus, the coverage of asset values is normally deficient. Third, there are quite often disclosure problems in releasing this type of data for research use.

The second major source of wealth data consists of estate tax records. These, too, are administrative records, but unlike wealth tax records they cover decedents, not the living. In the United States the use of estate tax data as a means of making wealth distribution estimates was largely developed by Robert Lampman and James Smith.[2] There are five main problems associated with this source of data. First, the sample is limited to the top of the wealth distribution (decedents with gross estates of $60,000 or more in 1969). Second, asset coverage is limited, with consumer durables and household inventories omitted. In addition, there is a tendency for assets, particularly business equity, to be undervalued for tax reasons. Third, very limited demographic detail is available on the decedent and none on his (or her) family. Fourth, developing full population estimates from the sample of decedents depends on assumptions about relative mortality rates (though the overall size distribution estimates are fairly robust with respect to different assumptions). Fifth, it is difficult to determine the effect of inter vivos transfers (gifts before death) and the establishment of trust funds on the size distribution of wealth estimated from this data source.

The third major source of wealth data comes from direct surveys of households. This might come from a full census or from a sample survey. Perhaps the best known example of this type in the United States before 1969 is the Federal Reserve Board's 1962–63 Survey of Financial Characteristics of Consumers.[3] As in all surveys, deficiencies arise because of the limited time and budget allocated to complete them. For this survey, 2,557 consumer units were given questionnaires to report their assets and liabilities, as well as other household information. The asset coverage is fairly complete, except for consumer durables. The main problem with this survey is the severe underreporting of liquid assets and installment debt.[4] For example, in comparison with Flow of Funds data (now called the Financial Accounts of the United States), only 51 percent of savings accounts, 55 percent of U.S. government securities, 39 percent of state and local government securities, and 58 percent of installment debt were reported in the survey. Another problem with this survey is that due to its relatively small sample size, wealth distribution estimates for subgroups of the population, particularly the poor and the rich, are not very reliable.

The fourth major source of wealth data derives from income flows. Essentially, the technique involves "capitalizing" interest, dividends, business profits, and the like into corresponding asset values. The work of Charles Stewart and Stanley Lebergott provides early examples of such estimates for the United States.[5] Up until 1980, the technique was used on aggregate income flow data. MESP, in effect, uses the same technique on a microdata base. There are both advantages and disadvantages to this technique.[6] First, the resulting asset estimates are only as reliable as the underlying income flow data. In Stewart, Lebergott, and the MESP database, the underlying income flows come from IRS tax returns. This is probably the most accurate source of income information in the United States, particularly for nonwage income. Moreover, the income data contained in the tax returns are probably more reliable than survey-based wealth data.

A second advantage is that the resulting wealth imputations automatically balance with the national balance totals, because the capitalizing ratio is the ratio of the national total for a given asset to the sample total of the corresponding income flow. Third, a possible disadvantage is that the resulting wealth estimates are sensitive to the yield ratios used. In Stewart, Lebergott, and the MESP database, it was implicitly assumed that the yield on each asset was the *same* for each income class, race, region of the country, and the like. If there were a systematic relation between yield and some demographic characteristics (for example, higher income classes may receive a higher dividend yield on stock equity than lower income ones), then a bias would be introduced into the wealth imputations. But the advantages seem to outweigh the disadvantages. Since a capitalization procedure is not "tied" to a particular survey or set of administrative records, it can be applied to any sample frame. Thus, as in the MESP database, full coverage of the population is possible. Also, the technique is a relatively open one, so that assets not normally covered by this approach, like consumer durables, can be added to the household portfolio. This approach thus makes possible full coverage of assets and liabilities.

The Formation of the MESP Database

The MESP database was formed by combining information from the 1970 Census Public Use sample with the IRS tax return data and by imputing asset and liability values based on income flows and other available household information. The sample frame of the MESP data base is the 1970 state 15 percent census 1 / 1000 Public Use Sample (PUS), which contains personal and household information for a randomly drawn sample of 63,457 households. Statistical matching procedures were used to add household information from three other data sets: the 1970 IRS Tax Model (IRS 70), the 1969 Tax Model (IRS 69), and the 1970 state 5 percent census 1 / 1000 Public Use Sample (PUSS). Asset and liability information was then imputed to each household based on its extended set of demographic and income data, and household asset and liability estimates were lastly adjusted to align with national balance sheet totals of household wealth.

The Statistical Matches

A statistical matching procedure developed by Ruggles and Ruggles and Ruggles, Ruggles, and Wolff was used to combine information from the two censuses and the two tax return files.[7] In all, three separate matches were performed. The first match was between the 1969 and 1970 IRS files. This was done because a special 1970 IRS file had been developed by the Social Security Administration containing the race and age of the head of household on each tax return,[8] as well as more detailed information on the deductions taken in each tax return, particularly mortgage and other interest payments, and state, local, sales, and property tax payments, than the 1969 IRS file. For the match, the two files were first divided into single and joint returns. The single filers were then divided into four cohort groups: males under 65, males 65 or over, females under 65, and females 65 or over. The joint filers were also divided into four cohorts: both under 65, both 65 or over, husband under 65 and wife 65 or over, and husband 65 or over and wife under 65. Each of these groups was then subdivided again, depending on the number of children in the family.

Tax returns within each of these finely divided groups were then matched between the IRS 69 and IRS 70 files, depending on how close the two records were with respect to the following thirteen items: adjusted gross income (AGI); and the ratios of wage and salary earnings to AGI, interest income to AGI, long-term capital gains to AGI, rental income to AGI, dividends to AGI, farm income to AGI, trust income to AGI, royalty income to AGI, business and professional earnings to AGI, pension income to AGI, property sale gains to AGI, and total deductions to AGI. Race, age, and itemized deductions were then transferred from the IRS 70 record to the corresponding IRS 69 record.

The second and major match was between this "augmented" IRS 69 file and the 1970 PUS file, containing income and earnings information for the year 1969. The purpose of this match was to combine the detailed in come information of the IRS 69 file with the detailed demographic informa tion of the PUS. Moreover, the PUS contains information on the value of owner occupied housing as well as stocks of durables held. Both sets of in formation were thus required to construct household balance sheets.

The two files were first divided into cohort groups on the basis of the fol lowing four (common) variables: marital status (single vs. married); gender (for singles); age of the head of household; and race of the head of household. Within each cohort group the two files were matched depending on how close the two records were with respect to the following six characteristics: number of children; homeowner vs. renter; wage and salary earnings; business earnings; farm income; and total income. The detailed income information, as well as data on itemized deductions, was then transferred from the IRS 69 file to the 1970 PUS file.

The last match was that of the PUS5 file to the PUS. The reason for this match was that only the PUS5 file had information on the televisions, radios, and clothes washers and dryers owned by each household. The two files were first divided into cohorts on the basis of the following five variables: marital status; age of the head of household; gender of the head of household; race of the head of household; and homeowner vs. renter status. Records from the two files were matched depending on how close they were with respect to the following five characteristics: number of children; value of property or gross monthly rental; wage earnings of the head of household; wage earnings of the spouse; and total family income. Information on the stocks of consumer durables was then transferred from the PUS5 file to the PUS.[9]

Alignment of Income Flows

Since tax returns were imputed to households in the PUS, some error was expected in the total income flows computed from this sample. This is docu mented in Table A2.1, which compares the MESP totals with those of the IRS Statistics of Income (SOI). The AGI and wage and salary totals were quite close. The interest, dividend, business and professional net income, and rental income totals were all higher in the unadjusted MESP file than in the

Table A2.1. Comparison of 1969 income flows between the unadjusted MESP totals and statistics of income

Income Type	National Totals (billions of dollars)		MESP/IRS	Percent Receiving the Item	
	MESP	IRS		MESP	IRS
Adjusted gross income	$629.60	603.6	1.04		
Wages and salary	573.1	499.0	1.15		
Interest	44.5	19.6	2.27	65.1	42.3
Dividends	38.4	16.9	2.27	30.7	16.0
Business and professional net income	42.6	30.4	1.40	32.7	8.0
Partnership net income	−17.2	2.0		5.7	2.7
Farm net income	−10.0	3.6		16.5	4.1
Rental income	4.0	2.6	1.54	20.6	8.4
Estates and trust income	−1.2	1.4		1.9	0.8

Source: Author's computation from the 1969 MESP file and the 1969 SOI.

Abbreviations: MESP, Measurement of Economic and Social Performance; SOI, Survey of Income.

IRS totals. The main reason for the discrepancy is evident from the second column of the table: the matching procedure assigned too many tax returns containing these income items to households in the PUS sample frame.[10]

The fix-up procedure was straightforward. In the case of interest, dividends, business and professional net income, and rental income, I randomly eliminated these entries so that the percent of households receiving each item in the MESP file was equal to the IRS percentage.[11] I then adjusted the remaining income entries by a constant multiple so that they would sum to the IRS total. In the case of partnership, farm, and trust income, where the signs for the totals differed, I used a somewhat different procedure. I randomly eliminated a certain percentage of positive entries and a certain (though different) percentage of negative entries, so that the percentage receiving the income item and the total income flow would equal the IRS total.[12]

Asset and Liability Imputations

The next step was to "build up" balance sheet information for each household based on the stock and flow data already contained in the (now adjusted) MESP

Table A2.2 Aggregate national balance sheet of household wealth for the United States, 1969, by category (billions of current dollars)

Category		Value
Assets	3,612.8	
Tangible Assets	1,220.3	
Owner-occupied housing		635.0
Other real estate		175.8
Automobiles		89.5
Other consumer durables		227.3
Inventories		92.7
Financial Assets	2,392.6	
Demand deposits and currency		104.9
Time and savings deposits		381.4
Federal securities		101.4
State and local governments securities		34.8
Corporate and foreign bonds, mortgages, open market paper, other instruments		85.6
Corporate stock		635.9
Farm business equity		218.1
Unincorporated nonfarm equity		314.5
Trust fund equity		132.8
Insurance and pension reserves		383.1
Liabilities	450.2	
Mortgage debt		276.6
Consumer credit		121.1
Other debt		52.5
Net Worth	3,162.6	

Source: Estimates prepared by Raymond Goldsmith in Richard Ruggles, "Statement for the Task Force on Distributive Impacts of Budget and Economic Policies of the House Committee on the Budget," mimeo, 1977. Consumer durables were split into autos and others from Bureau of Economic Analysis worksheets provided by John Musgrave.

database. The imputation procedures differed for different assets and liabilities. However, in all the procedures the resultant stock totals were aligned with the national balance sheet totals for the household sector (see Table A2.2).

Owner-Occupied Housing

House values were provided in the PUS, though they were coded in eleven intervals. The midpoints of each interval were used, except for the last, open-ended interval of $50,000 or more. For this we chose a value of $77,538 so that the total would agree with the aggregate balance sheet.

Consumer Durables

Ownership, though not values, was provided for the following set of durables in the PUS: number of automobiles (0, 1, 2, 3 or more), air conditioning unit, washing machine and clothes dryer, dishwasher, home food freezer, television, and radio. To construct a balance sheet for each household, it was necessary to increase the coverage of durables and to impute a dollar value for each durable owned by the household.

Estimates of the total value of consumer durables held by households were obtained from the Bureau of Economic Analysis (see Table A2.3). Moreover, from the 1960–61 Bureau of Labor Statistics Consumer Expenditure Survey (CES), information was provided about the annual expenditure by families on each of the following durables for 1960–1961: automobiles, washer / dryer combinations, refrigerators, other major appliances, small appliances, televisions, radios and phonographs, furniture, textiles, floor coverings, and housewares. For the imputation of consumer durable values, it was necessary to combine the information contained in these three sources of data. This was done in three successive steps. First, ownership of durables not included in the PUS inventory was imputed to households, and the purchase price and year of purchase of each durable were estimated for each household. Second, the current market value (as of 1969) of each durable was estimated by depreciating the purchase price of the durable according to its age and the life span of the durable. Third, the total value of durables held by households in the sample was aligned to the Bureau of Economic Analysis (BEA) net stock estimates.

In order to impute ownership of durables, I computed the percentage of households falling within predefined demographic categories who purchased each of eleven durables during the survey year on the basis of the CES. I initially used nine demographic characteristics: (1) urban / rural, (2) region, (3) gender of the household head, (4) race of the household head, (5) education of the household head, (6) marital status, (7) age of household head, (8) occupational status, and (9) family income. Using the nine-dimensional breakdown would have resulted in 43,336 ($2 \times 4 \times 2 \times 3 \times 3 \times 2 \times 7 \times 3 \times 7$) categories—far in excess of the 13,728 families in the CES. I therefore chose the three most important demographic characteristics out of the nine—

Table A2.3. Net stocks of consumer durables held by households in 1969 (billions of current dollars)

Category	Value
Automobiles	89.5
Other motor vehicles	9.5
Appliances	30.8
Radios, televisions, phonographs, etc.	30.9
Furniture	52.3
Textiles and other durable home furnishings (excluding china and utensils)	68.4
Other (including china and utensils, jewelry, books, and toys)	35.4
Total	316.8

Source: Bureau of Economic Analysis Worksheets, provided by John Musgrave. See Allan Young and John Musgrave, "Estimation of Capital Stock in the United States" (paper delivered at the Conference on Research in Income and Wealth, Toronto, Canada, 1976) for the methodology.

income, age, and urban/rural residence—and added a fourth category, homeowner/renter status.[13] This procedure resulted in a small enough number of cells to obtain reliable estimates of the proportion who purchased each durable by demographic group.[14]

I treated the proportion of each group purchasing each durable in 1960–1961 as the probability of each group's purchasing the good in calendar year 1960 and all successive years.[15] Let q_{ij} be the probability of demographic group j's purchasing durable i. I obtained information on L_i, the service life of each durable i (see Table A2.4). Thus, the probability r_{ij} that a person in group j owns durable i is $q_{ij}L_i$, under the assumption that no one in a group purchases a durable until its service life is over.[16] Probability r_{ij} was then computed for each household in the PUS on the basis of its demographic characteristics and for all durables except cars, television, radios, and washer/dryer units.[17] A number s_i between 0 and 1 was randomly picked (using a random number generator) from a uniform distribution for each household and each durable i. If $s_i < r_{ij}$, I assigned ownership of durable i to the household; otherwise no ownership was imputed. The age Ai of durable i was also imputed to households for all durables owned by the household (including those in the PUS inventory). Let $T_{ij} = 1/q_{ij}$. Tij then indicates the average length of ownership of durable i for demographic group j, where, if

Table A2.4. Service life (in years) of each of eleven consumer durables

Item	Service Life (years)
Automobiles	10
Televisions	9
Radios	9
Housewares	11
Small appliances	11
Textiles	10
Furniture	14
Floor coverings	10
Refrigerators	10
Washing machines / dryers	10
Other major appliances	10

Source: Allan Young and John Musgrave, "Estimation of Capital Stock in the United States," Table 1 (paper delivered at the Conference on Research in Income and Wealth, Toronto, Canada, 1976), 10.

$T_{ij} > L_i$, the good has zero value in the $T_{ij} - L_i$ years of possession. The age A_{ij} of good i is then given for each household by $A_i = s_i T_{ij} = s_i / q_{ij}$ (as long as $s_i < r_{ij}$).[18]

Table A2.5 compares the percentage of households who purchased each of the eleven durables in 1960–1961 according to the CES and my estimates of the percentage who purchased each durable in 1969 (that is, those durables whose age was less than or equal to 1). The imputed purchase estimates were quite close to the actual CES figures for all durables except autos and televisions. Automobile and television purchases in the imputation for calendar year 1969 were probably overstated because of the occurrence of multiple ownership of each item in the PUS.[19]

The next step was to impute the current market value of each durable. For this, the purchase price of each durable owned by households was estimated on the basis of regression analysis. Using the CES, I regressed family expenditure on each of the eleven durables, conditional on purchasing the durable, on the following set of variables common to the CES and PUS:[20] family income, years of schooling of the head of household; age of the head of household; family size; urban / rural / farm residence; region; gender of the head of household; race of the head of household; marital status; industry of employment of the head of household; occupation of the head of household; and homeowner / renter status.

Table A2.5. Comparison of the percentage of households purchasing durables and the average purchase price between the 1960–61 CES and the imputed value for the 1970 PUS

Durable	% of Households		Average Purchase Price (1961 dollars)		
	1960–61 CES	1969 PUS (Imputed)	CES	PUS	% Diff.
Textiles	76	70	44	70	59
Furniture	44	44	173	274	58
Floor coverings	30	25	87	183	110
Refrigerators	9	10	240	275	15
Washer / dryer units	10	9	193	207	7
Other major appliances	20	23	135	168	24
Small appliances	27	25	28	37	32
Housewares	70	56	19	41	116
Automobiles	24	40	1,234	1,561	26
Televisions	54	74	71	90	27
Radios and phonographs	44	41	76	148	95

Note: Sample sizes are CES 13,728; PUS 63,457.
Abbreviations: CES, Consumer Expenditure Survey; PUS, Public Use Sample.

The regression results were used to impute a purchase price to all households in the PUS owning durables, as follows: for each household owning durable i, I computed $p_i = xb_i$, where b_i are the regression coefficients for durable i and x the set of regressors. The estimated p_i is the mean purchase price (in 1961 dollars) of durable i for households with characteristics x. The variance was added back in by setting p^*_i, the purchase price of durable i, equal to $p_i + t\sigma$ where σ is the estimated standard error for the regression and t is a standard normal random variable whose value was obtained from a standard normal random number generator.[21]

Table A2.5 shows the mean purchase price of each of the eleven durables in the CES and the mean (imputed) purchase price for the same durables in the PUS. The PUS mean purchase prices were uniformly higher. This was to be expected, since the PUS imputations use 1969 incomes. (In fact, the mean income in current dollars was about 50 percent higher in 1969 than in 1961.)

To obtain the current market value V_i of durable i, I assumed a straight line depreciation schedule and computed Vi as follows:

$$V_i = (L_i - A_i) \, p^*_i / L_i$$

Table A2.6. Adjustment factors for the alignment of consumer durable totals in the PUS with the BEA totals

BEA Group	Adjustment Factor
Automobiles	0.99
Appliances (washer/dryer units, refrigerators, other major appliances, small appliances)	1.37
Televisions, radios, and phonographs	2.49
Furniture	4.04
Home furnishings (textiles, floor coverings, housewares)	2.80

Abbreviations: BEA, Bureau of Economic Analysis; PUS, Public Use Sample.

where A_i is the imputed age of durable i. In the case of autos and televisions, this valuation was done for each one owned by the household.

The final step was to reconcile my valuation of consumer durables with the aggregate BEA totals of household owned stocks (Table A2.2). There were two major sources of error in these estimates. First, they were still in 1961 dollars, though adjusted for 1969 incomes. Second, purchase decisions and expenditure behavior might have changed between 1961 and 1969.

To balance these estimates of the stock of household durables, I applied "adjustment factors," shown in Table A2.6, so that the stock of durables in the PUS sample would sum to the BEA totals. Automobile and major appliances required only minor adjustment. Furniture and home furnishings required a large adjustment, presumably because the CES coverage of these groups was considerably smaller than the BEA coverage. The television category required a large adjustment, probably because of the introduction of color televisions during the 1960s. The MESP coverage of consumer durables included all BEA categories except the "other durable" group (china, utensils, jewelry, books, toys, etc.). The PUS coverage thus amounted to $248.4 billion, or 78 percent of the BEA total.

Time Deposits, Bonds, Notes, and Other Interest-Earning Securities
Capitalization techniques were used for the valuation of the remaining assets in the household balance sheet. Ideally, information providing differential yields by demographic and income characteristics of households for different asset types would have been desirable. Thus, for example if we knew that high income households had an average yield of 8 percent on bonds, and

low income households an average yield of 6 percent, different capitalization ratios could be provided for low and high income households. Such information, however, was not available except for stock equity (see below). I therefore used uniform capitalization ratios for each of the remaining assets in the portfolio.

In the case of financial securities, interest on time and savings deposits was not distinguishable from that on bonds, notes, mortgages, and other financial securities in the tax return data. Time and savings deposits were therefore aggregated with the other financial securities to form one category. Moreover, state and local government bonds were excluded, since interest received from these bonds was nontaxable and, as a result, not recorded in the tax return in 1969. The average yield on this group of securities for 1969 was 3.4 percent (19.6 / 568.4), which was used to capitalize interest received into stock estimates. There were two offsetting biases in this procedure. First, the fact that savings accounts normally had lower interest rates than bonds and other securities implied that the imputation procedure was overstating the asset values of bond holders relative to those with savings accounts. I was therefore overestimating the financial security holdings of the upper income classes relative to the lower ones. Second, the fact that state and local government bonds were excluded implied that the financial security holdings of their owners, who were primarily upper income, were being understated.[22]

Corporate Securities
Dividends received from corporate equities were recorded in the IRS tax return data. The average yield was 2.7 percent (16.9 / 635.9), which I used to capitalize dividends into corporate stock estimates. In the case of this asset, some information was available on the relation of dividend yield to household income for 1969.[23] Dividend yields were found to vary inversely with income. However, average dividend yields by AGI class varied only from 2.78 to 2.51 percent.[24] This range was so small compared with the likely error in the imputation procedure that I ignored this correction.

Investment Real Estate Holdings
Net rental income was reported in the IRS tax return data. A simple capitalization procedure was not possible here, since some of the income reported was negative.[25] In general, gross rents and costs[26] rise with the value of the

property. Thus, the greater the discrepancy between gross rents and costs, the higher, in general, the value of the property. I therefore capitalized net rental income into real estate value proportional to the absolute value of net rental income. The average "yield" figure was 7.5 percent (13.2 / 175.8).

Unincorporated Nonfarm Business Equity

Net business and professional (including partnership) income was reported in the IRS tax return data. Like net rental income, both positive and negative entries occurred. I therefore used the same procedure as for real estate holdings, and capitalized the absolute value of net income into unincorporated nonfarm equity, using an average "yield" figure of 18.7 percent (58.8 / 314.5).

Farm Equity

I used the same procedure as above to capitalize the absolute value of farm net income into farm equity value. The average "yield" figure was 4.8 percent (10.5 / 218.1).

Mortgage Debt

Considerably more information was available for the imputation of home mortgage debt. In the PUS, both home value and length of time of ownership ("When Moved In") were provided for each household. From other sources, I obtained information on average interest rates for home mortgages, average maturity of home mortgages, and a price index for residential housing (see Table A2.7). Assuming an average down payment of 25 percent and using standard mortgage amortization tables, I computed the outstanding home mortgage for each homeowner on the basis of initial house value (current value multiplied by the price index) and time of ownership. The initial estimates resulted in a total household mortgage debt of 273.8, compared with the balance sheet total of 276.6. I then adjusted the estimates by 1 percent (276.6 / 273.8).

Other Household Debt

Interest payments for households itemizing their deductions were recorded in the IRS tax return data.[27] In the MESP file, 40.9 percent of all households recorded some interest payment. The SFCC reported that 56 percent of all

Table A2.7. Basic data for mortgage debt imputation

Period	Average Interest Rate on Home Mortgages[a] (%)	Price Index for Residential Structures[b] (1970 = 100)	Average Maturity[c] (months)
1946–1949	4.34	60.8	231
1950–1959	4.81	76.9	261
1960–1964	5.69	80.9	318
1965–1966	5.93	83.5	329
1967	6.56	87.7	334
1968	7.19	91.9	338
1969	8.26	100.0	338

Sources: a. "U.S. Department of Commerce, Bureau of Economic Analysis, *Business Conditions Digest* (February 1976), Table C.118, p. 109 (FHA mortgages).

b. U.S. Department of Commerce, Bureau of Economic Analysis, *National Income and Product Accounts of the United States, 1929–74,* Table 7-13, pp. 294–95.

c. For average maturity, I used a weighted average of FHA and conventional mortgages. Prior to 1964, the source was Guttentag and Beck, *New Series on Home Mortgage Yields,* NBER, 1970 (#92 General Series), Tables C-2 and C-3. After 1963, the source was Department of Housing and Urban Development, *Housing and Urban Development Trends: Annual Summary* (May 1970), Table A-61.

households in 1962 had some form of debt other than mortgage debt. I assumed that 56 percent of all households in 1969 had some consumer debt, and that the remainder (56% − 40.9% = 15.1%) were households that did not itemize their deductions. I randomly selected this remaining 15.1 percent from households that did not itemize deductions and capitalized the resulting interest flows into household debt, using an average interest rate of 7.3 percent (12.6 / 173.6).

Asset Coverage

Table A2.8 gives a summary of household information contained in the MESP database. A comparison with the aggregate balance sheet in Table A2.1 reveals the extent of its coverage. Owner-occupied housing, other real estate, and automobiles are fully covered. Seventy percent (158.9 / 227.3) of other consumer durables are included in the MESP database but there is no coverage of inventories. The MESP coverage of tangible assets thus amounts to 87 percent (1059.2 / 1220.3). Coverage of financial assets is also incomplete. Time and savings deposits, federal securities, bonds, mortgages, and other

Table A2.8. Summary of household information in the MESP database

Demographic Information
    Family and household size and composition
    Location of household
    Age, sex, race, education of each member

Labor Force Information
    Employment status of each member
    Industry and occupation of employment
    Time worked for each member

Income Information
    Wage and salary earnings
    Self-employment earnings (including partnership and unincorporated business income)
    Farm income
    Social Security income
    Pension income
    Welfare and public assistance transfers
    Royalties
    Interest
    Dividends
    Capital gains
    Rental income
    Trust income

Balance Sheet Information
    Tangible assets
        owner-occupied housing
        other real estate
        automobiles
        other consumer durables

Financial Assets
    time and savings deposits, bonds (except state and local government), corporate stock, farm business equity
    unincorporated nonfarm equity

Liabilities
    mortgage debt
    other household debt

securities, corporate stock, farm business equity, and unincorporated non-farm equity are fully covered. However, demand deposits and currency, state and local government securities, trust fund equity, and insurance and pension reserves are not included. The coverage of financial assets amounts to 73 percent (1736.9 / 2392.6), and that of total assets equals 77 percent (2796.1 / 3612.8). Liabilities are fully covered in the database.

Not present in the asset list are the following: household inventories (semi-durables); state and local government securities; cash surrender value of life insurance; DB pension wealth; and Social Security entitlements.

Summary Estimates of the Size Distribution of Household Wealth

This section presents estimates of the distribution of household wealth in the United States in 1969 from the MESP database. I divide the household portfolio into five categories: owner-occupied home (primary home only); automobiles and other consumer durables; financial assets, including time and savings deposits, federal securities, corporate and foreign bonds, mortgages, open market paper, other instruments (excluding state and local government bonds), and corporate stock; farm business equity, unincorporated non-farm equity, and investment real estate (including second homes); and debt, including mortgage debt, consumer debt, and other personal loans. Total assets are the sum of the first four categories. Net worth is equal to total assets less debt.

The full sample consists of 63,457 households and is representative of the U.S. population as a whole for 1969 (see Table A2.9). In 1969 mean assets per household were $44,000 and mean net worth was $40,000. The concentration of ownership, as measured by the Gini coefficient, varied predictably by type of asset.[28] The Gini coefficient for consumer durables was quite low, at 0.30, and that for owner occupied housing was 0.68. Financial securities were highly concentrated with a Gini of 0.91. Business equity was the most concentrated of all, as indicated by a Gini coefficient of 0.94. The distribution of total assets was more unequal than that of consumer durables but less unequal than that of financial securities or of business equity; its Gini coefficient was 0.69. The distribution of net worth was more unequal than that of total assets, indicating an overall negative correlation between assets and debt.

Table A2.9. 1969 summary statistics for the full sample

Number of households	63,457
Mean asset value per household (current $)	$44,029
Mean net worth per household (current $)	$39,926
Gini coefficients	
Own home	0.68
Consumer durables	0.30
Financial securities[a]	0.91
Business equity[b]	0.94
Total assets	0.69
Net worth	0.81

a. This category includes time and savings deposits, stocks, bonds, government securities, mortgages, and other financial securities.

b. This category includes both farm and nonfarm business equity and investment real estate.

Conclusions and Cautions

A word of caution should be noted in the use of this database, even though general tests of its reliability have proved positive.[29] With any new database, there are certain problems and limitations in its use. Some can be corrected for or overcome with additional work and some cannot. In any synthetic database created through statistical matching techniques, certain conditional joint distributions are not reliable. In this case, the joint distributions of non-common variables in the PUS file and the IRS file conditional on a common variable cannot be used for estimation purposes, because this is the information that is lacking (and the rationale for performing the match). For example, the covariance of education (a PUS variable) and stock equity (an IRS variable) conditional on income (a common variable) will not be reliable in the MESP database. However, the overall (unconditional) covariance of education and stock equity can be reliably estimated.[30]

Other deficiencies involve the estimation of household assets and liabilities. These estimates might be improved with additional work. With regard to owner-occupied housing, currently, house values are recorded in eleven interval codes; some attempt might be made to "smooth out" the distribution using a random number generator. The estimation procedure for consumer durables might be improved by using the later 1972–1973 Consumer Expenditure Survey; full coverage of durables might also be possible. It would also be desirable to add stocks of semidurables to the household portfolio using the 1972–1973 Consumer Expenditure Survey.

The category of currency and demand deposits should also be added to the household portfolio.[31] With regard to financial securities, some attempt might be made to split time and savings deposits from bonds, mortgages, and other financial instruments, since the two groups of assets are currently aggregated into one category. It would also be desirable to add a separate imputation for nontaxed state and local government bonds, though appropriate data may be difficult to locate. Trust fund equity is not currently included in the household portfolio, and it would, of course, be desirable to include this, since a portion of the wealth of the rich is held in this form. One possible source for this imputation is the entry "trust fund income," which is currently in the IRS tax return data. Before this can be undertaken, the problem of whom to assign the assets of a trust to—whether the current beneficiary, the remainderman, or possibly the trustee—must be resolved. Pensions, too, should be added to the household portfolio, but here again important conceptual issues must first be resolved. For example, should only vested pensions be assigned to households? Should only redeemable pensions be imputed? How should one handle partially funded pensions? Should Social Security be included in pensions? Finally, the assignment of the cash surrender value of life insurance policies to households poses less serious conceptual problems than that of pensions. Here, the problem of obtaining pertinent data makes this imputation very rough, if not impossible.

Despite its limitations and deficiencies, the MESP database is still the most complete in coverage of both households and assets of any now available up to 1983. Moreover, unlike survey or administrative data sets, the MESP database, thanks to its methodology, allows continual modification, improvement, and expansion of asset and liability estimates and coverage. It is hoped that future use will result in this database's gradual improvement as a research tool.

Estimation of Retirement Wealth

This appendix provides methodological details on the construction of estimates for both Social Security wealth (SSW) and defined benefit pension wealth (DBW). Two methodologies were employed in my work. An earlier one was used for the 1962 SFCC and the 1983 SCF files. These estimates were used in Chapters 6, 11, 12, and 13. A later method was developed for the 1983, 1989, 2001, 2007, 2010, and 2013 SCF. The estimates were made use of in Chapters 8, 11, 12, and 13.

The Later Methodology—the 1983, 1989, 2001, 2007, 2010, and 2013 SCF

The imputation of both DBW and SSW involves a large number of steps. The standard definitions of DBW and SSW are based on the conventional "ongoing concern" treatment in which it is assumed that employees will continue to work at their place of employment until their expected date of retirement.

Defined Benefit Pension Wealth

For a retiree (r) the procedure is straightforward. Let PB be the pension benefit currently being received by the retiree. The SCF questionnaire indicates how many pension plans each spouse holds and what the expected (or current) pension benefit is. The SCF questionnaire also indicates whether the pension benefits remain fixed in nominal terms over time for a particular beneficiary or are indexed for inflation. In the case of the former, DBW is given by:

$$DBW_r = \int_0^{109-A} PB(1-m_t)e^{-\delta t}\, dt \tag{A3.1a}$$

and in the latter case,

$$DBW_r = \int_0^{109-A} PB(1-m_t)e^{-\delta^* t}\, dt \tag{A3.1b}$$

where A is the current age of the retiree; m_t is the mortality rate at time t conditional on age, gender, and race; δ^* is the real annual discount rate, set to 2 percent; γ is the inflation rate assumed to be 3 percent per year; $\delta = \delta^* + \gamma$ is the nominal annual discount rate, equal to 5 percent; and the integration runs from zero to the number of years when the retiree reaches an arbitrary age limit of 109.

Estimates of DBW (as well as SSW) are quite sensitive to the choice of inflation rate and discount rate. I chose a 3 percent inflation rate because it is very close to the actual average annual change of the Consumer Price Index (CPI-U) from 1983 to 2013. Moreover, I choose a 5 percent nominal discount rate because it likewise is close to the actual average annual rate of return on liquid assets over the same period. These two choices lead to a 2 percent *real* discount rate (the difference between the two rates). A higher real discount rate will lead to lower estimates of DBW (and likewise SSW), and, conversely, a lower discount rate will lead to higher estimates of these two variables.[1]

Among current workers (w) the procedure is more complex. The SCF provides detailed information on pension coverage among current workers, including the type of plan, the expected benefit at retirement or the formula used to determine the benefit amount (for example, a fixed percentage of the average of the last five years' earnings), the expected retirement age when the benefits are effective, the likely retirement age of the worker, and vesting requirements. Information is provided not only for the current job (or jobs) of each spouse but for up to five past jobs as well. On the basis of the information provided in the SCF and on projected future earnings, future expected pension benefits (EPB$_w$) are then projected to the year of retirement or the first year of pension eligibility. Then the present value of pension wealth for current workers (w) is given by:

$$DBW_w = \int_{LR}^{109-A} EPB(1-m_t)e^{-\delta t}\, dt \tag{A3.2}$$

where RA is the expected age of retirement and $LR = A - RA$ is the number of years to retirement. The integration runs from the number of years to retirement, LR, to the number of years when the retiree reaches age 109.[2]

The calculations of DBW for current workers are based on employee response, including his or her stated expected age of retirement. A couple of
studies have looked at the reliability of employee-provided estimates of
pension wealth by comparing self-reported pension benefits with estimates
based on provider data. Using data from the 1992 wave of the Health and
Retirement study other researchers have found that individual reports of
pension benefits tended to differ from those based on provider information.[3]
However, the latter also calculated that the median values of DB plans from
the two sources were quite close (about a 6 percent difference). As a result,
for *average* values of pension wealth, employee-provided estimates of expected pension benefits seem to be fairly reliable.

Social Security Wealth

For current Social Security beneficiaries (r), the procedure is again straightforward. Let SSB be the Social Security benefit currently being received by
the retiree. Again, the SCF provides information for both husband and wife.
Since Social Security benefits are indexed for inflation, SSW is given by

$$SSW_r = \int_0^{109-A} SSB(1-m_t)e^{-\delta^* t}\,dt \qquad (A3.3)$$

where it is assumed that the current Social Security rules remain in effect
indefinitely.[4]

The imputation of SSW among current workers is based on the worker's
actual and projected earnings history estimated by a standard human
capital regression equation. Coverage is assigned based on whether the
individual expects to receive Social Security benefits and on whether the individual was salaried or self-employed. On the basis of the person's earnings
history, the average indexed monthly earnings (AIME) are computed. On the
basis of the rules current at the time of the survey year, the person's primary
insurance amount (PIA) is derived from AIME. Then,

$$SSW_w = \int_{LR}^{109-A} PIA(1-m_t)e^{-\delta^* t}\,dt \qquad (A3.4)$$

As with pension wealth, the integration runs from the number of years to
retirement, LR, to the number of years when the retiree reaches age 109.[5]

Estimates of SSW are based on reported earnings at a single point in time.
These estimates are likely to be inferior to those based on longitudinal work
histories of individual workers.[6] In fact, actual work histories show more

variance in earnings over time than an estimate based on a human capital earnings function projection. Moreover, they also show many periods of work disruption that cannot be completely captured here. In contrast, I do have *retrospective* information on work history provided by the respondent. In particular, each individual is asked to provide data on the total number of years worked full-time since age 18, the number of years worked part-time since age 18, and the expected age of retirement (both from full-time and part-time work). On the basis of this information, it is possible to approximate the total number of full-time and part-time years worked over the individual's lifetime and use these figures in the calculation of the individual's AIME.[7]

I can now define the different accounting measures to be used. Total pension wealth, PW, is the sum of defined contribution (DC) wealth and DBW:

$$PW = DCW + DBW \tag{A3.5}$$

Let NWX be marketable household wealth excluding DC wealth or "non-pension" wealth. Private augmented wealth PAW is then defined as the sum of NWX and total pension wealth:

$$PAW = NWX + PW \tag{A3.6}$$

Augmented household wealth, AW, is given by

$$AW = NWX + PW + SSW. \tag{A3.7}$$

Alternative Concepts of Retirement Wealth

Four alternative concepts of retirement wealth are developed in Chapter 8. Here I provide details on the first two of these: employer and employee contributions to DC pension plans.

Employer Contributions to DC Pension Plans
The SCF questionnaire indicates how many DC pension plans each spouse has (up to three per spouse). Information on the employer contribution to DC pensions plans is recorded in two ways, a flat dollar amount or as a percent of earnings.

For the first method, the survey data does not indicate whether the dollar contribution is indexed to inflation over time. In my calculations I assume that it is indexed to the CPI, which seems the more likely arrangement (if anything, this assumption will bias up the estimate). Let EMPAMT be the dollar amount of the employer contribution to the DC plan. Then, in this case, the present value of the stream of future employer contributions, $DCEMP_a$, is given by:

$$DCEMP_a = \int_0^{LR} EMPAMT(1-m_t)e^{-\delta^* t} \, dt. \tag{A3.8a}$$

The integration runs from the current year to LR, where RA is the expected age of retirement and $LR = A - RA$ is the number of years to retirement.[8]

In most cases, the employer contribution is given as a percent of earnings. If it is assumed that the proportion EMPPER is fixed over time, then in this case, $DCEMP_b$ is given by:

$$DCEMP_b = \int_0^{LR} EMPPER \cdot E_t^*(1-m_t)e^{-\delta^* t} \, dt \tag{A3.8b}$$

where E_t^* is the predicted earnings of the worker at time t in constant dollars.

Employee Contributions to DC Pension Plans

The computation of employee (worker) contributions to DC pension plans (DCEMPW), like DCEMP, is based on data provided in the SCF, which indicates what fraction of the employee's salary is currently contributed into the employee's DC account. As with DCEMP, it is assumed that the worker continues to work for the same employer until retirement and that the contribution rate remains unchanged over time. DCEMPW is defined in exactly analogous fashion to DCEMP except that in Equation A3.8a the term EMPAMT is replaced by EMPAMTW, which is the dollar amount of the *employee* contribution to the DC plan and is assumed to remain fixed in real terms over time; and in Equation A3.8b the term EMPPER is replaced by EMPPERW, which is the *employee* contribution to the DC plan as a percent of earnings and is assumed to be fixed over time.

More Details on the Estimation of Pension and Social Security Wealth

I generally follow the methodology laid out in the 1983 Survey of Consumer Finances codebook. However, even though estimates of both pension and Social Security wealth were provided in the 1983 SCF, I reestimate the values of both to be consistent with later years. The computations of retirement wealth are detailed here.

Defined Benefit Pension Wealth

DBW consists of two main components.[9]

(1) The present value of DB pensions from past jobs; that is, the sum of the present value of past DB job pensions for head and spouse.
(2) The present value of DB pensions from current jobs; that is the sum of the present value of current job nonthrift benefits for head and spouse. Expectations data are used for calculations.

The procedure is as follows. Pension coverage is first ascertained for current jobs. There are five possible categories: (1) covered and vested, anticipates benefits; (2) covered but not vested yet, anticipates benefits; (3) covered but not vested yet, does not anticipate benefits; (4) not covered but anticipates will be (the age when expected to be covered is ascertained); and (5) not covered, never will be.

For those who are covered by a pension plan or expect coverage, the person is asked how many distinct pension plans he or she is covered by. For each plan, the age at which the pension benefits are expected to be received is provided.

The actual expected annual retirement benefit is then determined by the following steps. First, the age at which the respondent will be vested in each plan is determined. Second, the age at which the respondent could retire with full benefits is ascertained. Third, the respondent was asked the nature of the formula used to determine the retirement benefits. There are six possibilities: (1) retirement formula based on age; (2) retirement formula based on years of service; (3) retirement formula based on meeting both age and years of service criteria; (4) retirement formula based on the sum or age and years of service; (5) retirement formula based on meeting either age or years of service criteria; and (6) other combinations or formulas.

Fourth, the age at which the respondent could retire with some benefits was asked. The same six choices of the formula used were then given. Fifth, the age at which the respondent expected benefits to start was then asked.

Sixth, the expected retirement benefit was computed depending on the type of formula. This consists of three possibilities.

(1) The annual pay in the final year of the job was computed. This variable, used in pension benefit calculations, is computed by projecting current pay to the year respondents say he/she will leave the job or retire. This projection is based on human capital earnings equations detailed below and a real discount rate of 2 percent. Wage growth is based on the historical change in the Bureau of Labor Statistics' mean hourly wages series for nonsupervisory workers for the period and of hours worked per week from 1979 to 2013.[10]

(2) In some cases, the respondent reported expected retirement benefits. This variable is the expected dollar retirement benefits in the first year of eligibility as answered by the respondent. For some observations the dollar amount was reported directly, but for others it was computed by multiplying reported benefits as a percentage of final earnings times the projected final earnings. The variable is given as an annual amount except when a lump sum is expected (in which case the lump sum amount is given).

(3) In other cases, the respondent reported expected retirement benefits as a percent of final pay. This variable is the expected retirement benefits in the first year of eligibility as answered by the respondent, expressed as a percent of their projected wages in their final year of work. For some observations the percent was reported directly, but for others it was computed by dividing the reported dollar benefit by the calculated projected final wage.

Seventh, on the basis of the responses above, the present value of pension benefits from each current and past plan applicable to both head and spouse is then computed. This variable is measured assuming an annual (or lump sum) pension benefit as given above, starting in the year of first benefits. Benefits for that and each succeeding year are adjusted for the probability of death and are discounted back to the survey year. For this, I use mortality rates by age, gender, and race in the computation of the present value of both DBW and SSW.[11] These are capped at 109 years. Spousal survival benefits are assumed to be opted for 75 percent the time and are randomly assigned when appropriate. Spousal survival benefits are also adjusted for death probabilities. Benefits are discounted at a real discount rate of 2 percent.

Eighth, pension wealth is also computed for those individuals currently receiving pension benefits from past jobs. This is based on the following responses: (1) number of years receiving benefits and (2) amount of pension benefit pay received in the year preceding the survey year. For pensions already being received, the nominal value of the pension is assumed to be fixed, and is indexed to the year it started by the actual price changes observed as measured by the CPI. The present value of pension benefits from each job is then measured assuming an annual pension benefit from the survey year onward. Benefits for that and each succeeding year (adjusted for probability of survival) are discounted back to the survey year. As before, I use mortality rates by age, gender, and race in the computation of the present value of both pensions and SSW. These are capped at 109 years. Spousal survival benefits are assumed to be opted for 75 percent of the time and are randomly assigned when appropriate. Spouse mortality tables are also used, and benefits are discounted a real discount rate of 2 percent.

Social Security Wealth

The present value of Social Security benefits is defined as: The sum of the present value of Social Security benefits for head and spouse. Social Security formulae and current receipts are used for calculations.

Among current Social Security benefit recipients, the steps are as follows: First, it is determined which kind of Social Security benefit is to be received. The possibilities are (1) retirement; (2) disability; (3) both retirement and disability; and (4) other kind. I use only types (1) and (3) in the calculation of SSW. Second, the respondent was asked the number of years receiving Social Security benefits. Third, both head and spouse were asked the amount received in the survey year.

Among future recipients, the steps are as follows. First, both head and spouse were asked to report the age at which they expected to receive Social Security benefits (zero if he or she does not expect benefits). Second, the number of years until the start of Social Security benefits is determined. Third, the respondent was asked the total number of years on Social Security jobs to current date. If this was not answered, then an estimate of Social Security coverage is used, summing over current and three possible past jobs. Fourth, an estimate of future years on Social Security jobs is computed from retirement years indicated by head and spouse.

Fifth, data on number of years on Social Security jobs, wage rates for each known job, estimates of retirement dates, and dates of starting benefits are used as inputs to Social Security formulae to compute benefits. Sixth, estimates of Social Security benefits are provided. A calculated value is based on current job wage. All persons are assumed to work continuously until their stated age of full-time retirement, and then part-time until their stated age of final retirement. All persons are assumed to retire no later than 72 or age plus one if currently over 72. Persons not currently working and over 50 are assumed not to work again. Wages are calculated by projecting current wages by the same method used to calculate final wages. This projection is based on human capital earnings equations detailed below and a real discount rate of 2 percent. Wage growth is based on the historical change in the Bureau of Labor Statistics' mean hourly wages series for nonsupervisory workers for the period and of hours worked per week from 1979 to 2013. Part-time years (if currently working full-time) are assigned wages equal to one half the projected full-time wages or the maximum amount allowable for full benefit receipt allowed by Social Security, whichever is smaller.

Seventh, the Social Security AIME used as the basis of computing the Social Security benefit base is computed. The variable is the average covered Social Security earnings per month (including zeros) for all years from 1937 or age 22 (whichever is later) to age 60. These are indexed by a Social Security wage index to the year the respondent is age 60. Years after 60 can be substituted at nominal value. The highest 35 years are used to compute the person's AIME. These procedures are mimicked using the SCF data on job earnings and future retirement plans to estimate an AIME value. Past and current job wages are projected back (and forward) to estimate earnings for each known year of work. As before, these projections are based on human capital earnings equations detailed below and a real discount rate of 2 percent. Wage changes are based on the historical change in the Bureau of Labor Statistics' mean hourly wages series for nonsupervisory workers for the period and of hours worked per week from 1979 to 2013. Other years of unknown jobs are filled in with terms from the closest known job to fill in the total number of Social Security covered years. Wages are then capped at the actual or projected Social Security maximum and minimum coverage amounts. The AIME is then computed using actual or projected Social Security wage indices. The variable is currently estimated for all persons projected to have future Social Security retirement benefits.

Eighth, the Social Security PIA is computed on an annual basis for the calculation of Social Security benefits. It is computed from the AIME. In 1982 the monthly PIA was computed as 90 percent of the first $254 of AIME plus 32 percent of the next $1274 plus 15 percent of the amount above that.

Calculations for future years up through 2013 use the formula for that year and for years after 2013 they take account of legislatively planned changes in this formula. The PIA is currently computed for all individuals projected to have future Social Security benefits.

Ninth, the present value of Social Security benefits is then computed assuming an annual benefit as given by the PIA estimate and starting in the year of first benefits (or the survey year). Benefits for that and each succeeding year (adjusted for probability of receipt) are discounted back to the survey year. As before, I use mortality rates by age, gender, and race in the computation of the present value of SSW. These are capped at 109 years. Benefits are discounted at a real discount rate of 2 percent.

Tenth, spousal benefits are also assumed at 50 percent of the primary benefit if a spouse is present. However, this variable will be zero if no spousal benefits are expected (such as when the individual's own benefits are larger than their spousal benefits). The age at which spousal benefits begin is estimated. Spouse mortality tables are also used for these calculations. The age at which widow's or widower's benefits first can be drawn is also estimated. It is an estimate of the age at which the individual could start to receive Social Security widow's or widower's benefits upon the death of the spouse. This variable will be zero if widow's benefits could never be drawn. An adjustment is also made if it appears that the recipient's benefits had been reduced because of work. Benefits are discounted at a real discount rate of 2 percent.

Human Capital Earnings Equations

The regression equations used to compute future and past earnings are as follows: Human capital earnings functions are estimated by gender, race, and schooling level. In particular, the sample is divided into 16 groups by the following characteristics: white and Asian versus African American and Hispanic; male and female; and less than 12 years of schooling, 12 years of schooling, 13 to 15 years of schooling, and 16 or more years. For each group, an earnings equation is estimated as follows:

$$\mathrm{Ln}(E_i) = b_0 + b_1 \, \mathrm{Log}(H_i) + b_2 \, X_i + b_3 \, X_i^2 + b_4 \, SE_i + \Sigma_j \, b_j OCCUP_{ij}$$
$$+ b_{10} \, MAR_i + b_{11} \, AS_I + \varepsilon_i, \tag{A3.9}$$

where ln is the natural logarithm; E_i is the current earnings of individual i; H_i is annual hours worked in the current year; X_i is years of experience at current age (estimated as age minus years of schooling minus 5); SE_i is a dummy variable indicating whether the person is self-employed or working for someone else; OCCUP is a set of five dummy variables indicating occupation of employment: (a) professional and managerial; (b) technical, sales, or administrative support; (c) service; (d) craft, and (e) other blue-collar, with farming the omitted category; MAR is a dummy variable indicating whether the person is married or not married; AS is a dummy variable indicating whether the person is Asian or not (used only for regressions on the first racial category); and ε is a stochastic error term. Future earnings are projected on the basis of the regression coefficients.[12]

Questions on Work History

Following is a sample of questions on work history drawn from the 1989 SCF codebook that is used to calculate the earnings profile of both head and spouse and to calculate the AIME for each:

1. Including any periods of self-employment, the military, and your current job, since you were 18, how many years have you worked full-time for all or most of the year?
2. Not counting your current job, have you ever had a full-time job that lasted for three years or more?
3. I want to know about the longest such job you had. Did you work for someone else, were you self-employed, or what?
4. When did you start working at that job?
5. When did you stop working at that job?
6. Since you were 18, have there been years when you only worked part-time for all or most of the year?
7. About how many years in total did you work part-time for all or most of the year?
8. Thinking now of the future, when do you expect to stop working full-time?
9. Do you expect to work part-time after that?
10. When do you expect to stop working altogether?

Questions on Defined Contributions Plans

1. Does your employer make contributions to this [Defined Contribu-
   tion] plan? Does the business make contributions to this plan?
2. What percent of pay or amount of money per month or year does
   your employer currently contribute?

The Earlier Methodology—The 1962 SFCC and the 1983 SCF

A slightly different methodology was employed to estimate DBW and SSW
than that used in Chapter 8 in order to ensure compatibility between the
1962 and 1983 wealth data. As in Chapter 8, the present value of DBW for
current retirees (r), DBWA, is given by:[13]

$$DBWA_r = \int_0^{LE} PBe^{-\delta t} \, dt \qquad (A3.10)$$

where PB is the pension benefit currently received by the retiree, LE is the
conditional life expectancy, and δ is the nominal discount rate, for which the
(nominal) ten-year U.S. Treasury Bill rate is used. For current Social Security beneficiaries,

$$SSWA_r = \int_0^{LE} SSBe^{-(g'-\delta^*)t} \, dt \qquad (A3.11)$$

where SSB is the currently received Social Security benefit, g' is the expected
real rate of growth of Social Security benefits over time for retirees, and δ^*
is the real discount rate, estimated as the (nominal) ten-year U.S. Treasury
Bill rate less the average rate of increase of the CPI over the previous ten
years.[14]

Among current workers (w) the procedure was more complex. For DBW
in 1962, a two-stage imputation was necessary. The first stage assigned pension coverage. The total number of covered workers was estimated for 1962[15]
and information was obtained on relative coverage rates by incomes class,
industry of employment, age, and sex of worker.[16] Based on these data, pension coverage was randomly assigned among workers.[17]

In the second stage, accumulated earnings (actually, AE1) from the start
of working life to the present were estimated for each covered worker (see
Equations A3.23 and A3.24). Covered workers in a given age cohort were

then assigned a percentile ranking n based on the distribution of AE1 for their cohort. It was assumed throughout that current workers retire at age 65.[18] Their expected pension benefit, EPB, was then given by,

$$EPB_n = PB_n e^{g''(65-A_c)} \text{ (1962 only)} \tag{A3.12}$$

where PB_n is the n-th percentile among pension benefits of beneficiaries of age 65 and g" is the expected real rate of growth of average pension benefits. Then pension wealth for current workers in the n-th percentile was given by:

$$DBWA_{w,n} = \int_0^{LD} EPB_n \, e^{gt} \cdot e^{-\delta^*(t+LR)} \, dt \tag{A3.13}$$

where $LR = 65 - A_c$ is the years to retirement and $LD = LE - 65$. For the 1983 SCF data, matters were much easier, since pension coverage and expected pension benefits were already provided for current workers.

The imputation of SSW among current workers was analogous to that of pension wealth. For the 1962 data, coverage was assigned based on employment status. Workers were again assigned a percentile ranking n based on the accumulated earnings (AE1) for their age group. The expected Social Security benefit at retirement (at age 65), ESSB, was given by

$$EESB_n = SSB_n \cdot e^{g(65-A_c)} \tag{A3.14}$$

where SSB_n is the n-th percentile of Social Security benefits among beneficiaries of age 65. Then:

$$SSWA_{w,n} = \int_0^{LD} ESSB_n \, e^{gt} \cdot e^{-\delta^*(t+LR)} \, dt \tag{A3.15}$$

where g is the expected real rate of growth in mean Social Security benefits for new retirees. The procedure for the 1983 data was identical, except that information on Social Security coverage for current workers was already provided.

I can now define the different accounting measures to be used. Let NWXB be marketable household wealth excluding defined contribution pension wealth, DCW.[19] Then:

$$NWB = NWXB + DCW. \tag{A3.16}$$

Total pension wealth, PWA, is given by:

$$PWA = DCW + DBWA. \tag{A3.17}$$

Augmented household wealth, AWB, is then given by

$$AWB = NWXA + PWA + SSWA. \tag{A3.18}$$

One other variable of interest here is human capital, defined as the present value of lifetime earnings, from the start of working life to retirement. Human capital earnings functions were estimated for each worker based on sex, race, and schooling to obtain $f_i(A)$, expected earnings for each worker i at age A, assuming no growth in average real earnings. Then, the present value of the stream of future earnings for individual i, $FE1_i$, is given by:

$$FE1_i = \int_{A_c}^{65} \left[f_i(A) \cdot E_i / f_i(A_c) \right] \cdot e^{(k - \delta^*)} dA \tag{A3.19}$$

where I used the alternative estimate of lifetime earnings, AE1, in which I adjusted lifetime earnings according to how current earnings deviated from the average (regression line) earnings for the age and demographic group of household head i and k is the expected rate of growth of mean labor earnings, for which values of 0.01 and 0.02 were used. Then, for workers,

$$HK_w = AE1 + FE1 \tag{A3.20}$$

Among retirees, human capital was imputed for Social Security beneficiaries only and was based on their percentile rank in the distribution of Social Security benefits. For a beneficiary in the n-th percentile, his (or her) estimated human capital at retirement (at age 65), EHK, is given by:

$$EHK_{r,n} = HK_n e^{-k^*(A_c - 65)} \tag{A3.21}$$

where HK_n is the n-th percentile of human capital among 64 year olds and k^* is the average real rate of growth of mean earnings since retirement. This procedure, by the way, captured the cohort effect on real earnings growth. Then,

$$HK_{r,n} = EHK_{r,n} \cdot e^{\delta^*(A_c - 65)} = HK_n \cdot e^{(\delta^* - k^*) \cdot (A_c - 65)} \tag{A3.22}$$

gives the present value of the individual's human capital.[20]

Human Capital Estimation

I used standard human capital earnings functions to estimate lifetime earnings.[21] Since I observed earnings for each household at one point in time, say

1962, it was necessary to make lifetime earnings estimates using cross-sectional data rather than longitudinal data. The procedure was as follows:

First, the sample was partitioned by the following characteristics:

(a) Race: whites and Asians ("whites," for short) versus others;
(b) Residence: urban and suburban ("urban," for short) versus rural;
(c) Occupation: professionals versus farmers versus others;
(d) Education: 0–11 years / 12 years / 13–15 years / 16 or more years.

Second, within each of these subgroups the current annual wage and salary earnings of the head of household was regressed on A and A^2 to obtain the average lifetime earnings profile for this group. Third, computations were performed from the regression results to estimate lifetime earnings up to current age for each racial, residential, schooling, and occupational group:

$$AE_i = \int_{A_0}^{A_c} f_i(A)e^{-g(A_c-A)}\,dA \tag{A3.23}$$

where AE_i is accumulated lifetime earnings for individual i from the end of schooling (A_0) to current age (A_c), $f_i(A)$ is the cross-sectional estimated age-earnings profile for the appropriate demographic group for i, and the earnings growth parameter $g_i = 0.0$, 0.01, 0.02, or 0.03.[22]

I also used an alternative estimate of accumulated earnings, AE1, in which I adjusted lifetime earnings according to how current earnings deviate from the average (regression line) earnings for the age and demographic group of household head i:

$$AE1_i = AE_i \cdot E_i / f_i(A_c) \text{ for } g = 0.0, 0.01, 0.02, \text{ or } 0.03. \tag{A3.24}$$

where E_i is the current earnings of individual i.[23]

Notes

1. Plan of the Book and Historical Backdrop

1. The chapter relies on publicly available data from the Current Population Survey, the Bureau of Labor Statistics, the National Income and Product Accounts, and other secondary sources. This chapter builds on previous work, presented in Edward N. Wolff, "The Stagnating Fortunes of the Middle Class," *Social Philosophy and Policy* 191, no. 4 (2002): 55–83; Wolff, ed., "Recent Trends in Living Standard in the United States," in *What Has Happened to the Quality of Life in the Advanced Industrialized Nations?* (Cheltenham, U.K.: Edward Elgar Publishing Ltd., 2004), 3–26; Wolff, "Rising Profitability and the Middle Class Squeeze," *Science & Society* 74, no. 3 (2010): 429–49; Wolff, "Inequality and Rising Profitability in the United States, 1947–2013," *International Review of Applied Economics* 29, no. 6 (2015): 741–69, available at http://www.tandfonline.com/doi/pdf/10.1080/02692171.2014.956704.

2. See http://www.nber.org/cycles/cyclesmain.html, accessed April 20, 2014. Though the "official" recession ended in 2009, I use the term "Great Recession" to refer to the period from 2007 to 2013 since household income remained relatively stagnant over these years.

3. The source for the GDP figures is http://www.bea.gov/iTable/index_nipa .cfm, accessed December 1, 2016.

4. U.S. Bureau of Labor Statistics, available at http://data.bls.gov/timeseries /LNS14000000, accessed December 1, 2016.

5. The data source is the U.S. Bureau of the Census, Current Population Survey, available at http://www.census.gov/hhes/www/income/histinc/, accessed December 1, 2016. Figures are in 2013 dollars unless otherwise indicated. It would actually be preferable to use *household* income rather than *family* income. Unfortunately, the official U.S. Bureau of the Census series on household income begins only in 1967, whereas family income data are available from 1947 onward. I also use the Census Bureau recommended consumer price index (CPI-U-RS) to deflate incomes over time. It should also be noted that CPS income data are "top-coded"— that is, have an upward bound in the public use sample. The upward bound varies

by year and income type. In recent years it is typically $100,000 for overall income but lower for certain income categories like interest and also lower in earlier year.

6. These figures are based on the U.S. Bureau of Labor Statistics (BLS) hourly wage series for production and nonsupervisory workers in private, nonagricultural industries. See U.S. Council of Economic Advisers, *Economic Report of the President, 2015,* available at http://www.gpo.gov/fdsys/pkg/ERP-2015/pdf/ERP-2015-table15.pdf, accessed December 1, 2016. This is the most widely used wage series. The BLS converts nominal wage figures to constant dollars on the basis of the Consumer Price Index (CPI-U).

7. These two are the National Income and Product Accounts wages and salaries per full-time equivalent employee (FTEE) and employee compensation (the sum of wages and salaries and employee benefits) per FTEE. Both series are deflated to constant dollars using the CPI-U price index. A third not shown here, employee compensation plus half of proprietors' income per person engaged in production, shows very similar time trends.

8. The data are taken from U.S. Bureau of the Census, *Statistical Abstract 2012,* Table 597, available at http://www.census.gov/prod/2011pubs/12statab/labor.pdf, accessed December 1, 2016.

9. U.S. Bureau of Labor Statistics, *Women in the Labor Force: A Databook,* February 2013, Table 4, available at http://www.bls.gov/cps/wlf-databook-2012.pdf, accessed December 1, 2016.

10. The data source is the U.S. Bureau of the Census, Current Population Survey, available at http://www.census.gov/hhes/www/income/histinc/, accessed December 1, 2016. These figures are based on unadjusted data.

11. The source is the World Top Incomes Database, available at http://topincomes.parisschoolofeconomics.eu/, accessed December 1, 2016.

12. The rates quoted here are for married couples, filing jointly. The data are from http://www.irs.gov/, accessed December 1, 2016.

13. The 39.6 percent rate in 2013 was effective for AGI above $400,000 for singles and above $450,000 for married couples.

14. In the case of an economy characterized by competitive input markets and constant returns to scale, it follows that wages and labor productivity should grow at exactly the same rate. In particular,

$$w = \partial X / \partial L = \varepsilon_L \, X / L$$

where w is the wage rate, X is total output, L is total employment, and ε_L is output elasticity of labor, which equals the wage share in this special case.

15. Results are shown for employee compensation per FTEE. Results are almost identical for employee compensation plus half of proprietors' income per Persons Employed in Production. The data source is U.S. Bureau of Economic Analysis, National Income and Product Accounts, available at http://www.bea.gov/bea/dn/nipaweb/SelectTable.asp, accessed October 22, 2015.

16. This definition of capital income excludes the pay of CEOs and other top management, bonuses, stock options, and the like, which are counted as labor compensation. If these components were included in capital income instead, the rise in the capital share since 1980 or so would be even greater than reported here.

17. From http://topincomes.parisschoolofeconomics.eu/.

18. The poverty rate series begins only in 1959.

19. Regression results for the corporate profit rate and corporate profit share are very similar because the two variables are highly correlated (a correlation coefficient of 0.89).

20. See Edward N. Wolff, *Poverty and Income Distribution,* 2nd ed. (New York: Wiley-Blackwell, 2009), chapter 3, for a discussion of rising income inequality and Engelbert Stockhammer, "Rising Inequality as a Cause of the Present Crisis," *Cambridge Journal of Economics* (2013), doi: 10.1093/cje/bet052 in regard to rising profit share.

21. William Lazonick, *Sustainable Prosperity in the New Economy?* (Kalamazoo, MI: W.E. Upjohn Institute for Employment Research, 2009).

22. See Dave Jamieson, "Union Membership Rate for U.S. Workers Tumbles to New Low," *Huffington Post,* May 4, 2015, available at http://www.huffingtonpost.com/2013/01/23/union-membership-rate_n_2535063.html, accessed December 5, 2016.

23. See David M. Gordon, *Fat and Mean: The Corporate Squeeze of Working Americans and the Myth of Managerial "Downsizing"* (New York: Free Press, 1996).

24. See Francine D. Blau and Lawrence M. Kahn, "International Differences in Male Wage Inequality: Institutions versus Market Forces," *Journal of Political Economy* 104, no. 4 (1996): 791–836.

25. A full analysis of the factors accounting for rising income inequality and a declining wage share is beyond the scope of the current volume. However, it is useful to mention two other important factors. The first is globalization. The emergence of China as a manufacturing export powerhouse and trade liberalization generally put downward pressure on U.S. wages, especially for less skilled workers. The second is the immigration of unskilled (including illegal) workers into the United States, which likely had a similar impact. For a more complete analysis, see Edward N. Wolff, "Inequality and Rising Profitability in the United States, 1947–2013," *International Review of Applied Economics* 29, no. 6 (2015): 741–69, available at http://www.tandfonline.com/doi/pdf/10.1080/02692171.2014.956704.

2. Trends in Household Wealth, 1962 to 2013

1. As noted below, though the "official" recession ended in June 2009, according to the National Bureau of Economic Research (NBER) definition, I refer to the period 2007 to 2013 as the Great Recession, since median income and wealth showed no recovery over these years.

2. This chapter is based on previous work: Edward N. Wolff, "The Distribution of Household Disposable Wealth in the United States," *The Review of Income and Wealth* series 29, no. 2, (June 1983): 125–46; Wolff, "Estimates of Household Wealth Inequality in the United States, 1962–83," *Review of Income and Wealth* series 33, no. 3 (September 1987): 231–56; Wolff, "Methodological Issues in the Estimation of the Size Distribution of Household Wealth," *Journal of Econometrics* 43, no. 1/2 (January/February 1990): 179–95; Wolff, "The Distribution of Household Wealth: Methodological Issues, Time Trends, and Cross-Sectional Comparisons," in *Economic Inequality and Poverty: International Perspectives*, ed. Lars Osberg (Armonk, NY: M. E. Sharpe, 1991), 92–133; Wolff, "Changing Inequality of Wealth," *American Economic Review Papers and Proceedings* 82, no. 2 (May 1992): 552–58; Wolff, "Trends in Household Wealth in the United States, 1962–1983 and 1983–1989," *Review of Income and Wealth* series 40, no. 2 (June 1994): 143–74; Wolff, "The Rich Get Increasingly Richer: Latest Data on Household Wealth during the 1980s," in *Research in Politics and Society* (Stamford, CT: JAI Press, 1995), 5:33–68; Wolff, *Top Heavy: A Study of Increasing Inequality of Wealth in America* (New York: The Twentieth Century Fund Press, 1995); Wolff, "Recent Trends in the Size Distribution of Household Wealth," *Journal of Economic Perspectives* 12, no. 3 (Summer 1998): 131–50; Wolff, "Recent Trends in Wealth Ownership, from 1983 to 1998," in *Assets for the Poor: The Benefits of Spreading Asset Ownership*, ed. Thomas M. Shapiro and Edward N. Wolff (New York: Russell Sage Press, 2001), 34–73; Wolff, ed., "Changes in Household Wealth in the 1980s and 1990s in the U.S.," in *International Perspectives on Household Wealth* (Cheltenham, U.K.: Edward Elgar Publishing Ltd., 2006), 107–50; Wolff, "Recent Trends in Household Wealth in the U.S.: Rising Debt and the Middle Class Squeeze," in *Economics of Wealth in the 21st Century*, ed. Jason M. Gonzales (Hauppauge, NY: Nova Science Publishers, Inc., 2011), 1–41; Wolff, "The Distribution of Wealth in the United States at the Start of the 21st Century," in *The Economics of Inequality, Poverty, and Discrimination in the 21st Century*, ed. Robert S. Rycroft (Santa Barbara, CA: ABC-CLIO, 2013), 38–56; Wolff, "The Asset Price Meltdown, Rising Leverage, and the Wealth of the Middle Class," *Journal of Economic Issues* 47, no. 2 (June 2013), 333–42; Wolff, "Household Wealth Trends in the United States, 1983–2010," *Oxford Review of Economic Policy* 30, no. 1 (2013): 21–43; Wolff, "The Asset Price Meltdown and Household Wealth over the Great Recession in the United States," in *Research in Economic Inequality* (Bingley, U.K.: Emerald Group Publishing Ltd., 2014), 22:1–42; Wolff, "The Middle Class: Losing Ground, Losing Wealth," in *Diversity and Disparities: America Enters a New Century*, ed. John R. Logan (New York: Russell Sage Foundation, 2014), 60–104; Wolff, "Wealth Inequality," *Pathways, The Poverty and Inequality Report*, Special Issue: State of the Union (2014): 34–41; Wolff, "Household Wealth Trends in the United States, 1962–2013: What Happened over the Great Recession?" NBER Working Paper no. 20733, December 2014. See also Edward N. Wolff, Lindsay A.

Owens, and Esra Burak, "How Much Wealth was Destroyed in the Great Recession?" in *The Great Recession,* ed. David B. Grusky, Bruce Western, and Christopher Wimer (New York: Russell Sage Foundation Press, 2011), 127–58.

3. The source for years 1989 to 2007 is Table 935 of the *2009 Statistical Abstract,* U.S. Bureau of the Census, available at http://www.census.gov/compendia /statab/. For years after 2007, the source is National Association of Realtors, "Median Sales Price of Existing Single-Family Homes for Metropolitan Areas," available at http://www.realtor.org/sites/default/files/reports/2012/embargoes /2012-q1-metro-home-prices-49bc10b1efdc1b8cc3eb66dbcdad55f7/metro -home-prices-q1-single-family-2012-05-09.pdf, both accessed October 17, 2014. The figures are based on median prices of existing houses for metropolitan areas only. All figures are in constant (2013) dollars unless otherwise indicated.

4. The Case-Schiller 20-City Composite Home Price NSA Index showed a rather different trend. It advanced by 35 percent from January 2001 to January 2004, and then by 33.5 percent from January 2004 to January 2007 (see https://fred.stlouisfed .org/series/SPCS20RSA, accessed December 9, 2016). It is not clear why the trends are so different between the two sources. However, the Case-Shiller index is based on data from the largest twenty metropolitan areas, whereas the National Association of Realtors index is much broader based, covering some 160 metropolitan areas. For my purposes here, the latter is a more reliable indicator of national housing price movements.

5. See http://www.nber.org/cycles/cyclesmain.html, accessed April 20, 2014. As noted previously, I use the term "Great Recession" to refer to the period from 2007 through 2013.

6. The source for the GDP figures is http://www.bea.gov/iTable/index_nipa .cfm, accessed December 1, 2016.

7. See U.S. Bureau of Labor Statistics at http://data.bls.gov/timeseries /LNS14000000, accessed December 1, 2016.

8. The Case-Shiller index shows a 27.9 percent drop from January 2007 to January 2010.

9. The Case-Shiller index indicates a 0.9 percent gain from January 2010 to January 2013.

10. The source for stock prices is Table B-96 of the *Economic Report of the President, 2013,* available at http://www.gpoaccess.gov/eop/tables13.html, with updates to 2013 from http://us.spindices.com/indices/equity/sp-composite-1500, both accessed October 17, 2014.

11. These figures are based on the BLS hourly wage series. The source is Table B-15 of the *Economic Report of the President, 2014,* available at http://www.gpo.gov /fdsys/pkg/ERP-2014/pdf/ERP-2014-table15.pdf, accessed October 17, 2014. The BLS wage figures are converted to constant dollars on the basis of the Consumer Price Index (CPI-U).

12. The figure is for civilian employment. The source is Table B-14 of the *Economic Report of the President, 2014,* available at http://www.gpo.gov/fdsys/pkg/ERP-2014/pdf/ERP-2014-table14.pdf, accessed October 17, 2014.

13. See Table B-12 of the *Economic Report of the President, 2014,* available at http://www.gpo.gov/fdsys/pkg/ERP-2014/pdf/ERP-2014-table12.pdf, accessed October 17, 2014.

14. These figures are based on the Federal Reserve Board's Financial Accounts of the United States (formerly, the Flow of Funds data), Table B.100, available at http://www.federalreserve.gov/releases/Z1/, accessed October 17, 2014.

15. Unfortunately, no data on educational loans are available before the 2004 SCF.

16. The computation of DB pension wealth is based on the present value of expected pension benefits upon retirement. See Chapter 8 for details.

17. See Constance F. Citro and Robert T. Michael, eds., *Measuring Poverty: A New Approach* (Washington, DC: National Academy Press, 1995).

18. See Dalton Conley, *Being Black, Living in the Red: Race, Wealth and Social Policy in America* (Berkeley: University of California Press, 1999).

19. See Seymour Spilerman, "Wealth and Stratification Processes," *American Review of Sociology* 26, no. 1 (2000): 497–524.

20. For a more extended discussion of the design of the list sample in the 2001 SCF, see Arthur B. Kennickell, "Modeling Wealth with Multiple Observations of Income: Redesign of the Sample for the 2001 Survey of Consumer Finances" (October 2001), available at http://www.federalreserve.gov/pubs/oss/oss2/method.html.

21. For a discussion of some of the issues involved in developing these weights, see the following: 1989 SCF, Arthur B. Kennickell and R. Louise Woodburn, "Estimation of Household Net Worth Using Model-Based and Design-Based Weights: Evidence from the 1989 Survey of Consumer Finances," Federal Reserve Board of Washington, April 1992, unpublished paper; 1992 SCF, Kennickell, Douglas A. McManus, and R. Louise Woodburn, "Weighting Design for the 1992 Survey of Consumer Finances," Federal Reserve Board of Washington, March 1996, unpublished paper; 1995 SCF, Kennickell and Woodburn, "Consistent Weight Design for the 1989, 1992, and 1995 SCFs, and the Distribution of Wealth," *Review of Income and Wealth* series 45, no. 2 (June 1999), 193–216; and 2001 SCF, Kennickell, "Modeling Wealth with Multiple Observations of Income."

22. See Appendix Table 2.1 for sample sizes by year and household characteristic.

23. On the other hand, the value of antiques, jewelry, art objects, and other "valuables" are included in the SCF in the category "other assets."

24. Another rationale is that if vehicles were included in the household portfolio, their "rate of return" would be substantially negative since they depreciate very rapidly over time (see Chapter 3 for calculations of the overall rate of return on the household portfolio).

25. Later on I do include these two components in what I call "augmented wealth." See Chapter 8 for a discussion and estimates of Social Security and defined benefit pension wealth.

26. FR does include "valuables" like artwork, which can be sold without significantly lowering a family's standard of living, as well as business assets that may be illiquid in the short term. As a result, FR is not a 100 percent pure concept since it includes some illiquid assets as well.

27. See Dorothy Projector and Gertrude Weiss, *Survey of Financial Characteristics of Consumers,* Federal Reserve Board Technical Papers (Washington, DC: Board of Governors of the Federal Reserve System, 1966).

28. See Wolff, "Estimates of Household Wealth Inequality in the United States, 1962–83," and Appendix 1 of this book for details on the adjustments.

29. See Appendix 1 of this book for details on adjustments made to the 1962 SFCC and the 1983 and 1989 SCF data files and Appendix 2 for details on the construction of the 1969 MESP data file. It should be noted that these four surveys were aligned to national balance sheet totals in order to provide consistency in the household wealth estimates, since they each use somewhat different sampling frames and methodologies. (The methodology for the 1983 SCF differs to some extent from that for the 1989 SCF, while the same methodology is used for SCF files for 1989 and onward). The 1992 SCF, the 1995 SCF, and the 1998 SCF also required some minor adjustments because they both showed serious discrepancies with the national balance sheet figures. My baseline estimates also exclude vehicles. Moreover, my calculations are based on the "public use" samples provided by the Federal Reserve Board, which are to some degree different from the internal files maintained by the Federal Reserve. As a result, my figures on mean and median net worth, as well as on wealth inequality, will in general be at a slight variance from the "standard" estimates provided by the Federal Reserve Board, which include the value of vehicles in their statistics (see, for example, Kennickell and Woodburn, "Consistent Weight Design for the 1989, 1992, and 1995 SCFs, and the Distribution of Wealth").

30. Unless otherwise indicated, all dollar figures are in 2013 dollars.

31. The percentage decline in median net worth from 2007 to 2010 was lower when vehicles were included in the measure of wealth—"only" 39 percent. The reason is that automobiles comprise a substantial share of the assets of the middle class. However, median net worth with vehicles remained virtually unchanged from 2010 to 2013.

32. The decline in mean net worth was also 16 percent when vehicles were included in net worth.

33. This is not to say that there was no major change in wealth inequality over these years. Indeed, on the basis of estate tax data, Wolff, *Top Heavy: A Study of Increasing Wealth Inequality in America* (New York: The New Press, 2002), documents a sharp reduction in wealth inequality from about 1969 to 1976 and then a sharp rise from 1976 to 1983. See Chapter 12 for details.

34. These years coincided with the last part of the Reagan administration and the first year of the George H. W. Bush administration. However, it is hard to think of specific policies of theirs that might have been responsible for the sharp spike in both income and wealth inequality, except, perhaps, the passage of the Tax Reform Act of 1986, which substantially lowered marginal tax rates on high income. This change put more disposable (after-tax) income into the hands of the rich, leading to greater savings and wealth accumulation.

35. This difference, by the way, shows the danger of relying on the share of the top 1 percent as a measure of inequality, as has been done in many studies, since it tracks differently over time than the Gini coefficient (see Figure 2.6).

36. Actually, the big slippage in the share of the top 1 percent occurred between 1998 and 2001. The main reason appears to be the "high tech" boom and bust, which sent stock prices in constant dollars up by 24 percent between 1998 and 2000 and then back to its 1998 level by 2001. House prices in real terms, on the other hand, rose by 12 percent between 1998 and 2001. There also appeared to be a sizeable drop in the share of households in the top 1 percent owning their own business, from 72 to 66 percent. Whereas the mean net worth of the top 1 percent increased by 13.5 percent, the mean value of unincorporated business equity and other real estate grew by only 6.2 percent.

37. It might seem somewhat surprising that wealth inequality remained relatively unchanged during the latter part of the George H. W. Bush administration, the Clinton administration, and the George W. Bush administration. As we shall see in Chapter 3, the stability in wealth inequality over these years was the result of a sharp rise in leverage (that is, the relative indebtedness) of the middle class.

38. The main culprit here in explaining the rather meager increase in the share of the top 1 percent was unincorporated business equity, whose mean value among the top percentile fell by 26 percent in real terms from 2007 to 2010, compared to a 16 percent overall decline in their mean net worth.

39. Once again, the large plunge in the shares of the top groups occurred between 1998 and 2001 and once again the proximate cause was the high tech boom and bust. There was also a decline in business equity among the top 1 percent, as noted earlier.

40. It should be noted that the income in each survey year (say 2013) is for the preceding year (2012 in this case).

41. It should be noted that the SCF data show a much higher level of income inequality than the CPS data. In the year 2000, for example, the CPS data show a share of the top 5 percent of 22.1 percent and a Gini coefficient of 0.462. The difference is primarily due to three factors. First, the SCF oversamples the rich, while the CPS is a representative sample. Second, the CPS data are top-coded (that is, there is an open-ended interval at the top, typically at $75,000 or $100,000), whereas the SCF data are not. Third, the income concepts differ between the two

samples. In particular, the SCF income definition includes realized capital gains whereas the CPS definition does not. The CPS data also show a large increase of inequality between 1989 and 2000, with the share of the top 5 percent rising from 18.9 to 22.1 percent and the Gini coefficient from 0.431 to 0.462.

42. The CPS data, in contrast, show little change in household income inequality, with the Gini coefficient falling slightly from 0.470 in 2006 to 0.468 in 2009. See http://www.census.gov/hhes/www/income/data/historical/household/2010/H04 _2010.xls. The work of Emmanuel Saez and Thomas Piketty, based on IRS tax data, revealed a sizeable decline in income inequality from 2007 to 2010. In particular, incomes at the 99.99th, 99.9th, and 99th percentile dropped sharply over these years. See the World Top Incomes Database, available at http://topincomes .parisschoolofeconomics.eu/, accessed October 24, 2014.

43. Also, see Chapter 12 for further discussion of the SZ series.

44. See http://www.forbes.com/forbes-400/.

45. The failure of the SCF to capture the very top of the wealth distribution pertains not just to the Forbes 400 but very likely to the wealth range from $100 million to $1 billion.

46. See Arthur B. Kennickell, "Ponds and Streams: Wealth and Income in the U.S., 1989 to 2007," Finance and Economics Discussion Series 2009–13 (Washington, DC: Federal Reserve Board, 2009).

47. Also of note on this score is a very recent paper by Jesse Bricker, Alice Henriques, Jacob Kimmel, and John Sabelhaus, "Measuring Income and Wealth at the Top Using Administrative and Survey Data," *Brookings Papers on Economic Activity,* 2016. The authors showed how very small changes in assumed capitalization rates and imputation techniques can generate enormous changes in estimated shares of top wealth groups in the SZ series. Based on their "preferred" series, they reported a 6.3 percent increase in the wealth share of the top 1 percent from 1989 to 2013, less than half the SZ figure of 14 percent from 1989 to 2012. As noted above, Zucman argues that the concentration of property income (dividends and interest) at the top is higher in the IRS tax data than in the SCF and trends upward more in the tax data than in the SCF. These facts would explain the discrepancy between the SZ series and the Bricker et al. results.

Another point of note is that both SZ and Bricker et al. included *pension reserves* as part of their definition of household wealth. Pension reserves were then allocated to the household level among retirees on the basis of whether someone in the household received a defined benefit pension benefit and among current workers on the basis of the labor force characteristics of the household. The methodology is peculiar for two reasons. First, as I argue in Chapter 8, if one counts the future flow of income from defined benefit plans as part of household wealth, by the same logic one must also include the future flow of Social Security income (that is, Social Security wealth). Second, if one were to include "defined benefit pension wealth" in household wealth the proper procedure is to compute the discounted stream of future pension benefits. The total value of this would not necessarily equal outstanding pension reserves, particularly if plans are underfunded.

48. P50 is median net worth and P99 is the wealth level at the 99th percentile.

49. Most studies of income inequality use the P50/P10 or P50/P20 ratio instead of the P50/P25 ratio. However, I am unable to use either, since P10 is always zero or negative and P20 was zero in 1962, 2010, and 2013.

50. In contrast, the share of the top 1 percent went up from 1962 to 1969.

51. It might seem odd that the share of total wealth gains accruing to the top quintile was greater over the full 1983–2013 stretch than in any of the four subperiods, The reason for this apparent anomaly is that the share of wealth gains received by a particular group like the top quintile is *not* additive over subperiods. This is so because:

$$\Delta w_{q,12} / \Delta w_{12} = (\Delta w_{q,1} + \Delta w_{q,2}) / (\Delta w_1 + \Delta w_2)$$

$$\neq [\Delta w_{q,1} / \Delta w_1 + \Delta w_{q,2} / \Delta w_2] / 2$$

where w refers to mean wealth, subscript q refers to quantile q, subscript 1 refers to period 1, subscript 2 refers to period 2, and subscript 12 refers to periods 1 and 2 combined. In other words, the *average* share of total wealth received by group q in period 1 and in period 2 does not necessarily equal the share of total wealth received by group q over the two time periods combined.

52. The category "vehicles" includes not only automobiles but also motor homes, RVs, airplanes, and boats.

53. The PSID results are from Fabian T. Pfeffer, Sheldon Danziger, and Robert F. Schoeni, "Wealth Disparities Before and After the Great Recession," *The Annals of the American Academy of Political and Social Science* 650 (November 2013): 98–123, and Pfeffer, Danziger, and Schoeni, "Wealth Levels, Wealth Inequality, and the Great Recession," Russell Sage Foundation (June 2014).

54. For example, Wolff, *Top Heavy;* Thomas Piketty and Emmanuel Saez, "Income Inequality in the United States, 1913–1998," *Quarterly Journal of Economics* 118, no. 1 (2003): 1–39; Piketty, *Capital in the Twenty-First Century* (Cambridge, MA: Harvard University Press, 2014).

3. Changing Portfolio Composition and the Rate of Return on Household Wealth

1. It may seem surprising that the share of housing in gross assets declined very little between 2007 and 2010, given the steep drop in housing prices, but the prices of other assets also fell over this period, particularly those of stocks and business equity.

2. Aggregate household balance sheet data from the Financial Accounts of the United States (FFA) show a similar reduction in the ratio of outstanding debt to gross assets among all households, from 23 to 18 percent. See Chapter 12 for details.

3. Also, for more details on the evolution of real estate in the household portfolio from 1983 to 1995, see Wolff, "Distributional Consequences of a National Land Value Tax on Real Property in the United States," in *Land Value Taxation: Can It and Will it Work?* ed. Dick Netzer (Cambridge, MA: Lincoln Institute of Land Policy, 1998), 61–104.

4. This trend is partly a statistical artifact because the homeownership rate among the bottom wealth quintile actually increased from 16.3 percent in 2007 to 26.5 percent in 2013. These results imply that many middle wealth households slipped into the bottom 20 percent over these years because of plummeting housing prices, while nonhomeowners moved up from the bottom quintile into one of the middle three wealth quintiles (these households were not affected by the collapse in home prices). All in all, the homeownership rate among the bottom 80 percent of the wealth distribution did decrease by 4.1 percentage points, from 61.8 percent in 2007 to 57.6 percent in 2013. Perhaps a more telling statistic is, as shown in Chapter 9, that the homeownership rate among the middle *income* quintile dropped by 5.7 percentage points from 68.9 percent in 2007 to 63.2 percent in 2013.

5. Consumer expenditures are obtained from the Bureau of Labor Statistics' Consumer Expenditure Survey, available at http://www.bls.gov/cex/, accessed January 28, 2016. Data on expenditures are available only by income class, not wealth class.

6. See the previous note for the data source for consumer expenditures.

7. This may not be surprising after all. The homeowners who fell under water were those who bought homes when prices were at an all-time high. The collapse in home prices put these homeowners underwater. However, *most* homeowners bought their homes well before the price collapse. As a result, they saw their home values first soar and then fall back. Most of these homeowners had homes that in 2010 were worth less than in 2005–2006 but much more than when they originally bought their homes.

8. One possible explanation for this finding is that the least educated group was also the oldest group, who probably bought homes in the more distant past. This fact could explain their low incidence of negative home equity.

9. On the basis of the 2007 SCF, the overall debt to net worth ratio continuously declined from 93 percent for the under 35 age group to 2 percent for the age 75 and over group (see Chapter 9).

10. In 2007, the average house value was $207,600 and the average mortgage debt was $72,400, resulting in an average home equity of $135,200. If house prices declined by 24 percent and mortgage debt remained fixed, then average home equity would have fallen to $85,400, for a decline of 37 percent.

11. The source is Federal Housing Finance Agency, *Foreclosure Prevention Report,* First Quarter 2009, available at http://www.fha.gov/AboutUS/Reports/Report Documents/2009IQ_FPR_N508.pdf, accessed June 11, 2016. This report analyzed data from Fannie Mae and Freddie Mac.

12. It should be noted that states differ in their regulations regarding recourse for mortgage delinquency. It is possible that delinquency rates were higher in no-recourse states. If this is the case and these states were not average in terms of characteristics like income, education, or race, then state regulatory differences might account to some extent for the pattern of delinquency by these characteristics. While this is an interesting question, it was not possible to analyze the issue because of a lack of information on state of residence.

13. See Edward N. Wolff, *Top Heavy: A Study of Increasing Inequality of Wealth in America*, newly updated and expanded edition (New York: The New Press, 2002).

14. See Chapter 5 for an updated econometric analysis of factors affecting wealth inequality trends.

15. There was generally a positive relationship between median net worth and house prices. Between 1983 and 1989, median net worth grew by 2.3 percent and median home prices rose by 7 percent (both in constant dollars); between 1995 and 1998, both were essentially unchanged; between 2007 and 2010, the former plunged by 47 percent and the latter by 25 percent. However, there were some exceptions to this pattern. Between 2001 and 2004, median wealth fell by 0.7 percent while home prices boomed by 17 percent, while from 2010 to 2013, house prices were up by 7.7 percent but median wealth fell by 1.2 percent. Overall, there was a positive and relatively strong correlation of 0.77 between the change in median net worth and the change in home prices over the nine periods between 1983 and 2013.

16. This assumes that the prices of "other assets" remain unchanged.

17. See Marshall Blume, Jean Crockett, and Irwin Friend, "Stockownership in the United States: Characteristics and Trends," *Survey of Current Business* 54, no. 11 (1974): 26.

18. See Appendix 2 of the book for more discussion of this study. Appendix Table A1.2 shows very little systematic variation of bond yields, stock yields, returns on unincorporated businesses, and returns on trust funds by income class in 1962, except for the bond yield for the top income class, which was considerably greater than that of other income classes.

19. Martin Feldstein and Shlomo Yitzhaki, "Are High Income Individuals Better Stock Market Investors?" NBER Working Papers 0948, 1982.

20. Barry Johnson, Brian Raub, and Joseph Newcomb, "A New Look at the Income-Wealth Connection for America's Wealthiest Decedents," IRS Statistics of Income Working Paper Series, 2013.

21. Emmanuel Saez and Gabriel Zucman, "Wealth Inequality in the United States since 1913: Evidence from Capitalized Income Tax Data," *Quarterly Journal of Economics* 131, no. 2 (May 2016): 519–78.

22. See Appendix Table 3.1 for the source data.

23. An earlier analysis was conducted by the author for the 1969–1975 period in the United States. For details, see Wolff, "The Distributional Effects of the 1969–75

Inflation on Holdings of Household Wealth in the United States," *Review of Income and Wealth,* series 25, no. 2 (June 1979): 195–207.

24. The 1983 data do not permit an estimation of indirect stock ownership, so I present the results for 1983 and 1989 separately from the other years.

25. Mean DC wealth among all households increased by $5,700 (in 2013 dollars) from 2007 to 2010, whereas the value of stocks and mutual funds alone declined by $15,300.

26. However, a full appraisal of retirement preparedness would also require a consideration of defined benefit pensions and Social Security. See Chapter 8 for details.

27. According to Chapter 5, net inheritance flows for middle-class households are quite small on an annual basis.

28. Results are different for mean net worth. In this case, mean wealth fell by 16 percent between 2007 and 2010. Based on the annual rate of return for all households, it would have fallen by 20 percent. This was offset by a positive annual savings rate of 1.2 percent on initial mean wealth. Saez and Zucman also reported a substantial dissavings rate for the bottom 90 percent of the wealth distribution over years 2007 to 2010—on the order of 5 percent on income. Their data series ends in 2012. (See Saez and Zucman, "Wealth Inequality in the United States since 1913.")

29. Results are similar for mean net worth. Mean wealth showed a slight increase from 2010 and 2013, according to the SCF. Based on the estimated rate of return for all households, mean net worth should have increased by 20 percent. In Chapter 5, I also use FFA data to analyze trends in household wealth from 2010 to 2013, with more sensible results.

4. International Comparisons of Household Wealth Inequality

1. See, for example, Anthony B. Atkinson, Lee Rainwater, and Timothy Smeeding, *Income Distribution in Advanced Economies: The Evidence from the Luxembourg Income Study (LIS)* (Paris: OECD, 1995); Brigitte Buhmann et al., "Equivalence Scales, Well-Being, Inequality, and Poverty: Sensitivity Estimates across Ten Countries Using the Luxembourg Income Study (LIS) Database," *Review of Income and Wealth* series 34, no. 2 (June 1988): 115–42; and Michael O'Higgins, Guenther Schmaus, and Geoffrey Stephenson, "Income Distribution and Redistribution: A Microdata Analysis for Seven Countries," *Review of Income and Wealth* series 35 (June 1989): 107–32.

2. This chapter updates results from Denis Kessler and Edward N. Wolff, "A Comparative Analysis of Household Wealth Patterns in France and the United States," *Review of Income and Wealth* series 37, no. 3 (September 1991): 249–66, which presents a comparison of wealth inequality in France and the United States; Wolff, "International Comparisons of Wealth Inequality," *Review of Income and Wealth* series 42, no. 4 (December 1996): 433–51, which compiles estimates of household wealth inequality for a number of OECD countries; Wolff, *Top Heavy:*

A Study of Increasing Inequality of Wealth in America, newly updated and expanded edition (New York: New Press, 2002), which portrays long-term time series on wealth inequality for Sweden, the United Kingdom, and the United States; and Wolff, "International Comparisons of Wealth: Methodological Issues and a Summary of Findings," in *International Perspectives on Household Wealth* (Cheltenham, U.K.: Edward Elgar Publishing Ltd., 2006), 1–16, which discusses methodological issues in international comparisons of wealth.

3. See the section Methodological Issues in Estimating the Distribution of Household Wealth for a discussion of some of the difficulties encountered when comparing wealth data from different sources.

4. Data from James Davies et al., "The World Distribution of Household Wealth," *Personal Wealth from a Global Perspective* (Oxford: Oxford University Press, 2008), 395–418; "The Global Pattern of Household Wealth," *Journal of International Development* 21, no. 8 (November 2009): 1111–24; and "Level and Distribution of Global Household Wealth," *Economic Journal* 121 (March 2011): 223–54.

5. See, for example, Atkinson, Rainwater, and Smeeding, *Income Distribution in Advanced Economies.*

6. Ibid.

7. See, for example, Edward N. Wolff, "The Size Distribution of Wealth in the United States: A Comparison among Recent Household Surveys," in *Wealth, Work, and Health: Innovations in Measurement in the Social Sciences,* ed. James P. Smith and Robert J. Willis (Ann Arbor, MI: University of Michigan Press, 1999), 209–32, for statistical analysis of this issue.

8. For some of the issues involved in developing these weights in the case of the SCF, see, for example, Arthur B. Kennickell and R. Louise Woodburn, "Consistent Weight Design for the 1989, 1992, and 1995 SCFs, and the Distribution of Wealth," *Review of Income and Wealth* series 45, no. 2 (June 1999): 193–216.

9. See Richard Hauser and Holger Stein, "Inequality of the Distribution of Personal Wealth in Germany, 1973–98," in *International Perspectives on Household Wealth,* ed. Edward N. Wolff (Cheltenham, U.K.: Edward Elgar Publishing Ltd., 2006), 195–224.

10. Arthur Kennickell, "A Rolling Tide: Changes in the Distribution of Wealth in the US, 1998–2001," in *International Perspectives on Household Wealth,* ed. Edward N. Wolff (Cheltenham, U.K.: Edward Elgar Publishing Ltd., 2006), 19–88; Wolff, "Changes in Household Wealth in the 1980s and 1990s in the U.S.," in *International Perspectives on Household Wealth* (Cheltenham, U.K.: Edward Elgar Publishing Ltd., 2006), 107–50.

11. René Morissette, Xuelin Zhang, and Marie Drolet, "The Evolution of Wealth Inequality in Canada, 1984–99," in *International Perspectives on Household Wealth,* ed. Edward N. Wolff (Cheltenham, U.K.: Edward Elgar Publishing Ltd., 2006), 151–92.

12. See section on Long-Term Time Trends in Personal Wealth Inequality.

13. See, for example, the analysis of Brandolini et al., "Household Wealth Distribution in Italy in the 1990s," in *International Perspectives on Household Wealth,* ed. Edward N. Wolff (Cheltenham, U.K.: Edward Elgar Publishing Ltd., 2006), 225–75.

14. See Wolff, *Top Heavy.*

15. See Anthony F. Shorrocks, "U.K. Wealth Distribution: Current Evidence and Future Prospects," in *International Comparisons of the Distribution of Household Wealth,* ed. Edward N. Wolff (New York: Oxford University Press, 1987), 29–50.

16. According to the original figures of James D. Smith, "Recent Trends in the Distribution of Wealth in the U.S.: Data Research Problems and Prospects," in *International Comparisons of the Distribution of Household Wealth,* ed. Edward N. Wolff (New York: Oxford University Press, 1987), 72–89, the share of net worth owned by the top 1 percent of wealth holders fell from 27.7 percent in 1972 to 19.2 percent in 1976. Marvin Schwartz, "Preliminary Estimates of Personal Wealth, 1982: Composition of Assets," *Statistics of Income Bulletin* 4 (Winter 1984–85): 1–17, reported a slightly higher share of net worth owned by the top percentile in 1976, 20.8 percent, and I use his figure rather than Smith's for this series.

17. This trend is confirmed in the estate tax figures. According to Schwartz, "Preliminary Estimates of Personal Wealth," the share of total personal wealth held by the top 2.8 percent of the nation's adult population was 28 percent in 1982, and, according to Schwartz and Barry Johnson, "Estimates of Personal Wealth, 1986," *Statistics of Income Bulletin* 9 (Spring 1990): 63–78, the share held by the top 1.6 percent of the adult population was 28.5 percent in 1986.

18. The U.S. series is based on marketable wealth for the household unit. Sources for the United Kingdom are: 1923–1975—Shorrocks, "U.K. Wealth Distribution," Tables 2.1 and 2.2; 1976–1990—Board of Inland Revenue, *Inland Revenue Statistics, 1993* (London: HMSO, 1993), Series C, Table 11.5. Results are based on marketable wealth for adult individuals. The 1923–1975 data are benchmarked to the Inland Revenue figure for 1976. Sources for Sweden are 1920–1975—Roland Spånt, "Wealth Distribution in Sweden: 1920–1983," in *International Comparisons of the Distribution of Household Wealth,* ed. Edward N. Wolff (New York: Oxford University Press, 1987), Tables 3.7, 3.8, and 3.11; 1975–1990—Statistics Sweden, *Income Distribution Survey in 1990* (Orebro, Sweden: SCB Publishing Unit, 1992), Table 49. The unit is the household and wealth is valued at market prices. The 1920–1975 data are benchmarked to the Statistics Sweden figure for 1975.

19. J. Roine and D. Waldenström compiled data on Sweden and the United Kingdom, see "Long-Run Trends in the Distribution of Income and Wealth," in *Handbook of Income Distribution,* vol. 2A, ed. A. B. Atkinson and F. Bourguignon (Amsterdam: North-Holland Press, 2015), available at: http://www.uueconomics

.se/danielw/Handbook.htm. I have used the same underlying data sources for the two series—wealth tax data for the former and estate duty data for the latter. I also add updated data for the United States from Chapter 13.

20. See Chapter 13 for more discussion of the long-term U.S. series and recent updates.

21. James Davies, "The Distribution of Wealth in Canada," in *Research in Economic Inequality,* vol. 4: Studies in the Distribution of Household Wealth, ed. Edward N. Wolff (Greenwich, CT: JAI Press, 1993), 159–80.

22. In Table 4.2, I use the older data for the United Kingdom from Anthony B. Atkinson, J. P. F. Gordon, and A. Harrison, "Trends in the Shares of Top Wealth-Holders in Britain, 1923–81," *Oxford Bulletin of Economics and Statistics* 51, no. 3 (1989): 315–32, rather than the newer data, because the older data are more comparable to the U.K. Series D and E.

23. See Section Chapter 13 for more details.

24. See Chapter 8 for more discussion of this effect.

25. The U.S. series, derived from Chapter 13, Table 13.7, is based on augmented wealth for the household unit. The sources for the United Kingdom are Inland *Revenue Statistics, 1993,* Series *D,* Table 13.6, and Series E, Table 13.7. Results are for adult individuals.

26. For details, see Denis Kessler and Edward N. Wolff, "A Comparative Analysis of Household Wealth Patterns in France and the United States," *Review of Income and Wealth* series 37, no. 3 (September 1991): 249–66.

27. Richard V. Burkhauser, Joachim R. Frick, and Johannes Schwarze, "A Comparison of Alternative Measures of Economic Well-Being for Germany and the United States," *Review of Income and Wealth* series 43, no. 2 (June 1997): 153–72.

28. John Bauer and Andrew Mason, "The Distribution of Income and Wealth in Japan," *Review of Income and Wealth* series 38, no. 4 (December 1992): 403–28.

29. See Bager-Sjogren and N. A. Klevmarken, "The Distribution of Wealth in Sweden, 1984–1986," in *Research in Economic Inequality,* vol. 4: Studies in the Distribution of Household Wealth, ed. Edward N. Wolff (Greenwich, CT: JAI Press, 1993), 203–24, especially Table 1.

30. See Atkinson, Rainwater, and Smeeding, *Income Distribution in Advanced Economies.*

31. See Davies et al., "The Global Pattern of Household Wealth," *Journal of International Development* 21, no. 8 (November 2009): 1111–24, and "Level and Distribution of Global Household Wealth," *Economic Journal* 121 (March 2011): 223–54.

32. See Davies et al., "The Global Pattern of Household Wealth."

33. The negative wealth shares reported for Denmark, Finland, Germany, and Sweden in the original data were discarded, together with the zero shares reported elsewhere, thus treating the cell values as missing observations.

34. Frank Cowell et al., "Wealth, Top Incomes and Inequality," in *Wealth: Economics and Policy,* ed. Kirk Hamilton and Cameron Hepburn (Oxford University Press, forthcoming).

35. Additional studies that use the HFCS data are Frank Cowell and Philippe van Kerm, "Wealth Inequality: A Survey," *Journal of Economic Surveys* 29, no. 4 (2015): 671–710, and Olympia Bover et al., "Eurosystem Household Finance and Consumption Survey: Main Results on Assets, Debt, and Saving," *International Journal of Central Banking* 12, no. 2 (2016): 1–13.

5. Deconstructing Wealth Trends, 1983–2013

1. Daphne T. Greenwood and Edward N. Wolff, "Changes in Wealth in the United States, 1962–1983: Savings, Capital Gains, Inheritance and Lifetime Transfers," *Journal of Population Economics* 5, no. 4 (1992): 261–88.

2. Edward N. Wolff, "Wealth Accumulation by Age Cohort in the U.S., 1962–1992," *Geneva Journal on Risk and Insurance* 24, no. 1 (January 1999): 27–49, for years 1962 to 1992 and Wolff, *Inheriting Wealth in America: Future Boom or Bust?* (New York: Oxford University Press, 2015) for years 1983 to 2007.

3. Note that the mean wealth of three middle wealth quintiles is not necessarily equal to median wealth. In 2007, for example, median wealth (in 2013$) was $115,100 while the latter was equal to $155,200. The reason that the latter was higher was that the middle three wealth quintiles incorporated the wealth of the fourth quintile, which was generally considerably higher than that of the middle quintile. However, the two series trended very closely over time in terms of percentage change.

4. Zucman presented convincing evidence that substantial wealth was transferred from domestic accounts to foreign ones over time ("offshoring"); see Gabriel Zucman, "The Missing Wealth of Nations: Are Europe and the U.S. Net Debtors or Net Creditors?" *Quarterly Journal of Economics* 128, no. 3 (2013): 1321–64. In principle, offshoring should not present a problem for the SCF data since the SCF asks questions to domestic respondents about asset holdings in foreign accounts. This problem appears more germane to aggregate data like the Financial Accounts of the United States, because these accounts are based on only domestically held assets.

5. John Sabelhaus and Karen Pence, "Household Saving in the '90s: Evidence from Cross-Section Wealth Surveys," *Review of Income and Wealth* series 25, no. 4 (1999): 435–53.

6. An alternative approach is to use actual panel data. In the case of the SCF, there were two panels conducted covering the periods 1983–1986 and 2007–2009. Unfortunately, the coverage is not sufficient to provide much historical analysis of trends in capital gains and savings over the full thirty-year time period. Another

source is the Panel Study of Income Dynamics (PSID). This is a panel data source that covers years 1984 to 2013. There are a number of problems that make the SCF data preferable. First, and most notably, the PSID is weak on wealth coverage of the top end of the wealth distribution, particularly the top 1 percent. Since an important objective of this study is to decompose wealth trends between the top percentile and the middle three wealth quintiles of the wealth distribution, the SCF is definitely preferable on this score.

Second, the decomposition analysis relies heavily on the portfolio composition of each wealth, income, and demographic group (in order to compute the average rate of return of the group, r_{ct}). Here, also, the SCF is by far a superior source compared to the PSID since the SCF questionnaire contains several hundred questions on assets and liabilities held by each household. In contrast, the PSID has only 17 to 19 questions in total (depending on the year) on this topic.

7. Though the standard SCF income measure includes realized capital gains, this component is excluded here since it is already partially captured in the term $r_{ct}W_{ct-1}$.

8. Marianne P. Bitler and Hilary W. Hoynes, "The State of the Social Safety Net in the Post–Welfare Reform Era," *Brookings Papers on Economic Activity* (Washington, DC: The Brookings Institute, 2010), and "The More Things Change, the More They Stay the Same: The Safety Net, Living Arrangements, and Poverty in the Great Recession," NBER Working Paper 19449; Philip Armour, Richard V. Burkhauser, and Jeff Larrimore, "Deconstructing Income and Income Inequality Measures: A Crosswalk from Market Income to Comprehensive Income," *American Economic Review* 101, no. 3 (2013): 173–77.

9. See is Chapter 12, Table 12.3 and Figure 12.2. The wealth concept is W2 minus all consumer durables.

10. The evidence presented in Chapter 3 suggests very little systematic variation in rates of return across wealth (or income) class (see Chapter 3, section on Rates of Return).

11. Generally speaking, for the population as a whole, total gifts given would equal total gifts received. However, there are two offsetting factors in the computation of net wealth transfers. First, since the simulations are performed over time, it is possible for an *inheritance* to be received over the period with no corresponding negative entry since the household is no longer in the population. Second, donations to charities and non-profits are subtracted in the calculation of net wealth transfers received. The net wealth transfer figures are adjusted so that the total *gifts* reported received in a given year for the full population are equal to the total *gifts* reported given (aligned to the greater of the two figures).

12. I use here the ratio of total personal savings to personal income from NIPA, rather than the ratio to personal *disposable* income, which is the more usual concept, in order to maintain consistency with the SCF data.

13. Net wealth transfers once again made a small contribution to the wealth changes of the top 1 percent. Net wealth transfers were negative for the first four periods, since gifts given to other households (plus charitable donations) were greater than gifts and bequests received by the top 1 percent. The flow was positive in the fifth period because of several large inheritances reported by these families over the 2010–2013 period.

14. See Chapter 12, Table 12.3 and Figure 12.2. The wealth concept is W2 minus all consumer durables. See Chapter 12 for details.

15. By construction, the contribution of capital gains to the overall percentage growth in mean net worth remains unchanged in the two decompositions, as does the contribution of net wealth transfers.

16. This ratio is similar to the P90/P50 ratio used in Chapter 2.

17. Note that a negative value in Panel IV indicates that the component *reduces* inequality whereas a positive value indicates that the component *increases* inequality.

18. The results in more detail are as follows: The overall annual rate of return over years 2001–2007 was 4.04 percent. If the return for the top 1 percent is set to this rate from its actual 3.92 percent, as in line IC, then the mean net worth of the top 1 percent increases from $21,492,000 to $21,646,000 in 2007 or by 0.7 percent (since the rate of return is now higher), and that of the middle falls from $168,700 to $152,200 or by 9.8 percent (since the return is now lower). As a result, the ratio between the two rises from 127.4 to 142.2 in 2007 or by 11.6 percent, as shown in lines IB and IC. Actual rates of return therefore reduced the rise in the ratio from 11.6 percentage points to 1.4 percentage points or by 88 percent.

19. The results in greater detail are as follows: The overall annual rate of return over years 2007–2010 was −7.28 percent. If the return for the top 1 percent is set to this rate from its actual −6.52 percent, as in line IC, then the mean net worth of the top 1 percent falls from $18,438,000 to $18,050,000 in 2010 or by 2.1 percent, and that of the middle advances from $106,900 to $118,6200 or by 10.9 percent. As a result the ratio between the two drops from 172.4 to 152.2 or by 11.7 percent, as shown in lines IIA and IIB.

20. I use this measure in the decomposition rather than total net wealth transfers since the actual level of net transfers depends heavily on the wealth level of a group.

21. It is of interest that most of the literature on gifts and inheritances emphasizes the fact that the very rich receive higher amounts than lower wealth groups (see Chapter 7, for example). However, in point of fact, when the outflows are also taken into account, the rich are net donors rather than net recipients.

22. The same analysis was redone using the simulated change in net worth on the basis of the survey data aligned to the FFA (from Table 5.2) for the 2010–2013 period. The new results are very similar to those based on the unadjusted SCF data for the contributions made by differentials in rates of return and the net wealth

transfer ratio (see the last column of Table 5.3). However, results differ for the gap in savings rates between the two groups. In this case, the simulated P99/P2080 ratio fell by 6.3 percent with a uniform savings rate instead of 3.7 percent with the SCF data (line IIE). This result implies that the savings rate differential made a larger contribution to the upswing in the P99/P2080 ratio than reported on the basis of the unaligned data (accounting for 277 percent of the increase compared to 206 percent from the unaligned results).

23. In fairness to Piketty it should be noted that for him, r is the net return to production and financial capital while g is the world output growth rate.

24. See the World Top Incomes Database, available at http://topincomes .parisschoolofeconomics.eu/.

25. This effect is compounded by the fact that savings rates are generally higher for higher income households than for lower income ones as we shall see in Chapter 9.

26. It would also be desirable to use the ratio of overall debt to total disposable personal income as an explanatory variable. However, data on disposable personal income is not available before 1945.

27. See Chapter 8 and Appendix 3 of the book for a discussion of Social Security wealth.

28. Ideally it would be desirable to "instrument" INCTOP1 since INCTOP1 and WTOP1 are likely to be co-determined. For example, a greater share of wealth held by the rich will lead to a higher concentration of property income among this group. However, a suitable instrument is not readily available.

29. Both RPENS and RSSW prove to be statistically insignificant. The estimated coefficient of RPENS is positive, as expected, but that of RSSW is negative.

30. This very strong result is not unrelated to the fact that variables SZWTOP1 and INCTOP1 are both based on IRS tax return data. In this case, in particular, an instrumental variables regression is called for.

31. First differences regressions were also tried. However, the results are much weaker. One additional variable that is introduced is the inflation rate, measured by the annual change in the CPI. The rationale is that there is a strong inverse correlation between household net worth and the debt-equity ratio. As a result, price inflation generally increases the wealth of the lower wealth percentiles relative to the upper percentiles and should lower wealth inequality. However, the estimated coefficient on this new variable is positive with WTOP1 as the dependent variable but negative with SZWTOP1 as the dependent variable. In both cases, the estimated coefficients are statistically insignificant.

32. Consumer expenditure data are from the Bureau of Labor Statistics' Consumer Expenditure Survey, available at http://www.bls.gov/cex/, various years, accessed January 28, 2016. Data on expenditures are available only by income class, not wealth class.

33. There was no Consumer Expenditure Survey in 1983, so I use 1984 data instead. It should also be noted that unlike later years the tabulation of expenditures

by income class was not available by income quintile but by fixed dollar income levels. Estimated mean expenditures of the middle quintile are based on interpolation between the two middle income classes.

6. Age-Wealth Profiles and the Life Cycle Model

1. This chapter draws on the following three articles: Wolff, "The Accumulation of Wealth Over the Life Cycle: A Microdata Analysis," *Review of Income and Wealth* 27, no. 2 (June 1981): 75–96; Wolff, "Life Cycle Savings and the Individual Distribution of Wealth by Class," in *Modelling the Accumulation and Distribution of Wealth*, ed. Denis Kessler and André Masson (Oxford: Clarendon Press, 1988), 261–80; and Wolff, "Social Security, Pensions, and the Life Cycle Accumulation of Wealth: Some Empirical Tests," *Annales d'Economie et de Statistique* no. 9 (January/March 1988): 199–216.

2. The LCM has also been generalized by introducing a bequest motive for households. If an individual wants to leave a bequest for children (or other heirs), the person will make sure that some wealth will be left at time of death. The bequest motive, like uncertain longevity, will therefore result in a non-zero net worth at time of death. Indeed, Modigliani and Brumberg recognized this possibility in their original paper. See Chapter 7 for a literature review of inheritances and bequests.

3. Modigliani and Blumberg, "Utility Analysis and the Consumption Function: An Interpretation of Cross-Section Data," in *Post Keynesian Economics*, ed. Kenneth K. Kurihara (New Brunswick, NJ: Rutgers University Press, 1954), 388–436.

4. Ando and Modigliani, "The 'Life Cycle' Hypotheses of Saving: Aggregate Implications and Tests," *American Economic Review* 53, no. 1 (March 1963): 55–84.

5. Tobin, "Life Cycle Saving and Balanced Growth," in *Ten Economic Studies in the Tradition of Irving Fisher*, ed. William Fellner (New York: Wiley, 1967), 231–56.

6. It should be emphasized that Tobin proposed this variant as just one possible life cycle wealth profile. Empirically, there was no aggregate or microdata evidence to support this particular profile. Tobin stressed that liquidity constraints imposed by the absence of perfect capital markets are one explanation for the absence of negative net worth at early ages.

7. See Anthony F. Shorrocks, "The Age-Wealth Relationship: A Cross-Section and Cohort Analysis," *Review of Economics and Statistics* 57 (May 1975): 155–63.

8. Shorrocks, "U.K. Wealth Distribution: Current Evidence and Future Prospects," in *International Comparisons of the Distribution of Household Wealth*, ed. Edward N. Wolff (New York: Oxford University Press, 1987), 29–50.

9. For an analysis, see B. Douglas Bernheim, "Life Cycle Annuity Valuation" (NBER Paper no. 1511, National Bureau of Economic Research, Cambridge, MA, December 1984); and "The Economic Effects of Social Security: Toward a Reconciliation of Theory and Measurement," *Journal of Public Economics* 33, no. 3 (1987): 273–304.

10. Harold Lydall, "The Life Cycle in Income, Saving, and Asset Ownership," *Econometrica* 23, no. 2 (April 1955): 131–50.

11. John Lansing and John Sondquist, "A Cohort Analysis of Changes in the Distribution of Wealth," in *Six Papers on the Size Distribution of Income and Wealth,* ed. Lee Soltow (New York: National Bureau of Economic Research, 1969).

12. John Brittain, *Inheritance and the Inequality of Material Wealth* (Washington, DC: Brookings Institution, 1978).

13. Also, see the data on age-wealth profiles for years 1983 to 2013 in Chapter 9.

14. See, for example, J. Freidman, "Asset Accumulation and Depletion among the Elderly" (paper presented at the Brookings Institution Conference on Retirement and Aging, 1982); and Daniel S. Hammermesh, "Consumption during Retirement: The Missing Link in the Life Cycle," *Review of Economics and Statistics* 66, no. 1 (February 1984): 1–7.

15. See Chapter 8 and Appendix 3 for details on the estimation of DBW and SSW.

16. Shorrocks, "The Age-Wealth Relationship."

17. Thad Mirer, "The Wealth-Age Relation among the Aged," *American Economic Review* 69, no. 3 (June 1979): 435–43.

18. Thad Mirer, "The Dissaving Behavior of the Retired Elderly," *Southern Economic Journal* 46, no. 4 (April 1980): 1197–205.

19. Peter A. Diamond and Jerry A. Hausman, "Individual Retirement and Savings Behavior," *Journal of Public Economics* 23 (1984): 81–114.

20. Freidman, "Asset Accumulation and Depletion Among the Elderly."

21. Hammermesh, "Consumption during Retirement."

22. Danziger et al., "The Life Cycle Hypothesis and the Consumption Behavior of the Elderly," *Journal of Post Keynesian Economics* 5, no. 2 (Winter 1982–83): 208–27.

23. Alan S. Blinder, Roger Gordon, and Donald Weiss, "Social Security Bequests and the Life Cycle Theory of Savings: Cross-Sectional Texts," in *Determinants of National Saving and Wealth,* ed. Franco Modigliani and Richard Hemming (New York: St. Martin's Press, 1983).

24. Michael Hurd, "Savings of the Elderly and Desired Bequests," *American Economic Review* 77, no. 2 (1987): 298–312; and Michael Hurd, "Mortality, Risk, and Bequests," *Econometrica* 57, no. 4 (1989): 779–813.

25. Michael Hurd, "Wealth Depletion and Life Cycle Consumption," in *Topics in the Economics of Aging,* ed. David A. Wise (Chicago: University of Chicago Press for the National Bureau of Economic Research, 1992), 135–60.

26. Axel Borsch-Supan, "Saving and Consumption Patterns of the Elderly: The German Case," *Journal of Population Economics* 5 (1992): 289–303.

27. Hammermesh, "Consumption during Retirement."

28. James Banks, Richard Blundell, and Sarah Tanner, "Is There a Retirement-Savings Puzzle?" *American Economic Review* 88, no. 4 (1998): 769–88; B. Douglas Bernheim, Jonathan Skinner, and Steven Weinberg, "What Accounts for the Vari-

ation in Retirement Wealth among U.S. Households?" *American Economic Review* 91, no. 4 (September 2001): 832–57.

29. Eric M. Engen, William G. Gale, and Cori E. Uccello, "The Adequacy of Household Saving," *Brookings Papers on Economic Activity* no. 2 (1999): 65–165.

30. Anthony B. Atkinson, "The Distribution of Wealth and the Individual Life Cycle," *Oxford Economic Papers* 23, no. 2 (July 1971): 239–54.

31. Nicholas Oulton, "Inheritance and the Distribution of Wealth," *Oxford Economic Papers* 28, no. 1 (March 1976): 86–101

32. James B. Davies and Anthony F. Shorrocks, "Assessing the Quantitative Importance of Inheritance in the Distribution of Wealth," *Oxford Economic Papers* 30 (1978): 138–49.

33. James B. Davies, "The Relative Impact of Inheritance and Other Factors on Economic Inequality," *Quarterly Journal of Economics* 96 (August 1982): 471–98.

34. James B. Davies and France St-Hilaire, *Reforming Capital Income Taxation in Canada* (Ottawa: Economic Council of Canada, 1987).

35. John Laitner, "Random Earnings Differences, Lifetime Liquidity Constraints, and Altruistic Intergenerational Transfers," *Journal of Economic Theory* 58 (1992): 135–70.

36. Betsy White, "Empirical Tests of the Life Cycle Hypotheses," *American Economic Review* 68, no. 4 (September 1978): 547–60; Laurence J. Kotlikoff and Lawrence H. Summers, "The Role of Intergenerational Transfers in Aggregate Capital Accumulation," *Journal of Political Economy* 90 (August 1981): 706–32.

37. James B. Davies and Anthony F. Shorrocks, "The Distribution of Wealth," in *Handbook on Income Distribution,* ed. Anthony B. Atkinson and Francois Bourguignon (Amsterdam: Elsevier Science, 1999), 1: 605–765.

38. Erik Hurst, "The Retirement of a Consumption Puzzle" (NBER Working Paper no. 13789, National Bureau of Economic Research, Cambridge, MA, February 2008).

39. Mariacristina de Nardi, Eric French, and John B. Jones, "Savings After Retirement: A Survey" (NBER Working Paper no. 21268, National Bureau of Economic Research, Cambridge, MA, June 2015).

40. Menaham E. Yaari, "Uncertain Lifetime, Life Insurance, and the Theory of the Consumer," *Review of Economic Studies* 32 (April 1965): 137–58.

41. Laurence J. Kotlikoff and Avia Spivak, "The Family as an Incomplete Annuities Market," *Journal of Political Economy* 89 (April 1981): 372–91.

42. James B. Davies, "Uncertain Lifetime, Consumption and Dissaving in Retirement," *Journal of Political Economy* 89 (June 1981): 561–78.

43. Mervyn A. King and Louis Dicks-Mireaux, "Asset Holdings and the Life Cycle," *Economic Journal* 92 (June 1982): 247–67.

44. Eytan Sheshinski and Yoram Weiss, "Uncertainty and Optimal Social Security Systems," *Quarterly Journal of Economics* 96 (May 1981): 189–206.

45. R. Glenn Hubbard, "Do IRA's and Keoghs Increase Saving?" *National Tax Journal* 37, (1984): 43–54.

46. Martin Feldstein, "Social Security, Individual Retirement and Aggregate Capital Accumulation," *Journal of Political Economy* 82, no. 5 (September/October 1974): 905–26.

47. Feldstein also argued that the availability of Social Security retirement income might induce workers to retire earlier than otherwise and this possibility might have a positive effect on private savings. No independent estimate of this effect on savings was provided.

48. Martin S. Feldstein and Anthony Pellechio, "Social Security and Household Wealth Accumulation: New Microeconomic Evidence," *Review of Economics and Statistics* 61 (August 1979): 361–68.

49. Blinder, Gordon, and Weiss, "Social Security Bequests and the Life Cycle Theory of Savings."

50. Diamond and Hausman, "Individual Retirement and Savings Behavior."

51. Laurence J. Kotlikoff, "Testing the Theory of Social Security and Life Cycle Accumulation," *American Economic Review* 69 (June 1979): 396–410.

52. Dean R. Leimer and Selig D. Lesnoy, "Social Security and Private Saving: New Time-Series Evidence," *Journal of Political Economy* 90 (June 1982): 606–21.

53. Martin S. Feldstein, "Social Security and Private Saving: Reply," *Journal of Political Economy* 90 (June 1982): 630–41.

54. Henry J. Aaron, *Economic Effects of Social Security* (Washington, DC: Brookings Institution, 1982).

55. R. Glenn Hubbard, "Uncertain Lifetimes, Pensions, and Individual Savings," in *Issues in Pension Economies,* ed. Zvi Bodie, John Shoven, and David Wise (Chicago: University of Chicago Press, 1986); President's Commission on Pension Policy, "Pension Coverage in the United States" (mimeo, Washington, DC, 1980).

56. Robert B. Avery, Gregory E. Elliehausen, and Thomas A. Gustafson, "Pensions and Social Security in Household Portfolios: Evidence from the 1983 Survey of Consumer Finances" (Federal Reserve Board Research Papers in Banking and Financial Economics, October 1985).

57. B. Douglas Bernheim, "Dissaving after Retirement: Testing the Pure Life Cycle Hypothesis," in *Issues in Pension Economies,* ed. Zvi Bodie, John Shoven, and David Wise (Chicago: University of Chicago Press, 1986).

58. As King and Dicks-Mireaux argued in "Asset Holdings and the Life Cycle," the use of actuarial values to compute retirement wealth builds in a tendency for total wealth to decline rapidly after retirement, because conditional life expectancy decreases with age.

59. Alan L. Gustman and Thomas L. Steinmeier, "Effects of Pensions on Saving: Analysis with Data from the Health and Retirement Study" (NBER Working Paper 6681, National Bureau of Economic Research, Cambridge, MA, August 1998).

60. Defined contribution pension plans consist of Individual Retirement Accounts (IRAs), Keogh plans, 401(k) plans, and the like. These plans are like savings accounts. However, they are especially designed to allow workers to save for retirement by providing tax-deferred savings (see Chapter 8 for more details).

61. James M. Poterba, Steven F. Venti, and David A. Wise, "401(k) Plans and Future Patterns of Retirement Saving," *American Economic Review Papers and Proceedings* 87, no. 2 (May 1998): 179–84; and Poterba, Venti, and Wise, "The Transition to Personal Accounts and Increasing Retirement Wealth: Micro and Macro Evidence" (NBER Working Paper 8610, National Bureau of Economic Research, Cambridge, MA, November 2001).

62. William G. Gale, "The Effects of Pensions on Wealth: A Re-evaluation of Theory and Evidence," *Journal of Political Economy* 106 (1998): 707–23.

63. Eric M. Engen and William G. Gale, "Debt, Taxes, and the Effects of 401(k) Plans on Household Wealth Accumulation" (mimeo, the Brookings Institution, May 1997).

64. Eric M. Engen and William G. Gale, "The Effects of 401(k) Plans on Household Wealth: Differences Across Earnings Groups" (mimeo, The Brookings Institution, August 2000).

65. Arthur B. Kennickell and Annika E. Sunden, "Pensions, Social Security, and the Distribution of Wealth" (mimeo, Federal Reserve Board of Washington, December 1999).

66. James Tobin and Walter Dolde, "Wealth, Liquidity, and Consumption," in *Consumer Spending and Monetary Policy: The Linkages,* Federal Reserve Bank of Boston Conference Series 5 (Boston: Federal Reserve Bank of Boston, 1971), 99–146.

67. R. Glenn Hubbard and Kenneth L. Judd, "Liquidity Constraints, Fiscal Policy, and Consumption," *Brookings Papers on Economic Activity* no. 1 (1986): 1–59; and "Social Security and Individual Welfare: Precautionary Saving, Liquidity Constraints, and the Payroll Tax," *American Economic Review* 77, no. 4 (1987): 630–46.

68. Steven P. Zeldes, "Optimal Consumption with Stochastic Income: Deviations from Certainty Equivalence," *Quarterly Journal of Economics* 104 (May 1989): 275–98.

69. A similar analysis and result were reported by Jonathan S. Skinner in "Risky Income, Life Cycle Consumption, and Precautionary Savings," *Journal of Monetary Economics* 22 (September 1988): 237–55.

70. See chapter 6 in Laurence J. Kotlikoff, *What Determines Savings?* (Cambridge, MA: MIT Press, 1989).

71. Michael Palumbo, "Uncertain Medical Expenses and Precautionary Saving Near the End of the Life Cycle," *Review of Economic Studies* 66, no. 2 (1999): 395–421.

72. Ricardo J. Caballero, "Earnings Uncertainty and Aggregate Wealth Accumulation," *American Economic Review* 81, no. 4 (September 1991): 859–71.

73. Nancy Ammon Jianakoplos, Paul L. Menchik, and F. Owen Irvine, "Saving Behavior of Older Households: Rate-of-Return, Precautionary and Inheritance Effects," *Economic Letters* 50, no. 1 (January 1996): 111–20.

74. Christopher D. Carroll, "How Much Does Future Income Affect Current Consumption?" *Quarterly Journal of Economics* 109, no. 1 (February 1994): 111–47.

75. Christopher D. Carroll and Andrew A. Samwick, "How Important Is Precautionary Saving?" *Review of Economics and Statistics* 80, no. 3 (August 1998): 410–19.

76. Pierre-Olivier Gourinchas and Jonathan A. Parker, "Consumption over the Life Cycle," *Econometrica* 70, no. 1 (January 2002): 47–89. A similar set of findings on the importance of including a precautionary savings motive was reported in Orazio Attanasio et al., "Humps and Bumps in Lifetime Consumption," *Journal of Business and Economic Statistics* 17, no. 1 (1999): 22–35.

77. Edward N. Wolff, "The Accumulation of Wealth over the Life Cycle: A Microdata Analysis," *The Review of Income and Wealth* series 27, no. 2 (June 1981): 75–96.

78. To call such an investigation a "test" would presume too much. The LCM and its successors fully acknowledge the role of factors other than age as determinants of the distribution of household wealth.

79. See Appendix 2 of this book for a description of the database.

80. One difficulty in using the MESP sample to test the LCM is that the model refers to the behavior of a family over time (longitudinal behavior), whereas the data are cross-sectional. Under the simplifying assumptions of the LCM, this difference does not matter because the interest rate is zero and earnings are constant over time and *between cohorts*. If any of these assumptions is violated, then the regression analysis conducted using the MESP sample (or any other sample) does not, strictly speaking, provide a valid test of the life cycle.

Shorrocks showed, in "The Age-Wealth Relationship," that under fairly general conditions allowing for differences in earnings between cohorts, a cross-sectional inverted U-shaped age-wealth profile is necessary but not sufficient to ensure an inverted U-shaped age-wealth profile over the lifetime. Thus, rejection of an inverted U-shaped cross-sectional age-wealth profile is sufficient to reject the LCM, but the converse is not true.

Mirer, "The Wealth-Age Relation among the Aged," suggested one way to adjust the cross-sectional regression for differences in cohort earnings. However, the adjustment he proposed was inadequate once it was allowed that the interest rate was different from zero and that earnings increased with age for a given cohort in addition to allowing for differences in cohort earnings. To show this, assume that for the under-65 population everyone starts work at age 20, retirees at age 65, and has a constant savings rates. (It is now necessary to drop the assumption of a constant lifetime consumption pattern.) Define:

$A = \text{age} - 20$
W_A = wealth (now) for those in cohort A
E_{tA} = earnings at time t for cohort A
r = interest rate (constant over time)
g = rate at which earnings grow for a given cohort over time (the same for each cohort)
h = rate at which starting earnings increase between successive cohorts.

Then:

$$W_A = \int_0^A s E_{tA}\, e^{r(A-t)}\, dt = s\, e^{rA} \int_0^A E_{tA}\, e^{-rt}\, dt.$$

Moreover, $E_{tA} = E_{0A}\, e^{gt}$, $E_{0A} = E^*\, e^{(45-A)h}$.
Then:

$$W_A = \frac{s E^* e^{45h}}{r - g}\left(e^{(r-h)A} - e^{(g-h)A}\right) \quad \text{if } g \neq r$$

$$= s E^* e^{45h}\, e^{(r-h)A} \cdot A \qquad \text{if } g = r.$$

Here, it can be seen that the slope of the cross-sectional profile depends critically on the parameters r, g, and h.

81. I use "NWB" for wealth here since the MESP measure of wealth includes all consumer durables, though it excludes household inventories. See Appendix 2 of this book for details.

82. A few cases were eliminated because of data errors.

83. A regression was also estimated on the model

$$\text{NWB}_i = \beta_0 + \beta_1 A_i + \beta_2 A_i^2 + \beta_3 A_i^3 + u_i$$

The Tobin variant would predict: $\beta_1 < 0$; $\beta_2 > 0$; and $\beta_3 < 0$. Though the signs of the coefficient estimators are in the predicted direction, none of them is statistically significant.

84. The exception is from interracial marriage, which may cause *individuals* classified in one household race category to switch into another.

85. The same regression is also estimated for the following five occupational groups: (1) professional, technical, managerial, and administrative workers; (2) clerical and sales workers; (3) craftsmen; (4) operatives; and (5) service and unskilled workers. There are two problems with this classification. First, many workers will switch occupational class over their lifetimes. Second, only a small portion of those older than 65 recorded their last occupations. However, the results

do show significant inverted U-shaped life cycle wealth profiles for group 1, professionals and administrators, and group 3, craftsmen, with the profile considerably more "humped" for the former. Moreover, when the regression is estimated for only professional and technical workers, the coefficients on A^2 and A^3, their t-values, and the R^2 and adjusted R^2 statistics are all higher than for the more inclusive group 1.

86. For retirees without Social Security benefits, AE is imputed according to their education, sex, and race. See Appendix 3 of this book for details on the estimation of lifetime earnings.

87. An alternative is to regress the logarithm of wealth on age and lifetime earnings, which has the algebraic effect of reducing the dependent variable wealth proportionately more for large values than for small values. When this procedure was applied, the R^2 climbed to 0.10 and the t-statistics all exceeded 7.5 for the urban white sample. Though this procedure certainly improves the fit of the LCM, there is no theoretical rationale at this stage of analysis for using the logarithm of wealth instead of wealth as the dependent variable. Moreover, such a procedure requires the elimination from the sample of households with zero or negative net worth.

88. The lifetime earnings form $AE1_3$ was chosen because it yielded the best results in Table 6.6.

89. Additional experimentation showed, not surprisingly, that the size of mortgage debt follows age rather closely, whereas other household debt is virtually unrelated to age.

90. This is perhaps to be expected since in the MESP sample total capital wealth is 74 percent of total household wealth.

91. For rural residents, farm ownership, which is a portion of capital wealth, is a very important asset (at least in 1969), and the change in the value of farms tends to follow the life cycle pattern.

92. See Atkinson, "The Distribution of Wealth and the Individual Life Cycle."

93. See Joseph E. Stiglitz, "Distribution of Income and Wealth Among Individuals," *Econometrica* 37, no. 3 (July 1969): 382–97.

94. This analysis is based on data from the 1962 SFCC and the 1983 SCF.

95. There is a notable dip in mean wealth for the 60–64 age group. This age cohort was born around 1900 and reached the typical age for the beginning of wealth accumulation at the time of the Great Depression. This factor likely accounts for the cohort's relatively low wealth holding in 1962.

96. See Appendix 3 for details.

97. In econometrics, a piece-wise linear function is a real-valued function defined on the real numbers or a segment thereof, whose graph is composed of straight-line sections.

98. The inclusion of lifetime earnings also implicitly controls for the other source of bias noted by Shorrocks, "U.K. Wealth Distribution," that is, the sample

selection effect induced by the positive correlation between wealth and longevity. This is because of the high correlation between wealth and lifetime earnings and, correspondingly, between lifetime earnings and life expectancy. Also, see Bern heim, "Life Cycle Annuity Valuation," in which it was found that this sample selection bias was relatively small in similar analyses of the LCM.

99. For retirees without Social Security benefits, HK and AE are imputed according to their education, sex, and race. See Appendix 3 for details.

100. In the results shown here, g, the rate of growth of real earnings, is set to 1 percent per year. Results are quite similar for g equal to 2 percent per year. AE and AE1 when included as an independent variable in place of HK are less statistically significant than HK, a result consistent with the LCM (results not shown).

101. The same set of regressions is also estimated using current annual earnings instead of lifetime earnings. The significance level of current earnings is even greater than that of AE1 or HK, and the overall explanatory power of the equation is also greater. In the NWB equation on the 1962 data, the R^2 is 0.087. The result is surprising since HK is already adjusted to reflect current earnings. The reason for this result is not apparent, since it seems to contradict standard formulations of the LCM.

102. Technically, the truncation of the sample on the top and also on the bottom introduces a sample selection bias, since the error term is now also truncated. To correct for the truncation bias, I use the two-stage procedure developed by Heckman, which entails the estimation of a probit model for high wealth holders and the inclusion of the inverse of the Mills ratio in a second stage regression of wealth on age and human capital. See James J. Heckman, "The Common Structure of Statistical Models of Truncation, Sample Selection and Limited Dependent Variables and a Simple Estimator for Such Models," *Annals of Economic and Social Measurement* 5 (1976): 475–92; and "Sample Selection Bias as a Specification Error," *Econometrica* 47 (1979): 153–62.

Though the inverse Mills ratio is statistically significant in the first stage regression, the second-stage regression coefficients are not appreciably different from those shown in Table 6.13. Also, see King and Dicks-Mireaux, "Asset Holdings and the Life Cycle," for more details on this procedure.

103. See Diamond and Hausman, "Individual Retirement and Savings Behavior," and André Masson, "A Cohort Analysis of Age-Wealth Profiles Generated by a Simulation Model of France (1949–1975)," *Economic Journal* 96 (1986): 173–90, for a discussion of the formal model underlying this form.

104. King and Dicks-Mireaux, "Asset Holdings and the Life Cycle"; Hubbard, "Do IRA's and Keoghs Increase Saving?"; Diamond and Hausman, "Individual Retirement and Savings Behavior."

105. Avery, Elliehausen, and Gustafson, "Pensions and Social Security in Household Portfolios."

7. Inheritances and the Distribution of Wealth

1. For my earlier work on the subject of wealth transfers, see *Inheriting Wealth in America: Future Boom or Bust?* (New York: Oxford University Press, 2015). Also see Daphne T. Greenwood and Edward N. Wolff, "Changes in Wealth in the United States, 1962–1983: Savings, Capital Gains, Inheritance, and Lifetime Transfers," *Journal of Population Economics* 5, no. 4 (1992): 261–88; Wolff, "Wealth Accumulation by Age Cohort in the U.S., 1962–1992: The Role of Savings, Capital Gains and Intergenerational Transfers," *Geneva Papers on Risk and Insurance* 24, no. 1 (January 1999): 27–49; Wolff, "Inheritances and Wealth Inequality, 1989–1998," *American Economic Review Papers and Proceedings* 92, no. 2 (May 2002): 260–64; Wolff, "The Impact of Gifts and Bequests on the Distribution of Wealth," in *Death and Dollars,* ed. Alicia H. Munnell and Annika Sundén (Washington, DC: Brookings Institution, 2003), 345–75; Wolff and Maury Gittleman, "Inheritances and the Distribution of Wealth or Whatever Happened to the Great Inheritance Boom?" *Journal of Economic Inequality* 12, no. 4 (December 2014): 439–68.

2. These results come into play in Chapter 5 when I analyze factors affecting trends in mean and median household wealth and overall wealth inequality.

3. See, for example, Wolff, "Household Wealth Trends in the United States, 1983–2010," *Oxford Review of Economic Policy* 30, no. 1 (2014): 21–43.

4. See Wolff, "Wealth Accumulation by Age Cohort in the U.S., 1962–1992: The Role of Savings, Capital Gains and Intergenerational Transfers," *Geneva Papers on Risk and Insurance* 24, no. 1 (January 1999): 27–49; and "The Impact of Gifts and Bequests on the Distribution of Wealth."

5. Robert B. Avery and Michael S. Rendall, "Estimating the Size and Distribution of Baby Boomers' Prospective Inheritances," in *1993 Proceedings of the Social Statistics Section* (Alexandria, VA: American Statistical Association, 1993), 11–19.

6. Alicia H. Munnell et al., "How Important are Intergenerational Transfers for Baby Boomers?" (Boston College Center for Retirement Research, Working Paper 2011–1, Chestnut Hill, MA, 2011).

7. The median value among all households is zero in every year.

8. See chapter 2 in Wolff, *Inheriting Wealth in America,* for a more extensive review of the literature, including the theoretical underpinnings of the bequest motive.

9. Dorothy Projector and Gertrude Weiss, *Survey of Financial Characteristics of Consumers,* Federal Reserve Board Technical Papers (Washington, DC: Board of Governors of the Federal Reserve System, 1966).

10. Morgan et al., *Income and Welfare in the United States* (New York: McGraw-Hill Book Company, 1962).

11. Robin Barlow, Harvey E. Brazer, and James N. Morgan, *Economic Behavior of the Affluent* (Washington, DC: The Brookings Institution, 1966).

12. Paul Menchik and Martin David, "Income Distribution, Lifetime Saving and Bequests," *American Economic Review* 73, no. 4 (1983): 673–90.

13. Michael D. Hurd and Gabriella Mundaca, "The Importance of Gifts and Inheritances among the Affluent," in *The Measurement of Saving, Investment, and Wealth,* ed. Robert E. Lipsey and Helen Stone Tice (Chicago: Chicago University Press, 1989), 737–63.

14. William G. Gale and John K. Scholz, "Intergenerational Transfers and the Accumulation of Wealth," *Journal of Economic Perspectives* 8 (1994): 145–60.

15. Jeffrey R. Brown and Scott J. Weisbenner, "Intergenerational Transfers and Savings Behavior," in *Perspectives on the Economics of Aging,* ed. David A. Wise (Chicago: University of Chicago Press, 2004), 181–204.

16. Denis Kessler and André Masson, "Les transferts intergenerationales: l'aide, la donation, l'heritage" (Paris: C.N.R.S. Report, 1979).

17. N. Anders Klevmarken, "On the Wealth Dynamics of Swedish Families 1984–1998" (paper presented at the 21st Arne Ryde Symposium on Non-Human Wealth and Capital Accumulation, Lund, Sweden, August 23–25, 2001).

18. John Laitner and Amanda Sonnega, "Intergenerational Transfers in the Health and Retirement Study Data" (Ann Arbor: Michigan Retirement Research Center, 2010).

19. Eleni Karagiannaki, "Recent Trends in the Size and Distribution of Inherited Wealth in the UK" (LSE STICERD Research Paper No. CASE / 146, London School of Economics, June 2011); and "The Impact of Inheritance on the Distribution of Wealth: Evidence from the UK" (LSE STICERD Research Paper No. CASE / 148, London School of Economics, June 2011).

20. Karagiannaki, "The Impact of Inheritance."

21. Thomas Piketty, "On the Long-Run Evolution of Inheritance: France 1820–2050," *Quarterly Journal of Economics* 126, no. 3 (2011): 1071–131. See also Piketty, *Capital in the Twenty-First Century* (Cambridge, MA: Harvard University Press, 2014).

22. Anthony B. Atkinson, "Wealth and Inheritance in Britain from 1896 to the Present" (Centre for Analysis of Social Exclusion Working Paper 178, London School of Economics, November 2013).

23. Rowena Crawford and Andrew Hood, "Lifetime Receipt of Inheritances and the Distribution of Wealth in England," *Fiscal Studies* 37, no. 1 (2016): 55–75.

24. See Chapter 2 for a description of the sample design of the SCF and data sources and methods and the definition of household wealth used in this study.

25. The discrepancy in the share of households reporting a wealth transfer ranged from 0 percentage points to 0.2 percentage points in the eight survey years, except for 1989 when the difference amounted to 0.4 percentage points.

26. Actually, the date of receipt is rounded off to the nearest fifth year in the Public Use version of the SCF, so that some error is introduced into the calculations. There is also no date of receipt provided for the category "other gifts and

inheritances." To be on the conservative side, I assume the wealth transfer in that case was received in the year of the survey. I also trimmed the sample by capping all gifts and inheritances at $20 million (there were two such transfers in the 2004 SCF from trust funds and one such in the 2007 SCF).

27. It should be noted that there is an ongoing debate in the literature about how past inheritances should be valued relative to current wealth. In particular, should the dividends, interest, and capital gains received on past inheritances be counted as part of inheritances or as part of savings? The basic procedure here is to use a "normal rate" of return, including dividends, interest, and capital gains, to capitalize assets received from wealth transfers. This amount is counted in the "inheritance portion" of current wealth. Returns on inherited assets above or below this normal rate are implicitly treated as part of savings (dissavings). This is, of course, a somewhat arbitrary division and represents a shortcoming of the analysis. In previous work I used three additional capitalization factors: a real rate of return of 2 percent; a real rate of return of 4 percent; and period-specific capitalization rates. As shown in Wolff and Gittleman, "Inheritances and the Distribution of Wealth," and Wolff, *Inheriting Wealth in America,* the results are quite similar among these alternative capitalization choices. As a result, I show results only for r equal to 3 percent here.

28. The year 2004 is particularly anomalous, when the share from trusts was 28 percent (and the share from inheritances was down to 66 percent). This reflected two very large transfers from trust funds in that year.

29. The time trend coefficient is estimated from a pooled sample for years 1989, 1992, 1995, 1998, 2001, 2004, 2007, 2010, and 2013 (sample size of 41,529).

30. Table 7.2 shows the results of unweighted regressions. The same five regressions were also estimated using Weighted Least Squares, where the weights in each year were normalized so they summed to the same amount. The regressions results were virtually the same as those reported on the basis of unweighted ordinary least squares.

31. Differences between the omitted category and all other categories are significant at the 1 percent level for all income, wealth, and demographic groups except in one instance.

32. The two-tailed z-test generally indicates a statistically significant decline in the share receiving a wealth transfer between 1989 and 2013 for income, wealth, and demographic groups. The time trend coefficients are also generally negative and significant.

33. Differences in mean wealth transfers between the omitted category and all other categories are significant at the 1 percent level for all income, wealth, and demographic groups except in a few instances. Differences in median transfers, however, are generally significant at the 1 percent level for income and wealth classes and educational group but not generally for racial groups or age classes.

34. The z-test for the difference in mean transfers between 1989 and 2010 is generally significant for income, wealth, and demographic groups but the time trend coefficients are generally not significant. The z-test for the difference in median transfers between 1989 and 2010, on the other hand, is generally not significant.

35. Differences in mean wealth transfers between the omitted category and all other categories are significant at the 1 percent level for all income, wealth, and demographic groups except in one instance.

36. The time trend coefficient is significant in only a few instances.

37. The mean net worth of the bottom wealth class is negative.

38. With three exceptions, the z-test for the difference in transfers as a share of net worth is statistically significant between the top income class and the lower income classes and between the top wealth class and the lower wealth classes.

39. Notably, the time trend coefficient is significant and negative for the top two income classes and for the top three wealth classes.

40. The time trend coefficient is significant (and positive) only for white households. The large decline recorded for Hispanic households appears to be due to a very high mean value of wealth transfers of $1,695,100 in 1989. This, in turn, seems to be a single outlier and the result of the small sample size of this group in 1989 (only thirteen cases).

41. Time trend coefficients are largely insignificant.

42. The time trend coefficient is significant and positive for the lowest two educational groups and significant and negative for college graduates.

43. See chapter 3 in Wolff, *Inheriting Wealth in America,* where two additional steps were added to the analysis. First, the analysis was redone allowing a range of responses of savings to transfers, but assuming that the elasticity of saving with respect to wealth transfers did not vary by wealth class. Second, the last-mentioned assumption was relaxed and the analysis was redone by assuming a higher elasticity of saving with respect to wealth transfers for higher wealth households. The results are not materially altered in these two cases.

44. As noted previously, the SCF combines wealth transfers received into five-year intervals preceding the survey year.

45. Gifts and donations are trimmed at $20 million in order to lessen the influence of outliers. In 1995, there was one donation of $50 million reported; in 2007, there was one gift of $50 million and one donation of $35 million; and in 2010, there was one donation of $61 million.

46. The two figures would not necessarily be exactly equal because the recipient side is based on an average of the preceding five years whereas the donor side is based on the preceding year alone. Moreover, gifts given to someone living outside the United States would not show up on the recipient side (U.S. population only). These may include remittances to residents of less-developed countries like

Mexico. On the other hand, gifts received from someone living abroad would not show up on the donor side.

47. The simulation results shown in chapter 5 of Wolff, *Inheriting Wealth in America,* also suggest substantial underreporting of gifts from the recipient side. In Chapters 5 and 9 of this volume, I adjust the data on gifts received to align with the amount recorded on the donor side.

48. I use this data in Chapters 5 and 9 in my analysis of the sources of growth in household wealth.

49. Differences in recipiency rates are significant at the 1 percent level for all income, wealth, and demographic groups except in a few instances—most notably, between the youngest and oldest age groups (results are not shown).

50. Differences in mean values are significant (typically at the 1 percent level) for all income, wealth, and demographic groups except in a few instances and most notably between the youngest and oldest age groups (results are not shown).

51. Karen E. Dynan, Jonathan Skinner, and Stephen P. Zeldes, "The Importance of Bequests and Life-Cycle Saving in Capital Accumulation: A New Answer," *American Economic Review* 92, no. 2 (2002): 274–78.

52. The frequency of bequests may also drop if parental wealth dips to zero or below. There is also the possibility that mortality rates may have gone up somewhat since wealth is one factor that affects longevity and older people may have become poorer. This factor would increase the number of bequests given, but not their dollar value.

8. The Role of Social Security and Private Pensions

1. Martin Feldstein, "Social Security, Individual Retirement and Aggregate Capital Accumulation," *Journal of Political Economy* 82, no. 5 (September / October 1974): 905–26.

2. For a more comprehensive review of the relevant literature, see chapter 3 in Wolff, *The Transformation of the American Pension System: Was It Beneficial for Workers?* (Kalamazoo, MI: W. E. Upjohn Institute for Employment Research, 2011).

3. This chapter draws from the following: Wolff, "The Effects of Pensions and Social Security on the Distribution of Wealth in the U.S." in *International Comparisons of Household Wealth Distribution* (New York: Oxford University Press, 1987), 208–47; Wolff, "Methodological Issues in the Estimation of Retirement Wealth," in *Research in Economic Inequality,* ed. Daniel J. Slottje (Stamford, CT: JAI Press, 1992), 31–56; Wolff, *Retirement Insecurity: The Income Shortfalls Awaiting the Soon-to-Retire* (Washington, DC: Economic Policy Institute, 2002); Wolff, "The Devolution of the American Pension System: Who Gained and Who Lost?" *Eastern Economics Journal* 29, no. 4 (2003): 477–95; Wolff, "The Transfor-

mation of the American Pension System," in *Work Options for Mature Americans,* ed. Teresa Ghilarducci and John Turner (Notre Dame, IN: University of Notre Dame Press, 2007), 175–211; Wolff, "The Adequacy of Retirement Resources among the Soon-to-Retire, 1983–2001," in *Government Spending on the Elderly,* ed. Dimitri B. Papadimitriou (Houndsmill, Hampshire, UK: Palgrave Macmillan, 2007), 315–42; Wolff, *The Transformation of the American Pension System;* Wolff, "U.S. Pensions in the 2000s: the Lost Decade?" *Review of Income and Wealth,* series 61, no. 4 (December 2015): 599–629, available at doi: 10.1111 / roiw.12123; and Christian Weller and Edward N. Wolff, *Retirement Income: The Crucial Role of Social Security* (Washington, DC: Economic Policy Institute, 2005). See Wolff, "Methodological Issues in the Estimation of Retirement Wealth," in particular for a discussion of some of the issues involved in the definition and estimation of retirement.

4. David E. Bloom and Richard B. Freeman, "The Fall in Private Pension Coverage in the United States," *American Economic Review Papers and Proceedings* 82 (1992): 539–58.

5. A. L. Gustman and T. L. Steinmeier, "The Stampede toward Defined Contribution Pension Plans: Fact or Fiction?" *Industrial Relations* 31 (1992): 361–69.

6. W. E. Even and D. A. Macpherson, "Why Did Male Pension Coverage Decline in the 1980s?" *Industrial and Labor Relations Review* 47 (1994): 429–53.

7. U.S. Department of Labor, Pension and Welfare Benefits Administration, "Coverage Status of Workers Under Employer Provided Pension Plans: Findings from the Contingent Work Supplement to the February 1999 Current Population Survey" (Washington, DC: U.S. Department of Labor, 2000).

8. Alicia H. Munnell and Pamela Perun, "An Update on Private Pensions" (IB #50, Center for Retirement Research at Boston College, Boston, MA, August 2006).

9. James M. Poterba, "Retirement Security in an Aging Population," *American Economic Review Papers and Proceedings* 104, no. 5 (2014): 1–30.

10. Alan L. Gustman, Thomas L. Steinmeier, and Nahid Tabataba, "How Do Pension Changes Affect Retirement Preparedness? The Trend to Defined Contribution Plans and the Vulnerability of the Retirement Age Population to the Stock Market Decline of 2008–2009" (Michigan Retirement Research Center Working Paper 2009–206, Ann Arbor, MI, October 2009).

11. This contrasts with my computations of a 47 percent share in 2001 and a 41 percent share in 2007 of age group 47–64.

12. James M. Poterba, Steven F. Venti, and David A. Wise. "401(k) Plans and Future Patterns of Retirement Saving," *American Economic Review Papers and Proceedings* 87, no. 2 (May 1998): 179–84; James M. Poterba, Steven F. Venti, and David A. Wise, "The Transition to Personal Accounts and Increasing Retirement Wealth: Micro and Macro Evidence" (NBER Working Paper 8610, National Bureau of Economic Research, Cambridge, MA, November 2001).

13. James M. Poterba et al., "Defined Contribution Plans, Defined Benefit Plans, and the Accumulation of Retirement Wealth," *Journal of Public Economics* 91, no. 10 (2007): 2062–86.

14. Eric M. Engen and William G. Gale, "The Effects of 401(k) Plans on Household Wealth: Differences across Earnings Groups" (mimeo, the Brookings Institution, Washington, DC, August 2000).

15. Arthur B. Kennickell and Annika E. Sunden, "Pensions, Social Security, and the Distribution of Wealth" (mimeo, Washington, DC, Federal Reserve Board of Washington, December 1999).

16. Victor Chernozhukov and Christian Hansen, "The Effects of 401(k) Participation on the Wealth Distribution: An Instrumental Quantile Regression Analysis," *Review of Economics and Statistics* 86, no. 3 (2004): 735–51.

17. Gary V. Engelhardt and Anil Kumar, "Pensions and Household Wealth Accumulation," *Journal of Human Resources* 46 (2011): 203–36.

18. See Martin S. Feldstein, "Social Security and the Distribution of Wealth," *Journal of the American Statistical Association* 71 (1976): 800–807.

19. Wolff, "The Effects of Pensions and Social Security on the Distribution of Wealth in the U.S."

20. Kathleen McGarry and Andrew Davenport, "Pensions and the Distribution of Wealth" (NBER Working Paper 6171, National Bureau of Economic Research, Cambridge, MA, September 1997).

21. Kennickell and Sunden, "Pensions, Social Security, and the Distribution of Wealth."

22. Gustman et al., "Pension and Social Security Wealth in the Health and Retirement Study" (NBER Working Paper No. 5912, National Bureau of Economic Research, Cambridge, MA, February 1997).

23. Alan L. Gustman and Thomas L. Steinmeier, "Effects of Pensions on Saving: Analysis with Data from the Health and Retirement Study" (NBER Working Paper 6681, National Bureau of Economic Research, Cambridge, MA, August 1998).

24. See Chapter 2 and Appendix 1 for technical details on the SCF.

25. The Federal Reserve Board also made its own estimates of both DB pension and SSW for 1983. I do not use these estimates in this chapter but provide my own to be consistent with the method of the other years. Moreover, pertinent data on pensions and Social Security for 1983 are rather limited for households under the age of 47. As a result, I do not provide estimates of pension and SSW for this age group in 1983.

26. See Appendix 3 of the book for details.

27. For further discussion of this point, see Wolff, "Methodological Issues in the Estimation of Retirement Wealth."

28. Kennickell and Sunden, "Pensions, Social Security, and the Distribution of Wealth."

29. I concentrate on years 1983 to 2013 in this chapter because I have consistent estimates of pension and SSW for these years. See Chapter 12 for long-term trends in retirement wealth.

30. I use the term "Great Recession" to refer to the period from 2007 through 2013.

31. I have chosen age 47 as a break point. By age 47 most workers have accumulated somewhere between 20 and 25 years of labor market experience and are on a fairly stable earnings path, so that projections of future earnings become reasonably reliable. Second, for those with a DB plan, most are fully vested by then and are likely to be able to project their future retirement benefit with some accuracy.

32. Figures on DBW cannot be estimated for households under age 47 in 1983 and, correspondingly, for all households as well.

33. The difference is not statistically significant, reflecting the large sampling variation from year to year.

34. All dollar figures are in 2013 dollars unless otherwise noted.

35. Median pension values are strongly affected by the share of households with pension wealth and, as a result, are not shown here for all households.

36. This relationship can, perhaps, be seen most clearly by a decomposition of the coefficient of variation. For any variable $X = X_1 + X_2$,

$$CV^2(X) = p_1^2 CV^2(X_1) + p_2^2 CV^2(X_2) + 2CC(X_1, X_2)$$

where CV is the coefficient of variation (the ratio of the standard deviation to the mean), CC is the coefficient of covariation, defined as the ratio of the covariance to X^2, $p_1 = E(X_1) / E(X)$, $p_2 = E(X_2) / E(X)$, and "E" is the expected (or mean) value. The interaction term principally reflects the correlation coefficient between DCW and DBW. The correlation coefficient also rose over time (from 0.07 in 1989 to 0.24 in 2007 among all households). The rising interaction term as a result also made a positive contribution to the growth in overall pension wealth inequality.

37. Results are shown for only the fiftieth percentile and above because below this point values are predominantly zero.

38. Results are shown for only the fortieth percentile and above because below this point values are predominantly zero.

39. I show trends in medians (8.5) separately from those in mean values (8.4) because for most variables the trends are quite different. Gini coefficients are shown in 8.6.

40. A small decline in both mean and median SSW for middle-aged households can be seen in the data for the period from 1983 to 1989. This decrease in SSW probably reflects the decline in average real wages over the period according to the BLS real hourly wage series, as well as the increase in the normal retirement age from 65 to 67 from the new Social Security legislation of the period.

41. The inequality of SSW first fell very substantially from 1989 to 2001, a trend that primarily reflected increasing Social Security coverage, and then rose sharply

from 2001 to 2007 though not enough to offset its fall during the 1990s. The change over 2000–2007 mainly reflected the rising spread in (annual) earnings and by implication, the rise in lifetime earnings inequality among this age group.

42. See note 37 for the algebraic decomposition.

43. The upward blip in 2007 reflects the housing bubble that ended in 2006.

44. Among older households, the primary reason for the rise in AW inequality was the increasing share of net worth in AW, which rose from 68 percent in 1989 to 76 percent in 2007. Since the *level* of inequality of NW is greater than that of retirement wealth, this shift resulted in higher inequality of AW in the later year. A secondary reason was the increase in the correlation between NWX and RW.

45. See Wolff, "Methodological Issues in the Estimation of Retirement Wealth."

46. See Appendix 3 for details on the method used to estimate DCEMP.

47. The calculations are performed for only age group 47 to 64. The value of pension wealth for retirees is not affected by the addition of DCEMP (or the other adjustments made below) since the value of their DC account is already set. Also, the value of DCEMP (and the other components described below) is too uncertain to estimate for young workers, since their work life is just beginning.

48. Some evidence of this is provided for the state of Michigan in Ngina Chiteji, "The Great Recession, DC Pensions, and the Decline in Retirement Savings" (mimeo, 2015). She indicated, for example, that 21 percent of respondents in the Michigan Recession and Recovery Study reported that their employers had reduced retirement contributions in 2012.

49. See Appendix 3 for details on the method used to estimate DCEMPW.

50. Because of a large number of missing values, it is not possible to show results for DCEMPW or PW** for 1983.

51. This process would require a household microsimulation model such as the MINT model that the Urban Institute and the Social Security Administration use (see, for example, Karen Smith, Eric Toder, and Howard Iams, "Lifetime Redistribution of Social Security Retirement Benefits" (mimeo, Washington, DC, Social Security Administration, 2001).

52. AWP cannot be computed for 1983 because DCEMPW is not available for this year.

53. Calculations could be performed for years 2007, 2010, and 2013 only because of the lack of comparable information for earlier years.

54. Results for age group 47–64 are highlighted in this section because this is the age group most affected by the transformation of the pension system and the pertinent data cover the period from 1983 to 2013.

55. Barry Bosworth, Gary Burtless, and Kan Zhang, "Later Retirement, Inequality in Old Age, and the Growing Gap in Longevity between Rich and Poor" (Washington, DC: Economic Studies at Brookings, 2016).

9. Wealth Differences among Socioeconomic Groups

1. Wolff, "Household Wealth Trends in the United States, 1962–2013: What Happened over the Great Recession?" (National Bureau of Economic Research, Cambridge, MA: NBER Working Paper No. 20733, December 2014).

2. Franco Modigliani and Richard Blumberg, "Utility Analysis and the Consumption Function: An Interpretation of Cross-Section Data," in *Post Keynesian Economics,* ed. Kenneth K. Kurihara (New Brunswick, NJ: Rutgers University Press, 1954), 388–436.

3. This section draws partly on Daphne T. Greenwood and Edward N. Wolff, "Relative Wealth Holdings of Children and the Elderly in the United States, 1962–1983," in *The Vulnerable,* ed. John Palmer, Timothy Smeeding, and Barbara Torrey (Washington, DC: The Urban Institute Press, 1988), 123–48; Robert Haveman et al., "Disparities in Well-Being among U.S. Children over Two Decades: 1962–1983," in *The Vulnerable,* 149–70; and Wolff, "Income, Wealth, and Late-Life Inequality in the U.S.," in *Annual Review of Gerontology and Geriatrics,* ed. Stephen Crystal and Dennis Shea (New York: Springer Publishing Co., 2002), 31–58.

4. This section draws in part on Maury Gittleman and Edward N. Wolff, "Racial Differences in Patterns of Wealth Accumulation," *Journal of Human Resources* 39, no. 1 (Winter 2004): 193–227; and Gittleman and Wolff, "Racial and Ethnic Differences in Wealth," in *Race and Economic Opportunity in the Twenty-First Century,* ed. Marlene Kim (New York: Routledge, 2007), 29–49.

5. This section draws in part on Wolff, "The Economic Status of Parents in Postwar America," in *Taking Parenting Public: The Case for a New Social Movement,* ed. Sylvia Hewlitt, Nancy Rankin, and Cornel West (Lanham, MD: Rowman and Littlefield, 2002), 59–82.

6. A "quantile" is a generic term referring to all percentiles groups, such as the second quintile or the top 5 percent.

7. See Chapter 3, specifically Table 3.10.

8. See Chapter 3, Table 3.8.

9. See chapter 5 in Wolff, *Inheriting Wealth in America: Future Boom or Bust?* (New York: Oxford University Press, 2015).

10. The unadjusted SCF data indicate negative growth in simulated mean wealth (−13 percent) for the second quintile and an annual savings rate of −44 percent, results that do not seem credible. Results for the third quintile on the basis of the unadjusted SCF data were similar (16 percentage point decline in mean wealth and a −49 percent savings rate).

11. Even the unadjusted SCF data indicate a robust 26 percent growth in mean wealth for the top percentile.

12. For this, I divide households into seven income groups on the basis of income intervals in 2013 dollars: under $15,000; $15,000–$24,999; $25,000–$49,999; $50,000–$74,999; $75,000–$99,999; $100,000–$249,999; and $250,000 or more.

13. This procedure assumes that, ceteris paribus, altering the distribution of income leaves mean NW by income class and other characteristics unchanged.

14. However, fully one-third of the households in this age group reported having a student loan outstanding.

15. As with racial minorities, the sample size is relatively small for age group 75 and over, so that the huge increase in the homeownership rate between 2001 and 2004 (almost 9 percentage points) may be ascribable to sampling variation (see Chapter 2, Appendix Table 2.1 for sample sizes).

16. As in 2007, the principal source of debt was mortgage debt, which comprised 70 percent of the total debt for the youngest age group in 2010. However, educational loans now amounted to 15 percent of their total liabilities, up from 9.5 percent in 2007, and 40 percent of households in this age group reported an outstanding student loan in 2010. Dissavings was also reflected in the decline in the homeownership rate, which fell from 40.8 percent in 2007 to 35.6 percent in 2013 among households under age 35 and from 66.1 to 61.7 percent for age group 35–44.

17. This pattern might also be partly a cohort effect since 401(k) plans and other defined contribution plans were not widely introduced into the workplace until after 1989.

18. See Chapter 3, Table 3.8.

19. As in 2007 and 2010, mortgage debt comprised the majority of overall debt of this age group, 64 percent, but student loans now comprised 20 percent of their total debt, up from 15 percent in 2010, and 41 percent of households in this age group reported an outstanding student loan in 2013.

20. This result might be largely due to sampling variability.

21. The methodology follows that described in Chapter 5.

22. I choose ages 55–64 as the base in these comparisons because wealth generally peaked for this age group except for a couple of years (see Table 9.5).

23. As shown in Table 9.5, the ratio of the mean wealth of the under-35 age group to *overall* mean wealth nosedived from 0.17 in 2007 to 0.11 in 2010.

24. I once again assume that, ceteris paribus, altering the age distribution leaves mean NW by age group and other characteristics unchanged.

25. It should be noted that these decompositions by various characteristics such as age and income are *not additive* because these characteristics are not statistically independent of each other. For example, the rise of mean and median income over time is due, in part, to the gradual aging of the population since older persons, in general, have higher income (as well as wealth) than younger ones.

26. The residual group, American Indians and Asians, is excluded here because of its small sample size.

27. It should be stressed that the unit of observation is the household, which includes families (two or more related individuals living together) as well as single adults. As is widely known, the share of female-headed households among

African Americans is much higher than that among whites. This difference partly accounts for the relatively lower income and wealth among African American households.

28. The 1988 income figure for black households appears to be an outlier. The low income for blacks in that year probably reflects the small sample size for blacks (and Hispanics as well) and the survey-to-survey sample variability (see Chapter 2, Appendix Table 2.1 for sample sizes).

29. The sample sizes of African Americans were relatively small in all years, as shown in Chapter 2, Appendix Table 2.1.

30. Also, see Gittleman and Wolff, "Racial Differences in Patterns of Wealth Accumulation," for additional evidence from the Panel Study of Income Dynamics (PSID).

31. As noted previously, there is a large amount of variation in the income and wealth figures for both blacks and Hispanics on a year-by-year basis. This is probably a reflection of the small sample sizes for these two groups and the associated sampling variability, as well as some changes in the wording of questions on race and ethnicity over the ten surveys (see Chapter 2, Appendix Table 2.1 for sample sizes).

32. In contrast, according the Current Population Survey (CPS) data, median household income among Hispanics grew by only 4.4 percent from 2003 to 2006 and that among non-Hispanic whites by 0.1 percent. It is not clear why there is such a large discrepancy between the SCF and CPS data.

33. One important reason for the wealth gap is differences in inheritances. According to the SCF data, 24.1 percent of white households in 1998 reported receiving an inheritance in 1998 or earlier in their lifetime, compared to 11 percent of black households, and the average bequest among white inheritors was $115,000 (present value in 1998), compared to $32,000 among black inheritors. Thus, inheritance differences appear to play a vital role in explaining the large wealth gap, particularly in light of the fact that black families appear to save more than white families at similar income levels (see, for example, Francine D. Blau and John W. Graham, "Black-White Differences in Wealth and Asset Composition," *Quarterly Journal of Economics* 105, no. 1 (May 1990): 321–39; Melvin L. Oliver and Thomas M. Shapiro, *Black Wealth, White Wealth* (New York: Routledge, 1997); and Gittleman and Wolff, "Racial Differences in Patterns of Wealth Accumulation."

34. Unfortunately, there are no data available to separate out actual declines in house prices for white, black, and Hispanic homeowners.

35. There was almost no change in the relative homeownership rates of the two groups—both experienced moderate losses—while the share of households with nonpositive NW actually increased more in relative terms for white households than black ones.

36. This follows the methodology laid out in Chapter 5.

37. This follows the methodology laid out in Chapter 5.

38. Once again, the high implicit savings rate estimated for this group may reflect the possibility that inter vivos gifts received by this group were under-reported.

39. The unadjusted SCF data indicates negative growth in simulated mean wealth (–15 percent) and an annual savings rate of –51 percent, results that do not seem credible.

40. The implicit savings rate is –31 percent on the basis of the unadjusted SCF data, which again does not seem believable.

41. Families with children were, on average, younger than those without children, so part of the differential in NW between these two groups is due to the higher wealth of older families.

42. Married couples with children were also getting older over the thirty years, which partly accounts for the rise in their *mean* NW but does not explain why their *median* NW fell so sharply.

43. In fact, according to Table 9.5, the homeownership rate peaked in 2004 at 69.1 percent.

44. See www.corelogic.com/research/foreclosure-report/national-foreclosure -report-may-2013.pdf. This total does not include so-called short sales (when the selling price of a home is less than the outstanding mortgage). Many homes were repossessed by banks and other financial institutions and some were probably sold to investors or speculators and became rental properties. Others may have been abandoned, condemned, or simply sat vacant.

45. For a more systematic analysis of the effects of homeownership on wealth accumulation, see Alexandra Killewald and Brielle Bryan, "Does Your Home Make You Wealthy?" *The Russell Sage Foundation Journal of the Social Sciences* 2, no. 6, (October 2016): 110–28.

46. The spread in rates of return was much smaller between income and educational groups.

10. Who Are the Rich? A Demographic Profile of High-Income and High-Wealth Americans

1. See Wolff, "Who Are the Rich? A Demographic Profile of High-Income and High-Wealth Americans," in *Does Atlas Shrug? The Economic Consequences of Taxing the Rich,* ed. Joel Slemrod (New York: Russell Sage Foundation and Harvard University Press, 2000), 74–113.

2. Thomas Piketty and Emmanuel Saez, "Income Inequality in the United States, 1913–1998," *Quarterly Journal of Economics* 118, no. 1 (2003): 1–39.

3. The industry classifications are provided directly in the SCF data and no further breakdown (except for 1983) is possible.

4. Though there are some problems with the "self-employed" category in the 1992 SCF data, I have tried to make the definition as consistent as possible with the 1983 SCF concept. The fact that the share of self-employed among all workers

shows only a modest increase between the two years suggests that the definitions are roughly comparable.

5. There was no separate category for professional workers in the 1992 SCF.

6. Data on wealth transfers are not available from the 1983 SCF. Details on the methodology used in the calculations are presented in Chapter 7.

7. I am ignoring miscellaneous assets in this breakdown.

8. I suspect that this results from a misclassification of a large portion of retirement income such as proceeds from defined contribution benefit plans like 401(k) plans.

9. On the other hand, see Joel Slemrod, "High-Income Families and the Tax Changes of the 1980s: The Anatomy of Behavioral Responses" (NBER Working Paper No. 5218, August 1995). Slemrod argued that a large part of the increase in reported self-employment income over this period was due to the conversion of corporations to Subchapter S corporations and partnerships for tax reasons. In particular, the 1986 Tax Reform Act caused the top marginal tax rate on personal income to fall below that on corporate earnings. Since income from S corporations and partnerships are treated as personal rather than corporate income, many corporations converted to S corporations. In this case, the purported rise in entrepreneurship might simply be due to a reclassification of income.

10. This "youthening" of the rich continued a trend for the 1977–1983 period, as noted in Joel Slemrod, "On the High-Income Laffer Curve" (Working Paper No. 93–5, University of Michigan Business School, The Office of Tax Policy Research, Ann Arbor, MI, March 1993).

11. The greater importance of finance and business services among the high-wealth group in 1992 in comparison to the high-income group probably reflects the stock market downturn of 1989, the 1991–1992 recession, and the ensuing shrinkage of the finance sector as a source of employment. The finance industry recovered after that in terms of employment.

12. The SCF combines these two income categories in the 2001 and the 2013 public use sample.

13. See Slemrod, "High-Income Families and the Tax Changes of the 1980s."

14. As discussed earlier, it is not possible to separate out rental, royalty, and trust income from self-employment income in the 2001 and 2013 SCFs.

11. The Persistence of Asset Poverty

1. The Census Bureau uses a set of money income thresholds that vary by family size and composition to determine who is in poverty. If a family's total income is less than the family's threshold, then that family and every individual in it is considered in poverty. The official poverty thresholds do not vary geographically, but they are updated for inflation using the Consumer Price Index (CPI-U). The official poverty definition uses money income before taxes and does not include

capital gains or noncash benefits (such as public housing, Medicaid, and food stamps). See https://www.census.gov/topics/income-poverty/poverty/guidance/pov erty-measures.html for more details.

2. See Wolff, "Wealth Holdings and Poverty Status in the United States," *Review of Income and Wealth* series 36, no. 2 (June 1990): 143–65.

3. See Robert Haveman and Edward N. Wolff, "The Concept and Measurement of Asset Poverty: Levels, Trends and Composition for the U.S., 1983–2001," *Journal of Economic Inequality* 2, no. 2 (August 2004): 145–69; and "Who Are the Asset Poor? Levels, Trends and Composition, 1983–1998," in *Inclusion in the American Dream: Assets, Poverty, and Public Policy,* ed. Michael Sherraden (New York: Oxford University Press, 2005), 61–86. In addition to showing overall trends in asset poverty, these two articles described both the pattern of asset poverty rates for various socioeconomic groups (e.g., race, age, schooling, and family structure) over the 1983–1998 period.

4. Mary Jo Bane and David T. Ellwood, "Slipping into and out of Poverty: The Dynamics of Spells," *Journal of Human Resources* 21, no. 1 (1986): 1–23.

5. Charles M. Beach, "Cyclical Sensitivity of Aggregate Income Inequality," *Review of Economics and Statistics* 59 (1977): 56–66; James R. Thornton, J. Agnello, and Charles R. Link, "Poverty and Economic Growth: Trickle Down Peters Out," *Economic Inquiry* 16 (1978): 385–94.

6. Patricia Ruggles and Robertson Williams, "Longitudinal Measures of Poverty: Accounting for Income and Assets over Time," *Review of Income and Wealth* 35, no. 3 (1989): 225–43.

7. For owner-occupied property, imputed rent is the imputed net income of the owner. It is calculated as the imputed output of housing services (space rent) less the expenses associated with owner-occupied housing, such as depreciation, maintenance and repairs, property taxes, and mortgage interest. In the national accounts the imputation is based on matching an owner-occupied property with an equivalent rental property to determine the rental value of the property.

8. I use "census income" for the calculations where U.S. Census income is equal to SCF income less capital gains, gifts, food stamps, and other nonmonetary assistance. I was able to identify capital gains directly, but gifts, food stamps, and other nonmonetary assistance are included in other categories and cannot be separately identified. The poverty line calculations are thus based on SCF income less capital gains. Poverty line definitions are based on income, size of family unit, householders 65 and over, and the number of related children under age 18.

9. Households include both families and unrelated individuals. The latter group is likely to have lower income than the former.

10. In Robert B. Avery et al., "Survey of Consumer Finances, 1983" (*Federal Reserve Bulletin* 1984, 679–92), the authors reported a similar homeownership rate, of 36 percent, for families with family income of $9,999 or less, based on the SCF. A further breakdown of homeownership rates revealed that among the elderly

poor, the rate was 63 percent, while among the nonelderly poor it was 30 percent. Homeownership also varied by geographical area. Among the urban poor, the rate was only 24 percent; in suburban areas it was 41 percent; and in rural areas the rate was 49 percent. Among the elderly poor living in rural areas, the homeownership rate was almost 75 percent.

11. The fact that the ratio of mean net worth between poor and nonpoor households is greater than the ratio of their mean incomes is partly a statistical artifact. Households are ranked by their income in the poverty rate calculation, and therefore the relative gap in their net worth has to be smaller than income unless income and wealth are perfectly correlated.

12. At first glance, it may seem odd that the overall ratio of debt between poor and nonpoor households was lower than the ratio of debt for each of the three age groups. However, this is *not* an error. The overall mean debt of poor households is a *weighted* average of the mean debt of poor households in each of the three age groups, similar to overall mean debt among the nonpoor. As a result, it is possible for the overall ratio to be lower (or higher) than that of each of the three subgroups.

13. It is interesting to look at the wealth holdings of the top 10 percent of the wealth distribution of poor families. In 1983 mean net worth of this group was $202,000, almost 25 percent greater than mean net worth of all the nonpoor, and their net worth was $187,000. For the upper wealth decile of the poor, home equity averaged $79,000, or 39 percent of mean net worth. Unincorporated business equity averaged $73,000, considerably above the mean value of this component for the nonpoor, and the mean value of investment real estate was $27,000. Together, unincorporated business equity and investment real estate comprised 49 percent of net worth of the upper decile, and 39 percent of them held one or the other investment. Thus, it appears that about 10 percent of the poor were relatively well off in regard to net worth, and 4 to 5 percent of the poor were "land poor" in the sense of having low income but owning a very high value of business assets.

14. For methodological details on the construction of estimates for both defined benefit pension wealth and Social Security wealth, see Appendix 3 and Wolff, "The Effects of Pensions and Social Security on the Distribution of Wealth in the U.S." in *International Comparisons of Household Wealth Distribution* (New York: Oxford University Press, 1987), 208–47. Note that the methodology used for the 1983 figures as shown in Table 11.5 differs from that used for the 2001 and 2013 estimates. As a result, I use the symbols DBWA and SSWA to refer to the 1983 estimates.

15. See Martin Feldstein, "Social Security, Individual Retirement and Aggregate Capital Accumulation," *Journal of Political Economy* 82, no. 5 (September / October 1974): 905–26.

16. It should be noted that the number of households currently receiving or expecting pension benefits in 1983 was less than the sum of the number of households

currently receiving benefits and the number expecting benefits, since a household may have one spouse currently receiving benefits and another expecting to receive benefits.

17. For 2001 and 2013, I compute a single value for DBW (pension wealth) and for SSW (Social Security wealth) on the basis of historical trends in real earnings, current legislated Social Security benefit formulae, and a 2 percent real discount rate. See Appendix 3 of this book for details.

18. See Chapter 8 for details.

19. These data are not available for 1962.

20. On the opposite side of the spectrum arises the issue of the relative number of poor people who have high wealth relative to their income. These can be thought of as the "land poor," who are rich in assets but poor in income. At a 3 percent annuity rate, only 15 percent of the poor in 1983 had an annuity-income ratio that exceeded 0.20 and only 6 percent had a ratio that exceeded 0.50. At a 5 percent annuity rate, 20 percent of poor families had an annuity-income ratio greater than 0.20 and 10 percent had a ratio greater than 0.50. At a 7 percent annuity rate, the respective percentages were 25 and 14. Thus, it appears that only a relatively small percentage of the poor had significant net worth, which confirms the findings reported in note 11.

21. This proposed revision is described in the report of the Panel on Poverty and Family Assistance, which was appointed by the Committee on National Statistics of the National Research Council of the National Academy of Sciences (see Constance F. Citro and Robert T. Michael, eds., *Measuring Poverty: A New Approach* (Washington, DC: National Academy Press, 1995).

22. Amartya Sen considered the needs standard (or poverty line) to have "some absolute justification of its own," as a level below which "one cannot participate adequately in communal activities, or be free of pubic shame from failure to satisfy conventions." *Inequality Reexamined* (Cambridge, MA: Russell Sage Foundation and Harvard University Press, 1992), 167.

23. In Robert Haveman and Melissa Mullikin, "Alternative Measures of National Poverty: Perspectives and Assessment," in *Ethics, Poverty and Inequality and Reform in Social Security,* ed. Erik Schokkaert (London: Ashgate Publishing Ltd., 2001) the authors discuss the advantages and disadvantages of these alternatives.

24. See, for example, Patricia Ruggles, *Drawing the Line: Alternative Poverty Measures and Their Implications for Public Policy* (Washington, DC: Urban Institute Press, 1990).

25. The most fundamental criticisms of the official measure focus on the basic social objective on which it rests; cash income may not be the most salient indicator of well-being or position. Similarly, in assessing poverty trends over time, perhaps the general trend in the overall level of living should be taken into account, as is the case with relative measures of poverty. Aside from taking exception to the

social objective that underlies the official measure, most other criticisms of it focus on the adequacy of the annual income measure of "economic resources." While the current cash income numerator of the poverty ratio may reflect the extent to which the family has cash income available to meet its immediate needs, it indicates little about the level of consumption spending potentially available to the family. For many families, annual income fluctuates substantially over time. Unemployment, layoffs, the decision to undertake mid-career training or to change jobs, health considerations, and especially income flows from farming and self-employment may all cause the money income of a household to change substantially from one year to the next. Even as an indicator of a family's ability to meet its immediate needs, the current cash income measure is flawed—it reflects neither the recipient value of in-kind transfers (e.g., food stamps and Medicaid, both of which are major programs in the United States supporting the economic well-being of low-income families), nor the taxes for which the family is liable. Although the Earned Income Tax Credit, a component of the tax system, has expanded into a major form of income support for the low income working population, the refundable payments from the credit are viewed as negative taxes and hence not included in the definition of income used in the official poverty measure. Similarly, whereas current cash income—and hence the official poverty measure—reflects financial flows in the form of interest and dividends from the assets held by individuals, the assets themselves are not counted, nor is the value of leisure (or voluntary nonwork) time reflected in the measure. (This is less the case for the NRC-proposed revision to the official poverty measure, as it attempts to account for some in-kind benefits in assessing the relationship of resources to needs.) The official poverty measure is also silent on the differences in the implicit value that families place on income from various sources. Income from public transfers, market work, and returns on financial assets are treated as being equivalent in contributing to the family's well-being.

26. These figures should not be confused with published poverty rate numbers, which are based on individual (that is, "head count") data.

27. The concept of asset poverty was first advanced by Melvin L. Oliver and Thomas M. Shapiro, *Black Wealth, White Wealth* (New York: Routledge, 1997).

28. Alternatively, one might define as poor households those whose income over a period of time *plus* their assets were not sufficient to maintain the required level of consumption for the stipulated period, as I did in Table 11.7. This would be a less demanding measure than the joint income / asset poverty measure.

29. Two strands of economics literature have studied the relationship between the resource flow (income) and resource stock (wealth) dimensions of economic well-being. Bron Weisbrod and W. Lee Hansen proposed an "income-net worth" measure of economic well-being in their article "An Income-Net Worth Approach to Measuring Economic Welfare," *American Economic Review* 58, no. 5 (1968): 1315–29.

In this framework, well-being was measured by adding to annual income the annual value of asset holdings when annuitized over the expected remaining years of lifetime. They presented estimates of the level and distribution of this value, which indicated substantially higher levels of well-being for older families, with more assets and fewer years over which to annuitize them. Later analysis refined the income-net worth measure and used it to measure the poverty of U.S. families. When measured over all families, the rate of income-net worth poverty was lower than the rate of income poverty, with substantial decreases in poverty rates for older families. See Marilyn Moon, *The Measurement of Economic Welfare: Applications to the Aged* (New York: Academic Press, 1977); Donald L. Lerman and James J. Mikesell, "Impacts of Adding Net Worth to the Poverty Definition," *Eastern Economic Journal* 14, no. 4 (1988): 357–70; and Michael S. Rendall and Alden Speare Jr., "Comparing Economic Well-Being among Elderly Americans," *Review of Income and Wealth* 39, no. 1 (1993): 1–21.

An alternative approach to understanding the links between income and savings (wealth holdings) has been stimulated by empirical observations that the ratio of wealth to permanent income increases monotonically with lifetime income, contrary to the prediction by the life cycle hypothesis of a constant ratio across families with varying lifetime incomes. James Ziliak empirically investigated these potential explanations, and concluded that eligibility for asset-tested transfer income accounted in part for the low level of liquid wealth for those with low permanent income, and that high labor market earnings partially explained why the wealth to permanent income ratio was higher than expected for families with high permanent income. See "Income Transfers and Assets of the Poor," *Review of Economics and Statistics* 85, no. 1 (February 2003): 63–76. These approaches both complement the joint income / asset poverty measures I use here, and suggest further research regarding the determinants of the probability of being joint asset-income poor relative to being either income or asset poor.

30. Caner and Wolff also analyzed the level and trend in asset poverty using data from the Panel Study of Income Dynamics. Asena Caner and Edward N. Wolff, "Asset Poverty in the United States, 1984–99: Evidence from the Panel Study of Income Dynamics," *Review of Income and Wealth* series 50, no. 4 (December 2004): 493–518; and "The Persistence of Asset Poverty in the United States, 1984–2001," in *Trends in Poverty and Welfare Alleviation Issues,* ed. Marie V. Lane (Hauppauge, NY: Nova Science, 2006), 51–80.

31. See Citro and Michael, *Measuring Poverty: A New Approach.*

32. The equivalence scale used here is the two-parameter scale recommended in Citro and Michael (ibid.) The scale equals $(A + 0.8 + 0.5*(C-1))^{0.7}$ for single-parent households and $(A + 0.5*(C-1))^{0.7}$ for all other households, with A and C representing, respectively, the number of adults and children in the family unit.

33. Note that net worth excludes Social Security and defined benefit pension wealth (that is, the present value of future expected Social Security and defined

benefit pension payments, respectively). Such future expected payments cannot be drawn against to finance current consumption. Defined contribution pensions, however, can be liquidated to support consumption, albeit with a penalty. The value of vehicles that may be owned is also excluded. The rationale for excluding vehicles is that for most families, particularly poor families, autos tend to be necessary for work-related transportation, and therefore not readily available for sale to meet consumption needs.

34. "Liquid resources" should not be confused with "liquid assets" as used in Chapter 3.

35. Both asset measures are defined more completely in the appendix to this chapter.

36. I have combined African Americans and Hispanics into a single group for two reasons. The first is the relatively small sample sizes for these two groups and the associated sampling variability. The second is some changes in the wording of questions on race and ethnicity over the ten SCF surveys. In particular, in the 1995 and 1998 surveys, the race question does not explicitly indicate non-Hispanic whites and non-Hispanic blacks for the first two categories, so that some Hispanics may have classified themselves as either whites or blacks. In the case of the former, there is no way to correct the classification.

37. See Franco Modigliani and Richard Blumberg, "Utility Analysis and the Consumption Function: An Interpretation of Cross-Section Data," in *Post Keynesian Economics,* ed. Kenneth K. Kurihara (New Brunswick, NJ: Rutgers University Press, 1954), 388–436.

38. The Great Recession "officially" ended in June 2009. See Chapters 1 and 2 for details.

39. Note that results for income-based poverty and joint income and asset poverty are similar and are not shown here.

40. It should be noted that since asset poverty for the base case (single males under the age of 65) remained virtually unchanged between 1983 and 2001 (see Table 11.10), the changes in coefficients reflect changes in the asset poverty propensity for these groups rather than for the base case.

12. Long-Term Trends in Aggregate Household Wealth

1. This chapter and Chapter 13 draw on three previous articles: Wolff, "Trends in Aggregate Household Wealth in the U.S., 1900–1983," *Review of Income and Wealth* series 35, no. 1 (March 1989): 1–30; Wolff, *Top Heavy: A Study of Increasing Inequality of Wealth in America* (New York: The Twentieth Century Fund Press, 1995); Wolff and Marcia Marley, "Long-Term Trends in U.S. Wealth Inequality: Methodological Issues and Results," in *The Measurement of Saving, Investment, and Wealth,* ed. Robert E. Lipsey and Helen Tice (Chicago: Chicago University Press, 1989), 765–843.

2. Raymond W. Goldsmith, Dorothy S. Brady, and Horst Mendershausen, *A Study of Saving in the United States* (Princeton, NJ: Princeton University Press, 1956); Goldsmith, *The National Wealth of the United States in the Postwar Period* (Princeton, NJ: Princeton University Press, 1962); Goldsmith, Robert E. Lipsey, and Morris Mendelson, *Studies in the National Balance Sheet of the United States* (Princeton, N.J.: Princeton University Press, 1963); Richard Ruggles and Nancy Ruggles, "Integrated Economic Accounts for the United States, 1947–1980," *Survey of Current Business* 62 (May 1982): 1–53; John Musgrave, "Fixed Reproducible Tangible Wealth in the United States: Revised Estimates," *Survey* of *Current Business* 66 (January 1986): 51–75; and the Federal Reserve Board's Financial Accounts of the United States (FFA), available at https://www.federalreserve.gov/releases/z1/current/html/default.htm. These sources are not entirely consistent in their choice of wealth concept, definition of assets and liabilities, or methodology. I have made adjustments to the published data where possible to improve comparability.

3. A more detailed description of the adjustments made for each asset category is provided in Wolff and Marley, "Long-Term Trends in U.S. Wealth Inequality," Appendix A. The adjusted aggregate household balance sheet data are available for the years 1922, 1929, 1939, 1945, 1949, 1953, 1962, 1969, 1972, 1979, 1981, 1983, 1989, 1992, 1995, 1998, 2001, 2004, 2007, 2010, and 2013. These correspond to the years for which distribution data are available. In addition, I include Goldsmith's aggregate estimates for the years 1900, 1912, and 1933.

4. The wealth concepts shown in Table 12.1 differ in subtle ways from the previous wealth concepts used in the paper. I have retained the original symbols. For example, W2 is close to NWA except that both trusts and pensions are valued as a portion of their corresponding reserves in the national balance sheet data. In contrast, in NWA (and NW) the value of trust equity and the outstanding value of defined contribution pension plans are reported directly by the respondent. Another difference is that W2 includes the value of all consumer durables whereas NWA includes the value of vehicles only.

5. See, for example, Chapter 8 and Appendix 3 of the book.

6. Raymond W. Goldsmith, Dorothy S. Brady, and Horst Mendershausen, *A Study of Saving in the United States* (Princeton, NJ: Princeton University Press, 1956); Goldsmith, *The National Wealth of the United States in the Postwar Period* (Princeton, NJ: Princeton University Press, 1962); Goldsmith, Robert E. Lipsey, and Morris Mendelson, *Studies in the National Balance Sheet of the United States* (Princeton, N.J.: Princeton University Press, 1963).

7. Ruggles and Ruggles, "Integrated Economic Accounts for the United States, 1947–1980."

8. See Appendix 12.1 for details on the construction of the balance sheets.

9. See Chapter 8 for a discussion of the erosion of defined benefit pensions in the United States and their replacement by defined contribution pensions.

10. For the GDP series, I use the GDP deflator as the price index, since it provides the best index for the whole national product. A comparison of the CPI and GDP deflator over the 1900–2013 period does reveal significant differences. For example, between 1900 and 1945, the GDP deflator and the CPI increased at almost the same rate; between 1945 and 1962, the GDP deflator rose almost a full percentage point per year faster than the CPI; between 1962 and 1969, the two were almost identical; between 1969 and 1983, the CPI increased by 0.3 percentage points per year faster than the GDP deflator; and from 1983 to 2013, the CPI rose by 0.5 percentage points faster. Over the full 1900–2013 period, the GDP deflator and CPI rose at almost exactly the same rate, 3 percent per year.

11. A better approach might be to use an equivalence class index, such as the poverty threshold, to compare family wealth. Such an index increases with family size, but less than proportionately, to reflect economies of consumption and the sharing of resources within the family unit. This approach was followed by Greenwood and Wolff to track changes in household wealth over the 1962–1983 period in the United States. I could not use this approach here, since it requires data on the distribution of wealth by family size. See Daphne T. Greenwood and Edward N. Wolff, "Relative Wealth Holdings of Children and the Elderly in the United States, 1962–1983," in *The Vulnerable,* ed. John Palmer, Timothy Smeeding, and Barbara Torrey (Washington, DC: The Urban Institute Press, 1988), 123–48.

12. See Appendix Table 12.1.

13. It is not possible to estimate median wealth from the FFA. As a result, it may also be the case that the 2010–2013 trend in median wealth from the SCF is valid while the trend in mean wealth is not. It is also of note, as discussed in Chapter 2, that the SCF trend in mean wealth over the 2010–2013 period aligns very well with another survey source, the Panel Study of Income Dynamics (PSID). However, this finding also raises questions about the validity of the PSID data for 2013.

14. Miscellaneous assets are excluded from W2 in the portfolio composition calculations.

15. It is also notable that the FFA data show a much smaller share of homes in total assets than the SCF figures do. For example, if I exclude consumer durables from W2 to get a wealth measure similar to NW in the SCF, the 2007 share of homes in total assets was 19 percent according to the FFA and 33 percent according to the SCF. As noted earlier, the FFA undervalues owner-occupied housing relative to the SCF (see Appendix Table 12.1).

16. The aggregate data provide total mortgage debt for the household sector. I estimated the value of mortgages held on owner-occupied housing by splitting total mortgage debt in proportion to the gross value of owner-occupied housing and that of other real estate.

17. This category includes deposits in financial institutions, money market funds, the cash surrender value of life insurance, and here the value of defined

contribution pensions plans like 401(k) plans and IRAs. This differs from the SCF definition of liquid assets as used in Chapter 3 in its inclusion of defined contribution pension plans.

18. Goldsmith, *Comparative National Balance Sheet.*

19. It is hard to make a direct comparison with these other two works since the definitions of wealth and income are so different, as are the periodizations. See Thomas Piketty, *Capital in the Twenty-First Century* (Cambridge, MA: Harvard University Press, 2014); Emmanuel Saez and Gabriel Zucman, "Wealth Inequality in the United States since 1913: Evidence from Capitalized Income Tax Data," *Quarterly Journal of Economics* 131, no. 2 (May 2016): 519–78.

20. Of course, this assessment is based only on the growth of average wealth. Whether this growth increased the national well-being also depends on how its distribution changed over time. Also, see Chapter 5 for more discussion of trends in savings rates.

21. All household balance sheet data except for trust accounts come from Goldsmith, Lipsey and Mendelsen, *Studies in the National Balance Sheet of the United States,* 42–85 and 118–19. Data for personal trusts for the pre-1945 years are from Goldsmith, Brody, and Mendershausen, *A Study of Saving in the United States,* 42–53, and for the 1945–1958 period from the Goldsmith, Lipsey, and Mendelsen, 120.

22. John C. Musgrave, "Fixed Reproducible Tangible Wealth in the United States: Revised Estimates," *Survey of Current Business* 66 (January 1986): 51–75. The data are taken from his revised series on tangible wealth (Table 10, p. 65, and Table 18, p. 73).

23. The accounts are available at: http://www.federalreserve.gov/releases/Z1/Current/data.htm. The data are drawn from the Table B.101, "Balance Sheet of Households and Nonprofit Organizations," and Table L.117, "Private and Public Pension Funds."

24. Richard Ruggles and Nancy Ruggles, "Integrated Economic Accounts for the United States, 1947–1980," *Survey of Current Business* 62 (May 1982): 1–53. See Table 2.40, "Household Sector Capital Accounts."

25. Richard T. Curtin, F. Thomas Juster, and James N. Morgan, "Survey Estimates of Wealth: An Assessment of Quality," in *The Measurement of Saving, Investment, and Wealth,* Studies of Income and Wealth, ed. Robert E. Lipsey and Helen Tice (Chicago: Chicago University Press, 1989), 473–548.

26. A comparison of aggregate wealth totals for 1962 and 1983 from national balance sheet data and household survey data is also discussed in Appendix 2 of this book in which the aggregate balance sheet figures are used to adjust the survey estimates for missing values and underreporting.

27. James D. Smith and Stephen D. Franklin, "The Concentration of Personal Wealth, 1922–1969," *American Economic Review* 64 (May 1974): 162–67.

28. Goldsmith, *Studies in the National Balance Sheet of the United States,* 5 and 181.

29. Ibid., 71.

30. Martin Feldstein, "Social Security, Individual Retirement and Aggregate Capital Accumulation," *Journal of Political Economy* 82, no. 5 (September/October 1974): 905–26.

31. Dean R. Leimer and Selig D. Lesnoy, "Social Security and Private Saving: New Time-Series Evidence," *Journal of Political Economy* 90 (June 1982): 606–21.

32. The Leimer and Lesnoy series was in 1972 dollars converted to nominal values using the CPI for the W4 series.

33. Aggregate Social Security wealth estimates for years 1989 to 2013 are derived from Chapter 8.

34. See Wolff, "Trends in Aggregate Household Wealth in the U.S., 1900–1983."

35. The FFA accounts are available at http://www.federalreserve.gov/releases/Z1/Current/data.htm. The data are drawn from the Table B.101, "Balance Sheet of Households and Nonprofit Organizations," and Table L.117, "Private and Public Pension Funds." This was possible for every asset and liability category with the sole exception of trust fund equity. In the FFA the assets in trust funds are consolidated into the corresponding asset category in the balance sheet (for example, corporate equities). I followed this convention in my adjusted FFA series. As a result, it was not possible to provide new estimates for the W1 series. In Table B.101, the line "pension entitlements" includes both defined contribution (DC) and defined benefit (DB) pension reserves. In my accounting framework, the value of DC pensions is included in liquid assets. My category "pension reserves" is restricted to reserves for only DB pensions. It was possible to split the total pension entitlements into these two components on the basis of data in Table L.117.

13. Long-Term Trends in the Concentration of Household Wealth

1. Data points from 1922 to 1983 are based on estate tax records. In addition, more detailed estimates are provided from microdata sources for the years 1962, 1969, 1983, 1989, 1992, 1995, 1998, 2001, 2004, 2007, 2010, and 2013 (see Chapter 2).

2. See Robert J. Lampman, *The Share of Top Wealthholders in National Wealth, 1922–56* (Princeton, NJ: Princeton University Press, 1962); Jeffrey G. Williamson and Peter A. Lindert, "Long-Term Trends in American Wealth Inequality," in *Modeling the Distribution and Intergenerational Transmission of Wealth,* ed. James D. Smith (Chicago: University of Chicago Press, 1980), 9–94; James D. Smith, "Recent Trends in the Distribution of Wealth in the U.S.: Data Research Problems and Prospects," in *International Comparisons of the Distribution of Household Wealth,* ed. Edward N. Wolff (New York: Oxford University Press, 1987), 72–89.

3. A more detailed explanation of the adjustments and imputations made to the size distribution data is given in Appendix B in Wolff and Marcia Marley,

"Long-Term Trends in U.S. Wealth Inequality: Methodological Issues and Results," in *The Measurement of Saving, Investment, and Wealth,* ed. Robert E. Lipsey and Helen Tice (Chicago: Chicago University Press, 1989), 765–843.

4. See 1969 MESP sample in Appendix 2 of the book and Wolff, "Estimates of the 1969 Size Distribution of Household Wealth in the United States from a Synthetic Database," in *Modeling the Distribution and Intergenerational Transmission of Wealth,* ed. James D. Smith (Chicago: University of Chicago Press, 1980), 223–71. See also Greenwood's 1973 database see in Daphne Greenwood, "An Estimation of U.S. Family Wealth and Its Distribution from Microdata, 1973," *Review of Income and Wealth* series 29, no. 3 (1983): 23–43.

5. The estate tax figures provide information for only the top wealth holders. There is no exact mapping between estimates of the share of top wealth holders and more inclusive inequality measures such as the Gini coefficient.

6. See Anthony B. Atkinson, "The Distribution of Wealth in Britain in the 1960's—The Estate Duty Method Reexamined," in *The Personal Distribution of Income and Wealth,* ed. James D. Smith (New York: Columbia University Press, 1975); and Anthony F. Shorrocks, "U.K. Wealth Distribution: Current Evidence and Future Prospects," in *International Comparisons of the Distribution of Household Wealth,* ed. Edward N. Wolff (New York: Oxford University Press, 1987), 29–50.

7. See Chapter 12, Table 12.1 for alternative wealth definitions.

8. Richard Ruggles and Nancy Ruggles, "Integrated Economic Accounts for the United States, 1947–1980," *Survey* of *Current Business* 62 (May 1982): 1–53. Although several alternative groupings were tried, it was not possible to exactly reproduce Smith's reported aggregate numbers using Ruggles and Ruggles's published data. The largest discrepancy was in the miscellaneous asset category.

9. I use year-end balance sheet data from Chapter 12 because midyear figures were not available for years 1922 to 1945.

10. In addition to the Lampman and Smith data, I included estate tax data figures for 1981 from Marvin Schwartz, "Trends in Personal Wealth, 1976–1981," *Statistics of Income Bulletin* 3 (Summer 1983): 1–26.

11. However, some trusts were not included at all in Smith's estate files. Thus, his numbers are below the "true" actuarial values. Lampman, on the other hand, assumed that there was extensive gift transfer to avoid taxes and adjusted the trust figures upward.

12. Table 13.3 reports concentration figures for total assets, whereas Table 13.1 reports them for net worth.

13. It should be noted that the concentration shares for W4 reported in Tables 13.3 and 13.4 depend both on the growth assumptions used in calculating aggregate Social Security wealth and on the assumed share of Social Security wealth held by the top one percent of wealth holders. The assumptions underlying the W4 concentration estimates are explained in Appendix 3 of the book.

14. This result is based on a comparison of Lampman's 1953 results and Schwartz's 1976 and 1981 estimates. Married women represented 18 percent of the sample in 1953, 16.8 percent in 1976, and 18 percent in 1981.

15. The adjustments are discussed in Appendix 1 of the book and in Wolff, "Estimates of Household Wealth Inequality in the United States, 1962–83," *Review of Income and Wealth* series 33, no. 3 (September 1987): 231–56. The estate tax data figures are my estimates of the share of the top 1 percent of households derived from Smith's data. For 1962, there are estimates from both sources.

16. William S. Cartwright and Robert Friedland, "The President's Commission on Pension Policy Household Survey 1979: Net Wealth Distribution by Type and Age for the United States," *Review of Income and Wealth* series 31, no. 3 (1985): 285–308.

17. The 1979 ISDP results are from Daniel B. Radner and Denton R. Vaughan, "Wealth, Income and the Economic Status of Aged Households," in *International Comparisons of the Distribution of Household Wealth,* ed. Edward N. Wolff (New York: Oxford University Press, 1987), 93–120. The 1979 Pension Commission survey estimates are from Cartwright and Friedland, "The President's Commission on Pension Policy Household Survey 1979." The 1962 SFCC and 1983 SCF are from Appendix 1 of the book.

18. Enrique J. Lamas and John M. McNeil, "Factors Associated with Household Net Worth" (paper presented at the meeting of the American Economic Association, New Orleans, LA, December 1986). The reliability of the SIPP and SCF surveys was discussed in Richard T. Curtin, F. Thomas Juster, and James N. Morgan, "Survey Estimates of Wealth: An Assessment of Quality," in *The Measurement of Saving, Investment, and Wealth,* ed. Robert E. Lipsey and Helen Tice (Chicago: Chicago University Press, 1989), 473–548.

19. The methodology is described in detail in Appendix 2 and Wolff, "Estimates of the 1969 Size Distribution of Household Wealth in the United States from a Synthetic Database"; Wolff, "Effect of Alternative Imputation Techniques on Estimates of Household Wealth in the U.S. in 1969," in *Accumulation et Repartition des Patrimoines,* ed. Denis Kessler, André Masson, and Dominque Strauss-Kahn (Paris: Economica, 1982), 147–80; and Wolff, "The Distribution of Household Disposable Wealth in the United States," *The Review of Income and Wealth* series 29, no. 2 (June 1983): 125–46.

20. The methodology is explained in Greenwood, "An Estimation of U.S. Family Wealth and Its Distribution from Microdata, 1973," and Daphne Greenwood, "Age, Income, and Household Size: Their Relation to Wealth Distribution in the United States," in *International Comparisons of the Distribution of Household Wealth,* ed. Edward N. Wolff (New York: Oxford University Press, 1987), 121–40.

21. Ibid., 126.

22. For details, see Appendix 1 of the book and Wolff, "Estimates of Household Wealth Inequality in the United States, 1962–83."

23. For details, see Appendix 2 of the book and Wolff, "Estimates of the 1969 Size Distribution of Household Wealth in the United States from a Synthetic Database," and "The Distribution of Household Disposable Wealth in the United States."

24. Radner and Vaughan, "Wealth, Income and the Economic Status of Aged Households."

25. Robert B. Avery and Arthur B. Kennickell, "U.S. Household Wealth: Changes from 1983 to 1986," in *Research in Economic Inequality*, ed. Edward N. Wolff (Greenwich, CT: JAI Press, 1993), 27–68.

26. Perhaps somewhat coincidentally, the share of total assets and net worth owned by the top 1 percent of *households* in 1962 computed on the basis of the SFCC lines up almost exactly with the share of total assets and net worth owned by the top one percent of *individuals* on the basis of the estate tax data. The same relation holds for 1969.

27. According to Smith's original figures, the share of net worth owned by the top 1 percent of wealth holders fell from 27.7 percent in 1972 to 19.2 percent in 1976 (see Smith, "Recent Trends in the Distribution of Wealth in the U.S."). Schwartz reported a slightly higher share of net worth owned by the top percentile in 1976, 20.8 percent, and I use his figure rather than Smith's for the "Combined Series" in column 6. See Marvin Schwartz, "Preliminary Estimates of Personal Wealth, 1982: Composition of Assets," *Statistics of Income Bulletin* 4 (Winter 1984–85): 1–17.

28. See Smith, "Recent Trends in the Distribution of Wealth in the U.S."

29. This trend is confirmed in the estate tax figures. According to Schwartz, the share of total personal wealth held by the top 2.8 percent of the nation's adult population was 28 percent in 1982, and, according to Schwartz and Johnson, the share held by the top 1.6 percent of the adult population was 28.5 percent in 1986. See Schwartz, "Preliminary Estimates of Personal Wealth, 1982"; and Schwartz and Barry Johnson, "Estimates of Personal Wealth, 1986," *Statistics of Income Bulletin* 9 (Spring 1990): 63–78.

30. As discussed in Chapter 2, the Gini coefficient for household wealth shows a different pattern. It rose slightly from 1989 to 2007, climbed sharply from 2007 to 2010, and then showed a very modest advance from 2010 to 2013. This comparison, by the way, highlights the problem of using concentration ratios as a measure of overall inequality.

31. Emmanuel Saez and Gabriel Zucman, "Wealth Inequality in the United States since 1913: Evidence from Capitalized Income Tax Data," *Quarterly Journal of Economics* 131, no. 2 (May 2016): 519–78. Wojciech Kopczuk and Emmanuel Saez, "Top Wealth Shares in the United States, 1916–2000: Evidence from Estate Tax Returns," *National Tax Journal* 57 (2004): 445–88.

32. Wojciech Kopczuk, "What Do We Know about the Evolution of Top Wealth Shares in the United States?" *Journal of Economic Perspectives* 29, no. 1 (Winter 2015): 47–66.

33. For details, see Chapter 8; Edward N. Wolff, "The Effects of Pensions and Social Security on the Distribution of Wealth in the U.S." in *International Comparisons of Household Wealth Distribution* (New York: Oxford University Press, 1987), 208–47; Wolff and Marley, "Long Term Trends in U.S. Wealth Inequality"; Wolff, "Methodological Issues in the Estimation of Retirement Wealth," in *Research in Economic Inequality*, ed. Daniel J. Slottje (Stamford, CT: JAI Press, 1992), 31–56.

34. The estimates shown here are based on the assumption that real average social security benefits grow by 2 percent per year over time.

35. It was not possible to add pension and Social Security wealth to the NW series shown in column 8. However, see Chapter 8 for more recent data on the inequality of augmented wealth.

14. Wealth Taxation

1. See Wolff, "Discussant Comment on Douglas Holtz-Eakin, 'The Uneasy Case for Abolishing the Estate Tax,'" *Tax Law Review* 51, no. 3 (1997): 517–21.

2. See Wolff, *Top Heavy: A Study of Increasing Inequality of Wealth in America* (New York: The Twentieth Century Fund Press, 1995). Much more recently, Thomas Piketty also proposed direct taxation of household wealth. See *Capital in the Twenty-First Century* (Cambridge, MA: Harvard University Press, 2014).

3. A related tax is the property tax, levied on the value of all real property (buildings and land). Though this is often overlooked in current debates on tax reforms, the property tax was the third-largest source of household tax revenue in 1985 and has been rising steeply in years since then. This tax is generally levied by local governments in this country and, as a result, will not be discussed in this chapter. Of the twenty-four OECD countries, all but Italy and Portugal had a separate tax on real property in the mid-1980s.

4. Gifts within three years of death were treated as transfers at death.

5. There are some complications that arise from capital losses and the carry-over of capital losses from previous years, particularly in regard to short-term capital gains.

6. Most of the information in this section was garnered from the Organization of Economic Cooperation and Development, *Taxation of Net Wealth, Capital Transfers and Capital Gains of Individuals* (Paris: OECD, 1988). The figures in this section are as of 1988 in most cases.

7. Japan also had a direct wealth tax for a short period after World War II.

8. In Switzerland, the wealth tax was actually a provincial (canton) tax, so that provisions varied among cantons.

9. There was a technical issue related to debts on excluded assets. Since the wealth tax was based on the total value of assets less debts, the appropriate treatment would have been to exclude debts on assets that were themselves excluded

from the tax base. However, because of the difficulty of assigning specific debts (such as bank overdrafts) to specific assets, countries varied in their treatment of this problem.

10. Actually, in the U.S. estate tax system, preferential treatment is given to a spousal transfer in the form of a complete exemption. There is also a special, additional tax levied on generation-skipping bequests.

11. U.S. Council of Economic Advisers, *Economic Report of the President* (Washington, DC: U.S. Government Printing Office, 2001), 422. The estimated total federal receipts from the estate and gift tax in the year 2000 was $27 billion, or 1.4 percent of total (estimated) tax revenue.

12. It should be noted that in the simulations all assets are appraised at market value (since this is the only valuation available).

13. The procedure was as follows: First, adjusted gross income (AGI) was estimated as the sum of all income items (excluding Social Security income). Second, the number of exemptions was computed. Third, the standard deduction was calculated. This was based on the filing status of the household and the number of persons age 65 or older in the household. Fourth, taxable income was calculated by taking AGI minus the number of exemptions multiplied by $2,000 and subtracting the standard deduction. Federal income tax was then computed on the basis of the appropriate tax tables. After the initial run, the estimation procedure could be calibrated. Total individual federal income taxes collected in 1989 amounted to $445.7 billion (the source is the Council of Economic Advisors, 1991, Table B-77). The tax estimation used here produced a total tax figure for all households of $526.4 billion (an 18 percent discrepancy). The tax estimates were subsequently reduced by 18 percent to align with the actual figure. With this system, taxes were then recomputed in the same way, except in treating household wealth as an additional taxable item in accordance with the details of each of the three plans shown in Table 14.2.

14. Data problems included the following: itemized deductions, particularly interest payments and state and local tax payments, could not be included in the analysis; capital gains could not be incorporated in family income; tax-exempt interest income was not excluded from AGI; and any adjustments to income were not included in the computation of AGI. It was assumed that the net effect of these omitted adjustments was approximately captured by the 18 percent adjustment to tax revenues.

15. The revenue effect estimated on the basis of the Swiss system (2.2 percent of total U.S. tax revenues) was not very far out of line with the actual experience of that country; in 1985, the Swiss wealth tax accounted for 2.3 percent of total tax revenues in Switzerland. On the other hand, the relative revenue effects estimated from the German and particularly the Swedish system were much greater than the actual wealth tax yields in those countries. There are four possible reasons for the discrepancy in results. First, total tax revenues were a higher proportion of

GDP in Germany (37 percent in 1988) and in Sweden (55 percent) than in the United States (30 percent). Second, household wealth holdings relative to income may have been lower in Germany and Sweden than in the United States. Third, there may have been substantial tax evasion and avoidance in the two European countries. Fourth, in the case of Sweden at least, there was a cap on the joint income and wealth tax, which limited liability for the wealth tax for a large proportion of wealthy Swedish families because of the very high marginal tax rates on income that existed in the 1980s.

16. However, as indicated in note 15, the incorporation of itemized deductions, tax preference items, and other income adjustments would have made the effective tax rates on income considerably less progressive.

17. OECD, *Taxation of Net Wealth, Capital Transfers and Capital Gains of Individuals*.

18. As of May 1, 2016.

19. I used a somewhat different procedure than for the 1989 data. First, I updated the income data, which are for 2012, to 2013 dollars on the basis of the CPI-U (a factor of 1.01465). Second, adjusted gross income (AGI) was estimated as the sum of all income items except Social Security income and capital gains minus contributions to IRAs, 401(k) plans, and other defined contribution pension plans. Third, for married couples whose income was more than $32,000 and for singles whose income was more than $25,000, 85 percent of Social Security income above these limits was added back to AGI. Fourth, the number of exemptions was computed. This was based on the filing status of the household and the number of persons sixty-five or older in the household. Fifth, the standard deduction was calculated. Sixth, taxable income was calculated by taking AGI minus the number of exemptions multiplied by $3,900 and subtracting the standard deduction, subject to limitations for high-income filers. Seventh, federal income tax was then computed on the basis of the appropriate tax tables. Eighth, a separate tax on capital gains was computed subject to a 15 percent cap on the tax rate. Ninth, the Earned Income Tax Credit (EITC) was then calculated. Net income tax was then set equal to the tax on taxable income plus the capital gains tax minus the EITC. After the initial run, the estimation procedure could be calibrated. Total individual federal income taxes collected in 2013 amounted to $1,316.4 billion (U.S. Council of Economic Advisers, *Economic Report of the President,* 2015, Table B-21). The tax estimation used here produced a total tax figure for all households of $1,515.5 billion (a 15 percent discrepancy). The tax estimates were subsequently reduced by 15 percent to align with the actual figure. However, as in the tax simulation for 1989, I still use the standard deduction instead of itemized deductions in the tax calculations and do not capture certain tax preference items such as interest income from state and local government bonds. As a consequence, the results still likely overstate the redistributional effects of the personal income tax system.

20. The source is the Council of Economic Advisers, *Economic Report of the President,* 2015, Table B-22.

21. The ceiling was actually raised to $100,000 in 1926 but then lowered back to $50,000 in 1932.

22. This was done in my 1995 book, Edward N. Wolff, *Top Heavy: A Study of Increasing Inequality of Wealth in America* (New York: The Twentieth Century Fund Press, 1995). There are currently too few countries with a wealth tax to replicate the earlier analysis.

23. Organization for Economic Cooperation and Development, *National Accounts, Detailed Tables, 1978–1990,* Vol. 2 (Paris: OECD, 1992). Technically, the savings rates are for the sector grouping households, nonprofit institutions, and unincorporated businesses. The sample of countries includes all those listed in Table 14.1 except Denmark, Iceland, Ireland, Luxembourg, and Turkey.

24. In *Capital in the Twenty-First Century,* Piketty proposed a unified wealth tax across countries to address the problem of capital flight.

25. Other, more subtle exclusions may be warranted as well. For example, provisions to protect old people living with low income in valuable family homes appear worthwhile. The law could, for example, postpone taxes on this wealth, incorporating them into estate taxes.

15. Summary of Principal Findings and Concluding Comments

1. Sabrina Tavernise, "Sweeping Pain as Suicides Hit a 30-Year High," *New York Times,* April 22, 2016, p. A1.

Appendix 1

1. Note that the acronym FFA is a holdover from this source's previous name, the Flow of Funds Accounts.

2. See Wolff, "Estimates of Household Wealth Inequality in the United States, 1962–83," *Review of Income and Wealth* 33, no. 3 (September 1987): 231–56.

3. See Dorothy Projector and Gertrude Weiss, *Survey of Financial Characteristics of Consumers,* Federal Reserve Board Technical Papers (Washington, DC: Board of Governors of the Federal Reserve System, 1966), Table A14.

4. It should be noted that there were no missing value problems in the version of the SFCC file released by the Federal Reserve Board since imputations for missing values had already been performed by the Federal Reserve Board.

5. It should be noted that the use of uniform adjustment factors (overall or by income class) leads to an understatement of the actual variance of these holdings within the population. However, in previous work, sensitivity analyses were conducted on the 1969 MESP file, in which a random error term was added to the average adjustment factor for each asset. The results showed that the inclusion of

such an error term had very little effect on estimates of the Gini coefficient and other measures of overall wealth inequality in the population. For details, see Wolff, "Effect of Alternative Imputation Techniques on Estimates of Household Wealth in the U.S. in 1969," in *Accumulation et Repartition des Patrimoines,* ed. Denis Kessler, André Masson, and Dominque Strauss-Kahn (Paris: Economica, 1982), 147–80.

6. For more details, see Wolff, "Estimates of the 1969 Size Distribution of Household Wealth in the United States from a Synthetic Database," in *Modeling the Distribution and Intergenerational Transmission of Wealth,* ed. James D. Smith (Chicago: University of Chicago Press, 1980), 223–71.

7. U.S. Bureau of Labor Statistics, *Consumer Expenditure Survey: Integrated Diary and Interview Survey Data, 1972–73,* Table 127, Bulletin no. 1978 (Washington, DC: U.S. Government Printing Office, 1978), 359. Household inventory items include food purchased for home use, tobacco, alcoholic beverages, and clothing and clothing materials.

8. Projector and Weiss, *Survey of Financial Characteristics of Consumers,* Table A31.

9. See ibid., Table A14.

10. See, for example, Wolff, "The Effects of Pensions and Social Security on the Distribution of Wealth in the U.S." in *International Comparisons of Household Wealth Distribution,* ed. Edward N. Wolff (New York: Oxford University Press, 1987), 208–47.

11. I define a new measure of household wealth, W2*, as W2 plus household inventories.

12. Results are similar for W5, the sum of W2 and pension and Social Security wealth.

13. The imputation procedures are described in detail in Robert B. Avery, Gregory E. Elliehausen, and Arthur B. Kennickell, "Measuring Wealth with Survey Data: An Evaluation of the 1983 Survey of Consumer Finances" (paper presented at the twentieth conference of the International Association for Research in Income and Wealth, Rocca di Papa, Italy, September 1987).

14. Richard T. Curtin, F. Thomas Juster, and James N. Morgan, "Survey Estimates of Wealth: An Assessment of Quality," in *The Measurement of Saving, Investment, and Wealth,* ed. Robert E. Lipsey and Helen Tice (Chicago: Chicago University Press, 1989), 473–548.

15. Avery, Elliehausen, and Kennickell, "Measuring Wealth with Survey Data."

16. Indeed, the converse issue arises for some of these categories—namely, should their reported values be adjusted downward to align with the national balance sheet totals? I assume, as I do for the 1962 SFCC, that there was no apparent incentive for respondents to overreport the value of their assets. Moreover, it is likely that respondent market value estimates of some items such as owner-occupied housing and other real estate would be better than aggregate estimates

based on perpetual inventory techniques. Therefore, as in the case of the 1962 SFCC, I make no adjustment for these items.

17. The imputations for inventories were based on U.S. Bureau of Labor Statistics, *Consumer Expenditure Survey.*

18. It is not possible to compare either the distribution of financial securities between the two years since savings bonds were included in the 1962 category but excluded in the later year or the distribution of insurance CSV or pension CSV between the two years because these items are imputed in the 1962 data.

19. The effect of alignment was relatively modest for these two databases because the degree of underreporting of wealth among the rich was not as significant as it was in other wealth surveys. For example, Curtin, Juster, and Morgan reported significant differences in coverage, particularly of the upper wealth strata, between the 1983 SCF, on the one hand, and the 1984 Panel Study of Income Dynamics and the 1984 Wealth Supplement to the SIPP, on the other hand. (See Curtin, Juster, and Morgan, *The Measurement of Saving, Investment, and Wealth.*) Thus, for those surveys with poor coverage of the upper wealth strata, alignment to aggregate national balance sheet totals is likely to substantially alter estimated wealth inequality.

Appendix 2

1. For details, see Wolff, "Estimates of the 1969 Size Distribution of Household Wealth in the United States from a Synthetic Database," in *Modeling the Distribution and Intergenerational Transmission of Wealth,* ed. James D. Smith (Chicago: University of Chicago Press, 1980), 223–71.

2. For a description of the methodology see Robert J. Lampman, *The Share of Top Wealthholders in National Wealth, 1922–56* (Princeton, NJ: Princeton University Press, 1962); James D. Smith and Stephen D. Franklin, "The Concentration of Personal Wealth, 1922–1969," *American Economic Review* 64 (May 1974): 162–67; and James D. Smith, "Trends in the Concentration of Personal Wealth in the United States, 1958–1976," *Review of Income and Wealth* series 30, no. 4 (December 1984): 419–28.

3. See Dorothy Projector and Gertrude Weiss, *Survey of Financial Characteristics of Consumers,* Federal Reserve Board Technical Papers (Washington, DC: Board of Governors of the Federal Reserve System, 1966).

4. Ibid., 61, and Appendix 1 in this volume for details.

5. Charles Stewart, "Income Capitalization as a Method of Estimating the Distribution of Wealth by Size Group," in *Studies of Income and Wealth,* Vol. 3 (New York: National Bureau of Economic Research, 1939), 95–146; and Stanley Lebergott, *The American Economy* (Princeton, NJ: Princeton University Press, 1976).

6. See, for example, Milton Friedman, "Discussion on Income Capitalization," in *Studies of Income and Wealth,* Vol. 3 (New York: National Bureau of Economic Research, 1939).

7. Richard Ruggles and Nancy Ruggles, "A Strategy for Matching and Merging Microdatasets," *Annals of Economic and Social Measurement* 3, no. 2 (April 1974): 353–71; Nancy Ruggles, Richard Ruggles, and Edward Wolff, "Merging Microdata: Rationale, Practice and Testing," *Annals of Economic and Social Measurement* 6, no. 4 (Fall 1977): 407–28.

8. This information is not normally included in the tax return, except when the filer is 65 years of age or older.

9. Since the overlap in demographic information between the two samples was so substantial, this match provided an ideal opportunity to test the reliability of the matching technique. To do this, I ran two sets of regressions, the first with variables from the 15 percent PUS and the second with a mix of variables from the two files. In 90 percent of the cases, the regression coefficients in the two sets were not statistically different (see Ruggles, Ruggles, and Wolff, "Merging Microdata," for more details).

10. We expected some upward bias, since the MESP sample is a sample of households, which may file more than one tax return.

11. This procedure probably resulted in a slight downward bias in the percentage of households receiving the respective income items (see note 12).

12. I determined the percentage of positive entries to keep (p_1) and the percentage of negative entries to keep (p_2) by solving the following simultaneous system:

$$p_1 P + p_2 N = T$$
and
$$p_1 q + p_2 r = s$$

where   P = total positive income in the MESP file;
        N = total negative income in the MESP file;
        T = total income from the IRS file;
        q = percent receiving positive income in the MESP file;
        r = percent receiving negative income in the MESP file;
        S = percent receiving the income item in the IRS file.

13. Technically, I might have performed a t-ratio test for the difference in means for choosing the pattern of aggregation for each durable. However, from cross-tabulation analysis, income, age, and residence seemed by far the predominant determinants.

14. An alternative technique would have been to use logit regression to estimate the probability of purchase of each durable as a function of all nine demographic characteristics. Time and cost constraints prevented us from pursuing this course.

15. This procedure introduces two offsetting biases. First, since real income grows over time, the probability of purchasing for a given household will increase between 1960 and 1969. However, the probability of purchasing a durable declines with the age of the head of household, since stocks of durables tend to be acquired

early in the life cycle and then gradually replaced (and perhaps upgraded) as the household ages.

16. This is, of course, a very rough assumption. I could have assumed that the decision to purchase durable i is independent of ownership of i to allow multiple purchases. The distribution of the number of times durable i is purchased in a given span of years would then be given by a binomial distribution.

17. These are the durables already included in the PUS inventory.

18. In the case of automobiles and televisions, where the PUS inventory indicates the household owns more than one, the age of each was estimated.

19. This would overstate the probability of purchasing each in a given year, since the decision to purchase the item is treated as independent of the ownership of that item.

20. My major findings are as follows: (1) Income is a positive determinant of the amount spent on each durable, while the percent of income spent on durables is negatively related to the income level. (2) The amount spent on durables is positively related to the rate of dissavings, particularly for the more costly durables. (3) Homeowners spend more on durables relative to income than renters. (4) Larger families have smaller expenditures on durables.

21. The only restriction was that if p^*_i was less than zero, p^*_i was set equal to zero.

22. I ignored the problem of differences in capital gains for different portfolios in the case of financial securities, as well as stocks. I also ignored the problem of both capital and ordinary gains in the case of the other assets. See Lebergott, *The American Economy,* for a discussion of this problem.

23. See Marshall Blume, Jean Crockett, and Irwin Friend, "Stockownership in the United States: Characteristics and Trends," *Survey of Current Business* 54, no. 11 (1974): 26.

24. The average yield by AGI class was as follows:

AGI Class	Average Dividend Yield (%)
Under $5,000	2.77
5,000–9,999	2.76
10,000–14,999	2.78
15,000–24,999	2.75
25,000–49,999	2.65
50,000–99,999	2.56
100,000+	2.51

25. There was the additional problem that not all investment real estate was rented. This will result in an overstatement in the concentration of investment real estate ownership, though there was no apparent systematic bias with respect to income or wealth.

26. The costs included such items as utilities, repairs and maintenance, mortgage interest, property taxes, and depreciation.

27. In 1969 taxpayers were allowed to deduct all interest payments from taxable income.

28. The Gini coefficient measure includes both holders and nonholders. The Gini coefficients were considerably lower for owners alone in most asset groups.

29. See Wolff, "Effect of Alternative Imputation Techniques on Estimates of Household Wealth in the U.S. in 1969," in *Accumulation et Repartition des Patrimoines,* ed. Denis Kessler, André Masson, and Dominque Strauss-Kahn (Paris: Economica, 1982), 147–80.

30. See Ruggles, Ruggles and Wolff, "Merging Microdata," for more details.

31. See Wolff, "Effect of Alternative Imputation Techniques," for one attempt.

Appendix 3

1. I also used a 3 percent real discount rate to estimate both DB pension and Social Security wealth. The general results contained in Chapter 5 are not materially altered by the use of this higher discount rate (results not shown). Another crucial choice is the selection of which mortality rates to use in the calculation of DBW and SSW. I have used here the standard data from the *Statistical Abstract of the United States* based on age, gender and race. (See U.S. Bureau of the Census, *Statistical Abstract of the United States: 1988,* 108th edition [Washington, DC: U.S. Government Printing Office, 1987].) However, there are also available unofficial life expectancy estimates for individuals by age, gender, and income class (and even by educational attainment). As is well known, higher-income (and more educated) individuals live longer on average than those with lower income (or less education). The use of mortality rates conditional on income (or education) will have the effect of increasing estimates of DBW and SSW of higher-income (and better educated) individuals *relative to* lower-income (and less educated) individuals.

2. The mortality rate m_t associated with the year of retirement is the probability of surviving from the current age to the age of retirement.

3. Alan L. Gustman and Thomas L. Steinmeier, "What People Don't Know about Their Pensions and Social Security: An Analysis Using Linked Data from the Health and Retirement Study" (NBER Working Paper No. 7368, National Bureau of Economic Research, Cambridge, MA, September 1999); and Richard W. Johnson, Usha Sambamoorthi, and Stephen Crystal, "Pension Wealth at Midlife: Comparing Self-Reports with Provider Data," *Review of Income and Wealth* 46 (2000): 59–83.

4. Separate imputations are performed for husband and wife. According to current and past rules, a spouse—say, the wife—is entitled to the greater of her own

SS benefit or 50 percent of her husband's SS benefit. An adjustment in the Social Security benefit is also made for the surviving spouse. According to current and past rules, a surviving spouse is entitled to the greater of her own Social Security benefit or her deceased husband's.

5. As with pension wealth, the mortality rate m_t associated with the year of retirement is the probability of surviving from the current age to the age of retirement. Also, note that I use δ^* in the equation since Social Security benefits are indexed to the CPI.

6. See, for example, Karen Smith, Eric Toder, and Howard Iams, "Lifetime Redistribution of Social Security Retirement Benefits" (mimeo, Social Security Administration, 2001) in which estimates are based on actual Social Security work histories.

7. Though I can approximate the *number* of years of full-time and part-time work for a given worker, I cannot determine when in his or her work history periods of nonemployment occurred.

8. It should be noted that past employer (and employee) contributions to DC plans are already included in the current market value of DCW.

9. A third though minor component is also provided: pensions from other nonspecified sources.

10. These figures are based on the U.S. Bureau of Labor Statistics (BLS) hourly wage series. The source is Table B-15 of the *Economic Report of the President, 2014,* available at http://www.gpo.gov/fdsys/pkg/ERP-2014/pdf/ERP-2014-table15.pdf [accessed October 17, 2014]. The BLS wage figures are converted to constant dollars on the basis of the CPI-U. I use the BLS series rather than one of the alternatives to project future wages because it likely corresponds closest to changes in the Social Security wage base over time due to the cap on Social Security earnings that enter the Social Security benefit formula.

11. U.S. Bureau of the Census, *Statistical Abstract of the United States.* Various years and table numbers were referenced. I use the mortality tables as of the survey year (or the one nearest to the survey year).

12. This implicitly assumes that deviations from the regression line in the current year are a result of a transitory component to current income only. This procedure follows the conventions of the 1983 SCF codebook.

13. I use "DBWA" for DB pension wealth here instead of "DBW" since the methodology used here is somewhat different than used in Chapter 5. Likewise, I use "SSWA: instead of "SSW" for Social Security wealth.

14. Separate imputations are performed for husband and wife and an adjustment in the Social Security benefit is made for the surviving spouse.

15. From Alfred M. Skolnik, "Private Pension Plans, 1950–74," *Social Security Bulletin* 39 (June 1976): 3–17; and Table 3.1.1 in Laurence J. Kotlikoff and Daniel E. Smith, *Pensions in the American Economy* (Chicago: University of Chicago Press, 1983).

16. President's Commission on Pension Policy, "Pension Coverage in the United States" and "Preliminary Findings on a Nationwide Survey on Retirement Income Issues" (mimeo, Washington, DC, 1980).

17. For simplicity, it was assumed that pension vesting is immediate.

18. In 1962 and 1983, 65 was the mandatory retirement age for most workers. It was also the normal retirement age as embodied in the Social Security and most private pension benefit formulae. Statistically, it has remained the modal retirement age since 1962, though the percent of the labor force retiring before age 65 has been increasing and the proportion retiring after 65 has been declining.

19. The net worth concept used in this section is, as in the case of the 1969 MESP data, NWB, which includes imputations for all consumer durables. See Appendix 1 and Appendix 2 for details.

20. There was, unavoidably, a considerable degree of inconsistency in the treatment of workers and retirees. In particular, uncertainties in the imputation of SSWA and DBWA were considerably greater for current workers, while those of HK much greater for retirees. This may bias the regression results, particularly since measurement errors were particularly severe for both workers and retirees close to retirement age. Some experimentation was done by arbitrarily introducing errors in variables for SSWA and DBWA for current workers and HK for retirees. The resulting regression results differed very little from those based on ordinary least squares.

21. See Jacob Mincer, *Schooling, Experience and Earnings* (New York: National Bureau of Economic Research, 1974).

22. The variable g measures the rate at which mean earnings increase over time. If mean earnings were constant over time, then earnings for a given age cohort would follow the cross-sectional function $f(A)$ over time as the cohort aged. However, for $g > 0$, earnings for a given cohort would change from both a movement along $f(A)$ and form a shift in the whole function by g.

23. Here, it was assumed that the ratio between individual and average earnings is maintained throughout the life cycle. Alternative forms for the computation of lifetime earnings are given in Mincer, *Schooling, Experience and Earnings*, and Lee Lillard, "Inequality: Earning vs. Human Wealth," *American Economic Review* 67, no. 2 (March 1977): 42–53. Mincer regressed the logarithm of earnings on A and A^2 to obtain a life cycle earnings profile. Lillard regressed dollar earnings on A, A^2, and A^3. Experiments using Mincer's approach and Lillard's approach produced very little difference in lifetime earnings estimates.

References

Aaron, Henry J. *Economic Effects of Social Security*. Washington, DC: Brookings Institution, 1982.

Ando, Albert, and Franco Modigliani. "The 'Life Cycle' Hypotheses of Saving: Aggregate Implications and Tests." *American Economic Review* 53, no. 1 (March 1963): 55–84.

Armour, Philip, Richard V. Burkhauser, and Jeff Larrimore. "Deconstructing Income and Income Inequality Measures: A Crosswalk from Market Income to Comprehensive Income." *American Economic Review* 101, no. 3 (2013): 173–77.

Arrondel, Luc, Muriel Roger, and Frédérique Savignac. "Wealth and Income in the Euro Area: Heterogeneity in Households' Behaviours?" European Central Bank Working Paper no. 1709, August 2014.

Atkinson, Anthony B. "The Distribution of Wealth and the Individual Life Cycle." *Oxford Economic Papers* 23, no. 2 (July 1971): 239–54.

———. "The Distribution of Wealth in Britain in the 1960's—The Estate Duty Method Reexamined." In *The Personal Distribution of Income and Wealth*, edited by James D. Smith, 227–320. New York: Columbia University Press, 1975.

———. "Wealth and Inheritance in Britain from 1896 to the Present." Centre for Analysis of Social Exclusion Working Paper 178, London School of Economics, London, U.K., November 2013.

Atkinson, Anthony B., J. P. F. Gordon, and A. Harrison "Trends in the Shares of Top Wealth-Holders in Britain, 1923–81." *Oxford Bulletin of Economics and Statistics* 51, no. 3 (1989): 315–32.

Atkinson, Anthony B., Lee Rainwater, and Timothy Smeeding. *Income Distribution in Advanced Economies: The Evidence from the Luxembourg Income Study (LIS)*. Paris: OECD, 1995.

Attanasio, Orazio, James Banks, Costas Meghir, and Guglielmo Weber. "Humps and Bumps in Lifetime Consumption." *Journal of Business and Economic Statistics* 17, no. 1 (1999): 22–35.

Avery, Robert B., Gregory E. Elliehausen, and Thomas A. Gustafson. "Pensions and Social Security in Household Portfolios: Evidence from the 1983 Survey of Consumer Finances." Federal Reserve Board Research Papers in Banking and Financial Economics, Washington, DC, October 1985.

Avery, Robert B., Gregory E. Elliehausen, and Arthur B. Kennickell. "Measuring Wealth with Survey Data: An Evaluation of the 1983 Survey of Consumer Finances." Paper presented at the twentieth conference of the International Association for Research in Income and Wealth, Rocca di Papa, Italy, September 1987.

Avery, Robert B., and Arthur B. Kennickell. "U.S. Household Wealth: Changes from 1983 to 1986." In *Studies in the Distribution of Household Wealth,* edited by Edward N. Wolff, 27–68. Greenwich, CT: JAI Press, 1993.

Avery, Robert B., and Michael S. Rendall. "Estimating the Size and Distribution of Baby Boomers' Prospective Inheritances." In *1993 Proceedings of the Social Statistics Section,* edited by American Statistical Association, 11–19. Alexandria, VA: ASA, 1993.

Bager-Sjogren, L., and N. A. Klevmarken. "The Distribution of Wealth in Sweden, 1984–1986." In *Studies in the Distribution of Household Wealth,* edited by Edward N. Wolff, 203–24. Greenwich, CT: JAI Press, 1993.

Bane, Mary Jo, and David T. Ellwood. "Slipping Into and Out of Poverty: The Dynamics of Spells." *Journal of Human Resources* 21, no. 1 (1986): 1–23.

Banks, James, Richard Blundell, and Sarah Tanner. "Is There a Retirement-Savings Puzzle?" *American Economic Review* 88, no. 4 (1998): 769–88.

Barlow, Robin, Harvey E. Brazer, and James N. Morgan. *Economic Behavior of the Affluent.* Washington, DC: Brookings Institution, 1966.

Bauer, John, and Andrew Mason. "The Distribution of Income and Wealth in Japan." *Review of Income and Wealth* 38, no. 4 (December 1992): 403–28.

Beach, Charles M. "Cyclical Sensitivity of Aggregate Income Inequality." *Review of Economics and Statistics* 59 (1977): 56–66.

Bernheim, B. Douglas. "Dissaving after Retirement: Testing the Pure Life Cycle Hypothesis." In *Issues in Pension Economies,* edited by Zvi Bodie, John Shoven, and David Wise, 237–80. Chicago: University of Chicago Press, 1986.

———. "The Economic Effects of Social Security: Toward a Reconciliation of Theory and Measurement." *Journal of Public Economics* 33, no. 3 (1987): 273–304.

———. "Life Cycle Annuity Valuation." NBER Working Paper no. 1511, National Bureau of Economic Research, Cambridge, MA, December 1984.

Bernheim, B. Douglas, Jonathan Skinner, and Steven Weinberg. "What Accounts for the Variation in Retirement Wealth among U.S. Households?" *American Economic Review* 91, no. 4 (September 2001): 832–57.

Bitler, Marianne P., and Hilary W. Hoynes. "The More Things Change, the More They Stay the Same: The Safety Net, Living Arrangements, and Poverty in the

Great Recession." NBER Working Paper no. 19449, National Bureau of Economic Research, Cambridge, MA, 2013.

———. "The State of the Social Safety Net in the Post–Welfare Reform Era." Brookings Papers on Economic Activity. Washington, DC: Brookings Institution, 2010.

Blau, Francine D., and John W. Graham. "Black-White Differences in Wealth and Asset Composition." *Quarterly Journal of Economics* 105, no. 1 (May 1990): 321–39.

Blau, Francine D., and Lawrence M. Kahn. "International Differences in Male Wage Inequality: Institutions versus Market Forces." *Journal of Political Economy* 104, no. 4 (1996): 791–836.

Blinder, Alan S., Roger Gordon, and Donald Weiss. "Social Security Bequests and the Life Cycle Theory of Savings: Cross-Sectional Texts." In *Determinants of National Saving and Wealth*, edited by Franco Modigliani and Richard Hemming, 89–122. New York: St. Martin's Press, 1983.

Bloom, David E., and Richard B. Freeman. "The Fall in Private Pension Coverage in the United States." *American Economic Review Papers and Proceedings* 82 (1992): 539–58.

Blume, Marshall, Jean Crockett, and Irwin Friend. "Stockownership in the United States: Characteristics and Trends." *Survey of Current Business* 54, no. 11 (1974): 16–40.

Board of Governors of the Federal Reserve System. *Balance Sheets for the U.S. Economy, 1946–1985.* Washington, DC: Author, 1986.

Board of Inland Revenue. *Inland Revenue Statistics, 1993.* London: HMSO, 1993.

Borsch-Supan, Axel. "Saving and Consumption Patterns of the Elderly: The German Case." *Journal of Population Economics* 5 (1992): 289–303.

Bosworth, Barry, Gary Burtless, and Kan Zhang. "Later Retirement, Inequality in Old Age, and the Growing Gap in Longevity between Rich and Poor." Washington, DC: Brookings Institution, 2016.

Bover, Olympia, Martin Schürz, Jiri Slacelek, and Federica Teppa. "Eurosystem Household Finance and Consumption Survey: Main Results on Assets, Debt, and Saving." *International Journal of Central Banking* 12, no. 2 (2016): 1–13.

Brandolini, Andrea, Luigi Cannari, Giovanni D'Alessio, and Ivan Fatella. "Household Wealth Distribution in Italy in the 1990s." In *International Perspectives on Household Wealth*, edited by Edward N. Wolff, 225–75. Cheltenham, U.K.: Edward Elgar Publishing Ltd., 2006.

Bricker, Jesse, Alice Henriques, Jacob Kimmel, and John Sabelhaus. "Measuring Income and Wealth at the Top Using Administrative and Survey Data." *Brookings Papers on Economic Activity* (2016): 261–312.

Brittain, John A. *Inheritance and the Inequality of Material Wealth.* Washington, DC: Brookings Institution, 1978.

Brown, Jeffrey R., and Scott J. Weisbenner. "Intergenerational Transfers and Savings Behavior." In *Perspectives on the Economics of Aging,* edited by David A. Wise, 181–204. Chicago: University of Chicago Press, 2004.

Buhmann, Brigitte, Lee Rainwater, Guenther Schmaus, and Timothy M. Smeeding. "Equivalence Scales, Well-Being, Inequality, and Poverty: Sensitivity Estimates across Ten Countries Using the Luxembourg Income Study (LIS) Database." *Review of Income and Wealth* 34, no. 2 (June 1988): 115–42.

Burkhauser, Richard V., Joachim R. Frick, and Johannes Schwarze. "A Comparison of Alternative Measures of Economic Well-Being for Germany and the United States." *Review of Income and Wealth* 43, no. 2 (June 1997): 153–72.

Caballero, Ricardo J. "Earnings Uncertainty and Aggregate Wealth Accumulation." *American Economic Review* 81, no. 4 (September 1991): 859–71.

Caner, Asena, and Edward N. Wolff. "Asset Poverty in the United States, 1984–99: Evidence from the Panel Study of Income Dynamics." *Review of Income and Wealth* 50, no. 4 (December 2004): 493–518.

———. "The Persistence of Asset Poverty in the United States, 1984–2001." In *Trends in Poverty and Welfare Alleviation Issues,* edited by Marie V. Lane, 51–80. Hauppauge, NY: Nova Science, 2006.

Carroll, Christopher D. "How Much Does Future Income Affect Current Consumption?" *Quarterly Journal of Economics* 109, no. 1 (February 1994): 111–47.

Carroll, Christopher D., and Andrew A. Samwick. "How Important Is Precautionary Saving?" *Review of Economics and Statistics* 80, no. 3 (August 1998): 410–19.

Cartwright, William S., and Robert Friedland. "The President's Commission on Pension Policy Household Survey 1979: Net Wealth Distribution by Type and Age for the United States." *Review of Income and Wealth* 31, no. 3 (1985): 285–308.

Chernozhukov, Victor, and Christian Hansen. "The Effects of 401(k) Participation on the Wealth Distribution: An Instrumental Quantile Regression Analysis." *Review of Economics and Statistics* 86, no. 3 (2004): 735–51.

Chiteji, Ngina. "The Great Recession, DC Pensions, and the Decline in Retirement Savings." Mimeo.

Citro, Constance F., and Robert T. Michael, eds. *Measuring Poverty: A New Approach.* Washington, DC: National Academy Press, 1995.

Conley, Dalton. *Being Black, Living in the Red: Race, Wealth and Social Policy in America.* Berkeley: University of California Press, 1999.

Cowell, Frank, Brian Nolan, Javier Olivera, and Philippe Van Kerm. "Wealth, Top Incomes and Inequality." In *Wealth: Economics and Policy,* edited by Kirk Hamilton and Cameron Hepburn. Oxford, U.K.: Oxford University Press, forthcoming.

Cowell, Frank, and Philippe van Kerm. "Wealth Inequality: A Survey." *Journal of Economic Surveys* 29, no. 4 (2015): 671–710.

Crawford, Rowena, and Andrew Hood. "Lifetime Receipt of Inheritances and the Distribution of Wealth in England." *Fiscal Studies* 37, no. 1 (2016): 55–75.

Curtin, Richard T., F. Thomas Juster, and James N. Morgan. "Survey Estimates of Wealth: An Assessment of Quality." In *The Measurement of Saving, Investment, and Wealth,* edited by Robert E. Lipsey and Helen Tice, 473–548. Chicago: Chicago University Press, 1989.

Danziger, Sheldon, J. Van der Gaag, Eugene Smolensky, and Michael K. Taussig. "The Life Cycle Hypothesis and the Consumption Behavior of the Elderly." *Journal of Post Keynesian Economics* 5, no. 2 (Winter 1982): 208–27.

Davies, James B. "The Distribution of Wealth in Canada." In *Studies in the Distribution of Household Wealth,* edited by Edward N. Wolff, 159–80. Greenwich, CT: JAI Press, 1993.

———. "The Relative Impact of Inheritance and Other Factors on Economic Inequality." *Quarterly Journal of Economics* 96 (August 1982): 471–98.

———. "Uncertain Lifetime, Consumption and Dissaving in Retirement." *Journal of Political Economy* 89 (June 1981): 561–78.

Davies, James B., and France St-Hilaire. *Reforming Capital Income Taxation in Canada.* Ottawa, Canada: Economic Council of Canada, 1987.

Davies, James, Susanna Sandström, Anthony Shorrocks, and Edward N. Wolff. "The World Distribution of Household Wealth." In *Personal Wealth from a Global Perspective,* 395–418. Oxford, U.K.: Oxford University Press, 2008.

Davies, James, Susanna Sandström, Anthony Shorrocks, and Edward N. Wolff. "The Global Pattern of Household Wealth." *Journal of International Development* 21, no. 8 (November 2009): 1111–24.

———. "Level and Distribution of Global Household Wealth," *Economic Journal* 121 (March 2011): 223–54.

Davies, James B., and Anthony F. Shorrocks. "Assessing the Quantitative Importance of Inheritance in the Distribution of Wealth." *Oxford Economic Papers* 30 (1978): 138–49.

———. "The Distribution of Wealth." In Vol. 1 of *Handbook on Income Distribution,* edited by Anthony B. Atkinson and Francois Bourguignon, 605–75. Amsterdam: Elsevier Science, 1999.

De Nardi, Mariacristina, Eric French, and John B. Jones. "Savings after Retirement: A Survey." NBER Working Paper no. 21268, National Bureau of Economic Research, Cambridge, MA, June 2015.

Diamond, Peter A., and Jerry A. Hausman. "Individual Retirement and Savings Behavior." *Journal of Public Economics* 23 (1984): 81–114.

Dilnot, A. W. "The Distribution and Composition of Personal Sector Wealth in Australia." *The Australian Economic Review* 1 (1990): 33–40.

Dynan, Karen E., Jonathan Skinner, and Stephen P. Zeldes. "The Importance of Bequests and Life-Cycle Saving in Capital Accumulation: A New Answer." *American Economic Review* 92, no. 2 (2002): 274–78.

Engelhardt, Gary V., and Anil Kumar. "Pensions and Household Wealth Accumulation." *Journal of Human Resources* 46 (2011): 203–36.

Engen, Eric M., and William G. Gale. "Debt, Taxes, and the Effects of 401(k) Plans on Household Wealth Accumulation." Mimeo, Brookings Institution, Washington, DC, May 1997.

———. "The Effects of 401(k) Plans on Household Wealth: Differences Across Earnings Groups." Mimeo, Brookings Institution, Washington, DC, August 2000.

Engen, Eric M., William G. Gale, and Cori E. Uccello. "The Adequacy of Household Saving." *Brookings Papers on Economic Activity* no. 2 (1999): 65–165.

Even, W. E., and D. A. Macpherson. "Why Did Male Pension Coverage Decline in the 1980s?" *Industrial and Labor Relations Review* 47 (1994): 429–53.

Feldstein, Martin S. "Social Security and the Distribution of Wealth." *Journal of the American Statistical Association* 71 (1976): 800–807.

———. "Social Security, Individual Retirement and Aggregate Capital Accumulation." *Journal of Political Economy* 82, no. 5 (September/October 1974): 905–26.

———. "Social Security and Private Saving: Reply." *Journal of Political Economy* 90 (June 1982): 630–41.

Feldstein, Martin S., and Anthony Pellechio. "Social Security and Household Wealth Accumulation: New Microeconomic Evidence." *Review of Economics and Statistics* 61 (August 1979): 361–68.

Fouquet, Annie, and Dominique Strauss-Kahn. "The Size Distribution of Personal Wealth in France (1977): A First Attempt at the Estate Duty Method." *Review of Income and Wealth* 30, no. 4 (1984): 403–18.

Freidman, J. "Asset Accumulation and Depletion Among the Elderly." Paper presented at the Brookings Institution Conference on Retirement and Aging, Washington, DC, 1982.

Friedman, Milton. "Discussion on Income Capitalization." In Vol. 3 of *Studies of Income and Wealth*. New York: National Bureau of Economic Research, 1939.

Gale, William G. "The Effects of Pensions on Wealth: A Re-evaluation of Theory and Evidence." *Journal of Political Economy* 106 (1998): 707–23.

Gale, William G., and John K. Scholz. "Intergenerational Transfers and the Accumulation of Wealth." *Journal of Economic Perspectives* 8 (1994): 145–60.

Gittleman, Maury, and Edward N. Wolff. "Racial and Ethnic Differences in Wealth." In *Race and Economic Opportunity in the Twenty-First Century*, edited by Marlene Kim, 29–49. New York: Routledge, 2007.

———. "Racial Differences in Patterns of Wealth Accumulation." *Journal of Human Resources* 39, no. 1 (Winter 2004): 193–227.

Goldsmith, Raymond W. *Comparative National Balance Sheet: A Study of Twenty Countries, 1688–1979.* Chicago: University of Chicago Press, 1985.

———. *The National Wealth of the United States in the Postwar Period.* Princeton, NJ: Princeton University Press, 1962.

Goldsmith, Raymond W., Dorothy S. Brady, and Horst Mendershausen. *A Study of Saving in the United States.* Princeton, NJ: Princeton University Press, 1956.

Goldsmith, Raymond W., Robert E. Lipsey, and Morris Mendelson. *Studies in the National Balance Sheet of the United States.* Princeton, NJ: Princeton University Press, 1963.

Good, F. J. "Estimates of the Distribution of Personal Wealth." *Economic Trends,* no. 444 (October 1990): 137–57.

Gordon, David M. *Fat and Mean: The Corporate Squeeze of Working Americans and the Myth of Managerial "Downsizing."* New York: Free Press, 1996.

Gourinchas, Pierre-Olivier, and Jonathan A. Parker, "Consumption over the Life Cycle." *Econometrica* 70, no. 1 (January 2002): 47–89.

Greenwood, Daphne. "Age, Income, and Household Size: Their Relation to Wealth Distribution in the United States." In *International Comparisons of the Distribution of Household Wealth,* edited by Edward N. Wolff, 121–40. New York: Oxford University Press, 1987.

———. "An Estimation of U.S. Family Wealth and its Distribution from Microdata, 1973." *Review of Income and Wealth* 29, no. 3 (1983): 23–43.

Greenwood, Daphne T., and Edward N. Wolff. "Changes in Wealth in the United States, 1962–1983: Savings, Capital Gains, Inheritance, and Lifetime Transfers." *Journal of Population Economics* 5, no. 4 (1992): 261–88.

———. "Relative Wealth Holdings of Children and the Elderly in the United States, 1962–1983." In *The Vulnerable,* edited by John Palmer, Timothy Smeeding, and Barbara Torrey, 123–48. Washington, DC: The Urban Institute Press, 1988.

Gustman, Alan L., Olivia S. Mitchell, Andrew A. Samwick, and Thomas L. Steinmeier. "Pension and Social Security Wealth in the Health and Retirement Study." NBER Working Paper no. 5912, National Bureau of Economic Research, Cambridge, MA, February 1997.

Gustman, Alan L., and Thomas L. Steinmeier. "Effects of Pensions on Saving: Analysis with Data from the Health and Retirement Study." NBER Working Paper 6681, National Bureau of Economic Research, Cambridge, MA, August 1998.

———. "The Stampede toward Defined Contribution Pension Plans: Fact or Fiction?" *Industrial Relations* 31 (1992): 361–69.

———. "What People Don't Know about Their Pensions and Social Security: An Analysis Using Linked Data from the Health and Retirement Study." NBER Working Paper no. 7368, National Bureau of Economic Research, Cambridge, MA, September 1999.

Gustman, Alan L., Thomas L. Steinmeier, and Nahid Tabatabai. "How Do Pension Changes Affect Retirement Preparedness? The Trend to Defined Contribution Plans and the Vulnerability of the Retirement Age Population to the Stock Market Decline of 2008–2009." Michigan Retirement Research Center Working Paper 2009–206, Ann Arbor, MI, October 2009.

Hammermesh, Daniel S. "Consumption During Retirement: The Missing Link In the Life Cycle." *Review of Economics and Statistics* 66, no. 1 (February 1984): 1–7.

Hauser, Richard, and Holger Stein. "Inequality of the Distribution of Personal Wealth in Germany, 1973–98." In *International Perspectives on Household Wealth,* edited by Edward N. Wolff, 195–224. Cheltenham, U.K.: Edward Elgar Publishing Ltd., 2006.

Haveman, Robert, and Melissa Mullikin. "Alternative Measures of National Poverty: Perspectives and Assessment." In *Ethics, Poverty and Inequality and Reform in Social Security,* edited by Erik Schokkaert. London: Ashgate Publishing Ltd., 2001.

Haveman, Robert, Barbara Wolfe, Ross Finnie, and Edward N. Wolff. "Disparities in Well-Being among U.S. Children Over Two Decades: 1962–1983." In *The Vulnerable,* edited by John Palmer, Timothy Smeeding, and Barbara Torrey, 149–70. Washington, DC: The Urban Institute Press, 1988.

Haveman, Robert, and Edward N. Wolff. "The Concept and Measurement of Asset Poverty: Levels, Trends and Composition for the U.S., 1983–2001." *Journal of Economic Inequality* 2, no. 2 (August 2004): 145–69.

———. "Who Are the Asset Poor? Levels, Trends and Composition, 1983–1998." In *Inclusion in the American Dream: Assets, Poverty, and Public Policy,* edited by Michael Sherraden, 61–86. New York: Oxford University Press, 2005.

Heckman, James J. "The Common Structure of Statistical Models of Truncation, Sample Selection and Limited Dependent Variables and a Simple Estimator for Such Models." *Annals of Economic and Social Measurement* 5 (1976): 475–92.

———. "Sample Selection Bias as a Specification Error." *Econometrica* 47 (1979): 153–62.

Hubbard, R. Glenn. "Do IRA's and Keoghs Increase Saving?" *National Tax Journal* 37 (1984): 43–54.

———. "Uncertain Lifetimes, Pensions, and Individual Savings." In *Issues in Pension Economies,* edited by Zvi Bodie, John Shoven, and David Wise, 175–210. Chicago: University of Chicago Press, 1986.

Hubbard, R. Glenn, and Kenneth L. Judd. "Liquidity Constraints, Fiscal Policy, and Consumption." *Brookings Papers on Economic Activity,* no. 1 (1986): 1–59.

———. "Social Security and Individual Welfare: Precautionary Saving, Liquidity Constraints, and the Payroll Tax." *American Economic Review* 77, no. 4 (1987): 630–46.

Hurd, Michael D. "Savings of the Elderly and Desired Bequests." *American Economic Review* 77, no. 2 (1987): 298–312.

———. "Wealth Depletion and Life Cycle Consumption." In *Topics in the Economics of Aging,* edited by David A. Wise, 135–60. Chicago: University of Chicago Press, 1992.

Hurd, Michael D., and Gabriella Mundaca. "The Importance of Gifts and Inheritances among the Affluent." In *The Measurement of Saving, Investment, and Wealth,* edited by Robert E. Lipsey and Helen Stone Tice, 737–63. Chicago: University of Chicago Press, 1989.

Hurst, Erik. "The Retirement of a Consumption Puzzle." NBER Working Paper no. 13789, National Bureau of Economic Research, Cambridge, MA, February 2008.

Internal Revenue Service. *Statistics of Income, 1962: Individual Income Tax Returns.* Publication no. 79. Washington, DC: U.S. Government Printing Office, 1965.

Jamieson, Dave. "Union Membership Rate for U.S. Workers Tumbles to New Low." *Huffington Post,* May 4, 2015. http://www.huffingtonpost.com/2013/01/23/union-membership-rate_n_2535063.html.

Jansson, K., and S. Johansson. *Formogenhetsfordelningen 1975–1987.* Stockholm: Statistka Centralbyran, 1988.

Jäntti, Markus. "Trends in the Distribution of Income and Wealth—Finland 1987–98." In *International Perspectives on Household Wealth,* edited by Edward N. Wolff, 295–326. Cheltenham, U.K.: Edward Elgar Publishing Ltd., 2006.

Jianakoplos, Nancy Ammon, Paul L. Menchik, and F. Owen Irvine. "Saving Behavior of Older Households: Rate-of-Return, Precautionary and Inheritance Effects." *Economic Letters* 50, no. 1 (January 1996): 111–20.

Johnson, Barry, Brian Raub, and Joseph Newcomb. "A New Look at the Income-Wealth Connection for America's Wealthiest Decedents." IRS Statistics of Income Working Paper Series, 2013.

Johnson, Richard W., Usha Sambamoorthi, and Stephen Crystal. "Pension Wealth at Midlife: Comparing Self-Reports with Provider Data." *Review of Income and Wealth* 46 (2000): 59–83.

Karagiannaki, Eleni. "The Impact of Inheritance on the Distribution of Wealth: Evidence from the UK." LSE STICERD Research Paper no. CASE/148, London School of Economics, London, U.K., June 2011.

———. "Recent Trends in the Size and Distribution of Inherited Wealth in the UK." LSE STICERD Research Paper no. CASE/146, London School of Economics, London, U.K., June 2011.

Kennickell, Arthur B. "Modeling Wealth with Multiple Observations of Income: Redesign of the Sample for the 2001 Survey of Consumer Finances." Survey of Consumer Finances Working Paper, Federal Reserve Board of Washington, Washington DC, October 2001. http://www.federalreserve.gov/pubs/oss/oss2/method.html.

———. "Ponds and Streams: Wealth and Income in the U.S., 1989 to 2007." Finance and Economics Discussion Series 2009-13, Federal Reserve Board of Washington, 2009.

———. "A Rolling Tide: Changes in the Distribution of Wealth in the US, 1998–2001." In *International Perspectives on Household Wealth,* edited by Edward. N. Wolff, 19–88. Cheltenham U.K.: Edward Elgar Publishing Ltd., 2006.

Kennickell, Arthur B., Douglas A. McManus, and R. Louise Woodburn. "Weighting Design for the 1992 Survey of Consumer Finances." Unpublished manuscript. Federal Reserve Board of Washington, March 1996.

Kennickell, Arthur B., and Annika E. Sunden. "Pensions, Social Security, and the Distribution of Wealth." Mimeo, Federal Reserve Board of Washington, December 1999.

Kennickell, Arthur B., and R. Louise Woodburn. "Consistent Weight Design for the 1989, 1992, and 1995 SCFs, and the Distribution of Wealth." *Review of Income and Wealth* 45, no. 2 (June 1999): 193–216.

———. "Estimation of Household Net Worth Using Model-Based and Design-Based Weights: Evidence from the 1989 Survey of Consumer Finances." Unpublished manuscript. Federal Reserve Board of Washington, April 1992.

Kessler, Denis, and André Masson. "Les transferts intergenerationales: l'aide, la donation, l'heritage." Centre National de la Recherche Scientifique Report, Paris, 1979.

———. "Personal Wealth Distribution in France: Cross-Sectional Evidence and Extensions." In *International Comparisons of the Distribution of Household Wealth,* edited by Edward N. Wolff, 141–76. New York: Oxford University Press, 1987.

Kessler, Denis, and Edward N. Wolff. "A Comparative Analysis of Household Wealth Patterns in France and the United States." *Review of Income and Wealth* 37, no. 3 (September 1991): 249–66.

Killewald, Alexandra, and Brielle Bryan. "Does Your Home Make You Wealthy?" *The Russell Sage Foundation Journal of the Social Sciences* 2, no. 6 (October 2016): 110–28.

King, Mervyn A., and Louis Dicks-Mireaux. "Asset Holdings and the Life Cycle." *Economic Journal* 92 (June 1982): 247–67.

Klevmarken, A. "The Distribution of Wealth in Sweden: Trends and Driving Factors." In *Steigende wirtschaftliche Unglei chheit bei steigendem Reichtum?,* edited by G. Chaloupek and T. Zotter, 29–44. Tagung der Kammer für Arbeiter und Ang estellte für Wien. Vienna: LexisNexis Verlag ARD Orac., 2006.

Klevmarken, N. Anders. "On Household Wealth Trends in Sweden over the 1990s." In *International Perspectives on Household Wealth,* edited by Edward N. Wolff, 276–94. Cheltenham, U.K.: Edward Elgar Publishing Ltd., 2006.

———. "On the Wealth Dynamics of Swedish Families 1984–1998." Paper presented at the 21st Arne Ryde Symposium on Non-Human Wealth and Capital Accumulation, Lund, Sweden, August 23–25, 2001.

Kopczuk, Wojciech. "What Do We Know about the Evolution of Top Wealth Shares in the United States?" *Journal of Economic Perspectives* 29, no. 1 (Winter 2015): 47–66.

Kopczuk, Wojciech, and Emmanuel Saez. "Top Wealth Shares in the United States, 1916–2000: Evidence from Estate Tax Returns." *National Tax Journal* 57, part 2 (2004): 445–88.

Kotlikoff, Laurence J. "Testing the Theory of Social Security and Life Cycle Accumulation." *American Economic Review* 69 (June 1979): 396–410.

———. *What Determines Savings?* Cambridge, MA: MIT Press, 1989.

Kotlikoff, Laurence J., and Daniel E. Smith. *Pensions in the American Economy.* Chicago: University of Chicago Press, 1983.

Kotlikoff, Laurence J., and Avia Spivak. "The Family as an Incomplete Annuities Market." *Journal of Political Economy* 89 (April 1981): 372–91.

Kotlikoff, Laurence J., and Lawrence H. Summers. "The Role of Intergenerational Transfers in Aggregate Capital Accumulation." *Journal of Political Economy* 90 (August 1981): 706–32.

Laitner, John. "Random Earnings Differences, Lifetime Liquidity Constraints, and Altruistic Intergenerational Transfers." *Journal of Economic Theory* 58 (1992): 135–70.

Laitner, John, and Amanda Sonnega. "Intergenerational Transfers in the Health and Retirement Study Data." Michigan Retirement Research Center, Ann Arbor, MI, November 2010.

Lamas, Enrique J., and John M. McNeil. "Factors Associated with Household Net Worth." Paper presented at the meeting of the American Economic Association, New Orleans, LA, December 1986.

Lampman, Robert J. *The Share of Top Wealthholders in National Wealth, 1922–56.* Princeton, NJ: Princeton University Press, 1962.

Lansing, John B., and John Sonquist. "A Cohort Analysis of Changes in the Distribution of Wealth." In *Six Papers on the Size Distribution of Income and Wealth,* edited by Lee Soltow, 31–74. New York: National Bureau of Economic Research, 1969.

Lazonick, William. *Sustainable Prosperity in the New Economy?* Kalamazoo, MI: W.E. Upjohn Institute for Employment Research, 2009.

Lebergott, Stanley. *The American Economy.* Princeton, NJ: Princeton University Press, 1976.

Leimer, Dean R., and Selig D. Lesnoy. "Social Security and Private Saving: New Time-Series Evidence." *Journal of Political Economy* 90 (June 1982): 606–21.

Lerman, Donald L., and James J. Mikesell. "Impacts of Adding Net Worth to the Poverty Definition." *Eastern Economic Journal* 14, no. 4 (1988): 357–70.

Lillard, Lee. "Inequality: Earning vs. Human Wealth," *American Economic Review* 67, no. 2 (March 1977): 42–53.

Lollivier, S., and D. Verger. "Le montant de patrimoine et ses disparites." INSEE Working Paper F9508, Paris, 1995.

Lydall, Harold. "The Life Cycle in Income, Saving, and Asset Ownership." *Econometrica* 23, no. 2 (April 1955): 131–50.

McGarry, Kathleen, and Andrew Davenport. "Pensions and the Distribution of Wealth." NBER Working Paper 6171, National Bureau of Economic Research, Cambridge, MA, September 1997.

Menchik, Paul, and Martin David. "Income Distribution, Lifetime Saving and Bequests." *American Economic Review* 73, no. 4 (1983): 673–90.

Mincer, Jacob. *Schooling, Experience and Earnings.* New York: National Bureau of Economic Research, 1974.

Mirer, Thad W. "The Dissaving Behavior of the Retired Elderly." *Southern Economic Journal* 46, no. 4 (April 1980): 1197–1205.

———. "The Wealth-Age Relation among the Aged." *American Economic Review* 69, no. 3 (June 1979): 435–43.

Modigliani, Franco, and Richard Blumberg. "Utility Analysis and the Consumption Function: An Interpretation of Cross-Section Data." In *Post Keynesian Economics,* edited by Kenneth K. Kurihara, 388–436. New Brunswick, NJ: Rutgers University Press, 1954.

Moon, Marilyn. *The Measurement of Economic Welfare: Applications to the Aged.* New York: Academic Press, 1977.

Morissette, René, Xuelin Zhang, and Marie Drolet. "The Evolution of Wealth Inequality in Canada, 1984–99." In *International Perspectives on Household Wealth,* edited by Edward N. Wolff, 151–92. Cheltenham, U.K.: Edward Elgar Publishing Ltd., 2006.

Morgan, James N., Martin H. David, William. J. Cohen, and Harvey E. Brazer. *Income and Welfare in the United States.* New York: McGraw-Hill Book Company, 1962.

Munnell, Alicia H., and Pamela Perun. "An Update on Private Pensions." Center for Retirement Research at Boston College, Working Paper No. 50, Chestnut Hill, MA, August 2006.

Munnell, Alicia H., Anthony Webb, Zhenya Karamcheva, and Andrew Eschtruth. "How Important Are Intergenerational Transfers for Baby Boomers?" Center for Retirement Research at Boston College Working Paper 2011–1, Chestnut Hill, MA, 2011.

Musgrave, John C. "Fixed Reproducible Tangible Wealth in the United States: Revised estimates." *Survey of Current Business* 66 (January 1986): 51–75.

O'Higgins, Michael, Guenther Schmaus, and Geoffrey Stephenson. "Income Distribution and Redistribution: A Microdata Analysis for Seven Countries." *Review of Income and Wealth* 35 (June 1989): 107–32.

Oliver, Melvin L., and Thomas M. Shapiro. *Black Wealth, White Wealth.* New York: Routledge, 1997.

Organization for Economic Cooperation and Development. *National Accounts, Detailed Tables, 1978–1990.* Vol. 2. Paris: OECD, 1992.

———. *Taxation of Net Wealth, Capital Transfers and Capital Gains of Individuals.* Paris: OECD, 1988.

Oulton, Nicholas. "Inheritance and the Distribution of Wealth." *Oxford Economic Papers* 28, no. 1 (March 1976): 86–101.

Palumbo, Michael. "Uncertain Medical Expenses and Precautionary Saving Near the End of the Life Cycle." *Review of Economic Studies* 66, no. 2 (1999): 395–421.

Pfeffer, Fabian T., Sheldon Danziger, and Robert F. Schoeni. "Wealth Disparities before and after the Great Recession." *The Annals of the American Academy of Political and Social Science* 650 (November 2013): 98–123.

———. "Wealth Levels, Wealth Inequality, and the Great Recession." Russell Sage Foundation Research Summary, New York, June 2014.

Piketty, Thomas. *Capital in the Twenty-First Century,* Cambridge, MA: Harvard University Press, 2014.

———. "On the Long-Run Evolution of Inheritance: France 1820–2050." *Quarterly Journal of Economics* 126, no. 3 (2011): 1071–1131.

Piketty, Thomas, and Emmanuel Saez. "Income Inequality in the United States, 1913–1998." *Quarterly Journal of Economics* 118, no. 1 (2003): 1–39.

Poterba, James M. "Retirement Security in an Aging Population." *American Economic Review Papers and Proceedings* 104, no. 5 (2014): 1–30.

Poterba, James M., Joshua Rauh, Steven Venti, and David Wise. "Defined Contribution Plans, Defined Benefit Plans, and the Accumulation of Retirement Wealth." *Journal of Public Economics* 91, no. 10 (2007): 2062–86.

Poterba, James M., Steven F. Venti, and David A. Wise. "401(k) Plans and Future Patterns of Retirement Saving." *American Economic Review Papers and Proceedings* 87, no. 2 (May 1998): 179–84.

———. "The Transition to Personal Accounts and Increasing Retirement Wealth: Micro and Macro Evidence." NBER Working Paper 8610, National Bureau of Economic Research, Cambridge, MA, November 2001.

President's Commission on Pension Policy. "Pension Coverage in the United States." Mimeo, Washington, DC, 1980.

———. "Preliminary Findings on a Nationwide Survey on Retirement Income Issues." Mimeo, Washington, DC, 1980.

Projector, Dorothy, and Gertrude Weiss. *Survey of Financial Characteristics of Consumers.* Federal Reserve Board Technical Papers. Washington, DC: Board of Governors of the Federal Reserve System, 1966.

Radner, Daniel B., and Denton R. Vaughan. "Wealth, Income and the Economic Status of Aged Households." In *International Comparisons of the Distribution of Household Wealth,* edited by Edward N. Wolff, 93–120. New York: Oxford University Press, 1987.

Rendall, Michael S., and Alden Speare Jr. "Comparing Economic Well-Being among Elderly Americans." *Review of Income and Wealth* 39, no. 1 (1993): 1–21.

Roine, J., and D. Waldenström. "Long-run Trends in the Distribution of Income and Wealth." In Vol. 2A of *Handbook of Income Distribution,* edited by A. B. Atkinson and F. Bourguignon. Amsterdam: North-Holland, 2015. http://www .uueconomics.se/danielw/Handbook.htm.

Ruggles, Nancy, Richard Ruggles, and Edward Wolff. "Merging Microdata: Rationale, Practice and Testing." *Annals of Economic and Social Measurement* 6, no. 4 (Fall 1977): 407–28.

Ruggles, Patricia. *Drawing the Line: Alternative Poverty Measures and Their Implications for Public Policy.* Washington, DC: Urban Institute Press, 1990.

Ruggles, Patricia, and Robertson Williams. "Longitudinal Measures of Poverty: Accounting for Income and Assets Over Time." *Review of Income and Wealth* 35, no. 3 (1989): 225–43.

Ruggles, Richard. "Statement for the Task Force on Distributive Impacts of Budget and Economic Policies of the House Committee on the Budget." Mimeo, 1977.

Ruggles, Richard, and Nancy Ruggles. "Integrated Economic Accounts for the United States, 1947–1980." *Survey of Current Business* 62 (May 1982): 1–53.

———. "A Strategy for Matching and Merging Microdatasets." *Annals of Economic and Social Measurement* 3, no. 2 (April 1974): 353–71.

Sabelhaus, John, and Karen Pence. "Household Saving in the '90s: Evidence from Cross-Section Wealth Surveys." *Review of Income and Wealth* 25, no. 4 (1999): 435–53.

Saez, Emmanuel, and Gabriel Zucman. "Wealth Inequality in the United States since 1913: Evidence from Capitalized Income Tax Data." *Quarterly Journal of Economics* 131, no. 2 (May 2016): 519–78.

Schervish, Paul G., and John J. Havens. "Millionaires and the Millenium: New Estimates of the Forthcoming Wealth Transfer and the Prospects for a Golden Age of Philanthropy." Social Welfare Research Institute of Boston College, Boston, MA, 1999.

Schwartz, Marvin. "Preliminary Estimates of Personal Wealth, 1982: Composition of Assets." *Statistics of Income Bulletin* 4 (Winter 1984): 1–17.

———. "Trends in Personal Wealth, 1976–1981." *Statistics of Income Bulletin* 3 (Summer 1983): 1–26.

Schwartz, Marvin, and Barry Johnson. "Estimates of Personal Wealth, 1986." *Statistics of Income Bulletin* 9 (Spring 1990): 63–78.

Sen, Amartya. *Inequality Reexamined.* Cambridge, MA: Russell Sage Foundation and Harvard University Press, 1992.

Sheshinski, Eytan, and Yoram Weiss. "Uncertainty and Optimal Social Security Systems." *Quarterly Journal of Economics* 96 (May 1981): 189–206.

Shorrocks, Anthony F. "The Age-Wealth Relationship: A Cross-Section and Cohort Analysis." *Review of Economics and Statistics* 57 (May 1975): 155–63.

———. "U.K. Wealth Distribution: Current Evidence and Future Prospects." In *International Comparisons of the Distribution of Household Wealth*, edited by Edward N. Wolff, 29–50. New York: Oxford University Press, 1987.

Skinner, Jonathan S. "Risky Income, Life Cycle Consumption, and Precautionary Savings." *Journal of Monetary Economics* 22 (September 1988): 237–55.

Skolnik, Alfred M. "Private Pension Plans, 1950–74." *Social Security Bulletin* 39 (June 1976): 3–17.

Slemrod, Joel. "High-Income Families and the Tax Changes of the 1980s: The Anatomy of Behavioral Responses." NBER Working Paper no. 5218, National Bureau of Economic Research, Cambridge, MA, August 1995.

———. "On the High-Income Laffer Curve." Working Paper no. 93–5, The Office of Tax Policy Research, University of Michigan Business School, Ann Arbor, MI, March 1993.

Smith, James D. "Recent Trends in the Distribution of Wealth in the U.S.: Data Research Problems and Prospects." In *International Comparisons of the Distribution of Household Wealth*, edited by Edward N. Wolff, 72–89. New York: Oxford University Press, 1987.

———. "Trends in the Concentration of Personal Wealth in the United States, 1958–1976." *Review of Income and Wealth* 30, no. 4 (1984): 419–28.

Smith, James D., and Stephen D. Franklin. "The Concentration of Personal Wealth, 1922–1969." *American Economic Review* 64 (May 1974): 162–67.

Smith, Karen, Eric Toder, and Howard Iams. "Lifetime Redistribution of Social Security Retirement Benefits." Mimeo, Social Security Administration, 2001.

Spånt, Roland. "Wealth Distribution in Sweden: 1920–1983." In *International Comparisons of the Distribution of Household Wealth*, edited by Edward N. Wolff, 51–71. New York: Oxford University Press, 1987.

Spilerman, Seymour. "Wealth and Stratification Processes." *American Review of Sociology* 26, no. 1 (2000): 497–524.

Statistics Sweden. *Income Distribution Survey in 1990.* Orebro, Sweden: SCB Publishing Unit, 1992.

———. *Income Distribution Survey in 1992.* Orebro, Sweden: SCB Publishing Unit, 1994.

Stewart, Charles. "Income Capitalization as a Method of Estimating the Distribution of Wealth by Size Group." In Vol. 3 of *Studies of Income and Wealth,* 95–146. New York: National Bureau of Economic Research, 1939.

Stiglitz, Joseph E. "Distribution of Income and Wealth Among Individuals." *Econometrica* 37, no. 3 (July 1969): 382–97.

Stockhammer, Engelbert. "Rising Inequality as a Cause of the Present Crisis." *Cambridge Journal of Economics* (2013). doi: 10.1093 / cje / bet052.

Tachibanaki, H. *Land Taxation Reform in Japan.* JEI Report no. 28A, Japan Economic Institute, Washington, DC, July 20, 1990.

Takayama, N. "Household Asset- and Wealthholdings in Japan." In *Aging in the United States and Japan: Economic Trends,* edited by Yukio Noguchi and David Wise, 85–108. Chicago: Chicago University Press, 1994.

Tavernise, Sabrina. "Sweeping Pain as Suicides Hit a 30-Year High." *New York Times,* April 22, 2016, A1.

Thornton, James R., Richard J. Agnello, and Charles R. Link. "Poverty and Economic Growth: Trickle Down Peters Out." *Economic Inquiry* 16 (1978): 385–94.

Tobin, James. "Life Cycle Saving and Balanced Growth." In *Ten Economic Studies in the Tradition of Irving Fisher,* edited by William Fellner, 231–56. New York: Wiley, 1967.

Tobin, James, and Walter Dolde. "Wealth, Liquidity, and Consumption." In *Consumer Spending and Monetary Policy: the Linkages,* Federal Reserve Bank of Boston Conference Series 5, 99–146. Boston: Federal Reserve Bank of Boston, 1971.

U.S. Bureau of the Census. *Historical Statistics of the United States, Colonial Times to 1970.* Part 2. Washington, DC: U.S. Government Printing Office, 1975.

——. *Statistical Abstract of the United States: 1988.* 108th edition. Washington, DC: U.S. Government Printing Office, 1987.

U.S. Bureau of Labor Statistics. *Consumer Expenditure Survey: Integrated Diary and Interview Survey Data, 1972–73.* Bulletin no. 1978. Washington, DC: U.S. Government Printing Office, 1978.

U.S. Council of Economic Advisers. *Economic Report of the President,* Washington, DC: U.S. Government Printing Office, 2001 and 2015.

U.S. Department of Labor, Pension and Welfare Benefits Administration. "Coverage Status of Workers under Employer Provided Pension Plans: Findings from the Contingent Work Supplement to the February 1999 Current Population Survey." Washington, DC: U.S. Department of Labor, 2000.

Weisbrod, Burton, and W. Lee Hansen. "An Income-Net Worth Approach to Measuring Economic Welfare." *American Economic Review* 58, no. 5 (1968): 1315–29.

Weller, Christian, and Edward N. Wolff. *Retirement Income: The Crucial Role of Social Security.* Washington, DC: Economic Policy Institute, 2005.

White, Betsy. "Empirical Tests of the Life Cycle Hypotheses." *American Economic Review* 68, no. 4 (September 1978): 547–60.

Williamson, Jeffrey G., and Peter A. Lindert. "Long-term Trends in American Wealth Inequality." In *Modeling the Distribution and Intergenerational Transmission of Wealth,* edited by James D. Smith, 9–94. Chicago: University of Chicago Press, 1980.

Wolff, Edward N. "The Accumulation of Wealth over the Life Cycle: A Microdata Analysis." *The Review of Income and Wealth* 27, no. 2 (June 1981): 75–96.

———. "The Adequacy of Retirement Resources among the Soon-to-Retire, 1983–2001." In *Government Spending on the Elderly,* edited by Dimitri B. Papadimitriou, 315–42. Houndsmill, U.K.: Palgrave Macmillan, 2007.

———. "The Asset Price Meltdown and Household Wealth over the Great Recession in the United States." In Vol. 22 of *Research on Economic Inequality,* "Economic Well-Being and Inequality: Papers from the Fifth ECINEQ Meeting, 2014," 1–42. Bingley, U.K.: Emerald Group Publishing Ltd., 2014.

———. "The Asset Price Meltdown, Rising Leverage, and the Wealth of the Middle Class." *Journal of Economic Issues* 47, no. 2 (June 2013): 333–42.

———. "Changes in Household Wealth in the 1980s and 1990s in the U.S." In *International Perspectives on Household Wealth,* 107–50. Cheltenham, U.K.: Edward Elgar Publishing Ltd., 2006.

———. "Changing Inequality of Wealth." *American Economic Review Papers and Proceedings* 82, no. 2 (May 1992): 552–58.

———. "The Devolution of the American Pension System: Who Gained and Who Lost?" *Eastern Economics Journal* 29, no. 4 (Fall 2003): 477–95.

———. "Discussant Comment on Douglas Holtz-Eakin, 'The Uneasy Case for Abolishing the Estate Tax.'" *Tax Law Review* 51, no. 3 (1997): 517–21.

———. "The Distribution of Wealth in the United States at the Start of the 21st Century." In *The Economics of Inequality, Poverty, and Discrimination in the 21st Century,* edited by Robert S. Rycroft, 38–56. Santa Barbara, CA: ABC-CLIO, 2013.

———. "Distributional Consequences of a National Land Value Tax on Real Property In the United States." In *Land Value Taxation: Can It and Will It Work?* edited by Dick Netzer, 61–104. Cambridge, MA: Lincoln Institute of Land Policy, 1998.

———. "The Distributional Effects of the 1969–75 Inflation on Holdings of Household Wealth in the United States." *Review of Income and Wealth* 25, no. 2 (June 1979): 195–207.

———. "The Distribution of Household Disposable Wealth in the United States." *The Review of Income and Wealth* 29, no. 2 (June 1983): 125–46.

———. "The Distribution of Household Wealth: Methodological Issues, Time Trends, and Cross-Sectional Comparisons." In *Economic Inequality and Pov-*

erty: International Perspectives, edited by Lars Osberg, 92–133. Armonk, NY: M.E. Sharpe, 1991.

———. "The Economic Status of Parents in Postwar America." In *Taking Parenting Public: The Case for a New Social Movement,* edited by Sylvia Hewlitt, Nancy Rankin, and Cornel West, 59–82. Lanham, MD: Rowman and Littlefield, 2002.

———. "Effect of Alternative Imputation Techniques on Estimates of Household Wealth in the U.S. in 1969." In *Accumulation et Repartition des Patrimoines,* edited by Denis Kessler, André Masson, and Dominque Strauss-Kahn, 147–80. Paris: Economica, 1982.

———. "The Effects of Pensions and Social Security on the Distribution of Wealth in the U.S." In *International Comparisons of Household Wealth Distribution,* edited by Edward N. Wolff, 208–47. New York: Oxford University Press, 1987.

———. "Estimates of the 1969 Size Distribution of Household Wealth in the United States from a Synthetic Database." In *Modeling the Distribution and Intergenerational Transmission of Wealth,* edited by James D. Smith, 223–71. Chicago: University of Chicago Press, 1980.

———. "Estimates of Household Wealth Inequality in the United States, 1962–83." *Review of Income and Wealth* 33, no. 3 (September 1987): 231–56.

———. "Household Wealth trends in the United States, 1962–2013: What Happened over the Great Recession?" NBER Working Paper no. 20733, National Bureau of Economic Research, Cambridge, MA, December 2014.

———. "Household Wealth Trends in the United States, 1983–2010." *Oxford Review of Economic Policy* 30, no. 1 (2014): 21–43.

———. "The Impact of Gifts and Bequests on the Distribution of Wealth." In *Death and Dollars,* edited by Alicia H. Munnell and Annika Sundén, 345–75. Washington, DC: Brookings Institution, 2003.

———. "Income, Wealth, and Late-Life Inequality in the U.S." In Vol. 22 of *Annual Review of Gerontology and Geriatrics,* edited by Stephen Crystal and Dennis Shea, 31–58. New York: Springer Publishing Co., 2002.

———. "Inequality and Rising Profitability in the United States, 1947–2013." *International Review of Applied Economics* 29, no. 6 (2015): 741–69. http://www.tandfonline.com/doi/pdf/10.1080/02692171.2014.956704.

———. "Inheritances and Wealth Inequality, 1989–1998." *American Economic Review Papers and Proceedings* 92, no. 2 (May 2002): 260–64.

———. *Inheriting Wealth in America: Future Boom or Bust?* New York: Oxford University Press, 2015.

———. "International Comparisons of Wealth Inequality." *Review of Income and Wealth* 42, no. 4 (December 1996): 433–51.

———. "International Comparisons of Wealth: Methodological Issues and a Summary of Findings." In *International Perspectives on Household Wealth,* 1–16. Cheltenham, U.K.: Edward Elgar Publishing Ltd., 2006.

———. "Life Cycle Savings and the Individual Distribution of Wealth by Class." In *Modelling the Accumulation and Distribution of Wealth,* edited by Denis Kessler and André Masson, 261–80. Oxford: Clarendon Press, 1988.

———, "Methodological Issues in the Estimation of Retirement Wealth." In Vol. 2 of *Research in Economic Inequality,* edited by Daniel J. Slottje, 31–56. Stamford, CT: JAI Press, 1992.

———. "Methodological Issues in the Estimation of the Size Distribution of Household Wealth." *Journal of Econometrics* 43, no. 1 / 2 (January / February 1990): 179–95.

———. "The Middle Class: Losing Ground, Losing Wealth." In *Diversity and Disparities: America Enters a New Century,* edited by John R. Logan, 60–104. New York: Russell Sage Foundation, 2014.

———. *Poverty and Income Distribution.* 2nd ed. New York: Wiley-Blackwell, 2009.

———. "Recent Trends in Household Wealth in the U.S.: Rising Debt and the Middle Class Squeeze." In *Economics of Wealth in the 21st Century,* edited by Jason M. Gonzales, 1–41. Hauppauge, NY: Nova Science Publishers, Inc., 2011.

———. "Recent Trends in Living Standard in the United States." In *What Has Happened to the Quality of Life in the Advanced Industrialized Nations?,* 3–26. Cheltenham, U.K.: Edward Elgar Publishing Ltd., 2004.

———. "Recent Trends in the Size Distribution of Household Wealth." *Journal of Economic Perspectives* 12, no. 3 (Summer 1998): 131–50.

———. "Recent Trends in Wealth Ownership, from 1983 to 1998." In *Assets for the Poor: The Benefits of Spreading Asset Ownership,* edited by Thomas M. Shapiro and Edward N. Wolff, 34–73. New York: Russell Sage Press, 2001.

———. *Retirement Insecurity: The Income Shortfalls Awaiting the Soon-to-Retire.* Washington, DC: Economic Policy Institute, 2002.

———. "The Retirement Wealth of the Baby Boom Generation." *Journal of Monetary Economics* 54, no. 1 (January 2007): 1–40.

———. "The Rich Get Increasingly Richer: Latest Data on Household Wealth during the 1980s." In Vol. 5 of *Research in Politics and Society,* 33–68. Stamford, CT: JAI Press, 1995.

———. "Rising Profitability and the Middle Class Squeeze," *Science & Society* 74, no. 3 (July 2010): 429–49.

———. "The Size Distribution of Wealth in the United States: A Comparison among Recent Household Surveys." In *Wealth, Work, and Health: Innovations in Measurement in the Social Sciences,* edited by James P. Smith and Robert J. Willis, 209–32. Ann Arbor, MI: University of Michigan Press, 1999.

———. "Social Security, Pensions, and the Life Cycle Accumulation of Wealth: Some Empirical Tests." *Annales d'Economie et de Statistique,* no. 9 (Janvier / Mars 1988): 199–216.

———. "The Stagnating Fortunes of the Middle Class." *Social Philosophy and Policy* 191, no. 4 (2002): 55–83.

———. *Top Heavy: A Study of Increasing Inequality of Wealth in America.* New York: The Twentieth Century Fund Press, 1995.

———. *Top Heavy: A Study of Increasing Inequality of Wealth in America.* Updated and expanded edition. New York: The New Press, 2002.

———. "The Transformation of the American Pension System." In *Work Options for Mature Americans,* edited by Teresa Ghilarducci and John Turner, 175–211. Notre Dame, IN: University of Notre Dame Press, 2007.

———. *The Transformation of the American Pension System: Was It Beneficial for Workers?* Kalamazoo, MI: W.E. Upjohn Institute for Employment Research, 2011.

———. "Trends in Aggregate Household Wealth in the U.S., 1900–1983." *Review of Income and Wealth* 35, no. 1 (March 1989): 1–30.

———. "Trends in Household Wealth in the United States, 1962–1983 and 1983–1989." *Review of Income and Wealth* 40, no. 2 (June 1994): 143–74.

———. "U.S. Pensions in the 2000s: The Lost Decade?" *Review of Income and Wealth* 61, no. 4 (December 2015): 599–629. doi: 10.1111 / roiw.12123.

———. "Wealth Accumulation by Age Cohort in the U.S., 1962–1992: The Role of Savings, Capital Gains and Intergenerational Transfers." *Geneva Papers on Risk and Insurance* 24, no. 1 (January 1999): 27–49.

———. "Wealth Holdings and Poverty Status in the United States." *Review of Income and Wealth* 36, no. 2 (June 1990): 143–65.

———. "Wealth Inequality." *Pathways, The Poverty and Inequality Report.* Special Issue (2014): 34–41.

———. "Who Are the Rich? A Demographic Profile of High-Income And High-Wealth Americans." In *Does Atlas Shrug? The Economic Consequences of Taxing the Rich,* edited by Joel Slemrod, 74–113. New York: Russell Sage Foundation and Harvard University Press, 2000.

Wolff, Edward N., and Maury Gittleman. "Inheritances and the Distribution of Wealth or Whatever Happened to the Great Inheritance Boom?" *Journal of Economic Inequality* 12, no. 4 (December 2014): 439–68.

Wolff, Edward N., and Marcia Marley. "Long-Term Trends in U.S. Wealth Inequality: Methodological Issues and Results." In *The Measurement of Saving, Investment, and Wealth,* edited by Robert E. Lipsey and Helen Tice, 765–843. Chicago: Chicago University Press, 1989.

Wolff, Edward N., Lindsay A. Owens, and Esra Burak. "How Much Wealth Was Destroyed in the Great Recession?" In *The Great Recession,* edited by David B. Grusky, Bruce Western, and Christopher Wimer, 127–58. New York: Russell Sage Foundation Press, 2011.

Yaari, Menaham E. "Uncertain Lifetime, Life Insurance, and the Theory of the Consumer." *Review of Economic Studies* 32 (April 1965): 137–58.

Young, Allan, and John Musgrave. "Estimation of Capital Stock in the United States." Paper delivered at the Conference on Research in Income and Wealth, Toronto, Canada, 1976.

Zeldes, Steven P. "Optimal Consumption with Stochastic Income: Deviations from Certainty Equivalence." *Quarterly Journal of Economics* 104 (May 1989): 275–98.

Ziliak, James P. "Income Transfers and Assets of the Poor." *Review of Economics and Statistics* 85, no. 1 (February 2003): 63–76.

Zucman, Gabriel. "The Missing Wealth of Nations: Are Europe and the U.S. Net Debtors or Net Creditors?" *Quarterly Journal of Economics* 128, no. 3 (2013): 1321–64.

Acknowledgments

As is customary, I would like to express my gratitude to the foundations and institutions that helped fund my research on this topic: the National Science Foundation, the U.S. Department of Health and Human Services, the Alfred P. Sloan Foundation, the Russell Sage Foundation, the Ford Foundation, the Levy Economics Institute of Bard College, the W. E. Upjohn Institute for Employment Research, the Institute for New Economic Thinking, and the C. V. Starr Center for Applied Economics at New York University.

Index

Page numbers followed by f indicate figures. Page numbers followed by t indicate tables.